Enabling Blockchain Technology for Secure Networking and Communications

Adel Ben Mnaouer
Canadian University Dubai, UAE

Lamia Chaari Fourati
University of Sfax, Tunisia

A volume in the Advances in Information Security,
Privacy, and Ethics (AISPE) Book Series

Published in the United States of America by
IGI Global
Information Science Reference (an imprint of IGI Global)
701 E. Chocolate Avenue
Hershey PA, USA 17033
Tel: 717-533-8845
Fax: 717-533-8661
E-mail: cust@igi-global.com
Web site: http://www.igi-global.com

Library of Congress Cataloging-in-Publication Data

Names: Ben Mnaouer, Adel, 1962- editor. | Fourati, Lamia Chaari, 1972-
   editor.
Title: Enabling blockchain technology for secure networking and
   communications / Adel Ben Mnaouer and Lamia Chaari Fourati, editors.
Description: Hershey, PA : Information Science Reference, [2021] | Includes
   bibliographical references and index. | Summary: "This book consolidates
   the recent research initiatives directed towards exploiting the
   advantages of Blockchain technology for benefiting several areas of
   applications from security and robustness to scalability and
   privacy-preserving. The central focus of this book is investigate
   several current topics, such as Blockchain for IoT and its derivatives,
   applications of Blockchain for security and privacy across various
   domains, Blockchain for Identity Management, Integration of Artificial
   Intelligence and Blockchain, Blockchain and energy efficiency
   challenges"-- Provided by publisher.
Identifiers: LCCN 2020018698 (print) | LCCN 2020018699 (ebook) | ISBN
   9781799858393 (hardcover) | ISBN 9781799858409 (paperback) | ISBN
   9781799858416 (ebook)
Subjects: LCSH: Blockchains (Databases) | Computer networks--Security
   measures. | Digital communications--Security measures.
Classification: LCC QA76.9.B56 E53 2021 (print) | LCC QA76.9.B56 (ebook)
   | DDC 005.8/24--dc23
LC record available at https://lccn.loc.gov/2020018698
LC ebook record available at https://lccn.loc.gov/2020018699

This book is published in the IGI Global book series Advances in Information Security, Privacy, and Ethics (AISPE) (ISSN: 1948-9730; eISSN: 1948-9749)

British Cataloguing in Publication Data
A Cataloguing in Publication record for this book is available from the British Library.

For electronic access to this publication, please contact: eresources@igi-global.com.

Advances in Information Security, Privacy, and Ethics (AISPE) Book Series

Manish Gupta
State University of New York, USA

ISSN:1948-9730
EISSN:1948-9749

MISSION

As digital technologies become more pervasive in everyday life and the Internet is utilized in ever increasing ways by both private and public entities, concern over digital threats becomes more prevalent.

The **Advances in Information Security, Privacy, & Ethics (AISPE) Book Series** provides cutting-edge research on the protection and misuse of information and technology across various industries and settings. Comprised of scholarly research on topics such as identity management, cryptography, system security, authentication, and data protection, this book series is ideal for reference by IT professionals, academicians, and upper-level students.

COVERAGE

- Computer ethics
- Telecommunications Regulations
- Tracking Cookies
- Information Security Standards
- CIA Triad of Information Security
- Technoethics
- Global Privacy Concerns
- IT Risk
- Security Information Management
- Risk Management

IGI Global is currently accepting manuscripts for publication within this series. To submit a proposal for a volume in this series, please contact our Acquisition Editors at Acquisitions@igi-global.com or visit: http://www.igi-global.com/publish/.

Titles in this Series

For a list of additional titles in this series, please visit: www.igi-global.com/book-series

701 East Chocolate Avenue, Hershey, PA 17033, USA
Tel: 717-533-8845 x100 • Fax: 717-533-8661
E-Mail: cust@igi-global.com • www.igi-global.com

This work is dedicated to our family members who have been deprived of our company many times while we are busy editing this book.

Table of Contents

Section 1
Blockchain Tools, Modeling, and Structural Extensions

Detailed Table of Contents

Section 1
Blockchain Tools, Modeling, and Structural Extensions

    lamia Chaari Fourati, Higher Institute of Computer Science and Multimedia of Sfax, Tunisia
    Taher Layeb, Higher Institute of Computer Science and Multimedia of Sfax, Tunisia
    Achraf Haddaji, ENET'COM, Tunisia
    Samiha Ayed, University of Technology of Troyes, France
    Wiem Bekri, ENET'COM, Tunisia

Blockchain technology is considered the most relevant technology after the internet that revolutionizes many application domains. The first generation of BC technology, BC 1.0, is used for cryptocurrency purposes; the second generation, BC 2.0, as represented by Ethereum, is an open and decentralized platform empowering the running of decentralized applications (DApps) on top of BC as a new computing paradigm. Ethereum as a BC 2.0 leader has a large development community. Its open-source feature leads to the development of several emulation tools, simulators, TestNets, and security verification tools dedicated to Ethereum-based system performance analysis. Making an adequate decision regarding the choice of the most appropriate Ethereum tool responding to the requirement of a specific system or application still requires more investigation from researchers. In this regard, this chapter presents the characteristics of the most-used Ethereum simulators, emulators, and TestNets and provides comparative studies between Ethereum simulators, TestNets, and security verification tools.

    lamia Chaari Fourati, Higher Institute of Computer Science and Multimedia of Sfax, Tunisia
    Taher Layeb, Higher Institute of Computer Science and Multimedia of Sfax, Tunisia
    Achraf Haddaji, Higher Institute of Computer Science and Multimedia of Sfax, Tunisia
    Samiha Ayed, University of Technology of Troyes, France
    Wiem Bekri, ENET'COM, Tunisia

During this last decade, the blockchain (BC) paradigm is being required in several use cases and scenarios in particular for security, privacy, and trust provisioning. Accordingly, the research community and developers developed several emulation tools and frameworks for BC-based systems performance analysis. Making an adequate decision regarding the choice of the most suitable tool that can be used to develop and validate the performances of a specific BC-based system or application still requires more investigation. In this context, this chapter describes and highlights the most features and characteristics of the BC platforms and tools within the Hyperledger framework. The goal is to illustrate the advantages and the limitations of several BC tools and development environments within Hyperledger. In addition, this chapter provides an insight into BC 3.0 as the new generation of BC that meets the requirements of the smart application.

Chapter 3

Rim Moussa, University of Carthage, Tunisia
Alfredo Cuzzocrea, University of Calabria, Italy

Bitcoin is the most well-known cryptocurrency. It was first released in 2009 by Satoshi Nakamoto. Bitcoin serves as a decentralized medium of digital exchange, with transactions verified and recorded in the blockchain. The latter is a public immutable distributed ledger that operates without the need of a trusted record keeping authority or a central intermediary. It provides OLTP capabilities with both atomic transactions and data durability guarantees for blockchain transactions. Blockchain ledgers were not designed to perform analytics questions. The availability of the entire bitcoin transaction history, stored in its public blockchain, offers interesting opportunities for analyzing the transactions to obtain insights on users/entities patterns and transactions patterns. For these purposes, the authors need to store and analyze cryptocurrency transactions in a data warehouse. In this chapter, they investigate public blockchain datasets, and they overview different data models for setting up a data warehouse appliance of cryptocurrencies.

Chapter 4

Regio A. Michelin, Cybersecurity CRC, Australia & University of New South Wales,
    Australia
Roben Castagna Lunardi, Federal Institute of Education, Science and Technology of Rio
    Grande do Sul (IFRS), Brazil
Henry Cabral Nunes, Pontifical Catholic University of Rio Grande do Sul, Brazil
Volkan Dedeoglu, CSIRO, Australia
Charles V. Neu, University of Santa Cruz do Sul, Brazil
Avelino Francisco Zorzo, Pontifical Catholic University of Rio Grande do Sul, Brazil
Salil S. Kanhere, University of New South Wales, Australia

Blockchain has emerged as a technology that can change the way people and systems interact, providing mechanisms that ensure integrity and ownership of the data produced without reliance on a trusted third-party. Appendable-block blockchain is a novel instantiation that suits for solutions that require a high transaction throughput. Appendable-block blockchains focus on data produced by nodes instead of a relation (transaction) between two entities. This new kind of blockchain can improve how data are stored and managed in distributed systems. This chapter introduces the notion of appendable-block blockchain and exemplifies its applicability in multiple practical domains. Additionally, the authors provide a discussion on the security aspects of this new blockchain. Finally, the chapter presents current issues and possible future directions for appendable-block blockchains.

## Chapter 5

Tokenizing assets through the use of blockchain is the next big thing in digital currency markets. Securing the assets in the world of the internet is challenging as most of them can easily be copied and sold in the secondary market. Protecting the rights of the asset owner is one of the challenging research areas. NFTs (non-fungible tokens) are very useful in representing the ownership of unique items for any assets. NFTs ensure that an asset can have only one official owner at any point in time with the help of Ethereum-based blockchain network. Ethereum NFTs can ensure that no one can modify the ownership rights or copy and paste the digital assets. NFTs are a boon to the artists, musicians, and others who want to create impressive digital assets. The objective of this chapter is to take you to the world of NFTs and to explain how the NFTs are going to impact digital transactions in a bigger way in the future. This chapter covers the introduction, technical aspects, security impacts, use cases, and successful implementations of NFTs in various realms.

Section 2
Blockchain Applied to IoT, VANETs, and FANETs

## Chapter 6

Recently, the internet of things (IoT) has gained popularity as an enabling technology for wireless connectivity of mobile and/or stationary devices providing useful services for the general public in a collaborative manner. Mobile ad-hoc networks (MANETs) are regarded as a legacy enabling technology for various IoT applications. Vehicular ad-hoc networks (VANETs) and flying ad-hoc networks (FANETs) are specific extensions of MANETs that are drivers of IoT applications. However, IoT is prone to diverse attacks, being branded as the weakest link in the networking chain requiring effective solutions for achieving an acceptable level of security. Blockchain (BC) technology has been identified as an efficient method to remedy IoT security concerns. Therefore, this chapter classifies the attacks targeting IoT, VANETs, and FANETs systems based on their vulnerabilities. This chapter explores a selection of blockchain-based solutions for securing IoT, VANETs, and FANETs and presents open research directions compiled out of the presented solutions as useful guidelines for the readers.

## Chapter 7

During this last decade, the blockchain (BC) paradigm has been required in several use cases and scenarios in particular for security, privacy, and trust provisioning. Accordingly, several studies proposed the use of BC technology to secure and to assure the trustworthiness of unmanned aerial vehicles (UAVs). In this context, this chapter highlights several applications and scenarios for the deployment of UAVs within diverse smart systems. In addition, it illustrates the advantages of the integration of the BC within UAVs-based smart systems. This integration reveals new challenges and future research directions that are discussed in this chapter.

Chapter 8

Sasikumar R., K. Ramakrishnan College of Engineering, India

Karthikeyan P., Thiagarajar College of Engineering, India

Thangavel M., Siksha 'O' Anusandhan (Deemed), India

In the internet era, data is considered to be the primary asset, and the host or applications in a network are vulnerable to various attacks. Traditional network architectures have centralized authority to provide authentication, authorization, and access control services. In this case, there is a possibility of data mishandling activities from the valuable information available in the given network application. To avoid this type of mishandling, a new technology came into existence known as blockchain. Implementing blockchain technology in the internet of things (IoT) will ensure data integrity, stability, and durability. The authors present a detailed investigation of various IoT applications with blockchain implementation. Blockchain-based mechanisms will improve the security aspects in the traditional network applications related to IoT like insurance policies claiming, personal identification, and electronic health records.

Section 3
Effective Blockchain Adoption in Manufacturing

Chapter 9

Kamalendu Pal, City, University of London, UK

The internet of things (IoT) is ushering a new age of technology-driven automation of information systems into the manufacturing industry. One of the main concerns with IoT systems is the lack of privacy and security preserving schemes for controlling access and ensuring the safety of the data. Many security issues arise because of the centralized architecture of IoT-based information systems. Another concern is the lack of appropriate authentication and access control schemes to moderate the access to information generated by the IoT devices in the manufacturing industry. Hence, the question that arises is how to ensure the identity of the manufacturing machinery or the communication nodes. This chapter presents the advantages of blockchain technology to secure the operation of the modern manufacturing industry in a trustless environment with IoT applications. The chapter reviews the challenges and threats in IoT applications and how integration with blockchain can resolve some of the manufacturing enterprise information systems (EIS).

Modern manufacturing logistics and supply chain have transformed into highly complex value-creating business networks. It has become increasingly challenging to cross-check the source of raw materials and maintain visibility of products and merchandise while moving through the value chain network. This way, the high complexity of manufacturing business processes and the continuously growing amount of information lead to extraordinary demand to find an appropriate data processing architecture for the global manufacturing industry. The internet of things (IoT) applications can help manufacturing companies track, trace, and monitor products, business activities, and processes within the respective value chain networks. Combining with IoT, blockchain technology can enable a broader range of different application scenarios to improve value chain transparency. This chapter presents a hybrid (i.e., IoT, blockchain, service-oriented computing) data processing architecture for the manufacturing industry.

Section 4
Effective Use of Blockchain and IoT in E-Healthcare Systems

Blockchain is one of the trendy technologies in the current era. All industries are merging blockchain with their production line to benefit from its features such as security and decentralized data. One of the main problems in the healthcare system is the lack of interoperability (i.e., data should be patient-centered and not institution-centered). Healthcare information systems, in the current state, cannot communicate. Each organization works within its boundaries and owns its data. To make this shift, many challenges should be solved such as data privacy, standards, scalability, and others. Blockchain can solve these problems by giving the patients control over their data; therefore, they can share it with any institution for a time period. It is expected that blockchain will improve healthcare data management. In this chapter, the authors study the opportunity of blockchain to leverage biomedical and healthcare applications and research. Blockchain also contributes to the medication manufacturing area.

Growing organizations, institutions, and SMEs demand for transformation in all the aspects of their businesses along with the progression in time and technology. When it comes to healthcare, the growth should be heightened to higher levels with necessity. The need of providing quality of service (QoS) in healthcare is taking significant place, allowing health institutions and medical compliances to develop an ecosystem with cutting-edge technology with the same reliability but better productivity and performance.

Moreover, the healthcare systems are aiming for a more patient-centric strategy. Healthcare systems work on complicated and traditional methods, oftentimes administered via teams of professionals who manage data and supportive mechanisms of the system. Blockchain could streamline and automate those methods, conserving weeks of effort in the company's production line to increase the overall revenue and discover new opportunities. This chapter aims to illustrate blockchain technology along with its state-of-the-art applications in healthcare.

Preface

Nowadays, data/telecommunication networks and the Internet are used at an unprecedented large scale. However, this widespread usage is leading to an increase of both trusty and malicious users of these networks. Therefore, sensitive, and confidential data are continuously under the threat of cybersecurity attacks targeting public government institutions, private industries, corporate companies and of course, personal human privacy that has been recently devastated with near-zero hope of repair. Moreover, these recent years have witnessed a large-scale proliferation of a great variety of Internet-connectivity-enabled devices such as the so-called Internet of Things (IoT) ("things" empowered with wireless communication and computing capabilities and IP addressing being connected to the Internet) that are serving the public and private sector with useful applications (in healthcare, manufacturing, smart-irrigation, education, entertainments, etc.). Add to that the advent of the drone/UAV technologies that may incorporate IoT devices and may fly in solo or swarm formation (as Flying Ad-hoc Networks (FANETs)) while being connected to the Internet via different connection paradigms. Along with that, Vehicular Ad hoc Networks (VANETs) as vehicular variants of Mobile Ad-hoc Networks (MANETs) are reaching a mature state and their connectivity to the Internet has led to the recent hot topic concept of connected and autonomous vehicles that are fully loaded with IoT devices. Furthermore, the 4th Industrial Revolution (4IR) that is branded as a full fusion of advances in artificial intelligence (AI), robotics, the Internet of Things (IoT), genetic engineering, quantum computing, and more, is in full bloom and in full disruptive mode touching and affecting almost every industry, in almost every country while evolving at an exponential rather than a linear pace.

With all these proliferations and interleaving of technologies which are all relying on the Internet for ensuring the communication between their different elements and components are widening the gate of cybersecurity attacks and effective destructive or lucrative exploits by malicious and well-versed experts. These new generations of perpetrators are well-aware and well-informed about the weaknesses and vulnerabilities of the above technologies and of their weak links, are getting more and more ferocious, in their attacks day by day.

As a hope of beefing up the security of the above technologies among others, the Blockchain (BC) technology has been widely identified as a potential savior that has come to the rescue, since its inception by the anonymous Satoshi Nakamoto (2008) in his white paper. Indeed, the success of BC has been acclaimed worldwide and a huge number of researchers got passionate in inventing frameworks, tools, platforms for accommodating, implementing and adapting the BC technology in several fields of use to obtain finally, the long-awaited solution for ensuring provably secure and tamper-proof transactions.

Blockchain is a novel paradigm introduced to overcome these issues, which permits the verification of the illegibility of any transaction among several entities including businesses, machines, IoT devices, vehicular nodes and individuals. Indeed, Blockchain can be considered as a Distributed Ledger Technology (DLT) recording and securing transactions in a Peer-to-Peer (P2P) network as an alternative to using a centralized server as a mediator.

This book is intended to present and highlight the latest technologies, advances, implementations, architectures, tools and applications related to the potential integration of Blockchain as an enabling technology for secure networking and communications. The book focuses on several topics that address recent concerns in the community, including architectures and protocols related to trust node identification, data integrity and privacy preservation, secure content dissemination. In addition, it emphasizes the application of the Blockchain technology for emerging networks such the Internet of Things (IoT), Industrial IoT, VANETs, FANETs and healthcare systems. It is interesting to note that the call for chapters has received a strong response from the community. We hope that the accepted twelve chapters will provide helpful insights to our readership on the several approaches of adopting Blockchain for securing the networking and communication tasks for many applications. We have classified the content in this editorial into four sections with a total of twelve chapters, as detailed below.

The first section, entitled "Blockchain Tools, Modeling, and Structural Extensions," includes four chapters, which are:

The first chapter, titled "Metrics, Platforms, Emulators, and TestNets for Ethereum," presents the metrics and the characteristics of the most commonly used Ethereum simulators, emulators and TestNets. It also provides comparative studies between Ethereum simulators, TestNets and security verification tools. The content of this chapter provides the readership with the required knowledge to take an adequate decision regarding the choice of the most appropriate Ethereum tools corresponding to a specific system or application requirements.

Chapter 2, "Platforms and Tools Within the HyperLedger Framework," describes and highlights features and characteristics of the BC platforms and tools within the Hyperledger framework. The authors assessed the advantages and the limitations of several BC tools and development environments within Hyperledger. Besides, this chapter provides an insight into BC 3.0 as the new generation of BC that meets the requirements of smart applications.

Chapter 3, "Extracting Insights From Bitcoin Transactions: Data Warehouse Modeling and Analytical Questions," discusses Bitcoin transactions modeling and analysis to obtain insights on transactions and on users/entities patterns. Accordingly, the authors suggest storing and analyzing crypto-currencies' transactions in a data warehouse. Moreover, this chapter investigates public Blockchain datasets and overviews different data models for setting up a data warehouse appliance of crypto currencies.

Chapter 4, "Appendable-Block Blockchains: Overview, Applications, and Challenges," proposes a novel Blockchain instantiation named "Appendable-block Blockchain" which consists in a Blockchain model designed to support constrained entities producing information. These entities are arranged in a multi-layer architecture, according to their capabilities and purpose on the solution. Appendable-block Blockchains focus on data produced by nodes instead of a relation (transaction) between two entities. In addition, the chapter exemplifies its applicability in multiple practical domains and provides a discussion on the security aspects of this new Blockchain.

Chapter 5, "The world of NFTs (Non-Fungible Tokens): The Future of Blockchain and Asset Ownership," gives a detailed overview on Non-Fungible Tokens, a useful paradigm for ensuring and securing ownership uniqueness of digitally represented assets using Ethereum based Blockchain networks. The chapter presents technical aspects and security impact of NFTs and highlights some use cases and successful implementations of NFTs in a variety of domains.

Section 2, entitled "Blockchain Applied to IoT, VANETs, and FANETs," includes Chapters 6 to 8:

Chapter 6, "A Survey of Blockchain-Based Solutions for IoTs, VANETs, and FANETs," sketches the potentialities of Blockchain technology for achieving an acceptable level of security and for providing countermeasures for threats and attacks in IoTs, VANETs and FANETs contexts. Indeed, this chapter classifies the attacks targeting IoT, VANETs and FANETs systems based on their vulnerabilities and explores a selection of Blockchain-based solutions for securing these emerging networks. In addition, the authors pinpoint open research directions compiled out of the presented solutions as useful guidelines for the readers interested in further researching this topic.

Chapter 7, "Blockchain Towards Secure UAV-Based Systems," emphasizes the benefits of the use of UAVs correlated with Blockchain technology in several applications and domains, in particular, for security, privacy and trust provisioning. In this context, this chapter highlights several applications and scenarios for the deployments of UAVs within diverse smart applications and illustrates the advantages of the integration of Blockchain within UAVs-based smart systems. In addition, the authors give a particular insight on challenges and future research directions regarding the integration between UAVs and Blockchain technologies.

Chapter 8, "Blockchain Technology for IoT: An Information Security Perspective," provides a detailed study on the effective use of the Blockchain Technology for securing the communication paradigms used in applications pertaining to Ubiquitous healthcare, transportation systems, Smart Cities and smart Supply-Chain.

The third section, entitled "Effective Blockchain Adoption in Manufacturing," is devoted to exploring Blockchain issues, architectures, and protocols applied to manufacturing in the context of smart factories. This section includes Chapters 9 and 10.

Chapter 9, "Blockchain With the Internet of Things Solutions and Security Issues in the Manufacturing Industry," presents a deep study focusing on Blockchain security issues in smart manufacturing industry. Indeed, this chapter presents the advantages of Blockchain technology to secure the operation of modern manufacturing industry in a trustless environment with IoT applications.

Chapter 10, "Blockchain Technology With the Internet of Things in Manufacturing Data Processing Architecture," presents a hybrid IoT, Blockchain and Service-Oriented Computing architecture for data processing in the manufacturing industry that enhances value-chain transparency by securing the underlying communication structures.

The fourth and last section, entitled "Effective Use of Blockchain and IoT in E-Healthcare Systems," deals with the integration of Blockchain with e-health systems and comprises Chapters 11 and 12.

Chapter 11, "Blockchain for Healthcare and Medical Systems," presents a comprehensive study of the potentials of Blockchain in supporting biomedical and healthcare applications and research. It gives a synthesis of ongoing research trends for Blockchain in the healthcare system and explores the contributions of Blockchain into the pharmaceutical and drug manufacturing. In addition, this chapter illustrates how Blockchain adoption can help secure the communication and raise the effectiveness of biomedical and healthcare applications.

Chapter 12, "Blockchain and Its Applications in Healthcare," explores and studies the main hurdles weaknesses and problems faced by the healthcare business and industry that can be solved effectively throughout the adoption of the Blockchain technology and explores and highlight successful use cases of such adoptions that lead to established commercial products.

REFERENCES

Nakamoto, S. (2008). *Bitcoin: A Peer-to-Peer Electronic Cash System*. https://bitcoin.org/bitcoin.pdf

Acknowledgment

The editors would like to offer special thanks to Ms. Nadia Charef for the tremendous help and assistance she did during the late crucial stage of handling reviews and revisions. She did a wonderful and professional Job. Special thanks go also to Dr. Maroua Abdelhafidh for her dedication to the project, help and assistance.

Special thanks and appreciation are also due to the valuable members of the review board for providing professional 2 to 3 rounds of reviews. Without their valuable effort this book would not have been a reality.

Section 1
Blockchain Tools, Modeling, and Structural Extensions

Chapter 1
Metrics, Platforms, Emulators, and TestNets for Ethereum

Iamia Chaari Fourati
Higher Institute of Computer Science and Multimedia of Sfax, Tunisia

Taher Layeb
Higher Institute of Computer Science and Multimedia of Sfax, Tunisia

Achraf Haddaji
ENET'COM, Tunisia

Samiha Ayed
University of Technology of Troyes, France

Wiem Bekri
ENET'COM, Tunisia

ABSTRACT

Blockchain technology is considered the most relevant technology after the internet that revolutionizes many application domains. The first generation of BC technology, BC 1.0, is used for cryptocurrency purposes; the second generation, BC 2.0, as represented by Ethereum, is an open and decentralized platform empowering the running of decentralized applications (DApps) on top of BC as a new computing paradigm. Ethereum as a BC 2.0 leader has a large development community. Its open-source feature leads to the development of several emulation tools, simulators, TestNets, and security verification tools dedicated to Ethereum-based system performance analysis. Making an adequate decision regarding the choice of the most appropriate Ethereum tool responding to the requirement of a specific system or application still requires more investigation from researchers. In this regard, this chapter presents the characteristics of the most-used Ethereum simulators, emulators, and TestNets and provides comparative studies between Ethereum simulators, TestNets, and security verification tools.

DOI: 10.4018/978-1-7998-5839-3.ch001

INTRODUCTION

Before Ethereum (Wood, G., 2014), BC applications designed to do limited things. The crypto-currencies were designed to operate as peer-to-peer digital currencies, nothing more, which caused a problem for developers. To fill this gap, the developer of Ethereum, Vitalik Buterin, came up with an Ethereum Virtual Machine (EVM) as an inventive approach. EVM is a Turing-complete software executed on the Ethereum network. EVM allows anybody to execute whatever program he or she wants independent from the programming language. The EVM simplifies the creation of BC-based applications and enables the build of thousands of different apps on one single platform. Furthermore, Ethereum has its crypto-currency named Ether and a currency to pay for computations and transactions fees called Gas. Ethereum is principally for developers to build and deploy their decentralized applications, taking into consideration all the different industries. Besides, Ethereum can be used to build DAOs (Decentralized Autonomous Organizations) that are fully autonomous without any leader. DAOs run purely by Ethereum programming code and smart contracts.

Since all these decentralized applications will run on the Ethereum platform, they will all benefit from the BC properties. These proprieties are:

- **Immutability:** changes cannot be made to any data by a third party.
- **Tamper-proof and corruption-free**: the apps built are based on the principle of consensus and this makes censorship virtually impossible
- **Secure**: all applications and transactions secured with cryptography, giving them strong protection against fraud and hacking.
- **Anonymity**: based on the asymmetric cryptography and hashing of BC data (digital cryptographic keys, transactions...).

Although, the advantages of using Ethereum platform to run Dapp, the performance analysis of Ethereum- based solution require the use of simulators, emulators and Testnets. In this context, several tools are developed and this chapter presents these tools. Indeed, the manifolds of this chapter could be summarized into three points:

- Providing a comprehensive comparative study of current and various Ethereum emulation tools dedicated to analyzing the performance of Ethereum-based systems, which is useful for the
- researchers to better comprehend Ethereum aspects and to select the s
- uitable tools that fit their needs and their applications.
- Discussing Ethereum Testnets tools and their usage.
- Analyzing the potentialities of Ethereum security verification tools.

The rest of this chapter organized as follows: The second section pinpoints the Ethereum architecture. The third section discusses intensively BC evaluation strategies and metrics. The fourth section highlights the popular simulators and emulators tools developed for Ethereum-based BC. This book chapter provides a particular focus on Ethereum security verification tools. The fifth section describes and compares the most known Ethereum Testnets. The sixth section assesses open issues and future research direction regarding the possible enhancement of BC platforms. The last section concludes this chapter and pinpoints the lesson learned through this chapter.

ETHEREUM ARCHITECTURE

The Ethereum BC main architecture is 4-layer including network layer, consensus layer, data layer and application layer.

- **At the application layer**, Ethereum clients execute in EVM smart contracts associated to Ethereum accounts. Ethereum expands the BC concept with smart contracts. Smart Contracts (SC) are the programs running on the Ethereum BC, developed using a high level programming language, such as Solidity. When developers deploy a SC to Ethereum, the contract will be compiled into EVM. To execute the SC, EVM parses the source code of the contracts into an opcode sequence defined by Ethereum. Then, each node on the Ethereum system will receive the SC bytecode and have a copy in their ledger. Each node in Ethereum BC needs an EVM to execute the contracts properly and process the transactions.

- **The data layer** holds the BC data structures including transactions, Blocks and events. A transaction is an interaction a sender and a recipient. A transaction is specified by several fields including: (i) nonce (is a counter for tracking the total number of transactions that have been initiated by the sender), (ii) recipient, (iii) value (the amount of money to be transferred (if applicable), (iv) input (bytecode or data corresponding to the purpose of the transaction), (v) gasPrice and gasLimit (the unit price and the maximum amount of gas the sender is ready to pay the winning miner of a block containing the transaction), and (vi) the sender signature. The execution of a transaction updates the states of the accounts involved and therefore the state of the BC. Miner has to package the transactions into blocks and then should join them to a chain. To add a new block, the following steps must be respected: (i) Transactions grouped in a block. (ii) Miners check if block transactions conform to the defined rules. (iii) Miners validate the added block by executing a consensus mechanism. (iv) A reward is given to miners who validate the block. (v) Finally, the verified transactions will be stored in the BC.

- **The consensus layer** assures a consistent state of the BC. Ethereum started using proof of work (PoW) as its consensus mechanism, but it is soon switching to proof of stake (PoS). PoW is a compute intensive based consensus protocol. PoW is open and entirely decentralized and is required for the validation of each block. In PoW, peers (miners) search to solve a difficult mathematical problem based on a cryptographic hash algorithm. The solution proves that a miner spends time and resources solving the mathematical puzzle. Therefore, miners paid for any valid blocks added into the BC. This serves as the miner's motivation for the execution of any mining task. The transactions inside that block are considered confirmed when a block is solved. The main advantages of PoW consensus are safety and stability and the PoW main disadvantages are low performance and high power consumption PoW are known as energy-hungry mining algorithms. PoS belong to capability-based consensus protocol. Regarding the PoS paradigm, the miners in PoS are called forgers and the mining process is known as forging. At the beginning of a forging round, only the peers holding assets may participate in the consensus, in place of using energy to answer PoW puzzles, a PoS miner is limited to mining a percentage of transactions and it asks users to prove ownership of a certain amount of currency. The advantage of PoS is low power consumption and PoS disadvantages are its complex implementation and its low security.

- **The network layer** articulates an Ethereum peer-to-peer network of nodes or clients and updates the state of the BC from the active nodes. Each node (i.e., client) stores a copy of the entire

BC. For node discovery and routing purposes, each node keeps a dynamic routing table, IP address, UDP/TCP ports. Ethereum uses the RLPx protocol to discover target clients and uses the Ethereum Wire Protocol to facilitate the exchange of Ethereum BC information between clients.

To serve Ethereum BC layers a dedicated environment is required. It includes the following components: databases for storing BC data; a web user interface to interact with applications; cryptographic mechanisms to support the consensus protocols; and Internet service to provide connectivity within the network layer.

Performance is among key factors limiting the use of BC systems when running complex smart contracts. In the next section, we will focus on the performance metrics for assessing Ethereum-based systems performances.

BC EVALUATION STRATEGIES AND METRICS

This section pinpoints the main BC evaluation strategies and associated metrics during the evaluation process. Generally, any BC-based system could be evaluated and analyzed from numerous perspectives: functional testing, usability, block analysis, integration, security analysis, smart contracts, networks, and performance evaluation that is the main scope of this chapter.

BC Evaluation Metrics

Performance evaluation and testing of BC-based systems could be described by the set of metrics that could be classified into three categories: (i) BC metrics and parameters (the number of processed transactions, the number of produced blocks, finality time, processing time, etc...). (ii) Peer-to-Peer (P2P) network metrics (the number of active peers, the number of hit/miss requests, the volume and structure of P2P traffic, etc...), and node metrics (memory, storage, CPU, network, etc...).

BC Metrics and Parameters

The consensus, the transactions type and size, and the block size are the main BC parameters. However, the transaction throughput, the chain size, the commit time or transactional latency and the finality time are the main BC performance metrics.

- **Consensus:** The consensus protocol is a P2P protocol executed by the miners or peers to secure and maintain the BC. Consensus is the distributed process by which a set of nodes offers guaranteed unique transactions order and validates the block of transactions. The consensus solves the problem of mutual trust among nodes in the network. The consensus algorithm is the core of the BC framework. Selecting the appropriate consensus algorithm or not directly influences the BC performance; an unsuitable consensus algorithm can hurt system operation. The consensus algorithm performance in private BC-platforms measured through quantitative analysis of throughput and latency within different numbers of transactions.
- **Transactions Type/Size**: Transaction size corresponds to the amount of data to be added in the next block. Inappropriate selection may have increased transaction fees in public BC.

- **Block size**: Corresponds to the size of the block that is measured in term of the number of the transactions to be included in the block. The maximum fixed limit of a block is 1 megabyte per block for Bitcoin. Blocks with high size may have a negative impact on the future Operational Expenses (OPEX).

- **Transaction throughput**: is the rate at which valid transactions are committed by the BC network during a fixed period, usually computed as the number of transactions per second (**TPS**). During a period of time from **Ti** to **Tj**, TPS of $peer_k$ can be calculated by the following equation, (we abbreviate transaction as Tx):

$$TPSk = \frac{Count\Big(Tx \, in\big(Ti, Tj\big)\Big)}{\big(Tj - Ti\big)} \Big(Txs \, per \, s\Big) \qquad (1)$$

Then, the throughput of N peers is the arithmetic average computed by:

$$TPS = \frac{\sum_k TPSk}{N} \Big(Txs \, per \, s\Big) \qquad (2)$$

- **Chain size**: The prospect of BC is that it provides a complete and permanent record of every value transfer transacted on the chain. Therefore, theoretically, there is no limit regarding the chain size. A chain that is too long significantly decreases its distribution time to allow the new node to start the operation.

- **Network-wide latency (transactional Latency or commit time called also Average Response delay)**: corresponds to the amount of time required for a transaction to take effect to be used across the network. Precisely, it is the difference between the time when transaction is firstly sent to the network and the time when it is confirmed (be committed in a block and the block is accepted by all peers). During a period of time from **Ti** to **Tj**, the action of each transaction firstly sent to the peer is noted as Tx_{input} and the action when Tx is confirmed is noted as $Tx_{confirmed}$. Therefore, the Average Response Delay of $peer_k$ can be computed according the following equation:

$$ARDk = \frac{\sum_{Tx}\Big(t\big(Txconfirmed\big) - t\big(Txinput\big)\Big)}{Count\Big(Tx \, in\big(Ti, Tj\big)\Big)} \qquad (3)$$

The response delay of all smart contracts corresponds to the average and is computed as

$$ARD = \frac{\sum_k ARDk}{N} \Big(Txs \, / \, s\Big) \qquad (4)$$

- **Finality time**: Is the instant when a transaction is committed and can no longer be reversed. Defined within a consensus algorithm and a threshold should be carefully selected during the evaluation.

Network Metrics and Parameters

This subsection introduces network metrics that influences the performance of BC-based systems. The network metrics are correlated to the structure of underlying BC-related packets (service, data, etc.). Inefficient selection of this parameter may cause unnecessary traffic overheads.

- **Volume of P2P traffic**: Corresponds to the cumulative traffic amount generated by active nodes in the system. In case of public BC, the volume of P2P traffic is high, which may increase OPEX and may have a tremendous negative effect on connection quality and on energy consumption.
- **Packet loss ratio:** is the ratio between lost and sent packets related to BC operation. High packed loss lead to high delay and low TPS.

Node Metrics

Node hardware (CPU/GPU, memory) utilized within BC has an important effect on the involvement in the BC operation, as well as on the OPEX and on the Capital Expenditures. In the following, this chapter presents the main node metrics influencing the BC performance.

- **Transaction per CPU/GPU**: CPU/GPU is the hardware utilized for BC-related data processing. Smart contracts execution consumes many CPU resources. The CPU consumption degree is related to the contract (if it includes or not: encryption, loops…). Besides that, the actions of block commitment and hash computing consume also CPU resources. To take in consideration the diversity of peers CPUs we need a metric to monitor the utilization of the CPU during the smart contracts execution, and therefore the Transactions per CPU is the adequate parameter that fits the mentioned goal. Thus, Transactions Per CPU of peer$_k$ during a period of time from **Ti** to **Tj**, can be calculated according the equation (Eq.5):

$$TPCk = \frac{Count\left(Tx\ in\left(Ti, Tj\right)\right)}{\int_{Ti}^{Tj} F * CPU\left(t\right)}\left(Txs / \left(GHzs\right)\right), \tag{5}$$

Where F is the CPU core frequency and CPU(t) is the CPU usage by the BC program at t. The whole utilization of CPUs in the network corresponds to the TPCk average (see Eq.6).

$$TPC = \frac{\sum_{k} TPCk}{N}\left(Txs / \left(GHz * s\right)\right) \tag{6}$$

- **Transaction per Memory Second**: To execute transaction's, the CPU interacts with the RAM. Then an amount of RAM is required for efficient transaction or block processing. Thus the transactions per Memory Second represents the memory utilization and is computed according the equation Eq.7:

$$TPMSk = \frac{Count\left(Tx\,in\left(Ti\,,Tj\right)\right)}{\int_{Ti}^{Tj} RMEM\left(t\right) + VMEM\left(t\right)}\left(Txs\,/\left(MB * s\right)\right), \tag{7}$$

Where VMEM(t) is the virtual memory and RMEM(t) is the real memory used by the BC program at instant t. The whole utilization of RAMs in the network is computed by Eq.8:

$$TPMS = \frac{\sum_k TPMSk}{N}\left(Txs\,/\left(MB * s\right)\right) \tag{8}$$

- **Transactions per Disk I/O**: The BC program requires a separate storage space in the hard disk for storing the data including the world state and it consumes the I/O resources to maintain the BC (e.g., contract execution, block committing.). Similar to the TPC and TPMS, the metric Transactions Per Disk I/O represents the utilization of I/O and it is computed by the following equation (Eq.9):

$$TPDIOk = \frac{Count\left(Tx\,in\left(Ti,Tj\right)\right)}{\int_{Ti}^{Tj} DISKR\left(t\right) + DISKW\left(t\right)}\left(Txs\,/\left(kilobytes\right)\right), \tag{9}$$

where DISKR(t) is the size of the data read from the disk in the second t and DISKW(t) is the size of the data written into the disk. The disks of all the peers, computed by Eq.10:

$$TPDIO = \frac{\sum_k TPDIOk}{N}\left(Txs\,/\left(kilobytes\right)\right) \tag{10}$$

- **Node metrics Connectivity:** Corresponds to the metrics related to the node connectivity when a selected communications technology is used; including channel quality, reliability, latency, etc.
- **Read latency**: is the time between the read request submission and the reception of the reply.
- **Read throughput**: it measures how many read operations completed during a period quantified as reads per second (RPS).

In conclusion, the presented metrics regarding the BC data and the resources consumption are important for the BC users or managers. However, for the BC developers, it is essential to define other metrics related to each step within the transaction life cycle (validating, executing, State-Update and Commit). In this regard, authors in (Zheng, P. and al, 2018, May) suggested the following metrics: Transaction Propagating Rate, RPC Response Rate, Contract Execution Time, State Updating Time, and Consensus-Cost Time.

BC Evaluation Strategies

Authors in (Chakraborty, P. and al, 2018, October) studied the motivations, challenges, and needs of BC Software (BCS) developers, analyzed the differences between BCS and non-BCS development and surveyed the software development practices of BC projects. The main conclusion related to their surveys is that the software development tools that are adjusted for non-BCS are not suitable for BCS development tasks. Therefore, there is a need of new or improved tools for BC-based systems, such as a customized IDE for Empirical Software Engineering BCS development tasks, testing support, dedicated simulators, debuggers for smart contracts, BC frameworks and BCS domain-specific design notations. These findings motivate the authors to study, investigate and compare the particularities and the technical insight of BC simulation tools, frameworks and development environments.

Currently, analytical modelling and simulations are the standard strategies for the behaviour and performance analysis of the majority of BC-based solutions. Analytical modelling could also be applied to the BC evaluation when a mathematical model has a closed-form solution. Simulation models could be considered as a subclass of mathematical models. In this case, the simulation would combine both logical and mathematical aspects of the system and attempt to replicate a real-life system behaviour using dedicated software. In general, simulation tends to be deployed when the analytical description cannot be formulated. Simulation attempts to estimate a system's behaviour and development over time by executing a model.

In general, simulators are classified according to their operation mode. A simulator is charged with reproducing a system performance and its progress in a period by running a model. By changing conditions and variables in the implemented simulation model, researchers can make predictions about the behaviour of the simulated system without the need for the actual implementation of the entire system.

A model includes a set of hypothesis about the operation of the system and categorized as follows (Faria, C., and Correia, M, 2019, July):

- A stochastic model, which has statistic distributions as input values and leads to probabilistic outputs.
- A deterministic model that does not utilize random or probabilistic variables.
- A static model, which represents a system at a particular moment whereas a dynamic model describes the system over a certain period.
- A Discrete-event model considers the system as a sequence of events with the possibility to jump in time from an event to another. A discrete-event simulation model is suitable to model a BC system since it changes states in time at discrete points.
- A continuous model can track the system states over time and gives some views for the future development of BC systems.

Besides simulations and analysis, emulation corresponds to another group of approaches used for evaluating the performance of the entire or part of the BC-based systems. Emulation is the process of imitating the behaviour of the real system that can be observed from the outside to match an existing target.

Emulation is more accurate compared to simulation. However, it requires many computational resources to achieve it at the same time. Therefore, the next section of this chapter mainly focuses on the Ethereum simulators and emulators existing tools.

SIMULATORS AND EMULATORS FOR ETHEREUM-BASED BLOCKCHAINS

As we mentioned before, Ethereum has a huge development community, which leads to the development of many Ethereum-based tools such as BlockBench, BlockSim, TruffleSuite, and Ethereum security verification tools.

Blockbench Simulator

Blockbench represents an evaluation framework for analyzing private BC platforms (Dinh, T. T. A. and al, 2017, May). It can be integrated into BC platforms using simple APIs and benchmarks against workloads that are based on synthetic and real smart contracts. Blockbench comes with macro benchmark workloads to evaluate the global performance and with microbenchmark workloads to evaluate the performance of individual layers. Besides, the platform's performance can be measured using different applications, which reflect the operations performed on the BC. Blockbench provides the possibility to compare the different platforms (in term of throughput, latency, scalability and fault-tolerance) and it permits to understand deeply the different system design choices. In the following, figure 1 pinpoints the Blockbench components.

Figure 1. Internal architecture of the BlockBench simulator

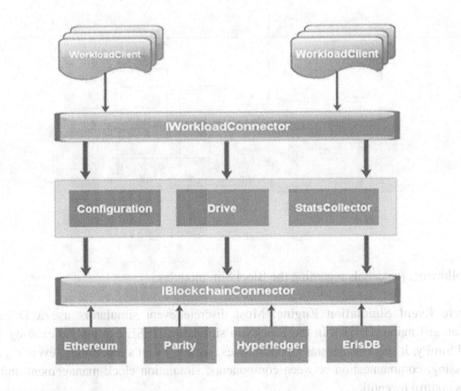

First, the BC is integrated into the framework's backend by implementing "IBlockchainConnector" interface, which contains operations for deploying application, invoking it by sending a transaction, and for querying the states of the BC. Then, users can utilize one of the existing workloads to evaluate the BC, or implement a new workload by using the "IWorkloadConnector" interface. Blockbench's main component is the Driver which takes as input a workload configurations defined by the user (such as number of operations, number of clients, threads, etc.), executes it on the BC and outputs running statistics that measure and evaluate performance metrics including throughput, latency, scalability, and fault tolerance.

BlockSim Simulator

BlockSim (Pandey, S. and al, 2019, May) (Faria, C., and Correia, M., 2019, July) is a discrete-event simulator implemented to simulate different BC models. BlockSim can track thousands of nodes and events that only change states. In addition, it assists in the design, implementation, and evaluation of BCs. BlockSim (Alharby, M., and van Moorsel, A, 2020). pursues a stochastic simulation model representing a random phenomenon by sampling from a probability distribution. This model is also dynamic modelling the system over a certain time interval. Figure 2 represents the architecture of the BlockSim tool. It shows the components, connectors and interfaces of the implementation.

Figure 2. Architecture of BlockSim simulator

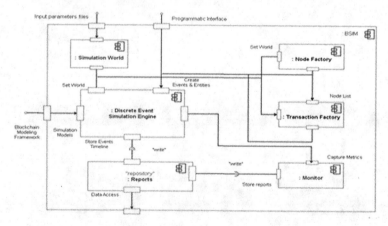

In the following, the details regarding the BlockSim modules:

- **Discrete Event Simulation Engine**: Most discrete event simulators use a Discrete Event Simulation Engine (DESE). In the BlockSim simulator, DESE exploits an existing framework called SimPy. It supports several functionalities, such as event's scheduling, event's queuing and processing, communication between components, simulation clock management and resources access control by entities.
- **Simulation World**: its principal role is to manipulate the input and configure the simulation's parameters that are necessary for the simulation models, which use the BC Modelling Framework. These parameters are classified as a set of files such as Configuration file, Delays file, Latencyfile,

and Throughput received and sent files. Then, users need to attribute these files to the simulation world and indicate the simulation start time and duration. Next, this component returns a variable world that will be shared to different components, providing the availability of all the attributes.

- **Transaction and Node Factory**: This module is responsible for generating transactions, which modelled as random phenomena. Then, when the simulation is running, a random node on a list broadcasts these transactions. Furthermore, the node factory creates the nodes used during the simulation. Users can fix the location, identifier and number of nodes.
- **Programmatic Interface**: It is the main interface accessible to users. They can write their model, use the existing ones to build their BC system, or change aspects of models already implemented using Python language and SimPy. This interface is also responsible for starting the simulation.
- **Monitor and Reports**: The monitor aims to detect metrics during the simulation such as blocks processed, transactions added to the queue, number of transactions each node broadcasts or receives, blocks and transactions propagation time. Thus, metrics can be easily updated by users and automatically collected and stored in the reports component.
- **Blockchain Modelling Framework**: Involves six layers including a node layer, a consensus layer, a ledger layer, a transaction and block layer, a network layer and a Cryptographic layer dedicated to defining cryptographic functions that will be used.

Table 1. Input Parameters/Outputs of BlockSim

Input Parameter	Output
Simtime (s): The length of the simulation time	**TPS**: Average number of transactions processed per second
Btime (s): The average time between two consecutive blocks	
Round (s): The time counter to move the simulator	**TPB**: Average number of transactions per block
Nn: The total number of nodes in the networks	**Latency**: Average confirmation time for transactions
Hi: The hash power of node i	
Bsize: The block size in Byte	**NumBlock**: total number of generated blocks
Bdelay (s): The average propagation delay of a block	**NumBlock-chain**: total number of blocks included in the global chain
Breward: The block reward	
Tn: The average amount of created transactions per second	**Num-discard-Bk**: total number of discarded blocks (stale blocks)
Tdelay (s): The average propagation delay of a transaction	
Tfee: The probability distribution of transaction fee	**Profit.Miner**: the profit gained by each miner
Tsize: The probability distribution of transaction size	
Runs: The number of simulation runs	

Truffle Suite

Truffle Suite (Trufflesuite, 2021). is another tool employed for evaluating private Ethereum-based BC. It includes a set of tools for BC emulation, transaction tracing and smart contacts. Besides, Truffle Suite is composed of three main modules taking into account different operational aspects.

1. **Truffle**: is the development environment integrating the compilation, testing, and smart contracts deployment. Truffle provides the development framework or virtual BC network. The smart contracts could be committed to the network via the truffle commands.
2. **Ganache**: It is the equivalent of the Ethereum wallet in the original Ethereum BC. It is a locally deployed BC simulator containing a graphical user interface that can simulate BC networks and live-test smart contracts without requiring setting up real test networks the values in the wallet fluctuate according to the actual Ethereum pricing.
3. **Drizzle**: is a collection of front-end libraries providing useful components for creating web applications that can seamlessly connect with smart contracts.

During, the setup process all the dependencies must be installed including Ganache, Node.js, Truffle, Atom with solidity Ethereum liner and drizzle. Node.js is a javascript runtime environment running javascript outside the browser, Atom is an editor dedicated to run everything from javascript to solidity. The atom with solidity liner acts as the editor for solidity code. Besides that, Truffle Suite supports development with Quorum, which is an enhanced Ethereum version with new features regarding transaction privacy. In addition, Truffle Suite support also development with other BC such as HyperLedger Fabric (Ban, T. Q. and al, 2019, February), Tezos (Anilkumar, V. and al, 2019, May) and Corda (Ismail, L. and al, 2019, March).

Ethereum Security Verification Tool

Recently, several studies highlighted the need for verifying smart contracts security. Indeed, Smart contracts provide the perfect security storm for the following reasons: (i) Smart contracts designed to store crypto-currency, when stolen it will be transferred irreversibly and it will be difficult to trace the operation. (ii) The money stored in these contracts is high, which make smart contracts a good target to attack incentive. (iii) Contract code stored publicly on the BC, which allows attackers to analyse the system that facilitates attacks. (iv) The Ethereum environment is antagonistic, with several actors including the miners involved in processing transactions and nodes involved in relaying. To fill this gap, several tools proposed to analyze Ethereum security such as Oyente, Remix, Securify, SmartCheck, F* Framework, Mythril, Gasper, VANDL, Rattle and Zeux.

*   **Oyente** (Luu, L. and al, 2016, October) According to the Ethereum community, Oyente recognized to be the most popular security analysis tool. It can analyze both smart contract bytecode and Solidity. It leverages symbolic execution to find potential security vulnerabilities, including timestamp dependence, transaction-ordering dependence, mishandled exceptions and reentrancy. Besides that, Oyente is the only tool that describes its verification method, which eliminates false positives. timestamp-
*   **Remix** (Remix, 2021). is a web-based IDE deployed to edit, compile and debug Solidity smart contracts straight from the browser via the same window. It does not require any setup, just visiting the Remix website. It includes a GUI where you edit code, starts new projects, connects to localhost and commit code. It provides the facility to choose the account and set the gas limit for every commit. Furthermore, it includes a testing environment and a debugger and it serves as a security tool that analyzes the solidity code, to assess potential vulnerability within coding patterns. Among the vulnerabilities detected by, Remix this chapter highlights the following: tx.origin us-

age, block hash usage, timestamp dependence, check effects (reentrancy), gas costly patterns, etc. Remix security testing tool relies on formal verification including theorem provers and deductive program verification.

- **Securify** (Securify, 2021)is another web-based security verification tool (based on the tool website: Securify is the first security analysis tool that provides smart contracts verification). Securify relies on static analysis checks and uses formal verification. The security issues that it supports are transaction reordering, insecure coding patterns, recursive calls, unexpected ether flows, and the use of untrusted input.

- **SmartCheck** (Tikhomirov, S. and al, 2018, May) is a web-based security-code-analysis-tool delivered by SmartDec team developed to check coding practices and to assess the severity level of vulnerabilities. SmartChek analysis run only for Solidity code. It is not specified which methodology used to recognize the vulnerabilities. DoS by external contract, reentrancy, gas costly patterns, locked money, tx.origin usage, timestamp dependency, and unchecked external call are mong the severe vulnerabilities identified by SmartCheck. Besides that, SmartCheck detects other low severity vulnerabilities, for example, compiler version not fixed, style guide violation, and redundant functions.

- **F* Framework** (Bhargavan, K. and al, 2016, October) is a framework dedicated to evaluating the runtime safety and the functional correctness of Ethereum smart contracts. F* Framework based on formal verification. It translates bytecode or Solidity into a functional programming language, after that it identifies the potential vulnerabilities.

- **Mythril** (Bhargavan, K. and al, 2016, October). is an experimental security analysis tool for Hedera, Quorum, Tron, Vechain, Roostock, and other EVM-compatible BCs. It detects security vulnerabilities in smart contracts that are built for Ethereum. Mythril uses symbolic execution, SMT solving and taint analysis to detect a variety of security vulnerabilities. Through a command-line interface, it can analyze bytecode and Solidity code. It can identify a large set of vulnerabilities, including unprotected functions, integer overflow/underflow, reentrancy, and tx.origin usage. Besides, t's also used (in combination with other tools and techniques) in the MythX security analysis platform.

- **Gasper** is a security tool introduced by Chen et al. (Chen, T. and al., 2017, February). It identifies gas costly programming patterns in a smart contract via a command-line interface. It runs analysis only for the bytecode. Moreover, they have discovered seven gas costly patterns. Gasper also relies on symbolic execution to cover all reachable code-blocks by disassembling its bytecode using a disassembler.

- **VANDL**(Brent, L. and al., 2018). uses Souffle (Jordan, H. and al., 2016, July) as the language to express the logic specifications regarding the security analysis. It includes five modules: (1) Vandal's analysis pipeline that transforms Ethereum Virtual Machine (EVM) bytecode to semantic logic relations; (2) Bytecode scraper retrieving EVM bytecode from the BC; (3) Disassembler that translates bytecode into opcodes; (4) Decompiler that translates low-level bytecode to register transfer language; and (5) Extractor that translates this register transfer language into logic semantic relations. Vandal can assess most of the security vulnerabilities, such as unchecked send, unsecured balance, re-entrancy and destroyable contract.

- **ZEUS:** (S Kalra, S. and al., 2018, February) verifies the safe programming practices related to vulnerable smart contracts. It combines a symbolic model checker with an abstract interpreter. ZEUS consists of three modules: policy builder, source code translator, and verifier. It has two inputs, that is, a security policy to verify the vulnerabilities of the smart contract source code written in Solidity. Firstly, ZEUS performs static analysis to check the smart contract code and the policy builder inserts the policy predicates as the declaration statements at the appropriate places in the source code. Secondly, the source code translator converts the source code with the policy assertions to LLVM(Low Level Virtual Machine) bytecode. Finally, the verifier identifies the assertion violations to recognize the vulnerable smart contracts. ZEUS can detect six security vulnerabilities in smart contracts covering unchecked send, re-entrancy bug, failed send, block/transaction state dependence, integer overflow/underflow, and transaction order dependence.

TESTNETS

Testnet (Hu, Y. C. and al., 2018, June) is an alternative to BC for testing. Testnet coins are different from Ether and are not supposed to have any value. Thanks to Testnet, application developers and BC testers can experiment their BC, without using real cryptocurrency or breaking the main BC. During tests, potential problems and vulnerabilities could be easly identified and treated by developers, which is very useful when creating crypto-currencies. Since its appearance, there are three Testnet versions. As a result of trading Testnet coins for real money, Testnet2 was the first Testnet update with a different genesis block. Testnet3 is the actual test network that introduces a third genesis block and solves problems of high difficulty and long time for verification of transactions. Furthermore, it contains blocks with edge-case transactions developed to test implementation compatibility. Testnets used in different BC platforms such as Bitcoin, Ethereum and Hyperledger. In the following, this chapter presents Ethereum Testnets.

Ethereum Public Testnets

Ethereum Testnets (Zhang, L. and al., 2019, August). are copies of the Ethereum BC practically identical to the Main Network (Mainnet) unless the fact that their Ether is worth-less. They have also different protocol features and characteristics. In the following, this section presents public Testnets.

Public Testnets are connected to the Internet and accessible to everyone via wallet interfaces. Ropsten, Kovan, and Rinkeby are the most popular public Testnet and past Testnets such as Olympic, Morden have been abandoned because they have been regularly attacked. In the following, some details regarding Ropsten, Kovan, Rinkeby, Gorli and Ganache CLI Testnets.

- **Ropsten** (Ropston, 2019): is a PoW Testnet for Ethereum supported by Geth and Parity. It runs the same protocol as Ethereum and is utilized for the test before deploying on the Main Network. Ropsten results are similar to Mainnet results because its consensus mechanism is PoW. Thus, any computer connecting to the Ropsten network can mine for test Ether, which makes transactions simulation more realistic.
- **Kovan** (Kovan, 2021): launched by the Parity team in March 2017 in response to the Ropsten spam attacks. It works only with the Parity node, so access is impossible for Geth users. In place of mining with PoW, Kovan uses PoA as a consensus mechanism. It prevents malicious actors to acquire large amounts of Ether and it provides Ether to authorized developers via a slow-release faucet service. It is the most used Testnet by Ethereum developers.

- **Rinkeby** (Rinkeby, 2021): is a PoA Testnet initiated by the Ethereum team in April 2017. It has the same advantages as Kovan with two modifications: it works only with Geth therefore it doesn't support Parity, and it uses a lightly different PoA consensus mechanism. Similar to Kovan and Rinkeby Ether are requested from an authorized faucet.
- **G˙orli** (Gorli, 2021): is the most recent Testnet set up started by the Parity team in September 2018. It utilizes PoA and it can support popular Ethereum clients such as Parity and Geth. G˙orli is compatible with all client implementations and it is robust enough to guarantee availability and reliability.
- **Ganache CLI**: Previously known as the TestRPC, Ganache CLI (Ganche, 2021) is a part of the Truffle Suite of Ethereum development tools. It is a NodeJS package that simulates full client behaviour and accelerates developing Ethereum applications. Including all popular RPC functions and features, GanacheCLI allows users to mine transactions instantly and to modify Gas price and mining speed. Ganache CLI is a fast and customizable (GanacheCli, 2021) BC emulator. It can be a desktop application and a command-line tool and it is supported by various operating systems such as Mac, Windows, and Linux.

Authors in (Hu, Y. C. and al., 2018, June) conducted extensive experiments on Ropsten, Rinkeby, and Kovan Ethereum Testnets to study interactions between smart contracts. They considered hierarchical interactions where one contract named custodian could deploy on-demand client contract, call their methods and access their data to perform updates. In the following table 2 and table 3 clarifies the main difference between most known public Ethereum Testnets.

Table 2. Brief Comparison between Public Ethereum Testnets.

TestNet	Consensus	Supported Clients	Avg. Block Times	M or F	Pros	Cons
Ropsten	PoW	Parity and Geth	14 sec	Mineable	Reproduces the current production environment. Can be used with both geth and parity	Vulnerable to spam attacks
Kovan	PoA	Parity	4 sec	Faucet	Immune to spam attacks.	It does not reproduce totally the production environment. Ether can't be mined
Rinkeby	PoA	Geth	15	Faucet	Immune to spam attacks.	It does not reproduce totally the production environment. Ether can't be mined
G˙orli	PoA	Multiclients		Faucet	Multi-clients	Unstable

Private Ethereum Testnets

Ethereum software enables a user to set up a private Ethereum chain that is separated from the main Ethereum chain. A private test network (Alphand, O. and al., 2018, April) is similar to a personal BC or user's own copy of Ethereum. User can mine or generate his own Ethereum from this network. In addition, private Testnets are very useful for teamwork and closed environments that simulate mining and transaction confirmations locally without the need to expose their network to the outside world and to avoid the risk of spam attacks. After a private Test network has been developed sufficiently, it can be exposed to the public. A private Testnet needs four components:

1. **Custom Genesis Block**: it is the zero block in a blockchain. Normally, it is hard coded into the clients, however on Ethereum, it is flexible.
2. **Data Directory**: it is the location where private chain data can be stored.
3. **Custom NetworkID**: it is a unique ID used in Ethereum networks composed of random numbers to shun syncing with other networks (Iyer, K., and Dannen, C., 2018).
4. **Disable Node Discovery**: it is a command line used to protect node against being discovered and accidentally added by developers.

Table 3. Brief Comparison between Ethereum Testnets.

TestNet	Language	Scalability	Speed	Security	Complexity	1	2	3
Ropsten	Go, Rust	Yes	Yes	Not immune to spam attacks	M	Y	Y	H
Kovan	Rust (Parity)	Yes	Yes	Immune to Spam attacks	Nm	X	X	L
Rinkeby	Go (Geth)	Yes	Yes	Immune to Spam attacks	Nm	X	X	L
G'orli	Go (Geth) Rust	Yes	Yes	Immune to Spam attacks	Nm	X	X	L
Ganache CLI	JavaScript	Nm	Nm	Nm	Nm	X	Y	L

Legend:; 1=Mining blocs; 2=Configuration; 3=Computing power; Y= supported; X=doesn't support; H=High; L=Low ; M=Medium; Nm=Not mentioned.

OPEN ISSUES AND FUTURE DIRECTIONS

In order to empower an efficient application of the Ethereum technology within different fields and domains, the Ethereum communities assessed several directions and issues for making practical and interoperable Ethereum networks and applications. In the following, we highlight some open issues and future direction regarding Ethereum platform and tools.

Scalability

The concern that limits the growth of public BC is scalability. The public network increases quickly in terms of data and participants due to the lack of restriction for a user to join the network, this lead to communication overhead since the number of block and transactions validations increases with the growth of the user's number, which puts a problem on the network scalability. Therefore, BC scalability should be always addressed and evaluated. Several new paradigms, concepts and approaches are introduced to fill this gap, but their validation still requires more investigations and analysis. Those approaches include:

- **Lighting network**: Lightning network is a layer on top of the BC network that lets users to perform transactions off-chain via channels without waiting for the block to be processed.
- **Sharding:** The nodes divided into shards, and the transactions are distributed among the shards in parallel for verification. Sharding enhances the transactions throughput with increasing number of shards. However, this concept is still under development and still require deep performance analysis with different existing BC networks.
- **Quantum money:** Authors in (Coladangelo, A., & Sattath, O., 2020) showed that SCs can be joint with quantum tools, in particular quantum lightning, to conceive a decentralized payment system solving the transactions scalability issue. The only approach related to quantum lightning relies on a computational assumption about multi-collision resistance of certain degree-2 hash functions. Discovering alternative constructions of quantum lightning, is an interesting open issue require more investigation. Smart contracts application to quantum cryptographic tasks is also unexplored.

Throughput

Before processing, every transaction in a BC network it requires peer-to-peer verifications. This task is time-consuming, especially in a public BC network involving a greater number of users, where every user validates the transaction. Subsequently, the throughput related to a BC network should be high enough to ensure the BC scalability. Developers and researchers have been working on increasing the performance of the BC technology when used at large-scale. New consensus mechanisms appeared with the goal to enhance the throughput of different BC platforms. In this context, the use of linked transactions instead of linked blocks is an interesting approach; however, this concept face challenges requiring more investigations.

Data Privacy

In the digital era of data transmission, data is shared online. Therefore, it is important that the data does not get into the wrong hands. This lead to a potential need for preserving privacy of the data The pseudo-anonymity property of the public BC network makes the transactions data visible to the public, which become a problem with sensitive data and with multi-party transactions in the network. To tackle this issue new methods appear such as the use of deterministic wallets, channels, and private network. Within private Ethereum networks, a group of trusted members has the authority to modify the network. To preserve privacy within Ethereum, authors in (Kumar, E. S., 2020) proposed two algorithms chaotic maps and the other on the diferential privacy to encrypt the edge weights of the transaction network, which in turn leads to addition of the noise into the data set before release to the public. Besides that, ensuring full privacy preserving Dapp on top of Ethereum is an open issue requiring more investigation.

Smart Contracts Vulnerabilities and Mitigations

Research on SC vulnerability is also vital, particularly as the usage of SCs expands. There is a need to design automated tools (e.g., using machine learning) identifying vulnerabilities in smart contracts, for the diverse SC languages and platforms in particular for Ethereum plateform. Machine learning can be used to check complex logic bugs and verify whether smart contract behaviors are expected. However, the challenging aspect in using machine learning is the lack of training datasets, to fill this gap, formal verification on smart contracts should be an interesting research direction that should be more explored.

LEARNED LESSONS AND CONCLUSION

BC systems are complex systems. That is why it is required to develop methods to evaluate these systems. Using simulators or emulators is one of the proposed solutions. Nevertheless, emulation causes a high power consumption, enormous overhead, and lack of scalability, therefore, an alternative approach is to use Testnets and simulators to evaluate a large-scale system in an unacceptable time. Besides that, in the real BC, participants must pay a transaction fee to encourage miners to validate the transactions and protect the network against spamming. A simulator considered as a replica of the original BC while maintaining its technology and functionalities. Transactions on the simulator are simulated (fake) with coins that do not have any real value. Furthermore, to evaluate a simulator, various metrics are taken into consideration. Indeed, the evaluation can be according to network characteristics (e.g. throughput, topology, latency, bandwidth, number of nodes) or BC system characteristics (e.g. number of miners, block size, block confirmation time, number of transactions per block, percentage of attacker nodes, percentage of failing nodes). This chapter presents a comprehensive study of Ethereum simulators useful for analyzing and evaluating Ethereum-based systems. Accordingly, the authors have considered in this chapter several emulators and simulators corresponding to BlockSim, BlockBench, TruffleSuite and several Ethereum security verification tools. Furthermore, Testnets are very useful for developers and researchers; therefore, the authors examined the most known and used Testnets dedicated to Ethereum platform with focus on their architectures. In this chapter, the authors compared simulators and Testnets by considering the most common metrics that put in evidence the simulators and Testnets performance (scalability, speed, security, complexity, fault tolerance, mining bloc, and configuration and computing power). Besides that, the authors recommend using Ethereum due to its advantages in terms of usability, security, currency and support and development tools. Ethereum uses the advanced encryption technologies for key generation such as elliptic curve and SHA 3. Furthermore, Solidity as Ethereum programming language is user friendly because it is a combination of Java script and C++. In addition, the Ethereum operation mode is permissionless and can work in both private and public modes that is crucial in testing. Furthermore, Ethereum has a huge community committing millions of transactions every week. The support provided by the community is very much beneficial to new developers.

Tables 4 and 5 recapitulate and summarize the most concepts and definitions within Ethereum platform, Ethereum simulators and emulators, and Ethereum Testnets.

Finally, the authors are convinced that the content of this book chapter will help researcher to select the suitable Ethereum tools required for their work.

Table 4.

Ethereum Emulators and Simulators and Security Verification Tools
Blockbench: is an evaluation framework for analyzing private BC platforms. It can be integrated into BC platforms using simple APIs and benchmarks against workloads based on synthetic and real SC.
BlockSim: is a discrete-event simulator simulating different BC models. It pursues a stochastic simulation model representing a random phenomenon by sampling from a probability distribution.
Truffle Suite: it evaluates private Ethereum-based BC. It includes a set of tools for BC emulation, transaction tracing and smart contacts. It is composed of Truffle, Ganache and Drizzle modules.
Oyente: is the popular Ethereum security analysis tool. It can analyze both SC bytecode and Solidity. **Remix:** is a web-based IDE deployed to edit, compile and debug Solidity smart contracts straight from the browser via the same window. It relies on formal verification. **Securify:** is a web-based security verification tool. It is the first security analysis tool that provides SCs verification. It relies on static analysis checks and uses formal verification.
SmartCheck: is a web-based security-code-analysis-tool. It checks coding practices and assesses the severity level of vulnerabilities. SmartChek analysis run only for Solidity code. **F* Framework:** is dedicated to evaluating the runtime safety and the functional correctness of Ethereum SCs. It translates bytecode or Solidity into a functional programming language, after that it identifies the potential vulnerabilities. **Mythril:** is an experimental security analysis tool for Hedera, Quorum, Tron, Vechain, Roostock, and other EVM-compatible BCs. It detects security vulnerabilities in smart contracts (SCs).
Gasper is a security tool that identifies gas costly programming patterns in a SC via a command-line interface. It runs analysis only for the bytecode. It relies on symbolic execution. **VANDL:** uses Souffle as the language to express the logic specifications regarding the security analysis. It can assess most of the security vulnerabilities, such as unchecked send, unsecured balance, re-entrancy and destroyable contract. **ZEUS:** verifies the safe programming practices related to vulnerable SCs. It combines a symbolic model checker with an abstract interpreter. It includes policy builder, source code translator, and verifier.

Table 5.

Public Ethereum Testnets
Ropsten: is a PoW Testnet supported by Geth and Parity [58]. It runs the same protocol as Ethereum and is utilized for the test before deploying on the Main Network.
Kovan: launched by the Parity in response to the Ropsten spam attacks. It works only with the Parity node. It uses PoA as a consensus mechanism. It is the most used Testnet by Ethereum developers.
Rinkeby: is a PoA Testnet. It has the same advantages as Kovan with two modifications: it works only with Geth and it uses a lightly different PoA consensus mechanism.
G´orli: is the recent Testnet . It utilizes PoA and it can support popular Ethereum clients such as Parity and Geth. G´orli is compatible with all client implementations and it is robust enough. **Ganache CLI:** Previously known as the TestRPC, Ganache CLI is a part of the Truffle Suite. It is a NodeJS package that simulates full client behaviour and accelerates developing Ethereum applications. Including all popular RPC functions and features.

REFERENCES

Alharby, M., & van Moorsel, A. (2020). *Blocksim: An extensible simulation tool for blockchain systems.* arXiv preprint arXiv:2004.13438.

Alphand, O., Amoretti, M., Claeys, T., Dall'Asta, S., Duda, A., Ferrari, G., ... Zanichelli, F. (2018, April). IoTChain: A blockchain security architecture for the In-ternet of Things. In *2018 IEEE Wireless Communications and Networking Conference(WCNC)* (pp. 1-6). IEEE.

Anilkumar, V., Joji, J. A., Afzal, A., & Sheik, R. (2019, May). Blockchain Simulation and Development platforms: Survey, Issues and Challenges. In *2019 International Conference on Intelligent Computing and Control Systems (ICCS)* (pp. 935-939). Academic Press.

Ban, T. Q., Anh, B. N., Son, N. T., & Van Dinh, T. (2019, February). Survey of Hyperledger Blockchain Frameworks: Case Study in FPT University's Cryptocurrency Wallets. In *Proceedings of the 2019 8th International Conference on Software and Computer Applications* (pp. 472-480). Academic Press.

Bhargavan, K., Delignat-Lavaud, A., Fournet, C., Gollamudi, A., Gonthier, G., Kobeissi, N., ... Zanella-Béguelin, S. (2016, October). Formal verification of smart contracts: *Short paper*. In *Proceedings of the 2016 ACM workshop on programming languages and analysis for security* (pp. 91-96). ACM.

Brent, L., Jurisevic, A., Kong, M., Liu, E., Gauthier, F., Gramoli, V., . . . Scholz, B. (2018). *Vandal: A scalable security analysis framework for smart contracts.* arXiv preprint arXiv:1809.03981.

Chakraborty, P., Shahriyar, R., Iqbal, A., & Bosu, A. (2018, October). Understanding the software development practices of blockchain projects: a survey. In *Proceedings of the 12th ACM/IEEE International Symposium on Empirical Software Engineering and Measurement* (pp. 1-10). 10.1145/3239235.3240298

Chen, T., Li, X., Luo, X., & Zhang, X. (2017, February). Under-optimized smart contracts devour your money. In *2017 IEEE 24th International Conference on Software Analysis, Evolution and Reengineering (SANER)* (pp. 442-446). IEEE.

Coladangelo, A., & Sattath, O. (2020). A quantum money solution to the blockchain scalability problem. *Quantum, 4,* 297.

Dinh, T. T. A., Wang, J., Chen, G., Liu, R., Ooi, B. C., & Tan, K. L. (2017, May). Blockbench: A framework for analyzing private blockchains. In *Proceedings of the 2017 ACM International Conference on Management of Data* (pp. 1085-1100). 10.1145/3035918.3064033

Faria, C., & Correia, M. (2019, July). BlockSim: Blockchain Simulator. In *2019 IEEE International Conference on Blockchain (Blockchain)* (pp. 439-446). 10.1109/Blockchain.2019.00067

Ganache. (2021). https://github.com/trufflesuite/ganache-cli

GanacheCli. (2021). https://docs.nethereum.com/en/latest/ethereum-and-clients/ganache-cli/

Goerli. (2021). https://goerli.net/

Hu, Y. C., Lee, T. T., Chatzopoulos, D., & Hui, P. (2018, June). Hierarchical interactions between ethereum smart contracts across testnets. In *Proceedings of the 1st Workshop on Cryptocurrencies and Blockchains for Distributed Systems* (pp. 7-12). Academic Press.

Ismail, L., Hameed, H., AlShamsi, M., AlHammadi, M., & AlDhanhani, N. (2019, March). Towards a Blockchain Deployment at UAE University: Performance Evaluation and Blockchain Taxonomy. In *Proceedings of the 2019 International Conference on Blockchain Technology* (pp. 30-38). Academic Press.

Iyer, K., & Dannen, C. (2018). The ethereum development environment. In Building games with ethereum smart contracts (pp. 19-36). Apress.

Jordan, H., Scholz, B., & Subotić, P. (2016, July). Soufflé: On synthesis of program analyzers. In *International Conference on Computer Aided Verification* (pp. 422-430). Springer.

Kalra, S. S., Goel, S., Dhawan, M., & Sharma, S. (2018, February). ZEUS: Analyzing Safety of Smart Contracts. In Ndss (pp. 1-12). Academic Press.

Kovan. (2021). https://kovan.etherscan.io/

Kumar, E. S. (2020). Preserving privacy in ethereum blockchain. *Annals of Data Science*, 1-19.

Luu, L., Chu, D. H., Olickel, H., Saxena, P., & Hobor, A. (2016, October). Making smart contracts smarter. In *Proceedings of the 2016 ACM SIGSAC conference on computer and communictions security* (pp. 254-269). ACM.

Pandey, S., Ojha, G., & Shrestha, B. (2019, May). BlockSIM: A practical simulationtool for optimal network design, stability and planning. In *2019 IEEE International Conference on Blockchain and Cryptocurrency (ICBC)* (pp. 133-137). 10.1109/BLOC.2019.8751320

Remix. (2021). https://remix.ethereum.org/

Rinkeby. (2021). https://www.rinkeby.io/

Ropston. (2019). *Testnet ropsten (eth) blockchain explorer*. https://ropsten.etherscan.io/

Securify. (2021). https://securify.ch

Tikhomirov, S., Voskresenskaya, E., Ivanitskiy, I., Takhaviev, R., Marchenko, E., & Alexandrov, Y. (2018, May). Smartcheck: Static analysis of ethereum smart contracts. In *Proceedings of the 1st International Workshop on Emerging Trends in Software Engineering for Blockchain* (pp. 9-16). Academic Press.

Trufflesuite. (2021). https://www.trufflesuite.com/

Wood, G. (2014). Ethereum: A secure decentralised generalised transaction ledger. *Ethereum Project Yellow Paper*, *151*(2014), 1-32.

Zhang, L., Lee, B., Ye, Y., & Qiao, Y. (2019, August). Ethereum Transaction Performance Evaluation Using Test-Nets. In *European Conference on Parallel Processing* (pp. 179-190). Springer.

Zheng, P., Zheng, Z., Luo, X., Chen, X., & Liu, X. (2018, May). A detailed and real-time performance monitoring framework for blockchain systems. In *2018 IEEE/ACM 40th International Conference on Software Engineering: Software Engineering in Practice Track (ICSE-SEIP)* (pp. 134-143). IEEE.

KEY TERMS AND DEFINITIONS

Block: A block contains a set of transactions, timestamp, a hash of the previous block, and a block number.

Blockchain: Is a data structure used to create a distributed and an open ledger that can record transactions between two entities. A BC is composed of blocks in a serialized manner.

Consensus: A set of algorithms ensure the consistency of BC.

Cryptocurrency: A kind of digital currency using encryption techniques.

Gas: Is a unit of measurement for computational steps. Every transaction is required to include a gas limit and a fee that it is willing to pay per gas.

IPFS: InterPlanetary File System is a decentralized filesystem. It uses DHT (distributed hash table) and Merkle DAG (directed acyclic graph) data structures. IPFS supports file versioning.

Ledger: Is a list of transactions. A database is different from a ledger. In a ledger, we can only add new transactions; however, in a database, we can add, modify, and delete transactions.

Merkle Tree: A data structure in hash-based cryptography, deployed in Bitcoin and Ethereum.

Mining: A peer-to-peer computer process used to secure and verify transactions.

Quantum Resistant Ledger (QRL): A technique to tackle the threats to cryptocurrency.

Smart Contracts: Self-executing contractual states stored on the BC.

Web3.js: A collection of libraries to interact with remote or local Ethereum node.

Chapter 2
Platforms and Tools Within the HyperLedger Framework

Iamia Chaari Fourati
Higher Institute of Computer Science and Multimedia of Sfax, Tunisia

Taher Layeb
Higher Institute of Computer Science and Multimedia of Sfax, Tunisia

Achraf Haddaji
Higher Institute of Computer Science and Multimedia of Sfax, Tunisia

Samiha Ayed
University of Technology of Troyes, France

Wiem Bekri
ENET'COM, Tunisia

ABSTRACT

During this last decade, the blockchain (BC) paradigm is being required in several use cases and scenarios in particular for security, privacy, and trust provisioning. Accordingly, the research community and developers developed several emulation tools and frameworks for BC-based systems performance analysis. Making an adequate decision regarding the choice of the most suitable tool that can be used to develop and validate the performances of a specific BC-based system or application still requires more investigation. In this context, this chapter describes and highlights the most features and characteristics of the BC platforms and tools within the Hyperledger framework. The goal is to illustrate the advantages and the limitations of several BC tools and development environments within Hyperledger. In addition, this chapter provides an insight into BC 3.0 as the new generation of BC that meets the requirements of the smart application.

DOI: 10.4018/978-1-7998-5839-3.ch002

INTRODUCTION

Nowadays, the BlockChain (BC) technology is considered the most relevant invention after the Internet. There are three phases or generations of the BC development: BC 1.0 as digital currency, BC 2.0 as digital economy, and BC 3.0 as a digital society. This diversity requires the analysis of the BC technological innovation aspects that necessitates the design, development, and deployment of BC emulation tools and BC dedicated environments and frameworks. Therefore, the development of BC related tools gained huge interests from the software development community. BC Software (BCS) development tasks, BC testing support, BC emulators and frameworks, as well as debuggers for smart contracts have certain particularities and specific technical aspects. These findings motivate the authors to study and compare the technical aspects of BC related tools within the Hyperledger framework.

The fact that the development of BC applications on a BC network is costly leading to the necessity of using a simulation platform to test the BC-based applications and systems before their real deployments. Besides that, the number of available BC tools and emulation platforms is rapidly increasing, which complicate the choice of suitable emulation platforms and tools that fulfil the user requirements. Therefore, researchers need advice and guidelines to select a suitable tool that fit their applications needs. To the best of our knowledge, although the high number of the developed BC tools and benchmarks, there are few studies dedicated to explaining the functionalities, usages and the best practices of the different Hyperledger emulation tools, benchmarking, frameworks and utilities. Accordingly, this book chapter will fill this gap and presents a comprehensive investigation related to platforms and tools for hyperledger-based systems performance analysis. Therefore, this study will provide a wide-ranging view of hyperledger plteforms and tools. Indeed, the manifolds of this chapter could be summarized into four points:

- Providing an overview regarding BC fundamentals
- Discussing and comparing the most known BC platforms.
- Analyzing the potentialities of Hyperledger benchmarks and tools to evaluate the performance of BC-based systems. Accordingly, a comparative investigation drew to guide the researchers in their choice of adequate Hyperledger tools.
- Highlighting potential open issues and future research directions that can be beneficial for the development and the deployment of BC-based solutions based on the use or exploitation of the Hyperledger framework.

The rest of this chapter organized as follows: The second section pinpoints the BC basic concepts corresponding to BC characteristics, structure and categories. The third section discusses and compares BC platforms. The fourth section provides basic knowledge's regarding Hyperledger frameworks and draws a comparative study between Hyperledger distributed ledgers and tools. The fifth section highlights potential open issues and future research directions related to the exploitation of the Hyperledger framework. Finally, the last section concludes this chapter and summarizes lessons learned via this chapter.

BLOCKCHAIN FUNDAMANTALS

BC, initiated from Bitcoin, is a continuously growing list of records, called blocks that are linked and secured via cryptography functions. A BC is a specific implementation of a Distributed Ledger (DL). A DL is essentially a distributed database of registrations or a public ledger that register transactions and events executed between peers. In practice, all the network nodes share the same copy of the database. Any change made on a node replicated to all the other nodes. Using BC eliminates the need for the third party for verification and does not require a central authority. Since the generation of Bitcoin, by Satoshi Nakamoto (Nakamoto.S, 2019) in 2009, the BC has been exploited in different areas rather than crypto-currencies such as e-finance, e-healthcare (Mettler, M. 2016, September), smart home, Internet of Things (IoT) (Dorri, A. and al, 2017, March), industry (Sikorski, J. and al, 2017), society (Aste, T. and al, 2017) and logistics.

BlockChain Characteristics

BC systems, with the characteristics of irreversibility, decentralization, and traceability, have attracted many attentions. Nevertheless, the constraint of BC-based systems is that the current BC performance is still weak. In the following, we highlight the main BC technology characteristics (Peters, G. and al, 2015):

- **Decentralized control**: a decentralized model that eliminates central authority.
- **Data transparency and audibility**: every transaction executed in a BC is saved and shared as a public copy to all the peers to trace and verify all previous transactions.
- **Distribute information:** every network node keeps a full copy of the BC to prevent that a centralized authority keeps all the information.
- **Decentralized consensus:** all the network nodes instead of a central entity assure the transaction's validation.
- **Secure:** the BC is a proof tampered system; this means that malicious actors cannot manipulate it.
- **Persistency**: concerning the inability of altering or deleting the transactions if they are recorded in the ledger.
- **Anonymity**: based on the asymmetric cryptography and hashing of BC data (digital cryptographic keys, transactions...).

Thanks to the mentioned properties, BC has quickly grown and widely been used in the last few years. Predictions ensure that global BC technology profits will testify to enormous growth in the coming years, with the market expected to increase to over 23.3 billion U.S. dollars in size by 2023 (Statista, 2020).

BlockChain Structure and Architecture

BC is a chain of blocks, which constitute the ledger that holds a permanent record of transactions accessing the distributed and decentralized BC network. Each block within the BC keeps a copy of the ledger containing all transactions details and the exchanged asset such as Ether and Bitcoin. All ledger copies updated and validated simultaneously. The ledger is composed of a set of blocks as shown in fig. 1.

Figure 1. Simple structure of a BlockChain

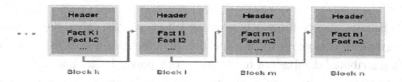

In the following, we define the main entities within a BC system.

- **Block:** used to record a set of transactions that occurred during a fixed period. Each block contains two parts: the body (content) and the header. The block header records the basic information (e.g., parent hash, hash, timestamp, Merkle-tree root, difficulty, nonce, etc.). The block content records the number of transactions and the transaction details. The body defines the transactions (called facts), that the database record. Facts can be monetary transactions or other types of data. The block header includes information concerning the block such as the timestamp and the transaction hash of the previous block. All the blocks form a chain of linked and ordered blocks. If a malicious user wants to attack the BC or to modify a transaction, it should modify all the blocks because their hashes link them.

- **Chain:** Chain includes several linked blocks. For illustration, in Bitcoin BC, each block identified with a hash value. Every newly generated block should record the hash value of the previous block, which known as a parent hash. Thus, we can search a sequence from the first block to the last block using the records related to the parent hash.

- **Transaction**: A transaction represents an operation of the ledger, such as transferring money (In the case of Bitcoin). BC includes two types of participant objects: objects that can only read facts and objects that can read and write facts that are named miners. Miner has to package the transactions into blocks and then should join them to a chain. To add a new block, the following steps must be respected: (i) Transactions grouped in a block. (ii) Miners check if block transactions conform to the defined rules. (iii) Miners validate the added block by executing a consensus mechanism. (iv) A reward is given to miners who validate the block. (v) Finally, the verified transactions will be stored in the BC.

- **Consensus:** The validation of blocks is one of the most important tasks within BC. Consensus algorithms (Bach, L. and al, 2018, May) have been designed for this aim, such as Proof of Work (PoW) (Gervais, A. and al, 2016, October), Proof of Stake (PoS) (Saleh, F., 2018), Proof of Capacity (PoC) (Pohrmen, F. H., and al, 2019) or Proof of Burn (PoB) (Karantias, K. and al, 2019).

Furthermore, to overcome certain BC limitation related to real-time aspects and scalability issues, many BCs enhancing their performance by modifying the system architecture and structure and by designing new consensus algorithms.

Besides that, fundamentally the BC architecture can be structured into four layers, which are the infrastructure layer, the platform layer, the distributed computing layer and the application layer. In the following, a brief description layer by layer of the BC architecture:

1. **The infrastructure layer**: includes the hardware components required to run the BC, such as storage, nodes, and network facilities. The nodes are the network participants. A typical BC network has three different types of nodes: light node (simple), full node, and mining. A light node in the network can just send and receive transactions and does not store a copy of the ledger neither validate a transaction. A mining node (known as a block generator) is a full node with the capability of mining. The storage component stores the ledger of the transaction records.
2. **The platform layer**: facilitates Remote Procedure Calls (RPC), REpresentational State Transfer (REST) API's and web Application Programming Interface (API) for the communication between the network participants.
3. **The distributed computing layer**: ensures local access to data, immutability, privacy, fault tolerance, authenticity, and security for the transaction data. It includes consensus protocols, transactions in the network. In addition, this layer is responsible for user authentication by using an encryption and hashing techniques for data privacy
4. **The application layer**: is the business logic for digital asset transactions and the execution of smart contracts. An application developed on top of a BC network can be accessed by the clients using the platform layer.

BlockChain Categories

There are three BC types: private or permissioned, public or permissionless, and consortium chains.

*   **Permissionless BC (public)**: is described as the new technology that permits sharing records to be shared by all network peers, owned and controlled by no one, updated by miners, and monitored by everyone. In permissionless BC, intermediaries or central authorities not required, and transaction records remain immutable once added to the BC. Decentralization is the main permissionless BC benefit. However, the speed limit regarding processing large volumes of transactions and the absence of a centralized authority to validate the existence, the ownership, and the value of items recorded on BC, and to report cyber-attacks are the main permissionless BC drawbacks.
*   **Permissioned BC (private):** refers to BC with restrictions in its control and membership procedures. In permissioned BC, an intrinsic configuration is required to define the roles of participants in which certain members can read, write information on the BC, or approve admission of new members. Since members have different access control authorizations, a permissioned BC considered partially decentralized. Besides that, a permissioned BC is not completely trustless; transactions could be rolled back by a centralized agency with override authority. The main advantage of a permissioned BC is to maintain privacy via an appropriate deployment of an access-control layer.
*   **Consortium BC:** The main difference between the private BC and the consortium BC is for private BC a single authority or organization has to look after the network, and for the consortium BC, multiple authorities and organization are the owners of the BC.

Table 1 pinpoints the major differences between the three BC categories.

Table 1. Brief comparison between BC categories

Parameters	Public	Private	Consortium
Read permission	Anyone	Invited users only	Depends
Write permission	Anyone	Approved users	Approved users
Ownership	Nobody	Single entity	Multiple entities
Participant	No	Yes	Yes
Transaction speed	Slow	Fast	Fast
Central Authority	Decentralized	Complete	Partial
Transaction Mutability	Cannot be tampered	Alteration is possible	Can be altered
Block Authentication	All	Specific organization	Selected nodes
Asset	Native Asset	Any Asset	Native Asset
Security	Proof of Stack	Pre-approved participants	Proof of Work
Identity	Anonymous	Known Identities	Pseudonymous

BLOCKCHAIN MAIN PLATFORMS

BC platforms provide the low-level implementation details related to ledger organization and transaction, consensus algorithms and incorporate a high level API to integrate for application developers. This ensures rapid design and deployment of BC applications. To date, there are several BCs platforms, the first part of this subsection introduces and compares Bitcoin, Ethereum, Hyperledger platforms and the second part pinpoints some of the leading platforms in the permissioned ledger space such as Corda, Quorum, and Multichain.

- **Bitcoin:** is the first generated BC. A crypto-currency serves as a digital financial asset. It uses public cryptography key, peer-to-peer networking and PoW to create and verify transactions. A new block created every 10 minutes (Vinayak, M., 2019). because the Bitcoin system is programmed as well. A fork becomes a stale block if it is not a part of the longest computationally chain. In Bitcoin, there are no balances, but there are Unspent Transaction Outputs (UTXO) in the BC. At any instant, some Bitcoins are received, they are saved as UTXO. When a client sends a Bitcoin, this means that a UTXO related to the receiver's address has been created. A transaction output made up of two main fields, the amount and a locking script. The locking script determines conditions to satisfy to spend the UTXO, and the smallest amount to be sent is called asatoshi (Novo, O, 2018).
- **Ethereum:** To facilitate the development of decentralized applications, Ethereum (Wood, G., 2014) is a distributed computing platform built on BC technology designed in 2013. It has a large development community and it is open-source. It supports a diversity of use-cases. Furthermore, Ethereum has its crypto-currency named Ether and a currency to pay for computations and transactions fees called Gas. Using Ethereum, Smart Contracts and Distributed Applications (DApps) built and executed without the need of a third party. Ethereum is not only a platform but also a Turing complete language used to create contracts and to build and publish distributed applications. Ethereum started using proof of work as its consensus mechanism, but it is soon switching

to proof of stake. Ethereum block creation time is remarkably lower than many other systems (Lee, W. M). Besides that, the new version of Ethereum client appears such as Parity (Parity, 2017) that provides another consensus protocol called PoA (Proof of Authority). With PoA, developers can build up consortium BC with higher throughput than the PoW chains of the legacy Ethereum version.

- **Hyperledger:** (Androulaki, E. and al, 2018, April) is an open-source created by the Linux Foundation to develop a suite of frameworks, tools and libraries for the industry. It follows the logic of Bitcoin script and UTXO as a reward. Hyperledger exploits the UTXO and the logic of script used by Bitcoin. It also uses Practical Byzantine Fault Tolerant (PBFT) as a consensus mechanism instead of the PoW algorithm. PBFT is a mechanism utilized generally in distributed networks and it is known to treat thousands of requests per second.

In general, the technical choices of BC technology include mainly four issues:

1. Permission design: whether permission needed or not to access the BC;
2. Choice of the consensus algorithm, i.e., how a new block is added to the BC;
3. Whether or not to use smart contracts, i.e., whether to use the BC as a virtual machine where programs representing business processes are running;
4. Whether or not to use a crypto-currency, i.e., whether the consensus algorithm and smart contract operations depend on an artificial currency or not.

Taking into consideration those technical choices, table 2 presents a Brief comparison between Bit-Coin, Ethereum and Hyperledger.

Table 2. Brief comparison between BitCoin, Ethereum and Hyperledger

Parameters	Hyperledger	Ethereum	BitCoin
Languages	Java	Golang Python	Golang C++
Crypto-currency	None, but can be implemented if required	Ether	Bitcoin
Consensus	PBFT (for Fabric)	Ethash(PoW) or Casper (PoS).	PoW
Network Type	Permissioned	Public	Public
Smart Contract Language	Yes (chaincode)	Yes (Solidity)	Limited
Confidentiality	Confidential Transactions	Transparent Transactions	Transparent Transactions
Transaction Mutability	Cannot be tampered	Alteration is possible	Can be altered
Compute-intensive	No	Partially	Yes
Throughput	High	Low	Very Low
Latency	100 ms(Fabric)	12 Second	10 Minutes
Immutability	Low	High	High
Privacy	High	Low	Low

During the last few years, new dedicated BC and ledgers appeared such as Hedera (Baird, L. and al, 2019), Corda (Brown, R. G. and al, 2016), Quorum (Quorum Whitepaper, 2020) and MultiChain BC plateforms. Most of BC platforms equally perform when considering relevant features, such as decentralisation, fraud resistance, trust, accountability, and so forth, due to their distributed and immutable nature. Consequently, another set of features should be considered for BC platform comparison such as simplicity, cost, size of the community, ease of learning, ease of use, level of support, performance, availability of training materials, security, reputation, history, updates or release of newer versions, ease of developing advanced features such as APIs, support of web development, type of software licenses .... In this context authors in (Nanayakkara, S. and al, 2021) presented a methodology for selection of a BC Platform to develop an enterprise system. The proposed methodology comprised of four stages; identification, selection, evaluation and validation. Initially, the available BC platforms will be identified followed by selecting a suitable BC platform using a Multi Attribute Rating Technique (SMART). Subsequently, the selected system should be evaluated in detail considering the system architecture, libraries, tools, domain-specific applications and capability analysis of the selected BC platform. In the following, this chapter will focus only on Hyperledger framework.

HYPERLEDGER FRAMEWORKS

Hyperledger BCs (Ban, T. Q. and al, 2019, February). introduced as a multi-ledger-based architecture for a private network to enable private and confidential transactions between participants within an organization. The multi-ledger-based architecture can be deployed in applications domains involving several collaborating organizations (such as collaborating universities, hospitals or banks) that require the guarantee of transactions confidentiality. In this regards, Hyperledger concentrates on permissioned BC frameworks affording complete support for organizations and companies that have their applications based on BC technology. Fig. 2 represents the greenhouse (Blummer, T. and al, 2018) of Hyperledger highlighting supported distributed ledgers, tools and libraries. Table 3 compares and highlights the main differences between distributed legers supported by hyperledger framework.

Figure 2. Hyperledger framework
(Blummer, T. and al, 2018)

Distributed Ledgers

Hyperledger Fabric

Hyperledger Fabric is a permissioned BC platform and one of the projects created by Linux Foundation (Mohammad, A. F., 2019). that includes leaders in banking, finance, supply chains, manufacturing, Internet of Things (IoT), etc. It contains numerous components such as committers, validators, endorsers, orderers and smart contracts. Hyperledger Fabric is a system with properties suitable for enterprise-class applications. It runs arbitrary smart contracts (Cachin, C, 2016, July). (called chain-code) implemented in Go/JAVA/NodeJS language. A Fabric network is composed of entities, peer nodes, ordering service nodes and clients, and each one has an identity furnished by a Membership Service Provider (MSP) generally associated with an organization. In the following, this chapter explains Hyperledger Fabric key components (Dhillon, V., and al, 2017) (Thakkar, P. and al, 2018, September):

- **Client application**: is in charge of creating transactions (invoke transactions) or broadcasting them in the network. The client sends a transaction proposal to one or more peers at the same time to collect proposal responses with endorsements and then broadcasts transactions to the ordering service and endorsers.
- **Peer**: is a node that is in charge of committing transactions to the BC, maintaining state updates and keeping a full copy of the ledger. Some nodes can be endorsing peers that aim to confirm a create chaincode transaction before committing it to the BC.
- **Chaincode** Hyperledger fabric makes use of smart contracts but usually refers to them as chain-code, which is a grouping of similar smart contracts. A chaincode containing smart contracts when deployed on network, those contracts are accessible as applications (Androulaki, E. and al, 2018, April).
- **Ordering Service Nodes (OSN) (or orderers):** are nodes that form together with the ordering service which order all transactions, create them as blocks of transactions, sign each block with its identity and then deliver them to peers using gossip-messaging protoco. In each transaction, the state updated and dependencies calculated during the execution phase. However, orders are ignorant of the application state and do not intervene in the execution nor in the validation of transactions.

The basic transaction flow is three-phases include execute-order-validate steps (Brandenburger, M., and al, 2018), which is represented in fig. 3 (rw-set: a read set and write set).

Figure 3. Execute-order-validate architecture of Fabric

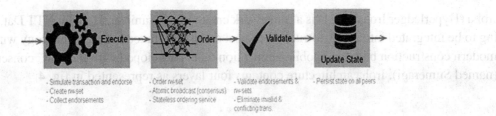

In the following, the details regarding the process related to each phase.

- In the Endorsement Phase, a client application simulates a transaction on selective peers and collects the state changes.
- In the Ordering Phase, the client broadcasts a transaction message to the Ordering Service which does not inspect the contents of the transaction to execute its operation. The transaction includes the read-write sets, the endorsing peer signatures and the Channel ID.
- In the Validation Phase, both endorsing and committing peers on a channel receive blocks from the network. In the beginning, the peer verifies Orderer's signature on the block, and each valid block is then decoded and all the transactions in the block are validated. However, if the endorsement policy is not fulfilled, then that transaction is marked as invalid.
- Finally, in the Ledger Update Phase, the ledger is therefore updated by adding the block to the local ledger. Next, the State Database (stat-eDB), which maintains the current state is updated with the write-sets of correct transactions. Updates are executed automatically for the block and applied on the StateDB.

Hyperledger Sawtooth

Hyperledger Sawtooth (Moriggl, P. and al, 2020) (Ampel, B., and al, 2019, July) is an open-source BC for developing networks and distributed ledger applications. Hyperledger Sawtooth proposes a modular architecture that has five components:

1. A peer to peer network used for transferring messages and transactions between nodes.
2. A distributed log that includes the list of transactions.
3. A smart contract logic layer for treating transactions.
4. A distributed state storage is used to store processing result.
5. A consensus algorithm is employed for producing consensus.

Moreover, Sawtooth isolates the core ledger system from the application environment. As a result, the application's development is simplified and the system becomes safe and secure. Hyperledger Sawtooth has many features. First, it has a flexible environment that allows developers to choose permissions, transaction regulations, consensus protocols, and many more according to their needs. In addition, Sawtooth includes an advanced parallel scheduler that orders transactions into parallel flows. Sawtooth-Ethereum integration project permits the interoperability of the Sawtooth platform to Ethereum. As a result, Ethereum smart contracts can be deployed to the Sawtooth platform with Seth transaction family.

Hyperledger Iroha

Iroha (Hyperledger Iroha, 2021) is a framework created by Suramitsu, Hitachi, NTT Dat, and Colu aiming to be integrated into an infrastructure project using distributed ledger technology with a simple and modern construction based on mobile application that is developed with the YAC consensus algorithm (named Sumeragi). Iroha architecture contains four layers as represented in fig. 4.

Figure 4. Hyperledger Iroha architecture

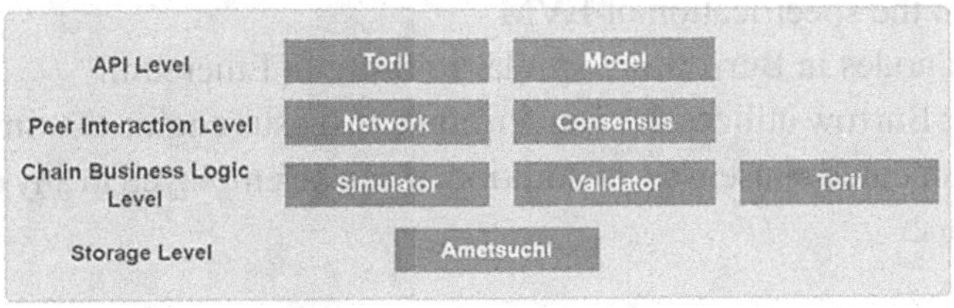

1. API level in which Torii (gate) offers the input and output interfaces for clients and model classes are considered as system entities.
2. Peer interaction level in which Network includes interaction with peers and the Consensus is responsible of agreeing peers on chain content in the network.
3. Chain business logic level in which the Simulator creates a momentary snapshot of storage to validate transactions. Then, Validator classes verify the business rules and the validity of transactions. Moreover, the Synchronizer synchronizes new peers in the system or disconnects them temporarily.
4. Storage level in which Ametsuchi is a ledger block storage composed of block store, a block index, and a world state view component.

Hyperledger Indy

Indy (Hyperledger Indy, 2021) is a distributed ledger that delivers tools, libraries, and reusable components aiming to generate decentralized digital identities across BC system or other distributed ledgers. Indy permits clients to share their authenticated identity with the organizations and groups in a secure, quick and easy way. The Indy code is dependent and generally associated with Sovrin Foundation, despite this Indy node can be used with a different network. Indy architecture is composed of three main layers. In the Data Model Layer, Indy allows client to send a transaction or a set of transactions. In addition, when claims are false, Indy applies a zero-knowledge proof of a revocation model. In the Execution Layer, a node can be either a client, which submits transaction proposals, or a validator, which orders the transactions and communicates with other nodes, or observer, which follows communication. The Indy consensus layer has its own distributed layer using Redundant Byzantine Fault Tolerance (RBFT) (Aublin, P. and al, 2013, July) and its Distributed Ledger Technology (DLT) administered by Sovrin (Sovrin, 2018).

Hyperledger Burrow

Burrow (Hyperledger burrow, 2021) is a private BC framework executing Ethereum Virtual Machine (EVM) smart contract. Burrow uses the Tendermint (Buchman, E., 2016) PoS principal consensus engine to provide transaction finality and high transaction throughput. Three main components construct a Burrow node: the permissioned EVM, the RPC gateway and the consensus engine. Burrow can be structured into three principal layers.

1. **Data Model Layer**: After being finalized by the consensus engine, transactions are then validated and addressed to the application state which regroups all accounts (contain smart contract code or

can be public-private key pair), the name registry and the validator. Moreover, blocks in Burrow is created in part to the specification of EVM.

2. **Execution Layer:** nodes in Burrow are similar to those in Ethereum.

3. **Consensus Layer**: Burrow utilizes the Tendermint consensus engine that implements peer-to-peer protocols and documented consensus. In addition, it can be employed in any environment and focus on sets of validators.

Hyperledger Tools

Hyperledger is constantly investing in building support tools that facilitate deployment, debugging, and design of any BC system, for both developers and users. Several tools allow easy and efficient access to BC. The most used among the tools are Hyperledger Composer, Hyperledger Explorer Hyperledger Cello, and Hyperledger Caliper.

Hyperledger Composer

Hyperledger Composer (Elrom, E., 2019) is the most developed and powerful Hyperledger tool. It is written in JavaScript and is the most active tool for development activity. It allows developers to quickly and easily define BC-based solutions, and then rapidly iterate through development cycles. Hyperledger Composer is built on top of Hyperledger Fabric for calling the Fabric APIs, it is really optional in the process of developing BC applications with Hyperledger Fabric. It can be said that it is a framework for Hyperledger Fabric. Migrating from Composer to other tools or developing without it are all valid options. Hyperledger Composer is efficient and sufficient for creating a proof-of-concept business model. Furthermore, three components make up Hyperledger Composer:

- **Business network archive (.bna):** These are source-code packages that define a business network. This module includes assets and the transactions related to these assets. Hyperledger Composer needs four files to be packaged together: (i) a network model file (.cto) defining the assets, transactions, and participants who can interact with these assets, (ii) an access control file (.acl) defining the permissions, a JavaScript file (.js), and a query file (.qry).
- **Hyperledger Composer Playground:** This used to configure and deploy network as well as test code without rolling out a BC.
- **REST API support:** This exposes functions to be used by front-end clients such as dapps.

Hyperledger Cello

Hyperledger Cello (Hyperledger Cello, 2018) developed to be a rich graphical user interface experience for Hyperledger solution. It allows easy hosting of BC, connected components and infrastructure according to external sites. It is a module-based BC tool and a service system. It is called BC as a Service (BaaS), it allows the user to maintain a BC network and infrastructure. Hyperledger Cello permits instant viewing of changes in the network, regardless of the size of the network. It allows both administrators and the operations side of your organization to deploy and manage BC as a service, allowing them to quickly maintain and reconfigure Fabric and Sawtooth deployments. The network administrator controls

Table 3. Brief comparison between Distributed Ledgers within Hyperledger Framework

Tools	Network Deployment	Interfaces	Consensus	Access Control	Operation Mode	Decentralization	Decentralized Identity	Compute-intensive	Usage	Transaction Hashes	Modularity	Flexibility	Scalability	Zero proof Knowledge	Latency
Indy	Need to Install Docker Using libindy-based CLI	Supported Indy SDK	Pluggable, RBFT	Not Defined	Distributed Identity Ledger	Distributed	Yes	No	Decentralized Identity Database Service for Businesses	Merkle Patricia Trie (SHA 256)	Average	Average	Average	No	Low
Burrow	Using Kubernetes tools	Supported RPC gateway	Tendermint	Supported by Ethereum	Permissioned Ethereum-based platform	Distributed	No	Partially	To run Ethereum smart contracts in a Hyperledger network	Patricia Tree (Ethereum)	Less	Average	Average	No	Low
Iroha	Need to install Docker	Supported by Torii a single RPC server.	Sumeragi (YAC), Voting-based	AC on chain business logic level. Role-based AC	Permissioned	Distributed	No	No	To optimize mobile application	Radix Merkle tree (SHA-3 512)	Less	High	Less	Yes	Low
Sawtooth	Need to install Docker, Ubuntu, or Kubern	Using REST API Separate between Core System and Application Level	Pluggable, PoET, Dev mode	Can change AC for both organization and smart contract by on-chain.	Permissioned or Permissionless	Partially	No	No	fishing industry supply chain	Radix Merkle tree (SHA512)	High	Average	High	No	Medium
Fabric	Need to install Docker Swarm	Based on SDK of Fabric to develop API or using Composer	Pluggable Trusted Solo, Crash fault tolerant Kafka, PBFT	Organization level AC on channels and attribute .Role-based AC in smart-contract	Permissioned	Partially	No	No	Networks Supply chain	Merkle tree (SHA256)	High	Average	Less	No	Low

the network by setting parameters such as the number of users on the network, the size of the network, and the authority of the users. The user can create smart contracts, verify the network and add new blocks to the network. BaaS is an offer that allows users to leverage cloud-based solutions to build, host and use their BC applications, smart contracts and BC-based features, while a cloud-based service provider manages all necessary infrastructure maintenance tasks and activities. Besides that, Hyperledger Cello allows you to manage multiple BC networks. Allows multiple BCs or nodes to synchronize with each other and it also offers analytics and tracking and capabilities.

Hyperledger Caliper

Hyperledger Caliper (Hyperldger Caliper, 2021). supported by the Linux Foundation used as a performance benchmark framework for permissioned BC. The key function of Hyperledger Caliper is to integrate different BC implementations such as Fabric, Composer, Iroha, Sawtooth, Indi and others into the evaluation system. Hyperledger Caliper is responsible for translation between the BC protocol and the caliper north bound interfaces (NBIs) for every BC platform to be tested. Using Caliper, we can send controlled workloads to the BC platform and measure the resulting transaction throughput and latencies. Caliper runs on the client machines and broadcasts transactions on the Fabric channel. It listens to block events from peers to check for transaction confirmations on the BC and assigns those transactions a completion timestamp. This tool generates HTML reports that contain some of the performance characteristics, such as throughput (tx/sec), success rate, latency, and CPU / Memory resource consumption based on listening to transaction timestamps. Using Caliper, the team working on BC applications can take continuous measurements while building smart contracts and transaction logic and use those measurements to track performance changes. The main advantage of using Hyperledger Caliper is that it supports many clients that can inject workloads in the BC network. However, this tool has certain limitation requiring changes to the Caliper code to be able to successfully launch controlled workloads at high send rates. In this regard, authors in (Baliga, A. and al, 2018, June) enhanced Caliper by:

- Equally balancing the load generated by the client across all the consortium peers within the consortium network.
- Modifying the client to spawn a new process that essentially splits the two functions into separate processes. A newly spawned process only listens to block events and inserts them in a messaging queue to be processed later by Caliper's main process, which eliminates the occurrence of failed transactions due to missed block events at higher transaction rates.

Hyperledger Explorer

Hyperledger Explorer (Hyperledger Explorer, 2021) provides a control panel to view transactions, block information node logs, statistics, smart contracts, and all other information about BCs. It allows invocation, deployments and querying blocks, users can query for specific blocks or transactions to see complete details. Besides, it gives its user the functionality to scroll through peruse data on the BC, and collect metrics about data as it is reported on blocks. Besides that, it can integrate with any authentication or authorization platform, commercial or open-source, to provide features that match user privileges.

BCVerifier

BCVerifier (Shimosawa, T. and al, 2020, November) is a tool dedicated to verifying Hyperledger Fabric Ledgers proposed to address three issues when it applied to enterprise systems: (i) local alteration of ledgers, (ii) short of endorsers faced especially with private data, and (iii) auditing requirements. From the issues, the authors have extracted six requirements. Indeed, local alteration derives the requirements (A) and (B), the endorsement issue leads to the requirements (C), (D) and (E) and the regulation issue derives the requirement (F):

(A) To check internal integrity of the ledger;
(B) To compare blocks with other peers/organizations;
(C) To check the read-write sets for transactions;
(D) To re-execute the transactions or equivalent logic;
(E) To access private data;
(F) To generate a report.

As mentioned in (Shimosawa, T. and al, 2020, November), BCverifier employs pluggable modules so that it can be adapted to check ledgers of various blockchain platforms. However, the version presented in (Shimosawa, T. and al, 2020, November) has modules only for Hyperledger Fabric. The BCverifier include five main modules:

- **Frontend**: The frontend module provides the user interface to the users. It may be CLI or GUI such as web interface while the presented implementation in (Shimosawa, T. and al, 2020, November) provides only CLI.
- **Data**: The data module abstracts the data representation in a ledger. The abstract model common to all the BC is a block and a transaction. A plugin for Hyperledger Fabric data represents a Fabric block, a hash function and a Fabric transaction.
- **Input**: The input module retrieves data from the ledger. The source can be a static file stored in a disk or some BC node connected by a network. Multiple sources, block sources, can be specified to compare the blocks from a source with those from another source.
- **Logic**: The logic module verifies blocks and transactions. It consists of three types of plugins: (i) a block verification plugin checks blocks, (ii) a transaction verification plugin checks transactions, which constitute platform-level checks, and (iii) the application plugin checks the semantics of the BC.
- **Output:** The output module produces a report in some file format. The first version of the tool produces a report in the JSON format, which contains the result from the logic components.

Besides that, BCverifier can verify in the ledger: immutability, consensus, and consistency in Hyperledger Fabric ledgers.

Shadow-Hyperledger

Shadow (Shadow documentation, 2021) is an open-source simulator able to run off-the-shelf software (e.g. Tor and Bitcoin) in a controlled, simulated network environment. Thus, a plugin to the shadow simulator must be created for every software run under simulation. Shadow plugin has been implemented in Hyperledger BC platforms allowing running simulations and measuring the performance and scalability. Fig.5 illustrates the Shadow-Hyperledger Framework.

Figure 5. Shadow-Hyperledger Framework

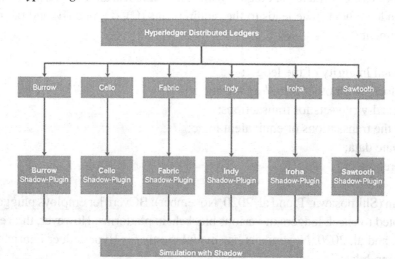

Hyperledger Libraries

TRANSACT, URSA, QUILT and ARIES are the main libraries supported by hyperledger framework. In the following, a brief description of the utilities and functionalities of these libraries.

TRANSACT

Transact is a library that manages the execution of smart contracts, this means that it regulates the planning of transactions and the storage of results in the world, but leaves consensus protocol, access rights, block management and other details specific implementation of BC technology. In other words, act Transact provides an extensible implementation for working with virtual machines that execute a smart contract program.

URSA

Ursa (Srpanj, 2019) is another project that originated from the Indy environment and is a stand-alone cryptographic library. The goal of this library is to offer a solution for all the cryptographic needs of the Hyperledger family and other sub projects and to avoid duplication of Cryptographic works. The library consists of two parts:

- **The Base Crypto library** offers more basic cryptographic operations such as signing using elliptic curve cryptography (ed25519 and secp256k1) and compression (blake2)

- **The z-mix** is a library for creating so-called Zero-Knowledge proof which allow party A to prove to party B the truth of the claim without B finding out the details of claims. Right now Fabric and Indy need to run evidence like this in their work, so it is a task z-mix to offer a flexible and secure implementation for drafting the relevant rules. ˘

QUILT

Hyperledger QUILT (Hyperledger Quilt, 2021) is the implementation of the inter-ledger protocol in Java. It provides a standardized and quality protocol for transaction redirection and interoperability, between ledger systems by implementing ILP, which is primarily a payments protocol and designed to transfer value across distributed ledgers and non-distributed ledgers. The tool enables easier communication between digital wallets, organizations, institutions, ˘ companies and supply chains that use the BC and allow them to run joint transaction.

ARIES

ARIES (Bernabe, J. B.) is the result of the ReliAble euRopean Identity EcoSystem (ARIES) H2020 research project aims to provide a stronger, more trusted, user-friendly and efficient authentication process though preserving a full respect to subject's and personal data privacy and protection. It ensures security aspects like credential management for privacy-respecting solutions and the reduction of identity theft, fraud, or wrong identity. Authentication processes ensured with the use of smart devices for biometrics acquisition (especially face) and electronic (using NFC) data. In other words, ARIES is an implementation of a decentralized key management system that allows connection within the peer network and sharing documents, messages and keys. The primary goal of this ˘tool is to enable interoperability between each system and the identity on the network using Decentralized Identity (DID). Moreover, digital identities within ARIES are generated with privacy preserving technologies and allowing citizens just to prove to be in possession of some attributes without exposing the rest of their data. A user manages multiple identities and credentials that are issued by Identity Providers (IdP) and presented to the Service Providers (SP) to access the offered services by them.

Besides that, ARIES approach considers a multi-domain interaction for eID management in order to achieve a distributed but unified eID ecosystem. Interaction with legacy non-ARIES IdPs can be also achieved by contacting those IdPs via standard protocols such as SAML, OAuth2, etc.

OPEN ISSUES AND FUTURE RESEARCH DIRECTIONS RELATED TO THE HYPERLEDGER FRAMEWORK EXPLOITATION

In order to empower an efficient application of the BC technology within different fields and domains, the BC communities assessed several directions and issues for making practical and interoperable BC networks. In the following, we highlight some open issues and future research direction regarding the exploitation of Hyperledger frameworks in order to fit the need of the smart systems-based applications.

Suitability to Smart Systems

BC 3.0 refers to the wide array of applications that do not take into consideration currency, money, financial markets, or other aspects of economic activity. These applications include health, art, science, education, identity, public goods, governance, and smart systems in general. The most auspicious application of the BC 3.0 technology is smart cities that aggregate several subsystems as smart mobility, smart governance, smart living, smart citizens, the smart use of natural resources, and smart economy. BC technology considered a promising technology that guarantees security, privacy and trustworthiness for the Internet of Every Things (IoET) including the Industrial Internet of Things (IIoT) known as (Industry 4.0), Internet of Medical Things (IoMT).... . However, old BC models (related to BC 1.0 and BC 2.0) could hardly fit the IoET requirements. The BC 3.0 technology provides new opportunities for redesigning the smart systems and the cyber-word in general, therefore, new BC tools and model should be developed under the BC 3.0 umbrella to consider the particularities of the application. Besides that the adoption of the BC 3.0 by real world applications require that the BC communicates with external entities, in this regards, there are still some issues to address related to: The external data reliability; How to reach consensus in case some of the nodes cannot reach the external data source; and who will administrate the third-party data sources? Therefore, The Hyperledger framework could be extended by several domains specific modules (defined under BC3.0 umbrella). In the current state, Hyperledger framework integrates hyperledger grids and hyperledger labs.

Standardization and Interoperability

The diversity of BC platforms and tools within hyperledger framework can face some interoperability issues. These BC platforms have different architectures, diverse consensus protocols and programming languages. Accordingly, this diversity will prohibit the interoperability between applications built with different BC platforms. Standardization will be the suitable solution to fill this gap and to allow communications between heterogeneous BC networks. In this regards, tools and platforms permitting cross BC communications appear. However, more work must done to develop specific standards BC platforms and consensus protocols.

LEARNED LESSONS AND CONCLUSION

The development of the BC's full potentials as an infrastructure technology requires a critical mass of investigators and the development of several tools and frameworks dedicated to assess the performance of BC networks. In this context, this chapter focused on the distributed ledgers and tools within the hyperledger framework. This chapter presents a comprehensive study of BC hyperledger framework useful for analyzing and evaluating BC based systems.

Tables 4 and 5 recapitulate and summarize hyperledger distributed tools and libraries.

Finally, the authors are convinced that the content of this book chapter will help researcher to select the suitable BC ledgers and tools within the hyperledger framework that fit their needs.

Table 4.

Hyperledger Libraries
TRANSACT: is a library that manages the execution of smart contracts.
URSA: is a stand-alone cryptographic library that offers a solution for all the cryptographic needs of the Hyper-ledger family and other sub projects to avoid duplication of Cryptographic works.
QUILT: is the implementation of the inter-ledger protocol in Java. It provides a standardized and quality protocol for transaction redirection and interoperability between ledger systems.
ARIES: it provide a strong, trusted, user-friendly and efficient authentication process though preserving a full respect to subject's and personal data privacy and protection.

Table 5.

Hyperledger Tools
Hyperledger Composer: is a set of collaboration tools for building BC business networks. It is built on top of Hyperledger Fabric for calling the Fabric APIs.
Hyperledger Cello: developed to be a rich graphical user interface experience for Hyperledger solution. It allows easy hosting of BC, connected components and infrastructure according to external sites.
Hyperledger Caliper: Supported by the Linux Foundation used as a performance benchmark framework for permissioned BC. It integrates different BC implementations.
Hyperledger Explorer: provides a control panel to view transactions, block information node logs, statistics, smart contracts, and all other information about BCs.
BCVerifier: dedicated to address three issues of Hyper-ledger Fabric Ledgers: (i) local alteration of ledgers, (ii) short of endorsers faced with private data, and (iii) auditing requirements.

REFERENCES

Ampel, B., Patton, M., & Chen, H. (2019, July). Performance modeling of hyperledger sawtooth blockchain. In *2019 IEEE International Conference on Intelligence and Security Informatics (ISI)* (pp. 59-61). IEEE.

Androulaki, E., Barger, A., Bortnikov, V., Cachin, C., Christidis, K., De Caro, A., ... Muralidharan, S. (2018, April). Hyperledger fabric: a distributed operating system for permissioned blockchains. In *Proceedings of the Thirteenth EuroSys Conference* (pp. 1-15). 10.1145/3190508.3190538

Aste, T., Tasca, P., & Di Matteo, T. (2017). Blockchain technologies: The foreseeable impact on society and industry. *Computer, 50*(9), 18–28. doi:10.1109/MC.2017.3571064

Aublin, P. L., Mokhtar, S. B., & Qu´ema, V. (2013, July). Rbft: Redundant byzantine fault tolerance. In *2013 IEEE 33rd International Conference on Distributed ComputingSystems* (pp. 297-306). IEEE.

Bach, L. M., Mihaljevic, B., & Zagar, M. (2018, May). Comparative analysis of blockchain consensus algorithms. In *41st International Convention on Information and Communication Technology, Electronics and Microelectronics (MIPRO)* (pp.1545-1550). 10.23919/MIPRO.2018.8400278

Baird, L., Harmon, M., & Madsen, P. (2019). Hedera: A public hashgraph network & Governing Council. *White Paper, 1.*

Baliga, A., Solanki, N., Verekar, S., Pednekar, A., Kamat, P., & Chatterjee, S. (2018, June). Performance characterization of hyperledger fabric. In 2018 Crypto Valley conference on blockchain technology (CVCBT) (pp. 65-74). IEEE.

Ban, T. Q., Anh, B. N., Son, N. T., & Van Dinh, T. (2019, February). Survey of Hyperledger Blockchain Frameworks: Case Study in FPT University's Cryptocurrency Wallets. In *Proceedings of the 2019 8th International Conference on Software and Computer Applications* (pp. 472-480). 10.1145/3316615.3316671

Bernabe, J. B., Torres, R., Martin, D., Crespo, A., Skarmeta, A., Fortune, D., ... Alamillo, I. (n.d.). *An Overview on ARIES: Reliable European Identity Ecosystem*. Academic Press.

Blummer, T., Sean, M., & Cachin, C. (2018). *An Introduction to Hyperledger*. Technical report, White paper.

Brandenburger, M., Cachin, C., Kapitza, R., & Sorniotti, A. (2018). *Blockchain and trusted computing: Problems, pitfalls, and a solution for hyperledger fabric.* arXivpreprint arXiv:1805.08541.

Brown, R. G., Carlyle, J., Grigg, I., & Hearn, M. (2016). Corda: an introduction. *R3 CEV.* Quorum Whitepaper: https://github.com/ConsenSys/quorum/blob/master/docs/Quorum%20Whitepaper%20v0.2.pdf

Buchman, E. (2016). *Tendermint: Byzantine fault tolerance in the age of blockchains* (Doctoral dissertation). Engineering Systems and Computing; University of Guelph, Canada.

Cachin, C. (2016, July). Architecture of the hyperledger blockchain fabric. In *Workshop on distributed cryptocurrencies and consensus ledgers* (Vol. 310, p. 4). Academic Press.

Dhillon, V., Metcalf, D., & Hooper, M. (2017). The hyperledger project. In *Blockchain enabled applications* (pp. 139–149). Apress.

Dorri, A., Kanhere, S. S., Jurdak, R., & Gauravaram, P. (2017, March). Blockchain for IoT security and privacy: The case study of a smart home. In *2017 IEEE international conference on pervasive computing and communications workshops (PerCom workshops)* (pp. 618-623). IEEE.

Elrom, E. (2019). Hyperledger. In *The Blockchain Developer* (pp. 299–348). Apress.

Gervais, A., Karame, G. O., Wüst, K., Glykantzis, V., Ritzdorf, H., & Capkun, S. (2016, October). On the security and performance of proof of work blockchains. In *Proceedings of the 2016 ACM SIGSAC conference on computer and communications security* (pp. 3-16). 10.1145/2976749.2978341

Hyperldger Caliper. (2021). *Documentation*. Available: https://github.com/hyperledger/caliper

Hyperledger Burrow. (2021). https://www.hyperledger.org/use/hyperledger-burrow

Hyperledger Cello. (2018). *Overview-Hyperledger Cello*. Available: https://cello.readthedocs.io/en/latest

Hyperledger Explorer. (2021). *A useful tool to view blocks, transactions on Hyperledger Fabric*. Available: https://www.hyperledger.org/use/explorer

Hyperledger Indy. (2021). https://www.hyperledger.org/use/hyperledger-indy

Hyperledger Iroha. (2021). https://github.com/hyperledger-archives/education/blob/master/LFS171x/docs/introduction-to-hyperledger-iroha.md

Hyperledger Quilt. (2021). Available: https://www.hyperledger.org/projects/quilt

Karantias, K., Kiayias, A., & Zindros, D. (2019). Proof-of-Burn. *International Conference on Financial Cryptography and Data Security*.

Mettler, M. (2016, September). Blockchain technology in healthcare: The revolution starts here. In *IEEE 18th international conference on e-health networking, applications and service (Healthcom)* (pp. 1-3). IEEE.

Mohammad, A. F. (2019). *Decision Analytics Using Permissioned Blockchain "Comm-ledger"* (PhD thesis). University of North Dakota.

Moriggl, P., Asprion, P. M., & Schneider, B. (2020). Blockchain Technologies Towards Data Privacy—Hyperledger Sawtooth as Unit of Analysis. In *New Trends in Business Information Systems and Technology* (pp. 299–313). Springer.

Nakamoto, S. (2019). *Bitcoin: A peer-to-peer electronic cash system*. Manubot.

Nanayakkara, S., Rodrigo, M. N. N., Perera, S., Weerasuriya, G. T., & Hijazi, A. A. (2021). A Methodology for Selection of a Blockchain Platform to Develop an Enterprise System. *Journal of Industrial Information Integration*, *23*, 100215. doi:10.1016/j.jii.2021.100215

Novo, O. (2018). Blockchain meets IoT: An architecture for scalable access management in IoT. *IEEE Internet of Things Journal*, *5*(2), 1184–1195. doi:10.1109/JIOT.2018.2812239

Parity. (2017). Error! Hyperlink reference not valid.*Parity documentation*. https://paritytech.github.io/wiki

Peters, G., Panayi, E., & Chapelle, A. (2015). Trends in cryptocurrencies and blockchain Technologies: A monetary theory and regulation perspective. *Journal of Financial Perspectives*, *3*(3).

Pohrmen, F. H., Das, R. K., & Saha, G. (2019). Blockchain-based security aspects in heterogeneous Internet-of-Things networks: A survey. *Transactions on Emerging Telecommunications Technologies*, *30*(10), e3741. doi:10.1002/ett.3741

Saleh, F. (2018). Blockchain without waste: Proof-of-stake. *Review of Financial Studies*.

Shadow Documentation. (2021). https://github.com/martmartinez91/shadow-hyperledger

Shimosawa, T., Sato, T., & Oshima, S. (2020, November). BCVerifier: A Tool to Verify Hyperledger Fabric Ledgers. In *2020 IEEE International Conference on Blockchain (Blockchain)* (pp. 291-299). IEEE.

Sikorski, J. J., Haughton, J., & Kraft, M. (2017). Blockchain technology in the chemical industry: Machine-to-machine electricity market. *Applied Energy*, *195*, 234–246. doi:10.1016/j.apenergy.2017.03.039

Sovrin. (2018). https://sovrin.org/wp-content/uploads/2018/03/Sovrin-Protocol-and-Token-White-Paper.pdf

Srpanj. (2019). *Guided Tour of Hyperledger Fabric and Hyperledger Indy*. https: //github.com/hyperledger/ursa

Statista, (2020) https://www.statista.com/statistics/647231/worldwide-blockchain-technology-market-size/

Thakkar, P., Nathan, S., & Viswanathan, B. (2018, September). Performance bench-marking and optimizing hyperledger fabric blockchain platform. In *2018 IEEE 26th International Symposium on Modeling, Analysis, and Simulation of Computer and Telecommunication Systems (MASCOTS)* (pp. 264-276). IEEE.

Vinayak, M. (2019). *FSCBlock: Designing financial smart contracts on permissioned and public blockchains* (Master's thesis). Department of Computer Science The University of Manitoba, Winnipeg, Canada.

Wood, G. (2014). Ethereum: A secure decentralised generalised transaction ledger. *Ethereum project yellow paper, 151*(2014), 1-32.

KEY TERMS AND DEFINITIONS

Burrow: Initially contributed by Monax and Intel, is a modular BC that was client-built to the specification of the Ethereum Virtual Machine (EVM). It uses the Tendermint PoS consensus engine.

Hyperledger Fabric: Contributed by IBM, designed to be a foundation for developing solutions with a modular architecture. It allows for plug-and-play components (consensus, membership services, and leverages containers) to host smart contracts that comprise the application logic of the system.

Indy: Contributed initially by the Sovrin Foundation, is a distributed ledger that delivers tools, libraries, and reusable components aiming to generate decentralized digital identities across BC system or other distributed ledgers.

Iroha: Designed for mobile development projects, is based on Hyperledger Fabric. It features modern, domain-driven C++ design and a new chain-based BFT consensus algorithm called Sumeragi.

Sawtooth: It was contributed by Intel and includes a novel consensus algorithm called Proof of Elapsed Time (PoET). It has potential in many areas, with support for both permissioned and permissionless deployments and recognition of diverse requirements. It is designed for versatility.

Chapter 3
Extracting Insights From Bitcoin Transactions:
Data Warehouse Modeling and Analytical Questions

Rim Moussa
University of Carthage, Tunisia

Alfredo Cuzzocrea
University of Calabria, Italy

ABSTRACT

Bitcoin is the most well-known cryptocurrency. It was first released in 2009 by Satoshi Nakamoto. Bitcoin serves as a decentralized medium of digital exchange, with transactions verified and recorded in the blockchain. The latter is a public immutable distributed ledger that operates without the need of a trusted record keeping authority or a central intermediary. It provides OLTP capabilities with both atomic transactions and data durability guarantees for blockchain transactions. Blockchain ledgers were not designed to perform analytics questions. The availability of the entire bitcoin transaction history, stored in its public blockchain, offers interesting opportunities for analyzing the transactions to obtain insights on users/entities patterns and transactions patterns. For these purposes, the authors need to store and analyze cryptocurrency transactions in a data warehouse. In this chapter, they investigate public blockchain datasets, and they overview different data models for setting up a data warehouse appliance of cryptocurrencies.

INTRODUCTION

Blockchains use cases are emerging in the financial services, such as supply chain, media, and many highly digitized industries. Blockchains are being used for distributed value exchange, based on cryptographically signed, irrevocable transactional records shared by all participants in a network. Each record contains a timestamp and reference links to previous transactions. The Bitcoin blockchain in particular

DOI: 10.4018/978-1-7998-5839-3.ch003

aims to remedy financial industry flaws. As motivated by Satoshi Nakamoto (Nakamoto, 2008), it is the first truly crypto-currency which does not discriminate its users based on citizenship or location, is available all time, and is secure with very low fees. It manages the life cycle of digitalized assets and immutably records operations in a distributed ledger. A digitalized asset can be any valuable object (e.g. crypto-currencies, securities, patient health records). Users trade electronically and more anonymously than via traditional electronic transfers. Bitcoins design keeps all transactions in a *public immutable distributed ledger*.

The Blockchain guarantees three main features – *Accessibility*, *Security*, and *Accountability*. Blockchain, being shared by all parties, makes data accessible for everyone involved. The data is stored on every computer, so that it is both decentralized and distributed. This enables a high level of security because intruders would need to access and alter the data on all linked computers at the same time in order to change one transaction. As a single, and fixed cache of information, Blockchain ensures accountability by everyone in the network.

While blockchain ledgers provide OLTP capabilities namely atomic transactions and data durability for transactions, they don't support On-Line Analytical Processing workloads (OLAP). OLAP performs multidimensional analysis of business data and provides the capability for complex calculations, trend analysis, and sophisticated data modeling. The capability to regularly generate time-scale and ergonomic reports on specific or aggregated money flows stored in the ledger is very important. The inability to easily build reports from the blockchain can reduce transparency and increase the difficulty of price discovery of BTC versus fiat currencies (e.g. US$, euro,...), as well as other fundamental analytical questions such as transactions and entities' patterns. Consequently, blockchain data must be ingested into a data warehouse system to be queried efficiently. Typically, Data Warehouses are implemented on relational stores. Achieving scalability and elasticity is a huge challenge for relational database management systems. Relational databases were designed to run on a single server in order to maintain the integrity of the table mappings and avoid the problems of distributed computing. The scalability, fit-to-data model, denormalization, and schema flexibility makes NoSQL stores a viable alternative option. NoSQL stands for "Not Only SQL". The most common types of NoSQL databases are key-value (e.g. Redis, Amazon DynamoDB), document (e.g. BaseX, MongoDB, CouchDB, ElasticSearch), column (e.g. BigQuery, Apache Drill, Cassandra, Apache HBase), and graph databases (e.g. Neo4j, Apache ArangoDB, JanusGraph, RedisGraph). Graph compute engines can be used in online analytical processing (OLAP) for bulk analysis (Chen, 2008).

This chapter describes different data models for setting up a data warehouse appliance for cryptocurrencies. For that purpose, we focus on the relational model, the nested-immutable model, and the graph model. For each model, we show typical queries which execute on the data warehouse.

Blockchain analytics specifically of Bitcoin blockchain should provide insight into a variety of economic indicators, illegal activities (e.g. ransoms, tracking sellers and buyers of illegal items, tracking laundering of large sums of money, gambling...).

The chapter is organized as follows, first we introduce key concepts of bitcoin transactions. Then, we present a sketch of Blockchain Relational Data Warehouse and detail integration workflows and typical business questions. After that, we present the nested-immutable model implemented by *Google* proposed as a cryptocurrency *warehouse* on *BigQuery*. We also present different graphs modeling and detail the insights they allow to extract. Finally, we conclude the chapter and present a research agenda.

BITCOIN TRANSACTIONS' KEY CONCEPTS

Bitcoin is a crypto-currency. The latter is a digital asset designed to work as a medium of exchange wherein individual coin ownership records are stored in a ledger existing in a form of a computerized database using cryptography to secure transaction records, to control the creation of additional coins, and to verify the transfer of coin ownership. Crypto-currencies use decentralized control as opposed to centralized digital currency and central banking systems. The core entities of a bitcoin blockchain are blocks, transactions, addresses, and users.

Transactions

Transactions allow managing funds, so funds can be either divided or aggregated only by being spent. A Bitcoin transaction allows multiple sending addresses (multi-input) and multiple receiving addresses (outputs). A transaction output comprises the recipient's Bitcoin address and number of Satoshis credited to that address. If the sum of the input values is larger than the amount that is to be paid, the payer designates a new address for the remaining change. Each non-coinbase transaction input must refer to an output of a previous transaction and contain a signature verifying ownership of Satoshis associated with that output. A coinbase transaction has no inputs and rewards the respective miners. The miners use it to collect the block reward for their work and any other transaction fees collected by the miner are also sent in this transaction. It provides the financial incentive for nodes to mine and is part of the coin minting process in Bitcoin.

Examples of Transactions are illustrated in Figure 1 and Figure 2.

Addresses

A Bitcoin address is generated based on a randomly selected key and is the only unique way of identification in the system. Due to the random property of Bitcoin addresses and the extremely low probability of key collisions in the enormous elliptic curve digital signature algorithm (ECDSA) key space, the number of Bitcoin addresses grows rapidly because different addresses can be generated for different transactions without address reuse. This address generation scheme provides adequate anonymity for Bitcoin transactions, making it difficult to track Bitcoin transactions conducted by real-world entities. According to (Gaihre et al., 2018) the majority of the users don't care about anonymity. Most of the addresses that are concerned about anonymity are rich addresses. The address is a hash over the public key of an asymmetric key-pair generated by the user. It can be shared publicly for receiving payments. However, the corresponding private key must be kept private in order to unlock and spend Bitcoins associated with addresses in the public blockchain. Users can use wallet software (e.g., BitcoinCore, blockchain.info) to generate an arbitrary number of public/private keys and to keep their private keys.

Many organizations and users reveal their addresses for business purposes or if they are looking for donations/tips or are related to known merchants. (e.g. the bitcoin address of https://wikileaks.org/ is 1HB5XMLmzFVj8ALj6mfBsbifRoD4miY36v). Also, addresses which start with the hex value 1dice belong to the gambling service known as satoshidice, and receive the bets. A Stock buyer address receives but never spends, and has a null Out-degree.

Linking addresses into clusters/entities provides a better insight into bitcoin users. The major heuristics for address linking are,

- **Multi-Input Transactions:** this heuristic is based on the fact that people use multiple addresses for transactions. All input addresses in the same transaction must be in the same set.
- **Change address:** in a transaction all of the Bitcoins of an individual are consumed and the change is returned to a new address called change address, one could link such addresses: input addresses and change address.
- **Output addresses in a Coinbase transaction:** Coinbase transactions can help identify entities that cooperate.

Services like *bitcoin mixing* or *tumbler* allow users to merge multiple unspent outputs from multiple addresses into one transaction with multiple destinations. This allows the obfuscation of the trail from the sender to the receiver.

Users

On a blockchain such as bitcoin, two parties can make an immutable and irreversible transaction that is for all time recorded on the ledger to be verified by anyone. Users include sellers and buyers as well as miners. The *miner* is a voluntary validator node, willing to dedicate some computational power to take part into the distributed consensus algorithm behind the Bitcoin blockchain security guarantees. Since validating new blocks, i.e. mining, is a computationally intensive task, rewards are proportionally assigned to miners.

Figure 1. The Genesis Transaction transfers 5,000,000,000 satoshis (50 BTC) to address 1A1zP1eP5QGe-fi2DMPTfTL5SLmv7DivfNa (1 Satoshi $=10^{-8}$ Bitcoin)

```
"hash":"4a5e1e4baab89f3a32518a88c31bc87f618f76673e2cc77ab2127b7afdeda33b"
"block_timestamp": "2009-01-03 18:15:05 UTC",
"is_coinbase": true,
"input_value": null,
"output_value": "5000000000",
"fee": "0"
"outputs": [
    {
      "addresses": ["1A1zP1eP5QGefi2DMPTfTL5SLmv7DivfNa"],
      "value": "5000000000"
    }
]
```

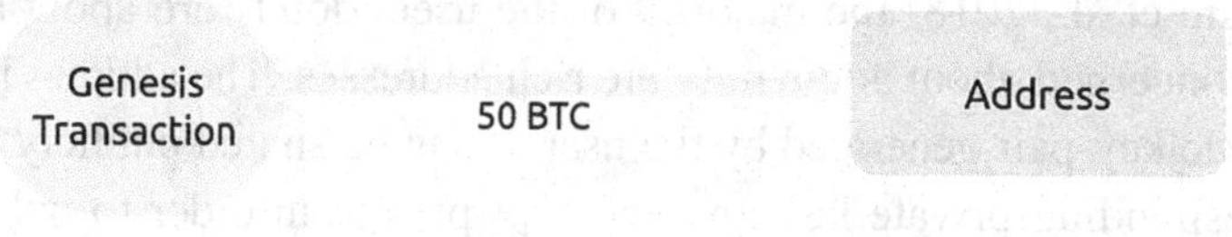

Genesis
Transaction   50 BTC   Address

Blocks

All Bitcoin transactions are stored in the blockchain that consists of a sequence of individual blocks. Blocks are for both storage as well as coin mining. The height of a block is its sequential number, or its distance from the first block. A block in the Bitcoin blockchain aggregates one or more transactions, provides a header with additional descriptive metadata (e.g., creation timestamp, sequential id), and also contains a hash-value, which is computed over selected header fields and a hash over the set of encapsulated transactions. The hash serves as a unique identifier for a block and is also used to refer to the previous (and next) block, which ensures that transactions within a block and the block sequence are non-mutable.

A RELATIONAL DATA WAREHOUSE APPLIANCE FOR BITCOIN TRANSACTIONS

Bitcoin data was about 5GB of stored data at the beginning of 2013 and reached over 250 GB at the beginning of 2020. Next, we briefly overview related work.

In (Kwok-Bun et al., 2019), the authors describe an experiment using three different methods for storing and querying Bitcoin data from SQL databases used for mostly teaching purposes, namely (i) Abe-Bitcoin: which reads the Bitcoin block file, transforms and loads the data into a relational database (Abe, 2013), (ii) BigQuery Bitcoin (Google, 2019): which is an on-line SQL interface for querying bitcoin data in SQL deployed on BigQuery/Google, and (iii) blockchainsql.io (Sphere 10 software, 2018): which is an on-line SQL interface for querying bitcoin data in SQL developed by an Australian software company Sphere 10.

In (Galici, 2020), the authors report the performance of ETL processes which scrap bitcoin datasets from different sources such as blockchair.com, blockcyper.com, blockchain.info, and chain.so. The target relational database design is simple, and many relevant information are not reported, such as multi-sign addresses and the relationship between output and input transactions.

In the sequel, we first propose a conceptual design of a relational data warehouse appliance for bitcoin transactions. Then, we describe the integration workflow.

Figure 2. Pizza Transaction: 131 input addresses participated in the pizza transaction and transferred 10,000 BTC to address 17SkEw2md5avVNyYgj6RiXuQKNwkXaxFyQ (1 Satoshi =10^{-8} Bitcoin)

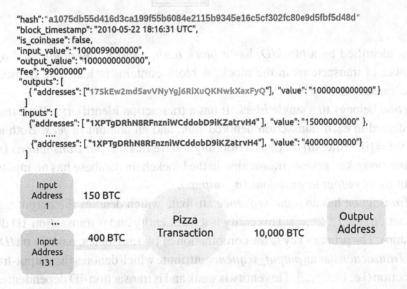

"hash":"a1075db55d416d3ca199f55b6084e2115b9345e16c5cf302fc80e9d5fbf5d48d"
"block_timestamp": "2010-05-22 18:16:31 UTC",
"is_coinbase": false,
"input_value": "1000099000000",
"output_value": "1000000000000",
"fee": "99000000"
"outputs": [
  { "addresses": ["17SkEw2md5avVNyYgj6RiXuQKNwkXaxFyQ"], "value": "1000000000000" }
]
"inputs": [
  { "addresses": ["1XPTgDRhN8RFnzniWCddobD9iKZatrvH4"], "value": "15000000000" },
  ....
  { "addresses": ["1XPTgDRhN8RFnzniWCddobD9iKZatrvH4"], "value": "40000000000"}
]

E/R Diagram and BTC Data Warehouse Relational Schema

Entity–relationship modeling was developed for database and design by Peter Chen and published in 1976. An entity–relationship model (or ER model) describes interrelated things of interest in a specific domain of knowledge. Figure 3 illustrates the ER diagram we propose for blockchain bitcoin transactions.

Figure 3. Entity/Relationship Diagram for the BTC database (with respect to Chen, crowsfeet and look across notation)

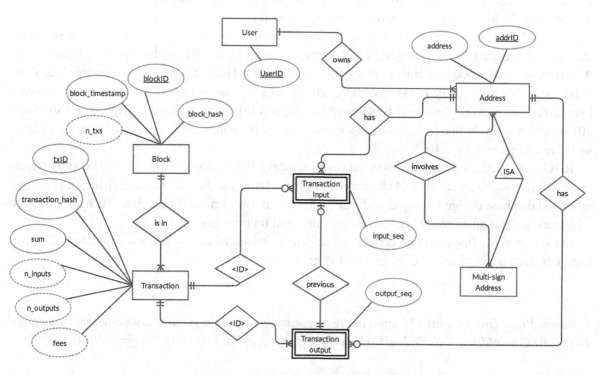

Each *block* is identified by a *blockID*, has a *block hash*, a *block timestamp*, and *n_trx*. The latter denotes the number of transactions in the block. A block contains at least one transaction, as it may contain multiple transactions.

Each *transaction* belongs to a single *block*. It has a transaction identifier: *txID*, a *transaction_hash*, an amount transferred in each transaction denoted *sum*, and an amount of *fees*. Both attributes are in Satoshi, (1 Satoshi $=10^{-8}$ Bitcoin). A transaction might have many *input transactions* (*n_inputs*).

The first transaction a.k.a. genesis transaction in the blockchain database has no inputs. Each transaction might output many *output transactions* (*n_outputs*).

Each *Input Transaction* has an *input sequence* attribute which denotes the output-transaction offset for a given transaction (i.e. 1st, 2nd,...). This entity is a weak entity and is transaction-ID dependent entity (i.e. ID relationship). The primary key is the combination of two attributes, namely *trxID* and *input_seq*.

Each *Output Transaction* has an *output_sequence* attribute which denotes the output-transaction offset for a given transaction (i.e. 1st, 2nd,...). This entity is weak and is transaction-ID dependent entity. It inherits TransactionID from Transaction entity, as primary key (i.e. ID relationship). An *Output Transaction* is either labeled *unspent output transaction* if it doesn't serve as input transaction in a new transaction or a *spent input transaction* if it serves as *input transaction* to a new transaction. This is materialized in the *previous relationship* involving *Transaction Input* and *Transaction output* entities.

Each Address is identified by an *addrID*. An address might be involved in multiple Multi-sign addresses. A Multi-sign address is a specialization of Address and involves many Addresses. Multisignature refers to requiring multiple addresses to authorize a Bitcoin transaction, rather than a single signature from one address. It has several applications such as dividing responsibility for possession of bitcoins among multiple people.

We obtain the logical schema for the BTC data warehouse schema illustrated in Figure 4.

Figure 4. Logical schema of the Bitcoin Transactions Relational Data Warehouse

```
multi_sign_address(msaID,addrID)
user(userID)
address(addrID,userID,address)
block(blockID,block-timestamp,block-hash,n-txs)
transaction(txID,tx hash,sum,n-inputs,fees,n-outputs,blockID)
transaction_input(txinID,input-seq,addrID,previous-tx-outID,previous-output-se
q,sum)
transaction_output(txoutID,output-seq,addrID,sum)
```

Compared to (Galici et al., 2020) proposed schema, our schema allows storing additional relevant information, such as *multi-sign addresses* and the relationship linking *output transaction* and *input transaction*.

BTC Dataset Integration Workflow

We use the dataset outsourced by Dani et al. (Dani et al., 2015) (described in Table 1). We use an *AWS EC2 instance* in order to download and decompress the dataset. We then import data into a *PostgreSQL* instance using PostgreSQL data import built-in functions. Table 2 shows the mapping between the dataset file and the corresponding external table. External tables are then used to build the BTC data warehouse as described in Table 3.

In Table 3, we summarize how we build the target tables. Notice that,

- The *User* table is built from *addr_sccs* et through selecting distinct values of attribute *userid* within *addr_sccs_et* external table.
- The *Address* table is built from both *address_et* and *addr_sccs_et* external tables.
- The *Block* table is equal to *block_hash_et*.
- A Multi-sign address is an address that exists in *tx_out_et* and it exists at least one related tuple in *multiple_et* relation. In order to generate the surrogate key *msaID*, we first group by *trxID* attribute, insert the resulting rows into a temporary relation with a sequence generating *msaID*. Then, we unflatten the grouping for each row in order to obtain multi_sign_address relation.
- The *Transaction* table is built from *tx_et* and *txh_et* tables. Notice that sum and fees columns are set to -1 and computed as follows: for each transaction *t*, *sum* attribute is calculated as the sum of

all the transaction inputs amounts which relate to transaction *t* minus the transaction output having the same address of input transaction (if any). Likewise, the fees attribute is the sum of all input transactions amounts minus the sum of all output transactions which relate to transaction *t*.

- Finally, the *Transaction input* table has the same schema as the external table *tx_in_et*, and the *Transaction output* table has the same schema as the external table *tx_out_et*.

Table 1. Details of a typical bitcoin transactions dataset (Dani et al., 2015)

File Name	Volume	Description and Format
bh.dat.gz	20MB	output file for block hashes (*blockID,hash,block_timestamp,n_txs*)
txh.dat.gz	12GB	output file for transaction hashes (*txID,hash*)
addresses.dat.gz	9.9GB	output file for address ID mapping to address strings (*addrID,address*)
tx.dat.xz	248MB	output file for transaction overview (mapping to block and number of inputs / outputs) (*txID,blockID,n_inputs,n_outputs*)
txin.dat.xz	7.1GB	output file for transaction inputs (*txID,input_seq, prev_txID, prev_output_seq,addrID,sum*)
txout.dat.xz	4.8GB	output file for transaction outputs (*txID,output_seq,addrID,sum*)
multiple.dat.gz	4MB	output file for transaction outputs with multiple addresses (multisign); the txout and txin file will only include the first address. This file includes all involved addresses data (*txID,output_seq,addrID*)
nonstandard.dat.gz	12MB	output file for nonstandard transaction outputs (*txID,output_seq*)
addr_sccs.dat.gz	1.6GB	separately generated (*addrID,userID*) address contraction dataset

Table 2. Mapping data files to external tables (staging area)

Data File	External Table
bh.dat	block_hash_et
txh.dat	txh_et
addresses.dat	address_et
tx.dat	tx_et
txin.dat	tx_in_et
txout.dat	tx_out_et
multiple.dat	multiple_et
nonstandard.dat	nonstandard_et
addr_sccs.dat	addr sccs_et

Relational Model Insights

Relational paradigm was proposed by Edgar Codd around 1969. It has since become the dominant database model for commercial applications. Using a relational data warehouse, such the one we describe above, we can aggregate transactions' data (alternatively addresses' data) and analyze along the temporal dimension; also search all transactions (alternatively addresses) matching specific predicates. Achieving scalability and elasticity is a huge challenge for relational databases. Relational databases were designed to run on a single server in order to maintain the integrity of the table mappings and avoid the problems of distributed computing. A distributed design of a relational database implies the design of a distributed schema which aims at reducing the execution time of frequent and complex queries, as well as an easy check of referential constraints. NoSQL databases designed to scale large amounts of data stored across shared-nothing servers with fast analytical querying are a natural fit for data warehouses. In the next section, we describe a cloud data warehouse utility designed by Google and available on Google Cloud Platform, which stores crypto-currencies transaction history on *BigQuery*.

Table 3. Target tables and corresponding algebraic expressions

Target Table	Algebraic Expression
user	$\Pi\{_{userid}\}$ addr_sccs_et
address	Π address_et $\rhd\lhd a_{address\_et.addrID=addr\_sccs\_et.addrID}$ addr_sccs_et {attributes-set} with attributes-set: address_et.addrID,addr_sccs_et.userID,address_et.address
Multi_sign_address	temp1 ← Π {trxID,addrID} tx_out_et $\rhd\lhd$ ($_{join-cond}$) multiple_et with join-cond: tx_out_et.txID=multiple_et.txID $\wedge$ tx_out_et.output_seq=multiple_et.output_seq temp2 ← GROUP temp1 BY trxID DO build-list(addrID) add msaID column unflatten in order to obtain (msaID,addrID) pairs
Transaction_input	tx_in_et
Transaction_output	tx_out_et
Transaction	Π tx_et $\rhd\lhd t_{x\_et.txID=txh\_et.txID}$ txh_et {attributes-set} with attributes-set: tx_et.txID,txh_et.hash,−1,tx_et.n-inputs,−1,tx_et.n-outputs,tx_et.blockID For each transaction t Do *trxo* is the transaction output which has an addrID equal to a transaction input addrID t.sum ← $\sum$ transaction_input.sum − trxo.sum t.fees ← $\sum$ transaction_input.sum − $\sum$ transaction output.sum
Block	block_hash_et

GOOGLE CRYPTO-CURRENCY DATA WAREHOUSE

As part of the *BigQuery Public Datasets program* (Google, 2019), *Google Cloud* released datasets consisting of the blockchain transaction history for multiple crypto-currencies such as *Bitcoin, Ethereum, Bitcoin Cash, Dash, Dogecoin, Ethereum Classic, Litecoin,* and *Zcash*. All datasets update every day via the Blockchain ETL ingestion framework. *BigQuery* is serverless, or more precisely a data warehouse as a service. It exposes a simple SQL client interface which enables users to run interactive queries.

BigQuery Architecture

Figure 5 illustrates BigQuery architecture. BigQuery employs a set of multi-tenant services driven by low-level Google infrastructure technologies like *Colossus, Dremel, Borg* and *Jupiter*.

- Data are stored in *Colossus* -Google's global storage system. *BigQuery* is an immutable data-base, i.e. it supports read-only use-cases. It stores data in a columnar format known as *Capacitor*. Each field of the BigQuery table i.e. column is stored in a separate *Capacitor file* which enables *BigQuery* to achieve a very high compression ratio and scan throughput. *BigQuery* leverages *Capacitor* to store data in *Colossus*. *Colossus* is Google's latest generation distributed file system and successor to GFS (Google File System). *Colossus* handles cluster-wide replication, recovery and distributed management.
- *Dremel* is a large multi-tenant cluster that executes SQL queries. Dremel turns SQL queries into multi-level serving trees. In a serving tree, a root server receives incoming queries from clients and routes the queries to the next level. The root server is responsible to return query results to the client. The leaves of the tree are called *slots* and do the heavy lifting of reading data from storage and any necessary computation. The branches of the tree are *mixers*, which perform the aggregation.
- BigQuery is orchestrated via *Borg* -Google's precursor to *Kubernetes*. *Borg* simultaneously runs thousands of *Dremel jobs* across one or more clusters made up of tens of thousands of machines. The *mixers* and *slots* are all run by *Borg*, which allocates hardware resources. In addition to as-signing compute capacity for *Dremel jobs*, *Borg* handles fault-tolerance.
- The petabit *Google's Jupiter network* is an ultra-fast network which can deliver terabytes of data in seconds directly from storage into compute for running Dremel jobs.

BigQuery (Tigani and Naidu, 2014; Lakshmanan and Tigani, 2019), has OLAP capabilities for big data. It consequently ingests, stores, and queries large datasets. It also implements Machine Learning algorithms. *BigQuery Machine Learning* (BQML) is a toolset that allows training and serving machine learning models directly in *BigQuery*. BQML supports the following types of models:

- *Linear regression* for forecasting for example, the total amount of transactions on a given day. Labels are real-valued (they cannot be +/- infinity or NaN).
- *Binary logistic regression* for classification; for example, determining whether a transaction is anomalous. Labels must only have two possible values.
- *Multiclass logistic regression* for classification. These models can be used to predict multiple pos-sible values such as whether an input is "low-value," "medium-value," or "high-value." Labels can have up to 50 unique values.
- *K-means clustering* for data segmentation; for example, identifying transactions or addresses seg-ments. K-means is an unsupervised learning technique, so model training does not require labels nor split data for training or evaluation.
- *Matrix Factorization* for creating recommendation systems.

- *Time series* for performing time-series forecasts.
- *Boosted Tree* for creating XGBoost based classification and regression models.
- *Deep Neural Network (DNN)* for creating TensorFlow based Deep Neural Networks for classification and regression models.
- *AutoML Tables* to create best-in-class models without feature engineering or model selection.

Bitcoin Tables in GCP BigQuery

The *GCP BigQuery* schema (Google, 2019) is denormalized, all of output transactions and input transactions of each transaction are stored into two arrays within the transaction relation. The goal of denormalization is workload performance tuning.

Figure 6 illustrates the BigQuery Database physical schema for bitcoin transactions.

Figure 5. Google BigQuery architecture

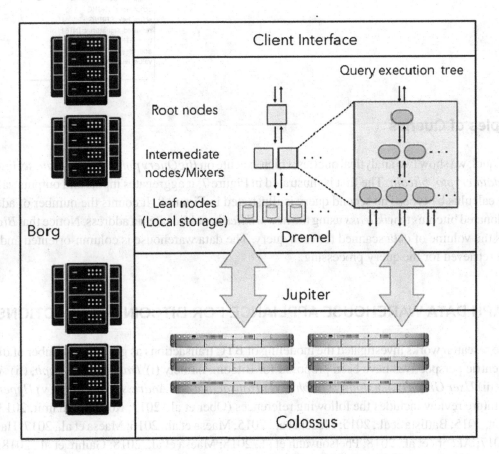

Figure 6. Bitcoin tables layouts in Google BigQuery

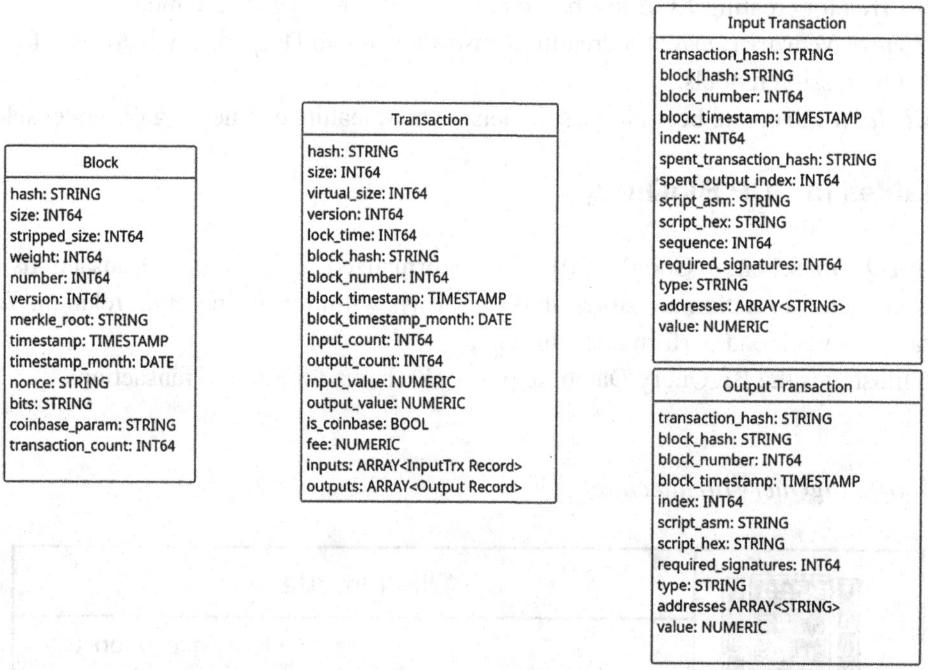

Examples of Queries

In the sequel, we show two analytical queries which execute on *BigQuery public bitcoin data set bigquery-public-data.crypto_bitcoin*. The first is illustrated in Figure 7, it aggregates inputs and outputs values for balance calculus by type. The second query is illustrated in Figure 8. It counts the number of addresses which donated bitcoins to *wikileaks* using the new *wikileaks* public bitcoin address. Notice that *BigQuery* displays the volume of data scanned for each query. The data warehouse is column-oriented and not all data are retrieved for the query processing.

A GRAPH DATA WAREHOUSE APPLIANCE FOR BITCOIN TRANSACTIONS

Multiple research works investigated the modeling of BTC transactions as graphs. A number of different graph-centric perspectives have been proposed for Bitcoin, namely (i) *Transaction Graph*, (ii) *Address Graph*, (iii) *User Graph* (a.k.a. *Entity Graph*), (iv) *Transaction and Address Graph*, and (v) *Hypergraph*. Our literature review includes the following references (Ober et al., 2013; Ron and Shamir, 2013; Zhao and Guan, 2015; Battista et al., 2015; Fleder et al., 2015; Maesa et al., 2016; Maesa et al., 2017; Haslhofer et al., 2017; Akcora et al., 2018; Phetsouvanh et al., 2018; Maesa et al., 2018; Gaihre et al., 2018; Goldsmith et al., 2019; Pontiveros et al., 2019; Maesa et al., 2019; Sharma and Bhatia, 2020; Lv et al., 2020).

Figure 7. This query executed on 7th of May 2021, runs over 1,280,189,454 tuples (88.2GB), and calculates the balance by type (1 Satoshi =10^{-8} Bitcoin)

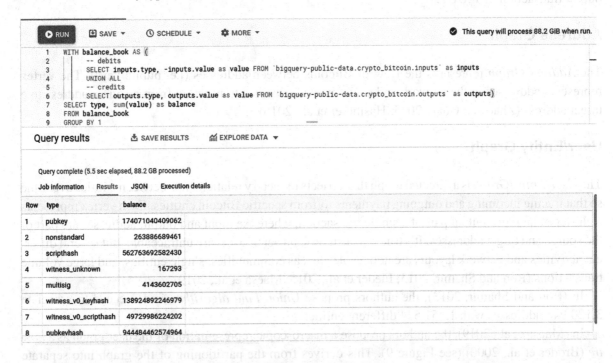

Figure 8. This query calculates the number of addresses which donate bitcoins to the new wikileaks bitcoin address '36EEHh9ME3kU7AZ3rUxBCyKR5FhR3RbqVo'(1 Satoshi =10^{-8} Bitcoin)

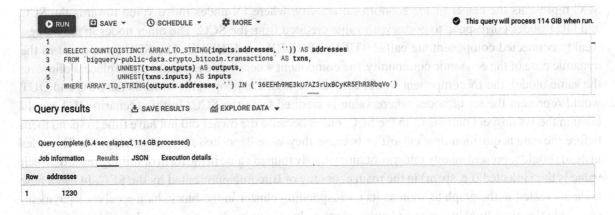

Transaction Graph

The *Transaction Graph* represents the flow of Bitcoins between transactions over time. Each vertex is a transaction and each directed edge includes the transferred Bitcoin value and a timestamp. The edge also is an output connecting two transactions with each other.

Pontiveros et al. (Pontiveros et al., 2019) propose a directed Transaction graph with different types of transactions for vertices, namely *Coinbase transactions* and *non-coinbase Transactions*. Each edge from a non-coinbase transaction T_i to a coinbase or non-coinbase transaction T_j, shows that $T_i.IN$ is an output transaction of $T_j.OUT$.

Address Graph

The *Address Graph* represents the flow of Bitcoins between addresses (i.e. public keys). The vertex represents addresses in the network and each directed edge is a transaction from a source address to a target address (Zhao and Guan, 2015; Haslhofer et al., 2016).

User/Entity Graph

The *User/Entity Graph* is a directed graph that reflects monetary relationships between entities over time so that tracing incoming and outgoing payments to/from specific Bitcoin entities. Each vertex represents a cluster of an input-output pair of a single transaction, where the input and output addresses are part of the source and target addresses. It's true that a significant set of users are untraceable, but several different activities and network layouts are noticeable such as communities, single entities, and large volume transactions (Ron and Shamir, 2013; Fleder et al., 2015; Maesa et al., 2019).

In (Ron and Shamir, 2013), the authors propose *Union-Find algorithm*, and succeed to associate 3,120,948 addresses with 1,851,544 different entities.

In (Maesa et al., 2019), the authors propose a macroscopic representation of the user graph as a *bow tie* (Broder et al., 2000) (see Figure 9). This derives from the partitioning of the graph into separate components according to the connectivity of its nodes, i.e. each node is assigned to a given component according to its reachable nodes set. The nodes in the biggest strongly connected component are called SCC. The remaining nodes reaching (resp. reached by) the ones in the SCC are called IN (resp. OUT). SCC represents the center of the economical activity, where IN nodes move value towards the SCC and OUT nodes correspond to nodes with value credited from the SCC. The other nodes in the biggest weakly connected component are called TUBE, TENDRIL, or FRINGE. The SCC component as the dynamic core of the economic community, the component where value exchanges take place. Following the same model, the IN component would contain the nodes moving value towards the SCC and OUT would represent the set of nodes where value is credited from the SCC. In this scenario OUT would contain the yet unspent outputs from the SCC, either because the owner did not have time to spend them before the data acquisition time cut-off or because they were deposited for cold storage. The IN nodes instead should represent mainly miners obtaining newly minted value in the form of mining rewards. Such value is then injected (i.e. spent) in the main economy of Bitcoin, represented by the SCC. In fact a new node is created in the graph as soon as its corresponding cluster in the blockchain receives a payment, so, inside the giant weakly connected component, value flows by design from nodes with no incoming arcs (that can only be part of IN) through multiple intermediate nodes until they reach nodes with no outgoing arcs (that can only be members of OUT). In this scheme TENDRIL FROM IN (TENDRIL TO OUT) are anomalies that send value to (receive value from) nodes not part of the main economy (i.e. outside the SCC). Similarly TUBE nodes transmit value from IN to OUT bypassing the SCC completely.

Figure 9. Bow tie

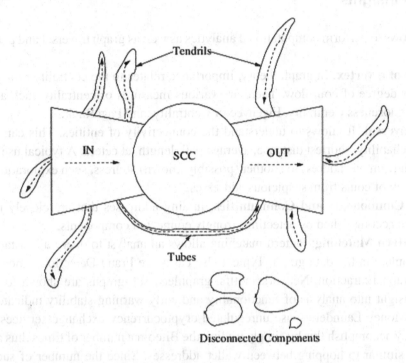

Graph of Transactions and Addresses

The Bitcoin network is a directed graph $G = (V, E, B)$ where V is a set of vertices, and $E \subseteq V \times V$ is a set of edges. $B = \{Address, Transaction\}$ represents the set of vertex types. For any vertex $u \in V$, it has a vertex type $\varphi(u) \in B$. For each edge e, $u, v \in E$ between adjacent nodes u and v, we have $\varphi(u) \neq \varphi(v)$, and either $\varphi(u) = Transaction$ or $\varphi(v) = Address$. That is, an edge $e \in E$ represents a coin transfer between an *address node* and *a transaction node*.

In (Akcora et al., 2018), each transaction with its input and output nodes represents a chainlet (subgraph). A *k-chainlet* $G_k = (V_k, E_k, B)$ is a subgraph of G with k nodes of type {*Transaction*}. A classification of 1-chainlets can be made in terms of x -the number of inputs, and y -the number of outputs, since there is only one transaction involved. *Merge 1-chainlet* matches transaction with $y = 1$ and $x > 1$, *Transition 1-chainlet* matches transaction with $x = y$, and *Split 1-chainlet* matches a transaction with $y > x$.

Hypergraph

Maesa et al. (Maesa et al., 2016) propose a weighted directed hypergraph $H = (A, T)$ with A is the set of all addresses; T is the set of transactions, which can be modeled as a set of ordered pairs (A_1, A_2) with $A_1, A_2 \subseteq A$, meaning that the addresses in A_1 are paying the addresses in A_2. To each transaction $s = (A_1, A_2) \in T$, they associate (i) a timestamp telling when the transaction took place, (ii) a distribution of amounts among the nodes in A_2 denoted as b_s. More formally, b_s is a function associating to each $a \in A_2$ a multiset of values in R. Indeed, notice that there can be transactions associated to the same $a \in A_2$ more than one single amount, and (iii) a fee φ_s (eventually 0) that associates to A_1 the voluntary taxes paid.

Graph Model Insights

Graph model allows to perform computational analytics as well as graph traversal and pattern matching,

- **Centrality of a vertex**: In graph theory, importance relates to the centrality of a vertex. It could be a higher degree of coin flow. There are various measures of centrality such as Betweenness Centrality, Closeness Centrality, Eigenvector Centrality, and PageRank.
- **Graph Traversal**: It allows to understand the connectivity of entities. This can be in terms of finding reachability, shortest distance, average path length, et cetera. A typical use case is exploring the path from one address to another (possibly known) address, such exploration could help to track the flow of coins from suspicious addresses.
- **Detecting Components and Communities**: finding addresses that are closely related to each other can be accomplished by detecting strongly connected components.
- **Graph Pattern Matching**: Pattern matching allows an analyst to query all instances of a given pattern/template in the data graph. Typical Use cases are Fraud Detection, Anomaly Detection, and Sub-graph Extraction. Network motifs, graphlets, sub-graphs are shown to provide an invaluable insight into analysis of functionality and early warning stability indicators in financial networks. Money Launderers use unregulated cryptocurrency exchange services to clean their money. They accomplish this by simply trading the Bitcoin a number of times thus adding degrees of privacy similar to hopping between wallet addresses. Since the number of such unregulated exchanges are few. A template matching to a launderers trail could be used to identify all such transactions matching this template and the addresses involved could be flagged for further monitoring (Maesa et al., 2016).

In Table 4, we summarize addressed business questions in related works adopting the graph data model.

Graph Model Scalability

Distribution is the ability to spread a database over multiple servers in order to be scalable. A graph database that distributes its data should be able to connect two vertices with an edge even when those two vertices are stored on two different servers. It will be difficult to design a partitioned graph for bitcoin transactions, since the partitioning must be dynamic and needs to be performed every time we refresh the data warehouse. The second alternative to graph databases is to use frameworks suitable for graph analytics, such as Google's Pregel (Malewicz et al, 2010) -a system for large-scale graph processing on distributed cluster of commodity machines, as well as Apache Giraph (Khayyat et al., 2017). Google's Pregel, Apache Giraph, Apache Spark Graph Frames do not use a graph database for storage, and are optimized for scanning and processing Big Graphs in batch mode.

FUTURE RESEARCH DIRECTIONS

Blockchain creates a decentralized and secure digital ledger of all transactions across a peer-to-peer network. Digital currencies like Bitcoin use decentralised blockchain to record an open and unalterable history of transactions. Vast amounts of transactional data are being generated on the blockchain. This

Table 4. Synopsis of insights obtained from graph data model

Research Work	Insights
(Ron and Shamir, 2013)	Authors isolate all the large transactions (with amount > 50,000 bitcoins), and analyze how these amounts were accumulated and then spent (investigation of long chains patterns).
(Ober et al., 2013)	Authors focus on metrics: they analyze Price per bitcoin and activity of entities over time; Exchange rate in USD at Mt. Gox (weighted average); Entity activity over time (linear scale); Entity activity over time (logarithmic scale); Total number of transactions (logarithmic scale); dormant coins (Bitcoins that have not been in use for a certain amount of time).
(Fleder et al., 2015)	Authors build an Address Graph, then a User Graph: Investigation of anonymity in the Bitcoin system, via linking bitcoin public keys to real people, and tracing user activity.
(Zhao and Guan, 2015)	Authors Investigate *Mt. Gox case* (on February 10, 2014, *Mt. Gox* issued a press release claiming that it had lost more than 850,000 BTC); they show that this case features double-spending, theft, money laundering and fraudulent transactions.
(Battista et al., 2015)	Authors analyze real money laundering processes. They define the *BitCone* or *cone* of a transaction S as the subgraph reachable from S within a given time limit T. They present a system for the visual analysis of flows in the Blockchain.
(Maesa et al., 2016)	Authors focus on the analysis of the outliers present in the in-degree distribution of the users graph. Anomalous patterns relate to Pseudo-Spasm-transactions (PS-transactions). Basically the behavior of the PS-transaction creator is to create a chain of transactions, where a transaction at each step pays a constant amount of 0.00001 BTC to some addresses and leaves the change in an intermediary address used as input for the next hop in the chain. A chain ends either when the funds in the last change address are used for a transaction without this particular structure or when the input funds are completely spent and no change address is used in the last transaction of the chain.
(Maesa et al., 2017)	Authors analyse the outliers in the in-degree distribution of the bitcoin users graph and find out that topological patterns are due to artificial users behaviors.
(Haslhofer et al., 2017)	Authors propose *GraphSense*, which allows users to explore transactions and follow the money flow, facilitates analytics by semantically enriching the transaction graph, supports path and graph pattern search, and guides analysts to anomalous data points.
(Akcora et al., 2018)	Authors propose a novel concept of *chainlets* (Bitcoin subgraphs), which allows to evaluate the local topological structure of the Bitcoin graph over time; impact of local topological structures on Bitcoin price dynamics. Network flows can be detailed in terms of successive chainlets. Granger causality test assesses whether one time series is useful in predicting another.
(Phetsouvanh et al., 2018)	Authors propose graph mining techniques to explore the relationships among wallet addresses suspected to be involved in a given extortion racket, exploiting the anonymity of the Bitcoin network to collect and launder money. They base their work on Ashley Madison blackmail campaign in 2015.
(Maesa et al, 2019)	Authors perform an analysis of the Bitcoin users graph, obtained by heuristic clustering of the Bitcoin transaction graph. The nodes are augmented with the users balance and the edges are weighted according to the Bitcoin value exchanged. Then they are classified into SCC, OUT, IN, TENDRIL, FRINGE, TUBE, DISCONNECTED. They also perform a temporal analysis, studying how the different components change over time.
(Goldsmith et al., 2019)	Authors analyze six hack subnetworks of bitcoin transactions known to belong to two prominent hacking groups
(Pontiveros et al., 2019)	Authors propose propose a new centrality measure named *mint centrality*. The measure uses the inherent tree structure of transactions in bitcoin and their relation to the corresponding set of coinbase transactions
(Sharma and Bhatia, 2020)	Authors analyze payments to Ransomware.
(Lv et al., 2020)	Authors analyze the entity information of bitcoin transactions on the chain to achieve the effect of de-anonymization.

requires sophisticated analysis due to anonymity in order to track money laundering and illegal funding of criminal activity. In this chapter, we overview different data models and analytics business queries investigated in each data model. Business queries related to transaction data, exchange and market data, mining, fees data, anonymous transactions, as well as pattern matching and community discovery. Graph models for bitcoin transactions offer more insights. The data integration in graph data models is more complex than for relational data model and nested-immutable data model.

Future research work includes *first* devising optimized data integration workflows adapted for graph models and ingestion of real-time data; *second* optimizing graph models to serve as real-time cryptocurrency data warehouse enabling both OLAP queries and pattern matching queries; *finally* combining benefits of the two models the relational and the graph model using multi-model and polystores technologies.

REFERENCES

Abe Developers. (2013). *Block browser for bitcoin and similar currencies.* https://github.com/bitcoin-abe/bitcoin-abe

Akcora, C. G., Dey, A. K., Gel, Y. R., & Kantarcioglu, M. (2018). Forecasting bitcoin price with graph chainlets. In *22nd Pacific-Asia Conference, PAKDD Proceedings, Part III. Volume 10939 of Lecture Notes in Computer Science.* Springer.

Battista, G. D., Donato, V. D., Patrignani, M., Pizzonia, M., Roselli, V., & Tamassia, R. (2015). Bitconeview: visualization of flows in the bitcoin transaction graph. *12th IEEE Symposium on Visualization for Cyber Security*, 1–8. 10.1109/VIZSEC.2015.7312773

BigQuery. (2020). *Google: Bitcoin in BigQuery: blockchain analytics on public data.* https://cloud.google.com/blog/products/gcp/bitcoin-in-bigquery-blockchain-analytics-on-public-data

Broder, A. Z., Kumar, R., Maghoul, F., Raghavan, P., Rajagopalan, S., Stata, R., Tomkins, A., & Wiener, J. L. (2000). Graph structure in the web. *Computer Networks*, *33*(1-6), 309–320. doi:10.1016/S1389-1286(00)00083-9

Chen, C., Yan, X., Zhu, F., Han, J., & Yu, P. S. (2008). Graph OLAP: Towards Online Analytical Processing on Graphs. *Eighth IEEE International Conference on Data Mining*, 103-112. 10.1109/ICDM.2008.30

Dani, K. (2018). *BTC dataset.* https://senseable2015-6.mit.edu/bitcoin/

Fleder, M., Kester, M.S., & Pillai, S. (2015). *Bitcoin transaction graph analysis.* CoRR abs/1502.01657.

Gaihre, A., Luo, Y., & Liu, H. (2018). Do bitcoin users really care about anonymity? an analysis of the bitcoin transaction graph. *IEEE International Conference on Big Data*, 1198–1207. 10.1109/Big-Data.2018.8622442

Galici, R., Ordile, L., Marchesi, M., Pinna, A., & Tonelli, R. (2020). Applying the ETL process to blockchain data. *prospect and findings. Inf.*, *11*(4), 204. doi:10.3390/info11040204

GCP. (2020). *Google Cloud Platform: Bitcoin Historical Data. Bitcoin data at 1-min intervals from select exchanges, Jan 2012 to April 2020.* https://www.kaggle.com/mczielinski/bitcoin-historical-data

Goldsmith, D., Grauer, K., & Shmalo, Y. (2019). *Analyzing hack subnetworks in the bitcoin transaction graph*. CoRR abs/1910.13415.

Google. (2019). *Introducing six new cryptocurrencies in BigQuery Public Datasets and how to analyze them*. https://cloud.google.com/blog/products/data-analytics/introducing-six-new-cryptocurrencies-in-bigquery-public-datasets-and-how-to-analyze-them

Haslhofer, B., Karl, R., & Filtz, E. (2016). O bitcoin where art thou? insight into large-scale transaction graphs. *12th International Conference on Semantic Systems - SEMANTiCS2016 and the 1st International Workshop on Semantic Change & Evolving Semantics (SuCCESS'16), Leipzig, Germany, Volume 1695 of CEUR Workshop Proceedings.*

Khayyat, Z., Abdelaziz, I., Sakr, S. M., & Orakzai, F.M. (2017). Large-Scale Graph Processing Using Apache Giraph. Springer.

Kwok-Bun, Y., Karthika, C., & Hema, G. (2019). Storing and querying bitcoin blockchain using sql databases. *Information Systems Education Journal, 17*, 24–41.

Lakshmanan, V., & Tigani, J. (2019). BigQuery: The Definitive Guide Data Warehousing, Analytics, and Machine Learning at Scale. O'Reilly Publishing.

Lv, X., Zhong, Y., & Tan, Q. (2020). A study of bitcoin de-anonymization: Graph and multidimensional data analysis. *5th IEEE International Conference on Data Science in Cyberspace, DSC 2020*, 339–345. 10.1109/DSC50466.2020.00059

Maesa, D. D. F. (2017). Detecting artificial behaviours in the bitcoin users graph. *Online Social Networks and Media, 3-4*, 63–74. doi:10.1016/j.osnem.2017.10.006

Maesa, D. D. F., Marino, A., & Ricci, L. (2016). An analysis of the bitcoin users graph: inferring unusual behaviours. *5th International Workshop on Complex Networks and their Applications*, 749–760. 10.1007/978-3-319-50901-3_59

Maesa, D. D. F., Marino, A., & Ricci, L. (2016). *Uncovering the bitcoin blockchain: An analysis of the full users graph. IEEE International Conference on Data Science and Advanced Analytics*, 537–546.

Maesa, D. D. F., Marino, A., & Ricci, L. (2018). The graph structure of bitcoin. *Proceedings of the 7th International Conference on Complex Networks and Their Applications*, 547–558. 10.1007/978-3-030-05414-4_44

Maesa, D. D. F., Marino, A., & Ricci, L. (2019). The bow tie structure of the bitcoin users graph. *Applied Network Science, 4*(1), 1–22. doi:10.100741109-019-0163-y

Malewicz, G., Austern, M. H., Bik, A. J. C., Dehnert, J. C., Horn, I., Leiser, N., & Czajkowski, G. (2010). Pregel: a system for large-scale graph processing. *Proceedings of the international conference on Management of data*, 135-146. 10.1145/1807167.1807184

Nakamoto, S. (2008). *A Peer-to-Peer Electronic Cash System*. https://bitcoin.org/bitcoin.pdf

Nathan, S., Govindarajan, C., Saraf, A., Sethi, M., & Jayachandran, P. (2019). Blockchain meets database: Design and implementation of a blockchain relational database. *Proc. VLDB Endow., 12,* 1539–1552. 10.14778/3342263.3342632

Ober, M., Katzenbeisser, S., & Hamacher, K. (2013). Structure and anonymity of the bitcoin transaction graph. *Future Internet, 5*(2), 237–250. doi:10.3390/fi5020237

Paik, H., Xu, X., Bandara, H. M. N. D., Lee, S. U., & Lo, S. K. (2019). Analysis of data management in blockchain-based systems: From architecture to governance. *IEEE Access: Practical Innovations, Open Solutions, 7,* 186091–186107. doi:10.1109/ACCESS.2019.2961404

Phetsouvanh, S., Oggier, F. E., & Datta, A. (2018). EGRET: extortion graph exploration techniques in the bitcoin network. *IEEE International Conference on Data Mining Workshops, ICDM Workshops, Singapore, Singapore,* 244–251. 10.1109/ICDMW.2018.00043

Pontiveros, B. B. F., Steichen, M., & State, R. (2019). Mint centrality: A centrality measure for the bitcoin transaction graph. *IEEE International Conference on Blockchain and Cryptocurrency,* 159–162.

Ron, D., & Shamir, A. (2013). Quantitative analysis of the full bitcoin transaction graph. *Lecture Notes in Computer Science., 7859,* 6–24.

Sharma, A., & Bhatia, A. (2020). *Bitcoin's blockchain data analytics: A graph theoretic perspective.* CoRR abs/2002.06403.

Sphere 10 Software. (2018). *Blockchain SQL.* http://blockchainsql.io/

Tigani, J., & Naidu, S. (2014). *Google BigQuery Analytics* (1st ed.). Wiley Publishing.

Zhao, C., & Guan, Y. (2015) A graph-based investigation of bitcoin transactions. *11th IFIP WG 11.9 International Conference,* 79–95.

KEY TERMS AND DEFINITIONS

BigQuery: Is a serverless, highly scalable, and cost-effective multi-cloud data warehouse provided as a service by Google Cloud Platform.

Bitcoin: Bitcoin is a digital currency that was created in January 2009. Bitcoin is commonly abbreviated as "BTC". Unlike fiat currency, bitcoin is created, distributed, traded, and stored with the use of a decentralized ledger system, known as a blockchain.

Blockchain: A system in which a record of transactions made in a cryptocurrency are maintained across several computers that are linked in a peer-to-peer network. The ledger is immutable, which means that the data entered is irreversible. This means that transactions are permanently recorded and viewable to anyone.

Cryptocurrency: A digital currency in which transactions are verified and records maintained by a decentralized system using cryptography, rather than by a centralized authority.

Data Warehousing: Is the process for collecting and managing data from varied sources to provide meaningful business insights.

FinTech: Financial technology (abbreviated FinTech) is the technology and innovation that aims to compete with traditional financial methods in the delivery of financial services.

Graph: A structure made of vertices and edges connecting vertices.

On-Line Analytical Processing: Abbreviated OLAP is a software for performing multidimensional analysis at high speeds on large volumes of data from a data warehouse, or a data mart.

Chapter 4
Appendable–Block Blockchains:
Overview, Applications, and Challenges

Regio A. Michelin
 https://orcid.org/0000-0002-6758-1466
Cybersecurity CRC, Australia & University of New South Wales, Australia

Roben Castagna Lunardi
Federal Institute of Education, Science and Technology of Rio Grande do Sul (IFRS), Brazil

Henry Cabral Nunes
Pontifical Catholic University of Rio Grande do Sul, Brazil

Volkan Dedeoglu
CSIRO, Australia

Charles V. Neu
University of Santa Cruz do Sul, Brazil

Avelino Francisco Zorzo
Pontifical Catholic University of Rio Grande do Sul, Brazil

Salil S. Kanhere
 https://orcid.org/0000-0002-1835-3475
University of New South Wales, Australia

ABSTRACT

Blockchain has emerged as a technology that can change the way people and systems interact, providing mechanisms that ensure integrity and ownership of the data produced without reliance on a trusted third-party. Appendable-block blockchain is a novel instantiation that suits for solutions that require a high transaction throughput. Appendable-block blockchains focus on data produced by nodes instead of a relation (transaction) between two entities. This new kind of blockchain can improve how data are stored and managed in distributed systems. This chapter introduces the notion of appendable-block blockchain and exemplifies its applicability in multiple practical domains. Additionally, the authors provide a discussion on the security aspects of this new blockchain. Finally, the chapter presents current issues and possible future directions for appendable-block blockchains.

DOI: 10.4018/978-1-7998-5839-3.ch004

INTRODUCTION

In recent years, blockchain technology has been used in different types of applications to solve, naturally, problems related to, for example, resilience, distributed processing, integrity and non-repudiation of produced information. Furthermore, different types of blockchain have also been developed to solve those problems using novel architectures, data structures, consensus algorithms or even the possibility to execute Turing machine code. Data blocks, for example, can be organised as the traditional Bitcoin block, using a Directed-Acyclic Graph, or using an appendable-block data structure.

The appendable-block capability, for example, changes the way that transactions are combined into a block. Our proposed blockchain architecture follows the traditional block definition in terms of splitting it in two different parts: (*i*) block header: this part contains the immutable information in the block. (*ii*) block payload: where the transactions are stored. However, in our architecture, the payload arranges the transactions using a linked list structure, and it defines a set of rules that enables an entity to send transactions to the block where the entity public key is stored.

The block header contains the required information to validate transactions ownership, and uniquely identify the block. It is composed of the block owner public key, sequential number identifier in the blockchain, previous block header hash, timestamp when the block was created, access policies, and expiration time.

The block payload can only contain transactions produced from the entity that holds the private key used to sign the transactions. The validation to append a new transaction, requires that the transaction must be signed by the entity private key, and the block expiration time was not reached. The signature is validated using the public key, stored in the block header, and thus the transaction is appended at the end of the payload section. Using a similar idea from traditional blockchain, where the first block points to the genesis block, and thus the following blocks are linked together, in the appendable-block blockchain the first transaction contains the block header hash data, and the following transactions are linked with the previous transaction's hash. This data structure enables the proposed blockchain to reduce the data fragmentation, as the transactions are grouped in blocks according to the entity that produces it.

This blockchain model was designed to support constrained entities producing information. These entities are arranged in a multi-layer architecture, according to their capabilities and purpose on the solution.

The rest of this chapter will present the different architectures that can be used to organize the appendable-block blockchain; a discussion on the different types of block data structures and explain the one used in the appendable-block blockchain; how consensus algorithms and smart contracts are used; and, finally, different applications that use appendable-block blockchain are presented.

ARCHITECTURES

Initially, as presented by Bitcoin (Nakamoto, 2008), blockchain was designed to operate over a completely distributed architecture, where all nodes can (also known as full nodes) have the same role in the management and in the operation of the blockchain. However, due to the characteristics of many applications, some proposals discussed the usage of blockchain in a more controlled environment. For example, for international bank transfers, Ripple (Armknecht *et al.*, 2015) proposed an architecture composed of different roles, where clients connect through servers. Clients mean light-nodes that control a key pair and request transactions. Servers can be different kinds of nodes: a proposer (who will try to insert a new transaction requested by a client), validator (a node that will validate or not a transaction in a consensus round) or a tracking node (a server that receives validate transactions).

Appendable-block blockchain was initially designed for a hierarchical Internet of Things (IoT) peer-to-peer network arranging different entities, *i.e.*, IoT nodes with different roles in the network. In a first proposal from Lunardi *et al.* (2018), these roles were divided into layers (see Figure 01):

1. Perception Layer: composed of devices, which produce information and interact with the physical world;
2. Transportation Layer: composed of gateways, which manage the access and control data and activity of devices;
3. Application Layer: composed of service providers, which request information from gateways.

Figure 1. Hierarchical Blockchain Architecture

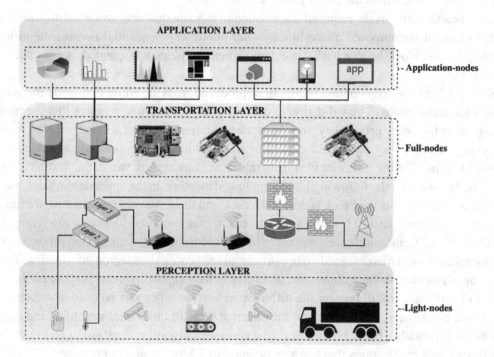

More generically, we can consider IoT devices as **light-nodes** in a blockchain, which produce information. Each light-node has its own key pair and will use its private key to sign and request transactions (set of data) to be inserted into the blockchain. Unlike cryptocurrencies blockchains (*e.g.*, Bitcoin and Ripple), the information produced does not require an exchange between light-nodes. Consequently, the information produced by each light-node is independent of each other. This kind of independent information produced allows the designing of a unique data structure that will be discussed in Section 2.

Additionally, gateways can be represented as consensus-nodes or **full-nodes**, *i.e.*, nodes that will perform consensus and also maintain the blockchain. These full-nodes will allow (or not) the access of the light-nodes and perform insertion in the blockchain. Also, full-nodes are responsible for consensus algorithms and are responsible to reject and store (locally or at remote storage) the information produced by the light-nodes. However, each consensus algorithm will use a different approach, and the full-nodes can be used or not in the consensus procedure. More details and discussions of consensus algorithms are presented in Section 3.

Finally, service providers can be considered as blockchain **application-nodes** or servers that provide an interface to access the information of the blockchain by an external application. Due to hardware constraints in IoT environments, these nodes are independent of the full-nodes. These nodes are responsible for managing the connections from clients outside of the blockchain network. Also, it is important to note that these nodes cannot connect directly to light-nodes, but only to full-nodes. Consequently, light-nodes - possibly composed of limited hardware - are protected from direct external access. More discussion about applications is presented in Section 5.

BLOCKCHAIN DATA STRUCTURE

Blockchain technology can use different types of data structures. The first type was the traditional data structure, which was designed to support the Bitcoin network. It is characterised by its immutable blocks and transactions. After that, a different data structure was introduced by using the Directed Acyclic Graph (DAG). The novelty was the absence of blocks, and the way transactions are linked to each other in a DAG structure. After the DAG a third data structure was proposed by a group of researchers. The appendable-block data structure, which uses a chain of blocks, similar to the traditional blockchain block, but with a mutable (appendable) block that can accept the insertion of new transactions. The last structure allows a transaction to be appended into a block already inserted in the blockchain. This section provides an overview of these three different data structures presented in Figure 02.

Figure 2. Blockchain data structures (adapted from Zorzo et al., (2018))

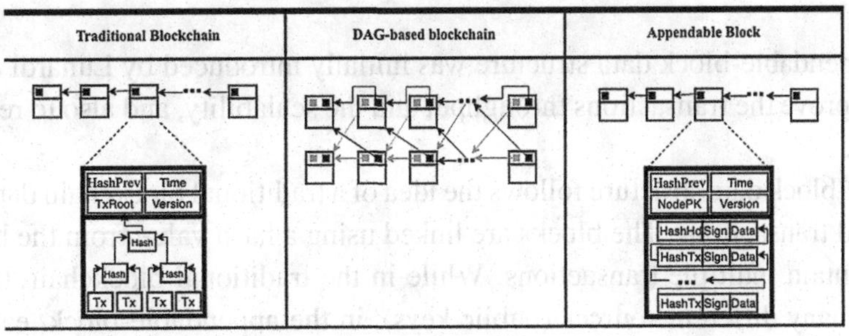

The traditional blockchain data structure was introduced by Nakamoto (2008) where he defines the Bitcoin blockchain. The initial focus of this model was to support a completely decentralised electronic cash for online payments. The electronic cash operations are represented by transactions that contain the amount of money to transfer, the sender and the receiver. Groups of these transactions are combined and inserted into blocks. Each block has a minimum set of metadata information, such as unique identification, a link to its predecessor and a timestamp. The nodes (users) have a unique encrypted address that is used to perform and sign transactions in this blockchain.

Traditionally the link between the blocks in a blockchain, follows the concept of a linked list, where the link between blocks is created by computing the block hash, and this value is inserted in the next block. Using the block hash and storing its value in the subsequent block grants to the blockchain the immutability property, because if any piece of data changes, the hash value will change and consequently the chain will break (Pervez *et al.*, 2018). Inside of the block, the transactions are arranged using a Merkle tree data structure, which gives to this data structure an efficient way to verify if a transaction is contained in the block. The main characteristic of this structure is to group the transactions ordered in the three leaves and compute transaction hashes in pairs, until they reach the root value. The Merkle tree allows to store multiple transactions, however it requires to follow the order and keep the root value. The traditional blockchain data structure, groups the transaction into the blocks as these transactions are sent to the network. This mechanism makes the transaction produced from the same source (identified by its public key), become fragmented, as each transaction could be stored in a different block.

The traditional data structure applied in most blockchains present some limitations such as data fragmentation, scalability and efficiency, which may restrict its utilisation in applications that require efficient micro transactions, such as Internet of Things (IoT) applications (Pervez *et al.*, 2018). On the other hand, DAG structures are emerging to revolutionise blockchain applications, especially in IoT environments, by offering optimised validation, high scalability, efficient provenance and multi-party involvement. DAG is composed of a network of different nodes that are able to approve transactions (Yang *et al.*, 2019). Each new transaction performed must be validated by at least two earlier transactions to be recorded on the blockchain network, building a distributed network of doubly-checked transactions. Thus, DAG structures do not require miners to perform transaction authorisation, providing a higher throughput with transactions going through almost directly. Moreover, as no miners are required, there are also no miners fees, thus reducing the costs associated with authenticating transactions. The most popular DAG based blockchain structures are Nxt, IOTA, Orumesh, DagCoin, Byteball, Nano and XDAG (Pervez *et al.*, 2018).

Appendable-Block Data Structure

The blockchain appendable-block data structure was initially introduced by Lunardi *et al.* (2018). This concept aims to improve the transactions throughput and the scalability, and also to reduce the information fragmentation.

The appendable-block data structure follows the idea of a traditional blockchain data structure, which relies on blocks and transactions. The blocks are linked using a hash value from the block predecessor. Each block can contain multiple transactions. While in the traditional blockchain the block contains transactions from many different sources (public keys), in the appendable-block, each block contains transactions only from a single source (only the owner of a public/private key pair can append transactions in its block). Based on this capability, every source can send transactions at any time, and its transactions are appended in the block of the corresponding public key, thus allowing different transactions from different sources, being appended into the blockchain at the same time. This characteristic improves the blockchain throughput, scalability and reduces the information fragmentation, as the transactions are grouped by its source. The appendable-block defines an expiration policy for each block, which prevents the block to grow continually. Once the expiration is achieved, it enforces the entity to create a new block.

In appendable-block blockchains, each block has two main parts: the Block Header and the Block Ledger. Block Header is composed of the identification and configuration data of the block, *i.e.*, it will maintain important information about the block. For example, in Figure 03, Block Header BH_k is composed of different fields. The hash of the previous block ($HashBH_{k-1}$) is used to ensure tamper-resistance to the blockchain. A unique index (k) helps to navigate and can be used as an index to easily access a block. An expiration value (Exp_k) ensures that a block can be closed after a number of interactions or at a specific timestamp (to avoid an infinite block). A timestamp ($Time_k$) is used to ensure that new blocks are not inserted in a specific order, avoiding blocks inserted in a long past or future. An access policy (Pol_k) represents the rules that a node is submitted. And the node public key (NPK_i) represents the owner of the data and can be used to validate all signatures produced by the device. Similar to the traditional blockchain data structure, Block Header is immutable, i.e., the data in the block header cannot be changed or modified.

Figure 3. Appendable-block blockchain data structure (Lunardi et al., (2019))

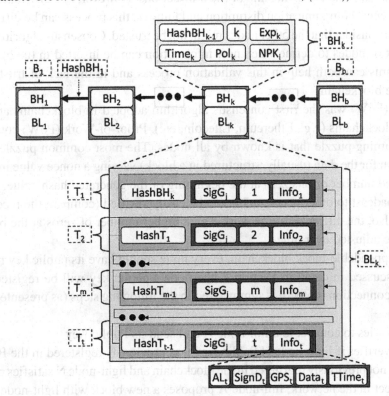

Block Ledger is composed of a set of transactions, but differently from traditional blockchain, new transactions can be linked to the last transaction in each block as long as the block expiration time has not been reached. In appendable-block blockchain each transaction is appended to the previous transaction, creating a hash chain (similar to the hash chain used to link the block headers). For example, in Figure 03, the last inserted transaction T_t was inserted in the Block Ledger BL_k using the hash of the previous transaction ($HashT_{t-1}$). Additionally, the transaction T_t is composed of the signature of the gateway ($SigG_j$) (or **full-node**) that processed the information ($Info_t$) and an index (t). The information processed ($Info_t$) was produced by the node (NPK_i) that is the owner of the block. This ownership is ensured by the signature of the device (or **light-node**) SignD$_t$ over all the other data in the (Info$_t$). The access level (AL$_t$) required to access the information of that information, the location (GPS$_t$), the information timestamp (TTime$_t$) and the data itself (Data$_t$).

Consequently, after a new Block Header is created, it is linked to the previous Block Header, preserving its integrity. Also, new information inserted in the Block Ledger is both signed and hashed, guaranteeing both integrity and non-repudiation.

CONSENSUS ALGORITHMS

Nodes should guarantee that the information stored in the blockchain is trusted and linked with other trusted information in the blockchain. In order to ensure that, nodes have to participate in a validation process to verify the data and the ownership of the transactions. However, in a distributed environment, sometimes with latency, communication disruption and failures, this process can be difficult to achieve. Also, a node should consider that the other nodes might not be trusted. Consensus algorithms is a protocol performed by a set of nodes to define when new information can be inserted in the blockchain. Thus, consensus algorithms can both help in this validation process and in the lack of trust in other nodes participating in the blockchain.

Proof-of-work (PoW) was the first consensus algorithm adopted in blockchains and is still being used in different blockchains (*e.g.*, Ethereum, Litecoin, etc). Proof-of-Work (PoW) consists of solving a resourcing consuming puzzle that is known by all nodes. The most common puzzle consists in the generation of a hash for the data (usually, structured in a block) varying a nonce value in order to obtain at least a predefined number of bits zero at the beginning of the generated hash value. After the block is created, it is broadcast to other peers, and it can be easily verified (compare the received hash with the block hash). Also, the difficulty of the work *e.g.*, a higher number of zeros at the beginning of the target hash), can be adjusted over time.

In the case of appendable-block blockchain, every node should have its public key registered in the blockchain. As discussed in detail in Section 2, the node's public key will be registered in a unique block header. The connection protocol is summarised in the following steps (as presented in Figure 04):

1. Light-node N tries to connect to a full-node A and send its Public Key
2. Full-node A verifies if light-node N Public Key was previously registered in the Blockchain
   a. If it was not previously registered in the blockchain and light-node N satisfies predefined rules to connect in the network, full-node A proposes a new block with light-node N Public Key
      i. To insert a new block, full-node A should send it to other gateways following a consensus algorithm
3. After a block with light-node N Public Key is inserted in the blockchain, full-node A and light-node N can establish an encrypted channel
4. After light-node N is connected to a full-node, they can exchange information
5. Any update from light-node N is a new transaction in the blockchain

More than the unreliable peer environment where a blockchain is executed, other aspects should be considered to choose a consensus algorithm, such as the hardware requirements (*e.g.*, computing power, memory and storage capabilities, and power consumption) and the architecture adopted (*e.g.*, number of

Figure 4. Connection protocol in IoT using appendable-block blockchain

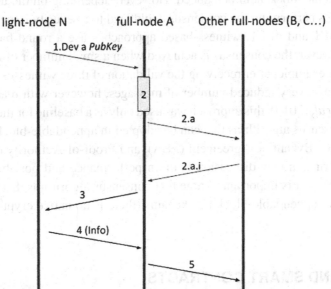

nodes performing the consensus and their connections). Consequently, in many scenarios - in particular, when nodes have limited hardware - Proof-of-Work is not the best option.

Appendable-block blockchains were designed for IoT environments based on a hierarchical P2P network. Many IoT devices have some limitations and some requirements that guide in the consensus algorithm that can be used. For example, high latency between the creation of information and its inclusion in the blockchain is not acceptable in many IoT applications (e.g., an actuator that needs to perform an action based on a set of sensor values). Consequently, voting based consensus algorithms are best fitted for this kind of blockchain, due to its small amount of processing required. Additionally, a voting-based approach can reduce the latency to insert information in the blockchain depending on how it is implemented. As presented by Lunardi *et al.* (2019), appendable-block blockchains adopted three main consensus algorithms: Practical Byzantine Fault Tolerance (PBFT), dBFT (delegated Byzantine Fault Tolerance), and Witness-based approaches.

PBFT was proposed by Castro & Liskov (1999) to achieve consensus in distributed systems. In a simplified way, this consensus is based on rounds that are started by a leader. The leader will send the information (or block) to all full-nodes (or gateways in IoT scenarios) participating in the network. After that, every full-node will vote if the information is valid or not. A consensus is achieved when more than ⅔ of the participating nodes vote that information (or a block) is valid. PBFT suffers from poor scalability due to a large number of messages exchanged, in particular if it is considered a large number of nodes. Moreover, achieving consensus in a dynamic environment can be a problem as active nodes can change their status during the consensus.

Proposed by Crain *et al.* (2017), dBFT is also based on rounds started by a leader. But differently to PBFT, the consensus is achieved using a set of nodes called delegates. These delegates are a limited number of full-nodes that will perform the consensus, and these delegates will propagate the information to other full-nodes. Consequently, the number of messages exchanged is reduced and also the latency to insert information in the blockchain is reduced. However, depending on the untrusted environment, a small number of nodes performing the consensus could lead to a security issue.

Similar to both PBFT and dBFT, witness-based approaches use a round-based voting process to insert information. However, the consensus is achieved when a small number of nodes (called witness) validate that block. For example, after receiving the validation of three witnesses, a block is considered valid. This approach has a very reduced number of messages, however with many security issues. As presented by Lunardi *et al.* (2019), this approach was used only as a baseline for the obtained throughput.

There are other consensus algorithms that can be adopted in appendable-block blockchains, such as BFT-SMART, Federated Byzantine Agreement (FBA), and Proof-of-Authority (PoA). However, each consensus algorithm brings a new discussion both on performance and possible security issues that should be addressed. Also, it is important to note that consensus algorithms that use rewards as incentives are not suitable for appendable-block blockchains (there is no native cryptocurrency in this kind of blockchains).

APPLICATIONS AND SMART CONTRACTS

Smart contracts are a significant development for blockchain technology, they consist of programs that exist on top of the blockchain and can be automatically triggered without the need of a central party controlling them. It allows versatility in the development of applications on top of the blockchain while also extending the blockchain benefits, such as non-repudiation, decentralization, security, and auditability to these applications. The appendable-block blockchain provides support for smart contracts using the model proposed in the work of Nunes *et al.* (2020) and Lunardi *et al.* (2020).

This context-based model has some key differences to other smart contract models, such as the ones used in Ethereum and Hyperledger Fabric. These differences arise from the distinct data structure, which allows the parallel insertion of transactions. This parallelism for transaction insertion is explored in the Context-based model to process smart contracts in parallel, which can significantly improve the performance and scalability. Although significant, those benefits do not apply to every application, where some can have its performance hindered. Hence it is critical to understand how the model works to correctly employ it.

In the model, there are two different types of blocks. The first one is the Pure-data block, which works like a normal block in the appendable-block blockchain. Thus, it stores data from the light-node which holds the private key to the block public key registered in the block header. The second type is the block with a context, this is a new type of block. The first modification is that the block has no public key attached to it, because of that any member of the network can attach transactions to it. We present the two types of blocks in Figure 05. Block B is a Pure Data block, it has a public key (PK i), and appends transactions normally to its data structure. Block B-1 and Block B+1 are both blocks with a context, their public key metadata is set to ∅.

The context of a block with context works as space where smart contracts can exist. For example, in Figure 05 the block B-1 has the Smart Contract I, II, and III within its context. While block B+1 has Smart Contract IV and V. The contexts are isolated one from another, and smart contracts inside one context cannot interact with smart contracts in another context. For example, Smart Contract I cannot interact with Smart Contract IV but can interact with Smart contract II, and III.

Figure 5. Context-based Smart contract example of blocks and context (Nunes et al., (2020))

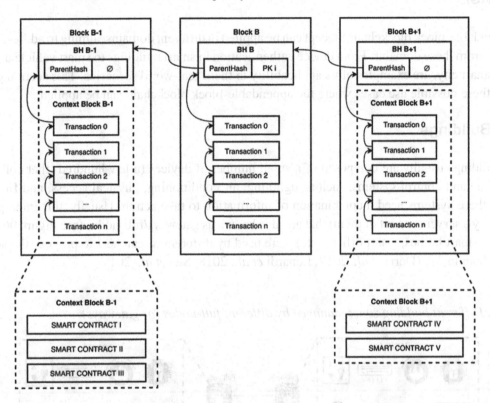

The processing of smart contracts works by appending bytecode for a Virtual Machine, such as the Ethereum virtual machine, in a transaction as the data payload. During the insertion of a new transaction in the blockchain, a node will extract the bytecode, execute it in the virtual machine with a context global state. A reference for this global state is stored in the last transaction inserted before this new one. This global state works as a snapshot of the state of all smart contracts stored in the context, the Merkel Patricia Trie is an example of how the state can be stored. This processing will result in a new state, which will have a reference to it attached to the new transaction before attaching it to the block.

The main advantage of this model is that transactions can be inserted into multiple blocks in parallel. Something not possible to attain in other blockchain data models. Although, context isolation can limit the performance and application of this model. The ideal application to work on this model can be divided into multiple blocks with context, thus having the possibility to divide into multiple parts that do not interact between them. Multiple blocks would allow multiple insertions of transactions at the same time, taking advantage of the parallelism. If the application cannot be divided into multiple parts, then most of the transactions would be destined to the same blocks. That would reduce the parallelism and hinder performance. Because of that, it is essential to understand the nature of the application and if it is possible to separate it in isolated parts for maximum performance.

USE CASES

The appendable-block blockchain concept can be applied in different domains, aiming to address various problems from these domains. From device authentication in smart buildings to smart vehicle data sharing in a smart city, are examples of its applicability in these real-world scenarios. This section presents some of these possible use cases where the appendable-block blockchain can be applied.

Smart Buildings

Smart buildings usually are composed of a small number of devices (a few hundred) that collect data and activate and control systems, such as lightning, air conditioning, physical access, and fire alarm. Some of these systems need a combination of information to take action. Usually, this intelligence is provided by a server (or a set of them) that are also known as gateways/full-nodes (see Figure 06). Smart buildings (smart homes, smart offices, etc) were used by different researchers to propose the adoption of blockchain in IoT (Dorri *et al.*, 2017; Lunardi *et al.*, 2018; She *et al.*, 2019).

Figure 6. Different building zones managed by different full-nodes (or gateways)

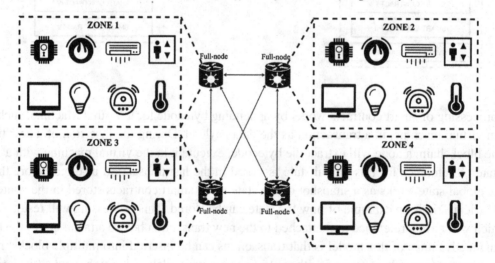

Smart buildings have some important characteristics that have to be taking into account to evaluate a system:

1. Communication delay is low (local area network);
2. Private and permissioned network;
3. Scenarios with a small number of devices;
4. Data usually is produced in an interval that varies from seconds to minutes;
5. Devices with low computing power.

Due to characteristic 1, packet losses and differences in the delay usually are lower than geo-distributed IoT scenarios. Additionally, voting based consensus algorithms, such as PBFT, can be used due to characteristics 2 and 3. Also, the blockchain should provide high throughput to be able to store all information produced (characteristic 4). Finally, due to characteristic 5, the blockchain should support and protect light-nodes.

The first effort to use appendable-block blockchain was presented by Lunardi *et al.* (2018). They evaluated an environment using real hardware to mimic a smart building. That work presents the hardware capabilities for devices (light-nodes) and gateways (full-nodes) to manage the collection and processing of IoT data. They show that constrained devices can be used in a hierarchical environment and can compute cryptography. Also, they present that appendable-block blockchain can be used in smart buildings.

Appendable-block blockchains can provide resilience to the information generated in smart buildings, at the same time that it ensures the integrity of the data produced. Additionally, Smart buildings can take advantage of some important characteristics of appendable-block blockchains: high throughput, hierarchical architecture (supporting light-nodes), possible parallel insertion (at the same time in different Block Ledgers), and configurable consensus algorithm. In particular, the appendable-block blockchains can be useful for sensors that produce information at a high rate. However, scenarios that require a token exchange (*e.g.*, Smart Grids) will require the development of smart contracts to create tokens and some security issues should be addressed, such as double-spending.

Smart Cities

The smart cities environment encompasses new technologies that collaborate producing and exchanging information to improve the quality of life of its citizens. The source of the information managed in the smart city is a wide range of heterogeneous IoT devices (sensors, actuators, smartphones, smart vehicles). The information is used by different service providers such as intelligent transportation and emergency services. Intelligent transportation systems in a smart city rely on the collected information to improve the safety and efficiency of its services. In the same way, emergency services such as police and ambulance, require acquired information from many different sources to take actions. It is of paramount importance to ensure the availability, response time and confiability in the information as presented by Rathore *et al.* (2018). Ensuring these properties becomes a challenge when the system requires near real-time processing/response time and in particular due to the volume of managed information.

The volume of data managed by Intelligent Transportation Systems (ITS) is an important aspect to take into account by the smart city design architecture. Smart vehicles are responsible for producing a huge amount of data using their sensors such as Global Positioning System (GPS), dashboard cameras, Light Detection and Ranging (LIDAR). Aiming to improve the management of data produced from smart vehicles and sharing this data with service providers, Michelin *et al.* (2018) used the appendable-block data structure to define a framework called SpeedyChain. The framework provides a resilient, decentralised and with low latency to manage the transactions produced by vehicles.

Figure 07 depicts the architecture to manage the data produced by the smart vehicles. Every smart vehicle is registered and identified by its public key in the blockchain. The information produced by the vehicle's sensors is consolidated into transactions which are signed and sent to the nearest roadside infrastructure (RSI). The RSIs are responsible for maintaining the blockchain, once receiving the transactions, they validate the transaction signature and append it to the block identified by the vehicle public key. Additionally, the RSI synchronizes the blockchain copy with its RSIs peers, as the vehicles are moving around the smart city and generating data to different RSIs. The service providers at any time can query information available in the blockchain. This information is available near to real-time.

Figure 7. Smart city scenario (Michelin et al., (2018))

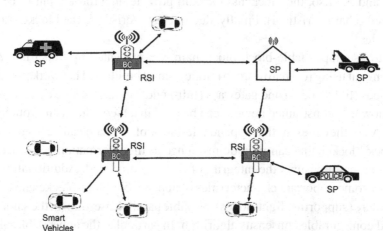

It was demonstrated in the experiments conducted by Michelin *et al*. (2018) research, that the processing time was under 30 milliseconds.

Appendable-block blockchain technology can address the data-sharing problem in smart cities. The capability to append transactions from multiple sources simultaneously in different blocks allows the information to become available to the service providers in real-time. Additionally, the peer-to-peer network model combined with hash and cryptography algorithms, introduced by the blockchain technology, grants the solution availability and confiability capabilities. Such properties are explored by Oham *et al*. (2021), where the blockchain technology tailors information access to restricted entities in the connected vehicle ecosystem, monitoring the internal state of the vehicle to identify cases of in-vehicle network compromise. In the same way, the appendable-block blockchain can enable the data sharing, availability and confiability properties to smart builds, service providers, emergency systems and energy management.

Supply Chain

Today's supply chains are complex networks with diverse business processes and interactions involving many stakeholders, such as primary producers, suppliers, manufacturers, distributors, retailers, regulatory bodies, and end consumers. The integration of IoT technology has enabled stakeholders to collect data and monitor business processes in real-time using sensor devices to improve the efficiency. However, this supply chain data is usually stored in data silos and not shared with other supply chain stakeholders. The geographic dispersion of stakeholders and the siloing of data make it harder to track the flow of products, information, and other interactions among the supply chain stakeholders. Furthermore, there is a growing consumer demand for provenance of products.

Recently, blockchain has been proposed as a promising solution to address the lack of visibility in supply chain data by providing a data recording and sharing platform with immutability, transparency, and traceability features (Malik *et al*., 2018; Malik *et al*., 2019). These proposals are based on consortium blockchains composed of traditional block structures and do not allow parallelisation of transaction insertions and smart contract executions.

Malik *et al*. (2019) proposed a hierarchical framework for blockchain-based supply chains with data, blockchain, and application layers. Supply chain stakeholders have gateway nodes that collect data from the associated IoT devices and other data sources at the data layer. At the blockchain layer, gateway nodes maintain a blockchain by generating new blocks and validating blocks generated by the other gateway nodes. Application layer provides an interface for data queries and applications executed on the blockchain data. The proposed framework uses a consortium blockchain with a traditional block structure, hence it does not allow appending new transactions to existing blocks and parallelization.

Since the supply chain data owned by a stakeholder is collected from data sources connected to its gateway nodes, and processed by the stakeholder, an appendable-block blockchain can improve the throughput and latency of the system by appending new transactions to existing blocks and executing context-based smart contracts on the data in parallel. For instance, consider a fresh food supply chain. The distributor transports products in temperature-controlled containers. The gateway node owned by the distributor collects the temperature data from a connected temperature sensor and generates a block for temperature data provided by that sensor device. The distributor may also generate a separate block for tracking location data provided by a GPS sensor. During the transportation of the products, new data can be appended to these blocks in parallel without the need for generating new blocks. Furthermore, context-based smart contracts can be executed on the data recorded on a block, without interacting with the data recorded on other blocks. For example, a smart contract can emit warning messages when the temperature reaches a threshold value on the block generated for the temperature sensor, while another smart contract can be executed on the block generated for the GPS sensor to emit a location notification message when the container reaches its destination. Similarly, other stakeholders generate blocks, append new transactions to the existing blocks and execute context-based smart contracts on the blocks.

Appendable-block blockchains can provide a platform for sharing supply chain data among the stakeholders. The integrity of the supply chain data is guaranteed by the blockchain structure. Furthermore, context-based smart contracts can be utilised for executing automated actions based on the data on context blocks. The parallelisation capability of appendable-block blockchains improves the transaction throughput and latency for supply chains that generate large amounts of data.

Data Preservation

Data preservation is a process to manage and store data in a safe and integer manner (Berman, 2008). Over the years, many solutions were developed, in particular to backup data. Currently, cloud-based solutions (Vitale *et al.*, 2018) is the most used approach. However, some distributed systems can have problems sharing and retrieving users' data. For example, many government systems do not provide an updated and global view of citizen data. Another common issue is the complete student curriculum, *i.e.*, every time that a student changes to another institution his data has to be somehow imported into a new system. Thus, blockchain can help in data preservation in distributed applications.

Appendable-block blockchain helps to organize that data from the same user in the same block. This feature changes how the data is viewed in the blockchain systems. Therefore, this kind of blockchain is centred on client information. In this way, all data is signed by the user. An advantage of this approach is that the same user can save its information in a non-conflicting way. Systems that validate and retrieve that information also can have a global and updated view from the user.

Appendable-block blockchain was designed for private/consortium architectures, where full-nodes manage who can access the information. Consequently, how the data are retrieved for different applications relies on the application-nodes. In this way, a system should be designed in a way that this application-nodes provides privacy for user data, and at the same time, deny access to that data when necessary. These features are not covered by current implementations of appendable-block blockchains. A discussion about data privacy will be presented in Section 6.

Lunardi *et al.* (2018) and Michelin *et al.* (2018) discussed the possibility of storing part of the data in cloud storages. This can introduce problems to the resilience of the solution, but it could help to reduce the size of the blockchain. A detailed discussion about security issues is presented in Section 6. Adopting or not a cloud-based storage, appendable-block blockchain can help to have an incremental change history in a set of data. This feature can help to recover information from a specific period of time stored in a tamper-resistance and distributed way.

Health Care

Health care is a complex environment that comprehends many entities and their relations, having to manage patients, staff, hospital, clinics, drugs, and many regulations. Health care environments have to handle sensitive user data, strict legislation, supply chain, sensors data, physical and cyber security, human resources, etc. Also, health care can have different operations based on the country's laws and policies. In this kind of environment, it is very hard to provide a solution that solves all these issues. Consequently, we present in this section a discussion about the most common and important of them.

Patients data is one of the most important aspects that health care systems have to deal with. This covers past diagnosis, laboratory tests, treatments, vaccination history, current and past diseases, etc. All this data is extremely important for patients' health and can be shared between different institutions (see Figure 08). However, in many systems, this information is not shared between hospitals and clinics. Also, it is hard for a patient to maintain all this information. Thus, blockchain emerged as a possible

Figure 8. Blockchain as a solution to track health history from patients

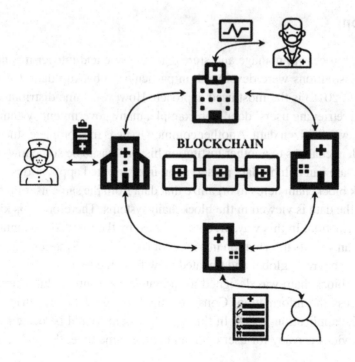

solution to deal with patients' data. Appendable-block blockchain, in special, can handle patients' data in a single block for each patient. Similarly to what was discussed previously, privacy is an important issue that should be taken into account during the design of the solution that will be used.

Also, every human resource (every staff from an institution) can be part of the system. Considering the adoption of smart contacts, the allocation of staff can be optimised by a system that monitors patients and sensors connected to them. A blockchain can be used both to store information and to execute optimization in the scheduling of treatments. Appendable-block blockchains can be used to both pure data blocks and to store/run smart contracts.

Moreover, other information can be used for health care systems. For example, there is a lack of discussion about the integration of gyms sensors, smart bands, and other fitness data that could be used in patients' health. Appendable-block blockchains could be used as a solution to integrate different information about the users. For example, a single blockchain shared between different entities that will store and use information about the same user.

Pharmacy and health insurance are important entities that could not be excluded from health care systems. Blockchain can help these two entities provide gamification and reward systems for patients that take care of their health. Lunardi *et al.* (2019b) proposed a system for gamification and rewarding using smart contracts focused on vaccination. This kind of application can help to propagate good practices in health care through both motivational and financial ways. Appendable-block blockchains do not provide coins or tokens by default, but they can be implemented through smart contracts. However, no solution was proposed for the tokenization in appendable-block blockchains.

Others

In this section, we briefly discuss other areas where appendable-block blockchain can be used. Robotics is an area where blockchain can collaborate in tackling a few common problems. First, it can solve security problems guaranteeing trust even on untrusted networks and assuring data integrity. The Second problem that it can solve is helping to give all participants of the network a common and global view. This can be used by individual robotic systems to make decisions based on the network state (Kapitonov *et al.*, 2019).

In a scenario where a global view and low latency is required the appendable-block blockchain can be a better fit than other blockchains. Each block can represent a robotic system, a sensor, an actuator or a group of parts. These blocks then receive transactions representing events or status. A robotic system can then consult the status and history of other robots in the blockchain and make decisions based on this global view. The appended information is guaranteed by the appendable-block blockchain, giving trust in the network. Additionally, the use of smart contracts can help in decision making and establishing a consensus between the robotic systems with all the parts of these decision processes registered in the blockchain.

Another important application is to update firmware from different hardware. Due to the characteristic of appendable-block blockchains, the same hardware type can use one smart contract context to validate the firmware used by different hardware. This application is especially important to ensure that the hardware of an equipment was not tampered by a malicious user. A smart contract can verify the correct operation of a group of devices by analysing their firmware and updating it when necessary.

Citizen identity validation and other governmental systems are also well suited for appendable-block blockchains. In this kind of environment, the government can maintain the full-nodes and control the access of the light-nodes (citizens), controlling the usage of identity in different domains, such as validation of virtual drive license to rent a car, passport and travel authorizations, usage of a health care system. Consequently, appendable-block blockchain has potential to be used to integrate different systems that require identification and needs to log historical data from citizens.

Data immutability is a property that makes blockchain technology suitable for enforcing data integrity. Based on this property, the blockchain was applied in the forensics domain. Michelin *et al.* (2020) proposes a framework to ensure the data integrity of the stored videos, allowing authorities to validate whether video footage has been tampered with. Such a solution provides video auditability and non-repudiation.

SECURITY ISSUES

Attacks and Vulnerabilities

Based on the appendable-block blockchain characteristics introduced in Section 2, some of the common blockchain attacks and vulnerabilities are not present in this type of blockchain. Some examples of attacks that are surpassed by the appendable-block blockchain are 51% (Gervais *et al.*, 2016), double spending (Karame *et al.*, 2012), and fork after withholding (Kwon *et al.*, 2017), as these attacks are mainly focused on the consensus algorithms and the fork resolution mechanism. The appendable-block blockchain was designed to run in IoT and hardware constrained devices, thus, the most common consensus algorithm (proof-of-work) was not an option to support this blockchain because of its high energy consumption.

Despite the appendable-block blockchain tackling some traditional blockchain vulnerabilities, there are still some vulnerabilities that could affect this blockchain. Attacks such as Deanonymization could succeed when executed against appendable-blockchain solutions. This attack is performed based on the peer connections and data sources. One possible mitigation on this issue was presented by Michelin *et al.* (2018) where the nodes are required to recreate a new key pair from time to time.

The Distributed Denial of Service (DDoS) attack is a widespread attack nowadays for network applications. Appendable-block blockchain also could be affected by this attack. There is no definitive solution to the DDoS attacks, however, among the best options to mitigate these attacks, are the combination of firewall and Intrusion Detection Systems (IDS) configuration with specific rules to block packages aiming to consume the network node resources.

Similar to DDoS attacks, which rely on the network, delay routing, eclipse and sybil attacks require the attacker to control/manipulate the communication in and out of the victim. As possible mitigation measures, to introduce a mechanism to establish trust between the peers, and/or combine with a peer reputation mechanism.

In addition to the presented attacks, appendable-block blockchain could also be susceptible to a malicious full-node attack. The compromised full-node can discard blocks and transactions received either from other full-nodes or from devices. This threat mitigation involves the consensus algorithm choice and definition, which require the participation of multiple full-nodes interacting to achieve the consensus.

It is important to highlight that these are the identified attacks to the appendable-block blockchain, the authors are still researching further attacks that can compromise this blockchain data model, as well different data models.

Privacy

Appendable-block blockchains were designed for private hierarchical architectures. Consequently, access to the information inserted in the blockchain relies on the full-nodes. All information is stored in blocks identified by Public Keys. Thus, with the correct behaviour of all nodes, there is no privacy problem in this architecture. However, malicious users can use mechanisms to explore failures and limitations to retrieve information about the users.

Appendable-block blockchains were designed to have an encrypted channel between peers and hierarchical communication between nodes. These measures reduce the probability of a collection of information in the middle of communication.

In the case of a light-node being tampered, the data produced by the light-node can be controlled and tampered. However, it will not affect the other light-nodes and their data. Light-nodes cannot access data from other light-nodes. All information is managed and controlled by full-nodes.

In the case of a full-node being tampered, all the information stored in the blockchain will be accessible by this malicious node. In the blockchain, the only link between a light-node and its data is their Public Key. In the case that data stored can contain personal information that can lead to a relation between the Public Key and its owner, special measures should be taken. For example, if an appendable-block blockchain will store sensitive information about a patient in a hospital, some encryption mechanisms should be used at the application level. This will ensure that no relevant information would be accessible by a malicious node.

In the case of an application-node being tampered, all information retrieved by it can be accessed by the malicious user. However, application-node, as the full-nodes, only knows the Public Key of the client. In the case of sensitive information being saved in the blockchain, the application should define an encryption mechanism for this data.

A possible solution that can help in privacy is adopting multiple Public Keys in order to make it harder to link the data produced by a single light-node. This approach is used in the context of smart vehicles in smart cities by Michelin *et al.* (2018). Although that solution is not properly evaluated, it can be used in appendable-block blockchains.

Trust

Public blockchains, such as Bitcoin and Ethereum, enable transactions between entities who do not necessarily trust each other, as the blockchain structure and the consensus mechanisms establish trust in the network. By contrast, appendable-block blockchains were designed for private networks with hierarchical architectures. Full-nodes and light-nodes are identified by their public keys and have the permission to generate transactions. Thus, they do not need to compete with each other to generate blocks using computationally expensive consensus mechanisms.

In appendable-block blockchains, the hash links between the block headers and the transactions in the block ledger guarantee the integrity of the data record. Furthermore, each transaction is signed by the light-node generating the data and the full-node generating the block. Thus, we can trust that the data was generated and appended to the block by the associated light-node and the full-node respectively, as long as the private keys of the nodes are secured.

Blockchain-based IoT applications heavily rely on sensor data that is generated external to the blockchain and blockchain mechanisms alone cannot guarantee the trustworthiness of the sensor data at its origin. This also holds for appendable-block blockchains, where data is sourced by individual sensor nodes (light-nodes). To improve the trust in the sensor data, trust and reputation mechanisms (Malil *et al.*, 2019; Dedeoglu *et al.*, 2019) can be implemented by the full-nodes before appending the data to blocks. Furthermore, since full-nodes have full control over block generation, a malicious full-node may choose not to append data provided by a light-node to its block. Thus, appendable-block blockchains do not guarantee trust in recording all data provided by light-nodes on the blockchain and further trust mechanisms are needed to guarantee data recording.

DISCUSSION AND FUTURE DIRECTIONS

Appendable-block blockchain is a prominent solution for distributed ledgers applications. Many aspects of its design help to store independent information in distributed environments, *i.e.*, information that is produced by a single user in shared management. Table 1 summarizes the main aspects of appendable-block blockchains.

Table 1. Main features of appendable-block blockchains

Features	Advantages	Shortcomings
Hierarchical Architecture	Limited hardware can participate as light-node; Control over who can access the network; Fewer nodes participating in the consensus; Access levels.	Not suitable for permissionless environments; Few nodes (full-nodes) control the blockchain.
Appendable-block data structure	Focused on data, instead of currency exchange; Lightweight data structure.	Currency exchange is not native.
Parallel data insertion	High throughput; Lower latency; Parallel execution of smart contracts.	Increased number of parallel communications.
Consensus not based on rewards	Suitable for limited hardware; Fast insertion of blocks and transactions; Less susceptible to double spending and similar attacks.	More messages exchanged; No incentives for fast validation during the consensus.
Context-based Smart Contracts	High execution throughput; Adaptable for each context.	Individual executions can have a higher response time; Performance depends on the application nature.

As presented previously, many scenarios can be benefited from one or more of appendable-block characteristics. Thus, low latency and high throughput can be helpful in many applications, such as smart environments. However, other scenarios can be challenging to use appendable-block blockchains. Especially, scenarios data are based on tokens or cryptocurrencies can be hard to implement due to how transactions are stored. For example, smart-grids with automated payment mechanisms for the power produced in a smart home. This payment, that can be understood as a cryptocurrency exchange, should be implemented at application level, possibly using smart contracts. Additionally, a fidelity program that has a reward mechanism to incentive the usage of that service is also not supported natively by appendable-block blockchains. There are a lot of other examples that use different types of exchange between two or more entities that are not well fitted to appendable-block blockchains.

Different work was presented to improve appendable-block blockchain, discussing different aspects, such as data structure, consensus algorithms and smart contracts. However, a lot more can be done to improve and provide additional features to appendable-block blockchains. One of the most neglected parts in appendable-block blockchains is the application layer. For example, application-nodes were not properly covered by appendable-block blockchain proposals. There is no research that focused on communication between application-nodes and external users. Another example is the need for better API and protocols to both communicate with full-nodes and to external access should be designed. Additionally, mechanisms to improve the data access and data persistence should be proposed to large scale systems.

Finally, there are some important issues that were not completely tackled by previous research in appendable-block blockchains. The most important are:

- Lack of a solution that supports end-to-end encryption for sensitive applications;
- Trust mechanisms that could be used for consensus algorithms;
- Design, and security analysis of external storage solutions;
- Patterns that help to define contexts and their relations;
- No zero-knowledge proof proposals or discussion;
- Secure application protocols to use appendable-block blockchains.

CONCLUSION

The appendable-block blockchain is a technology that was designed initially aiming at IoT networks to support constrained devices. This blockchain model provides a solution with high throughput and very low latency. To achieve these goals, the blockchain is focused on managing the data produced by the IoT network in a transaction structure to maintain information instead of currency exchange.

In this chapter, we presented an overview of the appendable-block blockchain concepts and their applicability. The presented use cases are a small set of possible applications in which this blockchain model could fit. However, many different scenarios and use cases could benefit from its properties. The design for the appendable-block blockchain, allows its customization to attend different requirements from several areas. This blockchain still presents a wide range of research opportunities such as consensus algorithms, communication protocols, ways to improve the solution scalability and security.

ACKNOWLEDGMENT

This research was achieved in cooperation with HP Brasil using incentives of Brazilian Informatics Law (Law n 8.248 of 1991). This study was financed in part by the Coordenação de Aperfeiçoamento de Pessoal de Nível Superior - Brasil (CAPES) - Finance Code 001. Avelino F. Zorzo is supported by CNPq (315192/2018-6) and FAPERGS. This work was supported by the INCT Forensic Sciences through the Conselho Nacional de Desenvolvimento Científico e Tecnológico (CNPq – process #465450/2014-8). Also, we thank the support from IFRS. The work has been supported by the Cyber Security Research

Centre Limited (CSCRC) whose activities are partially funded by the Australian Government's Cooperative Research Centres Programme.

REFERENCES

Angelis, S.D., Aniello, L., Baldoni, R., Lombardi, F., Margheri, A., & Sassone, V. (2018). PBFT vs Proof-of-Authority: Applying the CAP Theorem to Permissioned Blockchain. *ITASEC 2018*.

Armknecht, F., Karame, G. O., Mandal, A., Youssef, F., & Zenner, E. (2015). Ripple: Overview and outlook. In *International Conference on Trust and Trustworthy Computing* (pp. 163-180). Springer. 10.1007/978-3-319-22846-4_10

Berman, F. (2008, December). Got data? a guide to data preservation in the information age. *Communications of the ACM, 51*(12), 50–56. doi:10.1145/1409360.1409376

Bessani, A., Sousa, J., & Alchieri, E. E. P. (2014). State Machine Replication for the Masses with BFT-SMART. In *2014 44th Annual IEEE/IFIP International Conference on Dependable Systems and Networks*, (pp. 355-362). IEEE. 10.1109/DSN.2014.43

Castro, M., & Liskov, B. (1999). Practical Byzantine Fault Tolerance. *Third Symposium on Operating Systems Design and Implementation*, 173–186.

Crain, T., Gramoli, V., Larrea, M., & Raynal, M. (2017). *(Leader/Randomization/Signature)-free Byzantine Consensus for Consortium Blockchains*. CoRR, vol. abs/1702.03068.

Dedeoglu, V., Dorri, A., Jurdak, R., Michelin, R. A., Lunardi, R. C., Kanhere, S. S., & Zorzo, A. F. (2020). A Journey in Applying Blockchain for Cyberphysical Systems. In *2020 International Conference on COMmunication Systems & NETworkS (COMSNETS)* (pp. 383–390). IEEE 10.1109/COMSNETS48256.2020.9027487

Dedeoglu, V., Jurdak, R., Putra, G. D., Dorri, A., & Kanhere, S. S. (2019). A Trust Architecture for Blockchain in IoT. *16th EAI International Conference on Mobile and Ubiquitous Systems: Computing, Networking and Services*, 190–199. 10.1145/3360774.3360822

Dorri, A., Kanhere, S. S., Jurdak, R., & Gauravaram, P. (2017). Blockchain for IoT security and privacy: The case study of a smart home. In *2017 IEEE International Conference on Pervasive Computing and Communications Workshops* (pp. 618-623). IEEE. 10.1109/PERCOMW.2017.7917634

Gervais, A., Karame, G. O., Wüst, K., Glykantzis, V., Ritzdorf, H., & Capkun, S. (2016). *On the security and performance of proof of work blockchains. In 2016 ACM SIGSAC conference on computer and communications security*. ACM.

Kapitonov, A., Lonshakov, S., Berman, I., Castelló Ferrer, E., Bonsignorio, F. P., Bulatov, V., & Svistov, A. (2019). Robotic Services for New Paradigm Smart Cities Based on Decentralized Technologies. *Ledger, 4*.

Karame, G. O., Androulaki, E., & Capkun, S. (2012). *Double-spending fast payments in bitcoin. In 2012 ACM conference on Computer and communications security*. ACM.

Kwon, Y., Kim, D., Son, Y., Vasserman, E., & Kim, Y. (2017). Be selfish and avoid dilemmas: Fork after withholding (faw) attacks on bitcoin. In *2017 ACM SIGSAC Conference on Computer and Communications Security* (pp. 195-209). ACM 10.1145/3133956.3134019

Lunardi, R. C., Alharby, M., Nunes, H. C., Zorzo, A. F., Dong, C., & Moorsel, A. v. (2020). Context-based consensus for appendable-block blockchains. In *2020 IEEE International Conference on Blockchain (Blockchain)* (pp. 401-408). IEEE. 10.1109/Blockchain50366.2020.00058

Lunardi, R. C., Michelin, R. A., Neu, C. V., Nunes, H. C., Zorzo, A. F., & Kanhere, S. S. (2019). Impact of consensus on appendable-block blockchain for IoT. In *16th EAI International Conference on Mobile and Ubiquitous Systems: Computing, Networking and Services* (pp. 228–237). ACM. 10.1145/3360774.3360798

Lunardi, R. C., Michelin, R. A., Neu, C. V., & Zorzo, A. F. (2018). Distributed access control on IoT ledger-based architecture. In *2018 IEEE/IFIP Network Operations and Management Symposium* (pp. 1-7). IEEE. 10.1109/NOMS.2018.8406154

Lunardi, R. C., Nunes, H. C., Branco, V. D. S., Lipper, B. H., Neu, C. V., & Zorzo, A. F. (2019). Performance and Cost Evaluation of Smart Contracts in Collaborative Health Care Environments. *15th International Conference for Internet Technology and Secured Transactions*, 1-6.

Malik, S., Dedeoglu, V., Kanhere, S. S., & Jurdak, R. (2019). TrustChain: Trust Management in Blockchain and IoT supported Supply Chains. In *2019 IEEE International Conference on Blockchain (Blockchain)*, (pp. 184-193). IEEE. 10.1109/Blockchain.2019.00032

Malik, S., Kanhere, S. S., & Jurdak, R. (2018). Productchain: Scalable blockchain framework to support provenance in supply chains. In *2018 IEEE 17th International Symposium on Network Computing and Applications (NCA)* (pp. 1-10). IEEE.

Mazieres, D. (2015). The stellar consensus protocol: A federated model for internet-level consensus. *Stellar Development Foundation, 32*.

Michelin, R. A., Ahmed, N., Kanhere, S. S., Seneviratne, A., & Jha, S. (2020). Leveraging lightweight blockchain to establish data integrity for surveillance cameras. In *2020 IEEE International Conference on Blockchain and Cryptocurrency (ICBC)*, (pp. 1-3). IEEE

Michelin, R. A., Dorri, A., Steger, M., Lunardi, R. C., Kanhere, S. S., Jurdak, R., & Zorzo, A. F. (2018). SpeedyChain: A framework for decoupling data from blockchain for smart cities. In *15th EAI International Conference on Mobile and Ubiquitous Systems: Computing, Networking and Services* (pp. 145-154). EAI. 10.1145/3286978.3287019

Nakamoto, S. (2008). *Bitcoin: A Peer-to-Peer Electronic Cash System*. https://bitcoin.org/bitcoin.pdf

Nunes, H. C., Lunardi, R. C., Zorzo, A. F., Michelin, R. A., & Kanhere, S. S. (2020). Context-based smart contracts for appendable-block blockchains. In *IEEE International Conference on Blockchain and Cryptocurrency* (pp. 1-10). IEEE.

Oham, C., Michelin, R. A., Jurdak, R., Kanhere, S. S., & Jha, S. (2021). B-FERL: Blockchain based framework for securing smart vehicles. *Information Processing & Management, 58*(1), 102426. doi:10.1016/j.ipm.2020.102426

Pervez, H., Muneeb, M., Irfan, M. U., & Haq, I. U. (2018). A Comparative Analysis of DAG-Based Blockchain Architectures. In *2018 12th International Conference on Open Source Systems and Technologies*. 10.1109/ICOSST.2018.8632193

Rathore, M. M., Paul, A., Hong, W. H., Seo, H., Awan, I., & Saeed, S. (2018). Exploiting IoT and big data analytics: Defining smart digital city using real-time urban data. *Sustainable Cities and Society*, *40*, 600–610. doi:10.1016/j.scs.2017.12.022

She, W., Gu, Z., Lyu, X., Liu, Q., Tian, Z., & Liu, W. (2019). Homomorphic Consortium Blockchain for Smart Home System Sensitive Data Privacy Preserving. *IEEE Access: Practical Innovations, Open Solutions*, *7*, 62058–62070. doi:10.1109/ACCESS.2019.2916345

Vitale, F., Janzen, I., & Mcgrenere, J. (2018). Hoarding and Minimalism: Tendencies in Digital Data Preservation. In *2018 CHI Conference on Human Factors in Computing Systems* (pp. 1–12). ACM. 10.1145/3173574.3174161

Yang, S., Chen, Z., Cui, L., Xu, M., Ming, Z., & Xu, K. (2019). CoDAG: An Efficient and Compacted DAG-Based Blockchain Protocol. In *2019 IEEE International Conference on Blockchain* (pp. 314-318). IEEE. 10.1109/Blockchain.2019.00049

Zorzo, A. F., Nunes, H. C., Lunardi, R. C., Michelin, R. A., & Kanhere, S. S. (2018). Dependable IoT using blockchain-based technology. In *2018 Eighth Latin-American Symposium on Dependable Computing* (pp. 1-9). IEEE.

KEY TERMS AND DEFINITIONS

Appendable-Block: Is a block definition that uses a linked list to arrange the transactions in a block, thus making the block capable of support appending new transactions at any time.

Blockchain: Is a sequence of block linked to each other by a hash value obtained from the previous block.

Blockchain Data Structure: Is the data organisation applied to create a structure for blocks (typically linked list) and the transactions inside each block.

IoT: The internet of things is a concept in which an object is capable of data processing and network communication.

PBFT: Practical Byzantine fault tolerance is a consensus algorithm that relies on the election of a leader and running voting among the nodes.

PoW: Proof-of-work is one of the most popular consensuses algorithms used in some blockchain implementation and rely on devices performing some typically CPU intensive computation tasks.

Smart Contract: Is a piece of code that can be embedded in the blockchain, allowing a remote execution when invoked.

Chapter 5
The World of NFTs (Non–Fungible Tokens):
The Future of Blockchain and Asset Ownership

Ramakrishnan Raman

(iD) https://orcid.org/0000-0001-8934-8625

Higher Colleges of Technology, UAE

Benson Edwin Raj

Higher Colleges of Technology, UAE

ABSTRACT

Tokenizing assets through the use of blockchain is the next big thing in digital currency markets. Securing the assets in the world of the internet is challenging as most of them can easily be copied and sold in the secondary market. Protecting the rights of the asset owner is one of the challenging research areas. NFTs (non-fungible tokens) are very useful in representing the ownership of unique items for any assets. NFTs ensure that an asset can have only one official owner at any point in time with the help of Ethereum-based blockchain network. Ethereum NFTs can ensure that no one can modify the ownership rights or copy and paste the digital assets. NFTs are a boon to the artists, musicians, and others who want to create impressive digital assets. The objective of this chapter is to take you to the world of NFTs and to explain how the NFTs are going to impact digital transactions in a bigger way in the future. This chapter covers the introduction, technical aspects, security impacts, use cases, and successful implementations of NFTs in various realms.

INTRODUCTION TO BLOCKCHAIN AND BITCOINS

Blockchain has the huge potential to challenge the way the businesses are working in digital realm. In 2008, the first blockchain was conceptualized by Nakamoto where it's evolved and applied in many domains

DOI: 10.4018/978-1-7998-5839-3.ch005

beyond cryptocurrencies. In the whitepaper released by Nakamoto in 2009, he provided technological aspects of blockchain with how the decentralization and trust works together. This paper focused on the usage of cryptocurrencies as an alternative to the fiat currency. Blockchain is a P2P DLT (Peer-to-Peer Digital Ledger Technology) which is secured and record transactions across many computers commonly known as nodes. In other words, blockchain is a platform where people are allowed to perform transactions without the centralized control or trusted arbitrator. P2P networks take care of managing these records and along with a time-stamping server.

A blockchain is a collection of blocks. Each block contains the transaction data, the timestamp of the transaction and the crypto key. For example, in the bitcoin blockchain network, each block can have basic information about the transaction such as receiver, sender and the value of the bitcoin. Each block in a blockchain is references the content of the previous block which are cryptographically secured together. The blockchain uses asymmetric cryptography for securing the transactions. A user can generate a random private key and use it to derive a public key. The address of the user is generated using the private key and the amount also stored. The user can sign transactions from his address using his private key. The public key will be used for the verification of the origin. If the user loses the private key is equivalent to losing crypto-money in his/her account. Users can maintain digital wallets to manage their funds. The batches of transactions in the blockchain are approved by all the participants in the node. Every transaction in the ledger is added to the chain makes it difficult to tamper or revise the data. Any new transactions to the blockchain network need to get approval from all the nodes or in other words, "consensus" to add the transaction to the existing chain. Hence, the blockchain transactions are trusted, shared, public but with no single user control (Beck, R. and C. Müller-Bloch., 2017). The following four pillars of blockchain technology ensure this technology is creating ripple effects in the various sectors from financial to manufacturing to education.

- Immutability ensures the transaction data in blockchain environment are immutable
- Finality gives the assurance that the transactions cannot be cancelled or altered once completed
- Consensus a fault-tolerant mechanism that is used in computer and blockchain systems to achieve the necessary agreement on a single data value or a single state of the network among distributed processes or multi-agent systems. (Investopedia)
- Provenance allows businesses to collate, verify and validity of the key data in the blockchain platform.

Here is the quick summary of how does the blockchain works:

1. The transaction request is the first step in blockchain
2. To represent this transaction, a block will be created
3. This transaction block is sent to all the nodes in the blockchain network. Each block consists of the data, the previous block hash, and the current block hash.
4. The nodes once received the block, it starts validating the block using a consensus method.
5. After successful validation and approval from 51% of the network nodes, the block will be added to the existing blockchain environment.

Many of us believe, bitcoin and blockchain are same. However, we need to understand that the blockchain is the underlying technology for cryptocurrencies such as bitcoins. Bitcoin is the first real world application for blockchain. Bitcoin is a decentralized digital currency powered by a huge, distributed network of computers or nodes. This digital currency can be owned, sent, received or stored in a secured digital wallet, is a physical or digital device that facilitates the trading of bitcoin and allows users to track ownership of coins (Investopedia). It is important to note that there is no bank or financial intermediary involved in any bitcoin transactions. There are broadly two types of Bitcoins: Bitcoin Cash (BCH) and Bitcoin (BTC). BCH transactions comes with a much lower fee for transaction which allows for borderless currency exchange. The balances in the bitcoin tokens are secured by public and private key combination. These keys ensure the transactions are cryptographically secured. According to Investopedia, Bitcoin has around 12,000 nodes as of January 2021 and the numbers are increasing sharply.

The next generation of blockchain implementations like Ethereum is an open and decentralized network, secured using a consensus algorithm called Proof-Of-Work. It has introduced the concept of smart contracts, a piece of software code that runs on all participating blockchain nodes. A smart contract is a program which runs on a Blockchain, a collection of code and data that has been stored at a specific address on its Blockchain. A type of pre-programmed account with pre-defined functions.

Smart contracts leads to the building of permission-able and permission-less blockchain infrastructure for business transactions. Based on this, blockchain architecture has evolved into 3 types. They are public blockchain architecture, private blockchain architecture and the consortium blockchain architecture.

- In the public blockchain, anyone can participate in the blockchain network. The examples for public blockchain includes Bitcoin, Litecoin and Ethereum.
- In the private blockchain, only the administrators can define who join and access the data in the blockchain network.
- The consortium blockchain is the combination of public and private blockchain network which has the total control over the way it works. This is also called as "Enterprise Blockchain network".

This helps the businesses to simplify the human interactions and stakeholder's collaboration on several industries which includes Supply chain management, financial payments, borderless currency exchanges and energy markets. In 2017, many companies launched ICO (Initial coin offering) to raise their capital and sell shares in the form of Ethereum tokens. However, many of the ICOs failed to deliver their promise and saw a huge drop in the cryptocurrencies values.

The following diagram illustrates the evolution of blockchain and bitcoins clearly (Accenture, 2018)

To summarize, the usage of digital cryptocurrencies for the businesses are increasing like never before and this leads to the concept of using NFT (Non-fungible Tokens) for protecting digital assets. The next section provides brief overview of NFT.

INTRODUCTION TO NON-FUNGIBLE TOKENS (NFT)

Fungibility is defined as "any item that can be replaced with another identical item or mutually interchangeable". Typical example is the currency exchange where the value of your currency is same whether it's replaced with a similar value currency or it resides in your bank account. However, think of the amount of digital assets we own in the form of arts, photography, articles, domain names, event-tickets and any in-game unique items. Protecting these digital assets are challenging in the internet market. The need of

Figure 1. History of Blockchain

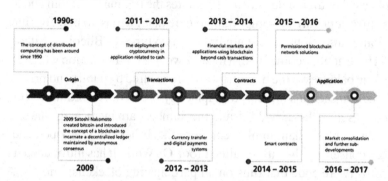

blockchain technology is vital to protect our digital assets. Blockchain technology provides coordination layer (Regner, Urbach and Schweizer, 2019) for digital assets to control ownerships and permissions.

The introduction of smart contracts in Ethereum enables users to build Ethereum token systems which are generally referred as Ethereum sub-currencies. By combining smart contracts and tokens, Ethereum opened up the possibility to build a wide array of possible decentralized projects (NFT Yearly report, 2020).

According to Wikipedia, "A non-fungible token (NFT) is a unit of data stored on a digital ledger, called a blockchain, that certifies any digital file to be unique. An NFT functions like a cryptographic token, but unlike cryptocurrencies such as Bitcoin, are not mutually interchangeable, in other words, not fungible"

NFTs (Non-fungible tokens) are very useful in representing the ownership of unique items whether it is digital or physical assets. According to one of the authors from New York Times (Kevin Roose, 2021), An NFT is created or minted from digital objects that represents both tangible and intangible items that includes arts, GIF images, virtual avatars. Design sneakers and music. NFTs ensure that an asset can have only one official owner at any point of time as the underlying mechanism uses Ethereum based Blockchain network. As Blockchain has its unique properties of decentralization, transparency, and Immutability, Ethereum NFTs can ensure that no one can modify the ownership rights or copy and paste the digital assets. Verifying the ownership and managing the transportability of the NFTs are governed by the usage of smart contracts in Ethereum platform. One of the key differences between Cryptocurrencies and Non-Fungible Tokens is that every NFT is completely and not directly interchangeable with any other asset by identity, value, and/or utility. Every Non-Fungible Token contains metadata which are unique in nature, these attributes can include size, artist name, scarcity etc. (Dan Kelly et.al 2020)

The decades of digitalization have created tons of digital assets for the individuals and industries. These digital assets are owned by the product owners. For example, the amazing painting created by the artist and sharing it in the internet can easily be copied or replicated in the market without the creator's consent. This is the true reality of the internet today. There is no easier way to verify the ownership of digital assets in the secondary market as the ownership records are maintained by the selling company.

Whereas, every NFT have owner and can be easily verified in the public domain. The problem for event management companies is bigger in terms of digitization, control over secondary market transaction, independence, security, transparency and automation of ticket sales. The organization build their own infrastructure. On the other hand, event tickets created using NFT can be traded on any Ethereum blockchain platform. Sometimes, there are geographical restrictions hinder the sale or resale of digital assets. This can be sorted by using NFTs where the digital asset owners can sell their creative work anywhere as Ethereum can be easily accessed in a global market. For the music industry, the composers often lose their share of royalties even their work is resold multiple times. The music streaming companies, retains major portion of the profits from the sales (Etherum.org, 2021). With NFTs, composers can retain ownership rights at any time and can claim the royalties directly in the secondary market. Hence, it's clear that NFTs has a major breakthrough in terms of managing digital or physical asset ownership easier in the current internet methodology.

Each token in NFT has unique identifier and has the optional metadata which clearly indicates the information about the NFT owner. The NFTs are not interchangeable or transferable on the same value. NFTs live in the Ethereum blockchain platform and anyone can buy or sell in Ethereum based market. For the NFT owners, they can easily prove it, no one can modify the data and can sell or hold it as long as they wish. For the creators of NFT, they can easily prove they are the creator. Moreover, the NFTs provide the way to determine the scarcity, earn royalties and sell on the NFT markets without intermediaries. NFTs have added lots of advantages for their creators by providing the way if earning royalties when they are sold from one person to another. The well-structured smart contracts build into the NFTs can ensure the royalties for the creators.

To summarize, the NFTs have following four characteristics (Diego Geroni, 2021):

- Every single NFT is unique
- Not replaceable with similar tokens
- Uses ERC-721 and ERC-1155 standards
- The scarcity of the NFT increases their values

The objective of this chapter is to provide clear understanding of NFTs including their technical aspects, security impact, use cases and successful implementations in various domains.

TECHNICAL OVERVIEW OF NFT

After the initial breakthrough of Blockchain technology, the concept of executing smart contracts in the blockchain nodes by Ethereum became the game changer in the industry. Ethereum, is a permissionless blockchain protocol that allows users to create and deploy programs in its infrastructure. The growth of Ethereum community leads to the various implementation of smart contracts. To support the interoperability, the community has agreed to have an application-level standard called Ethereum Request for Comments (ERCs). The ERC-721 (William Entriken et.al 2018), is a Non-Fungible Token Standard that implements an API for tokens within Smart Contracts. The most popular interface ERC-20 specified the standard interface to design and deploy fungible tokens in Ethereum infrastructure. These fungible tokens were later used to facilitate ICOs for crowdfunding. Also, ERC-20 tokens can be traded in regular and decentralized exchanges.

In 2017, EIP (Ethereum Improvement Proposals) has introduced a standard to deal with non-fungible tokens (NFTs) namely ERC-721. This standard interface clearly distinguishes the need for the introduction of non-fungible from the fungible tokens. Unlike ERC-20 for fungible tokens, ERC-721 standard has clearly specified that every NFT should have unique id and should be transferrable but cannot be divided or merged (Dragos I.Musan, 2020).

ERC-721 hosts multiple functions that enable the communication between NFTs such as finding the owner of the token, approving the transfers and validating the approved addresses.

All NFTs have the following attributes as defined in ERC-721 standards:

- tokenID – Unique identifier for each created token (uint256)
- contractAddress – Unique address of the owner

So, for any ERC-721 NFT, the combination of (contractAddress, tokenID) is globally unique. ERC-721 provides functionalities such as transfer tokens, get the current token balance, get the owner of a specific token and the total supply of the token available on the network. Also, it has other functionalities like approving the transactions and the amount from third party account.

ERC-721 has following methods to provide various functionalities as below:

- *function balanceOf(address _owner) external view returns (uint256)*
  - To get the token balance of the address owner at any instance
- *function ownerOf(uint256 _tokenId) external view returns (address)*
  - To get the details of the created token using tokenID attribute
- *function safeTransferFrom(address _from, address _to, uint256 _tokenId, bytes data) external payable*
  - To safely transfer the token from one address to another address with actual data in bytes
- *function safeTransferFrom(address _from, address _to, uint256 _tokenId) external payable*
  - Overloaded method to safely transfer the token from one address to another address without actual data
- *function transferFrom(address _from, address _to, uint256 _tokenId) external payable*
  - To transfer the token from one address to another address in unsafe manner
- *function approve(address _approved, uint256 _tokenId) external payable*
  - To approve or grant another entity permission to transfer a token on the owner's behalf.
- *function setApprovalForAll(address _operator, bool _approved) external*
  - To set the approval for another entity permission to transfer a token
- *function getApproved(uint256 _tokenId) external view returns (address)*
  - To get the approval for another entity permission to transfer a token
- *function isApprovedForAll(address _owner, address _operator) external view returns (bool)*
  - To check the validity of all the approved operators for the owner to transfer a token

ERC-721 has the following built-in events:

- *event Transfer(address indexed _from, address indexed _to, uint256 indexed _tokenId);*
  - To initiate the transfer of a token from one address to another address
- *event Approval(address indexed _owner, address indexed _approved, uint256 indexed _tokenId);*
  - To trigger or intimate when the token transfer is approved
- *event ApprovalForAll(address indexed _owner, address indexed _operator, bool _approved);*
  - To enable bulk approval for multiple tokens by the third party on owner's behalf.

Apart from the functions proposed in ERC-721, the standard allows the users to achieve interesting results as per EIPS-721.

- Disallow transfers if the contract is paused
- Blacklist certain address from receiving NFTs
- Disallow unsafe transfers
- Charge a fee to both parties of a transaction
- Read only NFT registry

One of the popular NFT-based organization, CryptoKitties created NFTs using ERC-721 standards that is indivisible and unique. CryptoKitties are built on Ethereum network and all the transactions are fueled by "Ether" one of the kind of cryptocurrency from Ethereum. They have added some interesting events to their ERC-721 implementation as below:

```python
# Using the Pregnant and Birth Events ABI to get info about new Kitties.
ck_extra_events_abi = [
    {
        'anonymous': False,
        'inputs': [
            {'indexed': False, 'name': 'owner', 'type': 'address'},
            {'indexed': False, 'name': 'matronId', 'type': 'uint256'},
            {'indexed': False, 'name': 'sireId', 'type': 'uint256'},
            {'indexed': False, 'name': 'cooldownEndBlock', 'type': 'uint256'}],
        'name': 'Pregnant',
        'type': 'event'
    },
    {
        'anonymous': False,
        'inputs': [
            {'indexed': False, 'name': 'owner', 'type': 'address'},
            {'indexed': False, 'name': 'kittyId', 'type': 'uint256'},
            {'indexed': False, 'name': 'matronId', 'type': 'uint256'},
            {'indexed': False, 'name': 'sireId', 'type': 'uint256'},
            {'indexed': False, 'name': 'genes', 'type': 'uint256'}],
        'name': 'Birth',
        'type': 'event'
    }]
# We need the event's signature to filter the logs
ck_event_signatures = [
    w3.sha3(text="Pregnant(address,uint256,uint256,uint256)").hex(),
    w3.sha3(text="Birth(address,uint256,uint256,uint256,uint256)").hex(),
]
# Here is a Pregnant Event:
#https://etherscan.io/tx/0xc97eb514a41004acc447ac9d0d6a27ea6da305ac8b877dff37e
```

```
49db42e1f8cef#eventlog
pregnant_logs = w3.eth.getLogs({
    "fromBlock": w3.eth.blockNumber - 120,
    "address": w3.toChecksumAddress(ck_token_addr),
    "topics": [ck_extra_events_abi[0]]
})
recent_pregnants = [get_event_data(ck_extra_events_abi[0], log)["args"] for
log in pregnant_logs]
# Here is a Birth Event:
# - https://etherscan.io/tx/0x3978028e08a25bb4c44f7877eb3573b9644309c044bf087e
335397f16356340a
birth_logs = w3.eth.getLogs({
    "fromBlock": w3.eth.blockNumber - 120,
    "address": w3.toChecksumAddress(ck_token_addr),
    "topics": [ck_extra_events_abi[1]]
})
recent_births = [get_event_data(ck_extra_events_abi[1], log)["args"] for log
in birth_logs]
```

Also, it is essential to understand the concept of "Gas" in Ethereum which plays important role in the smart contracts' execution. Gas refers to the unit that measures the amount of computational effort required to execute specific operations on the Ethereum network (Etherum.org). Each Ethereum transaction requires enough computational resources to execute, and this requires a fee. Gas fees helps to keep the Ethereum network safe and secure. As each transaction requires a fee to execute on the network, this indirectly discourage external actors from spamming the network. Also, Gas acts as a fundamental unit of computation in Ethereum. To prevent infinite loops or other parts of the code that waste computational resources, each transaction required to set a limit on the number of steps required for transaction execution. The following diagram illustrates the usage of Gas in Ethereum network:

Figure 2. Gas usage in Ethereum
(Adopted from Ethereum EVM)

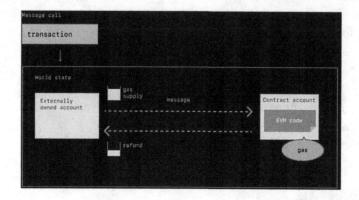

There are other standards available for tokens which includes ERC-1155 and IBC to support combo tokens (both fungible and non-fungible) and semi-fungible token which is not in the scope of this chapter. The concept of "colored coins" were used to represent the real-world assets on the Bitcoin blockchain (Wang, 2017). With the creation of ERC-721, the idea of "color coins" has been realized for the first time. Apart from this, ERC-721 tokens find it applicability in the following areas:

- Gaming: Expressing the unique properties of in-game user customization or any other utility
- Collectibles: Perfect fit for collectible items as described in the CryptoKitties example above
- VR Real estate: creating unique real-estate digital models and trade them with ERC-721 tokens.

For stateless data communication, NFT application needs to build on the commonly used internet standards like TCP/IP, HTTP, HTML/CSS and REST (Restful State Transfer). HTTP is required to deal with request between different computers and HTML/CSS is required to display content on the web.

For interoperability, the common data format and a permissioned API for reading or writing the data is essential. NFT application uses JSON format for data exchange. The following shows the ERC721 Metadata JSON Schema: (EIP-721)

```
{
    "title": "Asset Metadata",
    "type": "object",
    "properties": {
        "name": {
            "type": "string",
            "description": "Identifies the asset to which this NFT represents"
        },
        "description": {
            "type": "string",
            "description": "Describes the asset to which this NFT represents"
        },
        "image": {
            "type": "string",
            "description": "A URI pointing to a resource with mime type image/* representing the asset to which this NFT represents. Consider making any images at a width between 320 and 1080 pixels and aspect ratio between 1.91:1 and 4:5 inclusive."
        }
    }
}
```

NFT applications needs to be built on the Ethereum Blockchain network which is public and permissionless that supports smart contracts. In addition, there is a larger Ethereum community and has more than 60K nodes without a single point of failure. Hence, the applications build on Ethereum will be supported with basic pillars of Blockchain which includes trust, transparency, integrity, non-repudiation and availability.

The applications developed in Java are compiled to byte code using Java Virtual Machines (JVM). In the same manner, Ethereum has developed its own programming language called "Solidity" which has similar syntax like JavaScript and the program developed in Solidity will be compiled to byte codes using Ethereum Virtual Machine (EVM).

A successful research and implementation of NFT for finance domain has developed a decentralized app (DApp) and presented their results in (Dragos I, 2020). Their *DApp* platform has two main features:

- Leasing – Gives user the provision to lease their NFT in the market
- Lending – Enables users to use their NFTs as a collateral for loans

They have used the OpenZeppelin contracts library for creating smart contracts. Mainly, they used two interfaces for this purpose: IERC721 and IERC721Receiver

- IERC721 is an interface with function definitions for building ERC-721 compliant smart contracts used for interacting with the addresses of the smart contracts of the tokens.
- IERC721Receiver is an interface mainly used to implement security features into the smart contracts.

The core aspect of ERC-721 NFT is the owner of the token can be uniquely identified by their block-chain account address (BCA). The participant nodes in the blockchain communicates with the blockchain through a BCA which is a combination of private and public keys. The use of physical unclonable functions (PUFs) in the hardware of the semi-conductor devices was proposed (Javier et.al 2021) to associate digital and physical ids. Also, by using the new attribute in ERC-721, the token can be traced in the same blockchain network. Also, this paper presented the possibility of extending ERC-721 standard to suit with their area of research related to Internet of Things (IoT). This gives lot of confidence for the NFT community to customize ERC-721 standards to their own use cases.

One of the successful implementations of prototype for event-ticketing applications (Regner, Urbach and Schweizer, 2019) using NFTs has suggested the following tools as well:

- *Truffle* – Contains tools for the deployment of smart contracts
- *Mocha and ganache-cli* – Provides local Ethereum blockchain network for testing
- *Infura* – Provides access to public Ethereum test networks like Ropsten

NFT minting platforms were introduced in recent years that allows anyone to deploy smart contracts for NFTs without having any technical or development skills (Ruben Merrie, 2021). Few of the platforms are listed here:

- *Digital Art Chain* – Allow users to mint NFTs by just uploading any digital image
- *Marble cards* – Allows users to create any digital cards using any URL
- *Mintable* – Allows regular people to create their own NFTs
- *Rarible and Cargo* – Bulk NFTs creation and rich media to help artist and musicians
- *OpenSea* – Allows to mint NFTs for free of cost

ERC-721 standard is currently the most used standard for creating NFTs in digital art and virtual games. And it's used by hundreds of DApps for creating millions-of-tokens. According to Redomski, the creator of the NFTs, pointed out that the NFTs are expensive and in-efficient to deploy large databases of items. This is considered as one of the important limitations as NFTs are fast growing in the digital market.

To overcome these limitations, Redomski created his own standard for NFTs called *ERC-1155*. With this new standard, the users can create infinite number of fungible and non-fungible tokens in a single smart contract in contrast to ERC-721. This will greatly reduce the number of tokens running in all the machines all over the world which leads to wastage of processing power, electricity and storage space. Further, Redomski claims ERC-1155 can be easily handled by all blockchain platforms especially for gaming industry. The following diagram highlights the comparison of ERC-721 and ERC-1155 standards on various critical factors.

Figure 3. Comparison of ERC-721 and ERC-1155

	ERC-721	ERC-1155	
Token Creation	Only one token in a single contract	Multiple tokens in a single contract	
Limitation	Can only create NFTs	Can create both Fungible and Non Fungible Contracts	
Cost	Expensive	Cheaper	
Ease of Use	Allows single operation for each transaction	Allows multiple operations in a single transaction	
Storage Requirement	More	Less	
Efficiency	Low	High	

BENEFITS AND OPERATIONAL CHALLENGES IN NFT

One of the whitepapers released by Deloitte (Patrick Laurant et.al,) has identified the benefits of using NFT in financial industry. Nevertheless, these lists of benefits applicable to all the domains.

- *Greater liquidity* – Using NFT for owning the assets can give more freedom for the creators to sell their assets in the secondary market of their choice to liquidate their token. The sellers benefitted from "liquidity premium" adding more value for their assets.
- *Faster and cheaper transactions* – Since, most of the transaction are completed with smart contracts the process can be easily automated. This may reduce the administrative burden, intermediary influences, and lower transaction fees.
- *Greater transparency* – NFTs are built on Blockchain concepts, which ensures the immutable records of ownership. This helps to have greater transparency in the transaction in three ways: to know whom you are dealing with, to know your rights and to know the previous owner of the asset, if any.
- *More accessibility* – NFT transaction will be in the Blockchain environment which ensure 24X7 availability with almost no downtime for accessibility. Few companies trying to solve this issue by adding security compliance and audit mechanism at the token level.
- *Trustworthiness:* The NFT metadata is accurate and it's very hard to create counterfeit NFTs as these are built on the pillars of Blockchain we discussed in section 1.

The following operational challenges are highlighted (Julia, 2018) when using tokens for business transactions.

- *Security compliance* – As blockchain based platforms are decentralized by default, it's hard to verify the security regulation across the globe.
- *Infrastructure issue* - The development of NFTs largely depends on the underlying infrastructure that deals with the scalability and the transaction fees. This has the direct impact on the speed of the execution.
- Many of the people are spending time in virtual world, the gap between centralized world and decentralized world is widening.
- *User experience* – The mainstream adoption of NFT is still under progress. Many of the users will be trading or dealing with NFT tokens without having the internal knowledge of how it's working.

Apart from the discussed challenges, the following points highlights few of the legal issues (Adam Cherinchaw et.al, 2021) when considering NFTs for business transactions:

- *Data Hosting and storage* – NFT and the digital asset it represents are always stored separately. The NFT is connected to a digital asset via a link. When the asset is removed from the hosted server, the link will be broken. This creates a greater challenge for the creators to recover the token leads to data loss.
- *Gaining royalties* – NFTs depends on the smart contracts to get the royalties each time it is resold. However, these automated resales of payments can happen only if it's sold in the same platform. Many of the countries law and jurisdictions (including US, UK and EU), does not recognize the resale rights and it leads to great loss for the creators.
- *Data protection laws* – The data protection laws across the globe gives the individual the rights to remove the personal data. But, as NFTs are built on the blockchain platform, the records are immutable, and this possess greater challenge in data privacy.
- *Intellectual Property (IP) rights* – There is a limited awareness of legal restrictions on copyrighted work for the people participating in NFTs. This may leads to potential infringement liability.
- *Anti-money laundering (AML)* – Any transaction that deals with cryptocurrency or token exchanges raises potential legal issues across the globe. This applies to NFT and the platform may be misused if not governed legally.
- *Technology lifespan* – Currently NFTs are built on Ethereum blockchain platform which is very robust at this moment. But, in the future there may be competent players emerge.

USE CASES FOR NFT

NFTs are gaining popularity recent days with their emergence of usage in multiple industries. Here is the list of most common use-cases where NFTs can have major impact:

- Digital Assets ownership
- Virtual gaming industry
- Domain naming services

- Banking and Finance industry
- Event ticketing management
- Fashion
- Licenses and certifications
- Sports
- Collectibles
- Music

Digital Assets Ownership

Maintaining the ownership of digital assets is one the challenging realms for the current scenario. Most of the selling platforms take a huge share of profits from the actual creators of the digital assets. When the same asset is sold in the secondary market, the content creators never get royalties or sometimes they get a small percentage of share. Many of the digital creations can be easily copy and pasted through various tools and methods and ownership data can be diminished on the internet. Collectibles are one of the popular applications in NFTs where most of the sales are happening. The platforms like OpenSea allows people to buy and sell the digital collectibles for online games or football clubs. NFTs bring more traditional collector items like cards, coins and stamps in to the Blockchain (cryptoslate.com). For the artists, copyright infringements is a major challenge. NFTs provide a solution for this by providing proof of ownership and authenticity. The platforms such as SuperRare, MarketsPlace and Rarible allows users to create original digital artworks and sell it on the NFTs based Ethereum blockchain market.

Virtual Gaming Industry

One of the booming use cases for NFTs are gaming industry as many of the game developers adopted the use of tokenized in-game items that can be easily transferred or exchanged with P2P market places and trading platforms. Also, this helps the players to keep their statistics and achievement in the games in the blockchain platform. Verification of ownership of gaming items and redeem the values seamlessly through NFT platform is becoming common across the game industry. NFT has created a new economy as players now have the potential to earn money by building and developing their own in-game digital assets. Also, this mutually-benefitting business model between players and developers earn royalties from the secondary markets. The digital asset ownership of any in-game assets created by the players remain in the system even though the players are not active on the particular game (Ruben Merrie, 2021). Some of the popular NFT game platforms are: Axie Infinity, Gods Unchained and My Crypto Heroes.

- Axie Infinity - One the first games in the Ethereum blockchain platform that created the digital pet community that allows create, buy and sell digital assets.
- Gods Unchained – Digital collectible card game where cards are issued as NFTs
- My Crypto Heroes – A Japanese based game where in-game items are delivered as Ethereum based NFTs

Domain Name Service

Though, the usage of NFTs for Domain Name Services are limited. Ethereum has introduced the concept of using NFTs for DNS on its own style "Ethereum Name Service (ENS)". Using ENS, it's easier for anyone to remember the NFT address and allows anyone to transfer the Cryptocurrency (ETH or other coins) by just using the ENS. With ENS, it's not required for the domain registry. Apart from storing the cryptocurrencies, the owner can include Twitter handles and email addresses. (Etherum Name Services, 2021)

Banking and Finance Industry

Applying blockchain technology to the traditional banking transaction to overcome the shortcomings has recently emerged as Decentralized Finance (DeFi). DeFi uses decentralized protocols to leverage trading and finance through ERC-20 standards for NFTs (Dragos I.Musan, 2020). The total value of 44.16 billion USD has been locked in DeFi as per DeFi pulse.

Figure 4. The total value locked (USD) in DeFi
(adopted from DeFi Pulse website)

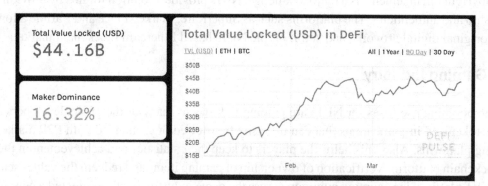

The NFT backed loans and leasing is one of the popular areas for DeFi. The NFT can be used as a collateral as well. NFT creators can allow fractional ownership [eth.org] where they allow investors the opportunity to own a part of their NFTs. These factionalized NFTs can be traded not only in Ethereum marketplace but also in Decentralized Exchanges (DEXs) like Uniswap. Uniswap is a smart contract based Automated Market Maker that dynamically calculates and adjust exchange rates for trading ERC-20 tokens (Dragos I.Musan, 2020). Decentralized Lending Pools (DLP) are another interesting DeFi application where anyone can liquidate the pool of ERC-20 tokens. DLP helps in instant borrowing, deposits and collateral features. Currently, ETHLend is one of the successful implementations for P2P loans and liquidity. Flash loans are type of new loans particularly in Ethereum DeFi solution which enable instant borrowing with no collateral and no risk of default. Flash loans are very useful in arbitrage, wash trading, collateral swapping and flash minting (Dragos I.Musan 2020).

Event Ticketing Management

The ticket in an event management system represents a token to attend any event such as cultural, adventure, entertainment or sports. The ticket comes in various forms either as a digital or physical entity. The tickets are usually sold directly by the event organizers in the primary market. However, the same tickets are also sold in noticeably with huge difference in the base price. Using QR codes or bar codes will encode the information. However, they are not tamper-proof that anyone duplicate the original tickets and sale in the secondary market. This has created a huge loss in the event management industry. Here are some of the challenges the event management companies face in ticket handling (Regner, Urbach and Schweizer, 2019)

- Limited scalability
- Lack of Trust
- No or less control over the secondary markets
- Agents or intermediaries' dependency
- Lack of transparency
- No way to validate the authenticity of the tickets

Using NFTs for ticket management system has the potential to overcome the challenges listed above. Each ticket can be created with unique id using NFT which deployed in Ethereum Blockchain infrastructure (Regner, Urbach and Schweizer, 2019). Hence, the tickets possess the basic properties of blockchain which includes immutability, transparency, integrity, and availability. With the help of smart contracts, event management companies have a full control over the price in both primary and secondary markets. The customers who purchased the tickets have the ability to trace the authenticity and validity of the event ticket. Based on their research observation, here is the key takeaway:

- Using NFTs for ticket management system helps to overcome the weakness of the existing system such as susceptibility to fraud, secondary market control and validation of ticket ownership.

Fashion

Counterfeiting fashion accessories is one of the common events in the fashion industry. NFTs can help consumers easily verify the ownership of the accessories and other relevant details.

Licenses and Certifications

The education industry issues digital certificates for the course completion or degree attainment. This certificate can be easily counterfeit in the market. The use of NFTs for issuing certificates or license will greatly reduce the burden of manual verification.

Sports

Counterfeit tickets and the collectibles create nuances in the sports industry. The ticket managing can be easily done with NFTs for protecting the ticket ownership and blocking the tickets in the secondary market. Tokenization of successful athletes is also on rising trend. The NFT value of the athletes rise with their performance in each event.

Collectibles

After the successful business idea implemented by CryptoKitties in 2017, many companies started the initiative to invite the online users to collect rare digital items. The collectibles industry is one of the most promising and sales oriented NFT applications. Since, the NFTs maintain their uniqueness, they play important role in providing solution for digitalizing the collectible market. As copyright and proof of ownership are the built-in nature of NFTs, this makes the perfect fit for collectibles industry. Here are some of the examples where NFTs are used in collectibles:

- Cryptostamp Project – An initiative from the Austrian postal service to link NFTs in collecting stamps
- NBA – An NFT based blockchain based trading card system that offers basketball game highlights.
- Terra Virtua platform – Allows to collect 3D animated collectibles from The God Father, Top Gun, Sunset Boulevard and Lost in Space.

Music

Copyright and pirating is one of the major issues in the Music industry. The piracy in this industry can cause financial damages to the artists in millions of dollars. Music files can be linked to NFTs to avoid the problems. Only the creator can claim the rights to access the files. The music files cannot be re-distributed or duplicated in NFTs. This approach brings great benefits to the musicians as they get an opportunity to reach their audience without intermediaries.

As the NFT ecosystem is rapidly developing, here are the list of few top NFT projects implemented successfully:

- **OpenSea** – One of the best and biggest marketplace to purchase NFT art and collectibles. The users can purchase items using cryptocurrencies such as ETH.
- **Async**.art – An NFT platform where users can create, buy and sell tokens. Also, it allows to buy a "layers" of digital art work.
- **Cryptokitties** – One of the successful NFT implementations to create, buy and sell digital cats. This project gives the spotlight for NFT marketplace.
- **Ethereum Name Services (ENS)** – The platform allows users to register for NFT based Domain names and the same can be tradable in the NFT marketplace.

There is a greater number of NFT projects currently. Refer to the additional reading section to explore.

CONCLUSION

We have covered the various important aspects to enable the readers to get the glimpse of NFTs. Ethereum blockchain has got a remarkable place in the global-wide adoption of blockchain concepts for multiple use cases beyond using it only for cryptocurrency transaction. Also, it's very clear that NFTs are going to be the future of Blockchain as the world is gearing up for digital revolution. Beyond digital assets, NFTs have its advantages in traditional banking and investment industry. The entertainment and the recreation industry have quickly adapted to the rapid changes in the business by using blockchain for its business transactions.

The NFT ecosystem has experienced boom during 2020 in terms of volume traded and liquidity. NFT can no longer be in the speculative industry and it will slowly get into the mainstream business as a value generation industry. Gaming and crypto-art industries are still very favorable for using NFTs for their transaction at present and in the future. The NFTs could create a new digital economy in the market.

According to the NFT yearly report 2020, NFT ecosystem is evolving fast with its full potential reaching the individual creatives, artists, musicians, film makers and few major game industries such as NBA, Atari. The world of NFT will be soon become mainstream and will be revolutionary for the digital industry.

The recent google trends report on the people who searched for the terms "NFT" or "Non-Fungible Tokens" have increased tremendously in recent days. This shows the influence and the visibility NFT is increasing day-by-day. The following diagrams shows this trend (Source: Google Trends)

Figure 5. Google Trends - "Non Fungible Tokens" - keyword search

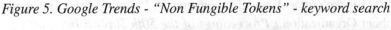

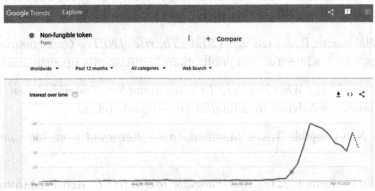

Figure 6. Google Trends - "NFT" keyword search

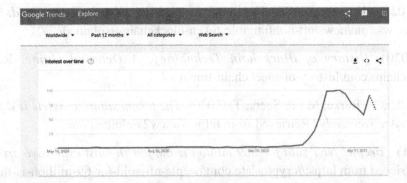

To summarize, NFTs is gaining momentum in bringing the digital and the physicals worlds as close as possible with its "true ownership" as the key component feature. (Dan Kelly et.al 2020)

The recent auction of Twitter CEO Jack's first ever tweet has the highest bid at $2.5 million worth of NFTs. And, amazingly an art called "Every day: First 5000 days" created by Winklemann (popularly known as "Beeple" by his online persona) has been sold for $69 million worth of NFTs is the fourth most expensive artwork sold by a living artist to a Singapore-based NFT start-up. The following quote by Beeple shows how NFTs play a major role in the lives of digital asset owners (Shaurya Malwa, 2021):

Artists have been using hardware and software to create artwork and distribute it on the internet for the last 20+ years but there was never a real way to truly own and collect it. With NFTs that has now changed.

REFERENCES

Arcenegui, J., Arjona, R., Román, R., & Baturone, I. (2021). Secure Combination of IoT and Blockchain by Physically Binding IoT Devices to Smart Non-Fungible Tokens Using PUFs. *Sensors*.

Beck, R., & Müller-Bloch, C. (2017). Blockchain as Radical Innovation: A Framework for Engaging with Distributed Ledgers as Incumbent Organization.: *Proceedings of the 50th Hawaii International Conference on System Sciences*, 5390–5399. 10.24251/HICSS.2017.653

Cherinchaw, A., Vallabhaneni, P., & Lizaso, S. (2021). *The rise of NFTs – Opportunities and legal issues.* Retrieved from https://www.whitecase.com/publications/alert/rise-nfts-opportunities-and-legal-issues

Conti, R., & Schmidt, J. (2021), *What You Need To Know About Non-Fungible Tokens (NFTs).* Retrieved from https://www.forbes.com/advisor/investing/nft-non-fungible-token/

EIP-721. ERC-721 Non-Fungible Token Standard. (n.d.). Retrieved from https://eips.ethereum.org/EIPS/eip-721

Ethereum Blockchain Platform. (2021a). *Non-Fungible Tokens (NFT).* Retrieved from https://ethereum.org/en/nft/

Ethereum Blockchain Platform. (2021b). *Ethereum Name Service.* Retrieved from https://app.ens.domains/

Gornstein, L. (2021). *What is an NFT? The trendy blockchain technology explained.* Retrieved from https://www.cbsnews.com/news/nft-nonfungible-token-blockchain-explained/

Iredale, G. (2020). *History of Blockchain Technology: A Detailed Guide.* Retrieved from https://101blockchains.com/history-of-blockchain-timeline/

Laurant, P., Chollet, T., Burke, M., & Seers, T. (2020). *The tokenization of assets is disrupting the financial industry. Are you ready?* Retrieved from https://www2.deloitte.com/

Malwa, S. (2021). *'Beeple' NFT sold for $69 million is the fourth most expensive artwork sold by a living artist.* Retrieved from https://cryptoslate.com/beeple-nft-sold-for-69-million-is-the-fourth-most-expensive-artwork-sold-by-a-living-artist/

Merrie, R. (2021). *The big five NFT use cases*. Retrieved from https://cryptoslate.com/the-big-five-nft-use-cases

Musan, D. I. (2020). *NFT.finance Leveraging Non-Fungible Tokens* [Unpublished master's dissertation]. Imperial College, London, UK.

Regner, F., Urbach, N., & Schweizer, A. (2019). NFTs in Practice – Non-Fungible Tokens as Core Component of a Blockchain-based Event Ticketing Application. *ICIS 2019 Proceedings*, 1. Retrieved from https://aisel.aisnet.org/icis2019/blockchain_fintech/blockchain_fintech/1

Roose, K. (2021). *Buy This Column on the Blockchain! Why can't a journalist join the NFT party, too?* Retrieved from https://www.nytimes.com/2021/03/24/technology/nft-column-blockchain.html

KEY TERMS AND DEFINITIONS

Decentralized Finance (DeFi): An alternative banking solution that uses open source technology mainly cryptocurrencies and blockchain for day-to-day banking transactions.

Digital Wallet: A crypto-wallet to store crypto-currency and tokens.

Ethereum Request for Comments (ERC): The standard proposed by Ethereum Blockchain to ensure interoperability of the digital tokens in its platform to provide the list of rules to be followed by token implementation.

Ethereum Virtual Machine (EVM): The smart contracts source code developed in the Ethereum platform needs to be compiled into a byte code by using EVM. Ethereum uses its own high-level JavaScript like programming language called "Solidity."

Immutability: The property in which the transactions once added in the Blockchain network cannot be modified or altered.

Minting: The process of creating NFTs by writing an NFT contract or using any of the available NFT creation platforms.

Non-Fungible Token: A digital token which has the unique identifier and metadata which cannot be shareable.

Smart Contracts: A small piece of code that runs on the Blockchain nodes to deploy business components.

APPENDIX: LIST OF NFT PROJECTS

CryptoKitties. https://www.cryptokitties.co

0xcert ERC-721 Token. https://github.com/0xcert/ethereum-erc721

Su Squares. https://tenthousandsu.com

Decentraland. https://decentraland.org

CryptoPunks. https://www.larvalabs.com/cryptopunks

DMarket. https://www.dmarket.io

Enjin Coin. https://enjincoin.io

Ubitquity. https://www.ubitquity.io

Propy. https://tokensale.propy.com

CryptoKitties Deployed Contract. https://etherscan.io/address/0x06012c8cf97bead5deae237070f9587
    f8e7a266d#code

Su Squares Bug Bounty Program. https://github.com/fulldecent/su-squares-bounty

XXXXERC721. https://github.com/fulldecent/erc721-example

ERC721ExampleDeed. https://github.com/nastassiasachs/ERC721ExampleDeed

Curio Cards. https://mycuriocards.com

Rare Pepe. https://rarepepewallet.com

Auctionhouse Asset Interface. https://github.com/dob/auctionhouse/blob/master/contracts/Asset.sol

OpenZeppelin SafeERC20.sol Implementation. https://github.com/OpenZeppelin/zeppelin-solidity/blob/
    master/contracts/token/ERC20/SafeERC20.sol

Section 2
Blockchain Applied to IoT, VANETs, and FANETs

Chapter 6
A Survey of Blockchain-Based Solutions for IoTs, VANETs, and FANETs

Maroua Abdelhafidh
(iD) https://orcid.org/0000-0003-0626-5598
University of Sfax, Tunisia

Nadia Charef
Canadian University Dubai, UAE

Adel Ben Mnaouer
(iD) https://orcid.org/0000-0003-3617-7636
Canadian University Dubai, UAE

Lamia Chaari
University of Sfax, Tunisia

ABSTRACT

Recently, the internet of things (IoT) has gained popularity as an enabling technology for wireless connectivity of mobile and/or stationary devices providing useful services for the general public in a collaborative manner. Mobile ad-hoc networks (MANETs) are regarded as a legacy enabling technology for various IoT applications. Vehicular ad-hoc networks (VANETs) and flying ad-hoc networks (FANETs) are specific extensions of MANETs that are drivers of IoT applications. However, IoT is prone to diverse attacks, being branded as the weakest link in the networking chain requiring effective solutions for achieving an acceptable level of security. Blockchain (BC) technology has been identified as an efficient method to remedy IoT security concerns. Therefore, this chapter classifies the attacks targeting IoT, VANETs, and FANETs systems based on their vulnerabilities. This chapter explores a selection of blockchain-based solutions for securing IoT, VANETs, and FANETs and presents open research directions compiled out of the presented solutions as useful guidelines for the readers.

DOI: 10.4018/978-1-7998-5839-3.ch006

INTRODUCTION

Nowadays, Internet of Things (IoT) (Stoyanova et al.2020) has experienced tremendous opportunities and potential interest from various applications allowing a seamless connection of multiple and diverse devices to the internet in order to exchange efficiently collected data.

With the growth of IoT applications, a rise of Mobile Ad Hoc Networks (MANETs) (Tripathy et al.2020), Vehicular Ad Hoc Networks (VANETs) (Hamdi et al.2020) and Flying Ad Hoc Networks (Mukherjee et al.2018) applications is recognized. MANETs is a network of mobile nodes that are connected wirelessly and characterized by a dynamic network topology. FANET is another class of ad-hoc networks that is a subcategory of VANETs which is a sub form of MANET as illustrated in figure 1.

Figure 1. MANET, VANET, FANET and IoT

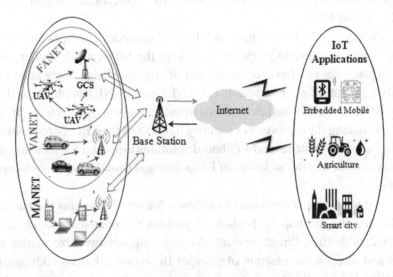

At present, IoT systems are often dependent upon a centralized architecture where information is sent from the connected devices and equipment to a proprietary cloud where the data is processed using analytics and then sent back to those tiny IoT devices to coordinate them as with all centralized systems. All devices are identified, authenticated and connected through cloud servers and the data collected by the devices is stored in the cloud for further processing (Ali et al.2018).

This centralized network architecture cannot be able to respond to the growing needs of the huge IoT ecosystems with the growth of connected devices that will be approximately 75.44 billion, as announced in (Alam2018). This gathered data, stored in centralized servers, can be tampered and consequently lacks traceability. Furthermore, through the current architecture, users have limited control over their data and are made to trust the cloud and have no choice but to rely on their promises of security. Accordingly, IoT security efforts mostly focus on securing point-to-point communication and fall short in addressing security during the lifecycle of data by thinking about this problem of trust. IoT devices need to confidently exchange data without having to rely on an intermediary which adds friction and costs reconciliation problems and all sorts of transactional challenges.

In this context, Blockchain (BC) (Lu2019) is a tailored technology for such problems. It has attracted a tremendous interest from various IoT applications thanks to its distributed nature that implies no single entity controls the ledger, but rather the participating peers together validate the authenticity of records. These records are organized in blocks which are linked together using cryptographic hashes (Ferrag et al.2018). All the BC peers have to validate each record to get added to a block (Reyna et al.2018) in order to be uploaded to the BC. This agreement is achieved through consensus algorithms such as Proof of Work (PoW), Proof of Stake (PoS), Delegated Proof-of-Stake (DPoS), and Proof-of-Authority (PoA). Accordingly, BC keeps track through the data records and achieves a sort of distributed trust that can drastically reduce the cost of verification and bootstrap IoT platform without assigning a lot of market power or much control to one single entity.

Due to this distribution of computing power of resources or IoT devices with BC and its high traceability and trust level, the system designed with BC is much more resilient to attackers.

This technology is currently revolutionizing several IoT applications but still in its early stage of research with VANETs and FANETs.

Several surveys (Wang et al.2020) (Wang et al.2019b) (Fernández-Caramés and Fraga-Lamas2018) (Ferrag et al.2018) have been already proposed to present the IoT security challenges and to explain the integration of BC technology. However, to the best of our knowledge, there is no work on efficient handling of security vulnerabilities of various IoT, VANET and FANET applications by leveraging the benefits offered by BC technology, that has been discussed recently in the literature. In addition, there is no relevant work highlighting the taxonomy of security threats and their BC-based solutions. Hence, our chapter is presenting a synthesis of several BC-based solutions proposed for securing the IoT, VANET and FANET systems considering the inclusion of Edge, Fog and Cloud computing layers in their overall proposed architectures.

The remainder of this chapter is organized as follows: Section II presents the basic concept of IoT, VANETs, FANETs, and BC technology. Section III reviews the related works on the IoT, VANETs, FANETs security vulnerabilities, threats and attacks and proposes two taxonomies of these threats. Section IV studies and discusses a selection of relevant BC-based solutions addressing these security vulnerabilities. Section V highlights future directions and suggests some open research areas related to the effective use of BC for securing the above systems. Section VI concludes the chapter and pinpoints some learned lessons.

To better clarify the acronyms, table 1 reports all the notations used in this chapter.

BACKGROUND

IoT Systems Basic Concepts

Internet of Things (IoT) (HaddadPajouh et al.2019) system represents a platform that combines software and hardware components connected to the internet enabling them to collect and exchange large amount of data. This data is analyzed and processed in order to perform an adequate action or some services offered to the end-user.

Various IoT definitions have been presented in the literature. Gupta et al. (Gupta and Quamara2020) highlighted a things-oriented definition of the IoT without defining the communication protocols by considering it as an interconnection of sensing and devices sharing information across platforms. Bodkhe et al. (Bodkhe and Tanwar2020) presented the IoT from the viewpoint of communication and environment so that devices should be connected in spaces using intelligent interfaces to connect, communicate within the user environment and context. Kavitha et al. (Kavitha and Ravikumar2021) detailed the IoT from a network context. Hence, the devices are connected through the Internet. In conclusion, the IoT is a hybrid infrastructure that associates the digital and physical worlds together through empowering physical things with communication and moderate computing capabilities to allow remote and possibly mobile, access, control and interrogation of these physical things through the Internet. Therefore, it is supposed to define the used entities and the interactions between them considering the communication architecture and scenarios. In an IoT system, it is important to ensure the security and privacy of the system especially with the increase of the number of IoT devices. As mentioned in (Bansal), the authors affirmed that this number will increase progressively to reach 75 billion by 2025. Accordingly, to address the IoT security characteristics, authors in (Hassan et al.2019) (Zarpelão et al.2017) (Sha et al.2018) explained the IoT security requirements (authentication of devices (El-Hajj et al.2019), confidentiality and integrity of data (Garg et al.2020), fault tolerance (Chakraborty et al.2019), heterogeneity (Paul and Jeyaraj2019), access control (Qiu et al.2020), etc), the various possible threats and attacks and they highlighted the proposed solutions.

Table 1. List of Acronyms

Acronym	Meaning	Acronym	Meaning
6LOWPAN	IPv6 over Low -Power Wireless Personal Area Networks	P2P	Peer-to-peer
AHD	Ad-hoc Domain	PoA	Proof-of-Authority
BC	Blockchain	PoET	Proof of Elapsed Time
BLE	Bluetooth Low Energy	PoS	Proof of Stake
DDoS	Distributed DoS	PoW	Proof of Work
DoS	Denial of Service	RFID	Radio Frequency Identification
DPoS	Delegated Proof-of-Stake	RSD	Roadside Domain
DTLS	Datagram Transport Layer Security	RSU	Roadside Unit
FANET	Flying Ah-doc Network	SDN	Software-Defined Networking
GCS	Ground Control Station	SSL	Secure Socket Layer
GPS	Global Positioning System	TLS	Transport Layer Security
HIP	Host Identity Protocol	UAV	Unmanned Aerial Vehicles
IoT	Internet of Things	V2I	Vehicle to Infrastructure
ITS	Intelligent Transportation System	V2V	Vehicle to Vehicle
IVD	In-Vehicle Domain	VANET	Vehicular Ah-doc Network
MANET	Mobile Ad-hoc Network	WEP	Wired Equivalent Policy
OBU	On-board Unit	WSN	Wireless Sensor Network

As addressed in (Dorri et al.2017b) (Dorri et al.2017a), IoT requires a distributed, auditable and scalable solution to ensure its security and privacy. The authors affirmed that the BC technology has the potential to achieve efficiently the IoT security requirements. It is considered as a distributed ledger where data is shared among peer nodes and builds a collective trust between them under a decentralized network. This unified and decentralized nature enables a security measure for IoT.

Blockchain Basic Concepts

Blockchain has been used to revolutionize many IoT applications and it represents a suitable technology that is able to provide a distributed secure ecosystem for the IoT (Kamran et al.2020). It offers a distributed management system in which all nodes can communicate, share information and all together manage the system by means of a distributed consensus among them. This peer-to-peer networking creates a distributed database synchronization which is an attractive feature for IoT to offer auditability and traceability.

As defined by Zheng et al. (Zheng et al.2017), the most important features that justify the increased use of BC technology in several industries and by a majority of researchers are its (i) decentralized infrastructure, (ii) immutability, (iii) ability to control new entries to the network and detect intrusion attempts by applying a decentralized consensus, (iv) It's auditability (to verify the transactions between peers transparently), and (v) their fault tolerance aspect in enabling data replicas records and avoiding data leakage.

Blockchain Structure

A Blockchain is composed of blocks containing the details of transactions within the network. Each block contains information about the current node and previous node, namely, the body and the header, respectively. The body includes the data in form of transactions and the number of transactions inside the block. The header contains a timestamp that indicates when the block was published and a Merkle tree that allows verifying the transactions stored within the body of the block. In addition, it involves the identifier of the previous block. This structure makes it similar to a linked list that ensures the immutability of the BC contents.

Types of Blockchain

Three types of BC, highlighting its privacy levels, are used in different scenarios by presenting various attributes. Table 2 shows a detailed comparison between these types.

- Public Blockchain (Tang et al.2019): is a distributed ledger system that allows to everyone to join the network, publish new blocks, read the transactions data and validate it. Public BCs are called permissionless in that it is very open and permit to anyone to have a copy of the BC. This type is required to manage a large number of anonymous nodes, so it is necessary to mitigate potential malicious behavior. Cryptocurrency networks are examples of such a BC including Bitcoin, Litcoin and Ethereum (Wood et al.2014).
- Private Blockchain (Pahlajani et al.2019): This BC is permissioned and is formed by a set of known transacting parties. All transactions will be validated and controlled by a selected set of nodes. Therefore, a private BC is not as tamper-resistant as a public BC. This type of BC is mainly for

enterprise, use cases and permissioned ledgers will replicate a high degree of confidentiality and accountability and transparency. Hyperledger (Cachin et al.2016) and Ripple (Pilkington2016) are the examples of the private BC.

Table 2. Comparison of Public, Private and Consortium Blockchains

Features	Public Blockchain	Private Blockchain	Consortium Blockchain
Nodes participation in consensus process	All nodes	Only particular participants	Selected nodes in various Organizations
Immutability	Yes	Partial	
Consensus Mechanism	PoS/PoW	multi-party consensus algorithm	
Permissionless	Yes	No	
Transaction speed	Slow	Fast	
Operations	Public read, write, share, validate	Restricted (Approved participants)	
Advantage	Best security of complete trustable transactions.	Emphasize the speed of the system. Highly scalable	● Mitigate some of the risks of a private Blockchain (by removing centralized control) ● Their smaller number of nodes gives them generally much more efficient performance than that of a public Blockchain.

- Consortium Blockchain (Gai et al.2019): called also federated BC. The most notable difference from public and private BC can be notified at the consensus level. It is performed by more than one central entity. Therefore, this system is flexible and decentralized, so that the visibility of the transactions can be limited to validators, searchable by authorized persons, or by all. As private BCs, a consortium BC does not include processing fees. Energy Web Foundation and IBM Food Trust are examples of such BC.

Smart Contracts

Smart contracts (Wang et al.2019a) are tiny computer programs stored inside the BC, used to manage transactions under specific conditions. Therefore, smart contracts are the digital equivalent of traditional contracts in the real world.

They are stored in the BC and inherit interesting properties like immutability and distribution. It is distributed by means that the output of the contract is validated by every node on the network. Tampering with smart contracts becomes almost impossible.

These contracts execute on Ethereum BC's platform that was created and designed to build decentralized applications. These applications are fully trustworthy and transparent because they run on BC. However, smart contracts are not controlled or modified even by developers after the deployment (Praitheeshan et al.2019).

Consensus Algorithms for Blockchain Development

Consensus algorithm is a strategy that a group of computers use to manage which nodes in the network get to set the state of truth that everyone else follows and agrees on. There are different applied consensus algorithms that each one has different properties or tradeoffs in terms of how secure the agreement is:

- Proof of Work (PoW) (Gervais et al.2016): It is the first consensus algorithm that has been developed. It is used to validate transactions and broadcast new blocks to the BC. It helps to protect the network against numerous different attacks. While PoW is a reliable and secure solution for managing decentralized ledger, it is also very resource intensive by consuming a lot of power.
- Proof of Stake (PoS) (Saleh2018): is designed to overcome the drawbacks of the proof of work algorithm. In the Proof of Stake algorithm, each block gets validated before another block is added to the ledger. Miners can participate in the mining process with their coins to stake.
- Proof of Elapsed Time (PoET) (Chen et al.2017): it is a modified form of PoS. Only approved parties selected based on their reputation can become validators. It can be used by private or permissioned BC networks.

Since the network requires identification of the miners, the consensus algorithm ensures a secure login into the system.

VANET Basic Concepts

Technology advancement and the emergence of smart cities have given rise to VANET technology (Lee and Atkison, 2021). VANET is a self organized ad-hoc network that consists of vehicles communicating through Peer-to-peer (P2P) communication or via multihop communication using Wireless technology. The vehicle in VANET contains an On-Board Units (OBU) to communicate with other vehicles and the Roadside Units (RSUs).

VANET is considered a subset of MANET. A major characteristic of VANET is that its topology changes more frequently compared to MANET due to the high speed of the vehicles. Other differences between the two types of network include the large scale of VANET deployment and unlimited power consumption of its node as opposed to MANET (Mokhtar and Azab, 2015).

Communication in VANET can be divided into three domains, namely the Roadside Domain (RSD), Ad-hoc Domain (AHD), and In-vehicle Domain (IVD). Communication at these domains can be classified according to three types of communication: Vehicle to Vehicle (V2V), Vehicle to Infrastructure (V2I), and Intra-Vehicle communication. V2V refers to the ad-hoc communication that occurs between vehicles. On the other hand, V2I describes the communication between vehicles and the RSUs. Intra-vehicle communication is used to define the internal communication of On-board Units (OBUs). VANET is an important technology to establish Intelligent Transportation Systems (ITS) and can play a critical role to enhance the safety and comfort level of drivers and transportation efficiency. VANETs can be used for effective traffic management, provide drivers access to road and environmental conditions, accident prevention and emergency awareness.

FANET Basic Concepts

Flying Ad-hoc Network (Chriki et al.2019) is a sub-class of VANET that is a subcategory of MANET where multiple Unmanned Aerial Vehicles (UAVs) are connected in wireless Ad-hoc Network to cover the monitored area. However, a FANET present specific features that differentiate it from other types of MANET network including the:

- Network connectivity: Connectivity within FANET can be often intermittent due to dynamic behavior of drones, which creates temporary disconnections. The communication link from the source to the destination may be unavailable for an indefinite period, which requires the reactivity of the network to find a backup path and avoid consequent losses to the application flows.
- Mobility model: In FANET, the mobility model depends on various parameters. It is dynamically modified due to the speed of drones, climatic conditions and many other geographical and topographical parameters.
- Strict and constrained deadline: Typically, FANETs are used for real-time applications. Therefore, the control and command messages must be processed in real time by the UAVs in order to avoid loss of control.

Despite the potential importance of FANET-based systems in monitoring and tracking applications, there are still some issues pertaining to stable networking due to the continuous dynamic behavior of drones. Furthermore, resource-constrained drones still need more innovative solutions to address the power scarcity that limits their flying time and consequently can negatively influence the monitoring efficiency. Moreover, various FANET-based systems suffer from security weaknesses that need effective solutions and further investigation. Accordingly, it is required to find a trade-off among security, stability, efficiency, and the network requirements

Similar to VANET, FANET presents three communication domains (Barka et al.2018) including the UAV to UAV communication, UAV to Ground Control Station (GCS) communication, and the hybrid communication.

IOTs, VANETs, AND FANETs: VULNERABILITIES, THREATS, AND ATTACKS

Although the rapid evolution of connected technologies, they are prone to various and critical security concerns. To tackle these challenges, a closer attention should be exclusively given to the emerging IoT, VANET and FANET related vulnerabilities. Accordingly, their related threats and consequent attacks can be highlighted and analyzed in order to define the adequate solutions to cope with these crucial security challenges.

In this section, each system's architecture is defined and explained. In addition, an overview that emphasizes on understanding different security challenges associated with each architecture layer is deeply addressed.

Vulnerabilities, Threats, and Attacks in IoT

IoT Security Architecture

There is no common architecture for the IoT and there are various IoT architecture presented in the literature (Aswale et al.2019) (Manogaran et al.2018). A few of them (Perwej et al.2019) proposed a four-layer architecture including the sensing layer, network layer, service layer and application-interface layer. The majority proposed three-layer architecture (Siegel et al.2017) composed of application, network and perception layers. Therefore, this architecture is considered to cover up the details of the IoT system and the IoT components, from devices, through the connecting network to the end-user through applications.

The perception layer consists of physical objects such as sensors and actuators, nodes, and devices. These devices gather the information from the environment and sense physical parameters. The collected data is then received by the network layer to send it to the application layer which in turn analyzes it in order to deliver specific services to the end-user.

Security vulnerabilities figure at each IoT architecture layer and cause different attacks. It is important to address the security issues in each layer and determine its related vulnerabilities in order to classify their targeted attacks. Alaba et al. (Alaba et al.2017) have surveyed the security threats such as the lack of privacy solutions for defining device location and the packet delay or loss and Distributed Denial of Service (DDoS) attack of Software-defined networking (SDN) architecture used for IoT application. In addition, they provided a taxonomy of IoT security attacks in the application domain (authentication, authorization, exhaustion of resources, and trust establishment), communication channel (MitM attacks, Eavesdropping), and data domain (Data privacy and confidentiality, Micro-probing, tampering of hard components, jamming, Collision, unfairness, exhaustion, replay, meta-data attacks, etc). Frustaci et al. (Frustaci et al.2017) have highlighted the various attacks against IoT system. They have classified them based on the IoT architecture layers (the perception layer including Node Tampering, malicious code injection, DoS attacks, routing attacks, and data transit attacks, the Transportation Layer including Routing Attacks and Data Transit Attacks, and the Application Layer presenting the Data Leakage, DoS Attack and Malicious Code Injection). The authors have investigated the proposed solutions for the highlighted attacks and they have concluded that the perception layer is the most vulnerable level of the IoT system due to the physical exposure of IoT devices, and their constrained resources.

Authors in (Kouicem et al.2018) have introduced the security requirements of various IoT applications (smart grids, healthcare, Transportation systems, smart cities, and manufacturing) in terms of authentication, confidentiality and privacy concerns. Moreover, they have revealed the security challenges for each application (Heterogeneity of communication standards, Scalability issues, Vulnerabilities related to information system technology, devices mobility, etc.). The authors have focused on IoT security solutions by discussing both classical approaches as well as new technologies.

Figure 2 illustrated the taxonomy of IoT security attacks present in each layer.

Perception Layer Vulnerabilities, Attacks and Solutions

This first layer is composed of IoT devices such as smartphones, Radio Frequency Identification (RFID) tags, sensors and actuators. These components sense, gather and measure various physical parameters. The collected data can be stored inside the devices or into a gateway to be processed and analyzed. The major functionalities of this layer are data sensing and data acquisition.

Due to the higher number of devices, their deployment security is an important challenge.

According to (Neshenko et al.2019), the vulnerabilities can be related to IoT devices, affect the confidentiality and the availability of the IoT system and make it victim to various malicious attacks that affect its security objectives and reduce its performance.

As the number of devices is continuously growing and operating autonomously in unattended environments, an attacker can access and manipulate it easily which causes physical damage to the devices and corrupts their control.

Several research works have addressed these vulnerabilities in order to understand their causes, and reveal their effects on the IoT system. Jiang et al. (Jiang et al.2020) have highlighted that the lack of the device encryption can lead to an illegitimate access to the sensed information to be easily extracted and modified. They have suggested security solutions such as proposing strong password-hashing algorithms, and providing transparent system file encryption to protect confidential data.

Nguyen et al. (Nguyen et al.2019) have affirmed that insufficient energy of the devices presents an IoT security challenge. Consequently, attackers try to shutdown the device and waste its limited energy by creating a series of legitimate messages. Therefore, the authors have revealed the importance of energy harvesting techniques to cope with power challenges (Azzabi et al.2017). In addition, they have affirmed that adequate authentication should be important to ensure IoT system confidentiality, interrupt malicious attackers to violate data integrity and save energy consequently.

On the other hand, common perception layer attacks have been elaborated in the literature as illustrated in table 3.

Table 3. Perception Layer attacks, effects and solutions

Attack	Effect	Proposed Solution
Node tempering and Jamming	● Access to sensitive information. ● DoS	● Physical Unclonable Functions based authentication (Aman et al.2017) ● CUTE Mote (Gomes et al.2017)
Sleep Deprivation Attack	Node shutdown	CUTE Mote (Gomes et al.2017)
Eavesdropping	Control data flow	Pervasive Authentication protocol and a Key establishment scheme (PAuthKey) (Porambage et al.2014)
Permanent Denial of Service (PDoS)	Resource Destruction	NetwOrked Smart object (NOS) Middleware (Sicari et al.2018)

Network Layer Vulnerabilities, Attacks and Solutions

This second layer, responsible for transmitting the collected data to the next layer, uses various transmission technologies such as ZigBee (Farahani2011), Bluetooth Low Energy (BLE) (DeCuir2013), 6LoWPAN (Al-Kashoash et al.2019), and LoRaWAN (de Carvalho Silva et al.2017).

At this level, IoT vulnerabilities can be caused by network or protocol weaknesses.

Various research works focus on the ZigBee protocol that ensures the secure communications between devices thanks to the use of symmetric keys shared between nodes (Rana et al.2018). In this context, khanji et al. (Khanji et al.2019) have addressed the various malicious actions employed to compromise

ZigBee-enabled IoT devices due to the unencrypted transmitted keys among nodes. Consequently, attackers can easily access the information and monitor the devices. DoS attack is the major resulting attack. Therefore, the authors have suggested deploying a secure key management process during the key installation to ensure the information confidentiality as highlighted also in (Harbi et al.2019) and (Pandharipande and Newsham2018).

When the Bluetooth technology is used, various vulnerabilities can help attackers to establish a connection with a victim. The authors in (Zeadally et al.2019) and (Antonioli et al.2020) have highlighted that the lack of authentication mechanism and insufficient protections when two devices are paired are the major Bluetooth vulnerabilities that allow an attacker to insert a rogue device between two paired Bluetooth devices and get access to the shared information.

It is recommended to examine the vulnerabilities of 6LoWPAN protocol. As addressed in (Bertin et al.2019), the use of malicious intermediary network nodes is a most known vulnerability of 6LoWPAN networks. It is based on verifying if the neighbor is a node that is authorized to access the Wireless Sensor Network (WSN). Various techniques have been suggested to deal with this vulnerability, including Encryption techniques like Datagram Transport Layer Security (DTLS), host identification technology like Host Identity Protocol (HIP) as affirmed by Benslimane et al. in (Benslimane et al.2018).

The LoRaWan protocol presents various security vulnerabilities leading to diverse attacks. The authors in (Yang et al.2018) (Butun et al.2018) (Butun et al.2019) (Noura et al.2020) have investigated the various LoRaWAN vulnerabilities and security issues including the transmission of different message without rekeying, caching and replay of ACK packets, transmission of falsified gateway beacons to repeatedly wake up sensors. Accordingly, this implies various attacks including replay, eavesdropping, DoS and battery exhaustion.

These network layer vulnerabilities increase the number of security network attacks as detailed in table 4.

Table 4. Network Layer attacks, effects and solutions

Attack		Effect	Proposed Solution
Denial/Distributed Denial of Service (DoS/ DDoS) (Sonar and Upadhyay2014)		● Delays data forwarding ● Prevent data to access its required destination	SDN based IoT framework (Yin et al.2018)
Routing Attack (Andrea et al.2015)	Sybil Attack	Malicious node redundancy	Trust aware Protocol (Airehrour et al.2019)
	Sinkhole Attack	Data Alteration	● Authentication ● Intrusion Detection (Glissa et al.2016)
	Wormhole Attack	Packet tunneling	Clustering based Intrusion Detection System (Shukla2017)
	Selective Forwarding attack	Disrupts routing paths and sends incomplete information.	● Hash Chain ● Authentication (Glissa et al.2016) (Pu and Hajjar2018)
Man in the Middle (MiTM)		Data Privacy violation	● Secure MQTT ● Inter-device Authentication (Singh et al.2015)
Replay Attack		● Network congestion ● DoS	Signcryption (Ashibani and Mahmoud2017)
RFID Unauthorized Access		Data Modification	SRAM based PUF (Singh et al.2015)

Application Layer Vulnerabilities, Attacks and Solutions

This third layer is responsible for the collected data analysis and processing. In addition, it is able to provide high-quality services to meet end-users' needs. Different IoT environments (i.e., smart city, healthcare, and industry) can be implemented within this level.

Andrea et al. (Andrea et al.2015) have focused on the security vulnerabilities present in the application layer. It includes the malicious software such as Trojan Horses, Spyware and Adware that infects the system by tampering data and causing DoS attacks. Accordingly, the authors in (Liu et al.2016) have developed a lightweight framework ensuring security techniques in order to eliminate Trojans hardware from IoT devices. They have employed a trusted communication between nodes with encrypted messages to prevent unauthorized parties from accessing the information and allow authorized nodes to verify the forwarded messages. Furthermore, IoT devices data can be victim to different categories of malware. Su et al. (Su et al.2018) have proposed a Lightweight Neural Network Framework that allows to detect accurately malwares from doubtful programs.

At this IoT architecture level, it is necessary to ensure data security by performing data authentication mechanisms, data confidentiality and integrity. The major prevalent data attacks (see table 5) in the IoT system (Aman et al.2018) include the data inconsistency due to the lack of data integrity either that is transmitted or stored in the database, and the unauthorized access to sensitive or confidential data in an unauthorized manner.

Table 5. Application Layer attacks, effects and solutions

Attack	Effect	Proposed Solution
Data Inconsistency	Data Inconsistency	Chaos-based privacy preserving cryptographic scheme along with Message Authentication Code (MAC) (Song et al.2017)
Unauthorized Access	● Lack of Data Privacy ● Confidential data disclosure in an unauthorized manner.	● Attribute-based encryption (ABE) (Zhang et al.2018) ● Improved Secure Directed Diffusion (ISDD) protocol (Sengupta et al.2019) ● Shared secret key with PUF (Gope and Sikdar2018)

Figure 2. Taxonomy of IoT Security Attacks

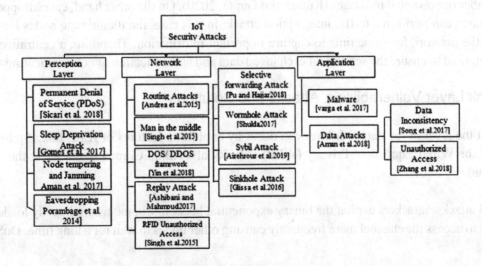

Vulnerabilities, Threats, and Attacks in VANETs

Ensuring security in VANETs is critical due to the sensitive nature of exchanged data, and threats to the privacy and security of users. Moreover, attaining security in VANETs can be challenging as a result of the large number of communication links, the ease to spoof valid IDs, network volatility, the need to achieve a trade-off between liability and privacy, delay sensitivity, large scalability, device heterogeneity in terms of communication and computation capabilities, and multi-hop communication. VANETs are vulnerable to attacks from several entities including: insider attacks such as compromised vehicles and outsider attacks. The attacks can be passive where an eavesdropper tries to capture information exchanged between communicating nodes. It can also be active, where the eavesdropper disguises as a legitimate vehicle and tries to alter the data exchanged (Mokhtar and Azab., 2015).

VANETs are prone to several security issues that differ according to the domain of communication (Hassija et al., 2020). In RSD, DDoS and routing attacks are the most common security issues. In the AHD domain that includes both V2V and V2I, communication is vulnerable to routing and authentication attacks. Authentication attacks happen when attackers use fake IDs to send malicious data. Similarly attackers can use fake IDs in IVD to gain sensitive data or implant false data. The authors in (Mokhtar and Azab., 2015), (Kaur et al., 2018), and (Krishnan and Kumar, 2020) have surveyed VANETs' related security threats. The next subsections summarize the security attacks covered by the three surveys according to five layers, namely, the physical layer, the data link layer, the network layer, the transport layer, and the application layer. The next subsections also touch on some security solutions implemented to address the presented attacks.

Physical Layer Vulnerabilities, Attacks and Solutions

The most common attacks at the level of the physical layer include: jamming attacks, eavesdropping, and DoS, as have been already highlighted with IoT systems.

To solve the jamming attacks, Spread Spectrum Techniques (Hossain et al., 2021) are used to make it difficult to jam or detect a signal. DoS and eavesdropping are caused by malicious vehicles in the network. The presence of malicious vehicles poses threats to the available bandwidth for data transmission in VANET. In the absence of a centralized authority, the attackers can flood the network with a large number of unwanted messages (Kumar and Gupta, 2020). On the other hand, eavesdroppers at the physical layer can perform a traffic interception attack. In this case, the illegitimate nodes listen to the traffic in the network for some time to capture important information. Therefore, a centralized unit is usually required to ensure the security of exchanged data and authentication of communicating vehicles.

Data Link Layer Vulnerabilities, Attacks and Solutions

Attacks at the level of the data link layer can occur by exploiting features of IEEE 802.11p MAC protocol and the Wired Equivalent Privacy (WEP) security algorithm. Common attacks at the data link layer include:

- DoS attacks: attackers exploit the binary exponential backoff scheme where heavily loaded nodes tend to access the channel more frequently causing other nodes to wait for a long time. DoS attacks can also occur when a malicious node takes advantage of the Ready to Send/Clear mechanism by causing interferences to the CTS, data, and ACK packet.

- Privacy and message integrity issue due to the usage of WEP to secure communication in IEEE 802.11p standard.

To address the DoS attacks, a modification has been introduced to the binary exponential backoff scheme where the backoff time is set by the receiver. On the other hand, IEEE 802.11i/WAP has fixed the vulnerabilities in WEP.

Network Layer Vulnerabilities, Attacks and Solutions

The dynamic nature of communicating vehicles in VANETs is the challenge hindering the design of routing protocols that ensure robust and secured communication. Common security threats to VANETs at the network layer include DoS and masquerading attacks. Other attacks include:

- Routing Table Overflow Attacks: involve the creation of routes toward nonexistent nodes to overwhelm the implementation of routing protocol.
- Routing Cache Poisoning Attacks: this includes the malicious manipulation of existing entries in the routing table leading to either undefined subnets or to malicious sites.
- The black hole attack: in this kind of attack, a node advertises itself as a legitimate node. Thus, the node can intercept the packet and drop it.
- Byzantine: this can involve a single malicious node or a set of malicious nodes that create routing loops by forwarding packets over long routes or dropping them.
- Wormhole attacks: involve the collaboration of two nodes to forward data along other legitimate nodes, creating a tunnel to take control of exchanged data.
- Rushing attacks: the attackers can forward packets faster than the legitimate nodes. Therefore, the likelihood that the attacker is part of the selected route is high.
- Location disclosure attack: these attacks involve the collection and leakage of location information.
- GPS Spoofing attacks: the attackers send a false signal instead of the original satellite signal to divert vehicles from the intended trajectory.
- Sybil Attacks: the attacker steals the identity of multiple nodes in VANET to insert malicious data that affect the decision made by legitimate nodes.
- Timing Attacks: the attacker delays the transmission of data, rendering it invalid as it reaches the destination.

To address routing attacks, it is important to ensure the legitimacy of communicating nodes. This is usually achieved by a centralized unit that is responsible for the authentication of participating vehicles in the case of VANETs.

Transport Layer Vulnerabilities, Attacks and Solutions

Common attacks at the level of Transport layer include

- SYN Flooding Attack: the attacker floods vehicles or remote base stations with SYN messages. Therefore, the receiver wastes resources waiting for a half-opened connection, making it unresponsive to legitimate traffic.
- Session Hijacking: happens when a malicious node spoofs the IP address of a legitimate vehicle to hijack its session and perform DoS on a trusted vehicle.
- TCP ACK Storm: occurs after session hijacking where the malicious vehicle storms the trusted vehicle with messages, causing the legitimate vehicle to storm the vehicle whose session was hijacked with ACK packets.

Other attacks at the level of the transport layer which are also relevant to IoT communication include masquerade, man-in-middle, rollback, and replay attacks. To address security's threats at this level, ensuring encrypted end-to-end communication is important. Common solutions to secure end-to-end communication include protocols such as Secure Socket Layer (SSL) (Dastres and Soori2020), and Transport Layer Security (TLS) (Siriwardena2020) that rely on public key cryptography.

Application Layer Vulnerabilities, Attacks and Solutions

Application layer's attacks in VANETs include:

- Malicious Code Attacks: include sending virus, worm, spyware, and trojan horse to vehicles and remote base stations. These types of attacks lead to the destruction of vehicles' applications, interruption of their services' access, and gaining information about legitimate vehicles.
- Repudiation Attacks: involve the refusal to send or receive messages by the attackers.
- Message Tampering Attack: the attacker can modify the content of the message leading vehicles to adapt a different driving behavior.

Common protection mechanisms against application layer's attacks include firewall programs to provide authentication mechanisms and filter packets. To strengthen firewall's operation, Intrusion Detection Systems (Kosmanos et al.2020) are also used to detect spoofed behavior by illegitimate vehicles. Anti-spyware programs are also used to detect spywares. On the other hand, To provide an advanced level of security against data-tampering in VANETs, the authors in (Karimireddy and Bakshi, 2016) propose a hybrid security framework that employs (Rivest–Shamir–Adleman) RSA and (Advanced Encryption Standard) AES to encrypt exchanged messages.

Vulnerabilities, Threats, and Attacks in FANETs

Since FANET is considered as a type of Ad-hoc Network, it is victim to the same security attacks. In addition, it presents new features including the dynamic and distributed environment, the frequent change of network topology because of the high mobility of UAVs, the UAVs limited computing and memory capacities. Accordingly, new security issues can be revealed. It can be either by taking control of the UAVs, interrupting the communication between the UAVs and the GCS, or stealing the collected data that affects its confidentiality and integrity. Therefore, these security attacks can be presented for five security layers as shown in figure 3: Physical layer, Link layer, Network layer, Transport layer and Application layer.

Physical Layer Vulnerabilities, Attacks and Solutions

The majority of works (Sun et al.2019) (Wu et al.2019) (CHAARI et al.2020) focus on eavesdropping, jamming, Spoofing attacks, etc. However, various specific attacks can occur and compromise the UAV functionality including hardware, software attacks. Accordingly, several research works have been suggested to improve the UAVs security. Different techniques are investigated to determine the various UAV components vulnerabilities and understand the possible consequent attacks as explored in (Alhawi2021).

Hardware attacks, as defined by (He et al.2019), occur when an attacker can access the UAV autopilot components, damage or reprogram it, and corrupt the stored data. In addition these attacks threaten on-board sensors such as Global Positioning System (GPS) receivers (Eldosouky et al.2019), IR sensor, camera and radar (Petit et al.2015). These attacks menace the UAV control and affect the survivability of the UAV.

The authors in (Nichols et al.2019) have highlighted that insecure authentication and authorization, the use of malicious hardware, hardcoded passwords and compromised GPS system can allow attackers to access and take control of the UAV components.

On the other hand, Software attacks compromise the software used in the devices such as the operating systems, and open source pilot systems. The SQL injections and insecure authentication are the major UAV software vulnerabilities allowing attackers to extract sensitive information such as credentials and emails and access critical systems to upload malicious codes or firmware (Dahiya and Garg2019).

Various solutions were proposed in order to detect these anomalies such as machine learning techniques (Challita et al.2019), intrusion detection schema (Kacem et al.2017), (Sedjelmaci et al.2017), and hardening the web-based systems used to program the UAVs routes (Pfaff2018).

Table 6. Physical Layer attacks, effects and solutions

Attack		Effect	Proposed Solution
Hardware Attacks (He et al.2019)	GPS Spoofing (Eldosouky et al.2019)	UAV redirection to be effortlessly captured	Intrusion detection schema (Arteaga et al.2019) (Kacem et al.2017) (Sedjelmaci et al.2017)
	On-board Sensor Spoofing (Petit et al.2015)	Mode confusion: False data	Drone sensor spoofing detection (SSDGOF) algorithm (Meng et al.2020)
Software Attacks (He et al.2019) (Dahiya and Garg2019)		False data injection	Authorization and authentication (Iqbal2021)

Data Link Layer Vulnerabilities, Attacks and Solutions

In this layer, the management of links between nodes and the neighbor discovery should be performed rapidly in a dynamic environment in order to hide network topology.

Behzadan et al. (Behzadan2017) have highlighted that accessible network topology allows attackers to find the most vulnerable regions with the maximum connectivity loss between nodes. (Behzadan2016) have suggested the use of covert communications between nodes to hide the network topology from attackers. However, the obtained results demonstrated that the topology can still be determined due to timing analysis attacks. Chen et al. (Chen et al.2017a) have proposed a method to optimize the positioning of UAVs in order to allow an autonomous UAVs path planning by exploiting a finely structured radio map.

On the other hand, to disrupt the data routing process, attackers can inject false bandwidth information into UAV network routing messages causing higher or lower bandwidth than the link really provides (Wei et al.2014).

Network Layer Vulnerabilities, Attacks and Solutions

Various attacks targeting the network layer have been identified and investigated. They aim to disturb the communication between nodes by absorbing network traffic, including malicious nodes in the network, and diverting and controlling network traffic. To achieve these goals, several methods can be adopted by attackers.

Similar to the link layer, the routing layer is also affected by channel jamming and connection deceiving attacks, aiming to increase the lack of UAVs collaboration and hence will disrupt the UAVs' mission and applications. Furthermore, the network performance can be decreased by injecting false messages, or replaying outdated messages. Consequently, the routing information can be disclosed.

To secure the UAV communication in FANET, different solutions have been proposed. Mowla et al. (Mowla et al.2020) have proposed and developed a Reinforcement Learning (RL) mechanism with spatial retreat strategy to ensure a cognitive jamming detection in FANET using various criteria. A Local Learning Mode (LLM) value, calculated by an on-device detection mechanism, is forwarded to an edge server to determine the global learning model value. The latter can be downloaded by the drone to recognize the jamming attack. Zhang et al. (Zhang et al.2019a) have implemented a successive convex optimization methods to improve the security performance. Accordingly, they have controlled the transmission channel and designed a UAVs trajectory to increase the secrecy rate in the uplink and the downlink communications.

Application Layer Vulnerabilities, Attacks and Solutions

UAVs transfer a lot of information that should be secured. The same data attacks (Erroneous data, flood packets, Desynchronization) that have been already detailed with IoT and VANET can occur with FANET applications. To prevent data from being intercepted by the attackers, it should be well verified and protected. Common mechanisms used for such protection are: encryption, authentication and authorization schema, etc (Bhardwaj et al.2020).

BLOCKCHAIN-BASED SOLUTIONS FOR IOT, VANETs AND FANETs SECURITY

Blockchain-Based Solutions for IoT Security

Blockchain-Based Solution for IoT Perception Layer

In order to obtain more secure devices and reliable communication between them, BC technology is used to solve the privacy challenge in IoT devices that are vulnerable to expose user data. Efficient authorization and authentication methods are needed to protect devices from malicious actions and illegitimate access.

Figure 3. Taxonomy of FANET Security Attacks

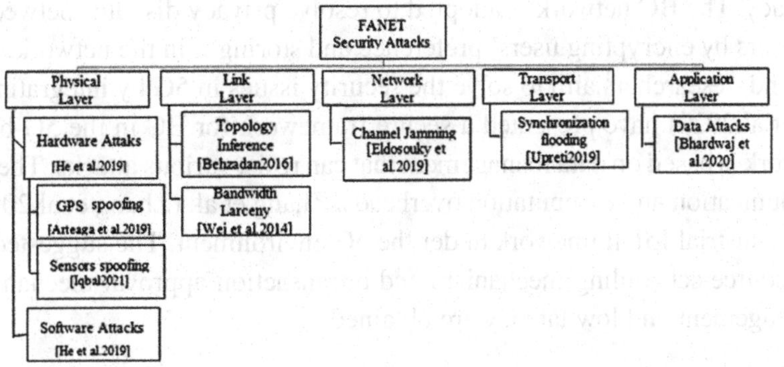

The authors in (Hammi et al.2018) have proposed a BC-based authentication mechanism for IoT called Bubbles-of-Trust. The IoT devices were grouped into clusters named bubbles. Before sharing data, devices are first authenticated. Ethereum is used to control the transactions between devices, validate the implemented public BC, and create secured virtual zones for secure communication. Khalid et al. (Khalid et al.2020) have combined the IoT system with a BC-enabled fog node used for the IoT devices registration and authentication. Each device should register using its corresponding BC-enabled fog node. Then, the information of these devices will be stored in the BC as blocks created for them and transmitted to other devices. Once a device authenticates, the BC-enabled fog node verifies its credentials and validates the authentication if the credentials are valid. Therefore, the device will be able to communicate with the other authenticated devices. Mohanta et al. (Mohanta et al.2019) have suggested a Ethereum BC-based system to establish a secure communication between edge devices and BC through gateways. Single smart contract is used to initialize the network, ensure devices' registration and authentication. The devices are identified by a pair of public/private key and Ethereum address.

Furthermore, key management and encryption methods are explored by several research works to keep the communication more secure and to allow the device authentication. Yazdinejad et al. (Yazdinejad et al.2019) have proposed an-IoT based solution where nodes are divided into clusters. A symmetric encryption is performed with the use of a shared key. The keys are created and distributed by the Cluster Head (CH) to its nodes members. The authors used the Proof-of-Authentication consensus algorithm (Maitra et al.2020) to validate new devices so that only the CH can verify the blocks to decide if the device can be trusted or not without executing the authentication process again.

Blockchain-Based Solution for IoT Network Layer

This layer allows the communication of the nodes and provides a method of propagating the data blocks to the rest of the network. Therefore, to ensure a secure and reliable communication process, the integration of BC is considered important as highlighted in (Zheng et al.2018b). The authors of (Ribeiro et al.2020) have focused on enhancing the LoRaWAN network server performance by coping with its centralized nature. They have proposed a private BC where smart contracts are employed for key management aspects. In the same context, Lin et al. (Lin et al.2017) have developed a trust mechanism that combines BC technology and LoRaWAN IoT technology to build an open and trusted system. This system aims to verify data transactions and their existence at an exact time in the network. In the work addressed in

(Cha et al.2018), the authors have proposed a BC Connected Gateway for BLE enabled IoT devices to maintain user privacy. The BC network is adopted to resolve privacy disputes between IoT application providers and its users by encrypting users' preference and storing it in the network.

On the other hand, researchers aim to solve the security issues in 5G by integrating BC technology. Bera et al. (Bera et al.2020) have presented a secure framework for BC in the 5G-based IoT environment. This framework is based on data management that can resist various attacks. The proposed scheme enables less communication and computation overheads. Zhang et al. (Zhang et al.2019) have designed a BC empowered Industrial IoT framework under the 5G environment. The suggested scheme includes a cross-domain resource scheduling mechanism and a transaction approval mechanism. Accordingly, secure service management and low latency are obtained.

Blockchain-Based Solution for IoT Application Layer

Since protecting user data is of utmost priority, therefore research has been focused on dealing with the aforementioned attacks.

Machado et al. (Machado and Fröhlich2018) have highlighted a three level split BC based architecture to ensure integrity of data stored in remote semi-trusted data storages. On the first level, they have introduced the PoT for Trustful Space Time Protocol (TSTP). The upper levels are responsible for maintaining integrity verification and data availability in semi trusted storages. In one such work, Rahulamathavan et al. (Rahulamathavan et al.2017) have proposed a BC based architecture by incorporating Attribute based Encryption (ABE) with it. Apart from supporting integrity and non-repudiation, the proposed scheme also preserves the privacy of transaction data. The proposed privacy preserving BC based architecture imposes access control to address confidentiality of shared data in the BC and thus provide end to end privacy preserving IoT systems. On the contrary, another work (Zheng et al.2018) has addressed a privacy preserving efficient medical data sharing scheme by utilizing ABE which hides all the attributes in the access control structure by utilizing the attribute bloom filter. The devices encrypt the data and send it to the server where only legitimate users satisfying the access control structure can decrypt the data. Sharma et al. (Sharma and Park2018) have proposed a novel BC based distributed cloud architecture. This architecture is able to gather, classify and interpret the huge amount of data at the edge of the network. This data is stored in the cloud that reduces the traffic load in the core network. Dorri et al. (Dorri et al.2019) have suggested a Lightweight Scalable BC (LSB) based scheme to achieve decentralization as well as end-to-end privacy and security. LSB is explored in a smart home with an overlay network. The latter is organized as clusters to ensure scalability and the public BC is managed by the CHs. Transactions are managed by a Distributed Throughput Management (DTM) scheme that guarantees the throughput and the system security.

Blockchain-Edge/Fog Computing Based Solutions for IoT Security

Other research works highlighted that the use of Edge/Fog Computing (E/FC) strategies with BC can provide more reliable and robust security (Bouachir et al.2020). As confirmed in (Uddin et al.2021), both the Edge and Fog computing systems facilitate the data processing with no need to be stored in the remote cloud. Accordingly, this solution is able to reduce the amount of data forwarded to the remote Cloud. Moreover, BC is required to ensure trust in a distributed Fog network and can be undertaken in highly decentralized environments. Li et al. (Li et al.2018) have proposed a distributed BC-based data storage scheme. Edge devices collect data from IoT devices, register it in the BC to be then forwarded to a Distributed Hash Table (DHT). Here, the BC is used as a trusted entity that manages and protects the stored data that can be accessible only in case of a successful user authentication. The work (Xu et al.2019) has focused on DDoS mitigation in Industrial IoT (IIoT) and have proposed a Multi-Level DDoS Mitigation Framework (MLDMF). It defended DDoS attacks at three levels, i.e. fog, cloud and edge computing levels. The fog, cloud and edge computing levels use a cluster of SDN controllers and applications, SDN-based IIoT gateways and big data along with intelligent computing respectively to analyze network traffic in order to detect and mitigate DDoS attacks. Authors in (Xiong et al.2018) have revealed that it would be very difficult for the resource-limited mobile devices to perform proof of work to reach consensus because of substantial resource requirements. Therefore, they propose a prototype for edge computing where the mobile devices would use the resources of the edge devices to perform complex proof of work operations. Li et al. 2019 (Li et al.2019) have proposed a distributed BC-based data storage scheme using certificateless cryptography. This secure proposed system uses edge devices which collect data from the IoT devices, register the data against that specific IoT device in the BC and finally forward the data to a Distributed Hash Table (DHT). The BC acts as a trusted third party by managing data storage, allowing data protection and also performing user authentication. Authors in (Sharma et al.2017) have designed a BC based distributed cloud architecture by incorporating SDN en-abled controller fog nodes at the edge of the network. This flexible architecture is capable of gathering, classifying and analyzing data streams at the edge of the network. This model also brings in an efficient way to offload data to the cloud and reduces delay and also traffic load in the core network. Uddin et al. (Uddin et al.2021) have highlighted that not all BC consensus mechanisms are suitable in a Fog ecosystem due to their limited resources. Hence, PoW is not suitable with Fog miners (Kumar et al.2019) instead of PoS and practical Byzantine Fault Tolerance (pBFT) consensus are appreciated for the Fog network.

Figure 4. Blockchain-based solutions for IoT Security Attacks

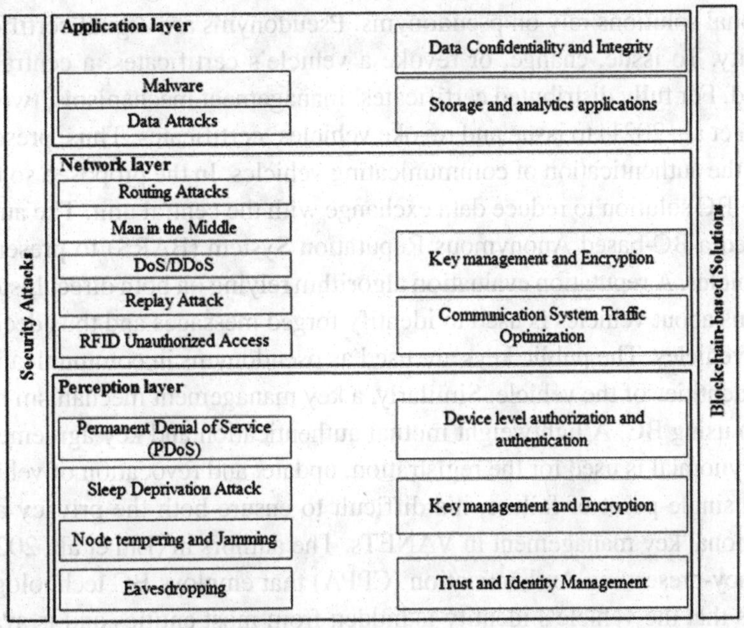

Blockchain-Based Solutions for VANETs Security

The security system used in VANETs must meet the following requirements: data authentication and integrity, data confidentiality, vehicle privacy and anonymity, information accessibility, data non-repudiation, data transfer integrity, vehicle traceability, scalability, efficiency and robustness, protection against forged messages, availability, anti-jamming, protection against impersonation, protection against tampering of in-transit on On-board traffic (Mokhtar and Azab., 2015). To address these requirements, several security solutions have been proposed. However, the main drawbacks of traditional solutions include dependence on a central authority, and low computation and storage capabilities of communicating devices. BC provides a distributed ledger to secure the communication of VANETs against single point of failure and data tempering.

Blockchain-Based Solution for VANETs Physical Layer

At the level of the physical layer, channel accessibility and security are critical factors to facilitate communication in VANETs. Thus, it is important to formulate a solution that guarantees secure communication channels and effective bandwidth utilization. In (Hassija et al., 2020), an advanced BC-based solution is used to store transactions, whereby a distributed Directed Acyclic Graph (DAG) is employed to connect vehicles and RSUs and ensure data immutability. Moreover, to ensure effective bandwidth utilization, an auction-based game-theoretic smart contract is used to govern the communication between requesting vehicles and RSUs.

Blockchain-Based Solution for VANETs Network Layer

Common protection against network layer attacks involves the authentication of communicating nodes and maintaining the privacy of their critical information such as location and identity. Key management mechanisms are important to ensure the legitimacy of communicating nodes. To achieve privacy in VANET, conventional solutions rely on pseudonyms. Pseudonyms are digital certificates used to hide the vehicles' identity. To issue, change, or revoke a vehicle's certificates, a centralized certification authority is required. For fully distributed certificates' management mechanisms, two different BCs are used in (Moussaoui et al., 2021) to issue and revoke vehicles' certificates. Thus, preserving the privacy of the vehicles and the authentication of communicating vehicles. In the proposed solution, vehicles act as the miners in the BC solution to reduce data exchange with the central unit. The authors in (Lu et al., 2018) have proposed a BC-based Anonymous Reputation System (BARS) to preserve the privacy of communicating vehicles. A reputation evaluation algorithm relying on both direct historical interactions and indirect opinions about vehicles is used to identify forged messages and thus decide the legitimacy of communicating vehicles. The public keys are used as pseudonyms in communications to hide information about real identities of the vehicle. Similarly, a key management mechanism has been proposed in (Ma et al., 2020) using BC. A lightweight mutual authentication and key agreement protocol based on the bivariate polynomial is used for the registration, update, and revocation of vehicles' public keys.

In addition to a single point of failure, it's difficult to ensure both the privacy and tractability of vehicles in conventional key management in VANETs. The authors in (Lin et al., 2020) have proposed a Conditional Privacy-preserving Authentication (CPPA) that employs BC technologies to address issues. CPPA implies that the vehicle's identity is hidden from most entities and is available for trusted entities to ensure tractability. BC is used to store vehicles' certificates to be retrieved by other vehicles and RSU for authentication purposes. A smart contract is used to manage the entities that can retrieve the certificates and track vehicles on the network. Moreover, a derivation key algorithm is adapted to reduce the number of pre-stored keys on vehicles' OBUs.

In (Li et al., 2020a), privacy of communicating vehicles' locations is achieved using a k-anonymous algorithm. To address the bottlenecks of a solution that relies on centralized authority to issue the digital certificates, BC is used to build a distributed ledged to store vehicle certificates based on a k-anonymous algorithm. Moreover, a trust management model is used to protect against malicious insiders' attacks. A similar solution is proposed in (Luo et al., 2019). To preserve the privacy of communicating nodes, the authors have suggested a BC enabled trust-based location protecting scheme with a trust management model based on Dirichlet distribution.

Blockchain-Based Solution for VANETs Application Layer

Ensuring data integrity and confidentiality is the main approach to address application layer's attacks in VANET. To provide protection of life-threatening information, the authors in (Shrestha et al., 2020) used a public distributed ledger to store the trustworthiness of nodes and exchanged messages. Moreover, a local BC is used per country to improve scalability and reduce latency. A similar solution is proposed in (El-Salakawy and Abu El-Kheir, 2020), where BC is used for the management of data exchanged to ensure secure communication. Exchanged data using the BC system include safety data and periodic beacons in order to reduce the overhead on the centralized storage unit. Alternatively, the authors in (Dwivedi et al., 2020) have proposed a BC-based decentralized system with an authentication protocol to ensure the legitimacy of communicating vehicles and a consensus mechanism to validate transactions. On the other hand, a fine-grained access scheme is proposed in (Li et al., 2020a). BC integrated with ciphertext-based encryption is used to manage the identity of communicating vehicles and store data. In addition, data access rights are established according to the requester's attribute. The aforementioned solutions help to enhance data immutability and protect against a single point of failure in traditional application security solutions for VANETs. Table 7 depicts the list of BC-based solutions proposed through the literature to address various security requirements in VANETs.

Blockchain-Edge/Fog Computing Based Solutions for VANETs Security

Edge/Fog computing (E/FC) is significant to address the computational constraint of vehicular networks. Employing a BC-based solution to preserve the privacy of vehicles or ensure the immutability of shared data impose a large demand on computational resources. The authors in (Zhang et al., 2018) have proposed a security architecture that consists of three layers, including the perception layer, the edge computing layer, and service layer. While BC is used at the perception and service to protect against data-tempering and the single point of failure, mobile edge computing is helpful to alleviate the computational demand on vehicles due to consensus algorithms. On the other hand, the authors in (Ayaz et al., 2021) have defined a BC-based voting solution that relies on the edge servers to control votes in the proposed Proof-of-Quality-Factor (PoQF) consensus algorithm. The authors in (Tan et al., 2020) have presented an integrated BC and edge computing that is useful to alleviate the computational burden on communicating vehicles and address the issue of interference between regular V2R exchanged data and control messages needed to ensure vehicles' authentication.

Table 7. Blockchain-based solutions for VANETs

Solution	Goal of Solution	Main Addressed Security and Privacy Requirements
(Hassija et al., 2020)	• Ensure Data Immutability • Efficient Bandwidth Utilization	• Data Confidentiality • Efficiency and Robustness
(Dwivedi et al., 2020)	Ensure data immutability	• Data authentication and integrity. • Vehicles' authentication.
(Shrestha et al., 2020)		• Data authentication and integrity • Data Confidentiality • Vehicles' authentication
(Lu et al., 2018)	• Privacy Preservation. • Key Management.	• Vehicle privacy and anonymity • Vehicles' authentication
(Luo et al., 2019)	Preserving Location Privacy	Vehicle privacy and anonymity
(Li et al., 2020a)		Vehicles' authentication
(Ma et al., 2020)	Key management	• Protection against impersonation • Data non-repudiation
(Moussaoui, 2021)		• Vehicles' authentication. • Scalability
(Lin et al., 2020)		• Vehicle privacy and anonymity • Vehicles' authentication • Vehicles' tractability
(Li et al., 2020b)	Access Control	• Data Confidentiality • Vehicle privacy and anonymity • Vehicles' authentication

Blockchain-Based Solution for FANETs Security

Besides the usefulness of FANETs in performing complex missions, it introduces communication security issues between multiple and heterogeneous drones. In this context, recently, BC is being typically introduced into the FANET network to not only manage the event messages and trustworthiness of nodes but also for secure, accurate delivery of data (Noor et al.2020) (Machado and Westphall2021).

Blockchain-Based Solution for FANET Physical Layer

Implementing BC-based solutions ensures the security of FANET devices and makes it impossible to disturb the UAVs hardware or software.

Islam et al. (Islam and Shin2019) have leveraged a BC-based secure data acquisition scheme for UAV swarm (BUS). In this scheme, data is collected and encrypted by IoT devices to be then sent to UAV that validates the transmitter's identity through a hash bloom filter and Digital Signature Algorithm (DSA). Consequently, the UAV forwards the data to the nearest server to prepare and store it in the BC. Simulations were conducted using MATLAB and Python to show the effect of π-hash bloom filters in the server and the UAV, respectively. The result of the simulation shows that BUS is successfully able to filter malicious devices completely. BUS was implemented and the result of experiments proved that utilizing UAV in the assistance of IoT devices ensures extended connectivity and reduces the energy consumption in IoT.

Allouch et al. (Allouch et al.2021) have proposed a lightweight BC-based security solution called Unmanned Traffic Management UTM-chain. The authors have explained and discussed the various UAVs security attacks. In the proposed system, during their flight, the drones constantly update their GPS location and destination address that reduces their vulnerability to GPS attacks. In addition, each UAV has a copy of the BC providing the flight path details which facilitates its flight even in case of communication jamming attack. ; thus, they can continue on its path in case of communication jamming.

Blockchain-Based Solution for FANET Network Layer

Tan et al. (Tan et al.2020) have proposed a secure key management scheme for FANETs that allows drones to generate and update their keys autonomously independently of any central authority. This approach is adapted with heterogeneous FANETs composed of a high-performance CH and other ordinary drones in the network. In order to enhance the scalability level of the proposed scheme, the CH is the only one responsible for the BC management and storage. The authors applied a new fair miner election approach that indicates the producer of the next block easily unlike the difficult process required in PoW consensus algorithm. Furthermore, the cluster key distribution, update process takes into account UAV migration between clusters and malicious UAV revocation tasks. These cluster keys management schemes can perform a secure communication within clusters by identifying impersonation, cloning and internal attacks. On the other hand, the authors have evaluated their scheme by revealing the energy consumption within clusters and comparing the consumption of CH UAVs and UAV members. In addition, the authors have evaluated the relationship between the average processing time of each transaction and the block size as well as the number of UAVs in the system.

Ghribi et al. (Ghribi et al.2020) have proposed a novel consensus-building mechanism for securing communication in a UAV network. This mechanism is based on the integration of BC with the public key cryptographic method of Elliptic Curve Diffe-Hellman (ECDH), a key derivation hash function SHA3 and One-Time Pad (OTP) encryption method. They have designed their scenario for a private BC-based UAV FANET that includes a Ground Control Station GCS, a leader UAV designated by the GCS, and UAV nodes. UAVs can communicate securely with one another using Elliptic-curve Cryptography (ECC) and thus have access to each other's public key.

Khullar et al. (Khullar et al.2020) have defined a decentralized architecture of FANET based on BC and using Practical Byzantine Fault Tolerance (PBFT) for consensus among nodes. They have used a gossip protocol for passing messages among neighboring nodes. For mobility management, authors applied a dynamic peer discovery algorithm so that nodes can disconnect from nodes flying away far from the current node and connect to close nodes. For that, they have used a shared routing table that is constantly updated with the latest location of the corresponding node. Moreover, in order to ensure a decentralized security approach, authors employed a modified version of RAFT consensus algorithm (Mingxiao et al.2017) based on dynamic leader election. The proposed architecture was evaluated by measuring the throughput presenting the valid transactions commitment rate that varies by a small amount and remains approximately constant. In addition, the network latency remains nearly constant with increase in the total number of nodes in the network and the message overload increases in the beginning with the increase in the total number of transmitted transactions but remains approximately constant afterwards.

Blockchain-Based Solution for FANET Application Layer

In FANET, the data integrity and confidentiality guarantee the consistency of collected data and its secure transmission and storage. Liang et al. (Liang et al.2017) have proposed a framework based on a public BC to ensure the secure communication between drones and the integrity of the collected data. They have implemented a prototype of a drone system composed by drones, control system, BC network, cloud database and server. The authors have validated their system using PoW and bitcoin.

Shetty et al. (Shetty et al.2019) have used Cryptographic Hash Functions to enable the integrity of the transmitted data. They have implemented a consensus mechanism in a block mining process to ensure data integrity.

Barka et al. (Barka et al.2019) have proposed a BC-based trust management solution for Unmanned Aerial System (BUAS) in FANET. They aimed to evaluate the trustworthiness of the exchanged messages between UAVs by the use of the Bayesian Inference (BI) approach (Rappel et al.2020) in order to define the truly occurring events and the trusted messages reporting them. To include the trust's offset into the BC by the appropriate GCS, authors combined Proof-of-Work and Proof-of-Stack miner selection. This solution was evaluated using NS-3 simulator and 3D random Waypoint UAV Mobility Model and proved that BUAS can enable high detection ratios exceeding the 95% for different dishonesty ratios with a minimum energy consumption and network overhead.

OPEN RESEARCH

This section provides the list of open research areas that still remain less investigated with regards to IoT, VANET and FANET security based on the major divisions made above:

- **The privacy and integrity of collected data:** The integration of BC with 5G/6G technologies including cloud computing, edge computing, Software Defined Networks, Network Function Virtualization, Network Slicing make the communication more secure against cybersecurity vulnerabilities (Haris and Al-Maadeed2020) (nguyen2020Blockchain).

Although numerous research efforts have been devoted to BC technology in IoT, VANET and FANET networks, researchers have not yet explored BC-enabled network softwarization (Hu et al.2020).

- **Deep Reinforcement Learning (DRL):** Deep-reinforcement learning techniques can be used to ensure stable communication. In addition, deep-reinforcement learning methods can be used to determine the optimal solution to avoid collisions during real-time path planning and navigation (Azar et al.2021).

In addition, future research works should develop new DRL techniques allowing with low computation without communication overhead in order to enhance the communication performance between nodes in IoT, VANETs and FANETs.

- **Integration of BC-E/FC:** The BC-E/FC integration becomes widely encouraged in various applications and it is still new in IoT, VANETs and FANETs applications. In fact, the synergy between

BC and E/FC can improve the system security and reliability. In addition, to protect the system database, it is recommended to deploy the BC in the cloud. Accordingly, through its cryptographic mechanisms and immutability, the BC can identify the vulnerabilities and protect the database from being altered by the attackers.

Various research works agree about the advantages of this integration, but researchers should take into account various challenges. The BC deployment can increase the system latency. This motivates researchers to find areas of harmony between BC latency, cloud latency in the three emerging IoT, VANETs and FANETs systems. Furthermore, the energy consumption represents a challenge related to BC-based system. In this context, it is highly motivating to propose new consensus algorithms that satisfy the high IoT, VANETs or FANETs systems security with efficient-energy results. Moreover, FANETs and VANETs require efficient mobility control due to the dynamic behavior of nodes (Wan et al., 2019). This issue can be solved by applying E/FC techniques but once the BC has been integrated, it figures again. Therefore, future research works should find solutions for this challenge while keeping the system latency and privacy.

CONCLUSION

With the emergence of IoT, VANET and FANET applications, diverse security vulnerabilities leading to several attacks on devices and collected data have been investigated in recent research works. Therefore, in this work, the basic concepts of IoT, VANET and FANET systems are presented to understand their main functionalities and features. Then, their specific security problems and the solutions proposed in the literature are discussed and a taxonomy of their attacks is defined. The proposed classification would help researchers find the most relevant attacks to their domain of interest. Besides, the comprehensive taxonomy is providing guidelines and hints for understanding the proposed solutions.

In addition, the study presented in this chapter emphasizes the emergence of BC technology as an indispensable and useful paradigm needed to build integrated and robust security solutions for IoT, VANET and FANET systems. Furthermore, BC provides efficient techniques and mechanisms to cope with centralized aspects of these systems. Finally, this chapter provides some open research areas on security issues in IoT, VANETs and FANETs for which BC based solutions are encouraged to be investigated.

REFERENCES

Airehrour, D., Gutierrez, J. A., & Ray, S. K. (2019). Sectrust-rpl: A secure trust-aware rpl routing protocol for the internet of things. *Future Generation Computer Systems*, *93*, 860–876. doi:10.1016/j.future.2018.03.021

Al-Kashoash, H. A., Kharrufa, H., Al-Nidawi, Y., & Kemp, A. H. (2019). Congestion control in wireless sensor and 6lowpan networks: Toward the internet of things. *Wireless Networks*, *25*(8), 4493–4522. doi:10.100711276-018-1743-y

Alaba, F. A., Othman, M., Hashem, I. A. T., & Alotaibi, F. (2017). Internet of things security: A survey. *Journal of Network and Computer Applications*, *88*, 10–28. doi:10.1016/j.jnca.2017.04.002

Alam, T. (2018). A reliable communication framework and its use in internet of things (iot). *CSEIT1835111*, *10*, 450–456.

Alhawi, O. M. (2021). *Finding Software Vulnerabilities in Unmanned Aerial Vehicles* (PhD thesis). University of Manchester.

Ali, M. S., Vecchio, M., Pincheira, M., Dolui, K., Antonelli, F., & Rehmani, M. H. (2018). Applications of blockchains in the internet of things: A comprehensive survey. *IEEE Communications Surveys and Tutorials*, *21*(2), 1676–1717. doi:10.1109/COMST.2018.2886932

Aman, M. N., Chua, K. C., & Sikdar, B. (2017). A light-weight mutual authentication protocol for iot systems. In *GLOBECOM 2017-2017 IEEE Global Communications Conference*, (pp. 1–6). IEEE. 10.1109/GLOCOM.2017.8253991

Aman, M. N., Sikdar, B., Chua, K. C., & Ali, A. (2018). Low power data integrity in iot systems. *IEEE Internet of Things Journal*, *5*(4), 3102–3113. doi:10.1109/JIOT.2018.2833206

Andrea, I., Chrysostomou, C., & Hadji Christofi, G. (2015). Internet of things: Security vulnerabilities and challenges. In 2015 IEEE symposium on computers and communication (ISCC), (pp. 180–187). IEEE.

Antonioli, D., Tippenhauer, N. O., & Rasmussen, K. (2020). Bias: Bluetooth impersonation attacks. In *2020 IEEE Symposium on Security and Privacy (SP)*, (pp. 549–562). IEEE. 10.1109/SP40000.2020.00093

Arteaga, S. P., Hernández, L. A. M., Pérez, G. S., Orozco, A. L. S., & Villalba, L. J. G. (2019). Analysis of the gps spoofing vulnerability in the drone 3dr solo. *IEEE Access: Practical Innovations, Open Solutions*, *7*, 51782–51789. doi:10.1109/ACCESS.2019.2911526

Ashibani, Y., & Mahmoud, Q. H. (2017). An efficient and secure scheme for smart home communication using identity-based signcryption. In *2017 IEEE 36th International Performance Computing and Communications Conference (IPCCC)*, (pp. 1–7). IEEE. 10.1109/PCCC.2017.8280497

Aswale, P., Shukla, A., Bharati, P., Bharambe, S., & Palve, S. (2019). *An overview of internet of things: architecture, protocols and challenges*. Information and Communication Technology for Intelligent Systems.

Ayaz, F., Sheng, Z., Tian, D., & Guan, Y. L. (2021). A Proof-of-Quality-Factor (PoQF)-Based Blockchain and Edge Computing for Vehicular Message Dissemination. *IEEE Internet of Things Journal*, *8*(4), 2468–2482. doi:10.1109/JIOT.2020.3026731

Azar, A. T., Koubaa, A., Ali Mohamed, N., Ibrahim, H. A., Ibrahim, Z. F., Kazim, M., Ammar, A., Benjdira, B., Khamis, A. M., Hameed, I. A., & Casalino, G. (2021). Drone deep reinforcement learning: A review. *Electronics (Basel)*, *10*(9), 999. doi:10.3390/electronics10090999

Azzabi, T., Farhat, H., & Sahli, N. (2017). A survey on wireless sensor networks security issues and military specificities. In *2017 International Conference on Advanced Systems and Electric Technologies (IC_ASET)*, (pp. 66–72). IEEE. 10.1109/ASET.2017.7983668

Barka, E., Kerrache, C. A., Benkraouda, H., Shuaib, K., Ahmad, F., & Kurugollu, F. (2019). Towards a trusted unmanned aerial system using blockchain for the protection of critical infrastructure. *Transactions on Emerging Telecommunications Technologies*, e3706. doi:10.1002/ett.3706

Barka, E., Kerrache, C. A., Hussain, R., Lagraa, N., Lakas, A., & Bouk, S. H. (2018). A trusted lightweight communication strategy for flying named data networking. *Sensors (Basel)*, *18*(8), 2683. doi:10.339018082683 PMID:30111732

Behzadan, V. (2016). *Real-time inference of topological structure and vulnerabilities for adaptive jamming against covert ad hoc networks*. PhD thesis.

Behzadan, V. (2017). *Cyber-physical attacks on uas networks-challenges and open research problems*. arXiv preprint arXiv:1702.01251.

Benslimane, Y., Benahmed, K., & Benslimane, H. (2018). Security mechanisms for 6lowpan network in context of internet of things: A survey. In *International Conference in Artificial Intelligence in Renewable Energetic Systems*, (pp. 49–69). Springer.

Bera, B., Saha, S., Das, A. K., Kumar, N., Lorenz, P., & Alazab, M. (2020). Blockchain-envisioned secure data delivery and collection scheme for 5g-based iot-enabled internet of drones environment. *IEEE Transactions on Vehicular Technology*, *69*(8), 9097–9111. doi:10.1109/TVT.2020.3000576

Bertin, E., Hussein, D., Sengul, C., & Frey, V. (2019). Access control in the internet of things: A survey of existing approaches and open research questions. *Annales des Télécommunications*, *74*(7), 375–388. doi:10.100712243-019-00709-7

Bhardwaj, V., Kaur, N., Vashisht, S., & Jain, S. (2020). Secrip: Secure and reliable intercluster routing protocol for efficient data transmission in flying ad hoc networks. *Transactions on Emerging Telecommunications Technologies*, e4068. doi:10.1002/ett.4068

Bodkhe, U., & Tanwar, S. (2020). Taxonomy of secure data dissemination techniques for iot environment. *IET Software*, *14*(6), 563–571. doi:10.1049/iet-sen.2020.0006

Bouachir, O., Grati, R., Aloqaily, M., & Mnaouer, A. B. (2020). Blockchain based solutions for achieving secure storage in fog computing. In Blockchain-enabled Fog and Edge Computing: Concepts, Architectures and Applications: Concepts, Architectures and Applications. Academic Press.

Butun, I., Pereira, N., & Gidlund, M. (2018). Analysis of lorawan v1. 1 security. *Proceedings of the 4th ACM MobiHoc Workshop on Experiences with the Design and Implementation of Smart Objects*, 1–6.

Butun, I., Pereira, N., & Gidlund, M. (2019). Security risk analysis of lorawan and future directions. *Future Internet*, *11*(1), 3. doi:10.3390/fi11010003

Cachin, C. (2016). Architecture of the hyperledger blockchain fabric. *Workshop on distributed cryptocurrencies and consensus ledgers*, 310.

Cha, S.-C., Chen, J.-F., Su, C., & Yeh, K.-H. (2018). A blockchain connected gateway for ble-based devices in the internet of things. *IEEE Access: Practical Innovations, Open Solutions*, *6*, 24639–24649. doi:10.1109/ACCESS.2018.2799942

Chaari, L., Chahbani, S., & Rezgui, J. (2020). Vulnerabilities assessment for unmanned aerial vehicles communication systems. In *2020 International Symposium on Networks, Computers and Communications (ISNCC)*, (pp. 1–6). IEEE.

Chakraborty, R. S., Mathew, J., & Vasilakos, A. V. (2019). *Security and fault tolerance in Internet of things.* Springer. doi:10.1007/978-3-030-02807-7

Challita, U., Ferdowsi, A., Chen, M., & Saad, W. (2019). Machine learning for wireless connectivity and security of cellular-connected uavs. *IEEE Wireless Communications, 26*(1), 28–35. doi:10.1109/MWC.2018.1800155

Chen, J., Yatnalli, U., & Gesbert, D. (2017a). Learning radio maps for uav-aided wireless networks: A segmented regression approach. In *2017 IEEE International Conference on Communications (ICC)*, (pp. 1–6). IEEE. 10.1109/ICC.2017.7997333

Chen, L., Xu, L., Shah, N., Gao, Z., Lu, Y., & Shi, W. (2017b). On security analysis of proof-of-elapsed-time (poet). In *International Symposium on Stabilization, Safety, and Security of Distributed Systems*, (pp. 282–297). Springer. 10.1007/978-3-319-69084-1_19

Cui, M., Zhang, G., Wu, Q., & Ng, D. W. K. (2018). Robust trajectory and transmit power design for secure uav communications. *IEEE Transactions on Vehicular Technology, 67*(9), 9042–9046. doi:10.1109/TVT.2018.2849644

Dahiya, S., & Garg, M. (2019). Unmanned aerial vehicles: Vulnerability to cyber attacks. In *International Conference on Unmanned Aerial System in Geomatics*, (pp. 201–211). Springer.

Dastres, R., & Soori, M. (2020). Secure socket layer (ssl) in the network and web security. *International Journal of Computer and Information Engineering, 14*(10), 330–333.

de Carvalho Silva, J., Rodrigues, J. J., Alberti, A. M., Solic, P., & Aquino, A. L. (2017). Lorawan—a low power wan protocol for internet of things: A review and opportunities. In *2017 2nd International Multidisciplinary Conference on Computer and Energy Science (SpliTech)*, (pp. 1–6). IEEE.

DeCuir, J. (2013). Introducing bluetooth smart: Part 1: A look at both classic and new technologies. *IEEE Consumer Electronics Magazine, 3*(1), 12–18. doi:10.1109/MCE.2013.2284932

Dorri, A., Kanhere, S. S., Jurdak, R., & Gauravaram, P. (2019). Lsb: A lightweight scalable blockchain for iot security and anonymity. *Journal of Parallel and Distributed Computing, 134*, 180–197. doi:10.1016/j.jpdc.2019.08.005

Dwivedi, S. K., Amin, R., Vollala, S., & Chaudhry, R. (2020). Blockchain-based secured event-information sharing protocol in internet of vehicles for smart cities. *Computers & Electrical Engineering, 86*, 106719. doi:10.1016/j.compeleceng.2020.106719

El-Hajj, M., Fadlallah, A., Chamoun, M., & Serhrouchni, A. (2019). A survey of internet of things (iot) authentication schemes. *Sensors (Basel), 19*(5), 1141. doi:10.339019051141 PMID:30845760

El-Salakawy, G., & Abu El-Kheir, M. (2020). Blockchain-based Data Management in Vehicular Networks. *2020 2nd Novel Intelligent and Leading Emerging Sciences Conference (NILES)*.

Eldosouky, A., Ferdowsi, A., & Saad, W. (2019). Drones in distress: A game-theoretic countermeasure for protecting uavs against gps spoofing. *IEEE Internet of Things Journal, 7*(4), 2840–2854. doi:10.1109/JIOT.2019.2963337

Farahani, S. (2011). *ZigBee wireless networks and transceivers*. Newnes.

Fernández-Caramés, T. M., & Fraga-Lamas, P. (2018). A review on the use of blockchain for the internet of things. *IEEE Access: Practical Innovations, Open Solutions*, 6, 32979–33001. doi:10.1109/ACCESS.2018.2842685

Ferrag, M. A., Derdour, M., Mukherjee, M., Derhab, A., Maglaras, L., & Janicke, H. (2018). Blockchain technologies for the internet of things: Research issues and challenges. *IEEE Internet of Things Journal*, 6(2), 2188–2204. doi:10.1109/JIOT.2018.2882794

Frustaci, M., Pace, P., Aloi, G., & Fortino, G. (2017). Evaluating critical security issues of the iot world: Present and future challenges. *IEEE Internet of Things Journal*, 5(4), 2483–2495. doi:10.1109/JIOT.2017.2767291

Gai, K., Wu, Y., Zhu, L., Qiu, M., & Shen, M. (2019). Privacy-preserving energy trading using consortium blockchain in smart grid. *IEEE Transactions on Industrial Informatics*, 15(6), 3548–3558. doi:10.1109/TII.2019.2893433

Garg, A., & Mittal, N. (2020). A security and confidentiality survey in wireless internet of things (iot). In *Internet of Things and Big Data Applications* (pp. 65–88). Springer. doi:10.1007/978-3-030-39119-5_5

Gervais, A., Karame, G. O., Wüst, K., Glykantzis, V., Ritzdorf, H., & Capkun, S. (2016). On the security and performance of proof of work blockchains. *Proceedings of the 2016 ACM SIGSAC conference on computer and communications security*, 3–16. 10.1145/2976749.2978341

Ghribi, E., Khoei, T. T., Gorji, H. T., Ranganathan, P., & Kaabouch, N. (2020). A secure blockchain-based communication approach for uav networks. In *2020 IEEE International Conference on Electro Information Technology (EIT)*, (pp. 411–415). IEEE. 10.1109/EIT48999.2020.9208314

Glissa, G., Rachedi, A., & Meddeb, A. (2016). A secure routing protocol based on rpl for internet of things. In *2016 IEEE Global Communications Conference (GLOBECOM)*, (pp. 1–7). IEEE. 10.1109/GLOCOM.2016.7841543

Gomes, T., Salgado, F., Tavares, A., & Cabral, J. (2017). Cute mote, a customizable and trustable end-device for the internet of things. *IEEE Sensors Journal*, 17(20), 6816–6824. doi:10.1109/JSEN.2017.2743460

Gope, P., & Sikdar, B. (2018). Lightweight and privacy-preserving two-factor authentication scheme for iot devices. *IEEE Internet of Things Journal*, 6(1), 580–589. doi:10.1109/JIOT.2018.2846299

Gupta, B., & Quamara, M. (2020). An overview of internet of things (iot): Architectural aspects, challenges, and protocols. *Concurrency and Computation*, 32(21), e4946. doi:10.1002/cpe.4946

HaddadPajouh, H., Dehghantanha, A., Parizi, R. M., Aledhari, M., & Karimipour, H. (2019). A survey on internet of things security: Requirements, challenges, and solutions. *Internet of Things*, 100129.

Hamdi, M. M., Audah, L., Rashid, S. A., Mohammed, A. H., Alani, S., & Mustafa, A. S. (2020). A review of applications, characteristics and challenges in vehicular ad hoc networks (vanets). In *2020 International Congress on Human-Computer Interaction, Optimization and Robotic Applications (HORA)*, (pp. 1–7). IEEE.

Hammi, M. T., Hammi, B., Bellot, P., & Serhrouchni, A. (2018). Bubbles of trust: A decentralized blockchain-based authentication system for iot. *Computers & Security*, *78*, 126–142. doi:10.1016/j.cose.2018.06.004

Harbi, Y., Aliouat, Z., Refoufi, A., Harous, S., & Bentaleb, A. (2019). Enhanced authentication and key management scheme for securing data transmission in the internet of things. *Ad Hoc Networks*, *94*, 101948. doi:10.1016/j.adhoc.2019.101948

Haris, R. M., & Al-Maadeed, S. (2020). Integrating blockchain technology in 5g enabled iot: A review. In *2020 IEEE International Conference on Informatics, IoT, and Enabling Technologies (ICIoT)*, (pp. 367–371). IEEE. 10.1109/ICIoT48696.2020.9089600

Hassan, W. H. (2019). Current research on internet of things (iot) security: A survey. *Computer Networks*, *148*, 283–294. doi:10.1016/j.comnet.2018.11.025

Hassija, V., Chamola, V., Gupta, V., & Chalapathi, G. S. (2020). *A Framework for Secure Vehicular Network using Advanced Blockchain. In 2020 International Wireless Communications and Mobile Computing*. IWCMC.

He, D. (2019). A survey on cyber security of unmanned aerial vehicles. *Chinese Journal of Computers*, *42*(05), 150–168.

Hossain, M. A., Md Noor, R., Azzuhri, S. R., Z'aba, M. R., Ahmedy, I., Yau, K. L. A., & Chembe, C. (2021). Spectrum sensing challenges & their solutions in cognitive radio based vehicular networks. *International Journal of Communication Systems*, *34*(7). Advance online publication. doi:10.1002/dac.4748

Hu, Q., Wang, W., Bai, X., Jin, S., & Jiang, T. (2020). Blockchain enabled federated slicing for 5g networks with ai accelerated optimization. *IEEE Network*, *34*(6), 46–52. doi:10.1109/MNET.021.1900653

Iqbal, S. (2021). A study on uav operating system security and future research challenges. In *2021 IEEE 11th Annual Computing and Communication Workshop and Conference (CCWC)*, (pp. 759–765). IEEE.

Islam, A., & Shin, S. Y. (2019). Bus: A blockchain-enabled data acquisition scheme with the assistance of uav swarm in internet of things. *IEEE Access: Practical Innovations, Open Solutions*, *7*, 103231–103249. doi:10.1109/ACCESS.2019.2930774

Jiang, X., Lora, M., & Chattopadhyay, S. (2020). An experimental analysis of security vulnerabilities in industrial iot devices. *ACM Transactions on Internet Technology*, *20*(2), 1–24. doi:10.1145/3379542

Kacem, T., Wijesekera, D., & Costa, P. (2017). Key distribution scheme for aircraft equipped with secure ads-b in. In *2017 IEEE 20th International Conference on Intelligent Transportation Systems (ITSC)*, (pp. 1–6). IEEE. 10.1109/ITSC.2017.8317719

Kamran, M., Khan, H. U., Nisar, W., Farooq, M., & Rehman, S.-U. (2020). Blockchain and internet of things: A bibliometric study. *Computers & Electrical Engineering*, *81*, 106525. doi:10.1016/j.compeleceng.2019.106525

Karimireddy, T., & Bakshi, A. G. (2016). A hybrid security framework for the vehicular communications in VANET. *2016 International Conference on Wireless Communications, Signal Processing and Networking (WiSPNET)*. 10.1109/WiSPNET.2016.7566479

Kaur, R., Singh, T. P., & Khajuria, V. (2018). Security Issues in Vehicular Ad-Hoc Network (VANET). *2018 2nd International Conference on Trends in Electronics and Informatics (ICOEI)*.

Kavitha, D., & Ravikumar, S. (2021). Iot and context-aware learning-based optimal neural network model for real-time health monitoring. *Transactions on Emerging Telecommunications Technologies*, *32*(1), e4132. doi:10.1002/ett.4132

Khalid, U., Asim, M., Baker, T., Hung, P. C., Tariq, M. A., & Rafferty, L. (2020). A decentralized lightweight blockchain-based authentication mechanism for iot systems. *Cluster Computing*, *23*(3), 1–21. doi:10.100710586-020-03058-6

Khanji, S., Iqbal, F., & Hung, P. (2019). Zigbee security vulnerabilities: Exploration and evaluating. In *2019 10th International Conference on Information and Communication Systems (ICICS)*, (pp. 52–57). IEEE.

Khullar, K., Malhotra, Y., & Kumar, A. (2020). Decentralized and secure communication architecture for fanets using blockchain. *Procedia Computer Science*, *173*, 158–170. doi:10.1016/j.procs.2020.06.020

Kosmanos, D., Pappas, A., Maglaras, L., Moschoyiannis, S., Aparicio-Navarro, F. J., Argyriou, A., & Janicke, H. (2020). A novel intrusion detection system against spoofing attacks in connected electric vehicles. *Array*, *5*, 100013. doi:10.1016/j.array.2019.100013

Kouicem, D. E., Bouabdallah, A., & Lakhlef, H. (2018). Internet of things security: A top-down survey. *Computer Networks*, *141*, 199–221. doi:10.1016/j.comnet.2018.03.012

Krishnan, P. R., & Kumar, P. A. R. (2020). Security and Privacy in VANET: Concepts, Solutions and Challenges. *2020 International Conference on Inventive Computation Technologies (ICICT)*. 10.1109/ICICT48043.2020.9112535

Kumar, A., & Gupta, N. (2020). A Secure RSU based Security against Multiple Attacks in VANET. *2020 3rd International Conference on Intelligent Sustainable Systems (ICISS)*.

Kumar, G., Saha, R., Rai, M. K., Thomas, R., & Kim, T.-H. (2019). Proof-of-work consensus approach in blockchain technology for cloud and fog computing using maximization-factorization statistics. *IEEE Internet of Things Journal*, *6*(4), 6835–6842. doi:10.1109/JIOT.2019.2911969

Lee, H., Eom, S., Park, J., & Lee, I. (2018). Uav-aided secure communications with cooperative jamming. *IEEE Transactions on Vehicular Technology*, *67*(10), 9385–9392. doi:10.1109/TVT.2018.2853723

Lee, M., & Atkison, T. (2021). Vanet applications: Past, present, and future. *Vehicular Communications*, *28*, 100310. doi:10.1016/j.vehcom.2020.100310

Li, B., Liang, R., Zhu, D., Chen, W., & Lin, Q. (2020). Blockchain-Based Trust Management Model for Location Privacy Preserving in VANET. *IEEE Transactions on Intelligent Transportation Systems*, 1–11. doi:10.1109/TITS.2020.3035869

Li, H., Pei, L., Liao, D., Chen, S., Zhang, M., & Xu, D. (2020). FADB: A Fine-Grained Access Control Scheme for VANET Data Based on Blockchain. *IEEE Access: Practical Innovations, Open Solutions*, *8*, 85190–85203. doi:10.1109/ACCESS.2020.2992203

Li, R., Song, T., Mei, B., Li, H., Cheng, X., & Sun, L. (2018). Blockchain for large-scale internet of things data storage and protection. *IEEE Transactions on Services Computing, 12*(5), 762–771. doi:10.1109/TSC.2018.2853167

Lin, C., He, D., Huang, X., Kumar, N., & Choo, K.-K. R. (2020). BCPPA: A Blockchain-Based Conditional Privacy-Preserving Authentication Protocol for Vehicular Ad Hoc Networks. *IEEE Transactions on Intelligent Transportation Systems*, 1–13.

Lin, J., Shen, Z., & Miao, C. (2017). Using blockchain technology to build trust in sharing lorawan iot. *Proceedings of the 2nd International Conference on Crowd Science and Engineering*, 38–43. 10.1145/3126973.3126980

Liu, C., Cronin, P., & Yang, C. (2016). A mutual auditing framework to protect iot against hardware trojans. In *2016 21st Asia and South Pacific Design Automation Conference (ASP-DAC)*, (pp. 69–74). IEEE. 10.1109/ASPDAC.2016.7427991

Lu, Y. (2019). The blockchain: State-of-the-art and research challenges. *Journal of Industrial Information Integration, 15*, 80–90. doi:10.1016/j.jii.2019.04.002

Lu, Z., Liu, W., Wang, Q., Qu, G., & Liu, Z. (2018). A Privacy-Preserving Trust Model Based on Blockchain for VANETs. *IEEE Access: Practical Innovations, Open Solutions, 6*, 45655–45664. doi:10.1109/ACCESS.2018.2864189

Luo, B., Li, X., Weng, J., Guo, J., & Ma, J. (2020). Blockchain Enabled Trust-Based Location Privacy Protection Scheme in VANET. *IEEE Transactions on Vehicular Technology, 69*(2), 2034–2048. doi:10.1109/TVT.2019.2957744

Ma, Z., Zhang, J., Guo, Y., Liu, Y., Liu, X., & He, W. (2020). An Efficient Decentralized Key Management Mechanism for VANET With Blockchain. *IEEE Transactions on Vehicular Technology, 69*(6), 5836–5849. doi:10.1109/TVT.2020.2972923

Machado, C., & Fröhlich, A. A. M. (2018). Iot data integrity verification for cyber-physical systems using blockchain. In *2018 IEEE 21st International Symposium on Real-Time Distributed Computing (ISORC)*, (pp. 83–90). IEEE. 10.1109/ISORC.2018.00019

Machado, C., & Westphall, C. M. (2021). Blockchain incentivized data forwarding in manets: Strategies and challenges. *Ad Hoc Networks, 110*, 102321. doi:10.1016/j.adhoc.2020.102321

Maitra, S., Yanambaka, V. P., Abdelgawad, A., Puthal, D., & Yelamarthi, K. (2020). Proof-of-authentication consensus algorithm: Blockchain-based iot implementation. In *2020 IEEE 6th World Forum on Internet of Things (WF-IoT)*, (pp. 1–2). IEEE.

Manogaran, G., Varatharajan, R., Lopez, D., Kumar, P. M., Sundarasekar, R., & Thota, C. (2018). A new architecture of internet of things and big data ecosystem for secured smart healthcare monitoring and alerting system. *Future Generation Computer Systems, 82*, 375–387. doi:10.1016/j.future.2017.10.045

Meng, L., Ren, S., Tang, G., Yang, C., & Yang, W. (2020). Uav sensor spoofing detection algorithm based on gps and optical flow fusion. *Proceedings of the 2020 4th International Conference on Cryptography, Security and Privacy*, 146–151. 10.1145/3377644.3377670

Mingxiao, D., Xiaofeng, M., Zhe, Z., Xiangwei, W., & Qijun, C. (2017). A review on consensus algorithm of blockchain. In 2017 IEEE international conference on systems, man, and cybernetics (SMC), (pp. 2567–2572). IEEE. doi:10.1109/SMC.2017.8123011

Mohanta, B. K., Sahoo, A., Patel, S., Panda, S. S., Jena, D., & Gountia, D. (2019). Decauth: decentralized authentication scheme for iot device using ethereum blockchain. In TENCON 2019-2019 IEEE Region 10 Conference (TENCON), (pp. 558–563). IEEE. doi:10.1109/TENCON.2019.8929720

Mokhtar, B., & Azab, M. (2015). Survey on Security Issues in Vehicular Ad Hoc Networks. *Alexandria Engineering Journal*, *54*(4), 1115–1126. doi:10.1016/j.aej.2015.07.011

Moussaoui, D., Kadri, B., Feham, M., & Ammar Bensaber, B. (2021). A Distributed Blockchain Based PKI (BCPKI) architecture to enhance privacy in VANET. *2020 2nd International Workshop on Human-Centric Smart Environments for Health and Well-Being (IHSH)*.

Mowla, N. I., Tran, N. H., Doh, I., & Chae, K. (2020). Afrl: Adaptive federated reinforcement learning for intelligent jamming defense in fanet. *Journal of Communications and Networks (Seoul)*, *22*(3), 244–258. doi:10.1109/JCN.2020.000015

Mukherjee, A., Keshary, V., Pandya, K., Dey, N., & Satapathy, S. C. (2018). Flying ad hoc networks: A comprehensive survey. Information and Decision Sciences, 569–580.

Neshenko, N., Bou-Harb, E., Crichigno, J., Kaddoum, G., & Ghani, N. (2019). Demystifying iot security: An exhaustive survey on iot vulnerabilities and a first empirical look on internet-scale iot exploitations. *IEEE Communications Surveys and Tutorials*, *21*(3), 2702–2733. doi:10.1109/COMST.2019.2910750

Nguyen, V.-L., Lin, P.-C., & Hwang, R.-H. (2019). Energy depletion attacks in low power wireless networks. *IEEE Access: Practical Innovations, Open Solutions*, *7*, 51915–51932. doi:10.1109/ACCESS.2019.2911424

Nichols, R., Mumm, H., Lonstein, W., Carter, C., & Hood, J. (2019). *Understanding hostile use and cyber-vulnerabilities of uas: Components, autonomy v automation, sensors, saa, scada and cyber attack taxonomy*. Unmanned Aircraft Systems in the Cyber Domain.

Noor, F., Khan, M. A., Al-Zahrani, A., Ullah, I., & Al-Dhlan, K. A. (2020). A review on communications perspective of flying ad-hoc networks: Key enabling wireless technologies, applications, challenges and open research topics. *Drones (Basel)*, *4*(4), 65. doi:10.3390/drones4040065

Noura, H., Hatoum, T., Salman, O., Yaacoub, J.-P., and Chehab, A. (2020). Lorawan security survey: Issues, threats and possible mitigation techniques. *Internet of Things*, 100303.

Novo, O. (2018). Scalable access management in iot using blockchain: A performance evaluation. *IEEE Internet of Things Journal*, *6*(3), 4694–4701. doi:10.1109/JIOT.2018.2879679

Pahlajani, S., Kshirsagar, A., & Pachghare, V. (2019). Survey on private blockchain consensus algorithms. In *2019 1st International Conference on Innovations in Information and Communication Technology (ICIICT)*, (pp. 1–6). IEEE. 10.1109/ICIICT1.2019.8741353

Pandharipande, A., & Newsham, G. R. (2018). Lighting controls: Evolution and revolution. *Lighting Research & Technology*, *50*(1), 115–128. doi:10.1177/1477153517731909

Paul, A., & Jeyaraj, R. (2019). Internet of things: A primer. *Human Behavior and Emerging Technologies*, *1*(1), 37–47. doi:10.1002/hbe2.133

Perwej, Y., Parwej, F., Hassan, M. M. M., & Akhtar, N. (2019). *The internet-of-things (iot) security: A technological perspective and review. International Journal of Scientific Research in Computer Science, Engineering and Information Technology (IJSRCSEIT).*

Petit, J., Stottelaar, B., Feiri, M., & Kargl, F. (2015). Remote attacks on automated vehicles sensors: Experiments on camera and lidar. *Black Hat Europe*, *11*, 995.

Pfaff, B. L. (2018). *Overwhelming the SAA System of Delivery UAVs by Drone Swarming* (PhD thesis). Wright State University.

Pilkington, M. (2016). Blockchain technology: principles and applications. In *Research handbook on digital transformations*. Edward Elgar Publishing. doi:10.4337/9781784717766.00019

Porambage, P., Schmitt, C., Kumar, P., Gurtov, A., & Ylianttila, M. (2014). Pauthkey: A pervasive authentication protocol and key establishment scheme for wireless sensor networks in distributed iot applications. *International Journal of Distributed Sensor Networks*, *10*(7), 357430. doi:10.1155/2014/357430

Praitheeshan, P., Pan, L., Yu, J., Liu, J., & Doss, R. (2019). *Security analysis methods on ethereum smart contract vulnerabilities: a survey.* arXiv preprint arXiv:1908.08605.

Pu, C., & Hajjar, S. (2018). Mitigating forwarding misbehaviors in rpl-based low power and lossy networks. In 2018 15th IEEE Annual Consumer Communications & Networking Conference (CCNC), (pp. 1–6). IEEE. doi:10.1109/CCNC.2018.8319164

Qiu, J., Tian, Z., Du, C., Zuo, Q., Su, S., & Fang, B. (2020). A survey on access control in the age of internet of things. *IEEE Internet of Things Journal*, *7*(6), 4682–4696. doi:10.1109/JIOT.2020.2969326

Rana, S., Halim, M. A., & Kabir, M. H. (2018). Design and implementation of a security improvement framework of zigbee network for intelligent monitoring in iot platform. *Applied Sciences (Basel, Switzerland)*, *8*(11), 2305. doi:10.3390/app8112305

Rappel, H., Beex, L. A., Hale, J. S., Noels, L., & Bordas, S. (2020). A tutorial on bayesian inference to identify material parameters in solid mechanics. *Archives of Computational Methods in Engineering*, *27*(2), 361–385. doi:10.100711831-018-09311-x

Reyna, A., Martn, C., Chen, J., Soler, E., & Dáz, M. (2018). On blockchain and its integration with iot. challenges and opportunities. *Future Generation Computer Systems*, *88*, 173–190. doi:10.1016/j.future.2018.05.046

Ribeiro, V., Holanda, R., Ramos, A., & Rodrigues, J. J. (2020). Enhancing key management in lorawan with permissioned blockchain. *Sensors (Basel)*, *20*(11), 3068. doi:10.339020113068 PMID:32485791

Saleh, F. (2018). Blockchain without waste: Proof-of-stake. *Review of Financial Studies*.

Sedjelmaci, H., Senouci, S. M., & Ansari, N. (2017). A hierarchical detection and response system to enhance security against lethal cyber-attacks in uav networks. *IEEE Transactions on Systems, Man, and Cybernetics. Systems*, *48*(9), 1594–1606. doi:10.1109/TSMC.2017.2681698

Sengupta, J., Ruj, S., & Bit, S. D. (2019). End to end secure anonymous communication for secure directed diffusion in iot. *Proceedings of the 20th international conference on distributed computing and networking*, 445–450. 10.1145/3288599.3295577

Sha, K., Wei, W., Yang, T. A., Wang, Z., & Shi, W. (2018). On security challenges and open issues in internet of things. *Future Generation Computer Systems, 83*, 326–337. doi:10.1016/j.future.2018.01.059

Sharma, P. K., Chen, M.-Y., & Park, J. H. (2017). A software defined fog node based distributed blockchain cloud architecture for iot. *IEEE Access: Practical Innovations, Open Solutions, 6*, 115–124. doi:10.1109/ACCESS.2017.2757955

Sharma, P. K., & Park, J. H. (2018). Blockchain based hybrid network architecture for the smart city. *Future Generation Computer Systems, 86*, 650–655. doi:10.1016/j.future.2018.04.060

Shrestha, R., Bajracharya, R., Shrestha, A. P., & Nam, S. Y. (2020). A new type of blockchain for secure message exchange in VANET. *Digital Communications and Networks, 6*(2), 177–186. doi:10.1016/j.dcan.2019.04.003

Shukla, P. (2017). Ml-ids: A machine learning approach to detect wormhole attacks in internet of things. In 2017 Intelligent Systems Conference (IntelliSys), (pp. 234–240). IEEE. doi:10.1109/IntelliSys.2017.8324298

Sicari, S., Rizzardi, A., Miorandi, D., & Coen-Porisini, A. (2018). Reato: Reacting to denial of service attacks in the internet of things. *Computer Networks, 137*, 37–48. doi:10.1016/j.comnet.2018.03.020

Siegel, J. E., Erb, D. C., & Sarma, S. E. (2017). A survey of the connected vehicle landscape—Architectures, enabling technologies, applications, and development areas. *IEEE Transactions on Intelligent Transportation Systems, 19*(8), 2391–2406. doi:10.1109/TITS.2017.2749459

Singh, M., Rajan, M., Shivraj, V., & Balamuralidhar, P. (2015). Secure mqtt for internet of things (iot). In *2015 fifth international conference on communication systems and network technologies*, (pp. 746–751). IEEE.

Singh, P., Nayyar, A., Kaur, A., & Ghosh, U. (2020). Blockchain and fog based architecture for internet of everything in smart cities. *Future Internet, 12*(4), 61. doi:10.3390/fi12040061

Siriwardena, P. (2020). Securing apis with transport layer security (tls). In *Advanced API Security* (pp. 69–79). Springer. doi:10.1007/978-1-4842-2050-4_3

Sonar, K., & Upadhyay, H. (2014). A survey: Ddos attack on internet of things. *International Journal of Engineering Research and Development, 10*(11), 58–63.

Song, T., Li, R., Mei, B., Yu, J., Xing, X., & Cheng, X. (2017). A privacy preserving communication protocol for iot applications in smart homes. *IEEE Internet of Things Journal, 4*(6), 1844–1852. doi:10.1109/JIOT.2017.2707489

Stoyanova, M., Nikoloudakis, Y., Panagiotakis, S., Pallis, E., & Markakis, E. K. (2020). A survey on the internet of things (iot) forensics: Challenges, approaches, and open issues. *IEEE Communications Surveys and Tutorials, 22*(2), 1191–1221. doi:10.1109/COMST.2019.2962586

Su, J., Vasconcellos, D. V., Prasad, S., Sgandurra, D., Feng, Y., & Sakurai, K. (2018). Lightweight classification of iot malware based on image recognition. In *2018 IEEE 42Nd annual computer software and applications conference (COMPSAC)*, (vol. 2, pp. 664–669). IEEE. 10.1109/COMPSAC.2018.10315

Sun, X., Ng, D. W. K., Ding, Z., Xu, Y., & Zhong, Z. (2019). Physical layer security in uav systems: Challenges and opportunities. *IEEE Wireless Communications, 26*(5), 40–47. doi:10.1109/MWC.001.1900028

Tan, H., & Chung, I. (2020). Secure Authentication and Key Management With Blockchain in VANETs. *IEEE Access: Practical Innovations, Open Solutions, 8*, 2482–2498. doi:10.1109/ACCESS.2019.2962387

Tan, Y., Liu, J., & Kato, N. (2020). Blockchain-based key management for heterogeneous flying ad-hoc network. *IEEE Transactions on Industrial Informatics*.

Tang, H., Shi, Y., & Dong, P. (2019). Public blockchain evaluation using entropy and topsis. *Expert Systems with Applications, 117*, 204–210. doi:10.1016/j.eswa.2018.09.048

Tripathy, B. K., Jena, S. K., Reddy, V., Das, S., & Panda, S. K. (2020). A novel communication framework between manet and wsn in iot based smart environment. *International Journal of Information Technology*, 1–11.

Uddin, M. A., Stranieri, A., Gondal, I., & Balasubramanian, V. (2021). A survey on the adoption of blockchain in iot: Challenges and solutions. *Blockchain: Research and Applications*, 100006.

Wan, L., Eyers, D., & Zhang, H. (2019). Evaluating the Impact of Network Latency on the Safety of Blockchain Transactions. *2019 IEEE International Conference on Blockchain (Blockchain)*. 10.1109/Blockchain.2019.00033

Wang, Q., Zhu, X., Ni, Y., Gu, L., & Zhu, H. (2020). Blockchain for the iot and industrial iot: A review. *Internet of Things, 10*, 100081. doi:10.1016/j.iot.2019.100081

Wang, S., Ouyang, L., Yuan, Y., Ni, X., Han, X., & Wang, F.-Y. (2019a). Blockchain-enabled smart contracts: Architecture, applications, and future trends. *IEEE Transactions on Systems, Man, and Cybernetics. Systems, 49*(11), 2266–2277. doi:10.1109/TSMC.2019.2895123

Wang, X., Zha, X., Ni, W., Liu, R. P., Guo, Y. J., Niu, X., & Zheng, K. (2019b). Survey on blockchain for Internet of Things. *Computer Communications, 136*, 10–29. doi:10.1016/j.comcom.2019.01.006

Wei, S., Ge, L., Yu, W., Chen, G., Pham, K., Blasch, E., Shen, D., & Lu, C. (2014). Simulation study of unmanned aerial vehicle communication networks addressing bandwidth disruptions. In *Sensors and Systems for Space Applications VII* (Vol. 9085, p. 90850O). International Society for Optics and Photonics.

Wood, G. (2014). Ethereum: A secure decentralised generalised transaction ledger. *Ethereum Project Yellow Paper, 151*(2014), 1–32.

Wu, Q., Mei, W., & Zhang, R. (2019). Safeguarding wireless network with uavs: A physical layer security perspective. *IEEE Wireless Communications, 26*(5), 12–18. doi:10.1109/MWC.001.1900050

Xiong, Z., Zhang, Y., Niyato, D., Wang, P., & Han, Z. (2018). When mobile blockchain meets edge computing. *IEEE Communications Magazine, 56*(8), 33–39. doi:10.1109/MCOM.2018.1701095

Xu, Y., Ren, J., Wang, G., Zhang, C., Yang, J., & Zhang, Y. (2019). A blockchain-based nonrepudiation network computing service scheme for industrial iot. *IEEE Transactions on Industrial Informatics*, *15*(6), 3632–3641. doi:10.1109/TII.2019.2897133

Yang, X., Karampatzakis, E., Doerr, C., & Kuipers, F. (2018). Security vulnerabilities in lorawan. In *2018 IEEE/ACM Third International Conference on Internet-of-Things Design and Implementation (IoTDI)*, (pp. 129–140). IEEE. 10.1109/IoTDI.2018.00022

Yazdinejad, A., Parizi, R. M., Srivastava, G., Dehghantanha, A., & Choo, K.-K. R. (2019). Energy efficient decentralized authentication in internet of underwater things using blockchain. In 2019 IEEE Globecom Workshops (GC Wkshps), (pp. 1–6). IEEE. doi:10.1109/GCWkshps45667.2019.9024475

Yin, D., Zhang, L., & Yang, K. (2018). A ddos attack detection and mitigation with software-defined internet of things framework. *IEEE Access: Practical Innovations, Open Solutions*, *6*, 24694–24705. doi:10.1109/ACCESS.2018.2831284

Zarpelão, B. B., Miani, R. S., Kawakani, C. T., & de Alvarenga, S. C. (2017). A survey of intrusion detection in internet of things. *Journal of Network and Computer Applications*, *84*, 25–37. doi:10.1016/j.jnca.2017.02.009

Zeadally, S., Siddiqui, F., & Baig, Z. (2019). 25 years of bluetooth technology. *Future Internet*, *11*(9), 194. doi:10.3390/fi11090194

Zhang, G., Wu, Q., Cui, M., & Zhang, R. (2019a). Securing uav communications via joint trajectory and power control. *IEEE Transactions on Wireless Communications*, *18*(2), 1376–1389. doi:10.1109/TWC.2019.2892461

Zhang, K., Zhu, Y., Maharjan, S., & Zhang, Y. (2019b). Edge intelligence and blockchain empowered 5g beyond for the industrial internet of things. *IEEE Network*, *33*(5), 12–19. doi:10.1109/MNET.001.1800526

Zhang, N., Mi, X., Feng, X., Wang, X., Tian, Y., & Qian, F. (2018). *Understanding and mitigating the security risks of voice-controlled third-party skills on amazon alexa and google home.* arXiv preprint arXiv:1805.01525.

Zhang, X. D., Li, R., & Cui, B. (2018). A security architecture of VANET based on blockchain and mobile edge computing. *2018 1st IEEE International Conference on Hot Information-Centric Networking (HotICN)*.

Zheng, D., Wu, A., Zhang, Y., & Zhao, Q. (2018a). Efficient and privacy-preserving medical data sharing in internet of things with limited computing power. *IEEE Access: Practical Innovations, Open Solutions*, *6*, 28019–28027. doi:10.1109/ACCESS.2018.2840504

Zheng, Z., Xie, S., Dai, H., Chen, X., & Wang, H. (2017). *An overview of blockchain technology: Architecture, consensus, and future trends. In 2017 IEEE international congress on big data (BigData congress)*. IEEE.

Zheng, Z., Xie, S., Dai, H.-N., Chen, X., & Wang, H. (2018b). Blockchain challenges and opportunities: A survey. *International Journal of Web and Grid Services*, *14*(4), 352–375. doi:10.1504/IJWGS.2018.095647

KEY TERMS AND DEFINITIONS

Blockchain: A decentralized system based on a peer-to-peer network. Each network object keeps a copy of the ledger to avoid having a single point of failure. This technology can be explored in many use cases and used as a secure way to manage and protect all kinds of data.

FANET: A sub-category of the MANET that involves the deployment of a set of drones and ground stations through an ad hoc wireless network.

Internet of Things: Intelligent and autonomous connected objects that communicate with each other via the Internet. It encompasses the areas of the current Information Technology (IT) and uses other technologies such as Cloud Computing, Big data, or even the Blockchains.

MANET: A wireless network and without central entity (unlike a centralized or cellular communication network). It is based on the nodes ability to cooperate and form a network between them.

Security and Privacy: Set of policies and practices adopted to prevent and monitor unauthorized access or modification of an IT operation. It ensures the efficient system functioning.

VANET: A sub-category of MANET which is addressed for traffic management by intelligent transportation systems.

Vulnerabilities and Attacks: Malicious actions exploiting a weakness in a system to achieve a specific goal. These goals could be illegally gaining access to the system, interrupting or disrupting a service, or exploiting system resources.

Chapter 7
Blockchain Towards Secure UAV-Based Systems

Iamia Chaari Fourati

Higher Institute of Computer Science and Multimedia of Sfax, Tunisia

Mohamed Fourati

Higher Institute of Computer Science and Multimedia of Sfax, Tunisia

Bilel Najeh

Higher Institute of Computer Science and Multimedia of Sfax, Tunisia

Aicha Idriss

Higher Institute of Computer Science and Multimedia of Sfax, Tunisia

ABSTRACT

During this last decade, the blockchain (BC) paradigm has been required in several use cases and scenarios in particular for security, privacy, and trust provisioning. Accordingly, several studies proposed the use of BC technology to secure and to assure the trustworthiness of unmanned aerial vehicles (UAVs). In this context, this chapter highlights several applications and scenarios for the deployment of UAVs within diverse smart systems. In addition, it illustrates the advantages of the integration of the BC within UAVs-based smart systems. This integration reveals new challenges and future research directions that are discussed in this chapter.

INTRODUCTION

During this last decade, the world witnessed an increasing in the number of Unmanned Aerial Vehicles (UAVs) (Hentati, and Fourati, 2020) with different sizes, models, functionalities, and sensing and communication capabilities responding to the global demand in different domains. Indeed, UAVs are being useful in complex mission and critical scenarios in particular for hostile areas supervision involving multi and cooperative UAVs. In addition, the typical UAV applications in 5G and beyond are mobile

DOI: 10.4018/978-1-7998-5839-3.ch007

relay, aerial internet of things (IoT) data collector, aerial base station, aerial mobile user, aerial helper for traffic offloading or traffic caching. Besides that, the use of multi-UAVs in collaboration with terrestrial networks affords new ways for diverse context such as civilian, military, environmental, commercial, agriculture, smart city, healthcare, disaster monitoring, and telecommunication systems...However, UAVs based system face several technical challenges including cooperative computation offloading, QoE requirements, collision avoidance, mobility management, multi-node task scheduling, failure recovery, and security provisioning. The standard scenario of UAVs network is to have one or multi flying UAVs, which are supervised and managed by the user, via a ground control station (GCS) through a communication link (Krichen et al., 2018). MAVLINK is the standardized communication protocol between an UAV and a GCS and between UAVs. However, this protocol have several vulnerabilities (Chaari & al, 2018). BlockChain (BC) based solutions are the adequate paradigm that could mitigate vulnerabilities, threats and attacks within UAVs based systems. Accordingly, this chapter highlight the importance and the effectiveness of BC for securing UAVs communication. Indeed, the manifolds of this chapter could be summarized into three points:

- Providing a deep investigation regarding the various applications of BC technology in UAV systems. Indeed, this chapter discusses challenges pertaining UAVs scenarios, pinpoints how BC can enhance UAVs utility in each scenario and illustrates how certain BC features can help to overcome UAV security, trust and privacy issues.
- Giving a wider outlook to the readers, on how the correlation between BC and UAV technology can enhance the security level for smart systems environments.
- Highlighting potential open issues and future research directions that can be beneficial for the development and the deployment of BC-based UAV systems.

The rest of this chapter organized as follows: The second section overviews the fundamentals of UAVs with focus on UAVs communication systems, UAVs emerging applications and UAVs attacks. The third section presents the basic concepts related to BC technology with an insight on BC platforms, BC consensus and the role played by BC to enhance the UAVs-based systems security, privacy and trust. The fourth section discusses intensively various applications and scenarios of deploying BC within UAVs based systems. The fifth section affords the readers with a holistic vision of the ongoing research in BC-based UAV systems and assesses involved challenges, possible research opportunities, and future directions. Finally, the last section concludes this chapter and summarizes the lessons learned through this chapter.

UAVs FUNDAMENTALS

UAVs Communication Systems

Certain UAVs applications, such as surveillance of hostile areas, necessitate collaboration and synchronization between UAVs network and other types of networks for example Wireless Sensors Network (WSN), 5G networks, LEO satellite networks to enhance UAVs connectivity and coverage. Thus, a typical UAVs communication system will incorporate several networking technologies offering connectivity between UAVs and a GCS. In general, a continuous bidirectional link must be established between UAVs and a GCS to collect all the details about the aircraft status, real-time telemetry data and to send the suitable commands during flight. The downlink, from the UAV to the GCS, is dedicated to telemetry. It contains flight data collected by the UAV such as the geographical position and the video streaming captured by the camera during flight. However, the uplink, from the GCS to UAV reserved to commands that are sent to interact with the UAV (e.g. changing the direction of the UAV, reducing the UAV speed…). The communication between UAV and GCS should operate in a protected spectrum due to the critical implemented functions. Furthermore, to enhance robustness and reliability a backup link via satellite should be implemented. Besides that, advanced security mechanisms should be employed to avoid ghost control scenario in which the UAVs are monitored by unauthorized agents. The main communication protocols for data exchanging between GCS and UAV are either MAVLINK protocol or the STANAG 4586 protocol. Contrary to MAVLink, STANAG protocol is not an open source protocol. MAVLink is a lightweight an open source protocol deployed for bidirectional communications between cooperative UAVs or between a GCS and UAVs. MAVlink define two categories of messages: (1) Commands and control messages sent by the GCS to the UAV to execute specific actions by the autopilot. (2) Telemetry and state information messages transmitted from the UAV to the GCS. A detailed list of MAVLink messages is available in (Mavlink, 2021). For interoperability issue, MAVLink define higher-level protocols known as "microservices" that are used to exchange various types of data, including parameters, trajectories, images, missions, other files. Recently, advanced UAVs-based architectures proposed, these architectures include cloud layer or software defined networking (SDN) layer or integrated ground and space networks.

The main goal of the use of SDN controllers is to provide network programmability via the separation of control and data planes. SDN controllers allow the monitoring of UAVs mission features. Indeed, an SDN controller considers the global UAV context to manage UAVs systems, to avoid collisions, to optimize UAVs' mobility, and to establish secure and reliable communication path. Besides that, the SDN controller carries out all control functions, is the responsible of selecting relay nodes and effectively scheduling the UAVs tasks with the goal of running the required mission with security and quality of Experience (QoE) support. Figure 1, illustrates UAVs architectures.

Figure 1. UAVs Architectures

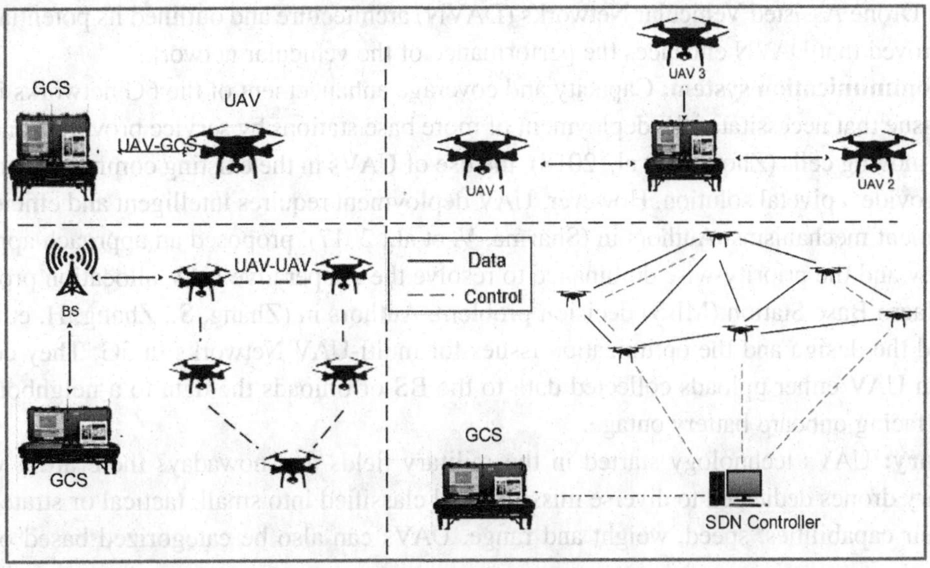

UAVs Emerging Applications

Over the past few years, a growing interest has been marked in the deployment of UAVs in various applications. The typical UAV applications in 5G and beyond are a mobile relay, an aerial internet of things (IoT) data collector, an aerial base station, aerial mobile user, aerial helper for traffic offloading or traffic caching. Besides that, the use of multi-UAVs in collaboration with terrestrial networks afford new ways for diverse context such as civilian, military, environmental, agriculture, smart city, disaster monitoring, and telecommunication systems...

- **Civilian applications:** UAVs initially conceived and de-ployed for military use, nowadays are utilized in numerous civilian applications (Shakhatreh, H. et al., 2019).. The use of single UAV is established and its related products are available to consumers, while civilian services and applications based on swarms UAVs or on collaboration between terrestrial networks and UAVs are still subject of research.
- **Agriculture applications:** In the agriculture field, UAVs are used for diverse use cases such as soil erosion monitoring, crop maturity measurement and Wildlife management. Authors in (Boursianis, A. D. et al., 2020) highlighted the importance of both IoT and UAVs toward the development of smart farming.
- **Disaster monitoring**: During a natural disaster, the response time of disaster management is key in saving the lives in the affected areas. UAVs have been used in diverse disaster management scenarios. For disaster special authorizations are granted to UAVs to manage quickly the situation. Authors in (Erdelj, M., et al., 2017), (Erdelj, M., & Natalizio, E., 2016, February). reviewed the UAVs latest advances for first response to disaster management and outlined the suitable network architectures. Authors in (Erdelj, M. et al, 2017). focused on the joint role that multi-UAV and WSN systems play for natural disaster management.
- **Smart transportation**: UAVs opens up new opportunities for advanced applications related to smart transportation such as fast and accurate data collection from UAV video including extracting traffic parameters detecting vehicles. Furthermore, UAVs can enhance vehicle-to-vehicle connectivity, interworking efficiency, infrastructure coverage. Authors in (Shi, W. et al., 2018). proposed Drone Assisted Vehicular Networks (DAVN) architecture and outlined its potential services and proved that DAVN enhances the performance of the vehicular network.
- **Telecommunication system:** Capacity and coverage enhancement of the 6G networks is the biggest issue that necessitates the deployment of more base stations by service providers and in some cases moving cells (Zhou, Z. et al., 2018), the use of UAVs in the existing communication system can provide a pivotal solution. However, UAV deployment requires intelligent and efficient UAVs placement mechanisms. Authors in (Sharma, V. et al., 2017). proposed an approach applying the entropy and the priority-wise dominance to resolve the cooperative UAV allocation problem and the Macro Base Station (MBS) decision problem. Authors in (Zhang, S., Zhang, H. et al., 2019) treated the design and the optimization issues for multi-UAV Networks in 5G. They considered that an UAV either uploads collected data to the BS or offloads the data to a neighboring UAV when facing onboard battery outage.
- **Military:** UAVs technology started in the military fields and nowadays there are a variety of military drones dedicated to diverse missions and classified into small, tactical or strategic based on their capabilities, speed, weight and range. UAVs can also be categorized based on the au-

tonomy or on the specific roles they are meant to play in military operations. In (Schneider, J., & Macdonald, J., 2016) authors explored tactical level barriers to the adoption of UAVs in the battlefield.

- **Healthcare & COVID-19:** There are some powerful applications for drones in the healthcare domain such as remote patient data collection, carrying emergency equipment or medication. In addition, during the public health emergency, such as the COVID-19 outbreak, UAVs can offer many benefits. Drone can be used for crowd surveillance to ensure social distancing, for spraying disinfectants in the contaminated regions and for delivery of medical supplies and other essentials.

UAVs Attacks

The diversity of UAVs applications and usage as well the complex and the sophisticated missions and tasks performed by UAVs, make UAVs vulnerable to various threats and attacks. Cyber-attacks against UAVs can result to several issues such as UAVs charge depletion, forcing the landing of the UAV in a different location, or even crashing of the UAV to cause financial loss. In the following, this chapter classifies UAVs attacks into three categories: (1) Attacks against communication link between UAV and GCS, (2) attacks against cooperative UAVs, and (3) attacks prohibiting UAVs functionalities.

Attacks Prohibiting Communications Between UAVs and GCS

Several attacks could prohibit the communication between UAVs and GCS. In the following this chapter highlights the most known attacks:

- **Jamming:** Wireless signal jamming may interrupt the links between GCSs and UAVs, and damage the system availability. To execute this attack in a UAV system, the jammer sends fake signals in the same frequency but with a higher power to jam real signals. This loss of control signal makes the UAV to enter into a lost link state.
- **Maldrone**: is a virus, which, once installed on the UAV, it enables the attacker to take control of the UAV. It acts as a proxy for the UAVs flight controller enabling the injection of the desired values for UAVs /GCS communications.
- **Trojans**: Trojan is a malicious program or software that monitors the UAV. It destroys files and damages hard drives in the GCS system to get remote access to the UAV.
- **Eavesdropping**: The eavesdropping is specified as unauthorized real-time interception of UAV communication allowing an attacker to detect all the commands sent from the GCS to the UAV. The attack also allows the attacker to gain a copy of the required data. In terms of UAV, the attacker would eavesdrop to learn the way the packets in the network are designed and then use this knowledge to launch a harmful active attack.
- **Man-In-The-Middle attack**: All the exchanged messages between the UAVs and the GCS transit via the attacker; and the attacker will control communications between UAVs and GCS. Besides, the attacker also secretly collects confidential data that can be used by the attackers to behave as though they are legitimate users.
- **Flooding attack**: exhausts the network bandwidth and it consumes UAVs and GCS resources such as computational and battery power.

- **Replay attack**: enables adversary nodes to record legitimate control messages, store and retransmit them later.

Attacks Prohibiting Communications Between UAVs

Multi-UAVs are often deployed to carry out cooperative missions. However, the communication links between involved UAVs is vulnerable to security attacks disturbing the coordination between the UAVs. Below examples of such attacks:

- **Dispatch System Attack**: The UAVs route is predefined in advance to acheive the designated tasks. The attacker would launch an attack on the dispatching system that makes the system not follow the right allocated missions assigned to the UAV by mislead the UAV or make it crash to other UAVs. This attack can be launched via the injection of Trojans in the system.
- **ADS-B Attack:** To ensure smooth navigation and collision-free, UAVs implement the Automatic Dependent Surveillance Broadcast (ADS-B) module. ADS-B also provides an overview of the air traffic, which avoid collision by broadcasting between UAVs current location of each UAV its altitude, speed, unique identifier, etc. This ADS-B messages are sent via wireless links in plain text format that makes the messages vulnerable to a variety of attacks such as injecting fake messages to the other UAVs, deleting or altering the current messages.
- **Byzantine attack**: aims to create routing loops, and to forward packets via non-optimal paths, or to drop selectively packets.
- **Wormhole attack:** involves two attackers performing a colluding attack. One attacker records packets at a particular location and replays them to another attacker in order to analyze or simply drop them to cause anomalies by using a high-speed private network.
- **Blackhole attack**: The attacker attempts to advertise that it has a fresh route. By generating forge control packets, the adversary node may succeed in becoming part of the network route. Then, once chosen as an intermediate node, the attacker drops the packets instead of processing them.
- **Rushing attack**: The attacker node has the ability to send discovery messages much faster and in a very offensive manner comparing with the other nodes. The main constraint in this type is that the attacker node must sent the discovery messages before the other nodes begin sending their own discovery messages so that the receiver node cannot exploit their functions correctly expect the attacker node.
- **TCAS Induced Collision (TCAS)**: TCAS is a system that is designed to avoid collisions within UAVs. However, TCAS face a problem called TCAS Induced Collision that occurs in a heavy network environment. An attacker can altering the traffic data and forcing conditions that lead to a TCAS Induced Collision.

Attacks Prohibiting UAVs Functionalities

Certain attacks launched in the UAV impact the UAV functioning. In this category of attacks, the attacker aim to take full control of the UAV. It can either target the UAV components present in the UAV or the communication network present in the UAV system itself. Several attacks could prohibit UAVs functionalities such as Hijacking, alteration, exploitation of recorded video, GPS spoofing and DoS attacks.

- **Hijacking:** An adversary may be hijacked UAVs due to unsafe settings or software vulnerabilities; therefore, the adversary will exploit hijacked UAVs to complete internal attacks or to get fully control of UAVs.

- **Alteration Attack:** Hijacked UAVs or external adversaries can launch an alteration attack that corresponds to message injection, deletion, or modification. The content due to an alteration attack is poisoned content, which can classified as three types: (i) inauthentic content has a valid signature produced by an inauthentic key, (ii) corrupted content has an invalid signature, and (iii) fake content is produced by hijacked UAVs. Besides that, alteration attacks include message forgery (the attacker can create multiple virtual identities for transmitting fake messages using different forged positions), GPS spoofing (GPS used to define the position of the UAVs using waypoints message to fly to a false location), and identity spoofing

- **Exploitation of Recorded Video**: The GCS in some situation first requests the recorded video, an attack can be launched, provided that the attacker can access the flight controller to obstruct the system and to replace the original video with a manipulated one.

- **Denial of Service attacks (DoS):** DoS results is that the UAV become unresponsive to the GCS, and vice versa, due to the violation of the system's availability. The DoS attack can be carried out by overloading the processing units, depleting the batteries, flooding the communication channels, etc. The DoS attack can alter the commands given by the flight controller by making the system crash, land, drift and shut down the UAV while it is still functioning

- **GPS Spoofing**: In this attack, a fake GPS signal is generated. The signal can be artificially created or it could be pre-recorded past legitimate GPS signals. The attacker deceives the GPS receiver by successfully broadcasting the spoofed GPS signals from satellites that are higher in power than the legitimate GPS signals.

Although the diversity of attacks that can prohibit the UAVs tasks and mission and that can lead to harmful consequences for certain UAVs-based applications, there are different strategies and approaches to overcome these attacks and to ensure a secure-UAVs based environments. Blockchain (BC) is among the relevant technologies making the UAVs safer with great accuracy and ease of control. Multi-UAV communication is a suitable candidate for BC implementation. In the following section, this chapter highlights BC fundamentals.

BLOCKCHAIN FUNDAMENTALS

BC is a distributed and immutable ledger (database) that manages the growing list of digital records and provides a secure, trust and private approach for all the nodes on the network. This distributed database is consistent without the need for a central entity. The access to the ledger is rapid and transparent to all the participants of the BC network. BC adopts a consensus mechanisms and Smart Contract (SC) to reach an agreement among all the nodes on the BC and uses hash cryptographic primitives to ensure security and privacy. A BC consists of three main components:

- **BC Network**: It consists of a huge number of nodes, and each node on the network has the same status or information to avoid a single point of failure.

- **BC Transaction**: It is the process of data exchange between the nodes on the network. It includes the sender and receiver address for the authentication process. It identifies the transaction amount with the transaction identity number. Each transaction is broadcasted on the BC.
- **Global Ledger:** A global ledger is used to store the transaction history at each node on the BC network. Each node has its ledger that conserves the data from the first block to the latest block of the BC network.

BC Plateforms

Nowadays, several BC platforms exist. The most known platforms are Bitcoins, Ethereum and HyperLedger, Quorum, Corda, Multichain and Hebdra.

- **BitCoin**: Bitcoin is the first and the most famous application for the BC. Nakamoto defined bitcoin as a purely peer-to-peer version of electronic cash permitting online payments to be sent directly from one node to another node without going through a financial institution (Nakamoto. S., 2008). The digital asset carried by the network is also denoted bitcoin. As already implied, Bitcoin is a BC-based system. Peers ensure the trustworthiness of the system through the validation of transactions and hashing them into a chain of blocks. The validation of transaction is based on PoW consensus.
- **Ethereum**: is a distributed computing platform facilitating the development of decentralized applications. It has a large development community and it is open-source. Ethereum has its cryptocurrency named Ether and a currency to pay for computations and transactions fees called Gas.. Ethereum is not only a BC platform but also a Turing complete language used to create contracts and to build and publish distributed applications. Ethereum started using PoW as its consensus mechanism, but it is soon switching to proof of stake.
- **Hyperledger**: is an open-source created by the Linux Foundation to develop a suite of frameworks, tools and libraries for the industry. It follows the logic of Bitcoin script and UTXO as a reward. Hyperledger exploits the UTXO and the logic of script used by Bitcoin.
- **Hebdera** (Baird, L. et al, 2019): directed by a council of leading enterprises, across multiple industries. Hebdera platform built on the hashgraph distributed consensus algorithm (Baird, L., 2016). The hashgraph consensus algorithm guarantees near-perfect efficiency in bandwidth usage that enable processing hundreds of thousands of transactions per second in a single shard. In both BC and hashgraph ledgers, any user can create a transaction and put it into a container to be spread throughout the distributed network. In BC, "blocks" of containers form a single long chain. When two blocks created at the same moment, the network nodes will choose only one chain to continue and discard the other. In hashgraph, every container of transactions is incorporated into the ledger that which is more efficient than BCs. Furthermore, BC fails if the new containers arrive too quickly because new branches sprout faster than they can be pruned. There is no harm in the hashgraph data structure growing quickly. Every member can create transactions and containers whenever they want to allow more powerful mathematical guarantees. Compared to other platforms using coordinators or leaders, Hashgraph is resilient to Distributed Denial of Service (DDoS) attacks. Besides that, hashgraph ensures both fair ordering and fair Access. In addition, the hashgraph algorithm accomplishes being fast, efficient, inexpensive and timestamped.

- **Corda** (Brown, R. G. et al, 2016): is a distributed ledger platform made of mutually distrusting nodes that permits a single global database to record the state of agreements between people and institutions. Is a massive open-source environment testing tools providing a broad range of functionality, including unit tests and integration tests for both small and huge projects and is specialized for use with regulated financial institutions, thereby reducing the cost of financial services. Corda permits an analysis of the interoperability between different parties with personal BC systems. The main Corda characteristics are automated smart contracts and timestamping of documents to ensure validity and uniqueness.

- **Quorum**(Quorum, 2021): has been developed by J.P. Morgan for financial use-cases, and adopted for any type of industry. It is a permissioned BC based on the Ethereum Go implementation protocol. Quorum supports the RAFT and IBFT Consensus algorithms. Older version of Quorum supported QuorumChain, a basic m-of-n voting based consensus. Current version supports "Raft-based" and Istanbul BFT consensus algorithms. Raft is a consensus algorithm used for managing replicated state machines or logs that is useful for consortia where there the consortia members are known and provisioned into the system. RAFT offers faster block times and does not create unnecessary empty blocks. Istanbul BFT is a Byzantine fault tolerant state machine replication based consensus algorithm. The main designs goal of Quorum is to simplify the development of Ethereum's BC applications in enterprises. Quorum has almost the same functionality as Ethereum. However, it brings several enhancements: (i) regarding permissions management of network and peers; (ii) transaction and contract privacy, indeed it is possible to create private contracts and transactions whose payload is only visible to participants included the transaction parameters; and (iii) voting-based consensus protocols.

- **MultiChain** (Multichain, 2021): developed by Coin Sciences for permissioned BCs in the financial industry and for multi-currency exchanges in a consortium. It is an open source platform which is a fork of the Bitcoin BC aiming at compatibility with the Bitcoin ecosystem as much as possible. Unlike Bitcoin, MultiChain allow users to configure several parameters including the chain privacy, the permissions to access the network, the maximum block size and the mining incentive. Multichain consensus mechanism is called "mining"; the mining is processed by a set of identified block validators. There is a single validator per block, working in a round-robin scheduling strategy. MultiChain supports a variety of programming languages such as Python, Ruby or JavaScript, C#, PHP.

In summary, many BC systems and platforms exist. The BC performance is among key factors limiting the use of BC systems when running complex smart contracts. The BC performances is correlated with the used consensus protocols. The following subsection presents briefly the main consensus protocols categories.

BlockChain Main Consensus Protocols

A transaction in the BC is considered valid after the network participants have reached a consensus using a consensus algorithm. Consensus protocols used in the BCs can be classified into three main categories: (i) compute-intensive, (ii) non-computing capabilities, and (iii)voting. We provide a temporal evolution of these algorithms with a retrospective analysis to highlight the underlying issues.

Compute-Intensive Based Consensus Protocols

This category include Proof of Work-based protocols. PoW is the most famous consensus algorithm which is first introduced in Bitcoin. PoW is open and entirely decentralized and is required for the validation of each block. In this mechanism, peers (miners) search to solve a difficult mathematical problem based on a cryptographic hash algorithm. The solution proves that a miner spends time and resources solving the mathematical puzzle. Therefore, miners paid for any valid blocks added into the BC. This serves as the miner's motivation for the execution of any mining task. The transactions inside that block are considered confirmed when a block is solved. The main advantages of PoW consensus are safety and stability and the PoW main disadvantages are low performance and high power consumption PoW are known as energy-hungry mining algorithms.

Capability-Based Consensus Protocol

The high-energy consumption of compute-intensive-based consensus protocol is due to its competitive approach between miners to win the right to mine the next block. To fill this gap, several consensus protocols proposed to select a miner based on non-computing capability. The capability of a miner evaluated via other factors such as the contribution of the miner to the community, the amount of crypto-currency owned by that miner, the miner trust level, or the amount of storage owned by the miner. Different capability-based protocols are introduced below:

- **Proof of Stake (PoS)** was proposed in 2011 and used by the cryptocurrency in 2012. . Regarding the PoS paradigm, the miners in PoS are called forgers and the mining process is known as forging. At the beginning of a forging round, only the peers holding assets may participate in the consensus, in place of using energy to answer PoW puzzles, a PoS miner is limited to mining a percentage of transactions and it asks users to prove ownership of a certain amount of currency. The advantage of PoS is low power consumption and PoS disadvantages are its complex implementation and its low security.
- **Delegated Proof of Stake (DPoS)** was proposed in 2014 by Larimer. In DPoS forgers selected based on election rather than on the amount of staked coins owned. In DPoS a group of nodes called delegates and known as witnesses are elected via a voting process. A node can vote multiple witnesses with a single vote for each witness. The first N witnesses with the highest votes are then selected for the mining process to avoid a single witness from mining all the blocks.
- **Proof of Stake Velocity (PoSV)**: PoSV was proposed by Ren in 2014 to address the economic issue in PoS where a node may not perform transactions in order to increase its chance of being selected as the next forger. PoSV is an attempt to encourage financial flow in the network. However, if the counter parties exchange cryptocurrency with each other just for the purpose of reinitialization the coin age, then the economy will not get benefit from this financial flow.
- **Proof of Burn (PoB)**: PoB proposed in 2014 by Ian Stewart to address the problem of high-energy consumption in PoW and the issue of retrievable staked coins encouraging malicious users in PoS. In PoB, the miners need to burn the coins by sending them to an irretrievable address, known as eater address. The eater address has a public key associated with no private key making it impossible to retrieve the coins from that account. The coins once sent are removed from the network

and cannot be further used, which discourages the malicious miners from mining an invalid block, as a miner will spend coins to mine a block.

- **Proof of Space (PoSpace):** PoSpace also known as proof of capacity (PoC) was proposed in 2015 by Dziembowski et al to address the issue of rich getting richer and the issue of high energy consumption in the computation-based protocols. PoSpace is a two-step process: (1) plotting and (2) mining. The plotting step is a one-time process, in which the hard disk of the miner is plotted using hash values to ensure the storage space dedicated by the miner.

- **Proof of Importance (PoI):** PoI introduced in 2018 to address the issue of reduced transaction flow existing in the PoS. In PoI, a miner with the highest value of importance score in the network is selected to mine the next block. The importance score of a miner is computed based on three factors: (1) the number of crypto tokens vested by a miner, (2) number and size of transactions performed by a miner and (3) the participants with whom the miner perform transactions. In order to be eligible for the mining process, a miner needs to have a minimum threshold number of vested tokens, which we call vesting amount.

- **Proof of Authority (PoAuthority)** is a reputation-based consensus protocol where the reputation of the miner is at stake instead of coins. A validator (known as authorities) performs the role of a miner in PoAuthority. In order to be a validator, the authority must have good reputation.

- **Proof of Elapsed Time (PoET)**: PoET as a cost-efficient consensus protocol developed in 2016 by Intel. In PoET, minors will be selected based on time. Each verification node sleeps after creation of a random wait time and the node completes the waiting time first receives a chance to propose the next block. Having to depend on Intel is the major drawback of this consensus mechanism.

Voting-Based Consensus Protocols

The voting-based consensus protocols use a voting system to elect a miner for generating a block which resolve the high-energy consumption issue of compute-intensive-based protocols and address the problem of the rich getting richer in capability-based protocols. Voting-based protocols includes two subcategories: (1) Byzantine Fault Tolerance (BFT)-based and (2) Crash Fault Tolerance (CFT)-based. BFT-based consensus prevents the cases of failing node and malicious node and CFT-based consensus prevents only against the case of failing/crashing nodes.

Role of BlockChain Within UAVs Based Systems

Data security and privacy are the main concern in UAV communication. Existing fog and cloud-based centralized solutions provide security but suffer from having a single point of failure. The centralized approaches are susceptible to various cyber-attacks including eavesdropping, masquerade, linking, fabrication, jamming, and access control attacks. BC is a relevant solution to the above-mentioned issues. It ensures privacy, security and trust between the different stakeholders. Trust is provided since all participants' identities are verified, their privacy is guaranteed, and data storage is secured. In addition, BC prevents transactions from security risks and cyber frauds. The hashing algorithm used within BC are strong enough that does not let its reverse hash calculation. Using BC require UAV identity checking for any drone involved in a specific mission. Smart contracts mastered the trust requirement; it permits to maintain the trust between the peer nodes of the BC. Besides that, each BC characteristics has an advantage within the UAVs-based systems. In this regards, table 1 highlights and recapitulates BC characteristics and their potential in UAVs-based systems.

Table 1. BC characteristics and their potential in UAVs-based systems

BC Characteristics	Impacts of BC Characteristics in UAVs-based Systems
Decentralization	It overcomes the necessity of third-party to preserve trust in the UAV network. The deployed cryptographic primitives secure the UAV data. Decentralization solves the issue of single point failure.
Transparency	To maintain data integrity, the BC data is publicly available to all its peer nodes; within the UAV communication, making the data visible to all peers including UAVs, GCS, and users helps in taking appropriately real-time decisions.
Immutability	Immutability restricts the UAVs or peers to modify the recorded critical data.
Security and Privacy	BC secures UAV communication network by distributing the same data between all the peers in encrypted form, it would be difficult for an attacker to modify all instances of the encrypted data. Besides that, uses access control mechanisms and authentication procedures to provide data privacy and security.
Trust	The trust among the peer nodes (UAVs) in a BC network achieved using consensus mechanisms and smart contracts.
Traceability	Traceability is extreme important in identifying the malevolent nodes within UAVs network, BC keeps the complete information about the transaction, which guarantees the traceability characteristics.

In addition, the implementation of BC in UAV network prevents from various cyber-attacks as follows.

- **Data fabrication attack:** the use of consensus mechanisms and the immutability property of BC prevent from the data fabrication attack.
- **Eavesdropping attack**: the BC technology offers transaction and identity security with digital signature algorithms and cryptographic measures, which prevent from eavesdropping attack.
- **Distributed DoS attack:** BC is a full decentralized, it distributes the same content to a large number of nodes, which makes it difficult for malicious UAVs to execute DoS attack.
- **Jamming attack:** The SC concept in BC prevents from such attacks by letting only relevant data entered into the BC network.

BLOCKCHAIN SECURING UAVS-BASED-SYSTEMS

The distributed nature of a large-scale drone network faces many challenges, such as vulnerability to security threats and privacy leakage. To address these issues, the utilization of the BC technology to empower UAVs network has been adopted in several contexts and scenarios. In the following, this chapter pinpoints several systems and networks integrating UAVs and BC technologies.

Blockchain Assisted 5G/6G-UAV Networks

5G or 6G (Advanced cellular networks) and UAVs have a mutual relationship. Indeed, each technology can serve and offer advantages to the other technology. 5G or 6G technology is a promising solution providing connectivity between UAVs, between UAVs and the GCSs, or between groups of UAVs.

From the other side, UAVs can serve 5G or 6G networks. Thanks to their low-cost and flexible mobility, UAVs can serve as mobile switching centers or mobile base stations that improves the cellular network coverage and offers support for 5G infrastructure. Both UAVs and Cellular networks will be used to serve smart systems and smart applications such as the smart city scenario. In this case, other technologies are involved such as cloud computing and the fog/edge computing for data processing and storage. This heterogeneous communication environment is sensitive to trust and security issues. BC can be used to certify the identity of UAVs and to integrate UAVs with fog and cloud by ensuring data integrity and securing communication. Authors in (Aloqaily, M. et al, 2021) proposed design guidelines for BC-assisted 5G-UAV networks, with a focus on the smart city scenario. Figure 2 illustrates the system architecture integrating 5G, UAVs and BC as proposed by (Aloqaily, M. et al, 2021). BC authenticates communications among drones by tracking all their transactions, verifying data integrity and making verified data available to all network nodes. Service providers and UAVs need to execute smart contracts. In addition, authors in (Gupta, R. et al., 2021) proposed BC-based secure 6G-UAV network supporting various applications such as precision agriculture, surveillance, live streaming, law enforcement, traffic monitoring, and search and rescue... The proposed architecture by (Gupta, R. et al., 2021) is structured into five layers including (i) data sensing layer, (ii) communication layer, (iii) UAV layer, (iv) BC layer, and (v) application and control layer.

Figure 2. System Architecture Integrating BC-5G-UAVs
(Aloqaily, M. et al, 2021)

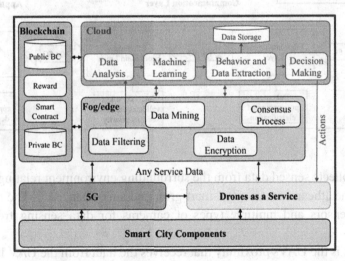

Recently, several other researchers contributed to this issue; in the following, this chapter highlights novel contributions related to the integration of BC with the cellular network to enable UAVs based systems:

Authors in (Han, T. et al., 2021) discussed the benefits to UAVs-enabled environments of using mobile edge computing with 5G communication networks; BC technology discussed as a novel approach ensuring the security of the whole environment. Authors in (Jian, X. et al., 2021) highlighted the role played by BC technology to empower trusted networking for UAVs in the B5G Era. In the same context, authors in (Wu, Y. et al., 2021) studied privacy considerations supporting 5G-enabled drone communications.

Besides, authors in (Gupta, R. et al., 2021) presented BC and AI integrated secure UAV networking architecture using 5G or 6G communications underlying diverse smart application scenarios providing security, transparency, reliability, intelligence, trust, flexibility, and efficiency to the UAV communication systems. The proposed communication architecture composed of five diverse layers (as illustrated in figure 3) including the UAV layer, edge-AI layer, application layer, BC layer, and communication layer.

Figure 3. System Architecture Integrating BC-5G-UAVs
(Gupta, R. et al., 2021)

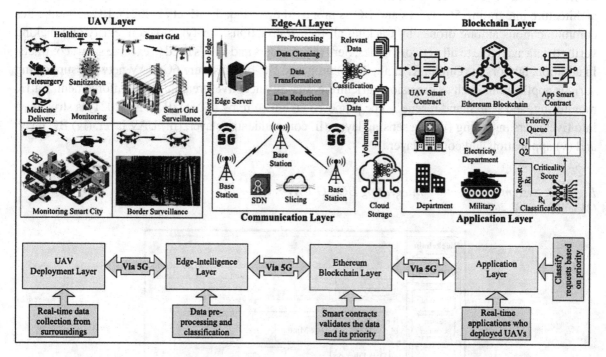

- **UAVs Layer**: collects sensed data from the surrounding environment relating to specific application scenarios (healthcare, smart city, smart grid, and surveillance…). The drones are equipped with multiple sensors and multiple types of cameras for data sensing from the surrounding environment.
- **Edge-AI Layer**: is the UAVs proximity that receives the data from the UAV layer. Edge-AI Layer assures the data storage, the data pre-processing and the dynamic decision and is mainly composed of high-end servers and storage. It integrates AI algorithms for data classification, Intrusion detection and decision-making.
- **Blockchain layer**: is a secure, immutable and transparent shared ledger. It stores the relevant data received from the edge-AI layer after pre-processing. It does not allow any data modification. Data are visible to all BC participating members. BC secures the data communication between the UAV layer and the application layer.
- **Communication layer:** This layer is responsible for providing connectivity and data exchange between UAVs and the GCS. Nowadays, the suitable networking technology is 5G or 6 G (ultra-

low latency, ultra-high reliability, high availability, high throughput and bandwidth, ultra density). Besides that 5G and 6G architecture are based on software-defined networking, virtualization, and network slicing, which facilitate UAVs network communication management.

- **Application layer:** This layer consists of diverse applications such as healthcare, smart grid, smart transportation, smart factories... In general, the communication layer should integrate network slicing-priority-based approaches to manage the quality of services and the quality of experiences related to the requirements of the diverse supported applications.

UAV Networks Based on Integration of SDN and Blockchain

The SDN paradigm separates the control plane from the data plane; SDN architecture has significant advantages in terms of scalability, flexibility, and programmability. SDN technology is very suitable for UAV networks. However, a centralized control plane will cause a single point of failure. A decentralized control based on the BC platform plane can be used to enhance the SDN networks robustness and to overcome the fragility of the SDN centralized control plane. In this context, authors in (Hu, N.et al., 2021) suggested a software-defined UAV network integrating SDN and BC technology. Figure 4 presents the suggested architecture by (Hu, N.et al., 2021), where the control plane is composed of multiple GCSs forming consortium BCs and adopting the practical Byzantine fault tolerance (PBFT) consensus algorithm. All GCSs share and synchronize control data based on the BC. The wireless links between ground stations and UAVs are via hyper-OpenFlow providing spectrum allocation, programmable traffic forwarding, event notification, and statistical reporting. To avoid malicious control nodes, an identity authentication mechanism is used between the data and the control planes.

Figure 4. UAV Networks based on Integration of SDN and Blockchain
(Hu, N.et al., 2021)

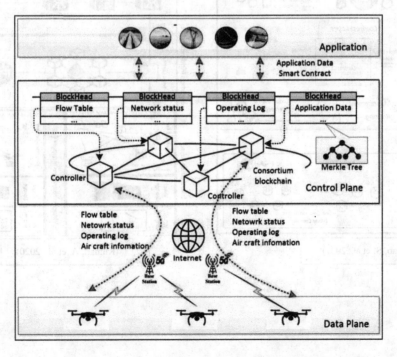

In the same context, authors in (Liao, S. et al., 2021) proposed the use of smart contracts and BC to ensure trusted collaboration between controllers of software-defined internet of drones (SD-IoD) dedicated to monitoring and supervising smart cities. Accordingly, the manifolds of their contributions are:

- A novel SD-IoD (see figure 5) architecture that enhances the support for flexibility and heterogeneity of IoD for environment monitoring;
- A new controller consortium BC for securing efficient cooperation and drone controllers interoperability including a new cryptographic currency cooperation coin and a new consensus mechanism proof of security guarantee (PoSG);
- A novel incentive mechanism to boost controllers to maintain their security and provide safer services to other controllers.

Figure 5 highlighted two architectures proposed by (Liao, S. et al., 2021) and (Kumari, A. et al., 2020).

Figure 5. Architecture of the BC-based Software Defined Internet of Drones
(Liao, S. et al., 2021)

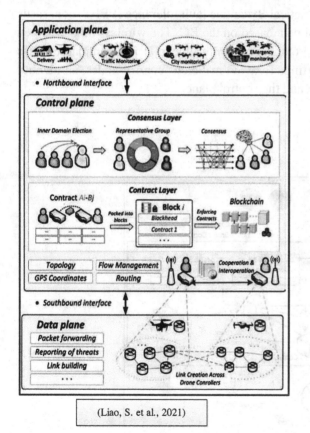

(Liao, S. et al., 2021)

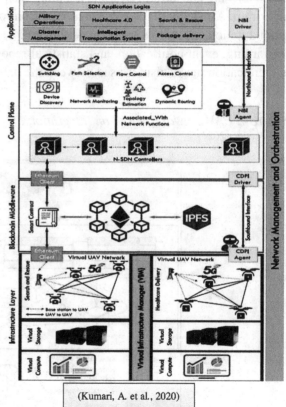

(Kumari, A. et al., 2020)

The SD-IoD architecture includes the application plane, control plane and data plane. The application plane integrates a variety of UAVs-assisted applications such as UAV delivery, UAV-assisted traffic monitoring system and UAV disaster relief in emergencies. SD-IoD. The control plane comprises drone controllers that are responsible for running control strategies and maintaining the network view. Each drone service provider manages task drones and multiple drone controllers. In addition, this plane includes two layers consensus layer and the contract layer as illustrated in figure 5. The data plane includes network devices such as provider's switches and various UAVs.

UAV Networks Based on Blockchain Toward Healthcare Systems

Healthcare is a vital concern for each nation growth and improvement. It is a critical and complex system involving several processes like medicines delivery, telemedicine practices and remote health monitoring. The healthcare ecosystem good governance makes it trustable, efficient, and effective. Besides that, Healthcare is a critical real-time application, where the delay and connectivity are the major constraints. In this regard, within the Healthcare 4.0 context, new researches proposed systems based on the integration of BC and UAVs toward an efficient and secure healthcare ecosystem. Indeed, authors in (Aggarwal, S. et al., 2021) studied the challenges and potentialities of BC-based UAVs for Healthcare 4.0 with a focus on designing a distributed P2P platform for UAVs that ensures integrity, confidentiality, identity management, and privacy preservation in healthcare 4.0. Besides that, during the coronavirus pandemic (COVID-19) UAVs represent a talented technology for fighting (COVID-19). Indeed, drones used to transport goods, medical supplies to a given target location in the quarantine areas, spraying disinfection and monitoring public space (such as absence mask identifying, maintaining social distance, infected case, scan identity…). Drone missions will rely on drone collaboration that necessitates that the UAVs be controlled in a decentralized fashion using the BC network. In this concern, authors in (Alsamhi, S. H. et al., 2021) proposed an architecture (see figure 6) integrating cooperative UAVs and BC to combat the COVID-19 pandemic.

Nowadays, outdoor health monitoring of ageing people is becoming a necessity authors in (Islam, A., & Shin, S. Y., 2019, July) proposed a BC-based secure scheme using UAV. In the proposed scheme, health data (HD) are gathered from user's wearable sensors and transmitted via UAVs to the nearest MEC server. Before to transmitting to MEC, HD are encrypted in order to provide protection against cyber threats. At the MEC, HD is diagnosed and if any abnormalities are found in the user's health, MEC server notifies the user and the nearest hospitals. When the processing is completed, HD are stored in BC with the consent of validators.

Blockchain Based Swarm UAV System Toward Crowd Monitoring

Intelligent UAV systems are becoming essential toward crowd monitoring to detect antisocial and abnormal behaviour. In this context, authors in (Xiao, W. et al., 2021) proposed a drone-swarm distributed monitoring system in a BC-powered network to monitor crowds, the architecture of the proposed system named USBCMS id represented by figure 7 and is structured into three layers: data layer, BC layer, and decision-making layer. The data layer collects monitoring data using the Internet of Things and swarms of UAV. The collected data transmitted via a 5G network to the edge cloud server (ECS) of the BC layer to storage the crowd monitoring data. Besides, the BC layer is also responsible for monitoring task distribution services. The decision-making layer integrates cognitive algorithm generated for data pre-processing and real-time analysis to detect violence in the crowd, estimate crowd quantity, and to analyze mass motion. The monitoring department (see figure 7) can access the monitoring data to monitor in real-time crowd status. In addition, smart contracts in USBCMS are two types: configuration contracts and functional contracts to monitor access transactions and data storage transactions.

Figure 6. BC-based Cooperative UAVs System to combat COVID-19
(Alsamhi, S. H. et al., 2021)

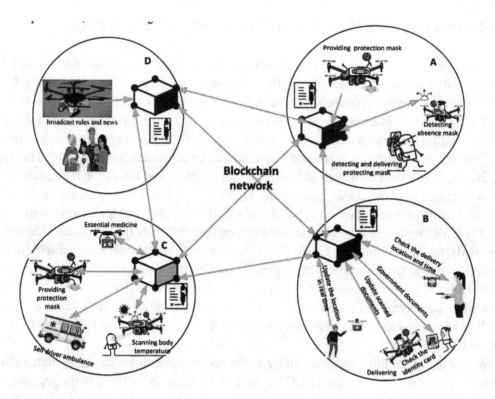

Blockchain-Based Task Offloading in UAVs Supporting Mobile Edge Computing

Nowadays, cloud providers offer task offloading as mobile edge computing (MEC) services for their customers. Several cloud providers use UAVs to cache data generated from IoT devices and forward this data to MEC servers. Authors in (Luo, S. et al., 2021) suggested a BC-based architecture of the decentralized offloading system. The architecture (illustrated in figure 8) includes three layers:

- **IoT layer**: The IoT devices usually have limited resources (memory, computational power, and energy storage), which needs the offloading task.
- **UAVs layer**: UAVs act as the offloading hubs for catching and forwarding the data from the IoT devices to the MEC servers to execute the offloaded tasks.
- **MEC servers layer**: In the MEC servers layer, a closed BC is set up among MEC servers for checking a service provider's honesty during a user data operation.

Figure 7. UAV Networks based on Integration of SDN and Blockchain
(Xiao, W. et al., 2021)

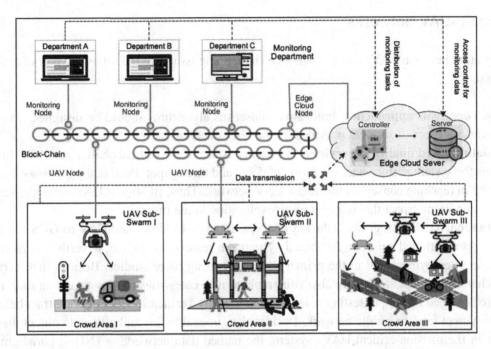

Figure 8. BC-Based Task Offloading in UAVs Supporting Mobile Edge Computing
(Luo, S. et al., 2021)

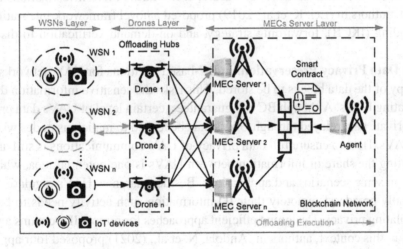

Edge computing resources need to be allocated efficiently between edge computing stations (ECSs) and UAVs in mobile networks. In this regards, authors in (Xu, H. et al, 2021) proposed a resource pricing and trading scheme based on Stackelberg dynamic game to allocate efficiently edge-computing resources between ECSs and UAVs. BC technology is integrated to record the entire resources trading process to protect security and privacy.

OPEN ISSUES AND FUTURE DIRECTIONS

Blockchain-UAV Networks

The integration between UAVs and BC still face challenging issues. In the following a brief description of such issues:

- **New consensus approaches**: Innovative consensus algorithms should be designed, considering the various types of services provided by the UAVs network.
- **Scalability and quality of services:** Scalability is one of the critical challenges of BC that influences the system performances in terms of delay and throughput. Poor scalability may lead to difficulty in reaching consensus forming a UAV network. Thus, BC-based UAV networks scalability is an important aspect that requires more exploration in the future.
- **Data security:** Data security is the key concern in UAVs-to-UAVs and UAV-to-GCS communication. As mentioned before, a BC-based system can resolve such issue, nevertheless its real-time efficient deployment still in the primary stage requiring more studies. Besides that, certain BC mechanisms and platforms are also vulnerable to new categories of threats and attacks. Besides, there is a need for proper testing solutions and security verification of smart contract before their deployment into the public network. Besides that, to enable fast and efficient content dissemination in the mission-critical-UAVs system, the named data networking (NDN) paradigm can be considered by adding caching mechanism within UAVs. However, this brings a new security challenge; for example, poisoned content can contaminate the cache on the routers and isolate valid content from the network. To countermeasure, such attacks more investigations are required. In this context, authors in (Lei, K. et al., 2019) proposed a novel framework integrating interest-key-content binding (IKCB), forwarding strategy, and on-demand verification to discover poisoned content.
- **Full UAVs Data Privacy Preservation**: In BC-based solutions for UAV networks, each UAV requires a copy of the data blocks to be stored. This risks the sensitive information dissemination to all participating UAVs. Although BC can guarantee a certain level of UAVs data privacy preservation, user private data relayed through UAVs may be leaked to malicious nodes who may compromise the UAVs. How to ensure full data privacy of UAV communications is still an open research issue. Limiting the share of information between UAVs is one potential idea, while this may not be possible in some scenarios and applications. Besides that, new UAVs regulations require UAV to periodically broadcast remotely their ID information such activity needs to be accomplished without violating privacy. Designing efficient approaches for remote ID remains an ongoing interest subject, in this context, authors in (Andola, N. et al., (2021) proposed four approaches to hide the UAV identity during the message exchanges using the BC, a non-interactive zero-knowledge proof with a bilinear map has been suggested to provide anonymity of UAV on the BC.
- **Energy efficiency:** UAVs are power-constrained devices with limited storage capacity and processing capabilities. BC-based UAV network requires more processing capabilities to execute SC and consensus algorithms on UAVs, which can generate a bottleneck in computation power. Miners (i.e., UAVs) consume a disproportionate amount of electricity when generating blocks; hence, existing UAVs may not have sufficient energy for blocks mining. Therefore, there is a need

for optimizing the UAV operations to avoid and reduce the bottleneck condition. In addition, there is a need for energy-efficient approaches and solutions.

- **Resource Constraints of UAVs**: Most existing UAVs have limited resources in terms of energy, computing, storage, size, and supported weight.... Consensus algorithms and encryption are required for BC systems; nevertheless, due to battery life and computational constraints, UAVs are in most cases incapable of computing-intensive tasks. Besides that, swarm and cooperative UAVs can gather gigabytes of data per second, whether the BC storage capacity can accommodate such a high data volume is still questionable, and how and whether to incorporate other storage resources such as edge or fog nodes with the UAV system remains an open challenge. In this context, recent works proposed Lightweight BC solutions to assist UAVs. Authors in (Wang, J. et al., 2021) developed and evaluated a lightweight BC to assist the swarm UAVs to enhance the routing security with constraints related to energy consumption and computation resources. Based on the traffic status, the swarm UAV A constructs consensus with Proof-of-Traffic (PoT).

- **Orchestration of various computing facilities**: Remote clouds, nearby edge and/or fog servers, UAVs, advanced cellular networks and other technologies, will become a necessity to integrate within BC-based UAVs communications, this leads to a new challenging issue regarding the orchestration of the diverse involved technologies.

- **Federated Learning (FL)**: Another interesting open issue is UAVs with Federated Learning (FL) functionalities. Indeed, advanced cellular networks offer the required infrastructure to run smart applications. UAVs can be used as relay devices close to end users to support edge servers and to forward messages. Implementing FL mechanisms in UAVs help in processing the collected data and sharing the learned model with the fog/cloud servers. However, this approach brings new constraints regarding UAV resources (computing, communication, and energy consumption, task scheduling that need more investigation. Authors in (Nguyen, D. C. et al., 2021) presented an overview on FLchain, an emerging paradigm in MEC empowered by the integration of BC and FL. FLchain enables scalable and secure edge intelligence in next-generation wireless networks. In addition, authors in (Pokhrel, S. R., 2021) suggested a joint FL and BC-based mobile computing system and developed an analytic framework to study the performance of data networking dynamics for LEOs constellation and a swarm of UAVs.

Blockchain Assisted 5G/6G-UAV Networks

The integration between advanced cellular network, UAVs and BC technologies empowers UAVs services and application via privacy, trust, security provisioning. This integration is useful in diversified application areas such as precision agriculture, healthcare, urban planning, military, sea communication, search and rescue and wildlife conservation... However, the integration of 6G and BC with the UAV network face new challenges. In the following, the assessed challenges:

- **Data type diversity**: Drones will exchange various types of messages within 5G/6G-UAVs networks, including data from the GCS to guide the UAVs to fulfil their tasks, data exchanged between UAVs, data gathered from IoT devices and data relayed from the cellular networks. This data type diversity requires the integration of advanced quality of services provisioning approaches. Besides that, some of the data may be too large to be stored in the BC efficiently or require frequent modification or deletion, off-chain BC storage should be deployed to solve this issue.

- **Implementing intelligent approaches**: Besides that, 6G communication technology would generate a gigantic amount of data, which necessitates big data analytics, machine learning deep learning, and techniques to process it into usable information. Therefore, the integration between UAVs, BC, cellular networks and intelligent approaches allows achieving a high intelligence and automation level that is the key to design advanced and novel services for smart systems. In this context, (Gumaei, A. et al, 2021) proposed a secure and intelligent 5G-enabled UAV identification and flight modes detection framework via integration of BC with a deep recurrent neural network (DRNN) and edge computing. Besides that, authors in (Gupta, R. et al., 2021) surveyed BC-based secure and intelligent UAV communication architecture underlying 5G network and artificial intelligence techniques. However, the contributions regarding this issue still limited and require more investigation.
- **Dense Networks:** The integration of a dense number of UAVs within cellular networks leads to various challenges such as channel selection, location identification, availability of a line of sight, and interference management.
- **Regulation and Standardization:** The regulation and the standardization activities related to the BC technology has not been completed yet by both IEEE and ITU as renowned standardization organizations. Thus, the integration of BC with the UAV is a big challenge facing both BC and UAVs. New proper rules, guidance and regulations should be established to decide which service providers may get access to the data in the BC and to regulate the safety and privacy related to the immersion of UAVs in smart systems. The mutual agreement should be defined to regulate the location and divisibility of services between the service providers. Without the BC technology standardization, it is relatively challenging to acquire BC in the real world for 5G/6G-UAVs networks.
- **Lack of 5G/6G infrastructure:** The integration of UAV, BC and 5G/6G can face UAV deployment issues due to the lack of 5G/6G communication infrastructure. The existing network devices and BC infrastructure may not be suitable for 6G communication systems due to high spectrum efficiency, extremely high data rates, frequency, and so on. First, the 6G infrastructure should be deployed, then, comes the UAV and BC integration. This would be a great challenge in terms of interconnectivity and costs.

CONCLUSION

UAVs play a prominent role in military and civilian usage, especially for complicated safety-critical missions and other diverse ranges of applications. Integrating UAVs with other advanced technologies such as BC technology, advanced cellular networks, fog and mobile edge computing, federated learning is a key concept to handle the needs and the requirements of smart applications. This chapter investigated and sketched the most relevant and recent BC-based UAVs solutions. Besides that, this chapter discussed various security concerns and attacks against UAV-based systems. In addition, this chapter assessed various open issues and research challenges regarding the integration of BC within UAVs.

REFERENCES

Aggarwal, S., Kumar, N., Alhussein, M., & Muhammad, G. (2021). Blockchain-Based UAV Path Planning for Healthcare 4.0: Current Challenges and the Way Ahead. *IEEE Network*, *35*(1), 20–29.

Aloqaily, M., Bouachir, O., Boukerche, A., & Al Ridhawi, I. (2021). Design guidelines for blockchain-assisted 5g-uav networks. *IEEE Network*, *35*(1), 64–71.

Alsamhi, S. H., Lee, B., Guizani, M., Kumar, N., Qiao, Y., & Liu, X. (2021). Blockchain for decentralized multi-drone to combat COVID-19 and future pandemics: Framework and proposed solutions. *Transactions on Emerging Telecommunications Technologies*, 4255.

Andola, N., Yadav, V. K., Venkatesan, S., & Verma, S. (2021). SpyChain: A Lightweight Blockchain for Authentication and Anonymous Authorization in IoD. *Wireless Personal Communications*, •••, 1–20.

Baird, L. (2016). *The swirlds hashgraph consensus algorithm: Fair, fast, byzantine fault tolerance.* Swirlds Tech Reports SWIRLDS-TR-2016-01, Tech. Rep.

Baird, L., Harmon, M., & Madsen, P. (2019). Hedera: A public hashgraph network & governing council. *White Paper, 1*.

Boursianis, A. D., Papadopoulou, M. S., Diamantoulakis, P., Liopa-Tsakalidi, A., Barouchas, P., Salahas, G., ... & Goudos, S. K. (2020). Internet of things (IoT) and agricultural unmanned aerial vehicles (UAVs) in smart farming: a comprehensive review. *Internet of Things*, 100187.

Brown, R. G., Carlyle, J., Grigg, I., & Hearn, M. (2016). Corda: an introduction. *R3 CEV*.

Chaari, L., Chahbani, S., & Rezgui, J. (2020, October). Vulnerabilities Assessment for Unmanned Aerial Vehicles Communication Systems. In *2020 International Symposium on Networks, Computers and Communications (ISNCC)* (pp. 1-6). IEEE.

Chen, J., Wang, W., Zhou, Y., Ahmed, S. H., & Wei, W. (2021). Exploiting 5G and Blockchain for Medical Applications of Drones. *IEEE Network*, *35*(1), 30–36.

Erdelj, M., Król, M., & Natalizio, E. (2017). Wireless sensor networks and multi-UAV systems for natural disaster management. *Computer Networks*, *124*, 72–86.

Erdelj, M., & Natalizio, E. (2016, February). UAV-assisted disaster management: Applications and open issues. In *2016 international conference on computing, networking and communications (ICNC)* (pp. 1-5). IEEE.

Erdelj, M., Natalizio, E., Chowdhury, K. R., & Akyildiz, I. F. (2017). Help from the sky: Leveraging UAVs for disaster management. *IEEE Pervasive Computing*, *16*(1), 24–32.

Gumaei, A., Al-Rakhami, M., Hassan, M. M., Pace, P., Alai, G., Lin, K., & Fortino, G. (2021). Deep Learning and Blockchain with Edge Computing for 5G-Enabled Drone Identification and Flight Mode Detection. *IEEE Network*, *35*(1), 94–100.

Gupta, R., Kumari, A., & Tanwar, S. (2021). Fusion of blockchain and artificial intelligence for secure drone networking underlying 5G communications. *Transactions on Emerging Telecommunications Technologies*, *32*(1), e4176.

Gupta, R., Nair, A., Tanwar, S., & Kumar, N. (2021). Blockchain-assisted secure UAV communication in 6G environment: Architecture, opportunities, and challenges. *IET Communications*.

Han, T., Ribeiro, I. D. L., Magaia, N., Preto, J., Segundo, A. H. F. N., de Macêdo, A. R. L., ... de Albuquerque, V. H. C. (2021). Emerging Drone Trends for Blockchain-Based 5G Networks: Open Issues and Future Perspectives. *IEEE Network*, *35*(1), 38–43.

Hentati, A. I., & Fourati, L. C. (2020). Comprehensive survey of UAVs communication networks. *Computer Standards & Interfaces*, *72*, 103451. doi:10.1016/j.csi.2020.103451

Hu, N., Tian, Z., Sun, Y., Yin, L., Zhao, B., Du, X., & Guizani, N. (2021). Building Agile and Resilient UAV Networks Based on SDN and Blockchain. *IEEE Network*, *35*(1), 57–63.

Islam, A., & Shin, S. Y. (2019, July). BHMUS: blockchain based secure outdoor health monitoring scheme using UAV in smart city. In *2019 7th international conference on information and communication technology (ICoICT)* (pp. 1-6). IEEE.

Jian, X., Leng, P., Wang, Y., Alrashoud, M., & Hossain, M. S. (2021). Blockchain-Empowered Trusted Networking for Unmanned Aerial Vehicles in the B5G Era. *IEEE Network*, *35*(1), 72–77.

Krichen, L., Fourati, M., & Fourati, L. C. (2018, September). Communication architecture for unmanned aerial vehicle system. In *International Conference on Ad-Hoc Networks and Wireless* (pp. 213-225). Springer. 10.1007/978-3-030-00247-3_20

Kumari, A., Gupta, R., Tanwar, S., & Kumar, N. (2020). A taxonomy of blockchain-enabled softwarization for secure UAV network. *Computer Communications*, *161*, 304–323.

Lei, K., Zhang, Q., Lou, J., Bai, B., & Xu, K. (2019). Securing ICN-based UAV ad hoc networks with blockchain. *IEEE Communications Magazine*, *57*(6), 26–32.

Liao, S., Wu, J., Li, J., Bashir, A. K., & Yang, W. (2021). Securing Collaborative Environment Monitoring in Smart Cities Using Blockchain Enabled Software-Defined Internet of Drones. *IEEE Internet of Things Magazine*, *4*(1), 12–18.

Luo, S., Li, H., Wen, Z., Qian, B., Morgan, G., Longo, A., ... Ranjan, R. (2021). Blockchain-Based Task Offloading in Drone-Aided Mobile Edge Computing. *IEEE Network*, *35*(1), 124–129.

MAVLINK. (2021). *MAVLink Common Message Set Specifications*. Available: https://mavlink.io/en/messages/common.html

Multichain. (2021). https://github.com/MultiChain/multichain

Nakamoto, S. (2008). *Bitcoin: A peer-to-peer electronic cash system*. https://bitcoin. org/bitcoin.pdf

Nguyen, D. C., Ding, M., Pham, Q. V., Pathirana, P. N., Le, L. B., Seneviratne, A., . . . Poor, H. V. (2021). *Federated learning meets blockchain in edge computing: Opportunities and challenges*. arXiv preprint arXiv:2104.01776.

Pokhrel, S. R. (2021). Blockchain Brings Trust to Collaborative Drones and LEO Satellites: An Intelligent Decentralized Learning in the Space. *IEEE Sensors Journal.*

Quorum. (2021). *Quorum Whitepaper.* https://github.com/ConsenSys/quorum/blob/master/docs/Quorum%20Whitepaper%20v0.2.pdf

Schneider, J., & Macdonald, J. (2016). *Technology and Adaptation on the Modern Battlefield: A Battlefield Perspective on the Adoption of Unmanned Aircraft.* Available at SSRN 2814202.

Shakhateh, H., Sawalmeh, A. H., Al-Fuqaha, A., Dou, Z., Almaita, E., Khalil, I., ... Guizani, M. (2019). Unmanned aerial vehicles (UAVs): A survey on civil applications and key research challenges. *IEEE Access: Practical Innovations, Open Solutions, 7,* 48572–48634.

Sharma, V., Srinivasan, K., Chao, H. C., Hua, K. L., & Cheng, W. H. (2017). Intelligent deployment of UAVs in 5G heterogeneous communication environment for improved coverage. *Journal of Network and Computer Applications, 85,* 94–105.

Shi, W., Zhou, H., Li, J., Xu, W., Zhang, N., & Shen, X. (2018). Drone assisted vehicular networks: Architecture, challenges and opportunities. *IEEE Network, 32*(3), 130–137.

Wang, J., Liu, Y., Niu, S., & Song, H. (2021). Lightweight blockchain assisted secure routing of swarm UAS networking. *Computer Communications, 165,* 131–140.

Wu, Y., Dai, H. N., Wang, H., & Choo, K. K. R. (2021). Blockchain-based privacy preservation for 5g-enabled drone communications. *IEEE Network, 35*(1), 50–56.

Xiao, W., Li, M., Alzahrani, B., Alotaibi, R., Barnawi, A., & Ai, Q. (2021). A Blockchain-Based Secure Crowd Monitoring System Using UAV Swarm. *IEEE Network, 35*(1), 108–115.

Xu, H., Huang, W., Zhou, Y., Yang, D., Li, M., & Han, Z. (2021). Edge Computing Resource Allocation for Unmanned Aerial Vehicle Assisted Mobile Network with Blockchain Applications. *IEEE Transactions on Wireless Communications.*

Zhang, S., Zhang, H., Di, B., & Song, L. (2019). Cellular UAV-to-X communications: Design and optimization for multi-UAV networks. *IEEE Transactions on Wireless Communications, 18*(2), 1346–1359.

Zhou, Z., Feng, J., Zhang, C., Chang, Z., Zhang, Y., & Huq, K. M. S. (2018). SAGECELL: Software-defined space-air-ground integrated movingcells. *IEEE Communications Magazine, 56*(8), 92–99.

KEY TERMS AND DEFINITIONS

6G Networks: In telecommunications, 6G is the sixth-generation standard currently under development for wireless communications technologies supporting cellular data networks. It is the planned successor to 5G and will likely be significantly faster and supporting such as virtual and augmented reality (VR/AR), ubiquitous instant communications, pervasive intelligence, and the internet of things.

Blockchain Network: It consists of a huge number of nodes, and each node on the network has the same status or information to avoid a single point of failure.

Blockchain Transaction: It is the process of data exchange between the nodes on the network. It includes the sender and receiver address for the authentication process. It identifies the transaction amount with the transaction identity number.

Consensus: A transaction in the blockchain is considered valid after the network participants have reached a consensus using a consensus algorithm.

Global Ledger: A global ledger is used to store the transaction history at each node on the blockchain network. Each node has its ledger that conserves the data from the first block to the latest block of the blockchain network.

Software-Defined Networking (SDN): Is an emerging architecture that is dynamic, manageable, cost-effective, and suitable for the high-bandwidth, dynamic nature of today's applications. SDN decouples the network control and forwarding functions enabling the network control to become directly programmable and the underlying infrastructure to be abstracted for applications and network services.

Unmanned Aerial Vehicles (UAVs): Commonly known as a drone, is an aircraft without a human pilot on-board. The flight of UAVs may operate under remote control by a human operator via a ground control station.

Chapter 8
Blockchain Technology for IoT:
An Information Security Perspective

Sasikumar R.
iD https://orcid.org/0000-0002-4656-6662
K. Ramakrishnan College of Engineering, India

Karthikeyan P.
iD https://orcid.org/0000-0003-2703-4051
Thiagarajar College of Engineering, India

Thangavel M.
iD https://orcid.org/0000-0002-2510-8857
Siksha 'O' Anusandhan (Deemed), India

ABSTRACT

In the internet era, data is considered to be the primary asset, and the host or applications in a network are vulnerable to various attacks. Traditional network architectures have centralized authority to provide authentication, authorization, and access control services. In this case, there is a possibility of data mishandling activities from the valuable information available in the given network application. To avoid this type of mishandling, a new technology came into existence known as blockchain. Implementing blockchain technology in the internet of things (IoT) will ensure data integrity, stability, and durability. The authors present a detailed investigation of various IoT applications with blockchain implementation. Blockchain-based mechanisms will improve the security aspects in the traditional network applications related to IoT like insurance policies claiming, personal identification, and electronic health records.

1. INTRODUCTION

The world recognizes Internet of Things (IoT) in the year 1999 by the British technology pioneer Kevin Ashton. It is the interconnected device, which is capable of gathering different types of data from various locations and communicate among themselves. It communicates and transfers data among the things in

DOI: 10.4018/978-1-7998-5839-3.ch008

peer to peer (P2P) manner. While enriching P2P communication, the workload among the things in the network will share with its neighbours. Involved devices may have differences in size, memory capacity, and processing capabilities. The main objectives of Internet-of-Things are 1) To gather valuable information from deployed location 2) Transform that information to centralized place without data loss 3) Above mentioned process is done without human intervention. IoT devices can be any devices that are capable of collecting and transforming data. For example, Smartwatches, Smartphones, Medical equipment, Environmental monitoring devices, Agricultural equipment, and many more. Communication among IoT devices is transmitted through a connected network topology.

Figure 1. IoT device example for Home automation

IoT is not a new technology; it is a combination of various traditional technologies like Wireless Sensor Network (WSN), Cloud computing, Big data analytics, Radio-Frequency Identification (RFID), Location-based services, and Automation. Internet of Things mainly deals with constraint devices. So it is unable to fulfil all the requirements like Storage capacity, Execution speed, Captured data Transferring capabilities, and Energy. In this case, Cloud computing will play a major part in IoT devices to provide a huge amount of memory for storage.

Every year millions of devices are connected through IoT across the globe. When thinking about millions of devices connected over the internet, People has to think about various issues with respect to information. Data integrity has to be improved and does redundancy should be minimized to maximize the storage capacity and increase the performance of data processing. Heterogeneity is one of the major issues while dealing with billions of devices, solution is cloud storage.

Constrained Application Protocol (CoAP) was proposed to solve the problem faced by constrained heterogeneous devices. To solve the energy consumption issues, Ultra Wideband technology has been used. With help of Blockchain technology, we can ensure the security and data reliability of IoT data.

1.1 Applications of IoT

Internet of Things comes forward in the day to day life activity, because of fast computing capabilities and accurateness of the result. In the following section, we are going to discuss some of the major applications of IoT (Lo.S.K et.al, 2019), which will take the majority of the part in our daily lifestyle.

a) Healthcare

A recent report from the United Nations predicted that there will be 2 billion older people by 2050, and many researchers report that around 89% of the senior people are living without help from their family. So it's very difficult for senior people to take care of themselves. IoT plays a major role in the Healthcare filed mainly for senior people, it provides medicals facilities as "Anywhere Anytime" to make them safe and comfortable in their life. For that purpose, many of the cheapest IoT sensors in the form of cost and size involved in this development. Most of the sensors are used as wearable, implanted, and ecological manner. RFID is one of the most important technologies used by IoT devices, for communicating with other devices, storing sensitive information, and tracking the living or nonliving objects in the world. An IoT sensor helps to identifying Glucose Level, Electrocardiogram Monitoring, Blood Pressure Monitoring, Body Temperature Monitoring and Oxygen Saturation Monitoring in Healthcare.

b) Transportation

IoT can change the current transport industry to the next level, making them by efficient use of data generated from sensors. It helps in the transportation industry by facilitating, traffic control system, Vehicle health monitoring, online reservation and booking system, Fleet management system, Self-controlling vehicle, and remote vehicle monitoring system. Some of the major benefits of IoT based transportation are: 1) It provides enhanced traveller experiences and accurate communication facilities. 2) It ensures safety to traveller by supporting weather monitoring facilities, vehicle to vehicle communication, current traffic, and health of vehicles. 3) Reduced energy utilization based on demand and supply mechanism. 4) This allows tracking real-time vehicle speed and location. 5) This ensures public safety assurance, disaster response, and rescue management.

c) Smart Cities

A smart city is considered by many researchers and corporate due to its inherent intelligence in trade with indescribable resource utilization and environment. Smart Cities require integrated intelligent sensors to operate efficiently (Jaoude et.al, 2019). Just imagine the integration of sensors to operate with energy consumption meter, water supply, traffic flows and parking, environmental pollution monitoring, security cameras on the street, supermarket, public transportation facilities, waste management system, and more.

d) Supply Chain Management

It is a process of tracking the raw materials from an organization to delivering a product to the customer. It enables the timely delivery of the product to the customer and improvement of accuracy. It reduces the investment cost for both manufacturers and retailers. SCM has three flow of its process: 1) Materials and Product flow 2) Information flow 3) Finance flow. Integration of IoT with supply chain management provides, where goods are available and how they are stored, when those goods will reach specified location, real-time inventory visibility, and monitoring. Some of the use cases are: Manufactures can detect faulty materials using IoT enabled cameras, Food retailers can check the temperature and humidity of place where food is currently available, Farmer can detect the soil condition to decide the optimum time to plant or harvest.

1.2 IoT Data Breach/Theft Attacks in Identified Applications

a) Smart Healthcare

IoT sensors play a major role in the smart healthcare application to monitor and take necessary action for patient health conditions. Those devices do their routine activities like patient health information collection and transforming those data to the storage location for taking necessary action. It is important to be acquainted with security requirements, vulnerabilities, and countermeasures. Here, it is possible to affect the overall process of healthcare by stealing/modifying the health data of the patient by the adversary (Tang.W et.al, 2019). Based on the above information attack can be classified into the following categories:

- **Denial of Services** – The attacker purposely creates unnecessary traffic in the communication channel to disturb the data transmission in the network. In the other side, accessing the protected information without having proper access rights. These activities will lead to insecurity for the patient information and improper treatment.
- **Router Attack** – Data transmission route plays a vital role in the medical field. In the Healthcare system, many of the sensors are based on wireless. During transmission, the attacker may create unnecessary traffic, which leads to unnecessary delay.
- **Selective Forwarding Attack** – This type of attack is very dangerous to the healthcare filed. In this type, the attacker will hack one or more sensors in the system. After compromising the sensor he/she will drop some of the packets, remaining information will pass on to the servers. This will misguide the treatment of the patient.

b) Transportation

IoT brings many advantages to the transportation system and also brings some challenges while implementing smart transportation (Wang.K et.al, 2018). Organization can track the following: Speed of the vehicle, live location using GPS, Transports idle condition. The following section includes challenges of Transportation:

- **Limited Connectivity** – Number of connectivity increases, many of the vehicles are not having capabilities to update their sensors software up-to-date, which leads to malfunctioning of devices.
- **Security breaches** – When increasing number of devices, it is tedious task to manage and monitor the entire devices. We must protect all the data generated by enormous number of appliances in the network.
- **Access control and Device authentication** - Access control mechanism should be adopted with users communicating with these sensors. This access control is based on a dynamic approach (i.e) User's List. Sensors must transmit data to authenticated devices in an encrypted format.
- **Network Attacks** –The attacker can stop the entire communication of the network. Due to network attacks transportation cost will increase, more fuel utilization, which reduces the safety of traveller.
- **Insufficient privacy protection** – Personal records are stored in the devices, it may be used by unauthorized users.

c) Smart Cities

Fast growth in the implementation of IoT helps to form the connected network in the smart cities, starting from smart meter to building, from traffic signals to parking lots and from garbage collection to the environmental pollution monitoring systems. There are many numbers of potential vulnerabilities and malicious activities (Falco.G et.al, 2018). Here we have pointed out common security threats and data breaches:

- **Eavesdropping** – Many numbers of sensors and its communication involved in the smart cities. Eavesdropping captures the network traffic and trying to listen to multiparty communication to trap the configuration information.
- **SQL Injection Attack** – Attacker trying to insert SQL query on the client request to the application for performing an insert or delete or modifying the original data available in the database.
- **Distributed Denial of Service** – The attacker tries to send multiple requests from end sensor/user to utilize the more bandwidth of the network for overloading. In such case, entire network will become slower.

d) Supply Chain Management

IoT is being used in many industries to secure supply chain management. Communication happening in the form of 1) interaction between device and supplier 2) supplier to supplier 3) device to device (Omitola et.al, 2018). Security is essential in any form of electronic communication including IoT devices and infrastructures. IoT devices and infrastructure may face several attacks, if those attacks are not handled appropriately it leads, danger to human, physical damages, and operational disturbances. The vulnerabilities of IoT based supply chain are:

- **People, Policy and Procedure vulnerability** – Policy and procedures are formulated by the organization. People involving in the process are trained to follow the framed policies and procedures. Inefficient approach and system take into security risk.

- **Software/firmware vulnerabilities** – All the components involved in the supply chain process are based on software. Software design, development, and deployment must be carefully intended. Errors in any one of the stages will allow the adversaries to access Supply Chain System.
- **Tampering proof of Work** –In between at any point of operation, the original information can be modified to misuse the entire operation.
- **Mal-hardware insertion** – In the assembly section of the product, the hardware may function improperly. It leads to disturbance of the entire process also it may happen due to internal attack.

1.3 IoT Security Essentials for Identified Applications

a) Smart Healthcare

One of the most important devices used by healthcare for data communication and storage is RFID. It enables communication between RFID-tags and RFID-readers. The following security requirements must be provide for communication.

1. **Mutual Authentication**- Before enabling communication between the sender and receiver, the process must ensure the mutual authentication between parties.
2. **Confidentiality and Anonymity**- The confidential information stored on the sensing device must be kept securely. Before transmitting, the information should be encrypted using any lightweight cryptography algorithms to ensure confidentiality.
3. **Self Healing** – Devices used for monitoring patient data may fail due to hardware failure or low energy. In this case, network devices should be capable to handle current situation.
4. **Computational Limitations** – IoT sensors are constrained devices, so these devices must be providing lightweight security mechanisms to minimize resource consumption and maximize security.
5. **Data Freshness** – Sensors and devices generated data must be a very recent one for providing better treatment.

b) Transportation System

Integration of transportation with IoT provides accurate communication facilities and location information, superior customer services, improved life of vehicle, accurate understanding and information of transits, autonomous vehicles, reduces traffic, and improved fuel utilization. To achieve the above advantages, the system needs following security essentials:

1. **Physical security, Access control, and Security measure** – Traffic and Vehicle management systems need proper Access-control mechanisms to restrict unauthorized access. Physical security is essential for both physical assets and digital assets.
2. **Developing Secure and Private Communication channel** – To avoid cyberattack on the public communication channel need to develop secure communication channel. In V2V communication, attacker can compromise the digital assets of the transport. To avoid such attacks need encryption-based communication channels.

c) Smart Cities

IoT technology and wireless connectivity together brings technology-enabled cities in the human lifecycle. This moves traditional city life into next-generation intelligent cities (Shen.M et.al, 2019). Following security requirements are necessary to implement smart cities:

1. **Firmware integrity and Security Boot** – Security boot is an approach, It utilizes cryptographic code for signing techniques. It ensures the code is executed by a device that data generated other authorized devices or trusted parties.
2. **Security Monitoring and Analysis** – In this approach, it captures the entire data from the end device to transforming information over the communication channel for analysis of the security violation. Once the malicious activities detected, the entire network policies should be executed to quarantines affected devices/users.
3. **Secure Authentication and Access Control** –The main objective of this Authentication should be to determine the right user on the right device at right time.
4. **Availability and Integrity** – Smart cities works based on real-time data. Without these data not possible to operate smart-city functionalities.

d) Smart Supply-chain

All major logistics providers and investors are faced with cybersecurity risk at securing the private data, investing time, resources. Due to security attacks, logistics providers and suppliers will face the loss of private information, increasing of investing cost, and increase process time. So it's time to address the cyber-security on supply-chain.

1. **Protection against Software/Firmware vulnerabilities** –Hackers could be embedded in their malware into this firmware; it works as spying on our device activity. So its role in the hardware industry to resist their hardware against malware and provide regular updates to their devices.
2. **Prevention against People/Policy/Procedure vulnerability** – Providing effective training to the staff on the latest cybersecurity risk and how to protect against them.
3. **Detection of malfunction hardware-** Devices may be executing vulnerable instruction due to failure condition or deployment of unauthorized devices inside network/software issue.
4. **Device Connectivity issue** – Before implementing any services on the network must be analyzed. Whenever adopting a new device to the network, the performance and security must be consulting with technology providers for moving devices in a too-long way.

1.4 Blockchain Technology Need in Identified Applications

This section describes how blockchain technologies provide a smart way for identified above applications (Miraz.M.H et.al, 2020).

a) Smart Healthcare

Implementing blockchain technology in the healthcare application will support to provide many advantages. It addresses for various attacks, availability and exchange of patient information.

- **Health Information Exchange and Interoperability** - In the traditional method of treatment, Electronics Health Records (EHR) limit within the particular sickbay alone, not easily share with others. As a result, a patient faces a lot of challenges in the sharing of authorized data to other consulting doctors (Zhou.T et.al 2019). Blockchain technology enables a new way of sharing authorized information worldwide. With the help of the distributed nature of blockchain technology, it provides patient information to consulting doctors even though it faces DoS attack. It ensures the availability of data at any point in time.
- **Secure and Trustable EHR sharing** - Blockchain enables timestamp-based data sharing and monitoring of clinical information with the help of Proof-of-Concept consensus protocols.
- **Information Privacy** – Even though blockchain is distributed in nature and information is publicly available, it uses the asymmetric strong cryptographic algorithm for ensuring the privacy of stored information. Private Keys helps to get data from blockchain for valid users. Mainly it uses homomorphic encryptions like Zero-Knowledge Proofs and zk-SNARKs.

b) Transportation Application

Blockchain has solutions to the transportation system faced over many decades; it supports organizational cost-saving and internet-based accurate tracking of transportation orders. Due to inefficient existing transportation methods, many companies are ready to join in blockchain-based transportation and logistics industry.

- **Reliability of Tracking** –Current systems do not support providing these data due to manipulation or false impression. Blockchain technology provides immutable data storage for increased reliability.
- **Tracking vehicle performance history** – The performance of vehicle can be monitor from unaltered transaction ledger.
- **Vehicle to Vehicle communication** – Many companies are already implementing v2v communication, which enables one vehicle can share its information to other for safety aspects and fuel efficiency. This information can be stored in the blockchain to enlarge the transportations industry to the next level.
- **Cut Costs and Eliminate Middlemen** – Quite possibly the most powerful methods of blockchain technology is "Smart-contract", which eliminates the middle man in the progress and self-executing instructions, based on the some conditions.

c) Smart Cities Application

Transformation of traditional cities into the next milestone with the help of the IoT. These systems require a database to store and manipulated the data generated by the above technology. In this case, blockchain will help well than a traditional database to improve the efficiency, security, and transparency of the operations.

- **Integrity over the information** – In this technology, integrity can be enforced by implementing the encryption technique over the communicating.
- **Direct communications** – Blockchain makes communication between the public and government/authorities directly without any intermediaries. This process will speed up communication, reduces waiting or approval times.
- **Increased Transparency and efficient management** – Entire operation happening in this progress will be transparent to the public and government, so no one can modify the value or process.
- **Real-Time information** – This technology enables the availability of real-time information over the network. In the distributed ledger, any authorized user can access real-time information with their identity.

d) Smart Supply Chain Management

Traditional supply-chain traceability methodology does not guarantee consistency, transparency, scalability, and accuracy of entire process. In the flow of supply-chain, every time resources move from one hand to another hand need to create a block on the blockchain to store material information, timestamp information, cost of a product from raw materials to product delivery. Blockchain technology provides more accuracy and transparency.

- **Interoperability** –Information sharing reduces delays and avoids fraudulent activities. All the progress in the supply chain can be tracked in real-time, it reduces the deficiency rate.
- **Tamper-proof Records and Smart-Contracts** – Anyone trying to tamper in supply chain records can detect easily. Smart contracts are automatically triggered based on need in the supply will reduce the waiting time and simplify the work.
- **Preventing Data-breach** – Supply chain has security risk at manufactured goods containment to stealing due to unproductive transparency. Blockchain technology helps to prevent implementing transparency from all corners.

2. BACKGROUND

Researchers say About 31 billion devices are connected via IoT in the year 2021. Every year this number will increase tremendously. Many research says, by the year 2025 one trillion devices will be connected to IoT. The author says this count will become very high if the internet world implements 5G technology. While discussing numerous devices generated data, it needs to be maintained with high security and privacy. In traditional methodologies, the centralized method used for maintaining that confidential information. It may be vulnerable to unauthorized access and data unavailability. Each node is possible of failure, it leads to data unavailability due to DoS attack. Cyberattack is the major problem, the originality of data can be modified by Attacker, and it creates very serious issues in the future. To address the above problems, blockchain technology play major role in that.

2.1 What Is Blockchain?

Blockchain technology is immutable, distributed in nature, and provides better reliability and availability of information. Blockchain is a public ledger, anyone can read the values of a block in a chain, but none of them will allow doing the modification. One member in the network will create a block for storing transactions, this block will be verified by other members on the same network. Once the network members agreed the above block will be added to the existing chain. Block stores various transaction details like timestamp, participating member's details. To distinguish one block from others, it uses a unique code called "hash". Hashes are a unique code generated by special cryptography algorithms. Initially this technology successfully implemented on the various Crypto-currencies. Table-1 lists outs the Applications where this technology has been applied for providing better performance. Here we mentioned familiar applications; it can extend many more applications too.

Table 1. Applications of blockchain technology

Sl No.	Name of the Applications
1.	Cryptocurrency
2.	Finance Sector's
3.	Internet of Things
4.	Smart Appliances
5.	Healthcare
6.	Government Land Registration Process
7.	Certification maintenance by Universities
8.	Supply-chain management sector

2.2 Working Principles of Blockchain

Blockchain is nothing but a sequence of blocks working together, helps to store data with immutable characteristics. To link or insert a new block to the chain following four activities to happen (Reiff, Feeb-2020). First, to create a block transaction should be happened, which states that some operation must take place in the event. Second, the above transactions must be approved by other members of the network. Third, once approved by the network members particular block will be inserted onto the existing chain with a unique identity. Fourth, this block will be reflected in every member's chain. Every block on the chain will get unique hash value, these hash not only depending on the current block transactions also it includes previous block hash value. Blockchain itself renews its structure for every 10 minutes.

2.3 Components Blockchain and Its Functionalities

A blockchain is a type of spreadsheet holding transaction details. The hash value is a combination of numbers and alphabets. In cryptocurrency, the size of the block will be 1MB. When a user creates a new transaction, that Tx will be recorded (called as mined) on a particular block with the help of consensus algorithms. A block on a blockchain can hold 4-7 transaction. The size of the block can be increase to a larger one; the block can hold more number of transactions in a block.

Table 2. Components in blockchain structure

Name of the Components	Description
Hash value of the Block	Hash value of the current Block
Previous Hash value	Hash value of the Previous Block
Nonce	Random number, Helps to achieve the target value
Block Number	It denotes the order of the block in the current chain
Timestamp	Date and Time of Block creation
Transaction Details	Transaction information

Each transaction has its unique identification number within this block. Figure-2 shows the structure of the Blockchain (Nofer.M et.al, 2017).

Every block contains the following particulars in it:

1. **Hash value of block:** By using hash algorithm this value is generated for every block. While generating a hash value for a particular block, it uses data in the block and previous block hash value.
2. **Previous hash value:** It maintains a hash value of the previous block in a network. The previous hash value of Genesis block is "00000000".
3. **Nonce:** Nonce is expanded as "Number only used once". It is a random number used by a blockchain to increase the difficulty level and helps for improving security.
4. **Timestamp:** Date and Time are monitored with the help of an internal clock. It ensures the transactions "proof of integrity". The transaction timestamp should be within some intervals. Otherwise completed work will be removed from the block.
5. **Transaction details:** It keeps the record of the transaction in a particular block.

Figure 2. Structure of blockchain

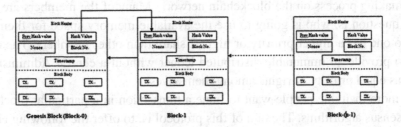

The initial block of any blockchain network is called "Genesis Block". When calculating a hash value for this block, it takes an argument for the hash algorithm is data of this block and "00000" as the previous hash value. Every block in the chain refers to the hash value of the previous block. Miners want to mine a new block need to satisfy the target value within the stipulated time. A consensus algorithm helps to mine a new block in the blockchain structure.

2.4 Merkle Tree

Blockchain has many numbers of blocks and each block has its transaction. In this case, it is very difficult to verify all the transactions. The verification process alone consumes more execution time and storage capacity. To resolve those issues, the Merkle tree has implemented in Blockchain technology. This mathematical model executes the verification process as soon as possible and produces with high accuracy. It uses some of the familiar hashing algorithms like MD5/SHA-3/SHA-256. Every transaction is paired with some other transaction to form the Merkle root, follows the concept of the binary tree. Each node must have two leaves and every transaction will generate its encrypted value using Hash algorithm. Once encrypted value achieved, then the leaves are paired to make a new root for those transactions. This process will be continued until the single root is achieved. This scenario will be shown in Figure-3.

Figure 3. Structure of Merkle Tree Root

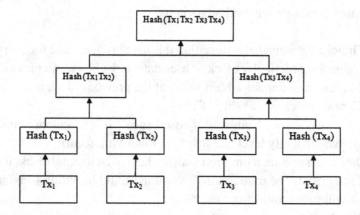

2.5 Consensus Protocols

It is a decision making process on the blockchain network. Many of the members are involved in this chain. Now the question is, who is going to use the available memory space for their transaction? In this structure, no one has a higher priority or highest share than other members. The objective of this technology is, to provide an immutable distributed ledger without a central Administrator/owner. So now everyone has equal priority or rights among themselves.

In this case, more than one people want to mine a transaction in a particular block, which will be resolved by consensus algorithms. The aim of this protocol is, to offer the following credentials to the members:

- Equal rights
- Co-Operation
- More members participation

- Decision making
- Conclusion

Various types of consensus algorithms available for blockchain technology. Algorithms can be decided depending upon the Application domain, Availability of resources, Time consideration, and processing speed. The performance of the mining process is measured based on the hash rate. Most familiar consensus algorithms are listed here (Lo.S.K et.al, 2019):

1. **Proof-of-Work(PoW)** - Anyone can mine a new block if miners will be capable of solving the puzzle within the stipulated period. More than one person solved the puzzle within the period, the mining process allowed based on their mining power.
2. **Proof-of-Stake(PoS)** –In this method, who has more coin with their wallet, chances of mining are very high.
3. **Byzantine Fault Tolerance-** During the voting time some nodes may become failure or malfunctioning. In this situation, this method will help us to continue the mining process without any delay.
4. **Proof-of-Activity(PoA)-** It inherits the characteristics of PoW and PoS.
5. **Proof-of-Capacity (PoC)-** Improved version of PoS. The nonce value is used for achieving the target hash value. With the help of transaction ID and nonce value can reach the target hash within the time duration.
6. **Proof-of-Burn-** Here miners will spend some amount for the transaction. This amount will be credited to the Eater side. On the Eater side, there is no private key to access those burnt coins. Once the miner mined the block can get some reward for mining the new block. In future miners able to get more money for this transaction. More number of algorithms explains in the Table 3.

The most common security threat for these consensus mechanisms is a 51% attack. In this type of attack will happen on the private network or the limited number of miners involved during mining process. And one more attack faced by any cryptocurrency is "Double spending" (Lee.Y et.al, 2020). Double spending, nothing but the same digital currency is spending for more than one transaction, to different purposes. To solve this issue, transactions will be placed in the mining pool for execution, (i.e) unconfirmed transactions. The first transaction will be validated, on the confirmation, it will be placed on the block. The second transaction will be invoked from the unconfirmed transaction, and then it will be rejected due to invalid.

2.6 Smart Contracts

The smart contract is a system protocol, which is digital facilitation to execute, verify, negotiation, and improving the performance of Blockchain technology without any intermediate authorities (Christidis.K et.al, 2016). Defined as "a computerized transaction protocol that executes the terms of a contract". This concept initially used by Bitcoin communities for transferring currencies. It needs permissioned, pre-written statement with an exact sequence of execution. Execution order must be mentioned very carefully, otherwise, execution will happen with the wrong answer. Generally, a contract has two attributes namely "state" and "value". It works like "IF…THEN" statement. Once the triggering statements are agreed by community members, it will be broadcast into the network and inserted into the particular block in the chain.

In addition to that, we can include the "WHEN" condition on the execution statements, can be Timestamp (or) particular state. According to the execution model of smart contracts stages are categorized into:

1. Discovery and Negotiation
2. Learning and self-description
3. Deployment and Development
4. Execution, Billing and Penalty services
5. Termination

Figure 4. Life-cycle of Smart contracts

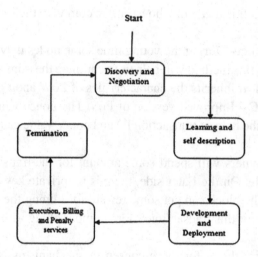

2.6.1 Challenges of Smart Contracts

Smart contracts work on distributed ledger, faces a lot of problems during executions of its predetermined instructions. Here, we have listed some of major issues:

1. **Mining order of transaction on the Block** - Every block has its own number of transactions in it. During simultaneous transaction, the miner can alter that order of transaction for writing on a block. It leads to invalidating the forthcoming valid transaction.
2. **Transaction leads to an unhandled exception** – Both caller and callee must be ensured the successful execution of the contract. If not checked properly, this will become the unhandled exception.
3. **Immutable bugs** - Stored information's are ineradicable. Suppose any improper implementation happened after the execution of contracts, it is unable to revoke the work.
4. **Performance issue** – Memory utilization is very high, possible to create bottleneck due to make multiple copies, Limited scalability.
5. **Privacy issue** – In this approach, both contract information and transaction data are publicly available.

2.7 Blockchain for IoT Applications

Blockchain is considered an innovative technology for smart healthcare domains. This technology helps to improve the availability, security, and privacy or transparency of healthcare system. IoT based health-care technology would be a more powerful and successful one. This technology helps to add force to traditional smart transportation systems. To eradicate fault or scam and improve security and privacy, IBM introduced blockchain-based transportation. A smart city uses digital technology to improve the effective functioning, share the information for quality improvement. Blockchain-based smart cities, sense and manage the data securely and effective utilization of resources in an economic way. The main objectives of supply-chain systems are to satisfy the customer requirements with quality and accuracy, cost reduction, traceability of products in a safer way. Blockchain technology facilitates for a supply-chain system with traceability, immutability, and distribution.

3. SECURITY CHALLENGES OF IOT AND INTEGRATION OF BLOCKCHAIN TECHNOLOGY

3.1 IoT Security Challenges in Healthcare

Dhillon et.al (2018) proposed innovative way of healthcare technologies helps the patient can have their healthcare services from their residence. To implement these facilities patient medical information must be recorded on the cloud environment for accessing remotely. To ensure authentication and efficiency the authors proposed ECC based multifactor authentication mechanism. A proposed system checks the timestamp to protect from integrity attacks, otherwise, communication data will be getting altered. By providing a unique private key to the communication parties system will protects from DoS and DDoS attacks. IoT based cloud storage is an open environment for all, it is easy for compromise attack, this architecture facilitates mutual authentication between Medical expert and cloud server to resist compromise attacks.

Duraiswamy et.al (2019) proposed security architecture for protecting patient data against cyber-attacks and improve performance. In this system, authentication helps to continuously monitor the patient even in the nonclinical situation. Architecture designed for protects from both passive and active attacks. Mutual authentication used to resist tampering or unauthorized access to patient records. A session key, unique pseudo-identity, sequence number, and hashing mechanism used for protection from various cyber-attacks.

Deebak et.al (2019) applied Anonymous Biometric Authentication Scheme for resolving privacy issue. Healthcare systems are vulnerable to an insider attack, forgery attack, user anonymity attack, and various cyber-attacks. One-way hash function approaches used to avoid legitimate user attack, for privacy concerns. The proposed system uses symmetric key based biometric to prevent illegal access to a user's identification. This session key is derived from the mathematical calculation as independently.

Tang.W et.al (2019) implements a data aggression scheme for collecting patient's medical information and provides confidentiality, protection against various cyber attacks. This system combines the "Boneh-Goh-Nissim Cryptosystem and Shamir Secret Sharing" to maintain data secrecy and fault tolerance. The proposed architecture provides fault tolerance of healthcare data using the shared secret key and sub secret key.

3.2 IoT Security Challenges in Smart Transportation

Wang.K et.al (2018) proposed a new approach for avoiding jamming and eavesdropping attack between sensors and remote controllers. This system simulated using two algorithms "stochastic algorithm with feedback and renewed intelligent simulated annealing". Here two antenna models used for transmission: Single antenna model and Multi-antenna model. Usually, Malicious jammers select optimal power strategies to increase the side effect of any sensors. Proposed architecture applies a stochastic algorithm with feedback algorithms to select an appropriate optimal strategy to avoid jamming and eavesdropping.

Riahi Sfar.A et.al (2019) enforces game theory-based approaches between actors to enable privacy and protect against various attacks. The main aim of this system is to protect against location tracking of vehicles and break forward secrecy. It consists of two actors involved in the data transformation. Players are "Data Holder" (DH) and "Data Requestor" (DR).

Chen.Q et.al (2019) proposed this model for reducing accident happens due to threads and physical individual protection. Proposed system use "Driver behaviours prediction & S2 module", this module designed based on biometric access control. An attacker can steal this biometric information from drivers, so to avoid these attacks proposed model uses the following machine learning algorithms: Hidden Markov Model, K-means clustering cross-validation, and support vector machine. Machine learning algorithm helps to become aware of authorized driver's characteristics and behavioural.

Eiza.M et.al (2017) describes and presented various threats and its countermeasures of automated vehicles. Automotive vehicles are operated with various sensors and electronics boards embedded with programming code. The attacker can exploit the systems through USB, Bluetooth, DSRC, OBD, and many more. To protect from various types of attacks providing one solution is not possible. So this operation can be done with multiple layers concepts. Secure OTA approach proposed for updating the most recent patches required by sensors.

3.3 IoT Security Challenges in Smart Cities

Falco.G et.al (2018) model uses, Heart of the smart cities is CCTV, electric grids, water networks, and transportation systems. All the sensors must be work properly and taken care should be done against cyber attacks. Many governments are feeling that smart city components are under high risk and difficult to identify which component affected by what types of vulnerabilities. To overcome these issues the authors proposed AI-based techniques to generate the automated generation of the tree to identify the risk and structures. The objective of the tree is to trace the affected device and leaves of the attacked system. The main advantage of this model is time consumption compared to manual tree generation.

Xu.C et.al (2019) proposes a strategy against DDoS attack in a smart city is SDNFV. The objective is to reduce the load of the Software-Defined Network. To protect against DDoS, attack model is defined into three modules "Attack trigger module", "attack detection module", and "attack backtracking module". Responsible for attack trigger module is, while abnormal transmission happens in the communication it sends an alert message to attack detection module. The attack detection module detects the traffic flow and forwarded it to the backtracking model. The backtracking module identifies the source generating DDoS attack.

Mohammad.N (2019) proposed a model to identify various cyber-security vulnerability and then assessed properties of those vulnerabilities. This system comprises of the three-layered model. In the first layer, ensures authentication and encryption process to avoid unauthorized access. But in this layer not protects from component level attacks. In addition to first layer activity, the second layer provides some of the tools and firewalls to protect and monitor malicious activity. The third layer called attack defense module plays an important role in cyber attacks. This model designed based on Markov Decision Process (MDP) because of the dynamic nature of attackers.

Badii.C et.al (2020) implements a framework called Snap4City. This framework provides full-stack security from IoT Devices to cloud storage including IoT edge. Authentication is ensured with the help of the Single Sign-On (SSO) module, which is a centralized approach. On the edge, the part has powerful processing capabilities, which take care connections and authentication works. Snap4City provides authentication and authorization using a user registry. This user registry managed by LDAP and CRM.

3.4 IoT Security Challenges in Supply-Chain Management

Omitola et.al (2018) used the iPhone/Apple supply chain for identifying vulnerabilities and attacks. The authors classified vulnerabilities into four categories depending upon the IoT ecosystem. Those are policy and procedure vulnerabilities, software vulnerabilities, network vulnerabilities, and gateway vulnerability. Likewise, attacks are classified into malicious insertion, exploitation of vulnerabilities, and Noncyber attacks. Insertion of malicious viruses can be done at any point in the supply chain lifecycle. These attacks are not possible to detect until proper observation of entire activities. The exploitation of malware may affect in the commercial sectors.

Chamekh.M et.al (2018) proposes a architecture to improve the issues of P2P communication using Merkel-Tree, it helps to improve scalability and key management. Proposed architecture designed using a hierarchical structure. In structure, each company can be built its own tree and nodes. While creating a node, each node will get a unique hash through that the hosting company can identify every node in the supply chain system. The tree structure has two identity Intra tree and Inter Tree. Each tree can be in a different phase in a different tree.

Hiromoto.R.E et.al (2017) designed a architecture using DANN. This machine-learning algorithm helps to analyze the behaviours of the system. These categories into two sub-networks, the First model represents normal data, and the second one used to become aware of abnormal behaviours caused by vulnerabilities. DANN is embedded with the hardware. It helps to monitor temperature instability, heat generation of components, component vibration including cryptography attacks. A Synchronous LGDM approach used to generate a data flow precedence graph helps to predict the balancing data flow in the supply chain.

Zhou.W et.al (2018) uses, RFID based framework for healthcare supply, to learn and progress automatically based on the environmental deviations. The reasons for motivating the authors to develop RFID based framework, healthcare appliances need to be track and trace from manufacturing to retailing for improving accuracy, protect from the theft of costly medical equipment and avoid from fake products. In this framework, the authors analyzed a simple RFID Reader authentication protocol. This protocol is lightweight and rapid execution, but not provides sufficient security.

3.5 Implementation of Blockchain Technology for IoT Enabled Healthcare Application

Xu.J et.al (2019) identified that Healthcare application implemented using IoT technology, it has storage constraints due to constrained devices, so it needs centralized third party storage devices for managing healthcare information, which makes user lose control over their data and leads to privacy leakage. It uses two chain mechanisms based on blockchain technology. One chain for keeping user information and another chain keeps doctor's data. To protect patient information used AES symmetric key-based encryption and for managing doctor's information, they used the asymmetric key-based Merkle tree approach. The advantage of this model ensures tamper resistant and avoids data crashes.

Griggs et.al (2018) identified from existing system, availability of EHR's does not guarantee, alteration of healthcare record and leakage are possible. In proposed model, Healthcare application is implemented on a smart contract using Ethereum, this approach is based on permissioned. Proposed model provides immutability, availability of EHR's is guaranteed, transparency. To ensure the privacy of patient information, this model doesn't make any association between patients and their data. Patients are still monitored remotely without compromising privacy.

Zhou.T et.al (2019) identified many issues on the traditional system. In existing, difficult to share EHR's of patients due to that information is stored in a distributed manner. Traditional system uses third-party and cloud-based storage structures for maintaining EHR, these approaches are vulnerable to various attacks. Proposed architecture, the encrypted medical data are stored in multiple blocks for ensuring privacy. Consensus identity-based Verifiable Random Function used for verification of node locally to avoid DDoS and Sybil attacks.

Zhang.A et.al (2018) pointed out, sharing of EHR are enrich accuracy of diagnosis. Security and privacy preservation are critical issues in the traditional system. The authors proposed a system depending on Private Blockchain and Consortium Blockchain. Private Blockchain is responsible for maintaining Personnel Health Information and the responsibility of consortium blockchain keeps secured index of PHI. Implementation of blockchain ensures immutability, so this model protects from the alteration of information. In the proposed model encrypted PHI is stored in a private blockchain. These records can be accessed only by authorized users, it ensures security on data.

3.6 Implementation of Blockchain Technology for IoT Enabled Smart Transportation System

Zheng.D et.al (2019) indicates that authentication and privacy are major concerns on VANET. In existing, it's difficult to control from internal forged and reply attacks. This advanced model used blockchain, to provide a solution for the above attack and also afford decentralized traceable vehicles. All the transactions are stored in the blockchain using a Hash algorithm. If an adversary/malicious tries to tamper the recorded data, he/she need to regenerate all the hashes in the network. So it is not possible to do the above work, it avoids tampering of Road Side Unit record. Each transaction has its transaction-id, vehicle communication happens using this id, the transaction with an inaccurate random number is discarded for protecting from reply attack.

Zeng.P et.al (2020) proposed a system for analysis and verification of security filed in smart traffic lights. In blockchain-based traffic, the information management system needs to prove the authenticity of the ledger to add new records since it avoids a ghost attack on the traffic system. Also, these distributed storage mechanisms avoid from various attacks.

Zhang.X et.al (2019) proposed a system based on Digital Signature using the ECC for ensuring reliability and integrity on VANET. The proposed architecture ensures the following security requirements: 1) Blockchain based system avoids malicious attacks in the centralized storage. 2) The digital signature-based authentication mechanism used for protecting from brute force. 3) All the vehicles need to verify before recording data on the storage, it guarantees the integrity. Liang.X et.al (2018) addresses the solution for IoT based smart cities security vulnerabilities. The blockchain technologies use public key algorithms ECC and SHA, it avoids leakage of information and cryptographic vulnerabilities.

3.7 Implementation of Blockchain Technology for IoT Enabled Smart Cities

Lee.Y et.al (2020) applies BC in home gateway, Gateway plays a major role, the gateway is vulnerable to various security threats such as reliability, availability, and cyber attacks. To address the above security vulnerabilities the authors proposed Blockchain technology to prevent DDoS attacks in smart home applications; it is not possible to attack all the nodes in the chain.

Xie.J et.al (2019) designed structure to smart city for improve the lifestyle of urban people using modern ICT. The characteristics of smart cities are: citizen's lifestyle improvement, effective utilization power consumption and transportation, environmental protection, traffic management, and many more. Here authors identified the following features of blockchain on smart-cities: Transparency and resource utilization protects from single point of failure and immutability nature.

Shen.M et.al (2019) proposed architecture called "SecureSVM". This architecture using a machine learning algorithm called SVM. To employ homomorphism cryptosystem for secure data sharing implements polynomial multiplication and comparison approaches. To protect from various threat model systems uses the "Known Cipher-Text Model" and "Known Background Model". This approach improves the efficiency and accuracy of the privacy system.

Biswas.K et.al (2016) presented a security framework for communication in smart cities. This framework has three different layers: Physical layer- is vulnerable to security attacks since the lack of encryption. Proposed architecture implements multiple vendors agreed on communications to avoid above security threats. In communication, the layer needs application-specific protocols for improved privacy. The final layer is the database layer, to protect from unauthorized manipulation of data, can use permissioned and permissonless blockchain.

3.8 Implementation of Blockchain Technology for IoT Enabled Supply Chain Management

Gao.Z et.al (2018) designed construction for maintaining supply chain hierarchies. But it is difficult to manage distributed nature and fraudulent activity. To ensure these, the authors proposed the "Two-step block consortium mechanism based on hybrid decentralized ledger". The proposed system needs two types of ledger 1)Reservation Ledger 2)Data Ledger to record the supply chain activity. RL is used to store users and helpers information whereas in DL stores the entire supply chain information. An attacker cannot modify or tamper the records since RL is implemented based on the PoW consensus algorithm. This system uses SSL enabled communication between two parties, it avoids from eavesdropping or tampering of the message.

Mao.D et.al (2019) proposed a model using smart contract-based consortium blockchain called FTSCON. It implements Online Double Auction algorithms for eliminating competition among merchants. This system uses the following mechanisms to improve the security. 1) To provide robust and scalable architecture uses p2p communication. 2) All the transactions are recorded on the block encrypted using the hash algorithm. 3) For privacy protection, this model uses only public key without revealing the private key.

Toma.C et.al (2018) dived the entire process into two parts. The first part consists of two smart-contracts; the first contract maintains a set of rules between product and seller, second contracts used to store exact information about the clients. The second part used to analyze the good's purchase information stored on the blockchain. With help of transaction key details are stored on blockchain. Once information recorded on the chain, in future it cannot modify, it prevents tampering of information.

Dasaklis.T.K et.al (2019) proposed a "forensics-by-design supply chain traceability framework with audit trails" for ensuring reliability, security, and resilience. Proposed system implements the token concept by using Bill-of-Material hierarchical list. Still, the proposed architecture needs to be addressed for assessing scalability in large scale applications.

4. SOLUTIONS AND RECOMMENDATIONS

This section provides how blockchain will help with the above application.

4.1 Benefits of Blockchain Technology Implementation for Smart Healthcare Application

Healthcare application requires high quality of services to provide better solutions and accuracy with the latest technological developments. Arya (2019) says the current approach does not provide sufficient security and flexibility on patient records and medical equipment. Novel technology helps in the following way:

- **Improving Medical Record Access**- Accessing a patient's medical history is difficult in the traditional healthcare system. Blockchain helps to access accurate medical history and reduce time consumption.
- **Securing Patients Health Records** – All information about the patients and other medical details will be stored in distributed with security.
- **Avoids Counterfeit Drugs** – In blockchain technology, all the information is secure and transparent. It helps to reduce the supply of counterfeit drugs and equipment to the patient and medical organization.

4.2 Benefits of Blockchain Technology Implementation for Smart Transportation System

Blockchain technology helps to eliminate the transparency issue in the transportation and logistics system (Chen.s et.al. 2020). This digital auditing guarantees accuracy and protects from the modification of recorded information. In addition to this:

- **Brings Trust and Data Transparency** – All the processes are transparent and accurate including price, ownership, and other processes.
- **Improved Traceability and Trackability** – Live transaction and location can be verified and tracked from anywhere. Transport status, location, and history of travel can be transparent.

- **Accelerated payment, better security, and reduction of fraud** – Automatic schedule can be done for the payment with help of smart contract.

4.3 Benefits of Blockchain Technology Implementation for Smart Cities

Blockchain technologies can be applied in smart cities in many aspects. In consideration with the categories benefits of blockchain technologies listed in the following:

- **Personal Data Storage** – With the rapid development of technology innovations, individual data also get increased rapidly. Blockchain technology helps to store and maintain personal data with security, transparency, and immutability.
- **Data Access Control** –Blockchain technology helps to provide an access control mechanism, which data requester can know they have access rights or not.
- **Effective Resource Utilization** - Recent years many countries face a lot of difficulties to use resources effectively. Blockchain technology provides solutions for the above difficulties.

4.4 Benefits of Blockchain Technology Implementation for Smart Supply-chain Management

The supply chain application covers many entities in the product lifecycle. Blockchain technologies help to maintain the product information from the raw material to delivery (Infopulse, 2019).

- **Transparent and controlled transactions** – It eliminates third-party involvement, and then result will be transparent and time-saving.
- **Preapproved Transaction Fees** – When making Swift based inter-bank transactions, the amount will be deducted only after completion of the transaction. But in the blockchain amount can be approved priorly.
- **Auditability and Reliability** - All the transaction details are maintained up to date on the blockchain.

4.5 Challenges of Blockchain Technology Implementation for Smart Healthcare Application

Many of the organization requests to implement blockchain-based healthcare technologies. But still, very few organizations are ready for implementation, due to new technology, and still difficult to understand the entire operation. Most of the people are not willing to share their Healthcare report to others. The following points discuss the additional challenges:

- **Storage Capability** – Healthcare organization includes Patients Healthcare Records, images, lab reports, and documents. New technology required huge storage capacity.
- **Data ownership Rules and Regulations** - In this technology eliminate the concept of a single owner of any data or information, so it leads to it difficult to frame the rules and regulations.

4.6 Challenges of Blockchain Technology Implementation for Smart Transportation System

Blockchain works efficiently when integration with smart contracts, it enforces communication clarity between parties, rules, and regulations. Still, it faces some of the challenges:

- **Infrastructure**- Blockchain-based specific infrastructure helps to improve the performance of the transportation system. Still, the specific infrastructure is in the investigation phase.
- **Computational Overheads** – The rapid growth of internet vehicles increases, it will create communication overhead. IoT based sensors are constrained devices, not capable to handle an increased number of vehicles and requests.

4.7 Challenges of Blockchain Technology Implementation for Smart Cities Application (Montori.F, 2018)

The following challenges are there to implement blockchain technology with smart cities.

- **Security and Privacy** – Blockchain provides privacy for the stored data, but these data cannot stay completely anonymous since distributed nature this technology.
- **Throughput**- This technology successfully implemented on crypto-currencies, but while focusing on throughput it supports a maximum of 7 transactions per second, in Ethereum supports 15 transactions per second. But this throughput is not sufficient in the current digital world;
- **High implementation cost** – The cost can be categories into two types. Design cost and Operational Cost, Design cost states that one-time implementation cost, and operational cost required to maintaining smart cities. All the aspects of blockchain technology require high cost.

4.8 Challenges of Blockchain Technology Implementation for Smart Supply-chain Management

All the technologies have to address challenges to adapt to any applications. Blockchain technology also has certain technological challenges while integrating with supply chain management (Mondal.S, 2019).

- **Technical issues** – Currently available infrastructure is only capable to store limited transaction details. This limits number of transactions and information storage. Another one is, digital technologies require constant updates.
- **Policymaking process**- All the industry/organization needs to support for this technology is short of policies, inadequate learning, and guidance platforms.

5. CONCLUSION

Blockchain technology comes with a decentralized and immutable environment. By default, this technology protects from tamper-proof, increases transparency, fast processing among multiple devices, and increased stability. With the help of millions of devices Internet of Things brings innovative technologies development to this world. By integrating Blockchain with IoT can monitor and track all the devices involved in many IoT based applications. Blockchain uses cryptographic algorithms for ensuring privacy and security to the world. Blockchain can afford valuable and resourceful in real-time applications while integrating with IoT. This technology brings consensus algorithms to ensure the work is done by authentication and protects from unauthorized activity. And another important concept is smart contracts, transactions can be created based on some constraints for reducing the intermediary, minimize time and cost consumption. Most familiar crypto-currencies like Etherum and Bitcoin face scalability issues and so it's difficult to handle IoT generated a large volume of data. The main limitation of blockchain technologies are, it requires a huge amount of energy and computing resources, very limited number of the transaction can be executed, in some situation economically and practically unviable.

REFERENCES

Abou Jaoude, J., & George Saade, R. (2019). Blockchain Applications – Usage in Different Domains. *IEEE Access : Practical Innovations, Open Solutions*, 7, 45360–45381.

Badii, C., Bellini, P., Difino, A., & Nesi, P. (2020). Smart City IoT Platform Respecting GDPR Privacy and Security Aspects. *IEEE Access: Practical Innovations, Open Solutions*, 8, 23601–23623. doi:10.1109/ACCESS.2020.2968741

Biswas, K., & Muthukkumarasamy, V. (2016). Securing Smart Cities Using Blockchain Technology. *IEEE International Conference on High Performance Computing and Communications*, 1392-1393.

Chamekh, M. (2018). Secured Distributed IoT Based Supply Chain Architecture. *IEEE International Conference on Enabling Technologies: Infrastructure for Collaborative Enterprises*, 199-202. 10.1109/WETICE.2018.00045

Chen, Q., Sowan, A. K., & Xu, S. (2018). A Safety and Security Architecture for Reducing Accidents in Intelligent Transportation Systems. *IEEE/ACM International Conference on Computer-Aided Design (ICCAD)*, 1-7. 10.1145/3240765.3243462

Chen, S., Liu, X., & Yan, J. (2020). *Processes, benefits, and challenges for adoption of blockchain technologies in food supply chains: a thematic analysis*. Inf Syst E-Bus Manage; doi:10.100710257-020-00467-3

Christidis, K., & Devetsikiotis, M. (2016). Blockchains and Smart Contracts for the IoT. *IEEE Access : Practical Innovations, Open Solutions*, 4, 2292–2303.

Dasaklis, T. K., Casino, F., Patsakis, C., & Douligeris, C. (2019). A Framework for Supply Chain Traceability Based on Blockchain Tokens. *Lecture Notes in Business Information Processing*, 362, vol-362. doi:10.1007/978-3-030-37453-2_56

Deebak, B.D., Al-Turjman, F., Aloqaily, M., & Alfandi, O. (2019). An Authentic-Based Privacy Preservation Protocol for Smart e-Healthcare Systems in IoT. *IEEE Access*. . doi:10.1109/ACCESS.2019.2941575

Dhillon, P., & Kalra, S. (2018). Multi-factor user authentication scheme for IoT-based healthcare services. *Journal of Reliable Intelligent Environments*, 4(3), 141–160. Advance online publication. doi:10.100740860-018-0062-5

Duraiswamy, S. (2019). End to end lightweight mutual authentication scheme in IoT-based healthcare environment. *Journal of Reliable Intelligent Environments*, 6(1), 3–13. Advance online publication. doi:10.100740860-019-00079-w

Falco, G., Viswanathan, A., Caldera, C., & Shrobe, H., (2018). A Master Attack Methodology for an AI-Based Automated Attack Planner for Smart Cities. *IEEE, 6*, 48360-48373.

Gao, Z., Xu, L., & Chen, L. (2018). CoC: A Unified Distributed Ledger Based Supply Chain Management System. *J. Comput. Sci. Technol., 33*, 237–248. . doi:10.100711390-018-1816-5

Griggs, Ossipova, O., Kohlios, C. P., Baccarini, A. N., Howson, E. A., & Hayajneh, T. (2018). Healthcare Blockchain System Using Smart Contracts for Secure Automated Remote Patient Monitoring. *Journal of Medical Systems, 42*(7), 130. Advance online publication. doi:10.100710916-018-0982-x PMID:29876661

Hashem Eiza, M., & Ni, Q. (2017). Driving with Sharks: Rethinking Connected Vehicles with Vehicle Cybersecurity. *IEEE Vehicular Technology Magazine, 12*(2), 45–51. doi:10.1109/MVT.2017.2669348

Hiromoto, R. E., Haney, M., & Vakanski, A. (2017). A secure architecture for IoT with supply chain risk management. *IEEE International Conference on IDAACS*, 431-435.

Infopulse (2019, Oct. 7). *Blockchain in Supply Chain Management: Key Use Cases and Benefits*. https://medium.com/@infopulseglobal_9037/blockchain-in-supply-chain-management-key-use-cases-and-benefits-6c6b7fd43094

Lee, Y., Rathore, S., Park, J. H., & Park, J. H. (2020). A blockchain-based smart home gateway architecture for preventing data forgery. *Hum. Cent. Comput. Inf. Sci., 10*(1), 9. doi:10.118613673-020-0214-5

Liang, X., Shetty, S., & Tosh, D. (2018). Exploring the Attack Surfaces in Blockchain Enabled Smart Cities. *IEEE International Smart Cities Conference*, 1-8. 10.1109/ISC2.2018.8656852

Lo, S. K. (2019). Analysis of Blockchain Solutions for IoT: A Systematic Literature Review. *IEEE Access : Practical Innovations, Open Solutions, 7*, 58822–58835.

Mao, D., Hao, Z., Wang, F., & Li, H. (2019). Novel Automatic Food Trading System Using Consortium Blockchain. *Arabian Journal for Science and Engineering, 44*(4), 3439–3455. doi:10.100713369-018-3537-z

Miraz, M.H. (2020). Blockchain of Things (BCoT): The Fusion of Blockchain and IoT Technologies. *Studies in Big Data, 60*.

Mohammad, N. (2019). A Multi-Tiered Defense Model for the Security Analysis of Critical Facilities in Smart Cities. *IEEE, 7*, 152585-152598.

Mondal, S., Wijewardena, K. P., Aruppuswami, S., Kriti, N., Kumar, D., & Chahal, P. (2019). Blockchain Inspired RFID-Based Information Architecture for Food Supply Chain. *IEEE IoT Journal, 6*(3), 5803–5813.

Montori, F., Bedogni, L., & Bononi, L. (2018). A Collaborative Internet of Things Architecture for Smart Cities and Environmental Monitoring. *IEEE IoT Journal, 5*(2), 592–605.

Nofer, M., Gomber, P., & Hinz, O. (2017). Blockchain Bus. *Inf Syst Eng, 59*, 183–187. doi:10.100712599-017-0467-3

Omitola, T., & Wills, G. (2018). Towards Mapping the Security Challenges of the Internet of Things (IoT) Supply Chain. *Procedia Computer Science, 126*, 441–450. doi:10.1016/j.procs.2018.07.278

Reiff, N. (2020, Feb. 1). *Blockchain Explained.* https://www.investopedia.com/terms/b/blockchain.asp

Riahi Sfar, A., Challal, Y., Moyal, P., & Natalizio, E. (2019). A Game Theoretic Approach for Privacy Preserving Model in IoT-Based Transportation. *IEEE Transactions on Intelligent Transportation Systems, 20*(12), 4405–4414. doi:10.1109/TITS.2018.2885054

Shen, M., Tang, X., Zhu, L., Du, X., & Guizani, M. (2019). Privacy-Preserving Support Vector Machine Training Over Blockchain-Based Encrypted IoT Data in Smart Cities. *IEEE Internet of Things Journal, 6*(5), 7702–7712.

Shen, M., Tang, X., Zhu, L., Du, X., & Guizani, M. (2019). Privacy-Preserving Support Vector Machine Training Over Blockchain-Based Encrypted IoT Data in Smart Cities. *IEEE IoT Journal, 6*(5), 7702-7712.

Tang, W. Ren, T., Deng, K., & Zhang, Y. (2019). Secure Data Aggregation of Lightweight E-Healthcare IoT Devices With Fair Incentives. *IEEE IoT Journal, 6*(5), 8714-8726.

Toma, C., Talpiga, B., Boja, C., Popa, M. I., & Zurini, M. (2018). Secure IoT Supply Chain Management Solution Using Blockchain and Smart Contracts Technology, Innovative Security Solutions for Information Technology and Communications. *Lecture Notes in Computer Science, 11359.* https://blog.usejournal.com/how-can-blockchain-healthcare-solution-benefits-hospitals-and-patients-43fa6ce485a3

Wang, K., Yuan, L., Miyazaki, T., Chen, Y., & Zhang, Y. (2018). Jamming and Eavesdropping Defense in Green Cyber–Physical Transportation Systems Using a Stackelberg Game. *IEEE Transactions on Industrial Informatics, 14*(9), 4232–4242. doi:10.1109/TII.2018.2841033

Xie, J., Tang, H., Huang, T., Yu, F. R., Xie, R., Liu, J., & Liu, Y. (2019). A Survey of Blockchain Technology Applied to Smart Cities: Research Issues and Challenges. *IEEE Communications Surveys and Tutorials, 21*(3), 2794–2830. doi:10.1109/COMST.2019.2899617

Xu, C., Lin, H., Wu, Y., Guo, X., & Lin, W. (2019). An SDNFV-Based DDoS Defense Technology for Smart Cities. *IEEE Access: Practical Innovations, Open Solutions, 7*, 137856–137874. doi:10.1109/ACCESS.2019.2943146

Xu, J., Xue, K., Li, S., Tian, H., Hong, J., Hong, P., & Yu, N. (2019). Healthchain: A Blockchain-Based Privacy Preserving Scheme for Large-Scale Health Data. *IEEE Internet of Things Journal, 6*(5), 8770–8781. doi:10.1109/JIOT.2019.2923525

Zeng, P., Wang, X., Li, H., Jiang, F., & Doss, R. (2020). A Scheme of Intelligent Traffic Light System Based on Distributed Security Architecture of Blockchain Technology. *IEEE Access: Practical Innovations, Open Solutions, 8*, 33644–33657. doi:10.1109/ACCESS.2020.2972606

Zhang, A., & Lin, X. (2018). Towards Secure and Privacy-Preserving Data Sharing in e-Health Systems via Consortium Blockchain. *Journal of Medical Systems*, *42*(8), 140. doi:10.100710916-018-0995-5 PMID:29956061

Zhang, X., & Chen, X. (2019). Data Security Sharing and Storage Based on a Consortium Blockchain in a Vehicular Ad-hoc Network. *IEEE Access: Practical Innovations, Open Solutions*, *7*, 58241–58254. doi:10.1109/ACCESS.2018.2890736

Zheng, D., Jing, C., Guo, R., Gao, S., & Wang, L. (2019). A Traceable Blockchain-Based Access Authentication System With Privacy Preservation in VANETs. *IEEE Access: Practical Innovations, Open Solutions*, *7*, 117716–117726. doi:10.1109/ACCESS.2019.2936575

Zhou, T., Li, X., & Zhao, H. (2019). Med-PPPHIS: Blockchain-Based Personal Healthcare Information System for National Physique Monitoring and Scientific Exercise Guiding. *Journal of Medical Systems*, *43*(9), 305. doi:10.100710916-019-1430-2 PMID:31410583

Zhou, W., & Piramuthu, S. (2018). IoT security perspective of a flexible healthcare supply chain. *Information Technology Management*, *19*(3), 141–153. doi:10.100710799-017-0279-7

KEY TERMS AND DEFINITIONS

Consensus Algorithm: Enforces teamwork and security among multiple nodes in distributed environment.

Electronic Health Records: Digital format of patient's medical information.

Immutability: The transactions of blockchain are consistent, unaltered, and unmodifiable.

Mining: Process of adding new block in a blockchain by solving mathematical problem.

Proof of Work: Submitted work need to be agreed by all other participants in a network.

Quality of Service: Can manage privacy, transparency, speed, and accuracy of blockchain transaction.

Smart Contract: Agreement based self-executing computer programs.

Smart Meter: Enabling two-way communication among sensors without human intervention.

Section 3
Effective Blockchain Adoption in Manufacturing

Chapter 9
Blockchain With the Internet of Things:
Solutions and Security Issues in the Manufacturing Industry

Kamalendu Pal

ⓘ https://orcid.org/0000-0001-7158-6481

City, University of London, UK

ABSTRACT

The internet of things (IoT) is ushering a new age of technology-driven automation of information systems into the manufacturing industry. One of the main concerns with IoT systems is the lack of privacy and security preserving schemes for controlling access and ensuring the safety of the data. Many security issues arise because of the centralized architecture of IoT-based information systems. Another concern is the lack of appropriate authentication and access control schemes to moderate the access to information generated by the IoT devices in the manufacturing industry. Hence, the question that arises is how to ensure the identity of the manufacturing machinery or the communication nodes. This chapter presents the advantages of blockchain technology to secure the operation of the modern manufacturing industry in a trustless environment with IoT applications. The chapter reviews the challenges and threats in IoT applications and how integration with blockchain can resolve some of the manufacturing enterprise information systems (EIS).

INTRODUCTION

As a result of changes in the economic, environmental, and business environments, the modern manufacturing industry appears to be riskier than ever before, which created a need for improving its supply chain privacy and security. These changes are for several reasons. First, the increasingly global economy both produces and depends on people's free flow, goods, and information. Second, disasters have increased in number and intensity during the recent decades. Natural disasters such as earthquakes, floods, or

DOI: 10.4018/978-1-7998-5839-3.ch009

pandemic (e.g., coronavirus) strike more often and have a more significant economic impact. Simultaneously, the number of human-made disasters such as industrial sabotage, wars, and terrorist attacks that affects manufacturing supply networks has increased (Colema, 2006). These factors have created significant challenges for manufacturers, the country, and the global economic condition. Simply put, manufacturers must deploy continuous improvement in business processes, which improve both supply chain activities execution and its security enhancement.

Besides, today's manufacturing industry (e.g., apparel, automobile) inclines to worldwide business operations due to the socioeconomic advantage of the globalization of product design and development (Pal, 2020). For example, a typical apparel manufacturing network consists of organizations' sequence, facilities, functions, and activities to produce and develop an ultimate product or related services. The action starts with raw materials purchase from selective suppliers and products produced at one or more production facilities (Pal, 2019). Next, these products are moved to intermediate collection points (e.g., warehouse, distribution centers) to store temporarily to move to the next stage of the manufacturing network and finally deliver the products to intermediate storages or retailers or customers (Pal, 2017) (Pal, 2018).

This way, global manufacturing networks are becoming increasingly complicated due to a growing need for inter-organizational and intra-organizational connectedness that enabled by advances in modern Information technologies (e.g., RFID, Internet of Things, Blockchain, Service-Oriented Computing, Big Data Analytics) (Okorie et al., 2017) and tightly coupled business processes. Also, the manufacturing business networks use information systems to monitor the operational activities in a nearly real-time situation.

The digitalization of business activities attracts attention from manufacturing network management purpose, improves communication, collaboration, and enhances trust within business partners due to real-time information sharing and better business process integration. However, the above new technologies come with different types of disruptions to operations and ultimate productivity. For example, some of the operational disruptions are malicious threats that hinder the safety of goods, services, and ultimately customers lose trust to do business with the manufacturing companies.

As a potential solution to tackle the security problems, practitioners and academics have reported some attractive research with IoT and blockchain-based information systems for maintaining transparency, data integrity, privacy, and security related issues. In a manufacturing data communication network context, the Internet of Things (IoT) system integrates different heterogeneous objects and sensors, which surround manufacturing operations and facilitates the information exchange within the business stakeholders (also known as nodes in networking term). With the rapid enlargement of the data communication network scale and the intelligent evolution of hardware technologies, typical standalone IoT-based applications may no longer satisfy the advanced need is for efficiency and security in the context of the high degree of heterogeneity of hardware devices and complex data formats. Firstly, burdensome connectivity and maintenance costs brought by centralized architecture result in its low scalability. Secondly, centralized systems are more vulnerable to adversaries' targeted attacks under network expansion (Pal & Yasar, 2020).

Intuitively, a decentralized approach based on blockchain technology may solve the above problems in a typical centralized IoT-based information system. Mainly, the above justification is for three reasons. Firstly, an autonomous decentralized information system is feasible for trusted business partners to join the network, improving the business task-processing ability independently. Secondly, multiparty coordination enhances nodes' state consistency that information system crashes due to being a single-point failure is avoidable. Thirdly, nodes could synchronize the whole information system state only by coping the blockchain ledger to minimize the computation related activities and improve storage load. Besides, blockchain-based IoT architecture for manufacturing information systems attracted researchers' attention (Pal, 2020) (Pal, 2021).

Despite the potential of blockchain-based technology, severe security issues have been raised in its integration with IoT to form an architecture for manufacturing business applications. This chapter presents different types of security-related problems for information system design purpose. Below, this chapter introduces first the basic idea of digitation of manufacturing business process. Next, the chapter presents the use of blockchain technology in IoT for manufacturing industry. Then, it discusses the future research directions that includes data security and industrial data breach related issues. Finally, the chapter presents the concluding remarks and future research directions.

DIGITATION OF MANUFACTURING BUSINESS PROCESS

The manufacturing (e.g., apparel, automotive) industry inclines to worldwide business operations due to the financial benefits of the globalization of product design and development. The connecting path from supplier to the customer can include several intermediaries, such as warehouse, wholesalers, and retailers, depending on the ultimate products and markets. Global apparel manufacturing networks are becoming increasingly complicated due to a growing need for inter-organizational and intra- critical strategic asset. Also, manufacturing business networks use information systems to monitor network activities(Pal, 2017) (Pal, 2020). Organizational connectedness, which enabled by advances in modern technologies and tightly coupled business processes. This way, in manufacturing business operational information has been a critical strategic asset.

An EIS is to acquire and manage data; and serve as a decision-making system within an enterprise. Therefore, the characteristics of an EIS can be analyzed in the context of decision-making purpose. Figure 1 has illustrated some of data generation sources (e.g., RFID scanner, sensor, security camera, intelligent machine) in a manufacturing environment, which is divided into different layers (e.g., perception layer, network layer, processing layer, application layer). With the evolution of manufacturing system, inputs, outputs, as well as system parameters can be changed with respect to time significantly. One can find that design variables have being increased exponentially with the evolution of manufacturing EIS. The information systems for modern manufacturing systems must accommodate the changes of the IT infrastructure (e.g., IoT, blockchain, SOC) as well as the changes and uncertainties in the system environments.

Evolution of IT Infrastructure

Primary functions of an EIS are (i) to acquire static and dynamic data from objects; (ii) to analyze data based on computer models; and (iii) to plan and control a system and optimize system performances using the processed data. The implementation of a manufacturing system paradigm relies heavily on available IT. In this sub-section, the IT infrastructure related to manufacturing is discussed. IoT has been identified as a critical technology with its great impact on manufacturing industry (Pal, 2021).

IoT becomes foundation for connecting things, sensors, actuators, and other smart technologies. IoT is an extension of the Internet, and IoT technology gives an immediate access to information about physical objects and leads to innovative services with high efficiency and productivity. The characteristics of IoT includes: (i) the pervasive sensing of objects; (ii) the hardware and software integration; and

(iii) many nodes. In developing an IoT, objects must be capable of interacting with each other, reacting autonomously to the changes of manufacturing environment (e.g., temperature, pressure).

Figure 1. A diagrammatic representation of manufacturing business process

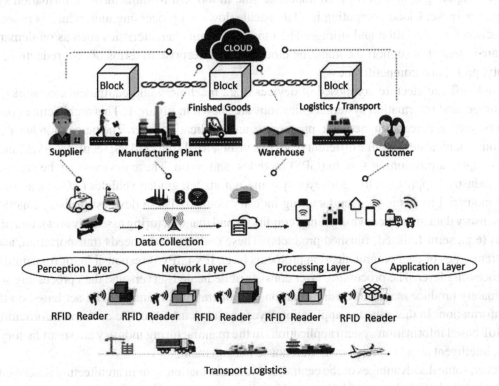

Radio Frequency Identification (RFID) technology has received massive attention from the manufacturing industry's daily operations as a critical component of the Internet of Things (IoT) world. In RFID-enabled manufacturing chain automation, an EPC (Electronic Product Code) is allocated to an individual item of interest and is attached to an RFID tag for tracking and tracing purpose. RFID tag-attached items are transported from one business activity to another or even move within the manufacturing partners. During the transportation process, individual partner interrogates RFID tags and add business-related contextual information into tags. In this way, involved business partners can check whether the items of interest have passed through the legitimate manufacturing network. If any inappropriateness is traced, such items may be classified as counterfeit products.

Also, the wireless sensor networks (WSNs) are used to provide cloud computing services to enterprises. WSNs are the most important infrastructure for the implementation of IoT. Various hardware and software systems are available to WSNs: (i) Internet Protocol version 6 (IPv6) makes it possible to connect unlimited number of devices, (ii) Wi-Fi and WiMAX provide high-speed and low-cost communication, (iii) Zigbee, Bluetooth, and RFID provide the communication in low-speed and local communication, and (iv) a mobile platform offers communications for anytime, anywhere, and anything. The importance of WSNs to industrial control systems have been discussed by researchers (Araujo et al., 2014). In the research field of WSNs, most ongoing work focuses on energy efficient routing, aggregation, and data management algorithms; other challenges include the large -scale deployment and semantic integration of massive data (Aberer et al., 2014), and security (Gandino et al., 2014).

Cloud computing is also playing an important role in modern manufacturing information system's automation purpose. Cloud computing is a large-scale, low-cost processing unit, which is based on the IP connection for calculation and storage. The most important characteristics such as on-demand self-service are essential to support a computing cloud for an enterprise in terms of cost reduction, system flexibility, profit, and competitiveness.

A simple IoT architecture composed of devices (e.g., machinery and equipment), networks, cloud-based storage, and information system applications are shown in Figure 1. This architecture consists of four layers, such as perception, network, processing, and application layer. The perception layer consists of electromechanical devices like different types of sensors, RFID tag readers, security surveillance cameras, geographical positioning system (GPS) modules, and so on. These devices may be accompanied by other industrial appliances like conveyor systems, automated guided vehicles (AGVs), and different types of industrial robots for a manufacturing industry context. These devices' primary function is to capture sensory data, monitor environmental conditions and manufacturing assembly areas, and transport materials (e.g., semi-finished, finished products). These collected data needs transportation, and there are different types of data communication protocols (e.g., IPv4, IPv6) responsible for transmitting data to the processing layer. The processing layer consists of dedicated servers and data processing software that ultimately produce management information, and operational managers can act based on the produced information. In this way, the application layer produces user-specific decision information. Few critical IoT based information system applications in the manufacturing industry are smart factory, smart robotics, intelligent supply chain, smart warehouse management.

However, some disadvantages of the centralized IoT information system architecture described above (Ali et al., 2019). A central point of failure could easily paralyze the whole data communication network. Besides, it is easy to misuse user-sensitive data in a centralized system; users have limited or no control over personal data. Centralized data can be tampered with or deleted by an intruder, and therefore the centralized system has lacks guaranteed traceability and accountability.

The vast popularity of IoT based information systems in the manufacturing industry also demands the appropriate protection of security and privacy-related issues to stop any system vulnerabilities and threats. Also, traditional security protections are not always problem-free. Hence, it is worth classifying different security problems classified based on objects of attack that are relevant to IoT based systems. This classification of security-related attacks would help industry-specific practitioners and researchers to understand which attacks are essential to their regular business operations. The different layer specific security related research is shown in Table 1, Table 2, and Table 3.

Blockchain technology is based on a distributed database management system that keeps records of all business-related transactional information that have been executed and shared among participating business partners in the network. This distributed database system is known as a distributed ledger technology (DLT). Individual business exchange information is stored in the distributed ledger and must be verified by most network members. All business-related transactions that have ever made are contained in the block. Bitcoin, the decentralized peer-to-peer (P2P) digital currency, is the most famous example of blockchain technology (Nakamoto, 2008).

Table 1. Perception layer attacks

Type of attack	Description
Tampering	Physical damage is caused to the device (e.g., RFID tag, Tag reader) or communication network (Andrea et al., 2015).
Malicious Code Injection	The attacker physically introduces a malicious code onto an IoT system by compromising its operation. The attacker can control the IoT system and launch attacks (Ahemd et al., 2017).
Radio Frequency Signal Interference (Jamming)	The predator sends a particular type of radiofrequency signal to hinder communication in the IoT system, and it creates a denial of service (DoS) from the information system (Ahemd et al., 2017).
Fake Node Injection:	The intruder creates an artificial node and the IoT-based system network and access the information from the network illegally or control data flow (Ahemd et al., 2017).
Sleep Denial Attack	The attacker aims to keep the battery-powered devices awake by sending them with inappropriate inputs, which causes exhaustion of battery power, leading to shutting down of nodes (Ahemd et al., 2017).
Side Channel Attack	In this attack, the intruder gets hold of the encryption keys by applying malicious techniques on the devices of the IoT-based information system (Andrea et al., 2015), and by using these keys, the attacker can encrypt or decrypt confidential information from the IoT network.
Permanent Denial of Service (PDoS)	In this attack, the attacker permanently damages the IoT system using hardware sabotage. The attack can be launched by damaging firmware or uploading an inappropriate BIOS using malware (Foundry, 2017).

The convergence of IoT with blockchain technology will have many advantages. The blockchain's decentralization model will have the ability to handle processing a vast number of transactions between IoT devices, significantly reducing the cost associated with installing and maintaining large, centralized data centers and distributing computation and storage needs across IoT devices networks. Working with blockchain technology will eliminate the single point of failure associated with the centralized IoT architecture. The convergence of Blockchain with IoT will allow the P2P messaging, file distribution, and autonomous coordination between IoT devices with no centralized computing model.

Blockchain technology offers a mechanism to record transactions, or any digital interaction designed to secure, transparent, highly resistant to outages, auditable, and efficient. In other words, blockchain technology has introduced an effective solution to IoT based information systems security. A blockchain enhances IoT devices to send inclusion data in a shared transaction repository with the tamper-resistant record. It improves business partners to access and supply IoT data without central control and management, which creates a digital fusion.

Software attacks are launched by an attacker taking advantage of the associated software or security vulnerabilities presented by an IoT system is shown in Table 3. This way, a malicious code can attack IoT-based infrastructure applications and create disruption (e.g., repeating the request of a new connection until the IoT system reaches maximum level) of an existing service for the global connectivity.

Blockchain technology offers a mechanism to record transactions, or any digital interaction design to secure, transparent, highly resistant to outages, auditable, and efficient. In other words, blockchain technology has introduced an effective solution to IoT based information systems security. A blockchain enhances IoT devices to send inclusion data in a shared transaction repository with the tamper-resistant record. It improves business partners to access and supply IoT data without central control and management, which creates a digital fusion.

Table 2. Network layer attacks

Type of attack	Description
Traffic Analysis Attack	Confidential data flowing to and from the devices are sniffed by the attacker, even without going close to the network to get network traffic information and attacking purpose (Andrea et al., 2015).
RFID Spoofing	The intruder first spoofs an RFID signal to access the information imprinted on the RFID tag (Ahemd et al., 2017). Using the original tag ID, the intruder can then send its manipulated data, posing it as valid. In this way, the intruder can create a problem for the business operation.
RFID Unauthorized Access	An intruder can read, modify, or delete data present on RFID nodes because of the lack of proper authentication mechanisms (Andrea et al., 2015).
Routing Information Attacks	These are direct attacks where the attacker spoofs or alters routing information and makes a nuisance by creating routing loops and sending error messages (Andrea et al., 2015).
Selective Forwarding	In this attack, a malicious node may alter, drop, or selectively forward some messages to other nodes in the network (Varga et al., 2017). Therefore, the information that reaches the destination is incomplete.
Sinkhole Attack	In this attack, an attacker compromises a node closer to the sink (known as sinkhole node) and makes it look attractive to other nodes in the network, thereby luring network traffic towards it (Ahemd et al., 2017).
Wormhole Attack	In a wormhole attack, an attacker maliciously prepares a low-latency link and then tunnels packets from one point to another through this link (Varga et al., 2017).
Sybil Attack	Here, a single malicious node claims multiple identities (known as Sybil nodes) and locates itself at different places in the network (Andrea et al., 2015). This leads to colossal resource allocation unfairly. • Man in the Middle Attack (MiTM): Here, an attacker manages to eavesdrop or monitor the communication between two IoT devices and access their private data (Andrea et al., 2015).
Replay Attack	An attacker may capture a signed packet and resend the packet multiple times to the destination (Varga et al., 2017). This keeps the network busy, leading to a DoS attack.
Denial/Distributed Denial of Service (DoS/DDoS) Attacks	Unlike DoS attack, multiple compromised nodes attack a specific target by flooding messages or connection requests to slow down or even crash the system server/network resource (Rambus).

Table 3. Software layer attacks

Type of attack	Description
Virus, Worms, Trojan Horses, Spyware and Adware	Using this malicious software, an adversary can infect the system to tampering data or stealing information or even launching DoS (Andrea et al., 2015).
Malware	Data present in IoT devices may be affected by malware, contaminating the cloud or data centres (Varga et al., 2017).

BACKGROUND OF BLOCKCHAIN TECHNOLOGY

The blockchain technology infrastructure has motivated many innovative applications in manufacturing industries. This technology's ideal blockchain vision is tamper evident and tamper resistant ledgers implemented in a distributed fashion, without a central repository. The central ideas guiding blockchain technology emerged in the late 1980s and early 1990s. A research paper (Lamport, 1998) published with the background knowledge of the Paxos protocol, which provided a consensus method for reaching an agreement resulting in a computer network. The central concepts of that research were combined and applied to the electronic cash-related research project by Satoshi Nakamoto (Nakamoto, 2008), leading to modern cryptocurrency or bitcoin-based systems.

Distributed Ledger Technology (DLT) Based Blockchain

The blockchain's initial basis is to institute trust in a P2P network bypassing any third managing parties' need. For example, Bitcoin started a P2P financial value exchange mechanism where no third-party (e.g., bank) is needed to provide a value-transfer transaction with anyone else on the blockchain community. Such a community-based trust is the main characteristic of system verifiability using mathematical modelling technique for evidence. The mechanism of this trust provision permits peers of a P2P network to transact with other community members without necessarily trusting each other. This behaviour is often referred to as the trustless behaviour of a blockchain system. The trustlessness also highlights that a blockchain network partner interested in transacting with another business entity on the blockchain does not necessarily need to know the real identity.

It permits users of a public blockchain system to be anonymous. A record of transactions among the peers is stored in a chain of a data structure known as blocks, the name blockchain's primary basis. Each block (or peer) of a blockchain network keeps a copy of this record. Moreover, a consensus, digital voting mechanism to use many network peers, is also decided on the blockchain state that all network stores' nodes. Hence, blockchain is often designed as distributed ledger-based technology. An individual instance of such a DLT, stored at each node (or peer) of the blockchain network and gets updated simultaneously with no mechanism for retroactive changes in the records. In this way, blockchain transactions cannot be deleted or altered.

Intelligent Use of Hashing

Intelligent techniques are used in hashing the blocks encapsulating transaction records together, which makes such records immutable. In other words, blockchain's transactions achieve validity, trust, and finality based on cryptographic proofs and underlying mathematical computation between different trading-peers (or partners), known as a hashing function. Encryption algorithms are used to provide confidentiality for creating hash function. These algorithmic solutions have the essential character that they are reversible in the sense that, with knowledge of the appropriate key, it must be possible to reconstruct the plaintext message from the cryptographic technique. This way hashing mechanism of a piece of data can be used to preserve the blockchain system's integrity. For example, Secure Hash Algorithm 256 (SHA256) is a member of the SHA2 hash functions currently used by many blockchain-based systems such as Bitcoin.

Figure 2. Immutable hashing mechanism in blockchain

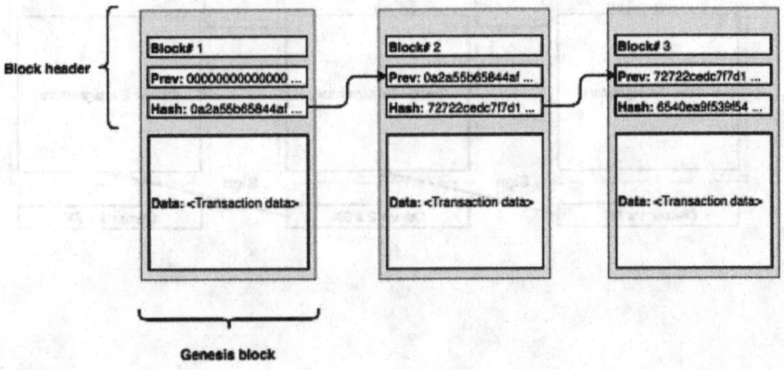

A simplified blockchain is shown in Figure 2. A block consists of four main fields (i.e., block number, previous hash (or prev), hash, data). Block number (e.g., #1, #2, #3) uniquely identify a block. The Prev field contains the previous block's (i.e., the block that comes before it) hash value. It is the way the chain of blocks stays together. The first block in a blockchain is often called the genesis block, is shown by its Prev field initialized to all zeros. The fourth field is the Merkle tree root, a data structure that keeps all the block's transaction-related information. Thus, the block body stores a record of all transactions categorized into input and output. It should be noticed that there is a technical difference between a transaction chain and a blockchain. Every block in a blockchain can contain multiple transaction chains, as shown in Figure 3. In turn, each transaction chain shows the value transferred from one peer of the network to another. Each such transaction chain is sometimes referred to as a digital coin or more usually as a token.

The communication among peer (or user) on blockchain uses a decentralized network in which an individual peer represents a node at which a blockchain client is installed. Once a peer performs a transaction with another peer or receives data from another user, it verifies its authenticity. Afterwards, it broadcasts the validated data to all other relevant nodes for business operation purpose.

Blockchain systems need acceptance and verification by all the chain peers, and this mechanism is known as a consensus. There are different algorithmic solutions available to cope with the distributed nature of this problem.

Distributed Consensus

These distributed consensus algorithms help the blockchain system users say regarding the overall state of the records preserved (or stored) in the blockchain network blocks. This section briefly introduces four of these algorithms, and they are – (i) Proof-of-Work (PoW), (ii) Proof of Stake (PoS), (iii) Practical Byzantine Fault Tolerance (PBFT), and (iv) Delegated Proof of Stake (DPoS).

Figure 3. Diagrammatic representation of transaction chain

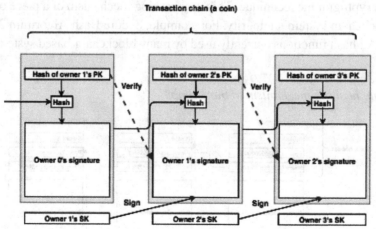

The PoW consensus algorithm is widely popularised by Bitcoin and assumes that all users vote with their "computing power" by solving consensus instances and creating the appropriate blocks. The PoS algorithm uses the existing way of achieving consensus in a distributed system. This algorithm needs the user to prove ownership of an amount of currency. It provides more efficient energy consumption in comparison to PoW. The PBFT consensus algorithm uses a state machine replication method to maintain with Byzantine faults. This algorithm uses an effective authentication method based on public-key cryptography. The DPoS uses a democratic technique to validate a block. It can confirm the transaction quickly.

The blockchain technology is proposed for many manufacturing use-cases where business needs data immutability and P2P consensus, and transaction confidentiality. There are different types of blockchain-based architectures available as industry-specific solution platforms.

Blockchain Technology Architecture in Manufacturing Industry

Blockchain is bringing new technological innovation to business operating models in the manufacturing industry. These business models eventually lead operational managers to develop new processes, which help automate manufacturing functions effectively. This trend is not the cheapest, most effective way to use something, but it is also presumably game-changing for manufacturing industries. As a result, changes occur in the manufacturing network's nature governing a business's relationships with its business partners. In turn, these blockchain-governed business models lead to significant shifts in the competitive structure of manufacturing companies.

Many researchers argue that blockchain technology's effects on manufacturing networks typify this process and usher new business practices using appropriate information systems architecture (Pal, 2020). Before discussing the effect of blockchain technology and its security-related issues, one should note that it is not the first time the manufacturing business network has undergone a revolution. The first occurred at the turn of the nineteenth century, followed by the twentieth century, and formed the manufacturing and distribution model throughout the twenty-first century. Information systems and their architectures play a dominating role in this revolutionary business transformation process. Hence, it is instructive to consider a simple blockchain architecture.

An overview of blockchain architecture is shown in Figure 4. In simple, blockchain can be of three different types: (i) public blockchain, (ii) private blockchain, and (iii) hybrid blockchain. A blockchain is permissionless when anyone is free to be involved in the process of authentication, verification and reaching consensus. A blockchain is permission where its participants are pre-selected. A few different variables could apply to make a permissionless or permission system into some form of hybrid.

The validation occurs to the next layer of the blockchain infrastructure, consensus, where nodes must agree on which transactions must be kept and validated in the blockchain. There are different security measures used to verify transactions within a blockchain system, the most known approaches to research a consensus today are PoW, PoS, and PBFT. Having a good consensus algorithm means better efficiency, safety, and convenience; nevertheless, which consensus an organization should choose depends on the use case.

The upper layer, the computer interface, allows blockchains to offer more functionality to the system. In this part, blockchain stores information on all the transactions that the users have made. For more advanced applications, one needs to store complex states which are dynamically changing, which means that the state shift from one to another once specific criteria are met in this system. These applications have given rise to smart contracts.

Smart contracts are the most transformative blockchain application, which could dramatically change how organizations work. The smart contracts can automate the transfer of assets when the negotiated conditions are met in this application; for example, when a shipment is delivered and verified, the contract will automatically enforce payments.

Figure 4. An overview of blockchain architecture

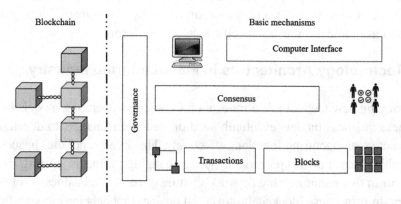

The governance layer (as shown in Figure 4) is human centered in blockchain architecture. Blockchain protocols are affected by inputs from different people who integrate new methods, improve the blockchain protocols, and patch the system.

In blockchain systems assets, monetary values are called tokens, and as stated by Nakamoto (Nakamoto, 2008), these are essential building blocks for the technology. The term tokenization means converting the rights and values of an asset into a digital token. Blockchain technology turns assets into a digitally encoded token that can be registered, tracked, and traded with a private key (Francisco & Swanson, 2017). It means that everything of value can be uploaded as a digital object in the blockchain system.

One of the critical aspects of blockchain technology is the decentralization of its operations. Decentralization means that each transaction in a blockchain transaction system does not need to be validated through a central trusted agency (e.g., bank or other financial organizations). This new validation technique implies that third parties resulting in higher costs and performance bottlenecks at the central services are no longer needed. It is here that consensus algorithms used to maintain data consistency in a distributed network. For an entity to operate in a decentralized network, an organization would be issued a digital identity that it could use in all business interactions.

In blockchain-based information systems, users are anonymous, but their account identifiers are not. Also, all asset transactions are publicly visible. Since blockchain technology users are unknown, it is essential to create trust in this system architecture. To build trust within a blockchain network enabled by four critical characteristics, as described below:

- **Ledger:** One of the essential characteristics of blockchain-based operation is distributed ledger technology (DLT). It is a decentralized technology to eliminate the need for a central authority or intermediary to process, validate or authenticate transactions. Manufacturing businesses use DLT to process, validate or authenticate transactions or other types of data exchanges.

- **Secure**: Blockchain technology produces a structure of data with inherent security qualities. It is based on principles of cryptography, decentralization, and consensus, which ensure trust in transactions. Blockchain technology makes sure that the data within the network of blocks is not tampered with and that the data within the ledger is attestable.
- **Shared**: Blockchain data is shared amongst multiple users of this network of nodes. It gives transparency across the node users in the network.
- **Distributed**: Blockchain technology can be geographically distributed. The decentralization helps to scale the number of nodes of a blockchain network to ensure it is more resilient to predators' attacks. By increasing the number of nodes, a predator's capability to impact the blockchain network's consensus protocol is minimized.

Also, for blockchain-based system architectures that permit anyone to anonymously create accounts and participate (called *permissionless* blockchain networks), these capabilities produce a level of trust amongst collaborating business partners with no prior knowledge of one another. Blockchain technology provides decentralization with the collaborating partners across a distributed network. This decentralization means there is no single point of failure, and a single user cannot change the record of transactions.

SECURITY-RELATED RESEARCH FOR BLOCKCHAIN TECHNOLOGY

Manufacturing businesses have leveraged blockchain technology and its built-in capabilities as an essential component within the software system architecture to provide more secure and dependable computation capability. However, ill-informed, or incorrect design decisions related to the choice and usage of a blockchain, and its components are probably the root cause of potential security risks to the system. For example, adversaries can exploit the envisioned design and verification limitations to compromise the system's security. The system becomes vulnerable to malicious attacks from cyberspace (Sturm et al., 2017). Some of the well-known attacks (e.g., Stuxnet, Shamoon, BlackEnergy, WannaCry, and TRITON) (Stouffer, 2020) created significant problems in recent decades.

The distributed manufacturing industry's critical issues are coordinating and controlling secure business information and its operational network. The application of cybersecurity controls in the operating environment demands the most significant attention and effort to ensure that appropriate security and risk mitigation are achieved. For example, manufacturing device spoofing and false authentication in information sharing (Kumar & Mallick, 2018) are significant problems for the industry. Besides, the heterogeneous nature of diversified equipment and the individualized service requirements make it difficult for blockchain-based P2P business operation (Leng et al., 2020).

In blockchain-based manufacturing business applications, trust and confidentiality among corporate partners play crucial roles in day-to-day operations (Ghosh & Tan, 2020). These issues also get compounded with individual products' personalization requirements across systems, which massively complicates the manufacturing and supply business activities (Mourtzis & Doukas, 2012). The other important issue is related to the manufacturing information system's data storage strategy. The fact is, it is easier to keep data and other files secure on a decentralized server than on a centralized one. With data stored across many computers in multiple locations, the risk of a single-entry point is mitigated and make fewer data accessible at each end. Decentralized platforms can even avoid holding sensitive information altogether, and it makes a better choice for manufacturing information system (Shen, 2002).

A literature survey shows that the techniques and methods of cybersecurity issues have been applied to the field of modern manufacturing information management systems, including traceability of operations (Mohamed & Al-Jaroodi, 2019), cyber-attacks to the digital thread (Sturm et al., 2017). Advanced virus on control system (e.g., Stuxnet) (12), device spoofing and false authentication in data sharing (Kumar & Mallick, 2018), interoperability among heterogenous equipment (Leng et al., 2020), confidentiality and trust between participants (Debabrata & Albert, 2020), information vulnerability and reliability across systems (Mourtzis & Doukas, 2012), and failure of critical nodes in centralized platforms (Shen, 2002).

Leveraging the advantages of integrating blockchain in IoT, academics and practitioners have investigated how to handle critical issues, such as IoT device-level security, managing enormous volumes of data, maintaining user privacy, and keeping confidentiality and trust (Pal, 2020) (Dorri et al., 2019) (Shen et al., 2019). In research work, a group of researchers (Kim et al., 2017) have proposed a blockchain-based IoT system architecture to prevent IoT devices' hacking problems. Besides, blockchain-based technologies are used to protect IoT application vulnerabilities.

Applications on the IoT Devices Management

In IoT, devices management relates to security solutions for the physical devices, embedded software, and residing data on the devices. Internet of Things (IoT) comprises "Things" (or IoT devices) that have remote sensing and data collecting capabilities and can exchange data with other connected devices and applications (directly or indirectly). IoT devices can collect data and process the data either locally or send them to centralize servers or cloud-based application back-ends for processing. A recent on-demand model of manufacturing that is leveraging IoT technologies is called Cloud-Based Manufacturing (CBM). It enables ubiquitous, convenient, on-demand network access to a shared pool of configurable manufacturing business processes information collection and use it service provision.

However, attackers seek to exfiltrate IoT devices' data using malicious codes in malware, especially on the open-source Android platform. Gu et al. (Gu et al., 2018) reported a malware identification system in a blockchain-based system named CB-MDEE composed of detecting consortium chain by test members and public chain users. The CB-MDEE system uses a soft-computing-based comparison technique and more than one marking function to minimize the false-positive rate and improve malware variants' identification ability. A research group (Lee et al., 2017) uses a firmware update scheme based on blockchain technology to safeguard the IoT system's embedded devices.

Applications on the IoT Access Management

Access control is a mechanism in computer security that regulates access to information system. The access control systems face many problems, such as third-party, inefficiency, and lack of privacy. These problems can be address by blockchain, the technology that received significant attention in recent years, and many potentials. Jemel and other researchers (Jemel & Serrhrouchni, 2017) report a couple of centralized access control systems problems. This study presents an access control mechanism with a temporal dimension to solve these problems and adapts a blockchain-based solution for verifying access permissions. The attribute-based Encryption method (Sahai & Waters, 2005) also has some problems, such as privacy leakage from the private key generator (PKG) (Hur & Noh, 2011) and a single point of failure as mentioned before. Wang and colleagues (Wang et al.,2018) introduce a framework for data sharing and access control to address this problem by implementing decentralized storage.

Recently, there has been a tremendous investment from the industries and significant interest from academia to solve significant research challenges in blockchain technologies. For example, consensus protocols are the primary building blocks of blockchain-based technologies. Therefore, the threats targeting the consensus protocols become a significant research issue in the blockchain (Pal, 2021), and impact of integrating artificial intelligence (AI) on both IoT and blockchain technology (Atlam et al., 2020).

BLOCKCHAIN SECURITY AND PRIVACY ISSUES

Blockchain technology offers an approach to storing information, executing transactions, performing functions, and establishing trust in secure computing without centralized authority in a networked environment (Minoli & Occhiogrosso, 2018). Although blockchain has received growing interest in academia and industry in recent years, blockchains' security and privacy continue to be at the centre of the debate when deploying blockchain in different industrial applications(Minoli & Occhiogrosso, 2018)(Pal, 2021).

Key Security Risk Areas of Blockchain

The main areas of security on blockchain technology are (i) Ledger, (ii) Consensus Mechanism, (iii) Networking Infrastructure, (iv) Identity Access Management, and (v) Cryptography. A diagrammatic representation is present in the risk areas in Figure 5.

- **Ledger:** The ledger uses to register all transactions and changes in the status of the data. The ledger distributed by intelligent design and shared between the blockchain participating nodes. Two challenging problems (or hazards) generally threaten the applicability of the ledger technology in blockchain applications: (a) unauthorized entry into the ledger; and (b) unauthorized (or improper, or illegal) operations on recorded ledger data.
- **Consensus Mechanism:** A consensus mechanism is a protocol (i.e., set of rules) to ensure that all the blockchain network participants comply with the agreed rules for day-to-day operations. It makes sure that the transactions originate from a legitimate source by having every participant consent to the distributed ledger's state. The public blockchain is a decentralized technology, and no centralized authority is in place to regulate the required act. Therefore, the network requires authorizations from the network participants to verify and authenticate any blockchain network activities. Several consensus mechanisms have introduced considering the requirements of secure digital transactions. However, proof of work (PoW), proof of stake (PoS), and delegated proof of stake (DPoS) are the few consensus protocols used by the industries. In this way, the blockchain relies on the distributed consensus mechanism to establish mutual trust. However, the consensus mechanism itself has a vulnerability, which attackers can exploit to control the entire blockchain. Although a few approaches, e.g., (Muhammad et al., 2018), are highlighted in blockchain-related research to deter and prevent security related attacks. Due to the inherent characteristics of openness, the PoW-based permissionless blockchain networks may not be completely secure.
- **Network Infrastructure:** The network infrastructure threats can detect in nodes being stopped by a malicious attacker using good anticipatory mechanisms. In August 2016, nearly 120,000 Bitcoin

(over US $60mn at the time) were stolen from Bitfinex (Nagaraj & Maguire, 2017). Based in Hong Kong, Bitfinex is one of the world's largest digital and cryptocurrency exchanges. The incident exploited security vulnerabilities within individual organizations. The blockchain network itself remained fully functional and operated as envisioned. The incident may have prevented a detailed end-to-end review of security, using scenarios, meaning there would have been a higher chance of identifying risks upfront and mitigating them at that point.

- **Identity Access Management:** Privacy in blockchain enables the client/user to perform transactions without leaking its identification information in the network. Also, blockchain technology uses numerous techniques to achieve the highest level of privacy and authenticity for transactions. As information comes from different users within the blockchain industrial ecosystem, the infrastructure needs to ensure every user privacy and authenticity. Blockchain-based information system often employs a combination of public and private key to encrypt and decrypt data securely.

Figure 5. Various Security Risk Areas of Blockchain

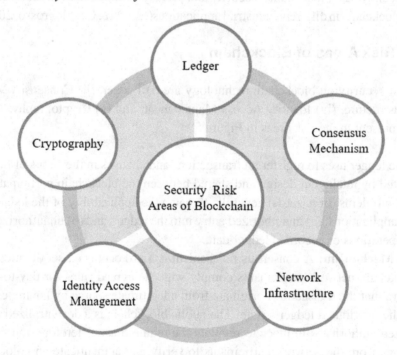

- **Cryptography:** The records on a blockchain are secured through cryptography. Network participants have their private keys assigned to the transactions they make and act as a personal digital signature. If a record is altered, the signature will become invalid, and the peer network will know right away that something has happened. However, there could be software bugs and glitches in cryptography coding. These could include developers' coding mistakes, inappropriate design, and an underlying defect in the cryptography routines.

Safety is an essential aspect of blockchain-based transaction processes. All the data within the blockchain ecosystem needs to be secured and tamperproof. The security ensures that there are no malicious nodes within the blockchain-based enterprise ecosystem. As mentioned earlier, the data inserted into a public ledger or inside the blockchain is distributed to individual users, and everyone maintains their local copy of the blockchain. In that local copy, that individual cannot tamper but upgrade the data and retransmit the network's data. However, for the transaction to be validated, the other nodes should be convinced that the broadcasted information is not malicious, and the system security is ensured.

THREAT MODELS FOR BLOCKCHAIN

This section explains the threat models that are considered by the blockchain protocols in IoT networks. Threat agents are mostly malicious attackers whose intention is to steal corporate vital information, disrupt system functionalities, or create problems for service provisions. Besides, attackers might also be inadvertent entities, such as developers of smart contacts who unintentionally create bugs and designers of blockchain-based system applications who make mistakes in the design or ignore some issues.

Threats facilitate various attacks on assets. Threats arise from vulnerabilities at the network, smart contracts, consensus protocol deviations or violations of consensus protocol assumptions, or application-specific vulnerabilities. Countermeasures safeguard the system from any attacks. These safeguard m involve various security and safety solutions and tools, incentives, reputation techniques, best practices, and so on. Threats and their agents cause risks. They may lead to a loss of monetary assets, a loss of privacy, a loss of reputation, service malfunctions, and disruptions of services and applications (i.e., availability issues).

Blockchain-based information systems owners wish to minimize the risk caused by threats that arise from threat agents. This section presents five types of attacks: *identity-based attacks*, *manipulation-based attacks*, *cryptanalytic attacks*, *reputation-based attacks*, and *service-based attacks*.

Identity-Based Attacks

The emergence of DLT based upon a blockchain data structure has given rise to new approaches to identity management, aiming to upend dominant approaches to providing and consuming digital identities. These new approaches to identity management (IdM) propose to enhance decentralization, transparency and user control in transactions that involve identity information. In identity-based attacks, the attacker forges identity to masquerade as an authorized user to access the system and manipulate it. Again, identity-based attacks can be broadly classified into four different types, and they are (i) Key attack, (ii) Replay attack, (iii)Impersonation attack, and Sybil attack.

- **Key attack:** In blockchain technology, certificates and identities are validated and protected in Hyperledger Fabric by asymmetric cryptography. How each participant chooses to store and protect their private key is up to them. A wide range of wallets and management methods available as Hyperledger Fabric requires no cohesive management scheme. An outside attacker obtaining private key(s) could lead to any number of attacks. To deal with this attack, LNSC (Lightning Network and Smart Contract) protocol (Huang et al., 2018) provides an authentication mechanism between the electric vehicles and charging piles. It uses elliptic curve encryption to calculate the hash functions, ensuring resiliency against the critical leakage attack.

- **Replay attack:** This attack aims to spoof two parties' identities, intercept their data packets, and relay them to their destinations without modification. To resist this attack, LNSC (Huang et al., 2018) uses the idea of elliptic curve encryption to calculate the hash functions. On the other hand, Benin (blockchain-based system for secure mutual authentication) (Lin et al., 2018) uses a fresh one-time public/private key pair.

- **Impersonation attack:** An attacker tries to masquerade as a legitimate user to perform unauthorized operations. As presented in Table II, three methods are proposed to protect against this attack. The elliptic curve encryption idea to calculate the hash functions is proposed by the LNSC protocol (Huang et al., 2018). Wang et al. (Wang et al., 2018) propose a distributed incentive-based cooperation mechanism, which protects the user's privacy and a transaction verification method. On the other hand, Benin (Lin et al., 2018) uses the concept of attribute-based signatures (i.e., legitimate devices can produce a valid signature, and hence any impersonation attempt will be detected when its corresponding authentication operation fails.

- **Sybil attack:** A Sybil attack is when an attacker creates multiple accounts on a blockchain to deceive the other blockchain participants. A successful Sybil attack increases the reputation of some agents or lowers the reputation of others by initiating interactions in the network. These attacks should not be an issue on a permissioned blockchain since the members are clearly identified and wallets are not normally used. TrustChain (i.e., capable of creating trusted transactions among strangers without central control) (Otte et al., 2017) addresses this issue by creating an immutable chain.

- **Whitewashing:** When an agent has a negative reputation, it can eliminate its identity and make a new one. There is no remedy to prevent this behaviour. However, it is suggested in (Otte et a., 2017) to give lower priorities to new identities agents when applying the allocation policy.

- **Service-based attacks:** The attacker try either to make the service unavailable or make it behave differently from its specifications. Under this category, we can find the following attacks:

- **DDoS/DoS attack:** A distributed denial-of-service (DDOS) attack is a prevalent type of network attack against a website, a communication network node, or even a membership service provider. The objective of this attack is to slow down or crash the system. The concentrated attack and subsequent shut down of the system result in a "denial of service" for legitimate users. Denial of Service (DoS) and DDoS are common security problems. DoS attacks on the connectivity of consensus nodes may result in a loss of consensus power, thus preventing consensus nodes from being rewarded. It involves sending a vast number of requests to cause the failure of the blockchain system. CoinParty (Ziegeldorf et al., 2018) proposes the idea of a decentralized mixing service. Liu et al. (Liu et al., 2018) employ a ring-based signature with the Elliptic Curve Digital Signature Algorithm (ECDSA). The resilience against DoS in BSeIn (Lin et al., 2018) is achieved by limiting the block size and using the *'multi-receivers'* encryption technique to provide confidentiality for authorized users.

FUTURE RESEARCH DIRECTIONS

The growth of IoT itself and its advancement in the industrial sector is putting a strain on the computing resources need to maintain the level of connectivity and data collection that IoT devices require (Chan, 2017). This is where service-oriented computing comes into the picture by acting as the backbone of everything IoT offers. Cloud computing, setting up virtual servers, launching a database instance, and creating data pipelines to help run IoT solutions become easier (Chan, 2017). Moreover, data security is an essential concern in such an environment where the cloud can improve security by providing proper authentication mechanisms, firmware, and software update procedures. Besides, the major data attacks that are prevalent in the IoT world today: (i) data inconsistency, which helps an attack on data integrity, leading to data inconsistency in transit or data stored in a central database is referred to as Data Inconsistency (ii) unauthorized access control; and with unauthorized access, malicious users can gain data ownership or access sensitive data., and (iii) data breach or memory leakage refers to disclosing personal, sensitive, or confidential data in an unauthorized manner.

The data breach has posed severe threats to user's personal information in recent years. Researchers are highlighting different aspects of data breach-related issues. One such work (Gope & Sikdar, 2018) on preventing data breach has proposed a lightweight privacy-preserving two-factor authentication scheme for securing the communication between IoT devices. In future, this research will review additional research in the IoT technology and data breach-related issues.

CONCLUSION

The current manufacturing industry operating environment has been extensively scrutinized to determine the primary needs of the enterprise information system's architecture purpose. It is encouraging that the emerging IoT infrastructure can support information systems of next-generation manufacturing enterprises appropriately. Anywhere, anytime, and anything, data collection systems are more than appropriate for gathering and sharing data among manufacturing supply chains resources. IoT technology-based information systems bring different opportunities to advance manufacturing businesses to sustain good system performance in a distributed and globalized environment. However, the application of IoT in executive information systems is at its primitive age; more research is needed in the areas (e.g., modularization, semantic integration, standardization) of encouraging technologies for safe, effective, reliable communication operational decision making.

The domain of global manufacturing communication systems is well suited to a hybrid (i.e., IoT and blockchain) information system architecture approach because of its distributed nature and operating characteristics. From an intelligent manufacturing management perspective, blockchain-based systems' most appealing traits are autonomy, collaboration, and reactivity. Blockchain-based systems can work without the direct intervention of humans or others. This feature helps to implement an automated information system in the global manufacturing industry.

REFERENCES

Aberer, K., Hauswirth, H., & Salehi, A. (2006). *Middleware Support for the Internet of Things.* Available: www.manfredhauswirth.org/research/papers/WSN2006.pdf

Adat, V., & Gupta, B. B. (2017). A DDoS attack mitigation framework for Internet of things. *2017 International Conference on Communication and Signal Processing (ICCSP)*, 2036–2041. 10.1109/ICCSP.2017.8286761

Ahemd, M. M., Shah, M. A., & Wahid, A. (2017). IoT security: a layered approach for attacks and defenses. *2017 International Conference on Communication Technologies (ComTech)*, 104–110. 10.1109/COMTECH.2017.8065757

Airehrour, D., Gutierrez, J. A., & Ray, S. K. (2019). Sectrust-rpl: A secure trust-aware rpl routing protocol for the Internet of things. *Future Generation Computer Systems*, *93*, 860–876. doi:10.1016/j.future.2018.03.021

Al-Turjman, F., & Alturjman, S. (2018). Context-sensitive access in industrial Internet of things (iiot) healthcare applications. *IEEE Transactions on Industrial Informatics*, *14*(6), 2736–2744. doi:10.1109/TII.2018.2808190

Alaba, F. A., Othman, M., Hashem, I. A. T., & Alotaibi, F. (2017). Internet of things security: A survey. *Journal of Network and Computer Applications*, *88*, 10–28. doi:10.1016/j.jnca.2017.04.002

Alccer, V., & Cruz-Machado, V. (2019). Scanning the industry 4.0: A literature review on technologies for manufacturing systems, Engineering Science and Technology. *International Journal (Toronto, Ont.)*, *22*(3), 899–919.

Ali, M. S., Vecchio, M., Pincheira, M., Dolui, K., Antonelli, F., & Rehmani, M. H. (2019). *Applications of blockchains in the Internet of things: A comprehensive survey*. IEEE Commun. Surv. Tutorials.

All, I. F. (2017). *The 5 Worst Examples of IoT Hacking and Vulnerabilities in Recorded History*. Academic Press.

Aman, M. N., Chua, K. C., & Sikdar, B. (2017). A lightweight mutual authentication protocol for IoT systems. *GLOBECOM 2017 - 2017 IEEE Global Communications Conference*, 1–6.

Andoni, M., Robu, V., Flynn, D., Abram, S., Geach, D., Jenkins, D., McCallum, P., & Peacock, A. (2019). Blockchain technology in the energy sector: A systematic review of challenges and opportunities. *Renewable & Sustainable Energy Reviews*, *100*, 143–174. doi:10.1016/j.rser.2018.10.014

Andrea, I., Chrysostomou, C., & Hadjichristofi, G. (2015). Internet of things: security vulnerabilities and challenges. *2015 IEEE Symposium on Computers and Communication (ISCC)*, 180–187. 10.1109/ISCC.2015.7405513

Araujo, J., Mazo, M., Anta, A. Jr, Tabuada, P., & Johansson, K. H. (2014, February). System Architecture, Protocols, and Algorithms for Aperiodic wireless control systems. *IEEE Transactions on Industrial Informatics*, *10*(1), 175–184. doi:10.1109/TII.2013.2262281

Ashibani, Y., & Mahmoud, Q. H. (2017). An efficient and secure scheme for smart home communication using identity-based encryption. *2017 IEEE 36th International Performance Computing and Communications Conference (IPCCC)*, 1–7.

Atlam, H. F., Alenezi, A., Alassafi, M. O., & Wills, G. B. (2018). Blockchain with Internet of things: Benefits, challenges, and future directions. *Int. J. Intell. Syst. Appl.*, *10*(6), 40–48. doi:10.5815/ijisa.2018.06.05

Atlam, H. F., Azad, M. A., Alzahrani, A. G., & Wills, G. (2020). A Review of Blockchain in Internet of Things and AI. *Journal of Big Data and Cognitive Computing*, 1-27.

Azzi, R., Chamoun, R. K., & Sokhn, M. (2019). The power of a blockchain-based supply chain. *Computers & Industrial Engineering*, *135*, 582–592. doi:10.1016/j.cie.2019.06.042

Boyes, H., Hallaq, B., Cunningham, J., & Watson, T. (2018). The industrial Internet of things (iiot): An analysis framework. *Computers in Industry*, *101*, 1–12. doi:10.1016/j.compind.2018.04.015

Cervantes, C., Poplade, D., Nogueira, M., & Santos, A. (2015). Detection of sinkhole attacks for supporting secure routing on 6lowpan for Internet of things. *2015 IFIP/IEEE International Symposium on Integrated Network Management (IM)*, 606–611. 10.1109/INM.2015.7140344

Cha, S., Chen, J., Su, C., & Yeh, K. (2018). A blockchain connected gateway for ble-based devices in the Internet of things. *IEEE Access: Practical Innovations, Open Solutions*, *6*, 24639–24649. doi:10.1109/ACCESS.2018.2799942

Chan, M. (2017). *Why Cloud Computing Is the Foundation of the Internet of Things*. Academic Press.

Chaudhary, R., Aujla, G. S., Garg, S., Kumar, N., & Rodrigues, J. J. P. C. (2018). Sdn-enabled multi-attribute-based secure communication for smart grid in riot environment. *IEEE Transactions on Industrial Informatics*, *14*(6), 2629–2640. doi:10.1109/TII.2018.2789442

Chen, G., & Ng, W. S. (2017). An efficient authorization framework for securing industrial Internet of things. TENCON 2017 - 2017 IEEE Region 10 Conference, 1219–1224. doi:10.1109/TENCON.2017.8228043

Chen, L., Lee, W.-K., Chang, C.-C., Choo, K.-K. R., & Zhang, N. (2019). Blockchain-based searchable encryption for electronic health record sharing. *Future Generation Computer Systems*, *95*, 420–429. doi:10.1016/j.future.2019.01.018

Choi, J., & Kim, Y. (2016). An improved lea block encryption algorithm to prevent side-channel attack in the IoT system. *2016 Asia-Pacific Signal and Information Processing Association Annual Summit and Conference (APSIPA)*, 1–4. 10.1109/APSIPA.2016.7820845

Colema, L. (2006). Frequency of man-made disasters in the 20the century. *Journal of Contingencies and Crisis Management*, *14*(1), 3–11.

De, S.J., & Ruj, S. (2017). Efficient decentralized attribute-based access control for mobile clouds. *IEEE Transactions on Cloud Computing*.

Dorri, A., Kanhere, S. S., Jurdak, R., & Gauravaram, P. (2019). *LSB: A Lightweight Scalable Blockchain for IoT Security and Privacy*. http://arxiv.org/ abs/1712.02969

Esfahani, A., Mantas, G., Matischek, R., Saghezchi, F. B., Rodriguez, J., Bicaku, A., Maksuti, S., Tauber, M. G., Schmittner, C., & Bastos, J. (2019). A lightweight authentication mechanism for m2m communications in industrial IoT environment. *IEEE Internet of Things Journal*, 6(1), 288–296. doi:10.1109/JIOT.2017.2737630

Fernndez-Carams, T. M., & Fraga-Lamas, P. (2018). A review on the use of blockchain for the Internet of things. *IEEE Access: Practical Innovations, Open Solutions*, 6, 32979–33001. doi:10.1109/ACCESS.2018.2842685

Ferran, M.A., Derdour, M., Mukherjee, M., Dahab, A., Maglaras, L., & Janicke, H. (2019). Blockchain technologies for the Internet of things: research issues and challenges. *IEEE Internet Things J.*

Forbes. (2019). Blockchain in healthcare: How it Could Make Digital Healthcare Safer and More Innovative. *Forbes*.

Frustaci, M., Pace, P., Aloi, G., & Fortino, G. (2018). *Evaluating critical security issues of the IoT world: present and future challenges. IEEE Internet Things*.

Gai, J., Choo, K., Qiu, K. R., & Zhu, L. (2018). Privacy-preserving content-oriented wireless communication in internet-of-things. *IEEE Internet of Things Journal*, 5(4), 3059–3067. doi:10.1109/JIOT.2018.2830340

Gandino, F., Montrucchio, B., & Rebaudengo, M. (2014). Key Management for Static Wireless Sensor Networks with Node Adding. *IEEE Transaction Industrial Informatics*.

Gibbon, J., (2018). *Introduction to Trusted Execution Environment: Arm's Trust zone*. Academic Press.

Glissa, G., Rachedi, A., & Meddeb, A. (2016). A secure routing protocol based on rpl for Internet of things. *IEEE Global Communications Conference (GLOBECOM)*, 1–7. 10.1109/GLOCOM.2016.7841543

Gomes, T., Salgado, F., Tavares, A., & Cabral, J. (2017). Cute mote, a customizable and trustable end-device for the Internet of things. *IEEE Sensors Journal*, 17(20), 6816–6824. doi:10.1109/JSEN.2017.2743460

Gope, P., & Sikdar, B. (2018). *Lightweight and privacy-preserving two-factor authentication scheme for IoT devices. IEEE Internet Things*.

Granville, K., (2018). *Facebook and Cambridge Analytica: what You Need to Know as Fallout Widens*. Academic Press.

Griggs, K. N., Osipova, O., Kohlios, C. P., Baccarini, A. N., Howson, E. A., & Hayajneh, T. (2018). Healthcare blockchain system using smart contracts for secure automated remote patient monitoring. *Journal of Medical Systems*, 42(7), 1–7. doi:10.100710916-018-0982-x PMID:29876661

Guan, Z., Si, G., Zhang, X., Wu, L., Guizani, N., Du, X., & Ma, Y. (2018). Privacy-preserving and efficient aggregation based on blockchain for power grid communications in smart communities. *IEEE Communications Magazine*, 56(7), 82–88. doi:10.1109/MCOM.2018.1700401

Guin, U., Singh, A., Alam, M., Caedo, J., & Skjellum, A. (2018). A secure low-cost edge device authentication scheme for the Internet of things. *31st International Conference on VLSI Design and 17th International Conference on Embedded Systems (VLSID)*, 85–90. 10.1109/VLSID.2018.42

Hei, X., Du, X., Wu, J., & Hu, F. (2010). Defending resource depletion attacks on implantable medical devices. *2010 IEEE Global Telecommunications Conference GLOBECOM 2010*, 1–5. 10.1109/GLO-COM.2010.5685228

Huang, J., Kong, L., Chen, G., Wu, M., Liu, X., & Zeng, P. (2019b). Towards secure industrial IoT: blockchain system with credit-based consensus mechanism. IEEE Trans. Ind.

Huang, X., Zhang, Y., Li, D., & Han, L. (2019a). An optimal scheduling algorithm for hybrid EV charging scenario using consortium blockchains. *Future Generation Computer Systems*, *91*, 555–562. doi:10.1016/j.future.2018.09.046

Huh, J.-H., & Seo, K. (2019). Blockchain-based mobile fingerprint verification and automatic log-in platform for future computing. *The Journal of Supercomputing*, *75*(6), 3123–3139. doi:10.100711227-018-2496-1

Huh, S.-K., & Kim, J.-H. (2019). The blockchain consensus algorithm for viable management of new and renewable energies. *Sustainability*, *11*(3184), 3184. doi:10.3390u11113184

Islam, S. H., Khan, M. K., & Al-Khouri, A. M. (2015). Anonymous and provably secure certificateless multireceiver encryption without bilinear pairing. *Secure. Commun. Netw.*, *8*(13), 2214–2231. https://onlinelibrary.wiley.com/doi/abs/10.1002/sec.1165

Kang, J., Xiong, Z., Niyato, D., Ye, D., Kim, D. I., & Zhao, J. (2019a). Toward secure blockchain-enabled Internet of vehicles: Optimizing consensus management using reputation and contract theory. *IEEE Transactions on Vehicular Technology*, *68*(3), 2906–2920. doi:10.1109/TVT.2019.2894944

Kang, J., Yu, R., Huang, X., Maharjan, S., Zhang, Y., & Hossain, E. (2017). Enabling localized peer-to-peer electricity trading among plug-in hybrid electric vehicles using consortium blockchains. *IEEE Transactions on Industrial Informatics*, *13*(6), 3154–3164. doi:10.1109/TII.2017.2709784

Kang, J., Yu, R., Huang, X., Wu, M., Maharjan, S., Xie, S., & Zhang, Y. (2019b). Blockchain for secure and efficient data sharing in vehicular edge computing and networks. *IEEE Internet of Things Journal*, *6*(3), 4660–4670. doi:10.1109/JIOT.2018.2875542

Karati, A., Islam, S. H., & Karuppiah, M. (2018). Provably secure and lightweight certificateless signature scheme for iiot environments. *IEEE Transactions on Industrial Informatics*, *14*(8), 3701–3711. doi:10.1109/TII.2018.2794991

Khan, F. I., & Hameed, S. (2019). Understanding security requirements and challenges in the Internet of things (iots): a review. *Journal of Computer Networks and Communications*.

Khan, M. A., & Salah, K. (2018). IoT security: Review, blockchain solutions, and open challenges. *Future Generation Computer Systems*, *82*, 395–411. doi:10.1016/j.future.2017.11.022

Kim, J.-H., & Huh, S.-K. (1973). A study on the improvement of smart grid security performance and blockchain smart grid perspective. *Energies*, 11.

Kim, S.-K., Kim, U.-M., & Huh, H. J. (2017). A study on improvement of blockchain application to overcome vulnerability of IoT multiplatform security. *Energies*, *12*(402).

Konigsmark, S. T. C., Chen, D., & Wong, M. D. F. (2016). Information dispersion for trojan defense through high-level synthesis. *ACM/EDAC/IEEE Design Automation Conference (DAC)*, 1–6. 10.1145/2897937.2898034

Kouicem, D. E., Bouabdallah, A., & Lakhlef, H. (2018). Internet of things security: A top-down survey. *Computer Networks*, *141*, 199–221. doi:10.1016/j.comnet.2018.03.012

Li, C., & Palanisamy, B. (2019). Privacy in Internet of things: From principles to technologies. *IEEE Internet of Things Journal*, *6*(1), 488–505. doi:10.1109/JIOT.2018.2864168

Li, R., Song, T., Mei, B., Li, H., Cheng, X., & Sun, L. (2019). Blockchain for large-scale Internet of things data storage and protection. *IEEE Transactions on Services Computing*, *12*(5), 762–771. doi:10.1109/TSC.2018.2853167

Li, X., Niu, J., Bhuiyan, M. Z. A., Wu, F., Karuppiah, M., & Kumari, S. (2018a). A robust ECC-based provable secure authentication protocol with privacy-preserving for industrial Internet of things. *IEEE Transactions on Industrial Informatics*, *14*(8), 3599–3609. doi:10.1109/TII.2017.2773666

Li, Z., Kang, J., Yu, R., Ye, D., Deng, Q., & Zhang, Y. (2018b). Consortium blockchain for secure energy trading in industrial Internet of things. *IEEE Transactions on Industrial Informatics*, *14*(8), 3690–3700.

Lin, C., He, D., Huang, X., Choo, K.-K. R., & Vasilakos, A. V. (2018). Basin: A blockchain-based secure mutual authentication with fine-grained access control system for industry 4.0. *Journal of Network and Computer Applications*, *116*, 42–52. doi:10.1016/j.jnca.2018.05.005

Ling, Z., Liu, K., Xu, Y., Jin, Y., & Fu, X. (2017). An end-to-end view of IoT security and privacy. *IEEE Global Communications Conference*, 1–7. 10.1109/GLOCOM.2017.8254011

Liu, C., Cronin, P., & Yang, C. (2016). A mutual auditing framework to protect iot against hardware trojans. *2016 21st Asia and South Pacific Design Automation Conference (ASP-DAC)*, 69–74. 10.1109/ASPDAC.2016.7427991

Liu, C. H., Lin, Q., & Wen, S. (2019b). *Blockchain-enabled data collection and sharing for industrial IoT with deep reinforcement learning. IEEE Transaction Industrial Informatics*. doi:10.1109/TII.2018.2890203

Liu, J., Zhang, C., & Fang, Y. (2018). Epic: A differential privacy framework to defend smart homes against internet traffic analysis. *IEEE Internet of Things Journal*, *5*(2), 1206–1217. doi:10.1109/JIOT.2018.2799820

Liu, Y., Guo, W., Fan, C., Chang, L., & Cheng, C. (2019a). A practical privacy-preserving data aggregation (3pda) scheme for smart grid. *IEEE Transactions on Industrial Informatics*, *15*(3), 1767–1774. doi:10.1109/TII.2018.2809672

Longo, F., Nicoletti, L., Padovano, A., d'Atri, G., & Forte, M. (2019). Blockchain-enabled supply chain: An experimental study. *Computers & Industrial Engineering*, *136*, 57–69. doi:10.1016/j.cie.2019.07.026

Lu, Y., & Li, J. (2016). A pairing-free certificate-based proxy re-encryption scheme for secure data sharing in public clouds. *Future Generation Computer Systems*, *62*, 140–147. doi:10.1016/j.future.2015.11.012

Machado, C., & Frhlich, A. A. M. (2018). IoT data integrity verification for cyber-physical systems using blockchain. *2018 IEEE 21st International Symposium on Real-Time Distributed Computing (ISORC)*, 83–90. 10.1109/ISORC.2018.00019

Makhdoom, I., Abolhasan, M., Abbas, H., & Ni, W. (2019). Blockchain's adoption in iot: The challenges, and a way forward. *Journal of Network and Computer Applications, 125*, 251–279. doi:10.1016/j.jnca.2018.10.019

Manditereza, K., (2017). *4 Key Differences between Scada and Industrial IoT*. Academic Press.

Manzoor, A., Liyanage, M., Braeken, A., Kanhere, S. S., & Ylianttila, M. (2019). Blockchain-Based Proxy Re-encryption Scheme for Secure IoT Data Sharing. *Clinical Orthopaedics and Related Research*.

Minoli, D., & Occhiogross, B. (2018). Blockchain mechanism for IoT security. *International Journal of Internet of Things*, 1-13.

Mondal, S., Wijewardena, K. P., Karuppuswami, S., Kriti, N., Kumar, D., & Chahal, P. (2019). Blockchain inspired RFID-based information architecture for food supply chain. *IEEE Internet of Things Journal, 6*(3), 5803–5813. doi:10.1109/JIOT.2019.2907658

Mosenia, A., & Jha, N. K. (2017). A comprehensive study of security of internet-of-things. *IEEE Transactions on Emerging Topics in Computing, 5*(4), 586–602. doi:10.1109/TETC.2016.2606384

Naeem, H., Guo, B., & Naeem, M. R. (2018). A lightweight malware static visual analysis for IoT infrastructure. *International Conference on Artificial Intelligence and Big Data (ICAIBD)*, 240–244.

ObserveIT. (2018). *5 Examples of Insider Threat-Caused Breaches that Illustrate the Scope of the Problem*. Author.

Okorie, O., Turner, C., Charnley, F., Moreno, M., & Tiwari, A. (2017). A review of data-driven approaches for circular economy in manufacturing. *Proceedings of the 18th European Roundtable for Sustainable Consumption and Production*.

Omar, A. A., Bhuiyan, M. Z. A., Basu, A., Kiyomoto, S., & Rahman, M. S. (2019). Privacy-friendly platform for healthcare data in cloud-based on blockchain environment. *Future Generation Computer Systems, 95*, 511–521. doi:10.1016/j.future.2018.12.044

Oztemel, E., & Gusev, S. (2018). Literature review of industry 4.0 and related technologies. *Journal of Intelligent Manufacturing*.

Pal, K. (2017). Building High Quality Big Data-Based Applications in Supply Chains. IGI Global Publication.

Pal, K. (2018). *Ontology-Based Web Service Architecture for Retail Supply Chain Management*. The 9th International Conference on Ambient Systems, Networks and Technologies, Porto, Portugal.

Pal, K. (2019). Algorithmic Solutions for RFID Tag Anti-Collision Problem in Supply Chain Management. *Procedia Computer Science, 151*, 929–934. doi:10.1016/j.procs.2019.04.129

Pal, K. (2020). *Information sharing for manufacturing supply chain management based on blockchain technology*. In I. Williams (Ed.), *Cross-Industry Use of Blockchain Technology and Opportunities for the Future* (pp. 1–17). IGI Global.

Pal, K. (2021). Applications of Secured Blockchain Technology in Manufacturing Industry. In Blockchain and AI Technology in the Industrial Internet of Things. IGI Global Publication.

Pal, K., & Yasar, A. (2020). Internet of Things and blockchain technology in apparel manufacturing supply chain data management. *Procedia Computer Science, 170*, 450–457. doi:10.1016/j.procs.2020.03.088

Park, N., & Kang, N. (2015). Mutual authentication scheme in secure Internet of things technology for comfortable lifestyle. *Sensors (Basel), 16*(1), 20. doi:10.339016010020 PMID:26712759

Porambage, P., Schmitt, C., Kumar, P., Gurtov, A., & Ylianttila, M. (2014). Pauthkey: A pervasive authentication protocol and key establishment scheme for wireless sensor networks in distributed IoT applications. *International Journal of Distributed Sensor Networks, 10*(7), 357430. doi:10.1155/2014/357430

Pu, C., & Hajjar, S. (2018). Mitigating forwarding misbehaviors in rpl-based low power and lossy networks. *2018 15th IEEE Annual Consumer Communications Networking Conference (CCNC)*, 1–6. 10.1109/CCNC.2018.8319164

Rahulamathavan, Y., Phan, R. C., Rajarajan, M., Misra, S., & Kondoz, A. (2017). Privacy-preserving blockchain-based IoT ecosystem using attribute-based encryption. *IEEE International Conference on Advanced Networks and Telecommunications Systems (ANTS)*, 1–6. 10.1109/ANTS.2017.8384164

Rambus. (n.d.). *Industrial IoT: Threats and countermeasures*. https://www.rambus.com/iot/industrial-IoT/

Reyna, A., Martn, C., Chen, J., Soler, E., & Daz, M. (2018). On blockchain and its integration with iot. challenges and opportunities. *Future Generation Computer Systems, 88*, 173–190. doi:10.1016/j.future.2018.05.046

Sfar, A. R., Natalizio, E., Challal, Y., & Chtourou, Z. (2018). A roadmap for security challenges in the Internet of things. *Digital Communications and Networks., 4*(2), 118–137. doi:10.1016/j.dcan.2017.04.003

Shen, M., Tang, X., Zhu, L., Du, X., & Guizani, M. (2019). Privacy-preserving support vector machine training over blockchain-based encrypted IoT data in smart cities. *IEEE Internet of Things Journal, 6*(5), 7702–7712. doi:10.1109/JIOT.2019.2901840

Shrestha, R., Bajracharya, R., Shrestha, A. P., & Nam, S. Y. (2019). *A new type of blockchain for secure message exchange in vanet*. Digital Communications and Networks. doi:10.1016/j.dcan.2019.04.003

Shukla, P. (2017). Ml-ids: A machine learning approach to detect wormhole attacks in the Internet of things. Intelligent Systems Conference (IntelliSys), 234–240. doi:10.1109/IntelliSys.2017.8324298

Sicari, S., Rizzardi, A., Miorandi, D., & Coen-Porisini, A. (2018). Reatoreacting to denial-of-service attacks in the Internet of things. *Computer Networks, 137*, 37–48. doi:10.1016/j.comnet.2018.03.020

Singh, M., Rajan, M. A., Shivraj, V. L., & Balamuralidhar, P. (2015). Secure MQTT for the Internet of things (IoT). *5th International Conference on Communication Systems and Network Technologies*, 746–751. 10.1109/CSNT.2015.16

Song, T., Li, R., Mei, B., Yu, J., Xing, X., & Cheng, X. (2017). A privacy-preserving communication protocol for IoT applications in smart homes. *IEEE Internet of Things Journal, 4*(6), 1844–1852. doi:10.1109/JIOT.2017.2707489

SOPHOS. (2015). *49 Busted in Europe for Man-In-The-Middle Bank Attacks.* https://nakedsecurity. sophos.com/2015/06/11/49-busted-in-europe-for-man-in-themiddle-bank-attacks/

Sreamr. (2017). *Streamr White Paper v2.0.* https://s3.amazonaws.com/streamr-public/ streamr-datacoin-whitepaper-2017-07-25-v1_0.pdf

Srinivas, J., Das, A. K., Wazid, M., & Kumar, N. (2018). *Anonymous lightweight chaotic map-based authenticated key agreement protocol for industrial internet of things. IEEE Trans.* Dependable Secure Comput.

Su, J., Vasconcellos, V. D., Prasad, S., Daniele, S., Feng, Y., & Sakurai, K. (2018). Lightweight classification of IoT malware based on image recognition. *IEEE 42nd Annual Computer Software and Applications Conference (COMPSAC), 2,* 664–669. doi:10.1109/TDSC.2018.2857811

Varga, P., Plosz, S., Soos, G., & Hegedus, C. (2017). Security Threats and Issues in Automation IoT. *2017 IEEE 13th International Workshop on Factory Communication Systems (WFCS),* 1–6. 10.1109/WFCS.2017.7991968

Vechain Team. (2018). *Vechain White Paper.* https://cdn.vechain.com/vechain_ico_ideas_of_ development_en.pdf

Waltonchain. (2021). *Waltonchain white paper v2.0.* https://www.waltonchain.org/en/ Waltonchain_White_Paper_2.0_EN.pdf

Wan, J., Li, J., Imran, M., Li, D., & e-Amin, F. (2019). A blockchain-based solution for enhancing security and privacy in smart factory. *IEEE Transaction.*

Wan, J., Tang, S., Shu, Z., Li, D., Wang, S., Imran, M., & Vasilakos, A. V. (2016). Software-defined industrial Internet of things in the context of industry 4.0. *IEEE Sensors Journal, 16*(20), 7373–7380. doi:10.1109/JSEN.2016.2565621

Wang, Q., Zhu, X., Ni, Y., Gu, L., & Zhu, H. (2019b). *Blockchain for the IoT and industrial IoT: a review.* Internet Things.

Wang, X., Zha, X., Ni, W., Liu, R. P., Guo, Y. J., Niu, X., & Zheng, K. (2019a). Survey on blockchain for Internet of things. *Computer Communications, 136,* 10–29. doi:10.1016/j.comcom.2019.01.006

Wurm, J., Hoang, K., & Arias, O., Sadeghi, A., & Jin, Y. (2016). Security analysis on consumer and industrial IoT devices. *21st Asia and South Pacific Design Automation Conference (ASP-DAC),* 519–524. 10.1109/ASPDAC.2016.7428064

Xiong, Z., Zhang, Y., Niyato, D., Wang, P., & Han, Z. (2018). When mobile blockchain meets edge computing. *IEEE Communications Magazine, 56*(8), 33–39. doi:10.1109/MCOM.2018.1701095

Xu, L. D., He, W., & Li, S. (2014). Internet of things in industries: A survey. *IEEE Transactions on Industrial Informatics, 10*(4), 2233–2243.

Xu, L. D., Xu, E. L., & Li, L. (2018). Industry 4.0: State of the art and future trends. *International Journal of Production Research*, *56*(8), 2941–2962. doi:10.1080/00207543.2018.1444806

Xu, Y., Ren, J., Wang, G., Zhang, C., Yang, J., & Zhang, Y. (2019). *A blockchain-based non-repudiation network computing service scheme for industrial IoT. IEEE Transaction Industrial Informatics.*

Yan, Q., Huang, W., Luo, X., Gong, Q., & Yu, F. R. (2018). A multi-level DDoS mitigation framework for the industrial Internet of things. *IEEE Communications Magazine*, *56*(2), 30–36. doi:10.1109/MCOM.2018.1700621

Yang, W., Wang, S., Huang, X., & Mu, Y. (2019a). On the Security of an Efficient and Robust Certificateless Signature Scheme for IIoT Environments. *IEEE Access: Practical Innovations, Open Solutions*, *7*, 91074–91079. doi:10.1109/ACCESS.2019.2927597

Yang, Y., Wu, L., Yin, G., Li, L., & Zhao, H. (2017). A survey on security and privacy issues in internet-of-things. *IEEE Internet of Things Journal*, *4*(5), 1250–1258. doi:10.1109/JIOT.2017.2694844

Yang, Z., Yang, K., Lei, L., Zheng, K., & Leung, V. C. M. (2019b). Blockchain-based decentralized trust management in vehicular networks. *IEEE Internet of Things Journal*, *6*(2), 1495–1505. doi:10.1109/JIOT.2018.2836144

Yao, X., Kong, H., Liu, H., Qiu, T., & Ning, H. (2019). An attribute credential-based public-key scheme for fog computing in digital manufacturing. *IEEE Trans. Ind. Inf.*

Yin, D., Zhang, L., & Yang, K. (2018). A DDoS attack detection and mitigation with software-defined Internet of things framework. *IEEE Access: Practical Innovations, Open Solutions*, *6*, 24694–24705. doi:10.1109/ACCESS.2018.2831284

Zhang, H., Wang, J., & Ding, Y. (2019b). Blockchain-based decentralized and secure keyless signature scheme for smart grid. *Energy*, *180*, 955–967. doi:10.1016/j.energy.2019.05.127

Zhang, N., Mi, X., Feng, X., Wang, X., Tian, Y., & Qian, F. (2018). *Understanding and Mitigating the Security Risks of Voice-Controlled Third-Party Skills on Amazon Alexa and Google Home.* Academic Press.

Zhang, Y., Deng, R., Zheng, D., Li, J., Wu, P., & Cao, J. (2019a). *Efficient and Robust Certificateless Signature for Data Crowdsensing in Cloud-Assisted Industrial IoT. IEEE Transaction Industry.* doi:10.1109/TII.2019.2894108

Zheng, D., Wu, A., Zhang, Y., & Zhao, Q. (2018). Efficient and privacy-preserving medical data sharing in the Internet of things with limited computing power. *IEEE Access: Practical Innovations, Open Solutions*, *6*, 28019–28027. doi:10.1109/ACCESS.2018.2840504

Zhou, R., Zhang, X., Du, X., Wang, X., Yang, G., & Guizani, M. (2018). File-centric multi-key aggregate keyword searchable encryption for industrial Internet of things. *IEEE Transactions on Industrial Informatics*, *14*(8), 3648–3658. doi:10.1109/TII.2018.2794442

Ziegeldorf, J. H., Morchon, O. G., & Wehrle, K. (2014). *Privacy in the Internet of Things: Threats and Challenges.* https://arxiv.org/abs/1505.07683

Chapter 10
Blockchain Technology With the Internet of Things in Manufacturing Data Processing Architecture

Kamalendu Pal

iD https://orcid.org/0000-0001-7158-6481

City, University of London, UK

ABSTRACT

Modern manufacturing logistics and supply chain have transformed into highly complex value-creating business networks. It has become increasingly challenging to cross-check the source of raw materials and maintain visibility of products and merchandise while moving through the value chain network. This way, the high complexity of manufacturing business processes and the continuously growing amount of information lead to extraordinary demand to find an appropriate data processing architecture for the global manufacturing industry. The internet of things (IoT) applications can help manufacturing companies track, trace, and monitor products, business activities, and processes within the respective value chain networks. Combining with IoT, blockchain technology can enable a broader range of different application scenarios to improve value chain transparency. This chapter presents a hybrid (i.e., IoT, blockchain, service-oriented computing) data processing architecture for the manufacturing industry.

INTRODUCTION

Modern manufacturing has got a long history of evolution for several hundred years. The first industrial revolution began in the last part of the 18th century (Lukac, 2015). It symbolized production systems powered by water and steam, followed by the second industrial revolution, which started in the early part of the 20th century with the characteristics of mass labour deployment and manufacturing systems based on electrical power. The third industrial revolution began in the early part of the 1970s with automatic production or manufacturing based on electronics and computer data communication technology.

DOI: 10.4018/978-1-7998-5839-3.ch010

The concept of Industry 4.0 was put forward for developing the German economy in 2011 (Pal, 2021). Industry 4.0 is characterized by cyber-physical systems (CPS) production based on heterogeneous data and knowledge integration. It is closely related to IoT, CPS, information and communication technology (ICT), enterprise architecture (EA), and enterprise integration (Pal, 2021).

In a typical manufacturing supply chain, raw materials purchase from suppliers and products manufactured at one or more production plants. Then the product move to intermediate storage (e.g., warehouse, distribution centres) for packing and shipping to retailers or customers. In this way, a manufacturing supply chain consists of business partners in the network, and these are the suppliers, transporters, manufacturers, distributors, retailers, and customers (Pal, 2019) (Pal, 2017). A diagrammatic representation of a manufacturing supply chain is shown in Figure 1.

In this way, a manufacturing supply chain creates a complex network of business processes. Due to globalization and business process decentralization, a manufacturing supply chain's efficient performance needs better visibility - defined as the capability to share on time and accurate data throughout the manufacturing supply chain network and coordination among supply chain business partners. In today's global business environment, companies recognize the strategic importance of well-managed manufacturing supply chains.

Manufacturers are trying to focus on the significance of changes taking place in enterprise integration initiatives (e.g., supply chains), and it is worth reviewing trends in production and operations management. Besides, the global extension of many supply networks means that their members are increasingly geographically dispersed, working across different time zones, many organizational boundaries, numerous types of organizational cultures, and related work practices. These teams are often brought together on short notice and coordinated in nearly real-time to complete a production project or a particular service within limited time and restricted resources. Very often, manufacturing supply chain business partners are engaged in many supply business activities simultaneously. In these situations, communications and real-time coordination between mobile and distributed supply chain members is complex, making the requirement for an efficient communication infrastructure that provides reliable on-demand access to both supply process information and related personnel more accurately.

Figure 1. Diagrammatic representation of a manufacturing supply chain network

Also, the change towards demand-driven production implies that not managing supplies but demands of the customer should trigger and influence the production processes. Consequently, logistics gets a new focus on optimizing the production process in a very dynamic environment. Besides, though there are different solutions and methods for regional business processes minimization (e.g., strategic manufacturing operations scheduling systems, inventory management systems, market trading optimization systems, and so on), generally, these local decisions do not assure the overall business optimization at the global level because of the conflicts between the local goals.

The manufacturing supply chain management (SCM) problem can be defined as the management of relationship across a supply chain network to find the synergy of intra- and inter-company business processes to optimize the overall business operation of the enterprise (e.g., quality assurance, cost minimization, and on-time delivery). The traditional simple integration techniques are not enough to assure global optimization due to their inherent complexity. For example, a researcher (Dreher, 1999) presented a complex VOLKSWAGEN index showing that an automobile is manufactured from 3000 up to more than 20000 parts. Also, researchers (Eschenbacher et al., 2000) shown the complexity of an integrated distributed production planning system for the same supply chain coordinated and controlled centrally would cause a lot of different problems: (i) bottlenecks of centrally control centres of production, (ii) planning in the complete supply chain can be very complex, (iii) confidential internal information must be provided to the individual centre, and (iv) data consistency is a significant issue in decentralized structures.

Manufacturers often use enterprise resource planning (ERP) to integrate procurement, production, distribution, inventory management, and sales systems. ERP evolved from early material requirements planning (MRP) and manufacturing resource planning (MRP II). ERP systems track a range of business resources, including raw materials, manufacturing capacity, inventory, and cash, plus commitments such as sales and purchase orders. Databases in ERP track and share this data across business functions and potentially to outside stakeholders.

Recent inclinations towards the convergence of wireless communications and Internet-based technologies can open new avenues of business operational data collaboration, minimizing the physical dispersion of manufacturing supply chain members. In this way, blockchain, a distributed database (or ledger) of transactions connected into blocks of unique data structure (known as node or block), promises to (i) enhance efficiency, speed, and security of ownership transfer of digital assets (ii) eliminate the requirement for central authorities to certify ownership and help to complete transactions, (iii) minimize administrative expenditure using agreements that can automatically activate, and create trusted actions based on computational algorithms (known as smart contract), and (iv) preventing fraud and corruption by using a transparent and publicly auditable ledger facility.

A significant challenge associated with blockchain adoption is finding out relevant use cases that would benefit from integrating blockchain technology with the Internet of Things (IoT) based information systems in the manufacturing industry. With recent advances in Radio Frequency Identification (RFID) technology, low-cost wireless sensor hardware, and computer network infrastructures, the Internet of Things (IoT) advance has attracted attention in connected manufacturing business activities and sharing operational business information more integrated way.

Spite the vast applicability of IoT-based applications in the manufacturing industry, and there are many challenges for deploying this technology. In the traditional manufacturing supply chain, new orders are sent to suppliers via fax or courier mail. The manufacturing supply chain can be deployed as a resource-interactive network that needs no hands-on operation combined with IoT. Each sensor in the manufacturing supply chain automatically collects the information required and automatically and efficiently performs its flow. However, IoT technology is still at the risk of a single point of failure, and there is a risk of leaking corporate privacy.

Blockchain technology emerges from the early research work of Satoshi Nakamoto (Nakamoto, 2008) on 'Bitcoin', a peer-to-peer (P2P) electronic currency system. This system permitted payments to be directly initiated by one party and send to the other without any intervention of a third-party financial institution (Rana et al., 2019). However, this technology is forming a stepping stone for trusted information exchange among business partners. The blockchain maintains the same ledger by different nodes or members in the blockchain network to complete a trusted transaction. In recent years, prominent public blockchain platforms (e.g., Ethereum, Hyperledger Fabric, Enterprise Operating System (EOS)) help industries to create decentralized applications using smart contract-based blockchain network. In this network, each node on the blockchain is responsible for allocating the ledger copy to all other participating nodes so that the data in the blockchain is tamper-proof.

In this way, blockchain integrated IoT architecture provides advantages of tamper-resistance information-sharing platforms. However, these architectures face many problems. For example, the explosion of data generated by IoT-based systems faces main challenges in data management, data mining, and security problems. Data management challenges are associated with many technology-specific essential issues. IoT sensors, machinery, and special-purpose devices generate huge data that need to process and stored appropriately in the manufacturing industry.

The rest of this chapter is organized as follows. Section 2 describes the overview of manufacturing network data management related technical issues. It also simply explains the paradigms of IoT technology and the blockchain used for business processes automation purposes. Section 3 presents the background knowledge of key technologies for automating the global manufacturing industry. Section 4 describes the challenges for blockchain-based IoT application. Section 5 presents the proposed three-layered framework for an information system. It includes data storage and consolidation policy-related research agendas, and this section also explains the emerging issues in blockchain-based information system's deployment. Section 6 review related research works. Section 7 explains the future research direction. Finally, Section 8 concludes by discussing relevant research issues.

BACKGROUND OF MANUFACTURING NETWORK DATA MANAGEMENT

It has become an important trend for the manufacturing industry to adopt decentralization as a new manufacturing paradigm. At the same time, data analysis advantages give more insights into manufacturing production lines, thus improving its overall productivity. It helps more efficient operations and facilities move from mass to customized production. Also, business processes automation improves the efficiency of industrial production. Detailed information on the constituent parts of manufacturing artefacts and their history are needed to streamline the dedicated manufacturing processes. In this way, digitalization helps to improve the efficiency of manufacturing systems. For example, sub-components of a manufacturing artefact traceability could be done through an RFID code that uses electromagnetic waves to identify and monitor tags attached to objects automatically. Information technology (IT) provides a new way to track the origin and flow of materials; therefore, it helps increase manufacturing operational information transparency. It provides the necessary infrastructure for the customization of product based on user requirements.

Data management challenge relates to many technology-specific essential issues. IoT sensors, machinery, and special-purpose-purpose devices generate massive data that need to be processed and stored in a manufacturing business. Business-specific data centre architecture for information systems also plays a crucial role. Few manufacturing businesses would invest in data storage sufficient to house all the IoT data collected from the network. Consequently, they need to prioritize data for operations or backup based on business uses and value. Data centres architecture are often distributed to improve processing efficiency and response time as IoT devices become more widely used for global business operational facilities.

Data mining applications play an essential role in IoT-based infrastructure. As different data types are available, data consists of traditional discrete data and streaming data generated from digital sensors in manufacturing plants, machinery, vehicles, and shipping packages. These real-time streaming of data provide temperature, humidity, location, and movement-related information of interest items. In this way, in the manufacturing industry, data mining applications provide correctional guidance to facilitate necessary actions.

IoT-based manufacturing chain information system's security is also a major challenging problem. A growing number and type of connected devices are introduced into IoT networks, the potential security threats escalate. Training developers may resolve security challenges to incorporate security solutions (e.g., intrusion prevention systems, firewalls) into products and operational services.

Figure 2. Overview of data management in a blockchain technology

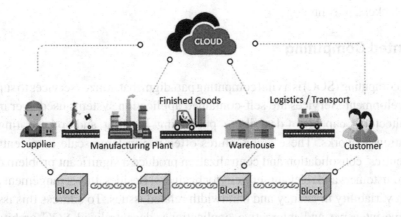

In this way, modern IoT-based infrastructure is often regarded as the catalyst for improving supply chain information sharing ability. Information sharing across manufacturing networks is based on linking unique identifications of objects – tagged using RFID transponders – with records in manufacturing business process-related information. The Electronic Product Code Information Services (EPCIS) plays an essential role in gathering and processing the collected data. IoT technology is used heavily in manufacturing business processes (e.g., inventory management, warehousing, and transportation of products, automatic object tracking) in supply chain management. With access to precise information, manufacturing supply chain operational managers can perform their analysis on a nearly real-time basis and take appropriate strategic decisions.

Despite making to the rapid development of IoT applications, the current IoT-centric architecture has led to many isolated data silos that hinder the full capabilities of appropriate data-driven business information systems. Besides, standalone IoT application systems face security and privacy-related technical issues. Blockchain technology can provide introduced an effective solution to IoT based information systems security. A blockchain enhances IoT devices to send data for inclusion in a shared transaction repository with the tamper-resistant record and enables business partners to access and supply IoT data without central control and management intervention. This chapter presents a blockchain-based design for the IoT applications that secure distributed data management to support transactions services within a multi-party global manufacturing network, as shown in Figure 2.

DECENTRALIZED MANUFACTURING AUTOMATION TECHNOLOGIES

The recent decade has seen the importance of disruptive innovations that have changed many manufacturing (e.g., apparel) business operations. In recent years, manufacturing companies are challenged to accomplish timely and accurate information exchange among the inventory-management applications and across the supply chain tiers. As a response to these challenges, the manufacturing industry initiated the inventory visibility and interoperability research projects, highlighting the requirements to establish interoperable data exchange standards among manufacturing business partners. It provides efficient operations and facilities with the shift from mass to customized production. This section presents some of the critical technologies which help to interoperable data exchange in the manufacturing industry. It includes a brief description of service-oriented computing, IoT based information systems, and an introduction to blockchain technology.

Service-Oriented Computing

Service-oriented computing (SOC) is a vital computing paradigm that utilizes services to support distributed applications' development. Services are self-contained application systems used over industry-specific middleware architectures, capable of describing, publishing, locating, and orchestrating over dedicated data communication networks. These architectures often use in large-scale data centre environment. However, data centres' consolidation and centralization produce a significant problem due to increased distance between customers and relevant services for business. Besides, this arrangement creates different outcomes in high variability in latency and bandwidth related issues. To address this issue, particularly regarding resource-intensive and interactive applications, decentralized SOC architectures, namely cloudlets, have emerged. Cloudlets are small-scale data centres situated near user applications and can mitigate low latency and high bandwidth guarantees. This chapter's research embraces this locality-aware data storage and processing trend and brings it to its full potential with a decentralized access control layer that ensures ownership and data sharing security.

IoT Based Information System

IoT technology's main backbone is a worldwide data communication network of interconnected smart objects. IoT technology's primary purpose is to share information acquired by smart objects, reflecting the manufacturing business activities, transportation, consumption, and other details of the manufacturing industry detail. The gathered information can be used for business-specific applications.

The prompt and effective decision depends on reasoning mechanisms and the quality and quality of business operational data. Every significant manufacturing business has been supported by the advancement of Information Technology (IT) and its applications. For example, the broad adoption of enterprise resource planning (ERP) and industrial business process automation made flexible manufacturing system feasible. It includes computer-aided design, computer-aided product development, and computer-aided process planning made computer integrated manufacturing practice. In developing enterprise information systems (EISs), more and more enterprises rely on IT software service providers to replace or advance their conventional systems. Hence, it makes sense to examine the IT infrastructure changes and evaluate their impacts on the evolution of manufacturing business process automation when a new IT solution (e.g., blockchain technology) becomes influential.

Blockchain Technology

Blockchain technology has attracted wide attention due to cryptocurrencies (e.g., bitcoin) (Nakamoto, 2008).In simple, blockchain is a distributed data structure comprising a chain of blocks. Blockchain technology acts as a distributed global record-keeping digital book (or ledger), which maintains all transactions records. Individually transactions are time-stamped and grouped into blocks where its cryptographic hash function identifies each block. The chain is formed of a linear sequence that each block references the hash of the previous block, creating a chain of blocks known as '*blockchain*'. Technically, a blockchain is managed by a network of nodes, and every node executes and records the transactions. A simple blockchain diagram is shown in Figure 3.

Blockchain technology is considered a strong foundation of research in cryptography, hashing, peer-to-peer (P2P) networks and consensus protocols. The initial excitement about Blockchain technology-enabled P2P transfers of digital currency to anybody in the world, crossing human-created boundaries (such as countries' borders) without intermediaries such as banks. This excitement heightened by realizing that P2P ability can be applied to other, non-crypto currency types of transactions. These transactions involve assets such as titles, deeds, music and art, secret codes, contracts between businesses, autonomous driver decisions, and artefacts resulting from many everyday human endeavours. A transaction record may contain other details based on the blockchain protocol and the application. In simple, a transaction in the blockchain is a transferable activity between different business partners.

A blockchain consists of a set of blocks, as shown in Figure 3, and an individual block encapsulates a hash of the previous block, which is creating a chain of blocks from the first, also called a genesis block the current block, where these blocks consist of transactions. These transactions mean an agreement between two participants, where the value of transfer may be of physical or digital assets, or it could be the completion of a task. The requested transaction is broadcasted to a P2P network consisting of computers, known as nodes, to validate the transfer. A node can be any electronic device (e.g., computer, phone, printer, or even smart machine) in a manufacturing business if connected to the Internet. All nodes have equal importance on a blockchain. Also, each node has a different type of tasks to perform in making a blockchain network. Technically, there are different types of blockchain nodes that have been identified and defined by the research community (Pal, 2020). In a simplistic sense, three types of nodes (i.e., Light Node, Full Node, and Mining or Forging node) are available for commercial information system implementation purpose.

Industry users of the blockchain-based information system network use mining nodes to create new blocks, verified by algorithmic software for their information, and ultimately add them to a distributed P2P network. Blockchain technology uses the consensus algorithm (Ferrag et al., 2018) to add a new block to the network and follow the steps as below:

1. Blockchain network user uses the cryptographic-based private key to sign a transaction and advertises the book to its peers.

2. Blockchain network peers validate the received transaction and advertise it over the blockchain network.
3. Involved users generally verify the transaction to meet a consensus algorithmic digital agreement.
4. The miner nodes add the valid transaction into a time-stamped block and broadcast it again into the blockchain network.
5. Next, verifying the advertised block and matching its hash with the previous block, the block in consideration adds to the blockchain network.

Figure 3. A diagrammatic representation of a blockchain

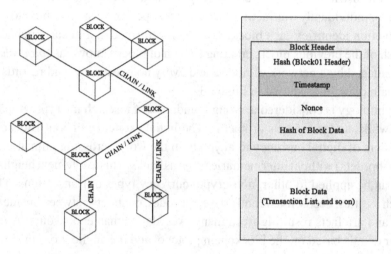

This way, consensus algorithms are one of the most important and revolutionary aspects of blockchain technology. Consensus algorithms use rules and verification methods to validate data that lets the blockchain network included devices agree about adding data to the blockchain network (Bashir, 2017).

One of the benefits of blockchain-based technology is to validate the block trustfulness in a decentralized, trustless business operating environment without the necessity of the trusted third-party authority. In a blockchain-based P2P network environment, it is challenging to reach a *consensus* on a newly generated block as the consensus may favour malicious nodes. This challenge can be mitigated by using dedicated *consensus* algorithms. Typical consensus algorithms are – proof of work (PoW), proof of stake (PoS), and practical byzantine fault tolerance (PBFT) (Bach et al., 2018).

- **Proof of Work (PoW)**: The creation of a newly generated block in a blockchain network is equivalent to the solution of a computationally difficult mathematical problem. The design and development of PoW process are time-consuming and costly, but once solved, other participants in the blockchain network can easily verify the solution. This way, 'Miners' solve a consensus problem, publish the solution to the network, and add the newly created block to the blockchain that will be spread over the chain to be verified by all participating nodes. This process can simultaneously take place in the different areas of the blockchain network. When peers decide to include a new block to the blockchain network, they must cross-check the branch size and choose the most accumulated work (the longest chain) that is considered to be the valid node (Gupta et al., 2018).

- **Proof of Stake (PoS)**: It attempts to create consensus in a different way than PoW. In the PoS, the originator of the next block is selected based on the different randomized combination of miners' resources and the duration that they hold their resources. Contrary to PoW miners that may not have a resource and only attempt to maximize profits by improving computational power, PoS miners defend the blockchain network to protect their wealth and profits. If the stake is higher than the transaction fees, participants can trust them to do their job correctly (Vashchuk & Shuwar, 2018).

- **Practical Byzantine Fault Tolerance (PBFT)**: The basic concept of PBFT originates from a story about a group of generals independently commanding a part of the Byzantine army surrounding a city they wanted to conquer. The most critical thing is that all generals reached a mutual decision to attack or retreat. The Byzantine problem attempt becomes even more complicated when disloyal generals vote for an irrelevant plan (Castro & Liskov, 2002). This consensus algorithm determines new blocks in rounds and selects the sponsor to advertise an uncorroborated block. The transaction validation includes three steps algorithm, and all network nodes vote (Castro & Liskov. 2002) (Joshi et al., 2018).

Classifying blockchains as *public* or *private* helps identify the main characteristics of many blockchain technologies. One of the essential characteristics of blockchain is the 'Distributed Ledger Technology (DLT). A ledge is a data structure that consists of an ordered list of transactions. For example, a ledger may record monetary transactions between business partners or good exchanged among known associate parties for the manufacturing industry. In blockchain technology, the ledger is replicated over all the nodes. Also, transactions are grouped into blocks that are then chained together. Therefore, the distributed ledger is a replicated append-only data structure. A blockchain begins with some initial states, and the ledger records the whole history of update operations made to the states.

In general, blockchain systems make use of cryptographic techniques (Menezes et al., 1997) to ensure the integrity of the ledgers. Integrity in this context means the ability to detect tampering of the blockchain data. This characteristic is crucial in public settings where there is no pre-established trust among business collaborators. However, integrity is also very important in private blockchains because the authenticated nodes can still act maliciously.

Some of the blockchains' promising applications are network monitoring and security services (e.g., including authentication, confidentiality, privacy, integrity, and provenance). All these services are crucial for the distributed applications, primarily due to the large amount of data being processed over the networks. Authentication helps to identify a user uniquely. Confidentiality guarantees that unauthorized users cannot read data. Privacy provides users with the ability to control who can access their data. Provenance allows efficient tracking of the data and resources along with their ownership and utilization. Integrity helps to verify that the data has not been modified or altered. The blockchain network needs to configure and optimize how the system's performance can be swifter if every node does not have to do every operation needed for a transaction on the chain.

Automated Transactions and Smart Contracts

An essential characteristic of blockchain technology is to automate smart contract. In a smart contract, the transactions will be executed only when the predefined conditions are accomplished (Dolgui et al., 2020). The 'contract' is defined in software and stored in the blockchain architecture. Once agreed between the parties, the 'contract' execution is entirely automated, with no need for third-party authorization and no possibility of modification. The steps of a smart contract are shown in Figure 4.

The contract terms agreed upon by manufacturing supply chain network participants are encoded in software written for a blockchain network. The contracts define the statement of obligations, advantages, and penalties, and the terms are enforced when the conditions for execution are satisfied. For example, in a cash-on-delivery smart contract, the contractual business partners realize automatic settlement when the procured items correctly arrive in the warehouse. This high degree of automation makes blockchain technology particularly suitable for multi-tier supplier networks with complex relationships; it is difficult to track the business's status and settle payments in this context.

Figure 4. Concept of blockchain contract

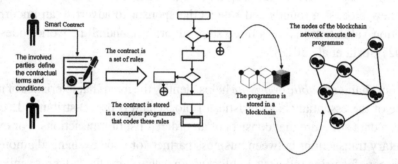

Blockchain technology, at its central, features an immutable distributed ledger, a decentralized network that is cryptographically secured. Blockchain technology can reduce operational costs, create immutable transformation records, and enable transparent ledgers where updates are nearly instantaneous.

Besides, the rapid inclination in the usage of IoT technology applications has led to the emergence of different IoT-based applications in manufacturing network – such as utility monitoring, transportation, and customer service. Some IoT applications also use blockchain-based techniques to incorporate user privacy and security in the development of applications. Despite IoT and blockchain-based applications integration advantages, this combination is not straightforward. The following section presents some of the challenges and the relevant solutions of using the blockchain-based technology that designs for IoT devices.

CHALLENGES FOR BLOCKCHAIN-BASED IoT APPLICATION

This section presents some of the crucial challenges and the related application solutions of deploying blockchain technology, which designs for the devices with permanent storage capability and computing capability on the minimal resources of IoT hardware. Some of the essential integration challenges can be found in the previous research works (Reyna et al., 2018) (Atlam et al., 2018).

Blockchain and IoT Integration Challenges

- **Scalability:** The blockchain size widens with an increasing number of connected devices because it needs to store all the transactional information and validate them. This is a significant integration disadvantage as IoT networks are expected to contain many nodes that can generate big data in real-time. Also, some of the recently implemented blockchain systems can only process a few transactions per second. It is one of the significant disadvantages of IoT (Zheng et al., 2017). To highlight the blockchain scalability issue, researchers reported blockchain storage optimization strategies to resolve the blockchain resource challenge using removing old transaction records (Bruce, 2014). Also, the same researchers worked on redesign blockchain based on IoT limits.

- **Security:** The increasing number of security-related attacks on IoT networks and their ultimate impacts make it essential to secure IoT devices with blockchain technology. This integration characteristic may create a severe problem when IoT-based applications do not operate appropriately and corrupted data arrive and remain in the blockchain. IoT devices need to be tested before their integration with blockchain because of the undetectable nature of this problem (Roman et al., 2013). They are often to be hacked since their constraints limit the firmware updates, stopping them from actuating over possible bugs or security breaches. Besides, it is challenging to update devices one by one, as required in global IoT deployments in the manufacturing industry. Hence, run-time up-grading and reconfiguration mechanisms are needed in the IoT devices to keep running over time (Reyna et al., 2018).

- **Anonymity and data privacy:** Privacy is an essential concern in IoT applications. Huge amounts of privacy-sensitive data can be generated, processed, and transferred between device applications. Blockchain technology presents an ideal solution to address identity management in IoT to protect the person's identity when sending personal data that protect user data privacy. Data privacy in transparent and public blockchain systems has already been discussed in conjunction with some available solutions. The blockchain transactions use particular and even dynamic addresses instead of identities. The user anonymity can be revealed by examing the transactions address advertised to every participant (He et al., 2018). The IoT devices secured data storage and authorization of access are a significant challenge since in order to accomplish it requires integrating security cryptographic solution to the device, considering limited resources.

- **Resource utilization and Consensus:** Trusted authority in centralized architectures make sure consensus integrity, while in the decentralized environment, nodes of the blockchain network need to reach consensus by voting, which is a resource-intensive process. IoT devices are attributed to relatively low computing capabilities and low power consumption, and low-bandwidth wireless connectivity. For example, blockchains that utilize PoW as a consensus mechanism need vast computational power and utilities a considerable amount of energy for the mining process. Computationally complex consensus algorithms are not applicable for IoT scenarios, and the limited resource should be allocated to find a possible agreement. However, PoS is more likely to be used in IoT, but none of these issues has yet been deployed in IoT as a commercial adoption (Atlam et al., 2018) (Danzi et al., 2018).

A distributed and decentralized blockchain architecture can reduce the overall cost of the IoT system in contrast to centralized architectures. However, a decentralized blockchain architecture suffers from a new type of resource-wasting, which poses challenges for its integration with IoT. Resource requirements depend on the blockchain network consensus algorithm. Typically, solutions to this problem are to delegate these tasks to an unconstrained device or another gateway device capable of catering for the functionality. Otherwise, off-chain solutions are also useable in this situation, and off-chain moves information outside the blockchain to minimize the high latency in the blockchain could provide the functionality (Reyna et al., 2018).

- **Smart contracts:** Devices can use smart contract techniques with addresses or guide them as application reaction to listening events. They provide a reliable and secure feature for the IoT, which record and manage their interactions. Working with smart contracts requires using oracles that consist of specific entities that provide real-world data in a trusted manner. Smart contracts should consider the heterogeneity and limitations presented in the IoT. Also, actuation mechanisms directly from smart contracts would help faster reactions with the IoT (Reyna et al., 2018).

- **Predictability:** Devices in manufacturing IoT applications require real-time communication with their operating environment, which means the time used by interactions between things should be predictable. Predictability is even more important for some specific applications based on IoT (Bui & Zorzi, 2011). For example, the transaction finality in blockchain under many consensus mechanisms (e.g., PoW, PoS) is probabilistic, and the confirmation confidence of the transaction in confusion is also probabilistic. It remains a fundamental challenge to incorporate predictability concerns in blockchain architecture (He et al., 2018).

- **Legal issues:** The blockchain integrates different people from many countries without any legal or compliance code to follow, making a severe concern for both manufacturers and service providers. As stated, the lack of regulations for private-key retrieval or reset or transaction reversion mechanisms creates problems. Some IoT applications envision a global, unique blockchain for devices, but it is unclear if this type of network is managed by manufacturers or open to users. In any case, blockchain will require legal regulation. These regulations will influence the future of blockchain and IoT and maybe disrupt the decentralized and accessible nature of blockchain by introducing a controlling, centralized participant such as a country (Governatori et al., 2018).

IoT designers should select a solution based on their restrictions and requirements, the diversity of solutions for blockchain integration with IoT, and different types of IoT devices and their applications. The next section presents the proposed architecture based on IoT, blockchain, and SOC technologies.

PROPOSED ENTERPRISE ARCHITECTURE

This section explains how service-oriented computing (SOC) technology will improve efficiencies, providing new business opportunities, address regulatory requirements, and improve transparency and visibility of global manufacturing activities. The IoT systems allow capturing real-time manufacturing business processes data from the plant-level operational environment. The enterprise architecture for distributed manufacturing (e.g., apparel) supply network used for the current research is shown in Figure 5. The architecture mainly consists of three layers: (i) IoT-based service, (ii) blockchain-based data control, and (iii) data storage and processing part.

IoT-Based Service Layer

The IoT technology development created many opportunities, such as interconnected and interoperable data collection and exchange devices. The data obtained from the IoT devices can make manufacturing more convenient through numerous types of decision-making at all its levels and areas of manufacturing business activities.

Blockchain-Based Data Controlling

The blockchain-based controlling part can potentially improve the IoT technology uses in the manufacturing industry. The manufacturing industry is part of a complex and information-intensive manufacturing supply chain comprising a set of globally connected and distributed organizations, including other critical infrastructures that support word trade, such as transport and international border management.

Manufacturing and its supply chain management are regarded as a domain where blockchains are good fits for various reasons. During the product's lifecycle, as it flows down the value chain (from production to consumption), the data produced in each step can be present as a transaction, therefore making a permanent history of the item of interest (i.e., product). Among other things, blockchain technology can effectively contribute to (i) record every single asset (from product to containers) as it flows through the manufacturing chain nodes, (ii) tracking order, receipts, invoices, payments, and any other official documents, and (iii) track digital assets (e.g., certifications, warranties, licenses, copyrights) in a unified way and parcels with physical assets, and others. Moreover, through its decentralized nature,

Figure 5. Enterprise information system architecture for manufacturing (e.g., apparel) business

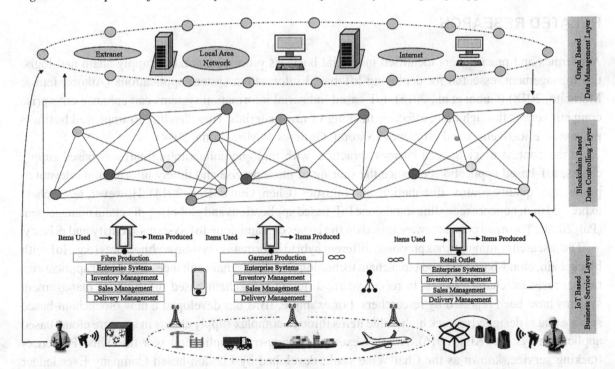

the blockchain can effectively share information regarding the manufacturing step, delivery, maintenance schemes of products between suppliers and vendors, bringing new collaboration opportunities in complex assembly lines.

The challenges in transportation modelling parameters, such as delays in delivery, loss of documentation, unknown source of products, errors, and so on, can be minimized and even avoided by blockchain implementation. The benefits of integrating the manufacturing supply chain with blockchain are enhanced environmental audit-related issues, minimize errors and delays, minimized transport costs, faster issue identification, increased trust (consumer and partner trust) and improved product transport and inventory management.

Data Management Layer

Industries use different blockchain platforms, and different data models are used on the platforms (e.g., Ethereum (Ethereum, 2021) adopted key-value data model, while a few of them, like R3 Corda (Corda, 2021) use relational data model). This characteristic emphasizes that any single blockchain platform not suitable for different types of data used in a wide range of manufacturing supply chain business applications. For example, geolocation data recorded from supply chain transport vehicles may not be efficiently queried using a key-value store. Also, even though blockchain platforms such as Hyperledger Fabric (Hyperledger, 2021) use for a pluggable storage model, service users must decide at development time which storage to use (e.g., either Level DB (Kim, 2016) (key-value store) or CouchDB (CoucDB, 2021) (document store). Thus, special techniques are required for supporting multiple types of data stores such as key-value, document, SQL, and spatial data stores simultaneously in the same blockchain system. In the proposed architecture, a generic graph-database model has been used.

RELATED RESEARCH

Academics and practitioners identified industrial business processes, notably supply chain and logistics management, essential for deploying IoT based information system applications (Atkore, Iera & Morabito, 2018) (Gubbi et al., 2013). IoT-based industrial information systems can enhance enterprise competitiveness through more effective tracking of raw materials' flow, leading to improved business processes' effectiveness and efficiency (Shroud, Ordieres & Miragliotts, 2014).

In the context of globalized business practice, with multiple collaborating-partners based supply chains, IoT-based applications enhance the sharing of more precise and timely information relevant to production, quality control, distribution, and logistics (Chen, Guo & Bao, 2014). However, researchers expressed their concern regarding standalone IoT-based applications and global supply chain management (Pal, 2020). The main concerns were raised on the issues of standalone IoT systems security and privacy.

The research community has proposed different hybrid information system architectures (e.g., IoT with blockchain, cloud-based IoT and blockchain technology). A blockchain enhances IoT-based applications tamper-resistant characteristics. In recent years, different blockchain-based information management systems have been reported by researchers. For example, IBM has developed a new blockchain-based service that is designed to track high-value items through complex supply chains in a secure cloud-based application system (Kim, 2016). Another exemplary industrial application is a fine-wine Provence-tracking service, known as the Chai Wine vault, developed by London-based Company Ever ledger

(Finextra, 2016) in a business partnership with fine-wine expert Maureen Downey. Blockchain-based digital identification tools for physical property and packaging have been reported for enhancing high-value parts for supply chain management (Arrear, 2017). An innovative anti-counterfeit application called Block Verify is designed and deployed to track anti-counterfeit products (Hulse apple, 2015) to create a sustainable business world. A start-up company from Finland (i.e., Kouvola) developed a smart tendering application for supply chain management in partnership with IBM. The reported application is built on an automatic blockchain-based smart contract (Banker, 2016). Another blockchain-based smart contract, called SmartLog, launched by Kouvola in recent years (AhIman, 2016).

In recent decades, due to globalization, manufacturing supply chain networks are going through an evolutionary change through the continued digitization of their business practices. These global manufacturing chains evolve into value-creating networks where the value chain becomes an essential source of competitive advantage. At the same time, developments are in progress to integrate blockchain technology with other innovative technological solutions (e.g., IoT-based applications, cloud-based solutions, and fog computing-based automation), leading to novel structures of modern manufacturing supply chains of collaboration and value-enhancing applications for the global apparel business. The reported research in this chapter is one of these value-creating applications, which explains the adoption of IoT-based item description and use in blockchain infrastructure to reap the combined advantages for future-generation apparel supply chain management.

This way, data and organize their transmission both nationally and globally is a requirement. It is still unclear how disparate blockchain technologies and systems will interoperate and integrate with other technological artefacts. This is compounded by unreliable and inefficient transmission standards and protocols that clog the arteries of information sharing between the exchange partners. Besides, an IoT environment is inherently dynamic, unpredictable, and affected by the ever-changing laws and regulations related to security and other interoperability requirements. Such sudden variability and random nature necessitate new laws and regulations in the manufacturing business world. In future, this research will review most of these issues.

FUTURE RESEARCH DIRECTIONS

Blockchain technology with the Internet of Things applications is getting importance in manufacturing industry automation. Besides, data privacy issues remain an essential challenge for regulatory bodies. The European General Data Protection Regulation (GDPR) lay the foundation for users to control their data and information about any devices involved in collecting and processing this data. The main objective is to provide individual entities must have the authoritative power and control over their data assets and to be able to transfer their data without any unmitigated risk. Blockchains gives the advantages of distributed ledger that can securely manage digital transactions, where the centralization of data is not needed. In future, this research will take the initiative that how blockchain technology can be used to develop an audit trail of data generated in IoT devices, providing GDPR rules to be verified on such a trail. This mechanism will help translate such rules into smart contracts to protect personal data transparently and automatically.

CONCLUSION

The economic disturbance caused by the ongoing pandemic due to coronavirus (i.e., COVID-19) are forcing myriad decisions on operation managers in the manufacturing supply chain management (SCM) team. It changes consumer buying patterns – the demand for a stable price, better service levels, which necessitate customer intelligence and varying supply and demand fulfilment related information. The COVID-19 situation has introduced significant stress on manufacturing supply chain networks; competing high street businesses are redesigning their SCM strategies. These strategies heavily depend on real-time information processing power that improves supply chain execution, reduces the operating costs of business, and improve market demand response. The Internet of Things (IoT) technology with blockchain-based information system architecture plays an important role in global manufacturing data sharing purpose.

Companies in the transportation and manufacturing industries can implement decentralized concepts for goods and transport containers tracking. Driven by the requirement for greater transparency in the manufacturing supply chain, which allows traceability from start to finish, comprehensive technical solutions are required. This is often a challenge for information technology (IT) solutions that focus on centralized solutions with complex access rights. Blockchain or derived concepts can remedy because they have already provided industrial solutions, which addressed these issues.

This chapter presents a hybrid enterprise information systems architecture consisting of IoT applications and a blockchain-based distributed ledger to support transaction services within a multi-party global manufacturing business network. The IoT is an intelligent global network of connected objects, which through unique address schemes, can help to collaborate with other business partners to achieve common objectives. The data obtained from the IoT applications along manufacturing business processes can make operational decision-making much more accessible. However, standalone IoT application systems face *security* and *privacy*-related problems. Finally, the chapter presents a research proposal outlining how blockchain technology can impact the IoT system's essential aspects of GDPR related issues and thus provide the foundation for future research challenges.

REFERENCES

AhIman, R. (2016). *Finish city partners with IBM to validate blockchain application in logistics*. https://cointelegraph.com/news/finish-city-partners-with-ibm-to-validate-blockchain-application-in-logistics

Atlam, H. F., Alenezi, A., Alassafi, M. O., & Wills, G. (2018). Blockchain with Internet of Things: Benefits, challenges, and future directions. *International Journal of Intelligent Systems and Applications*, *10*(6), 40–48. doi:10.5815/ijisa.2018.06.05

Atlam, H. F., Alenezi, A., Alassafi, M. O., & Wills, G. (2018). Blockchain with internet of things: Benefits, challenges, and future directions. *International Journal of Intelligent Systems and Applications*, *10*(6), 40–48. doi:10.5815/ijisa.2018.06.05

Bach, L., Mihaljevic, B., & Zagar, M. (2018). Comparative analysis of blockchain consensus algorithms. In *2018 41st International Convention on Information and Communication Technology, Electronics and Microelectronics (MIPRO)*. IEEE.

Banker, S. (2016). *Will blockchain technology revolutionize supply chain applications?* https://logisticsviewpoints.com/2016/06/20/will-block-chain-technology-revolutionize-supply-chain-applications/

Bashir, I. (2017). Mastering Blockchain. Packt Publishing Ltd, 2017.

Bruce, J. (2014). *The mini-blockchain scheme*. Academic Press.

Bui, N., & Zorzi, M. (2011). Health care applications: a solution based on the internet of things. In *Proceedings of the 4th international symposium on applied sciences in biomedical and communication technologies*. ACM.

Castro, M., & Liskov, B. (2002). Practical byzantine fault tolerance and proactive recovery. *ACM Transactions on Computer Systems*, *20*(4), 398–461. doi:10.1145/571637.571640

Chen, I., Guo, J., & Bao, F. (2014). Trust management for service composition in SOA-based IoT systems. *Proceedings of the IEEE Wireless Communications and Networking Conference (WCNC)*, 3444-3449.

Corda. (2021). https://www.corda.net

CouchDB. (2021). https://www.couchdb.apache.org

Danzi, P., Kalor, A. E., Stefanovic, C., & Popovski, P. (2018). Analysis of the communication traffic for blockchain synchronization of IoT devices. In *2018 IEEE International Conference on Communications (ICC)*. IEEE.

Dreher, D. (1999). *Logisttik-Benchmarking in der Automobile-Branche: ein Fuhrungsinstrument zur Steigerung der Wettbewerbsfahigkeit*. Keynote Speech at the International Conference on Advances in Production Management System – Global Production Management, Berlin, Germany.

Eschenbacher, J., Knirsch, P., & Timm, I. J. (2000). Demand Chain Optimization By Using Agent Technology. *Proceedings of the International Conference on Integrated Production Management*, 285-292.

Ethereum. (2021). https://www.ethereum.org

Ferrag, M. A., Derdour, D., Mukherjee, M., Derhab, A., Maglaras, A., & Janicke, H. (2018). Blockchain technologies for the internet of things: Research issues and challenges. *IEEE Internet of Things Journal*.

Finextra. (2016). *Everledger secures the first bottle of wine on the blockchain*. https://www.finextra.com/pressaritcle/67381/everledger-secures-the-first-bottle-of-wine-on-the-blockchain

Governatori, G., Idelberger, F., Milosevic, Z., Riveret, G., Sartor, G., & Xu, X. (2018). On legal contracts, imperative and declarative smart contracts, and blockchain systems. *Artificial Intelligence and Law*, *26*(4), 377–409. doi:10.100710506-018-9223-3

Gubbi, J., Buyya, R., Marusic, S., & Palaniswami, M. (2013). Internet of Things (IoT): A vision, architectural elements, and future directions. *Future Generation Computer Systems*, *29*(7), 1645–1660. doi:10.1016/j.future.2013.01.010

Gupta, D., Saia, J., & Young, M. (2018). Proof of work without all the work. In *Proceedings of the 19th International Conference on Distributed Computing and Networking*. ACM.

He, Q., Guan, N., Lv, M., & Yi, W. (2018). On the consensus mechanisms of blockchain/dlt for internet of things. In *2018 IEEE 13th International Symposium on Industrial Embedded Systems (SIES)*. IEEE. 10.1109/SIES.2018.8442076

Inera, A. (2017). *Bosch, Cisco, BNY Mellon, other launch new blockchain consortium*. https://www.reuters.com/article/us-blockchain-iot-idUSKBN15B2D7

Joshi, A. P., Han, M., & Wang, Y. (2018). A survey on security and privacy issues of blockchain technology. *Mathematical Foundations of Computing*, *1*(2), 121–147. doi:10.3934/mfc.2018007

Kim, N. (2016, July). IBM pushes blockchain into the supply chain. *Wall Street Journal*.

Larimer, D. (2018). *Delegated proof-of-stake consensus*. Academic Press.

Luigi, A., Antonio, I., & Morabito, G. (2010). The Internet of Things: A survey. *Computer Networks*, *54*(15), 2787–2805. doi:10.1016/j.comnet.2010.05.010

Lukac, D. (2015). The fourth ICT-based industrial revolution "Industry 4.0"??? HMI and the case of CAE/CAD innovation with EPLAN, in 23rd Telecommunication Forum Telfor (TELFOR), IEEE, 835-838.

Menezes, A. J., van Oorschot, P., & Vanstone, S. A. (1997). *The Handbook of Applied Cryptography*. CRC Press.

Nakamoto, S. (2008). *Bitcoin: A peer-to-peer electronic cash system*. Academic Press.

Pal, K. (2017). Supply Chain Coordination Based on Web Services. In H. K. Chan, N. Subramanian, & M. D. Abdulrahman (Eds.), *Supply Chain Management in the Big Data Era* (pp. 137–171). IGI Global Publication. doi:10.4018/978-1-5225-0956-1.ch009

Pal, K. (2019). Algorithmic Solutions for RFID Tag Anti-Collision Problem in Supply Chain Management. *The 9th International Symposium on Frontiers in Ambient and Mobile Systems (FAMS)*, 929-934.

Pal, K. (2020). Internet of Things and Blockchain Technology in Apparel Supply Chain Management. In H. Patel & G. S. Thakur (Eds.), *Blockchain Applications in IoT Security*. IGI Global Publication.

Pal, K. (2021). Applications of Secured Blockchain Technology in Manufacturing Industry. In Blockchain and AI Technology in the Industrial Internet of Things. IGI Global Publication.

Reyna, A., Martin, C., Chen, J., Soler, E., & Diaz, M. (2018). On blockchain and its integration with IoT, Challenges and opportunities. *Future Generation Computer Systems*, *28*, 173–190. doi:10.1016/j.future.2018.05.046

Roman, R., Zhou, J., & Lopez, J. (2013). On the features and challenges of security and privacy in distributed internet of things. *Computer Networks*, *5710*, 2266–2279.

Shrouf, F., Joaquin, B., Mere, O., & Miragliotta, G. (2014). Smart factories in Industry 4.0: A review of the concept and of energy management approached in production based on the Internet of Things paradigm. *Proceedings of the IEEE International Conference on Industrial Engineering and Engineering Management*, 679-701. 10.1109/IEEM.2014.7058728

Vashchuk, O. & Shuwar, R. (2018). *Pros and cons of consensus algorithm proof of stake. Difference in the network safety in proof of work and proof of stake*. doi:10.1145/3154273.3154333

World Economic Forum. (2015). *Deep shift technology tipping points and societal impact survey report*. http://www3.weforum.org/docs/WEF_GAC15_Technological_Tipping_Points_report_2015.pdf

Zheng, Z., Xie, S., Dai, H., Chen, X., & Wang, H. (2017). An overview of blockchain technology: Architecture, consensus, and future trends. In 2017 IEEE international congress on big data (BigData Congress). IEEE.

KEY TERMS AND DEFINITIONS

Block: A block is a data structure used to communicate incremental changes to the local state of a node. It consists of a list of transactions, a reference to a previous block and a nonce.

Blockchain: In simple, a blockchain is just a data structure that can be shared by different users using computing data communication network (e.g., peer-to-peer or P2P). Blockchain is a distributed data structure comprising a chain of blocks. It can act as a global ledger that maintains records of all transactions on a blockchain network. The transactions are time-stamped and bundled into blocks where each block is identified by its *cryptographic hash*.

Cryptography: Blockchain's transactions achieve validity, trust, and finality based on cryptographic proofs and underlying mathematical computations between various trading partners.

Decentralized Computing Infrastructure: These computing infrastructures feature computing nodes that can make independent processing and computational decisions irrespective of what other peer computing nodes may decide.

Immutability: This term refers to the fact that blockchain transactions cannot be deleted or altered.

Internet of Things (IoT): The internet of things (IoT), also called the internet of everything or the industrial internet, is now a technology paradigm envisioned as a global network of machines and devices capable of interacting with each other. The IoT is recognized as one of the most important areas of future technology and is gaining vast attention from a wide range of industries.

Provenance: In a blockchain ledger, provenance is a way to trace the origin of every transaction such that there is no dispute about the origin and sequence of the transactions in the ledger.

Supply Chain Management: A supply chain consists of a network of *key business processes* and facilities, involving end-users and suppliers that provide products, services, and information. In this chain management, improving the efficiency of the overall chain is an influential factor; and it needs at least four important strategic issues to be considered: supply chain network design, capacity planning, risk assessment and management, and performances monitoring and measurement. Moreover, the details break down of these issues need to consider in the level of individual business processes and sub-processes, and the combined performance of this chain. The coordination of these huge business processes and their performance improvement are the main objectives of a supply chain management system.

Warehouse: A warehouse can also be called a storage area, and it is a commercial building where raw materials or goods are stored by suppliers, exporters, manufacturers, or wholesalers, they are constructed and equipped with tools according to special standards depending on the purpose of their use.

Section 4
Effective Use of Blockchain and IoT in E-Healthcare Systems

Chapter 11
Blockchain for Healthcare and Medical Systems

Sanaa Kaddoura
Zayed University, UAE

Rima Grati
Zayed University, UAE

ABSTRACT

Blockchain is one of the trendy technologies in the current era. All industries are merging blockchain with their production line to benefit from its features such as security and decentralized data. One of the main problems in the healthcare system is the lack of interoperability (i.e., data should be patient-centered and not institution-centered). Healthcare information systems, in the current state, cannot communicate. Each organization works within its boundaries and owns its data. To make this shift, many challenges should be solved such as data privacy, standards, scalability, and others. Blockchain can solve these problems by giving the patients control over their data; therefore, they can share it with any institution for a time period. It is expected that blockchain will improve healthcare data management. In this chapter, the authors study the opportunity of blockchain to leverage biomedical and healthcare applications and research. Blockchain also contributes to the medication manufacturing area.

INTRODUCTION

Various countries are experiencing a rapid increase in the number of patients at hospitals and medical centers, making it hard to handle and manage through the existing infrastructure by available doctors and staff according to Tanwar et al. (2020). In fact, the recent technological breakthroughs bring up major updates and enhancements for healthcare centers to better capture the different challenges imposed with this increase. Healthcare systems are currently being directed with such vision in many aspects. It is expected that in 2030, healthcare systems will integrate different technologies to allow monitoring the health situation of each patient and allow accurate measurement of information that may help save the lives of patients and increase their well-being. Internet of Things (IoT) and wearable devices are key

DOI: 10.4018/978-1-7998-5839-3.ch011

enablers for this vision, leading to a higher quality of care for patients. Being tailored for individual's use, doctors are able to monitor each patient through his/her own IoT and wearable device, and thus treating more patients efficiently and accurately without the need to regularly visit clinics and hospitals, except in case of emergency. Patients are thus able to constantly update their doctors with their continuous changes to increase welfare and life-expectancy. This also reduces medical costs and helps in better utilization of resources in available healthcare.

This transformation towards a technological based healthcare system is expected to generate a massive amount of data that is created, stored, and accessed daily. However, this data is subject to multiple challenges imposed due to the nature of communication over the Internet. In fact, data security and privacy in healthcare systems are considered a top concern to be addressed when discussing healthcare data corresponding to patients. In 2018, over 13 million healthcare records were breached (Moro Visconti, 2020). Due to the sensitivity of healthcare data, healthcare data centers may be an attractive place to attackers who aim at financially benefiting from this information through selling it to a third-party provider. This raises the demand for a system that reserves healthcare data of the patients from any fraud. Saha el al. (2020) developed a new scheme that increases security and patients' data privacy against attackers. This approach showed efficiency in terms of computation cost with respect to other relevant approaches. Further, limitations on the patient's ownership of his/her medical data is a main concern as the patient is in need of a system that allows him/her to control access to this data.

Blockchain technology is one of the novel efforts that are being explored to solve this problem, which can offer an important solution that solves multiple challenges imposed by healthcare systems and hence provide better experience for users (De Aguiar et al., 2020). Blockchain can be defined as a decentralized and distributed digital ledger that allows recording transactions in a chain of immutable blocks linked together by cryptographic hashes. In a blockchain system, transactions are stored over multiple network participants whereby there is no need for a central authority to manage the transactions being done. The procedure starts by the user requesting a certain transaction which can be of any type of data including financial, health, or even a message. The user then provides a signature with his private key for this transaction, enabling other entities to verify the authenticity of this transaction using the public key of this user. The transaction is then sent to the entire network of peer-to-peer participants. Blockchain miners, a community of people responsible for ensuring the security of moving data over blocks in blockchain, select a batch of the available transactions to form a block. Each miner tries to find the correct hash output for the given batch of encoded transactions within this block. Whenever a blockchain miner is able to add a block of transaction to the blockchain, this block is considered complete, locking the ability to alter it. This necessitates recomputing the whole block and the blocks added after it. The complexity of this process protects the transactions from fraud and attacks as it involves high computational power to try different combinations of strings until the output string matches the stipulated requirements, hence, providing a highly secure aspect. Further, being a decentralized technology is also a key advantage, it hinders the action of malicious users through replicating data over multiple nodes and eventually malicious users should alter data across all nodes which are a hard task. For this reason, blockchain has been considered as a key solution to transform the current healthcare systems into a patient-centered systems through which the patient has his/her healthcare data records properly secured and shared everywhere at any time (Chen et al, 2019). A patient would then use mobile applications to record his/her data and send it to healthcare providers within seconds through the private blockchain network. This will enable patients to control and restrict the access over their data to only the concerned medical practitioners.

Figure 1 depicts a summary of the overall procedure. Blockchain aims to organize the process of healthcare while solving key issues in secure and privacy.

Figure 1. A Summary of Blockchain based Healthcare Systems

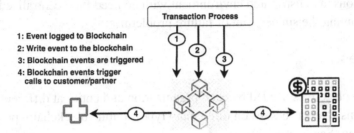

The main objective of this chapter is to gain a deeper understanding of blockchain technology and its potential improvements over healthcare systems. Section II discusses background information related to blockchain in terms of definition and types. It also presents the relation between blockchain with the healthcare systems and its limitations. Moreover, it describes how blockchain can support the current healthcare system. Section III discusses blockchain for medical health records privacy. Section IV presents ongoing research trends for blockchain in the healthcare system. In section V, the contributions of blockchain into the pharmaceutical and medications manufacturing is presented. Section VI shows how blockchain can help and contribute to biomedical and healthcare applications. Finally, section VII derives conclusions and Section VIII poses future research questions related to the contribution of blockchain in the healthcare domain.

BACKGROUND

In this section, some background information about blockchain technology in terms of its definition and types is discussed. In addition, the limitations of healthcare systems are presented to show how blockchain may help healthcare systems in tackling some of its challenges.

Blockchain: A Distributed Ledger Technology

According to Bashir (2018), blockchain is a peer-to-peer, distributed ledger technology (DLT) which is characterized with cryptographically secure, append-only, immutable and updateable-only mechanism done through consensus or agreement among peers. Blockchain uses a database which is consensually shared and synchronized between multiple independent computers available at different geographical areas. Each computer is known as a node or a peer, used to record certain transactions. While blockchain requires global consensus across all nodes to confirm a certain transaction, a DLT does not enforce global consensus because the latter allows achieving the consensus without having to validate the transaction' data across the entire blockchain.

Blockchain arranges data into blocks which can only be chained through appending them to each other without the ability to remove or modify any block. It allows transactions to have public entities that can check the authenticity of transactions. Any participant of the network is able to view the shared recordings across that network and can own a copy of it. Within seconds, the updates done on a certain ledger are directly apparent to all participants. A blockchain makes it possible for more than two entities to carry out transactions in a distributed environment with no need for a centralized trusted entity. This contributes to overcoming the single point of failure problem.

Blockchain Types

Due to the variety of objectives needed by each organization and entity at different scopes, blockchain has various types. This chapter focuses on three main types: Public blockchain, private blockchain and consortium blockchain (Sanka et al., 2021).

Public Blockchain

A public blockchain is a distributed and public ledger. It maintains the records of all the transactions by allowing anyone to join the blockchain network with read and write access permission. They are open to the public, and anyone can participate in the decision-making process as a node. Public blockchain allows any person to access information, submit transactions, and participate in the consensus procedure. Each entity that participates in contributing to the consensus procedure may or may not be rewarded for sharing its computational resources in the process of validating transactions and applying cryptographic hashes. All users of these permissionless ledgers maintain a copy of the ledger on their local nodes and use a distributed consensus mechanism to decide the eventual state of the ledger. Furthermore, the anonymity of the identity of each node is implemented to ensure a seamless protection. Key examples of public blockchain systems are Bitcoin, Ethereum, and Litecoin. Another popular example of public blockchain is cryptocurrency. Since anyone joins the network with read and write permission, all Bitcoin transactions are available to the public. You may see the sender' address, balance, and amount that has been transferred to the recipient' address. This brings up key advantages for public blockchains including:

- Open read and write: any person or entity can create transactions over the blockchain and anyone can access the transaction.
- Immutability: whenever the transaction is stored into blocks, it cannot be modified or deleted as there is no central entity that can control these actions.
- Security: the consensus mechanism or agreement ensures that all nodes in the network will approve on the same block that contains the created transactions.
- Scalability: The blockchain structure itself is replicated across the nodes. Thus, the network scalability is proportional to the miners who join or leave the network.

Private Blockchain

Private blockchain intersects with public blockchain through various similarities in terms of structure and mechanism. Both are the same in terms of technology, but with different roles. While public blockchain focus on transparency through providing access to everyone about each transaction, a private blockchain stipulates multiple rules to prevent misuse of information. A private blockchain is controlled by one organization which restricts access to this blockchain. This type of blockchain is mostly applied in database management and audit for certain organizations. Hence, this requires a trusted authority to work on the consensus. Private blockchain are considered permission-based blockchains allowing read and write access to be controlled by a certain entity or organization and access to blocks and transactions is usually restricted. The identity of users is needed to grant them access. This targets organizations that may not want all available users to access the details of each transaction. The owner of the private blockchain can then have a centralized access control on who can read or write to it. The owner needs to know the identity of involved users to define the permission rules about their type of access to data that can be committed to the ledger and what data can be retrieved from it.

The owner of a private blockchain should understand the responsibility of users so that the type of access should be granted for each user can be determined. In other words, users will be well known with their profiles shared with the owner of the private blockchain.

Private blockchain offers the following privileges:

- Permissioned access whereby a central entity controls access to the blockchain.
- Faster transactions: the lower number of miners available in a private blockchain makes a transaction faster to process.
- Scalability: the owner has the control over the number of miners added to the network on demand.

Examples on private blockchains include HydraChain and Quorum. Both of these blockchains have the option to run in a public mode if required, but they were developed with the purpose of providing a private blockchain.

Consortium Blockchain

Consortium blockchain, or semi-decentralized blockchain, is not granted to a single entity as a private blockchain; rather, it is granted to a group of approved individuals. It is a group of pre-defined nodes on the network. Therefore, it provides security inherited from public blockchains. Typically, consortium blockchains are associated with a group of collaborating organizations that aims to improve their businesses through leveraging blockchain technology. Nevertheless, this type of blockchain may allow certain participants to access or adopt a hybrid access method. It may allow everyone, or only participants, to access or adopt a hybrid access method. For instance, the root hash and its Application Program Interface (API) may be open to the public. Therefore, external entities can use this API to make a certain number of inquiries and obtain certain information related to blockchain status. Examples of consortium blockchains include: Hyperledger, and Corda.

Table 1 compares the three different types of blockchain in terms of participation, security, centralization, scalability, and efficiency (Sanka et al., 2021).

Limitations of Current Healthcare Systems

Most current healthcare systems maintain the records of patients on outdated systems, making the diagnosis a complex procedure and time-consuming for both doctors and patients. Thus, the implementation and maintenance of a patient-oriented healthcare system may incur high costs which the current healthcare system may not afford.

Table 1. Blockchain Types Comparison

Blockchain Type	Permission?	Security Level	Centralization
Public	Permission-less	High	Decentralized
Private	Permissioned	Fair	Centralized
Consortium	Permissioned	Good	Semi-centralized

Furthermore, current healthcare systems rely on centralized data storage as all records are stored in one central database (Khan & Hoque, 2016). This slows down the access to medical data and makes it prone to errors and lack of interoperability. Records that are available at various branches of the hospital can be lost and thus cannot be accessed by patients. Moreover, patients do not have a unified view of health data records that combines all their treatment history as well as healthcare centers may not have access to up-to-date patient's data if the records are located elsewhere. This makes data gathering and combining from multiple sources a very essential step before integrating any type of technology.

Systems impact patient care as doctors should be able to utilize available resources with an optimal vision to serve most patients while accommodating to the limitations of the systems which they operate on. This introduces clinical scenarios in which lab doctors cannot process patients' needs efficiently and thus increase the margin of error. This can be reflected in people's reaction towards healthcare and the high costs incurred by current health systems.

Blockchain Support for Current Healthcare Systems

Blockchain based healthcare systems have been in action worldwide. Blockchain has been enhancing the lives of patients and healthcare professionals. Further, the given blockchain implementations in healthcare domains are being enhanced to better use patients' data without compromising their privacy. Federated learning, homomorphic encryption and zero-knowledge proofs are examples on new components brought to existing blockchain technology. Popular use cases of blockchain in healthcare include the management of electronic medical records (EMRs), Drug/Pharmaceutical Supply Chain, Remote Patient Monitoring (RPM), Health Insurance Claims, Health Data Analytics (HDA), and clinical trials among others (Agbo et al., 2019). Blockchain can help healthcare systems in solving different challenges such as data privacy, redundancy decrease, transparency and trust, health data ownership and fewer errors due to decentralization. For this purpose, Albanese et al. (2020) developed an approach for trusted and decentralized management of dynamic consent in clinical trials based on blockchain technology.

Data Privacy

The property of immutability offered by blockchain technology helps in securing health stored on it, as the integrity of health data, once saved, cannot be modified or retrieved. Furthermore, the health data on the blockchain are encrypted and appended at a certain sequence that makes it harder to be attacked by malicious entities. Additionally, health data are saved on blockchain using cryptographic keys which help in protecting the identity of the patients. Yap et al. (2021) highlight privacy as a top priority due to the danger that may happen if the patient's data was breached. Any breach will affect the whole system, i.e. patients, stakeholders, and the miners who will lose their trust with it. The authors present the current state-of-the-art on blockchain-based medical healthcare system. Xia et al. (2017) proposed a lightweight blockchain-based framework with the aim of providing fast and secure transactions while preserving the autonomy of data over a cloud environment. The proposed framework controls access to the system, allowing only privileged users to have access to it. The system acts as a mediator between users and sensitive healthcare data.

Al Omar et al. (2019) proposed a blockchain-healthcare data management system to support accountability, anonymity and integrity. This is ensured by developing a protocol that encrypts data through different cryptographic mechanisms. The user will be able to log in through a secured channel to make any transaction. Guo et al. (2018) present an attribute-based signature (MA-ABS) scheme with multiple authorities with the aim of preserving the privacy of patients and maintaining the immutability of EHRs. The authors address collusion attacks through proposing a pseudorandom function seed is shared in every two authorities and preserved secretly. Moreover, in KeyGen, the private key of each authority is embedded into the private key of the patient. Given this strategy, the protocol resists $N-1$ corrupted authorities collusion attacks.

Redundancy Decrease

Blockchain ensures replicating transactions over multiple nodes, thus ensuring the availability of the health data stored on it. This contributes in building robust and resilient systems against data losses, data corruption and other data availability attacks (Abdu & Wang, 2021).

Transparency and Trust

Since blockchain ensures trust through allowing access to transactions by all minors, healthcare stakeholders may rely on it to develop their healthcare applications (Yaqoob et al., 2021).

Health Data Ownership

Using blockchain, patients will be able to control their data and its usage. Patients can monitor their health data which may be misused by other stakeholders and detect when such misuse occurs. Blockchain helps in achieving these requirements through cryptographic protocols and smart contracts (Ahmad et al., 2021).

Fewer Errors Due to Decentralization

According to Agbo et al. (2019), the decentralized nature of blockchain allows health practitioners and doctors to manage health data from different locations and by different entities, decreasing the errors that can be made on health systems and have controlled access over the same health records.

LITERATURE REVIEW FOR BLOCKCHAIN IN HEALTHCARE SYSTEMS

High research interests are being focused on enabling Blockchain in Healthcare systems. The first Subsection focuses on blockchain for patient-driven interoperability in healthcare (Bennet et al., 2017). The second subsection provides insights about the current emerging blockchain based solution for healthcare management systems.

Blockchain for Patient-Driven Interoperability

Blockchain technology aims at enabling peer-to-peer digital exchange of data and, hence, enabling patient-driven interoperability through allowing data to be in control of the patient (Gordon & Catalini, 2018). Health data thus can be available over multiple systems whenever the patient needs through sharing this data (Figure 2).

Figure 2. Blockchain for Patient-Driven Interoperability

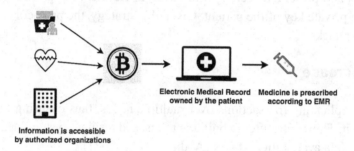

This gives patients a higher level of control over their data at any time. Several blockchain features can be exploited to enable a patient-centric interoperability including digital access rules, data aggregation, data liquidity, patient identity as well as data immutability (Chelladurai el al., 2021). Digital access rules associate all patients' data to his/her corresponding public key and thus allow the patient to assign access rules for each authority to the needed data. Data aggregation enables patients to connect to any institutional interface through his\her blockchain public key and thus reducing the overhead of sharing information again and again for every institution. Data liquidity allows patients to issue any time sensitive data that may help in better treating the patients. For example, a patient can announce on a public blockchain his/her allergy to some types of medicine. Whenever a certain emergency takes place, the healthcare staff will have this important information and will then be able to treat this patient with the type of medicine that fits him/her. Further, patients can use a multi-sig wallet or mobile device to manage their public key infrastructure along with their identity to protect their identity and ensure a trusted environment. As for data immutability, health data integrity is ensured through offering audit and append-only models by blockchain.

In fact, blockchain technology places patients at the center of the healthcare systems while enhancing system security, privacy and interoperability. For this purpose, many architecture and system designs based on blockchain for healthcare applications were proposed. Hussien et al. (2019) proposed a decentralized attribute-based signature (ABS) scheme for blockchain healthcare applications with the aim of preserving the privacy of the patient over the EHR system. The proposed approach relies on an on-chain and off-chain collaboration storage model which has been developed to ensure sharing data across multiple healthcare providers in a verifiable and immutable way. Guo et al. (2018) presents an ABS-based mechanism that allows different authorities in a decentralized EHR to maintain confidentiality of patient data.

Dagher et al. (2018) proposed a framework that uses smart contracts in an Ethereum blockchain to allow access control and artificial intelligence (AI) in EHR to provide a secure management system. Harshini et al. (2019) also consider using blockchain and AI in their work. The proposed framework is modelled with the constrained goal model (CGM) to meet multiple requirements. Uddin et al. (2018) proposed a tier that uses an end-to-end architecture with a patient center agent (PCA) using blockchain to maintain privacy of data streaming from body area sensors and stores them securely. The proposed architecture allows medical data to be shared in EHR among different health organizations while preserving privacy. Griggs et al. (2018) proposed a smart contract based IoT-RPM to manage medical devices and secure sensors. Ellouze et al. (2020) proposed a novel framework of modified blockchains for IoT devices that utilizes their distributed nature to provide secure management and analysis of big data in RPM. The additional security and privacy properties are based on big data analytics in RPM. Brogan et al. (2018) proposed an FHIR chain model to enhance the support for collaborative clinical decisions in the IoT-RPM through using blockchain technology and public-key cryptography. Pham et al. (2018) proposed a processing mechanism that aims to efficiently and moderately store medical device information in accordance with the health status of patients.

Zhou et al. (2018) proposed a MIStore blockchain to store medical insurance data with the aim of providing high-level credibility to individual patients. The data of patients' expenses are entered in the blockchain ledger to be protected by the tamper-resistant property. Wang et al. (2018) consider an artificial system based parallel healthcare system to improve accuracy and efficient. The proposed system utilizes consortium blockchain in order to link patients, healthcare providers and medical expert communities to comprehensive data sharing. Choudhury et al. (2019) proposed a permissioned blockchain based framework to reduce the administrative burden to ensure data integrity and privacy. Zhang et al. (2018) consider blockchain technology to develop a multi-level privacy preservation of location sharing of Telecare medicine information system (TMIS) in order to enable patients' access medical services or data from remote sites. Multi-level location sharing privacy is implemented on order-preserving symmetric encryption to be able to compare transactions to be applied directly to encrypted data without decryption.

Rathee et al. (2019) considers a healthcare blockchain based key management scheme for body sensor networks (BSNs). The proposed lightweight key management scheme for backup is based on BSNs and health blockchain. This development scheme contains storage keys entered into the ledger of blockchain to refuse statistical attacks. Agbo et al. (2019) design an architecture based on blockchain technology to meet the requirements of a healthcare system and address special needs to maintain storage of EHR with the goal of preserving patient's privacy. Zhang et al. (2017) provides a complete workflow for blockchain healthcare applications that considers multiple objectives including feasibility, capacity, user identification and authentication, interoperability and scalability. Zheng et al. (2018) proposes Byzantine fault tolerance (PBFT), a consensus mechanism for healthcare blockchain network, to simulate the response time for PBFT with continuous Markov chain (CTMC) model. Asamoah et al. (2017) proposed a blockchain system, MedShare, based on smart contracts, for data authenticity, auditing, and protection to support medical data exchange among multiple organizations with different backgrounds. The proposed model focused on determining data behavior and detecting cyberattacks of the entities offending behavior.

Rouhani et al. (2018) proposed a hyper ledger blockchain system with the aim of facilitating the efficient exchange of medical data between multiple entities, including patients and practitioners. Tian et al. (2019) introduce a blockchain based prototype system for medical data management through maintaining a shared key that can be rebuilt using legitimate parties prior to starting the diagnosis process. Rathore et al. (2020) develop a blockchain based system that focuses on implementing integrity of the patient's data, anonymity of patients, automation of workflows, audit and accountability. Drosatos et al. (2019) proposed a blockchain based data preservation system as a storage solution to ensure verifiability of data while maintaining user's privacy. McBee et al. (2020) proposed a framework for cross-domain image sharing in which blockchain functions are used to build a ledger of patient permissions for radiological studies.

Blockchain for Intelligent Healthcare Data Management

Sharing healthcare data managed by different organizations will help in deriving smart solutions that allow better understanding patterns and trends in public health and disease to ensure a higher quality of health care (Yaqoob et al., 2021). However, a big challenge for moving into intelligent healthcare solutions is the management of healthcare data available. In other words, gathering, storing, and analyzing personal healthcare while accounting for security and privacy concerns can be impossible without solutions that meet the patient and organizational concerns. Figure 3 shows how data should be synchronized from all types of organizations and entities such as hospitals, wearable device, and insurance companies among others to ensure a seamless workflow that achieves the highest levels of accuracy.

Figure 3. Intelligent Healthcare System combining multiple organizations close to the patient

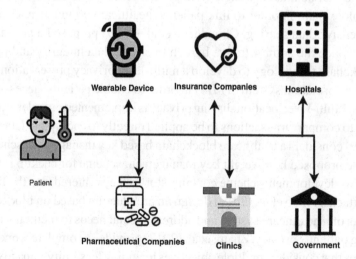

Introducing AI in various healthcare applications along with blockchain technologies introduces many powerful and resilient capabilities (Boulos et al., 2018). While deep learning and machine learning based solutions improve the advancement of automation, more data is needed to allow machine learning based solutions to predict patterns accurately (Mamoshina et al., 2018). Kuo et al. (2018) introduce Model-Chain, a framework that uses private blockchain to enable multiple institutions to contribute health data to train a machine-learning model to improve care while accounting for the privacy of health records. Wang et al. (2018) proposed a blockchain based parallel healthcare system (PHS), relying on artificial systems, and parallel execution (ACP) that captures multiple patients data attributes including patient's diagnosis, condition, and treatment process.

Maddux et al. (2017) described the opportunity of blockchain technology in the healthcare big data sector. This study mentioned data portability and distribution can be more secure using this technology. Blockchain stores every detail of a data distribution so interparty (data owners and researchers) communication develops in context with information validation, time proof, and identity justification etc. Yue et al. (2016) proposed a blockchain based Healthcare Data Gateway (HGD) architecture to enable patients to own, control and share data easily and securely without violating privacy. The proposed purpose-centric model access model allows the patient to control his\her data. Azaria et al. (2016) proposed MedRec as a decentralized record management system to handle EMRs, using blockchain technology. The proposed model leverages the unique blockchain properties such as authentication, confidentiality, accountability and data sharing- crucial considerations when handling sensitive information. The proposed model integrates multiple data sources such as local data storage solutions and provider's data while accounting for supply big data research. Zhang et al. (2018) study applying blockchain technology to clinical data sharing in the context of technical requirements defined in the "Shared Nationwide Interoperability Roadmap" from the Office of the National Coordinator for Health Information Technology (ONC). They analyze the ONC requirements and their implications for blockchain-based systems and then present FHIRChain, a blockchain-based architecture designed to meet ONC requirements. The authors demonstrate a FHIRChain-based decentralized app using digital health identities to authenticate participants in a case study of collaborative decision making for remote cancer care.

According to Gropper (2016) focus on the creation and use of blockchain-based identities to credential physicians and address the patient matching challenge facing health IT systems. The patients are supposed to have a digital wallet on their personal devices to create their blockchain-based IDs, which can then be used to communicate with the rest of the network. Instead of storing patient information, the proposed an approach that utilizes only blockchain-based ID and uses it to secure and manage access to patient data located in EHR systems.

BLOCKCHAIN FOR MEDICAL HEALTH RECORDS PRIVACY

One of the privacy concerns in healthcare systems is the electronic health records (EHR). Blockchain can be viewed as a solution for this problem. EHR is defined as a collection of electronic medical records for patients. EHR systems should ensure confidentiality, integrity, and availability (Shi et al., 2020). Many researches addressed the challenge of data privacy and security. Table 2 shows a comparison and analysis about some proposed systems in the literature. It is important to note that most of the mentioned systems use encryption techniques such as the cryptographic technology to increase both privacy and security. However, it is also well known that no security technique can ensure high level of privacy. Moreover, cryptography technology is also a computational cost. Table 2 shows some approaches in the literature that emphasized the problem of data security showing one contribution and one limitation for each.

It is important to note that all of these systems have guaranteed a certain level of security, privacy, anonymity, integration, and authentication requirements for a feasible and applicable system.

Table 2. Contributions and Limitations for EHR Systems illustrated in the literature

Research Paper	Main Technology	Contribution	Limitation
Al Omar el al. (2017)	PKE	Patients data protection and patients right of privacy	High computation due to the cryptography used
Zheng el al. (2018)	Cloud storage	Storage reduction for gigabytes dynamic data	Data is not protected due to a third party storage platform
Guo el al. (2018)	MA-ABS	Resistance to collusion attacks	High cost computation
Wang el al. (2018)	IPFS	Higher data throughput and lower prices in storage	Lack of strong privacy due to the cryptography used
Nguyen et al. (2019)	IPFS	High storage and data retrieval improvement	Leakage in personal information due to miners

BLOCKCHAIN CONTRIBUTION TO PHARMACEUTICAL AND MEDICATIONS MANUFACTURING

The integration of blockchain into the healthcare system spans over a wide number of applications and offers significant contributions (Haq et al., 2018). However, blockchain enhancements to the pharmaceutical and medications manufacturing focus on digitizing the drug supply chain which brings up multiple benefits which are discussed in this subsection.

Drug Supply Chain Digitization

Multiple possibilities are being envisioned to implement blockchain in pharmaceutical and medication systems, but one core pharmaceutical landscape is particularly the drug supply chain. Drug supply chain is very important as counterfeit medicines are increasing the burden over governmental and medical systems in terms of the economic cost of this global illegitimate market and endangering human lives that are prone to death if counterfeit drugs did not have the same active pharmaceutical ingredients or dosage levels as the realistic drug. Further, counterfeit drugs trade is very difficult to trace, with the World Health Organization announcing $75bn in 2010 for fake drug sales globally despite major international investigations whose aim is to reduce this type of trade – several moves are being done to overcome this great challenge. Governments are imposing multiple requirements on their supply chains to hinder the effect of counterfeit drugs in terms of integrity. The US introduced the Drug Supply Chain Security Act in 2013, giving the industry until 2023 to institute full, unit-level track-and-trace systems for products as they move through the supply chain. The U.S. Food and Drug Administration issued a series of guidance and policy documents concerning DSCSA to allow tracing all pharmaceutical products in the U.S. All trading partners in the drug supply chain should share an authorized "transaction information" regarding the exchange of pharmaceutical products. The trading partners should directly produce transaction information and collect and produce all transaction information data produced by the drug manufacturer via an interoperable electronic system.

However, as the challenge remains, pharmaceutical companies and distributors are keen to find other options for improving supply chain security, integrity and traceability. Being an evolving technology with various benefits, blockchain technology has been considered one a significant option to be considered by companies in that conversation. Yet the question on how to implement blockchain into the drug supply chain is a main question due to the complexities and solutions that can be considered in this regard.

The digitization of supply chains is attracting high research interests from multiple angles. In fact, supply chains are being generalized into various disciplines such as businesses, healthcare, environmental and farming among others. Hence, the identification of supply chain examples using blockchain exemplifies the breadth of blockchain technology application. Blockchain technology can support data collection, storage, and management, supporting significant product and supply chain information bringing up openness, transparency and security for all supply chain agents. Blockchain is offering various contributions at the level of drug supply chain digitization. First, it allows product identification as each product will be associated with a product identifier which is required to validate the needed information on the side chain. Second, it allows product tracing through requiring manufacturers and distributors to provide information in a shared ledger that allows automatic verification for important information. Moreover, it allows product verification by creating public solutions that entails verification of different combinations of information related to this drug. This helps better capture any illegitimate drug and notify the corresponding agencies about it.

Tseng et al. (2018) considered Gcoin blockchain as a base of the data flow of drugs to create transparent drug transaction data. The suggested regulation model of the drug supply chain can be changed to include a surveillance net model, and every unit that is involved in the drug supply chain would be able to participate simultaneously to prevent counterfeit drugs and to protect public health. Jamil et al. (2019) proposed a novel drug supply chain management using Hyperledger Fabric based on blockchain technology to handle secure drug supply chain records. The proposed system conducts drug record transactions on a blockchain to create a smart healthcare ecosystem with a drug supply chain with a support to launching a time-limited access to electronic drug records and patient electronic health records. We also carried out a number of experiments in order to demonstrate the usability and efficiency of the designed platform. Schöner et al. (2017) proposed LifeCrypter, a blockchain-based prototype system for tracking medical products through the supply chain with the aim of showing the benefit of the blockchain technology and illustrating how this prototype can guard patient lives with a patient-empowering blockchain solution.

Increasing the Safety and Transparency of the Pharmaceutical Supply Chain

With an estimation of 10-30% of medicine being fake in some countries, counterfeit drugs present a major and serious problem in the field of pharmacology producing different side effects to human health. According to WHO (World Health Organization), 30% of the total medicine sold in Africa, Asia, and Latin America is counterfeit. Being distributed through different complex networks represents one of the key challenges for governments and agencies that hinder capturing the increasing number of counterfeit drugs. An authentic supply chain is thus needed to ensure the safety of the pharmaceutical supply chain which can be enabled through blockchain technology.

With the help of smart contracts, blockchain allows real-time transactions to occur automatically in a secure manner. Blockchain can help connect stakeholders, eliminating some unwanted middlemen that may sell a non-authorized version of the medicine. Blockchain technology also helps to operate across borders so that users can operate everywhere, reaching underserved markets and hence enhancing the health of the communities.

Blockchain can help in producing precision medicine as genomic data components can be stored and shared over it which offers a higher level of security and trust than other traditional methods. Data cannot be altered over blockchain and this is a very important need in the medical field. Further, blockchain enables privacy and thus ensures that people's identities are accessed only by authorized users (Frost and Sullivan, 2019). Nørfeldt et al. (2019) proposed the concept of crypto-pharmaceuticals through which pharmaceutical products are connected in a patient-specific blockchain of individual dosage units. The proposed approach is based on the concept where each produced dosage unit has a unique information-rich pattern. A proof-of-concept application that can be used for integration of a pharmaceutical product into an IoT-based health-care system is introduced and a technical platform for integrating machine learning-based diagnosis with the patient's own data and leading to a safe manufacturing chain of fully serialized personalized products is produced. Blockchain's advanced features make it capable of providing a basis for complete traceability of drugs, from manufacturer to end consumer, and the ability to identify exactly where the supply chain breaks down during an issue. Blockchain covers different holes in pharmaceutical supply chains globally through providing a strong foundation of trustworthiness and safe practices for all patients and the community. Blockchain integrates these values by generating informative, real-time responses to events potentially impacting patient health, such as life-saving prescription medication debuts and product recalls.

Managing pharmaceutical production is another issue that blockchain can solve allowing public access to data announcements and thus offering higher safety for patients. Up to one million people are killed each year worldwide as a result of these types of errors, and better tracking through the supply chain would have a significant effect on the current pharmaceutical supply chain model (Bhardwaj, 2018).

Creating a greater sense of trust through blockchain and ensuring patients are safer will go far in creating a better relationship between pharmaceutical companies and the public. Additionally, product recalls will allow medicines to be returned much more efficiently through the supply chain than ever before. Patients want accurate results, and they want to know what they have done is helpful for future research. Using blockchain can make up-to-the-minute data available at any moment for all stakeholders.

BLOCKCHAIN CONTRIBUTION IN BIODMEDICAL AND HEALTHCARE APPLICATIONS

Blockchain has been also contributing for biomedical and healthcare applications (Kuo et al., 2017). This subsection goes over key contributions and improvements in Clinical Trials, medical record management and Internet of Medical Things (IoMT).

Improvements in Clinical Trials

Clinical trials play a key role in healthcare systems. However, clinical trials are coupled with different challenges including missing data, data dredging and endpoint switching hindering the full utilization of findings in this domain. Several efforts are being focused on clinical trials. Nugent et al. (2016) extend the idea of proving the existence of documents describing pre-specified endpoints over blockchain using smart contracts that resides at a specific address in a blockchain, and show that blockchain smart contracts provide a novel technological solution to the data manipulation problem, by acting as trusted administrators and providing an immutable record of trial history. Benchoufi et al. (2017) to implement a process allowing for collection of patients' informed consent, storing and tracking the consent in a secure, unfalsifiable and publicly verifiable way, and enabling the sharing of this information in real time. They design a proof-of-concept protocol consisting of a time-stamping sequence of steps using blockchain and then archive the consent through cryptographic validation in a transparent way. The proposed procedure ensures that the document cannot be corrupted on a dedicated public website.

Angeletti et al. (2017) present a secure way to control the flow of personal data for the case of recruitment of participants for clinical trials while ensuring the privacy of data of participating patients and providing useful and authentic data to the Clinical Research Institute. They provide a proof-of-concept implementation and study its performance based on a real-world evaluation. Wong et al. (2019) proposed a blockchain-based system to ensure immutability, traceability and trustworthiness of data collected in the clinical trial process. The authors use raw data from a real completed clinical trial, simulate the trial onto a proof of concept web portal service, and test its resilience to data tampering. Shae and Tsai (2017) proposed blockchain platform architecture for clinical trial and precision medicine and provide insights about the requirements needed to launch this platform. The objective of the proposed approach is to ensure data integrity and sharing which are two main challenges faced by clinical trials. Choudhury et al. (2017) proposed a novel data management framework based on permission blockchain technology using smart contracts with the aim of reducing the management burden, time, and enhancing data integrity and privacy in multi-site Clinical trials. They demonstrate how smart contracts and private channels can enable confidential data communication, protocol enforcement, and an automated audit trail and then evaluate the effectiveness of their in comparison with other approaches.

Improved Medical Record Management

The lack of interoperability in medical records systems prevents the realization of its benefits. The evolving concerns with respect to the security of medical data breaches, and the debates concerning data ownership, requires high research and development of efficient methods to administer medical records. With the increase of data generated by wearable devices, medical systems are expected to face a main challenge that corresponds to managing this increasing number of health data. Blockchain for medical record management will come to enable data integrity and transparency, automate data collection and other routine processes, and eventually improve data management. In addition to that, blockchain might also indirectly help solve another problem of medical record management system: access control granted by administrator. System administrators will control access of patient's data allowing authorized users only to view, edit or delete their information. Adopting blockchain will enforce data interoperability for easier patient identification (and many other purposes). Furthermore, updates in the medical record management are significantly changing in comparison with previous years and blockchain technology is the main driver of this change. The concept of Blockchain-based medical record management deployed by multiple companies (Moss et al., 2017). Estonia has secured more than one million citizens' records in a ledger in collaboration with Guardtime. According to Bau (2017), the system has proven that interoperability can be achieved and allowed easier tracking for health epidemics. Harshini et al. (2019) proposed a patient-driven model of record maintenance using Blockchain technology where smart contracts are incorporated to help in data exchange. He also considers using blockchain and AI in their work. The proposed framework is modelled with the constrained goal model (CGM) to meet multiple requirements. Vazirani et al. (2020) focus on showing how Electronic Medical Records can be managed by Blockchain, and how the introduction of this novel technology can create an interoperable infrastructure to manage records that leads to improved healthcare outcomes, while maintaining patient data ownership.

Internet of Medical Things (IoMT)

The internet of medical things (IoMT) is developed with the aim of improving healthcare services through providing customized medical solutions to people all over the world. The IoMT spans on different types of smart devices,including on-body and in-home segments among others. On-body segments are composed of health wearables and medical and clinical-grade wearables. Most of these devices are not regulated by health authorities but may be endorsed by experts for specific health applications based on informal clinical validation and consumer studie. In-home segment includes personal emergency response systems (PERS), remote patient monitoring (RPM) and telehealth virtual visits. Instead of consulting doctors and going to the hospital each time, doctors can remotely observe the data of the patient and process it in real time. The capabilities of IoMT allow more accurate diagnoses, less mistakes and lower costs of care. Paired with smartphone applications, this technology enables patients to send their health information to doctors in order to better surveil diseases and track and prevent chronic illnesses (Perez & Domingo-Palaoag, 2021). Further, this data can be shared with research organizations for intelligent decision making. While it is expected that IoMT devices will be between 20 and 30 billion by 2020, medical devices are moving away from restricted healthcare networks into public and thus posing increased security risks.

As IoMT can be considered as an important source of data, security and privacy are considered major concerns as this increasing growth of sensitive data should not be tampered or altered by malicious entities. One of the core technologies that offer such privileges for IoMT is blockchain which allows a peer-to-peer secure communication. According to Pilkington (2017), IoMT can help in tracking critical elements such as vital signs, electrocardiogram (ECG) and skin temperature through which blockchain can maintain and ensure collaborative patient health information sharing, and high quality of data reporting. Multiple works have considered blockchain within the scope of IoMT with various objectives. Dilawar et al. (2019) proposed a blockchain based IoMT security architecture to ensure the security of data transmission between connected nodes. With IoMT technology integrated to the patient-driven systems, Khezr et al. (2019) suggests that IoMT devices can be stored on blocks or to cloud storage and AI will help in dynamically creating those blocks in a way help in protecting sensitive data as blockchain and decentralized AI systems can cooperate to ensure a high level of security. Further, only authorized owners can seek access for this data and have it safely.

CONCLUSION

Blockchain is an advanced and recommended technology, which can be integrated into healthcare systems. This technology has massive profits such as data security, cost-saving in data access and storage, high privacy, speed, and central authorities. Hence, this chapter addressed the different types of blockchain, its limitations in the healthcare systems. Moreover, this chapter highlighted the main research topics that characterize the common issues of ongoing health-related systems and how real-world blockchain applications can help enhancing this domain.

OPEN RESEARCH DIRECTIONS IN BLOCKCHAIN AND HEALTHCARE

The studied domains could provide a basis for research directions to identify what enhancements can be done for blockchain-based healthcare systems. As blockchain technology has started to be used in a wider range of health applications, the volume of data generated in this era of the IoMT is growing significantly, limiting the functionality of blockchain systems to transactions' throughput and storage capacity. Hence, it is important for the blockchain system to be able to understand the transaction before adding it to the block in order to better utilize the given resources. Hence, one research direction can be transforming blockchain based healthcare systems to self-learners through utilizing intelligent and machine learning based solutions that can help in reducing redundant data storage and computation at later stages.

REFERENCES

Abdu, N. A. A., & Wang, Z. (2021, March). Blockchain for Healthcare Sector-Analytical Review. *IOP Conference Series. Materials Science and Engineering, 1110*(1), 012001.

Agbo, C. C., Mahmoud, Q. H., & Eklund, J. M. (2019, June). Blockchain technology in healthcare: a systematic review. In Healthcare (Vol. 7, No. 2, p. 56). Multidisciplinary Digital Publishing Institute.

Ahmad, R. W., Salah, K., Jayaraman, R., Yaqoob, I., Ellahham, S., & Omar, M. (2021). The role of block-chain technology in telehealth and telemedicine. *International Journal of Medical Informatics*, 104399.

Al Omar, A., Rahman, M. S., Basu, A., & Kiyomoto, S. (2017, December). Medibchain: A blockchain based privacy preserving platform for healthcare data. In *International conference on security, privacy and anonymity in computation, communication and storage* (pp. 534-543). Springer.

Albanese, G., Calbimonte, J. P., Schumacher, M., & Calvaresi, D. (2020). Dynamic consent management for clinical trials via private blockchain technology. *Journal of Ambient Intelligence and Humanized Computing*, 1–18.

Angeletti, F., Chatzigiannakis, I., & Vitaletti, A. (2017, September). The role of blockchain and IoT in recruiting participants for digital clinical trials. In *2017 25th International Conference on Software, Telecommunications and Computer Networks (SoftCOM)* (pp. 1-5). IEEE.

Asamoah, F., Kakourou, A., Dhami, S., Lau, S., Agache, I., Muraro, A., ... Sheikh, A. (2017). Allergen immunotherapy for allergic asthma: A systematic overview of systematic reviews. *Clinical and Trans-lational Allergy, 7*(1), 1–12.

Azaria, A., Ekblaw, A., Vieira, T., & Lippman, A. (2016, August). Medrec: Using blockchain for medi-cal data access and permission management. In *2016 2nd International Conference on Open and Big Data (OBD)* (pp. 25-30). IEEE.

Bashir, I. (2018). *Mastering Blockchain: Distributed ledger technology, decentralization, and smart contracts explained.* Packt Publishing Ltd.

Bau, T. (2017). *Why Estonia is a good place for eHealth (and why you should attend eHealth Tallinn).* https://www.himss.eu/himss-blog/why-estonia-good-place-ehealth-and-why-you-should-attend-ehealth-tallinn

Benchoufi, M., Porcher, R., & Ravaud, P. (2017). Blockchain protocols in clinical trials: Transparency and traceability of consent. *F1000 Research*, 6.

Bennett, B. (2017). Blockchain HIE overview: A framework for healthcare interoperability. *Telehealth Med. Today*, 2(3), 1–6.

Bhardwaj, G. (2018, April 25). Five use cases for blockchain in pharma. *Pharmaphorum.* https://pharmaphorum.com/views-and-analysis/five-use-cases-for-blockchain-in-pharma/

Boulos, M. N. K., Wilson, J. T., & Clauson, K. A. (2018). *Geospatial blockchain: promises, challenges, and scenarios in health and healthcare.* Academic Press.

Brogan, J., Baskaran, I., & Ramachandran, N. (2018). Authenticating health activity data using distributed ledger technologies. *Computational and Structural Biotechnology Journal*, 16, 257–266.

Chelladurai, U., & Pandian, S. (2021). A novel blockchain based electronic health record automation system for healthcare. *Journal of Ambient Intelligence and Humanized Computing*, 1–11.

Chen, H. S., Jarrell, J. T., Carpenter, K. A., Cohen, D. S., & Huang, X. (2019). Blockchain in healthcare: a patient-centered model. *Biomedical Journal of Scientific & Technical Research*, 20(3), 15017.

Choudhury, O., Fairoza, N., Sylla, I., & Das, A. (2019). *A blockchain framework for managing and monitoring data in multi-site clinical trials.* arXiv preprint arXiv:1902.03975.

Dagher, G. G., Mohler, J., Milojkovic, M., & Marella, P. B. (2018). Ancile: Privacy-preserving framework for access control and interoperability of electronic health records using blockchain technology. *Sustainable Cities and Society*, 39, 283–297.

De Aguiar, E. J., Faiçal, B. S., Krishnamachari, B., & Ueyama, J. (2020). A survey of blockchain-based strategies for healthcare. *ACM Computing Surveys*, 53(2), 1–27.

Dilawar, N., Rizwan, M., Ahmad, F., & Akram, S. (2019). Blockchain: Securing internet of medical things (IoMT). *Int. J. Adv. Comput. Sci. Appl*, 10(1), 82–89.

Drosatos, G., & Kaldoudi, E. (2019). Blockchain applications in the biomedical domain: A scoping review. *Computational and Structural Biotechnology Journal*, 17, 229–240.

Ellouze, F., Fersi, G., & Jmaiel, M. (2020, June). Blockchain for Internet of Medical Things: A Technical Review. In *International Conference on Smart Homes and Health Telematics* (pp. 259-267). Springer.

Frost & Sullivan. (2018). *The role of blockchain in precision medicine: Challenges, Opportunities, and Solutions.* https://ww2.frost.com/wp-content/uploads

Gordon, W. J., & Catalini, C. (2018). Blockchain technology for healthcare: Facilitating the transition to patient-driven interoperability. *Computational and Structural Biotechnology Journal*, 16, 224–230.

Griggs, K. N., Ossipova, O., Kohlios, C. P., Baccarini, A. N., Howson, E. A., & Hayajneh, T. (2018). Healthcare blockchain system using smart contracts for secure automated remote patient monitoring. *Journal of Medical Systems, 42*(7), 1–7.

Gropper, A. (2016, August). Powering the physician-patient relationship with HIE of one blockchain health IT. In *ONC/NIST use of Blockchain for healthcare and research workshop*. ONC/NIST.

Guo, R., Shi, H., Zhao, Q., & Zheng, D. (2018). Secure attribute-based signature scheme with multiple authorities for blockchain in electronic health records systems. *IEEE Access: Practical Innovations, Open Solutions, 6*, 11676–11686.

Haq, I., & Esuka, O. M. (2018). Blockchain technology in pharmaceutical industry to prevent counterfeit drugs. *International Journal of Computers and Applications, 180*(25), 8–12.

Harshini, V. M., Danai, S., Usha, H. R., & Kounte, M. R. (2019, April). Health record management through blockchain technology. In *2019 3rd International Conference on Trends in Electronics and Informatics (ICOEI)* (pp. 1411-1415). IEEE.

Hussien, H. M., Yasin, S. M., Udzir, S. N. I., Zaidan, A. A., & Zaidan, B. B. (2019). A systematic review for enabling of develop a blockchain technology in healthcare application: Taxonomy, substantially analysis, motivations, challenges, recommendations and future direction. *Journal of Medical Systems, 43*(10), 1–35.

Jamil, F., Hang, L., Kim, K., & Kim, D. (2019). A novel medical blockchain model for drug supply chain integrity management in a smart hospital. *Electronics (Basel), 8*(5), 505.

Khan, S., & Hoque, A. (2016). Digital health data: A comprehensive review of privacy and security risks and some recommendations. *Computer Science Journal of Moldova, 71*(2), 273–292.

Khezr, S., Moniruzzaman, M., Yassine, A., & Benlamri, R. (2019). Blockchain technology in healthcare: A comprehensive review and directions for future research. *Applied Sciences (Basel, Switzerland), 9*(9), 1736.

Kuo, T. T., Kim, H. E., & Ohno-Machado, L. (2017). Blockchain distributed ledger technologies for biomedical and health care applications. *Journal of the American Medical Informatics Association, 24*(6), 1211–1220.

Kuo, T. T., & Ohno-Machado, L. (2018). *Modelchain: Decentralized privacy-preserving healthcare predictive modeling framework on private blockchain networks*. arXiv preprint arXiv:1802.01746.

Maddux, D. (2017). *Cybersecurity and Blockchain in Healthcare*. Acumen Physical Solutions.

Mamoshina, P., Ojomoko, L., Yanovich, Y., Ostrovski, A., Botezatu, A., Prikhodko, P., ... Zhavoronkov, A. (2018). Converging blockchain and next-generation artificial intelligence technologies to decentralize and accelerate biomedical research and healthcare. *Oncotarget, 9*(5), 5665.

McBee, M. P., & Wilcox, C. (2020). Blockchain technology: Principles and applications in medical imaging. *Journal of Digital Imaging, 33*(3), 726–734.

Moss, J., Smith, C. & Davies, J. (2017). *Blockchain shows promise in healthcare*. Medical Industry Week, BMI Country Industry Reports.

Nguyen, D. C., Pathirana, P. N., Ding, M., & Seneviratne, A. (2019). Blockchain for secure ehrs sharing of mobile cloud based e-health systems. *IEEE Access: Practical Innovations, Open Solutions*, 7, 66792–66806.

Nørfeldt, L., Bøtker, J., Edinger, M., Genina, N., & Rantanen, J. (2019). Cryptopharmaceuticals: Increasing the safety of medication by a blockchain of pharmaceutical products. *Journal of Pharmaceutical Sciences*, *108*(9), 2838–2841.

Nugent, T., Upton, D., & Cimpoesu, M. (2016). Improving data transparency in clinical trials using blockchain smart contracts. *F1000 Research*, 5.

Perez, A. O., & Domingo-Palaoag, T. (2021, February). Blockchain-based Model for Health Information Exchange: A Case for Simulated Patient Referrals Using an Electronic Medical Record. *IOP Conference Series. Materials Science and Engineering*, *1077*(1), 012059.

Pham, H. L., Tran, T. H., & Nakashima, Y. (2018, December). A secure remote healthcare system for hospital using blockchain smart contract. In *2018 IEEE Globecom Workshops (GC Wkshps)* (pp. 1-6). IEEE.

Pilkington, M. (2017). Can blockchain improve healthcare management? *Consumer Medical Electronics and the IoMT*. https://ssrn.com/abstract=3025393

Rathee, G., Sharma, A., Saini, H., Kumar, R., & Iqbal, R. (2019). A hybrid framework for multimedia data processing in IoT-healthcare using blockchain technology. *Multimedia Tools and Applications*, 1–23.

Rathore, H., Mohamed, A., & Guizani, M. (2020). A survey of blockchain enabled cyber-physical systems. *Sensors (Basel)*, *20*(1), 282.

Rouhani, S., Butterworth, L., Simmons, A. D., Humphery, D. G., & Deters, R. (2018, July). MediChain TM: a secure decentralized medical data asset management system. In *2018 IEEE International Conference on Internet of Things (iThings) and IEEE Green Computing and Communications (GreenCom) and IEEE Cyber, Physical and Social Computing (CPSCom) and IEEE Smart Data (SmartData)* (pp. 1533-1538). IEEE.

Saha, S., Sutrala, A. K., Das, A. K., Kumar, N., & Rodrigues, J. J. (2020, June). On the design of blockchain-based access control protocol for IoT-enabled healthcare applications. In *ICC 2020-2020 IEEE International Conference on Communications (ICC)* (pp. 1-6). IEEE.

Sanka, A. I., Irfan, M., Huang, I., & Cheung, R. C. (2021). A survey of breakthrough in blockchain technology: Adoptions, applications, challenges and future research. *Computer Communications*.

Schöner, M. M., Kourouklis, D., Sandner, P., Gonzalez, E., & Förster, J. (2017). *Blockchain technology in the pharmaceutical industry*. Frankfurt School Blockchain Center.

Shae, Z., & Tsai, J. J. (2017, June). On the design of a blockchain platform for clinical trial and precision medicine. In *2017 IEEE 37th international conference on distributed computing systems (ICDCS)* (pp. 1972-1980). IEEE.

Shi, S., He, D., Li, L., Kumar, N., Khan, M. K., & Choo, K. R. (2020). Applications of blockchain in ensuring the security and privacy of electronic health record systems: A survey. *Computers & Security*, *97*, 101966.

Tanwar, S., Parekh, K., & Evans, R. (2020). Blockchain-based electronic healthcare record system for healthcare 4.0 applications. *Journal of Information Security and Applications*, *50*, 102407. doi:10.1016/j.jisa.2019.102407

Tian, H., He, J., & Ding, Y. (2019). Medical data management on blockchain with privacy. *Journal of Medical Systems*, *43*(2), 26.

Tseng, J. H., Liao, Y. C., Chong, B., & Liao, S. W. (2018). Governance on the drug supply chain via gcoin blockchain. *International Journal of Environmental Research and Public Health*, *15*(6), 1055.

Uddin, M. A., Stranieri, A., Gondal, I., & Balasubramanian, V. (2018). Continuous patient monitoring with a patient centric agent: A block architecture. *IEEE Access: Practical Innovations, Open Solutions*, *6*, 32700–32726.

Vazirani, A. A., O'Donoghue, O., Brindley, D., & Meinert, E. (2020). Blockchain vehicles for efficient medical record management. *NPJ Digital Medicine*, *3*(1), 1–5.

Visconti, R. M. (2020). Portfolio of Intangibles, Smart Infrastructural Investments, and Royalty Companies. In *The Valuation of Digital Intangibles* (pp. 449–490). Palgrave Macmillan. doi:10.1007/978-3-030-36918-7_18

Wang, S., Wang, J., Wang, X., Qiu, T., Yuan, Y., Ouyang, L., ... Wang, F. Y. (2018). Blockchain-powered parallel healthcare systems based on the ACP approach. *IEEE Transactions on Computational Social Systems*, *5*(4), 942–950.

Wong, D. R., Bhattacharya, S., & Butte, A. J. (2019). Prototype of running clinical trials in an untrustworthy environment using blockchain. *Nature Communications*, *10*(1), 1–8.

Xia, Q. I., Sifah, E. B., Smahi, A., Amofa, S., & Zhang, X. (2017). BBDS: Blockchain-based data sharing for electronic medical records in cloud environments. *Information*, *8*(2), 44.

Yap, K., Ali, E. E., & Chew, L. (2021). *The Need for Quality Assessment of mHealth Interventions*. Design and Quality Considerations for Developing Mobile Apps for Medication Management. doi:10.4018/978-1-7998-3832-6.ch004

Yaqoob, I., Salah, K., Jayaraman, R., & Al-Hammadi, Y. (2021). Blockchain for healthcare data management: Opportunities, challenges, and future recommendations. *Neural Computing & Applications*, 1–16.

Yue, X., Wang, H., Jin, D., Li, M., & Jiang, W. (2016). Healthcare data gateways: Found healthcare intelligence on blockchain with novel privacy risk control. *Journal of Medical Systems*, *40*(10), 1–8.

Zhang, P., Walker, M. A., White, J., Schmidt, D. C., & Lenz, G. (2017, October). Metrics for assessing blockchain-based healthcare decentralized apps. In *2017 IEEE 19th International Conference on e-Health Networking, Applications and Services (Healthcom)* (pp. 1-4). IEEE.

Zhang, P., White, J., Schmidt, D. C., Lenz, G., & Rosenbloom, S. T. (2018). FHIRChain: Applying blockchain to securely and scalably share clinical data. *Computational and Structural Biotechnology Journal, 16*, 267–278.

Zheng, K., Liu, Y., Dai, C., Duan, Y., & Huang, X. (2018, October). Model checking PBFT consensus mechanism in healthcare blockchain network. In *2018 9th International Conference on Information Technology in Medicine and Education (ITME)* (pp. 877-881). IEEE.

Zhou, L., Wang, L., & Sun, Y. (2018). MIStore: A blockchain-based medical insurance storage system. *Journal of Medical Systems, 42*(8), 1–17.

KEY TERMS AND DEFINITIONS

Biomedical: Biomedical sciences are a group of disciplines that use elements of natural science, structured science, or both to establish information, interventions, and technology for use in healthcare and public health.

Blockchain: Blockchain is a system used for storing data so that it is difficult or impossible to alter, hack, or trick it. A blockchain is a decentralized ledger of transactions distributed through the blockchain's entire network of computer systems.

Clinical Trials: Clinical trials are human clinical experiments that are used to assess the effectiveness of medical, surgical, or behavioral intervention.

Healthcare System: Is a group of individuals, organizations, and resources that provide health-care services to meet the needs of specific populations.

Internet of Medical Things: Clinical trials are human clinical experiments that are used to assess the effectiveness of medical, surgical, or behavioral intervention.

Interoperability: The ability of various information technology systems and software applications to communicate and share data correctly, efficiently, and reliably

Pharmaceutical Manufacturing: Pharmaceutical production refers to synthesizing pharmaceutical drugs on a large scale in the pharmaceutical industry. The production of drugs can be broken down into a sequence of unit operations.

Chapter 12
Blockchain and Its Applications in Healthcare

Maitri Rajesh Gohil
Dwarkadas J. Sanghvi College of Engineering, India

Sumukh Sandeep Maduskar
St. Francis Institute of Technology, India

Vikrant Gajria
Dwarkadas J. Sanghvi College of Engineering, India

Ramchandra Mangrulkar
(iD) https://orcid.org/0000-0002-9020-0713
Dwarkadas J. Sanghvi College of Engineering, India

ABSTRACT

Growing organizations, institutions, and SMEs demand for transformation in all the aspects of their businesses along with the progression in time and technology. When it comes to healthcare, the growth should be heightened to higher levels with necessity. The need of providing quality of service (QoS) in healthcare is taking significant place, allowing health institutions and medical compliances to develop an ecosystem with cutting-edge technology with the same reliability but better productivity and performance. Moreover, the healthcare systems are aiming for a more patient-centric strategy. Healthcare systems work on complicated and traditional methods, oftentimes administered via teams of professionals who manage data and supportive mechanisms of the system. Blockchain could streamline and automate those methods, conserving weeks of effort in the company's production line to increase the overall revenue and discover new opportunities. This chapter aims to illustrate blockchain technology along with its state-of-the-art applications in healthcare.

DOI: 10.4018/978-1-7998-5839-3.ch012

INTRODUCTION

Healthcare is one of the oldest and the most critical industries for mankind. The Healthcare sector is a complex system and consists of numerous components, including doctors, other staff, hospital management, pharmaceuticals, medical equipment manufacturing units, insurance/mediclaim providers, etc. Healthcare starts with the patient and doctor's relation and ends at the pharma conglomerates and the insurance institutions. The overview depicts a perspicuous image about the healthcare sector; however, an intricate set of factors are required to manage and operate the products, information and sometimes, the patient itself under different scenarios. In short, it is not just a single industry with specialized personnel. In fact, multiple industries are involved to safeguard human lives.

Unfortunately, access to healthcare across countries, communities, and individuals is not the same. It is influenced by socio-economic conditions as well as the health policies. A city is said to be healthy, when health services can be accessed in a timely manner to achieve the best possible health outcomes. Restrictions on the use of healthcare services can affect the overall well-being of a particular area/state and the country. An effective healthcare system not only functions as a backbone for human development, but also contributes to the country's overall economy and industrialization. However, ensuring the healthcare system robustness requires an extensive perception of the existing system and its drawbacks.

Businesses are witnessing significant transformation in their conventional business models and huge changes in every aspect as time and technology progress. Medicine and healthcare are one of those fields that need to keep up with the ever-changing technology for the ease and betterment of mankind. The quality of healthcare services can be improved by using the latest technology. Hence, in this field, the urgency of growth mandated by the emerging technology escalates to higher levels. Along with this, for customer satisfaction, healthcare is transitioning towards a more patient-centric approach, which requires focusing on two key factors: cost-effective treatments and appropriate healthcare facilities at all times.

The new and upcoming technology, namely, Blockchain gives a new value to the word 'trust' in commercial markets. It is simply a chain of blocks that traces all the activities as well as the transactions happening throughout a network. Blockchain technology comprises extremely secure, shared blocks of transactions called distributed ledgers which are distributed among thousands of computers in an agreed state of authenticity. Due to its decentralized system, no intervention or alteration is possible in blocks. Hence, security is high, and users can trust the platform for storing and sharing their data. Once equipped in all systems, it will be very easy to manage and keep track of all the data which cannot be changed.

The problems in healthcare systems can be handled competently by deploying blockchain. A blockchain-enabled healthcare system would allow sharing and analytics of important data for service providers and legal authorities assigned to manage that data. Hence, the data management processes will be improved, and their time complexity will be remarkably minimized. In the medical supply chain, the products from the companies are transferred through various checkpoints before it reaches the patient. It is a very complex process, as the medicines which are unused and in good condition can be sold to other customers and the expired stock is sent back to the company. Thus, it is a challenging task for the people involved in the process to keep track of the medicines and where they are being sold like retail shops, health systems, hospitals, or other organizations. In addition to easing the movement of physical products, a blockchain-enabled platform could greatly simplify how products are paid for and reimbursed as part of the contract administration process used by group purchasing organizations (GPOs), manufacturers and distributors. All these problems and some of the available use cases in the market are described in the chapter (Bell et al., 2018).

The chapter is divided into various sections. Section 2 introduces the healthcare process and gives insight into the current scenario. The third section delves into the existing systems in healthcare. Section 4 discusses the real-world cases, and the next section gives the future scope.

CURRENT SCENARIO OF HEALTHCARE

Healthcare is one of the most crucial and largest industries to maintain public health along with research and development of solutions on novel predicaments. It comprises institutions and firms concerned in the preparation and dealing of medicinal and pharmaceutical services. A good healthcare system must expedite the delivery of health services to patients. Currently, healthcare service provision can be tedious and prolonged due to legislative bodies and need for compliance. Hence, it gets infeasible to provide effective patient care even though the case is critical.

Due to the dependence on the several healthcare providers, there is an increasing need to implement new policies to deliver standardized healthcare assistance. Another abiding process that ends in high prices in the healthcare industry is the knowledge transaction. As victims don't hold all of their information, the risks of identity thefts, economic frauds, and falsifications in original data have risen. These days, despite having computational devices like computer workstations and smart systems at every health care bureau, systems are yet not capable of obtaining, interpreting and transferring data securely and seamlessly. Hence, the existing health care sector not only lacks advanced systems, but it also requires practices that are stable, transparent, keeping cost-efficiency and ease in operations.

A well-functioning health care system gets identified by its response to the regional population by following means:

- Enhancing the fitness level of societies.
- Protecting people from health issues.
- Defending people against the economic outgrowths of diseases.
- Implementing impartial passage to public-centered health care.
- Empowering people to play their roles in making decisions associated with their well-being and health care system.

Intermediaries play important roles to regulate the exchange of information, products, and services between individuals. Though, the principal challenge for intermediaries is product tracking and its validation in each stage of the supply chain. Let's take an example of a medicine. Firstly, the licensed pharma companies file a medical patent at the federal medical institution. Then, that patent undergoes several examinations by the institution. If passed, the federal body sanctions the company's approval. The company is obliged to the federal regulators (such as USFDA) for further procedures. Once the details admitted by these regulators, pharma companies start the primary production (but as a test solution). Once getting the result, it begins the final manufacturing under restricted environments. Each medical product labeled having detailed information for consumers. Clearance from judiciaries is essential for trade in the retail market. The retail market comprises drugstores where certified resellers sell these medicines only after an accredited doctor's prescription. This is a generalized scenario for any medicinal instrument practice.

Hospitals somewhat operate similar to this in the healthcare system. The primary components of a hospital are medical practitioners and patients. When a patient visits a hospital, the hospital system generates records of the patient. They also look for previous records to retrieve patient history. Then the information gets collected about the patient and its health issue. This profile is helpful for doctors and hospital systems to connect the treatment data with the patient's data. Many times, it stores this profile on a distributed network of hospitals. Network comprises health care systems like insurance firms, pharma companies, federal bodies for analysis of that data. For example, the United States has its restricted federal cloud where federal employee data is shared. They have given access to insurance firms, hospitals for faster access and allotment of services to federal employees. Over the globe, many hospitals have invested huge capital in data and operational systems for electronic health record (EHR) management, supply chain and functioning of the revenue cycle. Even after such provisions, interoperability, security of the information and inadequate process management result in the inefficiency of the existing systems. A report was published by a United Kingdom public health care system, the National Health Service (NHS). It showed that over 50% of entire hospital respondents for critical care, troubled because of access issues in patient history. In the United States of America, 78% of hospital officials stated that hospitals are still using traditional methods for their SCM (Supply Chain Management). It results not only in increased expenses, but it also causes integrity issues in the hospitals' data.

Along this, insurance companies track and analyze their customer services. Insurance companies based on patients as well as on their health records. Insurance is a contract in which the insurer compensates for losses from specified incidents. Insurance firms have to work under the guidelines of the regional administrative bodies. A supreme regulator appointed to oversee these firms in each state. According to the state laws, regulations can vary. Information collected from the insurer is useful for the company to follow them up. Unlawful activities can impact the rate of premium. Hence, an insurance company needs to protect itself first from such malicious activity to protect their customers' data. They also need to prevent cyber fraud. Another aspect is the number of policies a customer can have. For example, an insurance company has multiple instruments in the market such as life insurance, health cover or medical claim policy, term insurance. Customers can have one or more policies subscribed. There can be one customer and multiple insurance firms who have covered the same person. In such cases, managing the data on distinct systems gets complicated. Also, in the time of emergency, hospital authorities need more time to validate all the terms and conditions of each insurance firm to proceed further. To reduce this overload, insurance companies need to interlink the common facts about their customers in secure ways. Many companies have invested billions of dollars to find a solution to this issue. Solutions found till now, are more complex and difficult to manage. There is a threat not only to sensitive data disclosure but also the insurance firm's reputation. (Deloitte, n.d.)

The functioning of the healthcare industry has a significant issue - Interoperability. Interoperability defines the ability of the management and exchange of data between two or more information systems in a coordinated manner. HIE i.e., health information exchange allows the digital movement of healthcare information among disparate data nodes working under different compliance. For example, A US Citizen travelling in a European Union country may have the same medication necessities. However, the data management for the medical facilities, insurer and the federal identity of that person must be handled in a suitable manner according to interoperability standards of both regions. In the United States, HIPAA (Health Insurance Portability and Accountability Act) standardizes the safeguard of the citizen's health information whereas the EU has their own standards under GDPR (General Data Protection Regulation). These standards may sound easy to understand, but the pragmatic implementations are extremely convoluted and pricey. Additionally, the person or the federal agency should have a state-level provision or MoU (Memorandum of Understanding) to ensure that the data exchange should not violate the authentication and integration standards. Thus, the complexities occur in the real-time environment for parties involved in the interoperability of the healthcare data, as it is directly linked to the person registered in the system. These issues break into two main phases:

- Authentication of a patient
- Immutability of the information

The Authentication of a Patient

It is one of the most critical parts of healthcare services. Unfortunately, there is still the absence of a universal identification system for patients based on their data. Since 2009, major healthcare players are investing huge capital in this factor to enhance the authenticity of the system. Computational systems are susceptible to mismatching of the patient records. Due to this, patients may get irrelevant treatment and false medications. This may result in fatalities. Identifying the profile of an authentic patient and connecting it to its medical data is the need of the healthcare system. It has not matched with appropriate accuracy within the same healthcare service. Yet, the authenticity of third-party players remains as a major concern. Thus, the question arises - Can blockchain technology resolve this issue or not. Figure 1 depicts the medical data leak due to various reasons like hacking, theft, unauthorized access, etc.

Figure 1. Healthcare data theft reported by the HHS Department of US
(Source: HIPAA)

Reported Cases Currently Under Investigation by the Office of Civil Rights

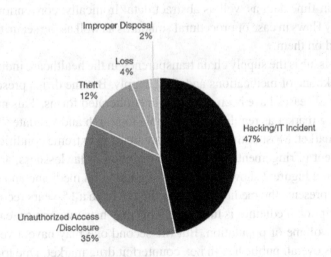

Base: 282 reported cases currently under investigation.
Source: https://ocrportal.hhs.gov/ocr/breach/breach_report.jsf

Immutability of the Information

From the healthcare perspective, immutability is the restriction applied to the electronic health records to seize unreasonable intervention in the data. There are three criteria in this factor:

- Interference
- Knowledge
- Accessibility of data

These factors relate to the business strategies. Any healthcare service provider won't expect a decline in the number of patients/customers. Every provider will strive to keep itself ahead in the industry. They will try to ensure their patients with a standard set of services and required privacy to their profiles. Immutability will thwart the exchange of patients' data to the unrelated alliances. This can be possible by following methods:

- Transparency in every transaction of the system done by the users
- Collaboration with only valid healthcare vendors and institutions. Allowed to those who want to take part in information exchange

In the exchange layer of the system, the transaction will happen in direct or passive manner. In direct manner, the information which has critical importance, stored in a secured and scalable system. Whereas, in case of passive transaction, the abstract data such as image, pictorial views, diagrams are stored with a pointer link. As an instance, the run-time system cannot store abstract data such as X-Ray records, CT Scan or Sonography results. These would be stored in a different environment which can be accessed by the authorized parties via interoperability methodologies. This should ensure the integrity and the validity of both run-time data as well as abstract data. Ironically, conventional healthcare information systems have many flaws in case of procedural standards as well as the security of the information stored or being processed on them.

Another major issue is the supply chain transparency in the healthcare industry. Pharmaceutical companies are the backbone of medications and drug supply. But the drugs prescribed by the doctor to the patient for specific diseases have been observed in adulterated forms. This number is growing in every drug manufacturing market as regulators are unable to search and validate the reliability of every drug being sold in the market. Most of the fake drugs are made in extreme conditions that are not suitable for production. Frequent infringements, due to the corruption or lawlessness, are proving to be dangerous to the general public. Figure 2 shows the average spending on medicine and medical drugs.

Above graph represents the medicine sales in the US from a 15-years record. Noticeably, after 2019, the trend of prescription medicines is tumbling. This may have two major reasons: One is the enhanced health quality per volume of population. But the second one may have a very negative impact on the economy as well as overall public health i.e., counterfeit drug market. Due to the increase in the growth of the fake drug market, pharma companies have a big challenge with patent rights and drug formulas leaked in public. The supply from pharma companies needs a secure supply chain to preserve their products' authenticity in the market. Numerous health organizations around the world are doing their own clinical research and drug testing with various experimental medicines and products. Hence, drug companies need a system to trace the prescription drugs as well as the sequential status of every stage in their supply chain. They need to stay connected to the pharmacies and wholesalers to ensure their brand distribution. The estimated growth of Healthcare fraud in various countries over a span of 5 years can be seen in Figure 3.

Figure 2. Estimated use and spending on medicine in the US 2009-2023
(Source: IQVIA Institute of Human Data Science)

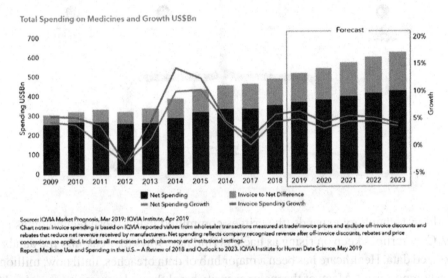

Figure 3. Estimated growth in Healthcare Fraud 2019-2024
(Source: Mordor Intelligence Inc.)

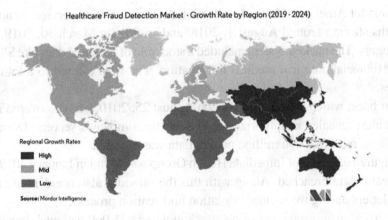

Compliances like HIPAA (Health Insurance Portability and Accountability Act), PIPEDA (Personal Information Protection and Electronic Documents Act) help to safeguard the patient data. But the major disadvantage of these compliances is the coordination of patient care between independent insurers and service providers. Hence, the need for a robust but autonomous body is there not only to protect the medical data and all the sensitive information regarding that but also to ease the operation without harming the existing flow of the system. Figure 4 gives an overview of the issues faced by the healthcare sector.

Figure 4. Current scenario of healthcare system: Issues
(Source: Deloitte Canada)

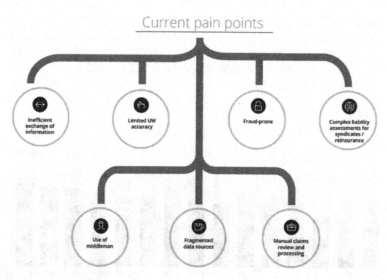

As the world of technology expands, the crimes committed using those technologies also increase exponentially. Cybercrimes keep on rising as hackers find new ways to break into the databases and acquire unauthorized data. Healthcare has been a major hub of data breaches, until now, millions of patient data have been compromised. Many of the major security breakthroughs weren't recognized for months. A few of the largest privacy violations (hacks) in healthcare that took place in the early part of 2019:

1. AMCA, short for American Medical Collection Agency, a billing services vendor, was hacked for eight months starting around August 1, 2018, and ending on March 30, 2019, compromising 25 million patients. The hacked system included a stockpile of personal data like SSN (Social Security Numbers), financial data and medical information. The firm catered to a lot of pathologies and laboratories.
2. A nine-year hack, which started probably on August 25, 2010, was discovered in April 2019 after an internal alert revealed unauthorized access on the company's servers. Dominion National, an insurance firm, reported 2.96 million patient data was violated
3. A misconfigured database of Inmediata Health Group was found in January 2019, with 1.57 million personal health data breached. Along with this the provider also accidentally mailed its patients the wrong letters during the security violation notification process.
4. In January 2019, an enormous spoofing attack violated 625,000 patients' data along with 2.5 million emails of the Oregon Department of Human Services. With the help of a targeted phishing attack, the hackers got hold of nine employees' credentials and thus access their emails, messages, and attachments.

The industry needs to improve its security strategy to keep up with the ever-increasing progressive hackers. Healthcare has entered the digital revolution lacking the skilled professionals and awareness among the system itself. Extensive and high-priced electronic health records platforms had also been organized without a careful study of the impact on the healthcare industry, along with knowledge, training, and analysis. To revive the losses of healthcare and strengthen it with better manners, the blockchain will be a very good choice. (Davis, 2019)

BLOCKCHAIN-ENABLED HEALTHCARE APPLICATIONS

A blockchain is generally regarded as a public ledger. However, this public digital ledger has the following key properties (Zheng, 2017):

1. Decentralized - Blockchain network is a peer-to-peer network. The "ledger" is distributed amongst all peers, which means that there is no single point of failure. Hence the blockchain network is not owned by any single entity.
2. Persistent - Blockchain is immutable. Once a transaction block has been generated, it can't be rolled back or deleted. Only valid transactions are added to the ledger by honest miners.
3. Anonymous - Users interact with the blockchain using self-generated identities, independent of any data related to their real-world identity. This often uses asymmetric cryptography techniques.
4. Auditable - Any new transaction has to refer to the previous history of transactions. This enables the network to audit and track all transactions. Invalid, or scammy transactions, may be added to the ledgers of dishonest miners. However, when broadcasted to the distributed network, the honest peers review the block and reject it within seconds, hence preventing further broadcast.

With the structure of blockchain and smart contracts in mind, it is easy to model a trustless infrastructure for pre-existing systems in the medical industry. Some of the possible applications of blockchain technology in the present centralized world are explored in this section:

Electronic Health Records (EHR) Data Management

Tracking and securing EHR can have many social and economic advantages. Patients often leave their data scattered across multiple clinics and hospitals. As time progresses, the risk of losing track of such data becomes more inevitable. Electronic Health Records (EHR) systems were never designed to work across multiple institutes. Hence a patient's log of medical history may be scattered across multiple institutes, making it difficult to track such records. Further, each institute may use a different EHR system making it difficult to integrate or interlope medical data from different institutes. An institute may use an EHR system with proprietary format to store the information which would make it difficult to integrate with some other institute's EHR system. This use of proprietary formatting of information is deliberate in some cases where the EHR developers have capitalistic motives, due to which patients and providers find difficulty in retrieving and sharing data. This problem is known as "health information blocking" (Dimitrov, 2019).

A sustainable healthcare system should prioritize the welfare of its patients, which includes keeping a well-tracked record of a patient's medical history while keeping into account certain records that should not be made available to the patient such as psychotherapy notes. As explained before, Blockchain is a secure public ledger, which makes it a perfect candidate for such applications. It makes sense to develop a solution based around "trustless" sharing of information from one EHR to another - a solution where the institutes need not trust the IT developers on storing such sensitive information. Such a trustless system would help in improving healthcare services for patients as well as in medical research since the medical history of patients would be available from several organizations/institutes in a coherent, uniform format.

Example:

This section describes an application related to managing EHR in a decentralized, fast, and secure manner in detail - MedRec (Ekblaw, 2016; Medrec, n.d.). MedRec is a prototype built on Ethereum blockchain for tackling four major issues related to EHR systems:

1. Fragmentation - Data is spread over multiple providers which makes it slow and difficult to retrieve a patient's medical history
2. System interoperability - One format does not suit all providers or EHR software solutions
3. Patient agency - Patients are often reluctant to spend time in retrieving data
4. Data quality and quantity - For advancements in medical research, it is preferred to have clean and bulk of data

MedRec provides on-chain permissions - so certain data can be hidden from patients - and data integrity logic to ensure safe storage of data. MedRec does not store EHRs directly on the Ethereum blockchain. Instead, metadata is stored on the blockchain in the form of "pointers" which may be used to locate the data and authenticate the user to access the data. Three smart contracts are defined for tracking of EHR data. Figure 5 illustrates the MedRec Architecture.

Figure 5. Contract structure of MedRec
(Source: Ekblaw, 2016)

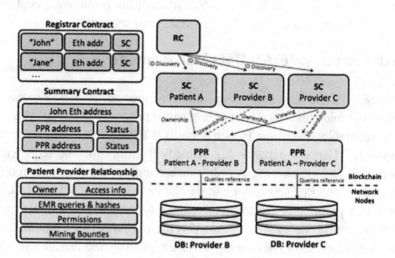

1. Registrar Contract

As mentioned before, MedRec allows using already existing IDs such as Social Security Numbers instead of cryptographic keys. This contract is used for mapping real-world identifiers to a user's Ethereum account. It also maps to an address (hash) on the blockchain where a special contract called Summary

Contract is stored. ID generation can be limited to certified institutions in this contract by setting up appropriate policies.

2. Patient-Provider Relationship Contract

For interaction between a medical institute and a patient, a Patient-Provider Relation (PPR) Contract is set up between the patient and provider's nodes. Think of this contract as the basis of the entire "trustless" model of storage of data. In the centralized world, the provider would have to trust the EHR developers for managing the data. Here, the provider trusts the smart contract - a piece of code. The PPR helps in storing an assortment of data pointers and associated permission rules. Each data pointer contains the location of data, the query string to fetch the data, and a hash value which is used to notify whether the record at the data source was updated or modified. These pointers are crafted and maintained by the provider. For sharing of data, a dictionary implementation (key-value pairs) maps the invitee's addresses to a similar list of queries that identify the portion of data that is allowed to be shared. This is helpful for hiding sensitive information from the patient. This is how storage, tracking, and permissions regarding data is implemented in PPR contracts.

3. Summary Contract

Lastly, the summary contact is used to track and search the medical record history. Each patient is given a summary contract which allows them to store the list of references to PPR contracts, with their respective statuses. Think of this contract as a patient's personal medical record book. It stores all the relationships the patient has with the medical hospitals or institutes that they have interacted with. This helps the patient to maintain an immutable, secure track of their medical history across multiple organizations.

Now that we've explained the architecture, let's see an example application of this project.

1. Patient Alice registers on the blockchain with her SSN using the Registrar Contract. This maps her SSN to an Ethereum address as well as her Summary Contract's address. This eliminates the need for trusting individual institutes on managing Alice's identity in their databases.
2. Alice goes to a Bob's Hospital which is a registered provider. Bob's Hospital stores Alice's data on their personal SQL database but uses a Patient-Provider contract which runs specific queries on the database to get the data in a format that is consistent across all providers.
3. Alice keeps track of the data stored at Bob's Hospital using her Summary Contract. The SC is updated with the PPR contract's address which was formed between Alice and Bob's Hospital. Alice can poll the contract to keep track of the PPR's status for real-time notifications about any new or updated records on the provider's database. Alice can accept, reject or delete relationships, deciding which relationships to providers in her history she acknowledges.

Personal Health Records (PHR) Data Management

With the advent of smart wearables like FitBit, Apple Watch, and similar medical IoT devices, personal life-log data such as oxygen level, stress, heart rate, and more data is incredibly easy to collect. Real-time analysis using Machine Learning is used to give users, medical professionals, and researchers relevant feedback about the data. This brings two issues: storage and security of this sensitive data. Blockchain can help by eliminating the middleman for storage of data, cuts the cost of developing and using such wearables (Dimitrov, 2019).

Example:

When designing a decentralized architecture, storing huge amounts of data in the blockchain is not a scalable solution. It will make querying and storage of data a slow process, which would demotivate stakeholders - patients and healthcare organizations - from adopting blockchain for storing PHR data. Hence, for personal data that is fed into a datastore at a high throughput, an alternative solution needs to be designed to make it anonymous and auditable.

We'll take an example of "A Ledger of Me". Ledger of Me is a reference system inspired by Medrec, which describes features that a PHR data management system should or must-have. Figure 6 gives its architecture. Unlike MedRec, where the stakeholders are two human entities - the patient and the healthcare provider, Ledger of Me architecture is based around the familiar principle of apps. These apps can be granted permission to read or write data belonging to a patient on external data sources. This concept is similar to today's centralized OAuth process. Think of how you allow apps to access your email, name, and other data after clicking the "Log In with Google" button. Ledger of Me designs a decentralized version of this system, where you control where the data is stored.

Figure 6. Architecture of "A Ledger of Me"
(Source: Leeming G et al)

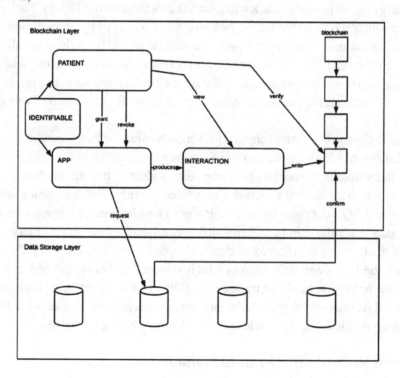

The patient can grant and revoke access to data by apps. Apps interact with data using smart contracts. Patients have full transparency over the interactions performed by an app over their data. Information about the core data models of the system is stored on the chain. An immutable history of actions performed by the user and the apps is stored on the blockchain - each action given a unique hash which can be used for identification and verification. Similar to MedRec, PHR is not stored on the blockchain directly, but it is represented in the system as pointers that reference external data sources. Only metadata such as data hash, URL, and other access information is stored on the blockchain (Leeming, 2019). Using a smart contract, one can describe the access control of data for an app on the chain, while the data is stored off-chain in a secure manner. If the application needs to be truly decentralized, there are decentralized storage options such as IPFS and Swarm.

To understand how this architecture would work in a decentralized world, consider a patient Alice who owns a health tracking device with multiple sensors. The device needs to store data to some datastore. How would Alice gain complete transparency and access control over this datastore?

First, the App on the device generates its own cryptographic account by generating a private and public key pair. Now the app can sign transactions on the blockchain. Alice has her own account on the blockchain network. Initially, Alice has a description of the data model in which she wants to store her sensitive healthcare data. She uses a smart contract to upload this model to the chain. The App on the device requests write access to this data model by making use of a smart contract specifically deployed for Alice. Once requested, Alice can grant or reject this permission. Once granted, the App gains credentials with appropriate permissions to write on the data store using a custom interface. For every write on the data store, the data store's interface writes a transaction to the blockchain, logging every interaction between the App and the data store. If the user no longer wants the app to write to the datastore, they can simply revoke the permission using the smart contract.

If a healthcare provider needs to access this PHR data, then they can do so by sending a read permission request to Alice's smart contract. Once Alice grants the permission, the healthcare provider can use the access credentials provided to access the data as long as the permission is not revoked. The takeaway so far is that blockchain may not be a scalable data warehouse, but it can be useful for building a trustless infrastructure for control over an individual's data.

Drug Supply Chain

In the pharmaceutical industry, the drug supply chain is too complex to track, leading to an ever-increasing number of cases of counterfeit drugs. Due to a lack of surveillance of the drugs, there are no proper statistics as to how many of such drugs are in circulation today. Amongst solutions like IoT based tracking of all drugs produced, blockchain can play a major role in the identification and verification of drugs. One possibility is to develop a smart contract for chain-of-custody logging of drugs based on unique identities (hashes) of pill containers. For additional surveillance, these containers can be equipped with integrated GPS for tracking in transit. Since blockchain is a public ledger, the identities of the drugs would lie in the public domain and hence can be verified by decentralized peers in the network.

Example:

A possible re-model of the supply chain using blockchain involves each drug or batch of drugs being uniquely identified by some code. This would be similar to how big corporates are tracking commercial goods such as Nestle's blockchain-based Zoégas coffee tracking. Typical stakeholders in the supply chain involve drug manufacturers, logistic service providers, distributors, hospitals/ pharmacies, and patients as the consumer. It is assumed that each of the stakeholders has an account on the blockchain network for signing their respective transactions. Blockchain can be implemented in the drug supply chain as described below:

1. Manufacturers Add Unique Identifiers to Manufactured Goods

The manufacturer adds a scannable code such as QR code or barcode to the manufactured goods. Scanning the code would provide essential information like timestamp, item name, item code, location, manufacturing, and expiry date. The same information is added to a smart contract deployed on a blockchain network, along with a status indicator. This returns a hash ID which can be used for tracing the medicine's supply chain in a transparent manner. Along with auditing the drugs, one can also store transportation-related information such as vehicle number, vehicle temperature, driver's license number, and so on. The initial state of the medicines is set to a state representing that the medicines have left for delivery from the manufacturer's end.

2. Distributors Deliver Drugs to Hospitals and Pharmacies

When the distributors receive the delivery, they can easily verify the medicines using the hash ID stored on the blockchain. Since blockchain is a public ledger, the distributor is assured that no tampering of data can take place and that the medicines indeed came from the manufacturer. On validating the medicines, the distributors would digitally sign a transaction that changes the medicine's status on the blockchain to the next state (received by the distributor).

3. Pharmacists Perform Necessary Checks

When pharmacists receive the drugs, it is incredibly easy to check the authenticity by using the hash ID and check the history of where the delivery has come from. This includes being able to verify the distributor and the manufacturer's identity. There would exist 2 scenarios of fraud. Firstly, if an illegal distributor tries to sell fake drugs, the transaction will be invalidated because of the fraudulent information that will be present on the blockchain about the drug. This means that the manufacturer's identity on the blockchain is absent, or the manufacturer is not a recognized/authorized manufacturer. Secondly, unauthorized individuals will not be able to sign transactions in this remodeled supply chain ecosystem without a valid private key. The manufacturer has to, and will, keep their private key safe so that no scammer can sign transactions on the blockchain personating as the manufacturer. In case the private key is compromised, the manufacturer can apply for a new account on some registry smart contract, similar to the one mentioned in Medrec (Blockchain for EHR). Therefore, pharmacists would get to know in real-time if any anomalies are found within the transactions. After approval of the received delivery, the pharmacist would change the status of the drugs to the next state (received by the pharmacist) by using their private key. (Soni, 2019; Pharma Logistics Editor, 2018; Tseng et al., 2018)

Insurance

Accessing insurance-related information is notoriously difficult and has been named among the biggest obstacles in providing effective healthcare today. Gathering an individual's medical information can be a tedious and time-consuming process. Additionally, due to no immediate return for such an uncomfortable process, consumers are more likely to pass on a policy. A well-organized and planned Blockchain-based medical record management system would help assure a sense of ease and security in the minds of the customers, resulting in an increase in coverage sales. With the use of blockchain, Deloitte reports that the entire application and insurance underwriting process can be brought down from an average of 45 days to near real-time, given that there is a bread-crumb trail of consumer's EHR and EMR data in a series of blockchains. Health insurers could easily obtain secured, verified patient information, hence providing a better customer experience and improving the insurance sales, as well as increasing the number of secured individuals in the country (Deloitte, 2016; IBM, n.d.).

Example:

Previous sections have already covered the application of blockchain in tracking patients' EHR and PHR for secure, authorized, and transparent control by the patient and access by healthcare providers in Subsections 1 and 2 of this section. This would help streamline the process of storage and retrieval of verified information of the patient, hence easing the process of buying insurance. Blockchain has proven to be a good information system. Alongside the EHR and PHR data, one can also keep a track of insurance-related information on the blockchain, linked to the same account used for EHR and PHR information, making blockchain a single point of truth for both patients and insurers. Similar to MedRec's PPR contracts, smart contracts can be designed for guiding the insurance providers to a patient's past claims, and for keeping track of any new claims submitted by the patient. Here is an example use case:

1. Patient Alice makes an insurance claim with Bob's insurance company by making use of an Insurance Claim smart contract. The transaction is signed using Alice's private key and can be verified by Bob at his end. This smart contract ensures a trustless process of making insurance claims. Alice does not have to trust any intermediate agent. This eliminates the risk of corruption in the claim filing process.
2. Bob has a Dapp which keeps polling the Insurance Claim start contract for any new claims. Once Alice's claim is verified by the network, Bob can retrieve Alice's public key and use a Claims History smart contract to find all of Alice's previous claims, along with the current claim, to check for any fraud. This data may be stored as data pointers with necessary access related metadata on the blockchain. Since multiple insurance providers use the same smart contract, Bob can retrieve verified copies of Alice's claims across multiple insurance providers.
3. Once the claim is approved, Bob changes Alice's claim to an approved state. Alice gets notified using her Dapp which keeps polling the Insurance Claim smart contract.

This seems very much alike to the previous section's contracts. However, here is a chance to go back to blockchain's origins - FinTech. Smart contracts, when they are invoked for some operation, can also accept some amount of the blockchain's currency - or "tokens". Suppose that, for approving Alice's insurance claim, Bob puts X amount of tokens in the smart contract. Now, the smart contract can immediately transfer these tokens to Alice's healthcare provider's account, without any intermediary in between. This eliminates the middleman for funds transfer - may it be the agent or the bank. This means lower cost of transfer of funds, transparent process of the insurance claim, and less chance of corruption in between.

CASE STUDIES

Many corporations are adopting the blockchain as the solution to the difficulties in the healthcare system. The main advantage is blockchain's inherent transparency and unalterable contracts. With the help of blockchain, all the competing companies that engage in diverse projects and potentials are superseded by computational power namely algorithms and computer functions, dropping the cost of business to the point of almost zero marginal cost. Today, the healthcare industry undergoes a broad spectrum of issues. Quality medical support is concentrated at a few major players regardless of high demands from public systems. Healthcare organizations often face poor diagnosis methods while having a high patient turnover. It generates an extreme load on healthcare staff, leading to poor health outcomes.

Due to legacy strategies, health care systems stagger rather than exploring new systems of doing things. It faces multiple issues in data accumulation, storage, and exchange. An extra tier of complexity is also combined for protecting centralized storage maintained by medical bodies. Thus, people have very restricted command over their data. But, a major risk is not viewed by people - Centralized warehouses are on high privacy issues. With blockchain technology, health institutions can now develop a decentralized architecture which will directly connect people with:

1. Health services
2. Medical services
3. Drug discovery and traceability
4. Mutual medical insurance
5. Health Consumption

A few of the industry implemented projects are mentioned below:

Project Allive

One of our use cases is on the Project Alive. This project is being developed to bring more transparency in patients' records and to connect the various stakeholders in the healthcare industry, Allive® aims to transform the healthcare industry. It is an intelligent healthcare ecosystem based on blockchain technology. It provides impartial, shareable, and precise knowledge assistance to patients, doctors, and health institutions. It has partnered with a high-end public blockchain project, Ontology®, that utilizes shared trust networks, built-in smart contracts and decentralized ledgers. It facilitates the partnership between distinct institutions and corporations. The system consists of decentralized applications with continuous functioning for the healthcare industry. It will help to provide a user-friendly, end-to-end solution to the public by connecting them with:

- Support teams
- Medical finance services
- Healthcare service providers
- Medical R&D institutions

To overcome the problems the healthcare industry encounters in data accumulation, its storage, exchange, and security, ALLIVE comprises three comprehensive healthcare service modules: Olife, Olivia and Oleaf (Bitcoinst, n.d.).

- OLIFE generates an encrypted, comprehensive profile for every patient which is self-perfection and available over the entire health data network. This module distributes the data in multiple locations, breaks data silos, allowing remote data transparency. Due to this, not only healthcare services could be more personalized instead of the traditional evidence-based medicine, but also the patients can understand themselves properly.

- OLIVIA is a major-hospital-qualified AI doctor which handles a combination of ML algorithms and medical data depositories to formulate a medical knowledge graph. It can provide particular information related to health, care and medical diagnoses to specific patients while also tailoring responses for unique scenarios at a fraction of the cost of visiting the doctors or other professionals. It can also provide customized suggestions about the meals of the patient in between the treatments.

- Finally, OLEAF complements the ecosystem for a healthy lifestyle by integrating the services such as general health administration, appointments of doctors, medicinal prescription submission, insurance procedures, in a decentralized way. For the nextgen healthcare delivery, it works as an on-chain hosting service for DAPPs, which deploys resources like IPFS file storage, bandwidth utilization, artificial intelligence, big data analysis.

Figure 7. Sectors Allive is active in
(Source: Allive)

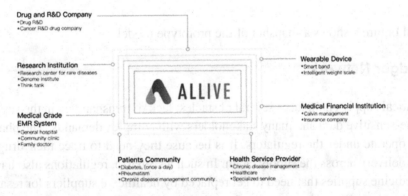

HealthSync With Oracle

Many of you may have encountered a health issue in your lives. Have you ever thought if there was a way of extracting medical history together in a way that ensures the right healthcare decisions are made at the right moment? You might be aware of the smart devices available in the form of wearables and health tracker apps and devices. However, it becomes difficult for companies to collect and preserve the person's medical data without compromising their confidentiality and sensitivity. As compliances like HIPAA and GDPR are actively monitoring the activities related to their citizens' data, companies are challenged to offer a flexible, accessible but secure platform to their customers for managing their health data. Another challenge faced by the companies is providing accurate, up-to-date, solicited health data to patients as well as doctors. That will help the consultants to advise the exact, possibly life-saving therapy.

Combining the cloud computing, the blockchain, and the Internet of Things (IoT), HealthSync is developing an elastic framework for healthcare foundations to share data and processes securely. It helps the institutions to share accurate information, preserving the sensitivity of the information. HNaaS is a

Blockchain/Distributed Ledger Technology powered network for healthcare data and applications. This data and applications span the complete range of health and medical data. HNaaS supports authentication, analytics, security, compliance, identification and applications. First, HNaaS sets policies and configures data and application layers. Next, it lodges security in each transaction. Lastly, it manages authorization, detection and compliance. As a protocol, HNaaS allows anyone with appropriate rights (which are assessed in the control layer) to transfer or communicate information. HealthSync builds, manages, operates, and maintains all networks.

With the help of the Oracle Blockchain Platform, HealthSync can easily implement patient monitoring and provide real-time accurate data to the distributed care team. The overview of how the system works is given below:

- Smart IoT devices collect the medical data through a cloud-based IoT set-up technology.
- This data is uploaded to a secure, permission-based Blockchain ledger. This will create an immutable, correct and up-to-date record of the patients' health.
- This stored information can be distributed to the various stakeholders of the healthcare chain such as healthcare providers, doctors, hospitals, etc., providing the most accurate health data to the healthcare personnel to provide accurate treatment. (HealthSync, n.d.; Oracle, n.d.; Cattermull, 2019)

Figure 8 and Figure 9 shows a snapshot of the prototype model.

The MediLedger Network

The pharmaceutical supply chain faces several obstacles; lack of transparency in the supply chain, unorganized but time-sensitive data and many stakeholders with complex demands. The pharma companies have to always operate under the regulators. It is because they need to trace their drugs, their storage shipments, and delivery across the supply chain. In such a scenario, regulations also have an important role to track medicine supplies that need to get replaced by healthcare suppliers for resale. The existing system of industry depends on the centralized database systems. Thus, the scaling and interoperability become complicated.

Figure 8. Snapshot of the System Prototype Monitoring
(Source: Oracle)

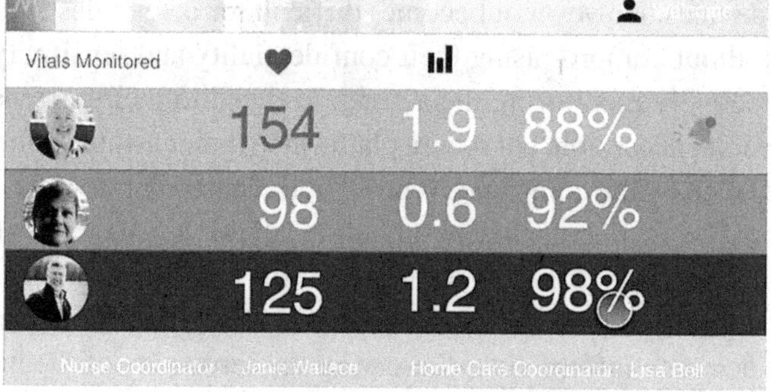

Figure 9. Snapshot of the System Prototype
(Source: Oracle)

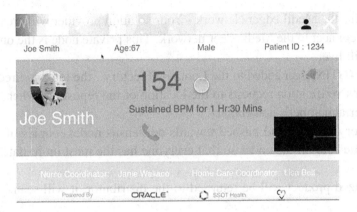

The new regulations require that all the returned prescription medicines must get verified by their unique product identifiers by the manufacturers before being resold. It also expected more interoperability in the industry. The MediLedger Network is a blockchain-based, open, decentralized network for the Pharmaceutical Industry to meet the track-and-trace demands of this additional set of regulations. Chronicles is the host of the project, a San Francisco-based firm. Chronicles operates a verification system that provides a secure and synchronized way to manage an 'industry phonebook' of Global Trade Item Numbers (GTINs).

The project aims to build an industry-owned, authorized blockchain network based on open standards and specifications. The MediLedger Network merges the Look-Up directory with an authorized messaging network. Companies can inquire and respond to their product identifier confirmation requests with the help of this Directory, which can be accessed through a blockchain. It allows only accredited companies to add their products in this directory and assign a unique identifier to every transfer of a drug product on it. This makes the system robust for a false entity to enter the process. As having authenticity and provenance before the transfer, MediLedger blockchain verifies every transaction, eliminating the requirement to do verification. Every item in the supply chain has proper provenance, or it doesn't move forward. Individual wholesalers also need not manage and keep track of enormous volumes of data like product lists, manufacturer addresses, as blockchain handles it all along with reducing errors (MediLedger, n.d.). It has an ability to:

- Maintains logs of transactions in an immutable manner.
- Supporting inter-industry business regulations without compromising private information, making it easy to verify the originality of products, contract terms.
- Preserves business analytics. Uses permission-based private messaging to share information with only authentic partners.
- Connect with trading partners and trusted service providers at the forefront of emerging solutions for the pharmaceutical industry today.

Product Verification System on the MediLedger Network

1. A company joins the MediLedger Network - Your solution provider will create a private node on your behalf to connect to the Mediledger network. This private node is the only place where your private data will live.
2. Your Products (GTINs) get added to the Lookup Directory - the lookup directory is like a phone book that points verification requests to the location of the repository where a manufacturer can respond to a serial number's authenticity.
3. Lookup directory updated and pushed towards consensus nodes- copies of the updated lookup directory will push to all the nodes so that everyone has the most up-to-date lookup directory at all times.
4. When a serialized product will be returned to the distributor, it will scan in the warehouse for verification.
5. Using the always up-to-date lookup directory, the verification message routed to the correct private node and the GTIN, serial number, lot number, and expiration date is verified.
6. It resells verified Product.
7. After a merger or acquisition, it can transfer responsibility for verifying GTINs from one manufacturer to another using smart contracts. The lookup directory updated and pushed to all nodes in the network.
8. The transferred GTIN is verified by the distributor with no delay or triggering an investigation.

Figure 10 is an architecture of the network.

Figure 10. Architecture of the MediLedger Project
(Source: MediLedger)

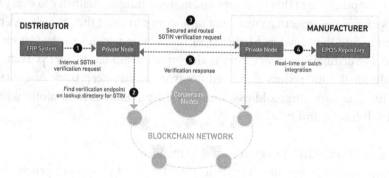

Blockchain Helping Corona

The pandemic that started at the end of 2019 has a disastrous impact across the globe. Massive data regarding COVID-19 or coronavirus keep cropping up from distinct points: social media, the press media, the digital media, and the most widespread one - the rumors. From the number of people affected in different regions to ever-changing safety procedures like preventive masks in public consumption of lukewarm water; COVID-19 data is up-to-date but undependable. Provinces are in misconception because of false information, resulting in severe damage to the safety and quality of an individual's life. However, forgetting the risk of its increase will be the carelessness of the community. Thus, it is very challenging to classify the rumors and the facts among this confusion. It became necessary to make the correct choices. The key to this is having precise data.

MiPasa, a project handled by a group of experts including health specialists, privacy experts, and software developers. MiPasa has partnered with various tech-giants like Oracle, Microsoft, and IBM to use data analytics to synthesize COVID-19 data sources. Using privacy methods and robust analytics available to business foundations, it became viable in accumulating accurate, updated data. The MiPasa Platform addresses disparities and identifies errors or misreporting before integrating reliable new data feeds. As a result, health administrators can react and devise solutions that can aid to suppress the outbreak or support recovery from the virus.

First, it accumulates data from various institutions to determine hot spots, information on individuals and state authorities, etc. and verifies the information before adding it to the database. Then, MiPasa ensures that this data is consistent with the original data. The public will do the last level of validation. They can report any inconsistencies in data. Thus, public health officials can analyze and respond to public sentiment. Hence, multiple administrators can validate the ever-changing, increasing data. Along with all this, MiPasa provides observations on the raw data collected. Although it works to merge all the public data, it does not distribute the private identifiable data. The platform supports decentralized identifiers to encode personal information. Hacera leverages a product known as Private-sea, which is based on zero-knowledge proofs, which use cryptography to allow data to be shareable between distinct entities without revealing sensitive information. All its components had deployed on various cloud platforms of its core partners. They had linked through a Hyper ledger-powered unbounded network. (Wolfson, 2020; MiPasa, n.d.).

Other Projects

The projects mentioned until now are only a few of the many implementations done in the industry. A lot of companies are investing in blockchain or undertaking projects in the medical world. One of the renowned companies, IBM, has partnered with a Chinese firm, Easysight Supply Chain Management. The project, called Yijian Blockchain Technology Application System, is a blockchain platform based on Hyper-ledger Fabric open-source blockchain framework. IBM Watson Health and the Food and Drug Administration (FDA) along with KPMG, Merck and Walmart are collaborating on a program that uses blockchain to identify, track and trace prescription medicines, vaccines distributed in the U.S. Another similar project is the BlockRx4 project which aims to provide visibility, verification, and validation of drug development using blockchain. In the United Kingdom (UK), Google's DeepMind plans to deploy blockchain technology for hospitals, the regulator National Health Service (NHS), and for patients to enable real-time tracking of personal health records. Novartis is using Blockchain and IoT to identify counterfeit medicines and also track temperature with live visibility for all members of the supply chain. Bill & Melinda Gates Foundation have funded a blockchain project for the developing nations. This project is undertaken by Factom, partnered with IPRD Solutions, to create secure medical records, accessed only by an allowed person with biometric verification in the developing nations.

CONCLUSION AND FUTURE SCOPE

Healthcare is one of the vital areas in the industry. A lot of firms are making enormous investments in blockchain to enhance the quality of services provided. There is a notable shift in healthcare, which persists to gain better competencies. Still, it needs to handle the migration of conventional systems towards emerging platforms without compromising the patients and their information. Blockchain is proving its ability by modifying the traditional medical systems with its essential properties: Persistence, anonymity, decentralization. Deployment of the blockchain will lessen the operational costs across the medical system. It will not only maintain data security but will also decrease the number of counterfeiters in the medical industry. Because of the distributed ledger, processing time will reduce in notable amounts. As soon as patients enrol, merged data will be accessible to the allowed parties. Individuals will have additional control over their data. Thus, it allows them to engage more in their well-being.

In the chapter, there are a lot of issues in the healthcare sector along with the ones mentioned, that might be resolved if the blockchain is implemented in a wide span of the globe. A large group of the population still don't have legal status for their identity. They don't receive healthcare aid due to lack of civil evidence. Hence, if this population gets a perpetual identity record based on blockchain health network, they would become a healthier group in global society in a short period.

Underdeveloped, especially countries having lowest income per capita have minimal access to the graded medications. Unfortunately, drugs or medicines in such countries are either ersatz or of below par quality. Such inhumane frauds result in the demise of over 250 thousand infants globally every year (Sample, 2019). A blockchain medical supply chain would permit every registered candidate member to review the entire supply. Blockchain could also protect the overseas funding and donation programs dedicated to healthcare and medical societies in underdeveloped countries. It would help in the transfer of endowment to the needful people. If thoroughly implemented, it will disrupt and revolutionize the healthcare market.

Blockchain may be an unfamiliar technology for the healthcare industry, but it will enrich public health soon. Its potential is dependent on the acceptance within the healthcare ecosystem. It will support the proper deployment of quality services and transparency in clinical preliminaries. That will build up the blockchain as the core foundation of the healthcare industry. Even though this new technology might have some flaws and conjectures related to its harmony with existing medical architecture and its cultural endorsement, blockchain will come to prominence in the near term.

REFERENCES

Azaria, A., Ekblaw, A., Vieira, T., & Lippman, A. (2016, August). Medrec: Using Blockchain For Medical Data Access And Permission Management. In *2016 2nd International Conference on Open and Big Data (OBD)* (pp. 25-30). IEEE. 10.1109/OBD.2016.11

Bell, L., Buchanan, W. J., Cameron, J., & Lo, O. (2018). *Applications Of Blockchain Within Healthcare.* Blockchain in Healthcare Today.

Bitcoinist. (n.d.). *Allive, an Intelligent Healthcare Blockchain Ecosystem, Partners with Ontology.* https://bitcoinist.com/allive-intelligent-healthcare-blockchain-ecosystem-partners-ontology/

Blockchain: The Indian Strategy. (2020). *NITI Aayog.* https://niti.gov.in/sites/default/files/2020-01/Blockchain_The_India_Strategy_Part_I.pdf

Cattermull, N. (2019, March 30). *Synchronized Patient Health Data With Blockchain Technology.* Oracle. https://blogs.oracle.com/blockchain/synchronized-patient-health-data-with-blockchain-technology

Davis, J. (2019, July 23). *The 10 Biggest Healthcare Breaches of 2019, So Far.* https://healthitsecurity.com/news/the-10-biggest-healthcare-data-breaches-of-2019-so-far

Deloitte. (2016). *Blockchain in Health and Life Insurance.* https://www2.deloitte.com/us/en/pages/life-sciences-and-health-care/articles/blockchain-in-insurance.html

Dimitrov, D. (2019). Blockchain Applications for Healthcare Data Management. *Healthcare Informatics Research, 25*(1), 51. doi:10.4258/hir.2019.25.1.51 PMID:30788182

Ekblaw & Azaria. (n.d.). *MedRec: Medical Data Management on the Blockchain.* https://viral.media.mit.edu/pub/medrec

HealthSync. (n.d.). https://www.healthsync.io/projects

IBM. (n.d.). *IBM Blockchain for Insurance.* https://www.ibm.com/blockchain/industries/insurance

Leeming, G., Ainsworth, J. D., & Cunningham, J. (2019). A Ledger of Me: Personalising healthcare using blockchain technology. *Frontiers in Medicine, 6,* 171. doi:10.3389/fmed.2019.00171 PMID:31396516

MediLedger. (n.d.). https://www.mediledger.com/

Mipasa. (n.d.). https://mipasa.org/

Oracle. (n.d.). *HealthSync Uses Oracle Blockchain Platform to Power More Intelligent Healthcare.* https://www.oracle.com/customers/healthsync-1-blockchain.html

Pharma Logistics Editor. (2018). *Blockchain: The Next Frontier for Pharmaceutical Supply Chains.* https://www.pharmalogisticsiq.com/logistics/articles/blockchain-the-next-frontier-for-pharmaceutical-supply-chains

Sample, I. (2019, March 11). *Fake drugs kill more than 250,000 children a year.* https://www.theguardian.com/science/2019/mar/11/fake-drugs-kill-more-than-250000-children-a-year-doctors-warn

Soni, K. (2019, November 12). *Blockchain in Pharma Supply.* Minddeft. https://minddeft.com/blog/blockchain-in-pharma-supply-chain/

Tseng, J. H., Liao, Y. C., Chong, B., & Liao, S. W. (2018). Governance on the drug supply chain via gcoin blockchain. *International Journal of Environmental Research and Public Health, 15*(6), 1055. doi:10.3390/ijerph15061055 PMID:29882861

Wolfson, R. (2020, April 4). *Blockchain Provides Trusted Data to Counter Spread of Coronavirus.* https://cointelegraph.com/news/blockchain-provides-trusted-data-to-counter-spread-of-coronavirus

Zheng, Z., Xie, S., Dai, H., Chen, X., & Wang, H. (2017, June). An Overview of Blockchain Technology: Architecture, Consensus, and Future Trends. In *2017 IEEE international congress on big data (BigData Congress)* (pp. 557-564). IEEE.

KEY TERMS AND DEFINITIONS

Decentralized System or Database: A kind of system configuration which involves multiple nodes in multiple locations, who don't have logical connection between them and work independently.

Electronic Health Record: The digital form of a patient's profile which includes his/her medical history, medications, and all types of ailments he/she has. It also includes important data for the medical administration regarding the demographics, current problems and progress notes of the patient by the medical practitioners under which patient is treated.

Ethereum: An open-source blockchain platform with smart contract features used for the cryptocurrency operations.

Federal Cloud: The cloud technology adoption by the government or federal institution to migrate their conventional information systems to the safe, secure and scalable environment. Generally, all the services or offerings by the government are distributed to the public via this channel.

Health Information Exchange: The management and secure sharing of the medical data of a patient between two or more health care institutions (pharmacies, insurers, hospitals, clinics, etc.) which facilitates different health services to the patient.

Hyperledger or Hyperledger brFaic: Is an industry-graded permissioned framework for distributed ledger dedicated for the development of blockchain-based solutions and applications. It is an open-source umbrella innovative by the Linux Foundation to encourage the innovations in IoT, blockchain for different industries.

Inter Planetary File System (IPFS): A distributed file system protocol used for peer-to-peer sharing of data. It utilizes content addressing technique to uniquely identify every file, connecting every node of the system in a global namespace.

OAuth (Open Authentication): An open-standard protocol for authorization which provides the individual users or the applications to obtain secure access of the information systems.

Public Ledger: A system which maintains member identities in a secure and pseudo version. It is a digital book-keeping service performed between its members with a mutual understanding for operations.

Smart Contract: The digital agreement record between two or more entities stored in a dedicated database, in immutable manner.

Supply Chain Management: A systemized approach for production and delivery of the products and services followed by the company – From obtaining raw material/information to the final delivery/deployment of the product or the services to the consumer.

Swarm: Is a distributed storage framework based on content distribution service protocols which works on the Ethereum blockchain technology.

Compilation of References

Abdu, N. A. A., & Wang, Z. (2021, March). Blockchain for Healthcare Sector-Analytical Review. *IOP Conference Series. Materials Science and Engineering, 1110*(1), 012001.

Abe Developers. (2013). *Block browser for bitcoin and similar currencies.* https://github.com/bitcoin-abe/bitcoin-abe

Aberer, K., Hauswirth, H., & Salehi, A. (2006). *Middleware Support for the Internet of Things.* Available: www.manfredhauswirth.org/research/papers/WSN2006.pdf

Abou Jaoude, J., & George Saade, R. (2019). Blockchain Applications – Usage in Different Domains. *IEEE Access : Practical Innovations, Open Solutions, 7,* 45360–45381.

Adat, V., & Gupta, B. B. (2017). A DDoS attack mitigation framework for Internet of things. *2017 International Conference on Communication and Signal Processing (ICCSP),* 2036–2041. 10.1109/ICCSP.2017.8286761

Agbo, C. C., Mahmoud, Q. H., & Eklund, J. M. (2019, June). Blockchain technology in healthcare: a systematic review. In Healthcare (Vol. 7, No. 2, p. 56). Multidisciplinary Digital Publishing Institute.

Aggarwal, S., Kumar, N., Alhussein, M., & Muhammad, G. (2021). Blockchain-Based UAV Path Planning for Healthcare 4.0: Current Challenges and the Way Ahead. *IEEE Network, 35*(1), 20–29.

Ahemd, M. M., Shah, M. A., & Wahid, A. (2017). IoT security: a layered approach for attacks and defenses. *2017 International Conference on Communication Technologies (ComTech),* 104–110. 10.1109/COMTECH.2017.8065757

AhIman, R. (2016). *Finish city partners with IBM to validate blockchain application in logistics.* https://cointelegraph.com/news/finish-city-partners-with-ibm-to-validate-blockchain-application-in-logistics

Ahmad, R. W., Salah, K., Jayaraman, R., Yaqoob, I., Ellahham, S., & Omar, M. (2021). The role of blockchain technology in telehealth and telemedicine. *International Journal of Medical Informatics,* 104399.

Airehrour, D., Gutierrez, J. A., & Ray, S. K. (2019). Sectrust-rpl: A secure trust-aware rpl routing protocol for the internet of things. *Future Generation Computer Systems, 93,* 860–876. doi:10.1016/j.future.2018.03.021

Akcora, C. G., Dey, A. K., Gel, Y. R., & Kantarcioglu, M. (2018). Forecasting bitcoin price with graph chainlets. In *22nd Pacific-Asia Conference, PAKDD Proceedings, Part III. Volume 10939 of Lecture Notes in Computer Science.* Springer.

Al Omar, A., Rahman, M. S., Basu, A., & Kiyomoto, S. (2017, December). Medibchain: A blockchain based privacy preserving platform for healthcare data. In *International conference on security, privacy and anonymity in computation, communication and storage* (pp. 534-543). Springer.

Alaba, F. A., Othman, M., Hashem, I. A. T., & Alotaibi, F. (2017). Internet of things security: A survey. *Journal of Network and Computer Applications, 88,* 10–28. doi:10.1016/j.jnca.2017.04.002

Alam, T. (2018). A reliable communication framework and its use in internet of things (iot). *CSEIT1835111*, *10*, 450–456.

Albanese, G., Calbimonte, J. P., Schumacher, M., & Calvaresi, D. (2020). Dynamic consent management for clinical trials via private blockchain technology. *Journal of Ambient Intelligence and Humanized Computing*, 1–18.

Alccer, V., & Cruz-Machado, V. (2019). Scanning the industry 4.0: A literature review on technologies for manufacturing systems, Engineering Science and Technology. *International Journal (Toronto, Ont.)*, *22*(3), 899–919.

Alharby, M., & van Moorsel, A. (2020). *Blocksim: An extensible simulation tool for blockchain systems.* arXiv preprint arXiv:2004.13438.

Alhawi, O. M. (2021). *Finding Software Vulnerabilities in Unmanned Aerial Vehicles* (PhD thesis). University of Manchester.

Ali, M. S., Vecchio, M., Pincheira, M., Dolui, K., Antonelli, F., & Rehmani, M. H. (2018). Applications of blockchains in the internet of things: A comprehensive survey. *IEEE Communications Surveys and Tutorials*, *21*(2), 1676–1717. doi:10.1109/COMST.2018.2886932

Ali, M. S., Vecchio, M., Pincheira, M., Dolui, K., Antonelli, F., & Rehmani, M. H. (2019). *Applications of blockchains in the Internet of things: A comprehensive survey.* IEEE Commun. Surv. Tutorials.

Al-Kashoash, H. A., Kharrufa, H., Al-Nidawi, Y., & Kemp, A. H. (2019). Congestion control in wireless sensor and 6lowpan networks: Toward the internet of things. *Wireless Networks*, *25*(8), 4493–4522. doi:10.100711276-018-1743-y

All, I. F. (2017). *The 5 Worst Examples of IoT Hacking and Vulnerabilities in Recorded History.* Academic Press.

Aloqaily, M., Bouachir, O., Boukerche, A., & Al Ridhawi, I. (2021). Design guidelines for blockchain-assisted 5g-uav networks. *IEEE Network*, *35*(1), 64–71.

Alphand, O., Amoretti, M., Claeys, T., Dall'Asta, S., Duda, A., Ferrari, G., ... Zanichelli, F. (2018, April). IoTChain: A blockchain security architecture for the In-ternet of Things. In *2018 IEEE Wireless Communications and Networking Conference(WCNC)* (pp. 1-6). IEEE.

Alsamhi, S. H., Lee, B., Guizani, M., Kumar, N., Qiao, Y., & Liu, X. (2021). Blockchain for decentralized multi-drone to combat COVID-19 and future pandemics: Framework and proposed solutions. *Transactions on Emerging Telecommunications Technologies*, 4255.

Al-Turjman, F., & Alturjman, S. (2018). Context-sensitive access in industrial Internet of things (iiot) healthcare applications. *IEEE Transactions on Industrial Informatics*, *14*(6), 2736–2744. doi:10.1109/TII.2018.2808190

Aman, M. N., Chua, K. C., & Sikdar, B. (2017). A lightweight mutual authentication protocol for IoT systems. *GLOBECOM 2017 - 2017 IEEE Global Communications Conference*, 1–6.

Aman, M. N., Chua, K. C., & Sikdar, B. (2017). A light-weight mutual authentication protocol for iot systems. In *GLOBECOM 2017-2017 IEEE Global Communications Conference*, (pp. 1–6). IEEE. 10.1109/GLOCOM.2017.8253991

Aman, M. N., Sikdar, B., Chua, K. C., & Ali, A. (2018). Low power data integrity in iot systems. *IEEE Internet of Things Journal*, *5*(4), 3102–3113. doi:10.1109/JIOT.2018.2833206

Ampel, B., Patton, M., & Chen, H. (2019, July). Performance modeling of hyperledger sawtooth blockchain. In *2019 IEEE International Conference on Intelligence and Security Informatics (ISI)* (pp. 59-61). IEEE.

Andola, N., Yadav, V. K., Venkatesan, S., & Verma, S. (2021). SpyChain: A Lightweight Blockchain for Authentication and Anonymous Authorization in IoD. *Wireless Personal Communications*, ●●●, 1–20.

Andoni, M., Robu, V., Flynn, D., Abram, S., Geach, D., Jenkins, D., McCallum, P., & Peacock, A. (2019). Blockchain technology in the energy sector: A systematic review of challenges and opportunities. *Renewable & Sustainable Energy Reviews, 100*, 143–174. doi:10.1016/j.rser.2018.10.014

Andrea, I., Chrysostomou, C., & Hadji Christofi, G. (2015). Internet of things: Security vulnerabilities and challenges. In 2015 IEEE symposium on computers and communication (ISCC), (pp. 180–187). IEEE.

Andrea, I., Chrysostomou, C., & Hadjichristofi, G. (2015). Internet of things: security vulnerabilities and challenges. *2015 IEEE Symposium on Computers and Communication (ISCC)*, 180–187. 10.1109/ISCC.2015.7405513

Androulaki, E., Barger, A., Bortnikov, V., Cachin, C., Christidis, K., De Caro, A., ... Muralidharan, S. (2018, April). Hyperledger fabric: a distributed operating system for permissioned blockchains. In *Proceedings of the Thirteenth EuroSys Conference* (pp. 1-15). 10.1145/3190508.3190538

Angeletti, F., Chatzigiannakis, I., & Vitaletti, A. (2017, September). The role of blockchain and IoT in recruiting participants for digital clinical trials. In *2017 25th International Conference on Software, Telecommunications and Computer Networks (SoftCOM)* (pp. 1-5). IEEE.

Angelis, S.D., Aniello, L., Baldoni, R., Lombardi, F., Margheri, A., & Sassone, V. (2018). PBFT vs Proof-of-Authority: Applying the CAP Theorem to Permissioned Blockchain. *ITASEC 2018*.

Anilkumar, V., Joji, J. A., Afzal, A., & Sheik, R. (2019, May). Blockchain Simulation and Development platforms: Survey, Issues and Challenges. In *2019 International Conference on Intelligent Computing and Control Systems (ICCS)* (pp. 935-939). Academic Press.

Antonioli, D., Tippenhauer, N. O., & Rasmussen, K. (2020). Bias: Bluetooth impersonation attacks. In *2020 IEEE Symposium on Security and Privacy (SP)*, (pp. 549–562). IEEE. 10.1109/SP40000.2020.00093

Araujo, J., Mazo, M., Anta, A. Jr, Tabuada, P., & Johansson, K. H. (2014, February). System Architecture, Protocols, and Algorithms for Aperiodic wireless control systems. *IEEE Transactions on Industrial Informatics, 10*(1), 175–184. doi:10.1109/TII.2013.2262281

Arcenegui, J., Arjona, R., Román, R., & Baturone, I. (2021). Secure Combination of IoT and Blockchain by Physically Binding IoT Devices to Smart Non-Fungible Tokens Using PUFs. *Sensors*.

Armknecht, F., Karame, G. O., Mandal, A., Youssef, F., & Zenner, E. (2015). Ripple: Overview and outlook. In *International Conference on Trust and Trustworthy Computing* (pp. 163-180). Springer. 10.1007/978-3-319-22846-4_10

Arteaga, S. P., Hernández, L. A. M., Pérez, G. S., Orozco, A. L. S., & Villalba, L. J. G. (2019). Analysis of the gps spoofing vulnerability in the drone 3dr solo. *IEEE Access: Practical Innovations, Open Solutions, 7*, 51782–51789. doi:10.1109/ACCESS.2019.2911526

Asamoah, F., Kakourou, A., Dhami, S., Lau, S., Agache, I., Muraro, A., ... Sheikh, A. (2017). Allergen immunotherapy for allergic asthma: A systematic overview of systematic reviews. *Clinical and Translational Allergy, 7*(1), 1–12.

Ashibani, Y., & Mahmoud, Q. H. (2017). An efficient and secure scheme for smart home communication using identity-based signcryption. In *2017 IEEE 36th International Performance Computing and Communications Conference (IPCCC)*, (pp. 1–7). IEEE. 10.1109/PCCC.2017.8280497

Ashibani, Y., & Mahmoud, Q. H. (2017). An efficient and secure scheme for smart home communication using identity-based encryption. *2017 IEEE 36th International Performance Computing and Communications Conference (IPCCC)*, 1–7.

Aste, T., Tasca, P., & Di Matteo, T. (2017). Blockchain technologies: The foreseeable impact on society and industry. *Computer, 50*(9), 18–28. doi:10.1109/MC.2017.3571064

Aswale, P., Shukla, A., Bharati, P., Bharambe, S., & Palve, S. (2019). *An overview of internet of things: architecture, protocols and challenges.* Information and Communication Technology for Intelligent Systems.

Atlam, H. F., Azad, M. A., Alzahrani, A. G., & Wills, G. (2020). A Review of Blockchain in Internet of Things and AI. *Journal of Big Data and Cognitive Computing*, 1-27.

Atlam, H. F., Alenezi, A., Alassafi, M. O., & Wills, G. B. (2018). Blockchain with Internet of things: Benefits, challenges, and future directions. *Int. J. Intell. Syst. Appl., 10*(6), 40–48. doi:10.5815/ijisa.2018.06.05

Aublin, P. L., Mokhtar, S. B., & Quéma, V. (2013, July). Rbft: Redundant byzantine fault tolerance. In *2013 IEEE 33rd International Conference on Distributed ComputingSystems* (pp. 297-306). IEEE.

Ayaz, F., Sheng, Z., Tian, D., & Guan, Y. L. (2021). A Proof-of-Quality-Factor (PoQF)-Based Blockchain and Edge Computing for Vehicular Message Dissemination. *IEEE Internet of Things Journal, 8*(4), 2468–2482. doi:10.1109/JIOT.2020.3026731

Azar, A. T., Koubaa, A., Ali Mohamed, N., Ibrahim, H. A., Ibrahim, Z. F., Kazim, M., Ammar, A., Benjdira, B., Khamis, A. M., Hameed, I. A., & Casalino, G. (2021). Drone deep reinforcement learning: A review. *Electronics (Basel), 10*(9), 999. doi:10.3390/electronics10090999

Azaria, A., Ekblaw, A., Vieira, T., & Lippman, A. (2016, August). Medrec: Using blockchain for medical data access and permission management. In *2016 2nd International Conference on Open and Big Data (OBD)* (pp. 25-30). IEEE.

Azaria, A., Ekblaw, A., Vieira, T., & Lippman, A. (2016, August). Medrec: Using Blockchain For Medical Data Access And Permission Management. In *2016 2nd International Conference on Open and Big Data (OBD)* (pp. 25-30). IEEE. 10.1109/OBD.2016.11

Azzabi, T., Farhat, H., & Sahli, N. (2017). A survey on wireless sensor networks security issues and military specificities. In *2017 International Conference on Advanced Systems and Electric Technologies (IC_ASET)*, (pp. 66–72). IEEE. 10.1109/ASET.2017.7983668

Azzi, R., Chamoun, R. K., & Sokhn, M. (2019). The power of a blockchain-based supply chain. *Computers & Industrial Engineering, 135*, 582–592. doi:10.1016/j.cie.2019.06.042

Bach, L., Mihaljevic, B., & Zagar, M. (2018). Comparative analysis of blockchain consensus algorithms. In *2018 41st International Convention on Information and Communication Technology, Electronics and Microelectronics (MIPRO)*. IEEE.

Bach, L. M., Mihaljevic, B., & Zagar, M. (2018, May). Comparative analysis of blockchain consensus algorithms. In *41st International Convention on Information and Communication Technology, Electronics and Microelectronics (MIPRO)* (pp.1545-1550). 10.23919/MIPRO.2018.8400278

Badii, C., Bellini, P., Difino, A., & Nesi, P. (2020). Smart City IoT Platform Respecting GDPR Privacy and Security Aspects. *IEEE Access: Practical Innovations, Open Solutions, 8*, 23601–23623. doi:10.1109/ACCESS.2020.2968741

Baird, L. (2016). *The swirlds hashgraph consensus algorithm: Fair, fast, byzantine fault tolerance.* Swirlds Tech Reports SWIRLDS-TR-2016-01, Tech. Rep.

Baird, L., Harmon, M., & Madsen, P. (2019). Hedera: A public hashgraph network & governing council. *White Paper, 1*.

Baird, L., Harmon, M., & Madsen, P. (2019). Hedera: A public hashgraph network & Governing Council. *White Paper, 1*.

Baliga, A., Solanki, N., Verekar, S., Pednekar, A., Kamat, P., & Chatterjee, S. (2018, June). Performance characterization of hyperledger fabric. In 2018 Crypto Valley conference on blockchain technology (CVCBT) (pp. 65-74). IEEE.

Ban, T. Q., Anh, B. N., Son, N. T., & Van Dinh, T. (2019, February). Survey of Hyperledger Blockchain Frameworks: Case Study in FPT University's Cryptocurrency Wallets. In *Proceedings of the 2019 8th International Conference on Software and Computer Applications* (pp. 472-480). Academic Press.

Banker, S. (2016). *Will blockchain technology revolutionize supply chain applications?* https://logisticsviewpoints.com/2016/06/20/will-block-chain-technology-revolutionize-supply-chain-applications/

Ban, T. Q., Anh, B. N., Son, N. T., & Van Dinh, T. (2019, February). Survey of Hyperledger Blockchain Frameworks: Case Study in FPT University's Cryptocurrency Wallets. In *Proceedings of the 2019 8th International Conference on Software and Computer Applications* (pp. 472-480). 10.1145/3316615.3316671

Barka, E., Kerrache, C. A., Benkraouda, H., Shuaib, K., Ahmad, F., & Kurugollu, F. (2019). Towards a trusted unmanned aerial system using blockchain for the protection of critical infrastructure. *Transactions on Emerging Telecommunications Technologies*, e3706. doi:10.1002/ett.3706

Barka, E., Kerrache, C. A., Hussain, R., Lagraa, N., Lakas, A., & Bouk, S. H. (2018). A trusted lightweight communication strategy for flying named data networking. *Sensors (Basel)*, *18*(8), 2683. doi:10.339018082683 PMID:30111732

Bashir, I. (2017). Mastering Blockchain. Packt Publishing Ltd, 2017.

Bashir, I. (2018). *Mastering Blockchain: Distributed ledger technology, decentralization, and smart contracts explained.* Packt Publishing Ltd.

Battista, G. D., Donato, V. D., Patrignani, M., Pizzonia, M., Roselli, V., & Tamassia, R. (2015). Bitconeview: visualization of flows in the bitcoin transaction graph. *12th IEEE Symposium on Visualization for Cyber Security*, 1–8. 10.1109/VIZSEC.2015.7312773

Bau, T. (2017). *Why Estonia is a good place for eHealth (and why you should attend eHealth Tallinn).* https://www.himss.eu/himss-blog/why-estonia-good-place-ehealth-and-why-you-should-attend-ehealth-tallinn

Beck, R., & Müller-Bloch, C. (2017). Blockchain as Radical Innovation: A Framework for Engaging with Distributed Ledgers as Incumbent Organization.: *Proceedings of the 50th Hawaii International Conference on System Sciences*, 5390–5399. 10.24251/HICSS.2017.653

Behzadan, V. (2016). *Real-time inference of topological structure and vulnerabilities for adaptive jamming against covert ad hoc networks.* PhD thesis.

Behzadan, V. (2017). *Cyber-physical attacks on uas networks-challenges and open research problems.* arXiv preprint arXiv:1702.01251.

Bell, L., Buchanan, W. J., Cameron, J., & Lo, O. (2018). *Applications Of Blockchain Within Healthcare.* Blockchain in Healthcare Today.

Benchoufi, M., Porcher, R., & Ravaud, P. (2017). Blockchain protocols in clinical trials: Transparency and traceability of consent. *F1000 Research*, 6.

Bennett, B. (2017). Blockchain HIE overview: A framework for healthcare interoperability. *Telehealth Med. Today*, *2*(3), 1–6.

Benslimane, Y., Benahmed, K., & Benslimane, H. (2018). Security mechanisms for 6lowpan network in context of internet of things: A survey. In *International Conference in Artificial Intelligence in Renewable Energetic Systems*, (pp. 49–69). Springer.

Bera, B., Saha, S., Das, A. K., Kumar, N., Lorenz, P., & Alazab, M. (2020). Blockchain-envisioned secure data delivery and collection scheme for 5g-based iot-enabled internet of drones environment. *IEEE Transactions on Vehicular Technology, 69*(8), 9097–9111. doi:10.1109/TVT.2020.3000576

Berman, F. (2008, December). Got data? a guide to data preservation in the information age. *Communications of the ACM, 51*(12), 50–56. doi:10.1145/1409360.1409376

Bernabe, J. B., Torres, R., Martin, D., Crespo, A., Skarmeta, A., Fortune, D., ... Alamillo, I. (n.d.). *An Overview on ARIES: Reliable European Identity Ecosystem.* Academic Press.

Bertin, E., Hussein, D., Sengul, C., & Frey, V. (2019). Access control in the internet of things: A survey of existing approaches and open research questions. *Annales des Télécommunications, 74*(7), 375–388. doi:10.100712243-019-00709-7

Bessani, A., Sousa, J., & Alchieri, E. E. P. (2014). State Machine Replication for the Masses with BFT-SMART. In *2014 44th Annual IEEE/IFIP International Conference on Dependable Systems and Networks,* (pp. 355-362). IEEE. 10.1109/DSN.2014.43

Bhardwaj, G. (2018, April 25). Five use cases for blockchain in pharma. *Pharmaphorum.* https://pharmaphorum.com/views-and-analysis/five-use-cases-for-blockchain-in-pharma/

Bhardwaj, V., Kaur, N., Vashisht, S., & Jain, S. (2020). Secrip: Secure and reliable intercluster routing protocol for efficient data transmission in flying ad hoc networks. *Transactions on Emerging Telecommunications Technologies,* e4068. doi:10.1002/ett.4068

Bhargavan, K., Delignat-Lavaud, A., Fournet, C., Gollamudi, A., Gonthier, G., Kobeissi, N., ... Zanella-Béguelin, S. (2016, October). Formal verification of smart contracts: *Short paper.* In *Proceedings of the 2016 ACM workshop on programming languages and analysis for security* (pp. 91-96). ACM.

BigQuery. (2020). *Google: Bitcoin in BigQuery: blockchain analytics on public data.* https://cloud.google.com/blog/products/gcp/bitcoin-in-bigquery-blockchain-analytics-on-public-data

Biswas, K., & Muthukkumarasamy, V. (2016). Securing Smart Cities Using Blockchain Technology. *IEEE International Conference on High Performance Computing and Communications,* 1392-1393.

Bitcoinist. (n.d.). *Allive, an Intelligent Healthcare Blockchain Ecosystem, Partners with Ontology.* https://bitcoinist.com/allive-intelligent-healthcare-blockchain-ecosystem-partners-ontology/

Blockchain: The Indian Strategy. (2020). *NITI Aayog.* https://niti.gov.in/sites/default/files/2020-01/Blockchain_The_India_Strategy_Part_I.pdf

Blummer, T., Sean, M., & Cachin, C. (2018). *An Introduction to Hyperledger.* Technical report, White paper.

Bodkhe, U., & Tanwar, S. (2020). Taxonomy of secure data dissemination techniques for iot environment. *IET Software, 14*(6), 563–571. doi:10.1049/iet-sen.2020.0006

Bouachir, O., Grati, R., Aloqaily, M., & Mnaouer, A. B. (2020). Blockchain based solutions for achieving secure storage in fog computing. In Blockchain-enabled Fog and Edge Computing: Concepts, Architectures and Applications: Concepts, Architectures and Applications. Academic Press.

Boulos, M. N. K., Wilson, J. T., & Clauson, K. A. (2018). *Geospatial blockchain: promises, challenges, and scenarios in health and healthcare.* Academic Press.

Boursianis, A. D., Papadopoulou, M. S., Diamantoulakis, P., Liopa-Tsakalidi, A., Barouchas, P., Salahas, G., ... & Goudos, S. K. (2020). Internet of things (IoT) and agricultural unmanned aerial vehicles (UAVs) in smart farming: a comprehensive review. *Internet of Things*, 100187.

Boyes, H., Hallaq, B., Cunningham, J., & Watson, T. (2018). The industrial Internet of things (iiot): An analysis framework. *Computers in Industry, 101*, 1–12. doi:10.1016/j.compind.2018.04.015

Brandenburger, M., Cachin, C., Kapitza, R., & Sorniotti, A. (2018). *Blockchain and trusted computing: Problems, pitfalls, and a solution for hyperledger fabric.* arXivpreprint arXiv:1805.08541.

Brent, L., Jurisevic, A., Kong, M., Liu, E., Gauthier, F., Gramoli, V., . . . Scholz, B. (2018). *Vandal: A scalable security analysis framework for smart contracts.* arXiv preprint arXiv:1809.03981.

Broder, A. Z., Kumar, R., Maghoul, F., Raghavan, P., Rajagopalan, S., Stata, R., Tomkins, A., & Wiener, J. L. (2000). Graph structure in the web. *Computer Networks, 33*(1-6), 309–320. doi:10.1016/S1389-1286(00)00083-9

Brogan, J., Baskaran, I., & Ramachandran, N. (2018). Authenticating health activity data using distributed ledger technologies. *Computational and Structural Biotechnology Journal, 16*, 257–266.

Brown, R. G., Carlyle, J., Grigg, I., & Hearn, M. (2016). Corda: an introduction. *R3 CEV.*

Brown, R. G., Carlyle, J., Grigg, I., & Hearn, M. (2016). Corda: an introduction. *R3 CEV.* Quorum Whitepaper: https://github.com/ConsenSys/quorum/blob/master/docs/Quorum%20Whitepaper%20v0.2.pdf

Bruce, J. (2014). *The mini-blockchain scheme.* Academic Press.

Buchman, E. (2016). *Tendermint: Byzantine fault tolerance in the age of blockchains* (Doctoral dissertation). Engineering Systems and Computing; University of Guelph, Canada.

Bui, N., & Zorzi, M. (2011). Health care applications: a solution based on the internet of things. In *Proceedings of the 4th international symposium on applied sciences in biomedical and communication technologies.* ACM.

Butun, I., Pereira, N., & Gidlund, M. (2018). Analysis of lorawan v1. 1 security. *Proceedings of the 4th ACM MobiHoc Workshop on Experiences with the Design and Implementation of Smart Objects*, 1–6.

Butun, I., Pereira, N., & Gidlund, M. (2019). Security risk analysis of lorawan and future directions. *Future Internet, 11*(1), 3. doi:10.3390/fi11010003

Cachin, C. (2016, July). Architecture of the hyperledger blockchain fabric. In *Workshop on distributed cryptocurrencies and consensus ledgers* (Vol. 310, p. 4). Academic Press.

Castro, M., & Liskov, B. (1999). Practical Byzantine Fault Tolerance. *Third Symposium on Operating Systems Design and Implementation*, 173–186.

Castro, M., & Liskov, B. (2002). Practical byzantine fault tolerance and proactive recovery. *ACM Transactions on Computer Systems, 20*(4), 398–461. doi:10.1145/571637.571640

Cattermull, N. (2019, March 30). *Synchronized Patient Health Data With Blockchain Technology.* Oracle. https://blogs.oracle.com/blockchain/synchronized-patient-health-data-with-blockchain-technology

Cervantes, C., Poplade, D., Nogueira, M., & Santos, A. (2015). Detection of sinkhole attacks for supporting secure routing on 6lowpan for Internet of things. *2015 IFIP/IEEE International Symposium on Integrated Network Management (IM)*, 606–611. 10.1109/INM.2015.7140344

Chaari, L., Chahbani, S., & Rezgui, J. (2020). Vulnerabilities assessment for unmanned aerial vehicles communication systems. In *2020 International Symposium on Networks, Computers and Communications (ISNCC)*, (pp. 1–6). IEEE.

Chaari, L., Chahbani, S., & Rezgui, J. (2020, October). Vulnerabilities Assessment for Unmanned Aerial Vehicles Communication Systems. In *2020 International Symposium on Networks, Computers and Communications (ISNCC)* (pp. 1-6). IEEE.

Chakraborty, P., Shahriyar, R., Iqbal, A., & Bosu, A. (2018, October). Understanding the software development practices of blockchain projects: a survey. In *Proceedings of the 12th ACM/IEEE International Symposium on Empirical Software Engineeringand Measurement* (pp. 1-10). 10.1145/3239235.3240298

Chakraborty, R. S., Mathew, J., & Vasilakos, A. V. (2019). *Security and fault tolerance in Internet of things*. Springer. doi:10.1007/978-3-030-02807-7

Challita, U., Ferdowsi, A., Chen, M., & Saad, W. (2019). Machine learning for wireless connectivity and security of cellular-connected uavs. *IEEE Wireless Communications*, 26(1), 28–35. doi:10.1109/MWC.2018.1800155

Chamekh, M. (2018). Secured Distributed IoT Based Supply Chain Architecture. *IEEE International Conference on Enabling Technologies: Infrastructure for Collaborative Enterprises*, 199-202. 10.1109/WETICE.2018.00045

Chan, M. (2017). *Why Cloud Computing Is the Foundation of the Internet of Things*. Academic Press.

Cha, S.-C., Chen, J.-F., Su, C., & Yeh, K.-H. (2018). A blockchain connected gateway for ble-based devices in the internet of things. *IEEE Access: Practical Innovations, Open Solutions*, 6, 24639–24649. doi:10.1109/ACCESS.2018.2799942

Chaudhary, R., Aujla, G. S., Garg, S., Kumar, N., & Rodrigues, J. J. P. C. (2018). Sdn-enabled multi-attribute-based secure communication for smart grid in riot environment. *IEEE Transactions on Industrial Informatics*, 14(6), 2629–2640. doi:10.1109/TII.2018.2789442

Chelladurai, U., & Pandian, S. (2021). A novel blockchain based electronic health record automation system for healthcare. *Journal of Ambient Intelligence and Humanized Computing*, 1–11.

Chen, G., & Ng, W. S. (2017). An efficient authorization framework for securing industrial Internet of things. TENCON 2017 - 2017 IEEE Region 10 Conference, 1219–1224. doi:10.1109/TENCON.2017.8228043

Chen, H. S., Jarrell, J. T., Carpenter, K. A., Cohen, D. S., & Huang, X. (2019). Blockchain in healthcare: a patient-centered model. *Biomedical Journal of Scientific & Technical Research*, 20(3), 15017.

Chen, T., Li, X., Luo, X., & Zhang, X. (2017, February). Under-optimized smart contracts devour your money. In *2017 IEEE 24th International Conference on Software Analysis, Evolution and Reengineering (SANER)* (pp. 442-446). IEEE.

Chen, C., Yan, X., Zhu, F., Han, J., & Yu, P. S. (2008). Graph OLAP: Towards Online Analytical Processing on Graphs. *Eighth IEEE International Conference on Data Mining*, 103-112. 10.1109/ICDM.2008.30

Chen, I., Guo, J., & Bao, F. (2014). Trust management for service composition in SOA-based IoT systems. *Proceedings of the IEEE Wireless Communications and Networking Conference (WCNC)*, 3444-3449.

Chen, J., Wang, W., Zhou, Y., Ahmed, S. H., & Wei, W. (2021). Exploiting 5G and Blockchain for Medical Applications of Drones. *IEEE Network*, 35(1), 30–36.

Chen, J., Yatnalli, U., & Gesbert, D. (2017a). Learning radio maps for uav-aided wireless networks: A segmented regression approach. In *2017 IEEE International Conference on Communications (ICC)*, (pp. 1–6). IEEE. 10.1109/ICC.2017.7997333

Chen, L., Lee, W.-K., Chang, C.-C., Choo, K.-K. R., & Zhang, N. (2019). Blockchain-based searchable encryption for electronic health record sharing. *Future Generation Computer Systems*, *95*, 420–429. doi:10.1016/j.future.2019.01.018

Chen, L., Xu, L., Shah, N., Gao, Z., Lu, Y., & Shi, W. (2017b). On security analysis of proof-of-elapsed-time (poet). In *International Symposium on Stabilization, Safety, and Security of Distributed Systems*, (pp. 282–297). Springer. 10.1007/978-3-319-69084-1_19

Chen, Q., Sowan, A. K., & Xu, S. (2018). A Safety and Security Architecture for Reducing Accidents in Intelligent Transportation Systems. *IEEE/ACM International Conference on Computer-Aided Design (ICCAD)*, 1-7. 10.1145/3240765.3243462

Chen, S., Liu, X., & Yan, J. (2020). *Processes, benefits, and challenges for adoption of blockchain technologies in food supply chains: a thematic analysis.* Inf Syst E-Bus Manage; doi:10.100710257-020-00467-3

Cherinchaw, A., Vallabhaneni, P., & Lizaso, S. (2021). *The rise of NFTs – Opportunities and legal issues.* Retrieved from https://www.whitecase.com/publications/alert/rise-nfts-opportunities-and-legal-issues

Choi, J., & Kim, Y. (2016). An improved lea block encryption algorithm to prevent side-channel attack in the IoT system. *2016 Asia-Pacific Signal and Information Processing Association Annual Summit and Conference (APSIPA)*, 1–4. 10.1109/APSIPA.2016.7820845

Choudhury, O., Fairoza, N., Sylla, I., & Das, A. (2019). *A blockchain framework for managing and monitoring data in multi-site clinical trials.* arXiv preprint arXiv:1902.03975.

Christidis, K., & Devetsikiotis, M. (2016). Blockchains and Smart Contracts for the IoT. *IEEE Access : Practical Innovations, Open Solutions*, *4*, 2292–2303.

Coladangelo, A., & Sattath, O. (2020). A quantum money solution to the blockchain scalability problem. *Quantum*, *4*, 297.

Colema, L. (2006). Frequency of man-made disasters in the 20the century. *Journal of Contingencies and Crisis Management*, *14*(1), 3–11.

Conti, R., & Schmidt, J. (2021), *What You Need To Know About Non-Fungible Tokens (NFTs).* Retrieved from https://www.forbes.com/advisor/investing/nft-non-fungible-token/

Corda. (2021). https://www.corda.net

CouchDB. (2021). https://www.couchdb.apache.org

Crain, T., Gramoli, V., Larrea, M., & Raynal, M. (2017). *(Leader/Randomization/Signature)-free Byzantine Consensus for Consortium Blockchains.* CoRR, vol. abs/1702.03068.

Cui, M., Zhang, G., Wu, Q., & Ng, D. W. K. (2018). Robust trajectory and transmit power design for secure uav communications. *IEEE Transactions on Vehicular Technology*, *67*(9), 9042–9046. doi:10.1109/TVT.2018.2849644

Dagher, G. G., Mohler, J., Milojkovic, M., & Marella, P. B. (2018). Ancile: Privacy-preserving framework for access control and interoperability of electronic health records using blockchain technology. *Sustainable Cities and Society*, *39*, 283–297.

Dahiya, S., & Garg, M. (2019). Unmanned aerial vehicles: Vulnerability to cyber attacks. In *International Conference on Unmanned Aerial System in Geomatics*, (pp. 201–211). Springer.

Dani, K. (2018). *BTC dataset.* https://senseable2015-6.mit.edu/bitcoin/

Danzi, P., Kalor, A. E., Stefanovic, C., & Popovski, P. (2018). Analysis of the communication traffic for blockchain synchronization of IoT devices. In *2018 IEEE International Conference on Communications (ICC)*. IEEE.

Dasaklis, T. K., Casino, F., Patsakis, C., & Douligeris, C. (2019). A Framework for Supply Chain Traceability Based on Blockchain Tokens. *Lecture Notes in Business Information Processing, 362,* vol-362. doi:10.1007/978-3-030-37453-2_56

Dastres, R., & Soori, M. (2020). Secure socket layer (ssl) in the network and web security. *International Journal of Computer and Information Engineering, 14*(10), 330–333.

Davis, J. (2019, July 23). *The 10 Biggest Healthcare Breaches of 2019, So Far.* https://healthitsecurity.com/news/the-10-biggest-healthcare-data-breaches-of-2019-so-far

De Aguiar, E. J., Faiçal, B. S., Krishnamachari, B., & Ueyama, J. (2020). A survey of blockchain-based strategies for healthcare. *ACM Computing Surveys, 53*(2), 1–27.

de Carvalho Silva, J., Rodrigues, J. J., Alberti, A. M., Solic, P., & Aquino, A. L. (2017). Lorawan—a low power wan protocol for internet of things: A review and opportunities. In *2017 2nd International Multidisciplinary Conference on Computer and Energy Science (SpliTech),* (pp. 1–6). IEEE.

De, S.J., & Ruj, S. (2017). Efficient decentralized attribute-based access control for mobile clouds. *IEEE Transactions on Cloud Computing.*

DeCuir, J. (2013). Introducing bluetooth smart: Part 1: A look at both classic and new technologies. *IEEE Consumer Electronics Magazine, 3*(1), 12–18. doi:10.1109/MCE.2013.2284932

Dedeoglu, V., Dorri, A., Jurdak, R., Michelin, R. A., Lunardi, R. C., Kanhere, S. S., & Zorzo, A. F. (2020). A Journey in Applying Blockchain for Cyberphysical Systems. In *2020 International Conference on COMmunication Systems & NETworkS (COMSNETS)* (pp. 383–390). IEEE 10.1109/COMSNETS48256.2020.9027487

Dedeoglu, V., Jurdak, R., Putra, G. D., Dorri, A., & Kanhere, S. S. (2019). A Trust Architecture for Blockchain in IoT. *16th EAI International Conference on Mobile and Ubiquitous Systems: Computing, Networking and Services,* 190–199. 10.1145/3360774.3360822

Deebak, B.D., Al-Turjman, F., Aloqaily, M., & Alfandi, O. (2019). An Authentic-Based Privacy Preservation Protocol for Smart e-Healthcare Systems in IoT. *IEEE Access.* . doi:10.1109/ACCESS.2019.2941575

Deloitte. (2016). *Blockchain in Health and Life Insurance.* https://www2.deloitte.com/us/en/pages/life-sciences-and-health-care/articles/blockchain-in-insurance.html

Dhillon, P., & Kalra, S. (2018). Multi-factor user authentication scheme for IoT-based healthcare services. *Journal of Reliable Intelligent Environments, 4*(3), 141–160. Advance online publication. doi:10.100740860-018-0062-5

Dhillon, V., Metcalf, D., & Hooper, M. (2017). The hyperledger project. In *Blockchain enabled applications* (pp. 139–149). Apress.

Dilawar, N., Rizwan, M., Ahmad, F., & Akram, S. (2019). Blockchain: Securing internet of medical things (IoMT). *Int. J. Adv. Comput. Sci. Appl, 10*(1), 82–89.

Dimitrov, D. (2019). Blockchain Applications for Healthcare Data Management. *Healthcare Informatics Research, 25*(1), 51. doi:10.4258/hir.2019.25.1.51 PMID:30788182

Dinh, T. T. A., Wang, J., Chen, G., Liu, R., Ooi, B. C., & Tan, K. L. (2017, May). Blockbench: A framework for analyzing private blockchains. In *Proceedings of the 2017ACM International Conference on Management of Data* (pp. 1085-1100). 10.1145/3035918.3064033

Dorri, A., Kanhere, S. S., Jurdak, R., & Gauravaram, P. (2017, March). Blockchain for IoT security and privacy: The case study of a smart home. In *2017 IEEE international conference on pervasive computing and communications workshops (PerCom workshops)* (pp. 618-623). IEEE.

Dorri, A., Kanhere, S. S., Jurdak, R., & Gauravaram, P. (2019). *LSB: A Lightweight Scalable Blockchain for IoT Security and Privacy.* http://arxiv.org/ abs/1712.02969

Dorri, A., Kanhere, S. S., Jurdak, R., & Gauravaram, P. (2017). Blockchain for IoT security and privacy: The case study of a smart home. In *2017 IEEE International Conference on Pervasive Computing and Communications Workshops* (pp. 618-623). IEEE. 10.1109/PERCOMW.2017.7917634

Dorri, A., Kanhere, S. S., Jurdak, R., & Gauravaram, P. (2019). Lsb: A lightweight scalable blockchain for iot security and anonymity. *Journal of Parallel and Distributed Computing, 134,* 180–197. doi:10.1016/j.jpdc.2019.08.005

Dreher, D. (1999). *Logisttik-Benchmarking in der Automobile-Branche: ein Fuhrungsinstrument zur Steigerung der Wettbewerbsfahigkeit.* Keynote Speech at the International Conference on Advances in Production Management System – Global Production Management, Berlin, Germany.

Drosatos, G., & Kaldoudi, E. (2019). Blockchain applications in the biomedical domain: A scoping review. *Computational and Structural Biotechnology Journal, 17,* 229–240.

Duraiswamy, S. (2019). End to end lightweight mutual authentication scheme in IoT-based healthcare environment. *Journal of Reliable Intelligent Environments, 6*(1), 3–13. Advance online publication. doi:10.100740860-019-00079-w

Dwivedi, S. K., Amin, R., Vollala, S., & Chaudhry, R. (2020). Blockchain-based secured event-information sharing protocol in internet of vehicles for smart cities. *Computers & Electrical Engineering, 86,* 106719. doi:10.1016/j.compeleceng.2020.106719

EIP-721. ERC-721 Non-Fungible Token Standard. (n.d.). Retrieved from https://eips.ethereum.org/EIPS/eip-721

Ekblaw & Azaria. (n.d.). *MedRec: Medical Data Management on the Blockchain.* https://viral.media.mit.edu/pub/medrec

Eldosouky, A., Ferdowsi, A., & Saad, W. (2019). Drones in distress: A game-theoretic countermeasure for protecting uavs against gps spoofing. *IEEE Internet of Things Journal, 7*(4), 2840–2854. doi:10.1109/JIOT.2019.2963337

El-Hajj, M., Fadlallah, A., Chamoun, M., & Serhrouchni, A. (2019). A survey of internet of things (iot) authentication schemes. *Sensors (Basel), 19*(5), 1141. doi:10.339019051141 PMID:30845760

Ellouze, F., Fersi, G., & Jmaiel, M. (2020, June). Blockchain for Internet of Medical Things: A Technical Review. In *International Conference on Smart Homes and Health Telematics* (pp. 259-267). Springer.

Elrom, E. (2019). Hyperledger. In *The Blockchain Developer* (pp. 299–348). Apress.

El-Salakawy, G., & Abu El-Kheir, M. (2020). Blockchain-based Data Management in Vehicular Networks. *2020 2nd Novel Intelligent and Leading Emerging Sciences Conference (NILES).*

Erdelj, M., & Natalizio, E. (2016, February). UAV-assisted disaster management: Applications and open issues. In *2016 international conference on computing, networking and communications (ICNC)* (pp. 1-5). IEEE.

Erdelj, M., Król, M., & Natalizio, E. (2017). Wireless sensor networks and multi-UAV systems for natural disaster management. *Computer Networks, 124,* 72–86.

Erdelj, M., Natalizio, E., Chowdhury, K. R., & Akyildiz, I. F. (2017). Help from the sky: Leveraging UAVs for disaster management. *IEEE Pervasive Computing, 16*(1), 24–32.

Eschenbacher, J., Knirsch, P., & Timm, I. J. (2000). Demand Chain Optimization By Using Agent Technology. *Proceedings of the International Conference on Integrated Production Management*, 285-292.

Esfahani, A., Mantas, G., Matischek, R., Saghezchi, F. B., Rodriguez, J., Bicaku, A., Maksuti, S., Tauber, M. G., Schmittner, C., & Bastos, J. (2019). A lightweight authentication mechanism for m2m communications in industrial IoT environment. *IEEE Internet of Things Journal*, 6(1), 288–296. doi:10.1109/JIOT.2017.2737630

Ethereum Blockchain Platform. (2021a). *Non-Fungible Tokens (NFT)*. Retrieved from https://ethereum.org/en/nft/

Ethereum Blockchain Platform. (2021b). *Ethereum Name Service*. Retrieved from https://app.ens.domains/

Ethereum. (2021). https://www.ethereum.org

Falco, G., Viswanathan, A., Caldera, C., & Shrobe, H., (2018). A Master Attack Methodology for an AI-Based Automated Attack Planner for Smart Cities. *IEEE, 6*, 48360-48373.

Farahani, S. (2011). *ZigBee wireless networks and transceivers*. Newnes.

Faria, C., & Correia, M. (2019, July). BlockSim: Blockchain Simulator. In *2019 IEEE International Conference on Blockchain (Blockchain)* (pp. 439-446). 10.1109/Blockchain.2019.00067

Fernández-Caramés, T. M., & Fraga-Lamas, P. (2018). A review on the use of blockchain for the internet of things. *IEEE Access: Practical Innovations, Open Solutions, 6*, 32979–33001. doi:10.1109/ACCESS.2018.2842685

Ferrag, M. A., Derdour, D., Mukherjee, M., Derhab, A., Maglaras, A., & Janicke, H. (2018). Blockchain technologies for the internet of things: Research issues and challenges. *IEEE Internet of Things Journal*.

Ferrag, M. A., Derdour, M., Mukherjee, M., Derhab, A., Maglaras, L., & Janicke, H. (2018). Blockchain technologies for the internet of things: Research issues and challenges. *IEEE Internet of Things Journal*, 6(2), 2188–2204. doi:10.1109/JIOT.2018.2882794

Ferran, M.A., Derdour, M., Mukherjee, M., Dahab, A., Maglaras, L., & Janicke, H. (2019). Blockchain technologies for the Internet of things: research issues and challenges. *IEEE Internet Things J*.

Finextra. (2016). *Everledger secures the first bottle of wine on the blockchain*. https://www.finextra.com/pressaritcle/67381/everledger-secures-the-first-bottle-of-wine-on-the-blockchain

Fleder, M., Kester, M.S., & Pillai, S. (2015). *Bitcoin transaction graph analysis*. CoRR abs/1502.01657.

Forbes. (2019). Blockchain in healthcare: How it Could Make Digital Healthcare Safer and More Innovative. *Forbes*.

Frost & Sullivan. (2018). *The role of blockchain in precision medicine: Challenges, Opportunities, and Solutions*. https://ww2.frost.com/wp-content/uploads

Frustaci, M., Pace, P., Aloi, G., & Fortino, G. (2017). Evaluating critical security issues of the iot world: Present and future challenges. *IEEE Internet of Things Journal*, 5(4), 2483–2495. doi:10.1109/JIOT.2017.2767291

Frustaci, M., Pace, P., Aloi, G., & Fortino, G. (2018). *Evaluating critical security issues of the IoT world: present and future challenges. IEEE Internet Things*.

Gaihre, A., Luo, Y., & Liu, H. (2018). Do bitcoin users really care about anonymity? an analysis of the bitcoin transaction graph. *IEEE International Conference on Big Data*, 1198–1207. 10.1109/BigData.2018.8622442

Gai, J., Choo, K., Qiu, K. R., & Zhu, L. (2018). Privacy-preserving content-oriented wireless communication in internet-of-things. *IEEE Internet of Things Journal*, 5(4), 3059–3067. doi:10.1109/JIOT.2018.2830340

Gai, K., Wu, Y., Zhu, L., Qiu, M., & Shen, M. (2019). Privacy-preserving energy trading using consortium blockchain in smart grid. *IEEE Transactions on Industrial Informatics, 15*(6), 3548–3558. doi:10.1109/TII.2019.2893433

Galici, R., Ordile, L., Marchesi, M., Pinna, A., & Tonelli, R. (2020). Applying the ETL process to blockchain data. *prospect and findings. Inf., 11*(4), 204. doi:10.3390/info11040204

Ganache. (2021). https://github.com/trufflesuite/ganache-cli

GanacheCli. (2021). https://docs.nethereum.com/en/latest/ethereum-and-clients/ganache-cli/

Gandino, F., Montrucchio, B., & Rebaudengo, M. (2014). Key Management for Static Wireless Sensor Networks with Node Adding. *IEEE Transaction Industrial Informatics*.

Gao, Z., Xu, L., & Chen, L. (2018). CoC: A Unified Distributed Ledger Based Supply Chain Management System. *J. Comput. Sci. Technol., 33*, 237–248. . doi:10.100711390-018-1816-5

Garg, A., & Mittal, N. (2020). A security and confidentiality survey in wireless internet of things (iot). In *Internet of Things and Big Data Applications* (pp. 65–88). Springer. doi:10.1007/978-3-030-39119-5_5

GCP. (2020). *Google Cloud Platform: Bitcoin Historical Data. Bitcoin data at 1-min intervals from select exchanges, Jan 2012 to April 2020.* https://www.kaggle.com/mczielinski/bitcoin-historical-data

Gervais, A., Karame, G. O., Wüst, K., Glykantzis, V., Ritzdorf, H., & Capkun, S. (2016). *On the security and performance of proof of work blockchains. In 2016 ACM SIGSAC conference on computer and communications security.* ACM.

Gervais, A., Karame, G. O., Wüst, K., Glykantzis, V., Ritzdorf, H., & Capkun, S. (2016, October). On the security and performance of proof of work blockchains. In *Proceedings of the 2016 ACM SIGSAC conference on computer and communications security* (pp. 3-16). 10.1145/2976749.2978341

Ghribi, E., Khoei, T. T., Gorji, H. T., Ranganathan, P., & Kaabouch, N. (2020). A secure blockchain-based communication approach for uav networks. In *2020 IEEE International Conference on Electro Information Technology (EIT)*, (pp. 411–415). IEEE. 10.1109/EIT48999.2020.9208314

Gibbon, J., (2018). *Introduction to Trusted Execution Environment: Arm's Trust zone.* Academic Press.

Glissa, G., Rachedi, A., & Meddeb, A. (2016). A secure routing protocol based on rpl for internet of things. In *2016 IEEE Global Communications Conference (GLOBECOM)*, (pp. 1–7). IEEE. 10.1109/GLOCOM.2016.7841543

Goerli. (2021). https://goerli.net/

Goldsmith, D., Grauer, K., & Shmalo, Y. (2019). *Analyzing hack subnetworks in the bitcoin transaction graph.* CoRR abs/1910.13415.

Gomes, T., Salgado, F., Tavares, A., & Cabral, J. (2017). Cute mote, a customizable and trustable end-device for the internet of things. *IEEE Sensors Journal, 17*(20), 6816–6824. doi:10.1109/JSEN.2017.2743460

Google. (2019). *Introducing six new cryptocurrencies in BigQuery Public Datasets and how to analyze them.* https://cloud.google.com/blog/products/data-analytics/introducing-six-new-cryptocurrencies-in-bigquery-public-datasets-and-how-to-analyze-them

Gope, P., & Sikdar, B. (2018). Lightweight and privacy-preserving two-factor authentication scheme for iot devices. *IEEE Internet of Things Journal, 6*(1), 580–589. doi:10.1109/JIOT.2018.2846299

Gope, P., & Sikdar, B. (2018). *Lightweight and privacy-preserving two-factor authentication scheme for IoT devices.* IEEE Internet Things.

Gordon, W. J., & Catalini, C. (2018). Blockchain technology for healthcare: Facilitating the transition to patient-driven interoperability. *Computational and Structural Biotechnology Journal, 16*, 224–230.

Gornstein, L. (2021). *What is an NFT? The trendy blockchain technology explained.* Retrieved from https://www.cbsnews.com/news/nft-nonfungible-token-blockchain-explained/

Governatori, G., Idelberger, F., Milosevic, Z., Riveret, G., Sartor, G., & Xu, X. (2018). On legal contracts, imperative and declarative smart contracts, and blockchain systems. *Artificial Intelligence and Law, 26*(4), 377–409. doi:10.100710506-018-9223-3

Granville, K., (2018). *Facebook and Cambridge Analytica: what You Need to Know as Fallout Widens.* Academic Press.

Griggs, K. N., Ossipova, O., Kohlios, C. P., Baccarini, A. N., Howson, E. A., & Hayajneh, T. (2018). Healthcare blockchain system using smart contracts for secure automated remote patient monitoring. *Journal of Medical Systems, 42*(7), 1–7.

Griggs, Ossipova, O., Kohlios, C. P., Baccarini, A. N., Howson, E. A., & Hayajneh, T. (2018). Healthcare Blockchain System Using Smart Contracts for Secure Automated Remote Patient Monitoring. *Journal of Medical Systems, 42*(7), 130. Advance online publication. doi:10.100710916-018-0982-x PMID:29876661

Gropper, A. (2016, August). Powering the physician-patient relationship with HIE of one blockchain health IT. In *ONC/NIST use of Blockchain for healthcare and research workshop.* ONC/NIST.

Guan, Z., Si, G., Zhang, X., Wu, L., Guizani, N., Du, X., & Ma, Y. (2018). Privacy-preserving and efficient aggregation based on blockchain for power grid communications in smart communities. *IEEE Communications Magazine, 56*(7), 82–88. doi:10.1109/MCOM.2018.1700401

Gubbi, J., Buyya, R., Marusic, S., & Palaniswami, M. (2013). Internet of Things (IoT): A vision, architectural elements, and future directions. *Future Generation Computer Systems, 29*(7), 1645–1660. doi:10.1016/j.future.2013.01.010

Guin, U., Singh, A., Alam, M., Caedo, J., & Skjellum, A. (2018). A secure low-cost edge device authentication scheme for the Internet of things. *31st International Conference on VLSI Design and 17th International Conference on Embedded Systems (VLSID)*, 85–90. 10.1109/VLSID.2018.42

Gumaei, A., Al-Rakhami, M., Hassan, M. M., Pace, P., Alai, G., Lin, K., & Fortino, G. (2021). Deep Learning and Blockchain with Edge Computing for 5G-Enabled Drone Identification and Flight Mode Detection. *IEEE Network, 35*(1), 94–100.

Guo, R., Shi, H., Zhao, Q., & Zheng, D. (2018). Secure attribute-based signature scheme with multiple authorities for blockchain in electronic health records systems. *IEEE Access: Practical Innovations, Open Solutions, 6*, 11676–11686.

Gupta, B., & Quamara, M. (2020). An overview of internet of things (iot): Architectural aspects, challenges, and protocols. *Concurrency and Computation, 32*(21), e4946. doi:10.1002/cpe.4946

Gupta, D., Saia, J., & Young, M. (2018). Proof of work without all the work. In *Proceedings of the 19th International Conference on Distributed Computing and Networking.* ACM.

Gupta, R., Kumari, A., & Tanwar, S. (2021). Fusion of blockchain and artificial intelligence for secure drone networking underlying 5G communications. *Transactions on Emerging Telecommunications Technologies, 32*(1), e4176.

Gupta, R., Nair, A., Tanwar, S., & Kumar, N. (2021). Blockchain-assisted secure UAV communication in 6G environment: Architecture, opportunities, and challenges. *IET Communications.*

HaddadPajouh, H., Dehghantanha, A., Parizi, R. M., Aledhari, M., & Karimipour, H. (2019). A survey on internet of things security: Requirements, challenges, and solutions. *Internet of Things*, 100129.

Hamdi, M. M., Audah, L., Rashid, S. A., Mohammed, A. H., Alani, S., & Mustafa, A. S. (2020). A review of applications, characteristics and challenges in vehicular ad hoc networks (vanets). In *2020 International Congress on Human-Computer Interaction, Optimization and Robotic Applications (HORA)*, (pp. 1–7). IEEE.

Hammi, M. T., Hammi, B., Bellot, P., & Serrhouchni, A. (2018). Bubbles of trust: A decentralized blockchain-based authentication system for iot. *Computers & Security*, 78, 126–142. doi:10.1016/j.cose.2018.06.004

Han, T., Ribeiro, I. D. L., Magaia, N., Preto, J., Segundo, A. H. F. N., de Macêdo, A. R. L., ... de Albuquerque, V. H. C. (2021). Emerging Drone Trends for Blockchain-Based 5G Networks: Open Issues and Future Perspectives. *IEEE Network*, 35(1), 38–43.

Haq, I., & Esuka, O. M. (2018). Blockchain technology in pharmaceutical industry to prevent counterfeit drugs. *International Journal of Computers and Applications*, 180(25), 8–12.

Harbi, Y., Aliouat, Z., Refoufi, A., Harous, S., & Bentaleb, A. (2019). Enhanced authentication and key management scheme for securing data transmission in the internet of things. *Ad Hoc Networks*, 94, 101948. doi:10.1016/j.adhoc.2019.101948

Haris, R. M., & Al-Maadeed, S. (2020). Integrating blockchain technology in 5g enabled iot: A review. In *2020 IEEE International Conference on Informatics, IoT, and Enabling Technologies (ICIoT)*, (pp. 367–371). IEEE. 10.1109/ICIoT48696.2020.9089600

Harshini, V. M., Danai, S., Usha, H. R., & Kounte, M. R. (2019, April). Health record management through blockchain technology. In *2019 3rd International Conference on Trends in Electronics and Informatics (ICOEI)* (pp. 1411-1415). IEEE.

Hashem Eiza, M., & Ni, Q. (2017). Driving with Sharks: Rethinking Connected Vehicles with Vehicle Cybersecurity. *IEEE Vehicular Technology Magazine*, 12(2), 45–51. doi:10.1109/MVT.2017.2669348

Haslhofer, B., Karl, R., & Filtz, E. (2016). O bitcoin where art thou? insight into large-scale transaction graphs. *12th International Conference on Semantic Systems - SEMANTiCS2016 and the 1st International Workshop on Semantic Change & Evolving Semantics (SuCCESS'16), Leipzig, Germany, Volume 1695 of CEUR Workshop Proceedings.*

Hassan, W. H. (2019). Current research on internet of things (iot) security: A survey. *Computer Networks*, 148, 283–294. doi:10.1016/j.comnet.2018.11.025

Hassija, V., Chamola, V., Gupta, V., & Chalapathi, G. S. (2020). *A Framework for Secure Vehicular Network using Advanced Blockchain. In 2020 International Wireless Communications and Mobile Computing*. IWCMC.

He, Q., Guan, N., Lv, M., & Yi, W. (2018). On the consensus mechanisms of blockchain/dlt for internet of things. In *2018 IEEE 13th International Symposium on Industrial Embedded Systems (SIES)*. IEEE. 10.1109/SIES.2018.8442076

HealthSync. (n.d.). https://www.healthsync.io/projects

He, D. (2019). A survey on cyber security of unmanned aerial vehicles. *Chinese Journal of Computers*, 42(05), 150–168.

Hei, X., Du, X., Wu, J., & Hu, F. (2010). Defending resource depletion attacks on implantable medical devices. *2010 IEEE Global Telecommunications Conference GLOBECOM 2010*, 1–5. 10.1109/GLOCOM.2010.5685228

Hentati, A. I., & Fourati, L. C. (2020). Comprehensive survey of UAVs communication networks. *Computer Standards & Interfaces*, 72, 103451. doi:10.1016/j.csi.2020.103451

Hiromoto, R. E., Haney, M., & Vakanski, A. (2017). A secure architecture for IoT with supply chain risk management. *IEEE International Conference on IDAACS*, 431-435.

Hossain, M. A., Md Noor, R., Azzuhri, S. R., Z'aba, M. R., Ahmedy, I., Yau, K. L. A., & Chembe, C. (2021). Spectrum sensing challenges & their solutions in cognitive radio based vehicular networks. *International Journal of Communication Systems*, *34*(7). Advance online publication. doi:10.1002/dac.4748

Hu, Y. C., Lee, T. T., Chatzopoulos, D., & Hui, P. (2018, June). Hierarchical interactions between ethereum smart contracts across testnets. In *Proceedings of the 1st Workshop on Cryptocurrencies and Blockchains for Distributed Systems* (pp. 7-12). Academic Press.

Huang, J., Kong, L., Chen, G., Wu, M., Liu, X., & Zeng, P. (2019b). Towards secure industrial IoT: blockchain system with credit-based consensus mechanism. IEEE Trans. Ind.

Huang, X., Zhang, Y., Li, D., & Han, L. (2019a). An optimal scheduling algorithm for hybrid EV charging scenario using consortium blockchains. *Future Generation Computer Systems*, *91*, 555–562. doi:10.1016/j.future.2018.09.046

Huh, J.-H., & Seo, K. (2019). Blockchain-based mobile fingerprint verification and automatic log-in platform for future computing. *The Journal of Supercomputing*, *75*(6), 3123–3139. doi:10.100711227-018-2496-1

Huh, S.-K., & Kim, J.-H. (2019). The blockchain consensus algorithm for viable management of new and renewable energies. *Sustainability*, *11*(3184), 3184. doi:10.3390u11113184

Hu, N., Tian, Z., Sun, Y., Yin, L., Zhao, B., Du, X., & Guizani, N. (2021). Building Agile and Resilient UAV Networks Based on SDN and Blockchain. *IEEE Network*, *35*(1), 57–63.

Hu, Q., Wang, W., Bai, X., Jin, S., & Jiang, T. (2020). Blockchain enabled federated slicing for 5g networks with ai accelerated optimization. *IEEE Network*, *34*(6), 46–52. doi:10.1109/MNET.021.1900653

Hussien, H. M., Yasin, S. M., Udzir, S. N. I., Zaidan, A. A., & Zaidan, B. B. (2019). A systematic review for enabling of develop a blockchain technology in healthcare application: Taxonomy, substantially analysis, motivations, challenges, recommendations and future direction. *Journal of Medical Systems*, *43*(10), 1–35.

Hyperldger Caliper. (2021). *Documentation*. Available: https://github.com/hyperledger/caliper

Hyperledger Burrow. (2021). https://www.hyperledger.org/use/hyperledger-burrow

Hyperledger Cello. (2018). *Overview-Hyperledger Cello*. Available: https://cello.readthedocs.io/en/latest

Hyperledger Explorer. (2021). *A useful tool to view blocks, transactions on Hyperledger Fabric*. Available: https://www.hyperledger.org/use/explorer

Hyperledger Indy. (2021). https://www.hyperledger.org/use/hyperledger-indy

Hyperledger Iroha. (2021). https://github.com/hyperledger-archives/education/blob/master/LFS171x/docs/introduction-to-hyperledger-iroha.md

Hyperledger Quilt. (2021). Available: https://www.hyperledger.org/projects/quilt

IBM. (n.d.). *IBM Blockchain for Insurance*. https://www.ibm.com/blockchain/industries/insurance

Inera, A. (2017). *Bosch, Cisco, BNY Mellon, other launch new blockchain consortium*. https://www.reuters.com/article/us-blockchain-iot-idUSKBN15B2D7

Infopulse (2019, Oct. 7). *Blockchain in Supply Chain Management: Key Use Cases and Benefits*. https://medium.com/@infopulseglobal_9037/blockchain-in-supply-chain-management-key-use-cases-and-benefits-6c6b7fd43094

Iqbal, S. (2021). A study on uav operating system security and future research challenges. In *2021 IEEE 11th Annual Computing and Communication Workshop and Conference (CCWC)*, (pp. 759–765). IEEE.

Iredale, G. (2020). *History of Blockchain Technology: A Detailed Guide.* Retrieved from https://101blockchains.com/history-of-blockchain-timeline/

Islam, A., & Shin, S. Y. (2019, July). BHMUS: blockchain based secure outdoor health monitoring scheme using UAV in smart city. In *2019 7th international conference on information and communication technology (ICoICT)* (pp. 1-6). IEEE.

Islam, S. H., Khan, M. K., & Al-Khouri, A. M. (2015). Anonymous and provably secure certificateless multireceiver encryption without bilinear pairing. *Secure. Commun. Netw., 8*(13), 2214–2231. https://onlinelibrary.wiley.com/doi/abs/10.1002/sec.1165

Islam, A., & Shin, S. Y. (2019). Bus: A blockchain-enabled data acquisition scheme with the assistance of uav swarm in internet of things. *IEEE Access: Practical Innovations, Open Solutions, 7,* 103231–103249. doi:10.1109/ACCESS.2019.2930774

Ismail, L., Hameed, H., AlShamsi, M., AlHammadi, M., & AlDhanhani, N. (2019, March). Towards a Blockchain Deployment at UAE University: Performance Evaluation and Blockchain Taxonomy. In *Proceedings of the 2019 International Conference on Blockchain Technology* (pp. 30-38). Academic Press.

Iyer, K., & Dannen, C. (2018). The ethereum development environment. In Building games with ethereum smart contracts (pp. 19-36). Apress.

Jamil, F., Hang, L., Kim, K., & Kim, D. (2019). A novel medical blockchain model for drug supply chain integrity management in a smart hospital. *Electronics (Basel), 8*(5), 505.

Jiang, X., Lora, M., & Chattopadhyay, S. (2020). An experimental analysis of security vulnerabilities in industrial iot devices. *ACM Transactions on Internet Technology, 20*(2), 1–24. doi:10.1145/3379542

Jian, X., Leng, P., Wang, Y., Alrashoud, M., & Hossain, M. S. (2021). Blockchain-Empowered Trusted Networking for Unmanned Aerial Vehicles in the B5G Era. *IEEE Network, 35*(1), 72–77.

Jordan, H., Scholz, B., & Subotić, P. (2016, July). Soufflé: On synthesis of program analyzers. In *International Conference on Computer Aided Verification* (pp. 422-430). Springer.

Joshi, A. P., Han, M., & Wang, Y. (2018). A survey on security and privacy issues of blockchain technology. *Mathematical Foundations of Computing, 1*(2), 121–147. doi:10.3934/mfc.2018007

Kacem, T., Wijesekera, D., & Costa, P. (2017). Key distribution scheme for aircraft equipped with secure ads-b in. In *2017 IEEE 20th International Conference on Intelligent Transportation Systems (ITSC),* (pp. 1–6). IEEE. 10.1109/ITSC.2017.8317719

Kalra, S. S., Goel, S., Dhawan, M., & Sharma, S. (2018, February). ZEUS: Analyzing Safety of Smart Contracts. In Ndss (pp. 1-12). Academic Press.

Kamran, M., Khan, H. U., Nisar, W., Farooq, M., & Rehman, S.-U. (2020). Blockchain and internet of things: A bibliometric study. *Computers & Electrical Engineering, 81,* 106525. doi:10.1016/j.compeleceng.2019.106525

Kang, J., Xiong, Z., Niyato, D., Ye, D., Kim, D. I., & Zhao, J. (2019a). Toward secure blockchain-enabled Internet of vehicles: Optimizing consensus management using reputation and contract theory. *IEEE Transactions on Vehicular Technology, 68*(3), 2906–2920. doi:10.1109/TVT.2019.2894944

Kang, J., Yu, R., Huang, X., Maharjan, S., Zhang, Y., & Hossain, E. (2017). Enabling localized peer-to-peer electricity trading among plug-in hybrid electric vehicles using consortium blockchains. *IEEE Transactions on Industrial Informatics, 13*(6), 3154–3164. doi:10.1109/TII.2017.2709784

Kang, J., Yu, R., Huang, X., Wu, M., Maharjan, S., Xie, S., & Zhang, Y. (2019b). Blockchain for secure and efficient data sharing in vehicular edge computing and networks. *IEEE Internet of Things Journal, 6*(3), 4660–4670. doi:10.1109/JIOT.2018.2875542

Kapitonov, A., Lonshakov, S., Berman, I., Castelló Ferrer, E., Bonsignorio, F. P., Bulatov, V., & Svistov, A. (2019). Robotic Services for New Paradigm Smart Cities Based on Decentralized Technologies. *Ledger, 4.*

Karame, G. O., Androulaki, E., & Capkun, S. (2012). *Double-spending fast payments in bitcoin. In 2012 ACM conference on Computer and communications security.* ACM.

Karantias, K., Kiayias, A., & Zindros, D. (2019). Proof-of-Burn. *International Conference on Financial Cryptography and Data Security.*

Karati, A., Islam, S. H., & Karuppiah, M. (2018). Provably secure and lightweight certificateless signature scheme for iiot environments. *IEEE Transactions on Industrial Informatics, 14*(8), 3701–3711. doi:10.1109/TII.2018.2794991

Karimireddy, T., & Bakshi, A. G. (2016). A hybrid security framework for the vehicular communications in VANET. *2016 International Conference on Wireless Communications, Signal Processing and Networking (WiSPNET).* 10.1109/WiSPNET.2016.7566479

Kaur, R., Singh, T. P., & Khajuria, V. (2018). Security Issues in Vehicular Ad-Hoc Network (VANET). *2018 2nd International Conference on Trends in Electronics and Informatics (ICOEI).*

Kavitha, D., & Ravikumar, S. (2021). Iot and context-aware learning-based optimal neural network model for real-time health monitoring. *Transactions on Emerging Telecommunications Technologies, 32*(1), e4132. doi:10.1002/ett.4132

Khalid, U., Asim, M., Baker, T., Hung, P. C., Tariq, M. A., & Rafferty, L. (2020). A decentralized lightweight blockchain-based authentication mechanism for iot systems. *Cluster Computing, 23*(3), 1–21. doi:10.100710586-020-03058-6

Khan, F. I., & Hameed, S. (2019). Understanding security requirements and challenges in the Internet of things (iots): a review. *Journal of Computer Networks and Communications.*

Khanji, S., Iqbal, F., & Hung, P. (2019). Zigbee security vulnerabilities: Exploration and evaluating. In *2019 10th International Conference on Information and Communication Systems (ICICS)*, (pp. 52–57). IEEE.

Khan, M. A., & Salah, K. (2018). IoT security: Review, blockchain solutions, and open challenges. *Future Generation Computer Systems, 82*, 395–411. doi:10.1016/j.future.2017.11.022

Khan, S., & Hoque, A. (2016). Digital health data: A comprehensive review of privacy and security risks and some recommendations. *Computer Science Journal of Moldova, 71*(2), 273–292.

Khayyat, Z., Abdelaziz, I., Sakr, S. M., & Orakzai, F.M. (2017). Large-Scale Graph Processing Using Apache Giraph. Springer.

Khezr, S., Moniruzzaman, M., Yassine, A., & Benlamri, R. (2019). Blockchain technology in healthcare: A comprehensive review and directions for future research. *Applied Sciences (Basel, Switzerland), 9*(9), 1736.

Khullar, K., Malhotra, Y., & Kumar, A. (2020). Decentralized and secure communication architecture for fanets using blockchain. *Procedia Computer Science, 173*, 158–170. doi:10.1016/j.procs.2020.06.020

Kim, N. (2016, July). IBM pushes blockchain into the supply chain. *Wall Street Journal.*

Kim, J.-H., & Huh, S.-K. (1973). A study on the improvement of smart grid security performance and blockchain smart grid perspective. *Energies, 11.*

Kim, S.-K., Kim, U.-M., & Huh, H. J. (2017). A study on improvement of blockchain application to overcome vulnerability of IoT multiplatform security. *Energies, 12*(402).

Konigsmark, S. T. C., Chen, D., & Wong, M. D. F. (2016). Information dispersion for trojan defense through high-level synthesis. *ACM/EDAC/IEEE Design Automation Conference (DAC)*, 1–6. 10.1145/2897937.2898034

Kosmanos, D., Pappas, A., Maglaras, L., Moschoyiannis, S., Aparicio-Navarro, F. J., Argyriou, A., & Janicke, H. (2020). A novel intrusion detection system against spoofing attacks in connected electric vehicles. *Array, 5*, 100013. doi:10.1016/j.array.2019.100013

Kouicem, D. E., Bouabdallah, A., & Lakhlef, H. (2018). Internet of things security: A top-down survey. *Computer Networks, 141*, 199–221. doi:10.1016/j.comnet.2018.03.012

Kovan. (2021). https://kovan.etherscan.io/

Krichen, L., Fourati, M., & Fourati, L. C. (2018, September). Communication architecture for unmanned aerial vehicle system. In *International Conference on Ad-Hoc Networks and Wireless* (pp. 213-225). Springer. 10.1007/978-3-030-00247-3_20

Krishnan, P. R., & Kumar, P. A. R. (2020). Security and Privacy in VANET: Concepts, Solutions and Challenges. *2020 International Conference on Inventive Computation Technologies (ICICT)*. 10.1109/ICICT48043.2020.9112535

Kumar, A., & Gupta, N. (2020). A Secure RSU based Security against Multiple Attacks in VANET. *2020 3rd International Conference on Intelligent Sustainable Systems (ICISS)*.

Kumar, E. S. (2020). Preserving privacy in ethereum blockchain. *Annals of Data Science*, 1-19.

Kumar, G., Saha, R., Rai, M. K., Thomas, R., & Kim, T.-H. (2019). Proof-of-work consensus approach in blockchain technology for cloud and fog computing using maximization-factorization statistics. *IEEE Internet of Things Journal, 6*(4), 6835–6842. doi:10.1109/JIOT.2019.2911969

Kumari, A., Gupta, R., Tanwar, S., & Kumar, N. (2020). A taxonomy of blockchain-enabled softwarization for secure UAV network. *Computer Communications, 161*, 304–323.

Kuo, T. T., & Ohno-Machado, L. (2018). *Modelchain: Decentralized privacy-preserving healthcare predictive modeling framework on private blockchain networks.* arXiv preprint arXiv:1802.01746.

Kuo, T. T., Kim, H. E., & Ohno-Machado, L. (2017). Blockchain distributed ledger technologies for biomedical and health care applications. *Journal of the American Medical Informatics Association, 24*(6), 1211–1220.

Kwok-Bun, Y., Karthika, C., & Hema, G. (2019). Storing and querying bitcoin blockchain using sql databases. *Information Systems Education Journal, 17*, 24–41.

Kwon, Y., Kim, D., Son, Y., Vasserman, E., & Kim, Y. (2017). Be selfish and avoid dilemmas: Fork after withholding (faw) attacks on bitcoin. In *2017 ACM SIGSAC Conference on Computer and Communications Security* (pp. 195-209). ACM 10.1145/3133956.3134019

Lakshmanan, V., & Tigani, J. (2019). BigQuery: The Definitive Guide Data Warehousing, Analytics, and Machine Learning at Scale. O'Reilly Publishing.

Larimer, D. (2018). *Delegated proof-of-stake consensus.* Academic Press.

Laurant, P., Chollet, T., Burke, M., & Seers, T. (2020). *The tokenization of assets is disrupting the financial industry. Are you ready?* Retrieved from https://www2.deloitte.com/

Lee, H., Eom, S., Park, J., & Lee, I. (2018). Uav-aided secure communications with cooperative jamming. *IEEE Transactions on Vehicular Technology, 67*(10), 9385–9392. doi:10.1109/TVT.2018.2853723

Lee, M., & Atkison, T. (2021). Vanet applications: Past, present, and future. *Vehicular Communications, 28*, 100310. doi:10.1016/j.vehcom.2020.100310

Leeming, G., Ainsworth, J. D., & Cunningham, J. (2019). A Ledger of Me: Personalising healthcare using blockchain technology. *Frontiers in Medicine, 6*, 171. doi:10.3389/fmed.2019.00171 PMID:31396516

Lee, Y., Rathore, S., Park, J. H., & Park, J. H. (2020). A blockchain-based smart home gateway architecture for preventing data forgery. *Hum. Cent. Comput. Inf. Sci., 10*(1), 9. doi:10.118613673-020-0214-5

Lei, K., Zhang, Q., Lou, J., Bai, B., & Xu, K. (2019). Securing ICN-based UAV ad hoc networks with blockchain. *IEEE Communications Magazine, 57*(6), 26–32.

Liang, X., Shetty, S., & Tosh, D. (2018). Exploring the Attack Surfaces in Blockchain Enabled Smart Cities. *IEEE International Smart Cities Conference*, 1-8. 10.1109/ISC2.2018.8656852

Liao, S., Wu, J., Li, J., Bashir, A. K., & Yang, W. (2021). Securing Collaborative Environment Monitoring in Smart Cities Using Blockchain Enabled Software-Defined Internet of Drones. *IEEE Internet of Things Magazine, 4*(1), 12–18.

Li, B., Liang, R., Zhu, D., Chen, W., & Lin, Q. (2020). Blockchain-Based Trust Management Model for Location Privacy Preserving in VANET. *IEEE Transactions on Intelligent Transportation Systems*, 1–11. doi:10.1109/TITS.2020.3035869

Li, C., & Palanisamy, B. (2019). Privacy in Internet of things: From principles to technologies. *IEEE Internet of Things Journal, 6*(1), 488–505. doi:10.1109/JIOT.2018.2864168

Li, H., Pei, L., Liao, D., Chen, S., Zhang, M., & Xu, D. (2020). FADB: A Fine-Grained Access Control Scheme for VANET Data Based on Blockchain. *IEEE Access: Practical Innovations, Open Solutions, 8*, 85190–85203. doi:10.1109/ACCESS.2020.2992203

Lin, C., He, D., Huang, X., Choo, K.-K. R., & Vasilakos, A. V. (2018). Basin: A blockchain-based secure mutual authentication with fine-grained access control system for industry 4.0. *Journal of Network and Computer Applications, 116*, 42–52. doi:10.1016/j.jnca.2018.05.005

Lin, C., He, D., Huang, X., Kumar, N., & Choo, K.-K. R. (2020). BCPPA: A Blockchain-Based Conditional Privacy-Preserving Authentication Protocol for Vehicular Ad Hoc Networks. *IEEE Transactions on Intelligent Transportation Systems*, 1–13.

Ling, Z., Liu, K., Xu, Y., Jin, Y., & Fu, X. (2017). An end-to-end view of IoT security and privacy. *IEEE Global Communications Conference*, 1–7. 10.1109/GLOCOM.2017.8254011

Lin, J., Shen, Z., & Miao, C. (2017). Using blockchain technology to build trust in sharing lorawan iot. *Proceedings of the 2nd International Conference on Crowd Science and Engineering*, 38–43. 10.1145/3126973.3126980

Li, R., Song, T., Mei, B., Li, H., Cheng, X., & Sun, L. (2018). Blockchain for large-scale internet of things data storage and protection. *IEEE Transactions on Services Computing, 12*(5), 762–771. doi:10.1109/TSC.2018.2853167

Liu, C., Cronin, P., & Yang, C. (2016). A mutual auditing framework to protect iot against hardware trojans. In *2016 21st Asia and South Pacific Design Automation Conference (ASP-DAC)*, (pp. 69–74). IEEE. 10.1109/ASPDAC.2016.7427991

Liu, C. H., Lin, Q., & Wen, S. (2019b). *Blockchain-enabled data collection and sharing for industrial IoT with deep reinforcement learning. IEEE Transaction Industrial Informatics*. doi:10.1109/TII.2018.2890203

Liu, J., Zhang, C., & Fang, Y. (2018). Epic: A differential privacy framework to defend smart homes against internet traffic analysis. *IEEE Internet of Things Journal, 5*(2), 1206–1217. doi:10.1109/JIOT.2018.2799820

Liu, Y., Guo, W., Fan, C., Chang, L., & Cheng, C. (2019a). A practical privacy-preserving data aggregation (3pda) scheme for smart grid. *IEEE Transactions on Industrial Informatics, 15*(3), 1767–1774. doi:10.1109/TII.2018.2809672

Li, X., Niu, J., Bhuiyan, M. Z. A., Wu, F., Karuppiah, M., & Kumari, S. (2018a). A robust ECC-based provable secure authentication protocol with privacy-preserving for industrial Internet of things. *IEEE Transactions on Industrial Informatics, 14*(8), 3599–3609. doi:10.1109/TII.2017.2773666

Li, Z., Kang, J., Yu, R., Ye, D., Deng, Q., & Zhang, Y. (2018b). Consortium blockchain for secure energy trading in industrial Internet of things. *IEEE Transactions on Industrial Informatics, 14*(8), 3690–3700.

Longo, F., Nicoletti, L., Padovano, A., d'Atri, G., & Forte, M. (2019). Blockchain-enabled supply chain: An experimental study. *Computers & Industrial Engineering, 136,* 57–69. doi:10.1016/j.cie.2019.07.026

Lo, S. K. (2019). Analysis of Blockchain Solutions for IoT: A Systematic Literature Review. *IEEE Access : Practical Innovations, Open Solutions, 7,* 58822–58835.

Luigi, A., Antonio, I., & Morabito, G. (2010). The Internet of Things: A survey. *Computer Networks, 54*(15), 2787–2805. doi:10.1016/j.comnet.2010.05.010

Lukac, D. (2015). The fourth ICT-based industrial revolution "Industry 4.0"??? HMI and the case of CAE/CAD innovation with EPLAN, in 23rd Telecommunication Forum Telfor (TELFOR), IEEE, 835-838.

Lunardi, R. C., Alharby, M., Nunes, H. C., Zorzo, A. F., Dong, C., & Moorsel, A. v. (2020). Context-based consensus for appendable-block blockchains. In *2020 IEEE International Conference on Blockchain (Blockchain)* (pp. 401-408). IEEE. 10.1109/Blockchain50366.2020.00058

Lunardi, R. C., Michelin, R. A., Neu, C. V., Nunes, H. C., Zorzo, A. F., & Kanhere, S. S. (2019). Impact of consensus on appendable-block blockchain for IoT. In *16th EAI International Conference on Mobile and Ubiquitous Systems: Computing, Networking and Services* (pp. 228–237). ACM. 10.1145/3360774.3360798

Lunardi, R. C., Michelin, R. A., Neu, C. V., & Zorzo, A. F. (2018). Distributed access control on IoT ledger-based architecture. In *2018 IEEE/IFIP Network Operations and Management Symposium* (pp. 1-7). IEEE. 10.1109/NOMS.2018.8406154

Lunardi, R. C., Nunes, H. C., Branco, V. D. S., Lipper, B. H., Neu, C. V., & Zorzo, A. F. (2019). Performance and Cost Evaluation of Smart Contracts in Collaborative Health Care Environments. *15th International Conference for Internet Technology and Secured Transactions,* 1-6.

Luo, B., Li, X., Weng, J., Guo, J., & Ma, J. (2020). Blockchain Enabled Trust-Based Location Privacy Protection Scheme in VANET. *IEEE Transactions on Vehicular Technology, 69*(2), 2034–2048. doi:10.1109/TVT.2019.2957744

Luo, S., Li, H., Wen, Z., Qian, B., Morgan, G., Longo, A., ... Ranjan, R. (2021). Blockchain-Based Task Offloading in Drone-Aided Mobile Edge Computing. *IEEE Network, 35*(1), 124–129.

Luu, L., Chu, D. H., Olickel, H., Saxena, P., & Hobor, A. (2016, October). Making smart contracts smarter. In *Proceedings of the 2016 ACM SIGSAC conference on computer and communictions security* (pp. 254-269). ACM.

Lu, Y. (2019). The blockchain: State-of-the-art and research challenges. *Journal of Industrial Information Integration, 15,* 80–90. doi:10.1016/j.jii.2019.04.002

Lu, Y., & Li, J. (2016). A pairing-free certificate-based proxy re-encryption scheme for secure data sharing in public clouds. *Future Generation Computer Systems, 62,* 140–147. doi:10.1016/j.future.2015.11.012

Lu, Z., Liu, W., Wang, Q., Qu, G., & Liu, Z. (2018). A Privacy-Preserving Trust Model Based on Blockchain for VANETs. *IEEE Access: Practical Innovations, Open Solutions*, *6*, 45655–45664. doi:10.1109/ACCESS.2018.2864189

Lv, X., Zhong, Y., & Tan, Q. (2020). A study of bitcoin de-anonymization: Graph and multidimensional data analysis. *5th IEEE International Conference on Data Science in Cyberspace, DSC 2020*, 339–345. 10.1109/DSC50466.2020.00059

Machado, C., & Fröhlich, A. A. M. (2018). Iot data integrity verification for cyber-physical systems using blockchain. In *2018 IEEE 21st International Symposium on Real-Time Distributed Computing (ISORC)*, (pp. 83–90). IEEE. 10.1109/ISORC.2018.00019

Machado, C., & Westphall, C. M. (2021). Blockchain incentivized data forwarding in manets: Strategies and challenges. *Ad Hoc Networks*, *110*, 102321. doi:10.1016/j.adhoc.2020.102321

Maddux, D. (2017). *Cybersecurity and Blockchain in Healthcare*. Acumen Physical Solutions.

Maesa, D. D. F., Marino, A., & Ricci, L. (2016). *Uncovering the bitcoin blockchain: An analysis of the full users graph*. *IEEE International Conference on Data Science and Advanced Analytics*, 537–546.

Maesa, D. D. F. (2017). Detecting artificial behaviours in the bitcoin users graph. *Online Social Networks and Media*, *3-4*, 63–74. doi:10.1016/j.osnem.2017.10.006

Maesa, D. D. F., Marino, A., & Ricci, L. (2016). An analysis of the bitcoin users graph: inferring unusual behaviours. *5th International Workshop on Complex Networks and their Applications*, 749–760. 10.1007/978-3-319-50901-3_59

Maesa, D. D. F., Marino, A., & Ricci, L. (2018). The graph structure of bitcoin. *Proceedings of the 7th International Conference on Complex Networks and Their Applications*, 547–558. 10.1007/978-3-030-05414-4_44

Maesa, D. D. F., Marino, A., & Ricci, L. (2019). The bow tie structure of the bitcoin users graph. *Applied Network Science*, *4*(1), 1–22. doi:10.100741109-019-0163-y

Maitra, S., Yanambaka, V. P., Abdelgawad, A., Puthal, D., & Yelamarthi, K. (2020). Proof-of-authentication consensus algorithm: Blockchain-based iot implementation. In *2020 IEEE 6th World Forum on Internet of Things (WF-IoT)*, (pp. 1–2). IEEE.

Makhdoom, I., Abolhasan, M., Abbas, H., & Ni, W. (2019). Blockchain's adoption in iot: The challenges, and a way forward. *Journal of Network and Computer Applications*, *125*, 251–279. doi:10.1016/j.jnca.2018.10.019

Malewicz, G., Austern, M. H., Bik, A. J. C., Dehnert, J. C., Horn, I., Leiser, N., & Czajkowski, G. (2010). Pregel: a system for large-scale graph processing. *Proceedings of the international conference on Management of data*, 135-146. 10.1145/1807167.1807184

Malik, S., Kanhere, S. S., & Jurdak, R. (2018). Productchain: Scalable blockchain framework to support provenance in supply chains. In *2018 IEEE 17th International Symposium on Network Computing and Applications (NCA)* (pp. 1-10). IEEE.

Malik, S., Dedeoglu, V., Kanhere, S. S., & Jurdak, R. (2019). TrustChain: Trust Management in Blockchain and IoT supported Supply Chains. In *2019 IEEE International Conference on Blockchain (Blockchain)*, (pp. 184-193). IEEE. 10.1109/Blockchain.2019.00032

Malwa, S. (2021). *'Beeple' NFT sold for $69 million is the fourth most expensive artwork sold by a living artist*. Retrieved from https://cryptoslate.com/beeple-nft-sold-for-69-million-is-the-fourth-most-expensive-artwork-sold-by-a-living-artist/

Mamoshina, P., Ojomoko, L., Yanovich, Y., Ostrovski, A., Botezatu, A., Prikhodko, P., ... Zhavoronkov, A. (2018). Converging blockchain and next-generation artificial intelligence technologies to decentralize and accelerate biomedical research and healthcare. *Oncotarget, 9*(5), 5665.

Manditereza, K., (2017). *4 Key Differences between Scada and Industrial IoT*. Academic Press.

Manogaran, G., Varatharajan, R., Lopez, D., Kumar, P. M., Sundarasekar, R., & Thota, C. (2018). A new architecture of internet of things and big data ecosystem for secured smart healthcare monitoring and alerting system. *Future Generation Computer Systems, 82*, 375–387. doi:10.1016/j.future.2017.10.045

Manzoor, A., Liyanage, M., Braeken, A., Kanhere, S. S., & Ylianttila, M. (2019). Blockchain-Based Proxy Re-encryption Scheme for Secure IoT Data Sharing. *Clinical Orthopaedics and Related Research.*

Mao, D., Hao, Z., Wang, F., & Li, H. (2019). Novel Automatic Food Trading System Using Consortium Blockchain. *Arabian Journal for Science and Engineering, 44*(4), 3439–3455. doi:10.100713369-018-3537-z

MAVLINK. (2021). *MAVLink Common Message Set Specifications*. Available: https://mavlink.io/en/messages/common.html

Ma, Z., Zhang, J., Guo, Y., Liu, Y., Liu, X., & He, W. (2020). An Efficient Decentralized Key Management Mechanism for VANET With Blockchain. *IEEE Transactions on Vehicular Technology, 69*(6), 5836–5849. doi:10.1109/TVT.2020.2972923

Mazieres, D. (2015). The stellar consensus protocol: A federated model for internet-level consensus. *Stellar Development Foundation, 32.*

McBee, M. P., & Wilcox, C. (2020). Blockchain technology: Principles and applications in medical imaging. *Journal of Digital Imaging, 33*(3), 726–734.

MediLedger. (n.d.). https://www.mediledger.com/

Menezes, A. J., van Oorschot, P., & Vanstone, S. A. (1997). *The Handbook of Applied Cryptography*. CRC Press.

Meng, L., Ren, S., Tang, G., Yang, C., & Yang, W. (2020). Uav sensor spoofing detection algorithm based on gps and optical flow fusion. *Proceedings of the 2020 4th International Conference on Cryptography, Security and Privacy*, 146–151. 10.1145/3377644.3377670

Merrie, R. (2021). *The big five NFT use cases*. Retrieved from https://cryptoslate.com/the-big-five-nft-use-cases

Mettler, M. (2016, September). Blockchain technology in healthcare: The revolution starts here. In *IEEE 18th international conference on e-health networking, applications and service (Healthcom)* (pp. 1-3). IEEE.

Michelin, R. A., Ahmed, N., Kanhere, S. S., Seneviratne, A., & Jha, S. (2020). Leveraging lightweight blockchain to establish data integrity for surveillance cameras. In *2020 IEEE International Conference on Blockchain and Cryptocurrency (ICBC)*, (pp. 1-3). IEEE

Michelin, R. A., Dorri, A., Steger, M., Lunardi, R. C., Kanhere, S. S., Jurdak, R., & Zorzo, A. F. (2018). SpeedyChain: A framework for decoupling data from blockchain for smart cities. In *15th EAI International Conference on Mobile and Ubiquitous Systems: Computing, Networking and Services* (pp. 145-154). EAI. 10.1145/3286978.3287019

Mingxiao, D., Xiaofeng, M., Zhe, Z., Xiangwei, W., & Qijun, C. (2017). A review on consensus algorithm of blockchain. In 2017 IEEE international conference on systems, man, and cybernetics (SMC), (pp. 2567–2572). IEEE. doi:10.1109/SMC.2017.8123011

Minoli, D., & Occhiogross, B. (2018). Blockchain mechanism for IoT security. *International Journal of Internet of Things*, 1-13.

Mipasa. (n.d.). https://mipasa.org/

Miraz, M.H. (2020). Blockchain of Things (BCoT): The Fusion of Blockchain and IoT Technologies. *Studies in Big Data, 60.*

Mohammad, A. F. (2019). *Decision Analytics Using Permissioned Blockchain "Comm-ledger"* (PhD thesis). University of North Dakota.

Mohammad, N. (2019). A Multi-Tiered Defense Model for the Security Analysis of Critical Facilities in Smart Cities. *IEEE, 7,* 152585-152598.

Mohanta, B. K., Sahoo, A., Patel, S., Panda, S. S., Jena, D., & Gountia, D. (2019). Decauth: decentralized authentication scheme for iot device using ethereum blockchain. In TENCON 2019-2019 IEEE Region 10 Conference (TENCON), (pp. 558–563). IEEE. doi:10.1109/TENCON.2019.8929720

Mokhtar, B., & Azab, M. (2015). Survey on Security Issues in Vehicular Ad Hoc Networks. *Alexandria Engineering Journal, 54*(4), 1115–1126. doi:10.1016/j.aej.2015.07.011

Mondal, S., Wijewardena, K. P., Aruppuswami, S., Kriti, N., Kumar, D., & Chahal, P. (2019). Blockchain Inspired RFID-Based Information Architecture for Food Supply Chain. *IEEE IoT Journal, 6*(3), 5803–5813.

Mondal, S., Wijewardena, K. P., Karuppuswami, S., Kriti, N., Kumar, D., & Chahal, P. (2019). Blockchain inspired RFID-based information architecture for food supply chain. *IEEE Internet of Things Journal, 6*(3), 5803–5813. doi:10.1109/JIOT.2019.2907658

Montori, F., Bedogni, L., & Bononi, L. (2018). A Collaborative Internet of Things Architecture for Smart Cities and Environmental Monitoring. *IEEE IoT Journal, 5*(2), 592–605.

Moriggl, P., Asprion, P. M., & Schneider, B. (2020). Blockchain Technologies Towards Data Privacy—Hyperledger Sawtooth as Unit of Analysis. In *New Trends in Business Information Systems and Technology* (pp. 299–313). Springer.

Mosenia, A., & Jha, N. K. (2017). A comprehensive study of security of internet-of-things. *IEEE Transactions on Emerging Topics in Computing, 5*(4), 586–602. doi:10.1109/TETC.2016.2606384

Moss, J., Smith, C. & Davies, J. (2017). *Blockchain shows promise in healthcare.* Medical Industry Week, BMI Country Industry Reports.

Moussaoui, D., Kadri, B., Feham, M., & Ammar Bensaber, B. (2021). A Distributed Blockchain Based PKI (BCPKI) architecture to enhance privacy in VANET. *2020 2nd International Workshop on Human-Centric Smart Environments for Health and Well-Being (IHSH).*

Mowla, N. I., Tran, N. H., Doh, I., & Chae, K. (2020). Afrl: Adaptive federated reinforcement learning for intelligent jamming defense in fanet. *Journal of Communications and Networks (Seoul), 22*(3), 244–258. doi:10.1109/JCN.2020.000015

Mukherjee, A., Keshary, V., Pandya, K., Dey, N., & Satapathy, S. C. (2018). Flying ad hoc networks: A comprehensive survey. Information and Decision Sciences, 569–580.

Multichain. (2021). https://github.com/MultiChain/multichain

Musan, D. I. (2020). *NFT.finance Leveraging Non-Fungible Tokens* [Unpublished master's dissertation]. Imperial College, London, UK.

Naeem, H., Guo, B., & Naeem, M. R. (2018). A lightweight malware static visual analysis for IoT infrastructure. *International Conference on Artificial Intelligence and Big Data (ICAIBD),* 240–244.

Nakamoto, S. (2008). *A Peer-to-Peer Electronic Cash System.* https://bitcoin.org/bitcoin.pdf

Nakamoto, S. (2008). *Bitcoin: A peer-to-peer electronic cash system.* Academic Press.

Nakamoto, S. (2008). *Bitcoin: A peer-to-peer electronic cash system.* https://bitcoin. org/bitcoin.pdf

Nakamoto, S. (2008). *Bitcoin: A Peer-to-Peer Electronic Cash System.* https://bitcoin.org/bitcoin.pdf

Nakamoto, S. (2019). *Bitcoin: A peer-to-peer electronic cash system.* Manubot.

Nanayakkara, S., Rodrigo, M. N. N., Perera, S., Weerasuriya, G. T., & Hijazi, A. A. (2021). A Methodology for Selection of a Blockchain Platform to Develop an Enterprise System. *Journal of Industrial Information Integration, 23,* 100215. doi:10.1016/j.jii.2021.100215

Nathan, S., Govindarajan, C., Saraf, A., Sethi, M., & Jayachandran, P. (2019). Blockchain meets database: Design and implementation of a blockchain relational database. *Proc. VLDB Endow., 12,* 1539–1552. 10.14778/3342263.3342632

Neshenko, N., Bou-Harb, E., Crichigno, J., Kaddoum, G., & Ghani, N. (2019). Demystifying iot security: An exhaustive survey on iot vulnerabilities and a first empirical look on internet-scale iot exploitations. *IEEE Communications Surveys and Tutorials, 21*(3), 2702–2733. doi:10.1109/COMST.2019.2910750

Nguyen, D. C., Ding, M., Pham, Q. V., Pathirana, P. N., Le, L. B., Seneviratne, A., . . . Poor, H. V. (2021). *Federated learning meets blockchain in edge computing: Opportunities and challenges.* arXiv preprint arXiv:2104.01776.

Nguyen, D. C., Pathirana, P. N., Ding, M., & Seneviratne, A. (2019). Blockchain for secure ehrs sharing of mobile cloud based e-health systems. *IEEE Access: Practical Innovations, Open Solutions, 7,* 66792–66806.

Nguyen, V.-L., Lin, P.-C., & Hwang, R.-H. (2019). Energy depletion attacks in low power wireless networks. *IEEE Access: Practical Innovations, Open Solutions, 7,* 51915–51932. doi:10.1109/ACCESS.2019.2911424

Nichols, R., Mumm, H., Lonstein, W., Carter, C., & Hood, J. (2019). *Understanding hostile use and cyber-vulnerabilities of uas: Components, autonomy v automation, sensors, saa, scada and cyber attack taxonomy.* Unmanned Aircraft Systems in the Cyber Domain.

Nofer, M., Gomber, P., & Hinz, O. (2017). Blockchain Bus. *Inf Syst Eng, 59,* 183–187. doi:10.100712599-017-0467-3

Noor, F., Khan, M. A., Al-Zahrani, A., Ullah, I., & Al-Dhlan, K. A. (2020). A review on communications perspective of flying ad-hoc networks: Key enabling wireless technologies, applications, challenges and open research topics. *Drones (Basel), 4*(4), 65. doi:10.3390/drones4040065

Nørfeldt, L., Bøtker, J., Edinger, M., Genina, N., & Rantanen, J. (2019). Cryptopharmaceuticals: Increasing the safety of medication by a blockchain of pharmaceutical products. *Journal of Pharmaceutical Sciences, 108*(9), 2838–2841.

Noura, H., Hatoum, T., Salman, O., Yaacoub, J.-P., and Chehab, A. (2020). Lorawan security survey: Issues, threats and possible mitigation techniques. *Internet of Things,* 100303.

Novo, O. (2018). Blockchain meets IoT: An architecture for scalable access management in IoT. *IEEE Internet of Things Journal, 5*(2), 1184–1195. doi:10.1109/JIOT.2018.2812239

Novo, O. (2018). Scalable access management in iot using blockchain: A performance evaluation. *IEEE Internet of Things Journal, 6*(3), 4694–4701. doi:10.1109/JIOT.2018.2879679

Nugent, T., Upton, D., & Cimpoesu, M. (2016). Improving data transparency in clinical trials using blockchain smart contracts. *F1000 Research, 5.*

Nunes, H. C., Lunardi, R. C., Zorzo, A. F., Michelin, R. A., & Kanhere, S. S. (2020). Context-based smart contracts for appendable-block blockchains. In *IEEE International Conference on Blockchain and Cryptocurrency* (pp. 1-10). IEEE.

Ober, M., Katzenbeisser, S., & Hamacher, K. (2013). Structure and anonymity of the bitcoin transaction graph. *Future Internet*, *5*(2), 237–250. doi:10.3390/fi5020237

ObserveIT. (2018). *5 Examples of Insider Threat-Caused Breaches that Illustrate the Scope of the Problem*. Author.

Oham, C., Michelin, R. A., Jurdak, R., Kanhere, S. S., & Jha, S. (2021). B-FERL: Blockchain based framework for securing smart vehicles. *Information Processing & Management*, *58*(1), 102426. doi:10.1016/j.ipm.2020.102426

Okorie, O., Turner, C., Charnley, F., Moreno, M., & Tiwari, A. (2017). A review of data-driven approaches for circular economy in manufacturing. *Proceedings of the 18th European Roundtable for Sustainable Consumption and Production*.

Omar, A. A., Bhuiyan, M. Z. A., Basu, A., Kiyomoto, S., & Rahman, M. S. (2019). Privacy-friendly platform for healthcare data in cloud-based on blockchain environment. *Future Generation Computer Systems*, *95*, 511–521. doi:10.1016/j.future.2018.12.044

Omitola, T., & Wills, G. (2018). Towards Mapping the Security Challenges of the Internet of Things (IoT) Supply Chain. *Procedia Computer Science*, *126*, 441–450. doi:10.1016/j.procs.2018.07.278

Oracle. (n.d.). *HealthSync Uses Oracle Blockchain Platform to Power More Intelligent Healthcare*. https://www.oracle.com/customers/healthsync-1-blockchain.html

Oztemel, E., & Gusev, S. (2018). Literature review of industry 4.0 and related technologies. *Journal of Intelligent Manufacturing*.

Pahlajani, S., Kshirsagar, A., & Pachghare, V. (2019). Survey on private blockchain consensus algorithms. In *2019 1st International Conference on Innovations in Information and Communication Technology (ICIICT)*, (pp. 1–6). IEEE. 10.1109/ICIICT1.2019.8741353

Paik, H., Xu, X., Bandara, H. M. N. D., Lee, S. U., & Lo, S. K. (2019). Analysis of data management in blockchain-based systems: From architecture to governance. *IEEE Access: Practical Innovations, Open Solutions*, *7*, 186091–186107. doi:10.1109/ACCESS.2019.2961404

Pal, K. (2017). Building High Quality Big Data-Based Applications in Supply Chains. IGI Global Publication.

Pal, K. (2018). *Ontology-Based Web Service Architecture for Retail Supply Chain Management*. The 9th International Conference on Ambient Systems, Networks and Technologies, Porto, Portugal.

Pal, K. (2019). Algorithmic Solutions for RFID Tag Anti-Collision Problem in Supply Chain Management. *The 9th International Symposium on Frontiers in Ambient and Mobile Systems (FAMS)*, 929-934.

Pal, K. (2021). Applications of Secured Blockchain Technology in Manufacturing Industry. In Blockchain and AI Technology in the Industrial Internet of Things. IGI Global Publication.

Pal, K. (2017). Supply Chain Coordination Based on Web Services. In H. K. Chan, N. Subramanian, & M. D. Abdulrahman (Eds.), *Supply Chain Management in the Big Data Era* (pp. 137–171). IGI Global Publication. doi:10.4018/978-1-5225-0956-1.ch009

Pal, K. (2019). Algorithmic Solutions for RFID Tag Anti-Collision Problem in Supply Chain Management. *Procedia Computer Science*, *151*, 929–934. doi:10.1016/j.procs.2019.04.129

Pal, K. (2020). *Information sharing for manufacturing supply chain management based on blockchain technology*. In I. Williams (Ed.), *Cross-Industry Use of Blockchain Technology and Opportunities for the Future* (pp. 1–17). IGI Global.

Pal, K. (2020). Internet of Things and Blockchain Technology in Apparel Supply Chain Management. In H. Patel & G. S. Thakur (Eds.), *Blockchain Applications in IoT Security*. IGI Global Publication.

Pal, K., & Yasar, A. (2020). Internet of Things and blockchain technology in apparel manufacturing supply chain data management. *Procedia Computer Science*, *170*, 450–457. doi:10.1016/j.procs.2020.03.088

Pandey, S., Ojha, G., & Shrestha, B. (2019, May). BlockSIM: A practical simulationtool for optimal network design, stability and planning. In *2019 IEEE International Conference on Blockchain and Cryptocurrency (ICBC)* (pp. 133-137). 10.1109/BLOC.2019.8751320

Pandharipande, A., & Newsham, G. R. (2018). Lighting controls: Evolution and revolution. *Lighting Research & Technology*, *50*(1), 115–128. doi:10.1177/1477153517731909

Parity. (2017). Error! Hyperlink reference not valid.*Parity documentation*. https://paritytech.github.io/wiki

Park, N., & Kang, N. (2015). Mutual authentication scheme in secure Internet of things technology for comfortable lifestyle. *Sensors (Basel)*, *16*(1), 20. doi:10.339016010020 PMID:26712759

Paul, A., & Jeyaraj, R. (2019). Internet of things: A primer. *Human Behavior and Emerging Technologies*, *1*(1), 37–47. doi:10.1002/hbe2.133

Perez, A. O., & Domingo-Palaoag, T. (2021, February). Blockchain-based Model for Health Information Exchange: A Case for Simulated Patient Referrals Using an Electronic Medical Record. *IOP Conference Series. Materials Science and Engineering*, *1077*(1), 012059.

Pervez, H., Muneeb, M., Irfan, M. U., & Haq, I. U. (2018). A Comparative Analysis of DAG-Based Blockchain Architectures. In *2018 12th International Conference on Open Source Systems and Technologies*. 10.1109/ICOSST.2018.8632193

Perwej, Y., Parwej, F., Hassan, M. M. M., & Akhtar, N. (2019). *The internet-of-things (iot) security: A technological perspective and review. International Journal of Scientific Research in Computer Science, Engineering and Information Technology (IJSRCSEIT)*.

Peters, G., Panayi, E., & Chapelle, A. (2015). Trends in cryptocurrencies and blockchain Technologies: A monetary theory and regulation perspective. *Journal of Financial Perspectives*, *3*(3).

Petit, J., Stottelaar, B., Feiri, M., & Kargl, F. (2015). Remote attacks on automated vehicles sensors: Experiments on camera and lidar. *Black Hat Europe*, *11*, 995.

Pfaff, B. L. (2018). *Overwhelming the SAA System of Delivery UAVs by Drone Swarming* (PhD thesis). Wright State University.

Pham, H. L., Tran, T. H., & Nakashima, Y. (2018, December). A secure remote healthcare system for hospital using blockchain smart contract. In *2018 IEEE Globecom Workshops (GC Wkshps)* (pp. 1-6). IEEE.

Pharma Logistics Editor. (2018). *Blockchain: The Next Frontier for Pharmaceutical Supply Chains*. https://www.pharmalogisticsiq.com/logistics/articles/blockchain-the-next-frontier-for-pharmaceutical-supply-chains

Phetsouvanh, S., Oggier, F. E., & Datta, A. (2018). EGRET: extortion graph exploration techniques in the bitcoin network. *IEEE International Conference on Data Mining Workshops, ICDM Workshops, Singapore, Singapore*, 244–251. 10.1109/ICDMW.2018.00043

Pilkington, M. (2017). Can blockchain improve healthcare management? *Consumer Medical Electronics and the IoMT*. https://ssrn.com/abstract=3025393

Pilkington, M. (2016). Blockchain technology: principles and applications. In *Research handbook on digital transformations*. Edward Elgar Publishing. doi:10.4337/9781784717766.00019

Pohrmen, F. H., Das, R. K., & Saha, G. (2019). Blockchain-based security aspects in heterogeneous Internet-of-Things networks: A survey. *Transactions on Emerging Telecommunications Technologies*, *30*(10), e3741. doi:10.1002/ett.3741

Pokhrel, S. R. (2021). Blockchain Brings Trust to Collaborative Drones and LEO Satellites: An Intelligent Decentralized Learning in the Space. *IEEE Sensors Journal*.

Pontiveros, B. B. F., Steichen, M., & State, R. (2019). Mint centrality: A centrality measure for the bitcoin transaction graph. *IEEE International Conference on Blockchain and Cryptocurrency*, 159–162.

Porambage, P., Schmitt, C., Kumar, P., Gurtov, A., & Ylianttila, M. (2014). Pauthkey: A pervasive authentication protocol and key establishment scheme for wireless sensor networks in distributed iot applications. *International Journal of Distributed Sensor Networks*, *10*(7), 357430. doi:10.1155/2014/357430

Praitheeshan, P., Pan, L., Yu, J., Liu, J., & Doss, R. (2019). *Security analysis methods on ethereum smart contract vulnerabilities: a survey.* arXiv preprint arXiv:1908.08605.

Pu, C., & Hajjar, S. (2018). Mitigating forwarding misbehaviors in rpl-based low power and lossy networks. In 2018 15th IEEE Annual Consumer Communications & Networking Conference (CCNC), (pp. 1–6). IEEE. doi:10.1109/CCNC.2018.8319164

Qiu, J., Tian, Z., Du, C., Zuo, Q., Su, S., & Fang, B. (2020). A survey on access control in the age of internet of things. *IEEE Internet of Things Journal*, *7*(6), 4682–4696. doi:10.1109/JIOT.2020.2969326

Quorum. (2021). *Quorum Whitepaper*. https://github.com/ConsenSys/quorum/blob/master/docs/Quorum%20Whitepaper%20v0.2.pdf

Rahulamathavan, Y., Phan, R. C., Rajarajan, M., Misra, S., & Kondoz, A. (2017). Privacy-preserving blockchain-based IoT ecosystem using attribute-based encryption. *IEEE International Conference on Advanced Networks and Telecommunications Systems (ANTS)*, 1–6. 10.1109/ANTS.2017.8384164

Rambus. (n.d.). *Industrial IoT: Threats and countermeasures*. https://www.rambus.com/iot/ industrial-IoT/

Rana, S., Halim, M. A., & Kabir, M. H. (2018). Design and implementation of a security improvement framework of zigbee network for intelligent monitoring in iot platform. *Applied Sciences (Basel, Switzerland)*, *8*(11), 2305. doi:10.3390/app8112305

Rappel, H., Beex, L. A., Hale, J. S., Noels, L., & Bordas, S. (2020). A tutorial on bayesian inference to identify material parameters in solid mechanics. *Archives of Computational Methods in Engineering*, *27*(2), 361–385. doi:10.100711831-018-09311-x

Rathee, G., Sharma, A., Saini, H., Kumar, R., & Iqbal, R. (2019). A hybrid framework for multimedia data processing in IoT-healthcare using blockchain technology. *Multimedia Tools and Applications*, 1–23.

Rathore, H., Mohamed, A., & Guizani, M. (2020). A survey of blockchain enabled cyber-physical systems. *Sensors (Basel)*, *20*(1), 282.

Rathore, M. M., Paul, A., Hong, W. H., Seo, H., Awan, I., & Saeed, S. (2018). Exploiting IoT and big data analytics: Defining smart digital city using real-time urban data. *Sustainable Cities and Society*, *40*, 600–610. doi:10.1016/j.scs.2017.12.022

Regner, F., Urbach, N., & Schweizer, A. (2019). NFTs in Practice – Non-Fungible Tokens as Core Component of a Blockchain-based Event Ticketing Application. *ICIS 2019 Proceedings*, 1. Retrieved from https://aisel.aisnet.org/icis2019/blockchain_fintech/blockchain_fintech/1

Reiff, N. (2020, Feb. 1). *Blockchain Explained.* https://www.investopedia.com/terms/b/blockchain.asp

Remix. (2021). https://remix.ethereum.org/

Reyna, A., Martn, C., Chen, J., Soler, E., & Dáz, M. (2018). On blockchain and its integration with iot. challenges and opportunities. *Future Generation Computer Systems*, *88*, 173–190. doi:10.1016/j.future.2018.05.046

Riahi Sfar, A., Challal, Y., Moyal, P., & Natalizio, E. (2019). A Game Theoretic Approach for Privacy Preserving Model in IoT-Based Transportation. *IEEE Transactions on Intelligent Transportation Systems*, *20*(12), 4405–4414. doi:10.1109/TITS.2018.2885054

Ribeiro, V., Holanda, R., Ramos, A., & Rodrigues, J. J. (2020). Enhancing key management in lorawan with permissioned blockchain. *Sensors (Basel)*, *20*(11), 3068. doi:10.339020113068 PMID:32485791

Rinkeby. (2021). https://www.rinkeby.io/

Roman, R., Zhou, J., & Lopez, J. (2013). On the features and challenges of security and privacy in distributed internet of things. *Computer Networks*, *5710*, 2266–2279.

Ron, D., & Shamir, A. (2013). Quantitative analysis of the full bitcoin transaction graph. *Lecture Notes in Computer Science.*, *7859*, 6–24.

Roose, K. (2021). *Buy This Column on the Blockchain! Why can't a journalist join the NFT party, too?* Retrieved from https://www.nytimes.com/2021/03/24/technology/nft-column-blockchain.html

Ropston. (2019). *Testnet ropsten (eth) blockchain explorer.* https://ropsten.etherscan.io/

Rouhani, S., Butterworth, L., Simmons, A. D., Humphery, D. G., & Deters, R. (2018, July). MediChain TM: a secure decentralized medical data asset management system. In *2018 IEEE International Conference on Internet of Things (iThings) and IEEE Green Computing and Communications (GreenCom) and IEEE Cyber, Physical and Social Computing (CPSCom) and IEEE Smart Data (SmartData)* (pp. 1533-1538). IEEE.

Saha, S., Sutrala, A. K., Das, A. K., Kumar, N., & Rodrigues, J. J. (2020, June). On the design of blockchain-based access control protocol for IoT-enabled healthcare applications. In *ICC 2020-2020 IEEE International Conference on Communications (ICC)* (pp. 1-6). IEEE.

Saleh, F. (2018). Blockchain without waste: Proof-of-stake. *Review of Financial Studies*.

Sample, I. (2019, March 11). *Fake drugs kill more than 250,000 children a year.* https://www.theguardian.com/science/2019/mar/11/fake-drugs-kill-more-than-250000-children-a-year-doctors-warn

Sanka, A. I., Irfan, M., Huang, I., & Cheung, R. C. (2021). A survey of breakthrough in blockchain technology: Adoptions, applications, challenges and future research. *Computer Communications*.

Schneider, J., & Macdonald, J. (2016). *Technology and Adaptation on the Modern Battlefield: A Battlefield Perspective on the Adoption of Unmanned Aircraft.* Available at SSRN 2814202.

Schöner, M. M., Kourouklis, D., Sandner, P., Gonzalez, E., & Förster, J. (2017). *Blockchain technology in the pharmaceutical industry.* Frankfurt School Blockchain Center.

Securify. (2021). https://securify.ch

Sedjelmaci, H., Senouci, S. M., & Ansari, N. (2017). A hierarchical detection and response system to enhance security against lethal cyber-attacks in uav networks. *IEEE Transactions on Systems, Man, and Cybernetics. Systems, 48*(9), 1594–1606. doi:10.1109/TSMC.2017.2681698

Sengupta, J., Ruj, S., & Bit, S. D. (2019). End to end secure anonymous communication for secure directed diffusion in iot. *Proceedings of the 20th international conference on distributed computing and networking*, 445–450. 10.1145/3288599.3295577

Sfar, A. R., Natalizio, E., Challal, Y., & Chtourou, Z. (2018). A roadmap for security challenges in the Internet of things. *Digital Communications and Networks., 4*(2), 118–137. doi:10.1016/j.dcan.2017.04.003

Shadow Documentation. (2021). https://github.com/martmartinez91/shadow-hyperledger

Shae, Z., & Tsai, J. J. (2017, June). On the design of a blockchain platform for clinical trial and precision medicine. In *2017 IEEE 37th international conference on distributed computing systems (ICDCS)* (pp. 1972-1980). IEEE.

Sha, K., Wei, W., Yang, T. A., Wang, Z., & Shi, W. (2018). On security challenges and open issues in internet of things. *Future Generation Computer Systems, 83*, 326–337. doi:10.1016/j.future.2018.01.059

Shakhateh, H., Sawalmeh, A. H., Al-Fuqaha, A., Dou, Z., Almaita, E., Khalil, I., ... Guizani, M. (2019). Unmanned aerial vehicles (UAVs): A survey on civil applications and key research challenges. *IEEE Access: Practical Innovations, Open Solutions, 7*, 48572–48634.

Sharma, A., & Bhatia, A. (2020). *Bitcoin's blockchain data analytics: A graph theoretic perspective.* CoRR abs/2002.06403.

Sharma, P. K., Chen, M.-Y., & Park, J. H. (2017). A software defined fog node based distributed blockchain cloud architecture for iot. *IEEE Access: Practical Innovations, Open Solutions, 6*, 115–124. doi:10.1109/ACCESS.2017.2757955

Sharma, P. K., & Park, J. H. (2018). Blockchain based hybrid network architecture for the smart city. *Future Generation Computer Systems, 86*, 650–655. doi:10.1016/j.future.2018.04.060

Sharma, V., Srinivasan, K., Chao, H. C., Hua, K. L., & Cheng, W. H. (2017). Intelligent deployment of UAVs in 5G heterogeneous communication environment for improved coverage. *Journal of Network and Computer Applications, 85*, 94–105.

Shen, M., Tang, X., Zhu, L., Du, X., & Guizani, M. (2019). Privacy-Preserving Support Vector Machine Training Over Blockchain-Based Encrypted IoT Data in Smart Cities. *IEEE IoT Journal, 6*(5), 7702-7712.

Shen, M., Tang, X., Zhu, L., Du, X., & Guizani, M. (2019). Privacy-Preserving Support Vector Machine Training Over Blockchain-Based Encrypted IoT Data in Smart Cities. *IEEE Internet of Things Journal, 6*(5), 7702–7712.

Shen, M., Tang, X., Zhu, L., Du, X., & Guizani, M. (2019). Privacy-preserving support vector machine training over blockchain-based encrypted IoT data in smart cities. *IEEE Internet of Things Journal, 6*(5), 7702–7712. doi:10.1109/JIOT.2019.2901840

She, W., Gu, Z., Lyu, X., Liu, Q., Tian, Z., & Liu, W. (2019). Homomorphic Consortium Blockchain for Smart Home System Sensitive Data Privacy Preserving. *IEEE Access: Practical Innovations, Open Solutions, 7*, 62058–62070. doi:10.1109/ACCESS.2019.2916345

Shimosawa, T., Sato, T., & Oshima, S. (2020, November). BCVerifier: A Tool to Verify Hyperledger Fabric Ledgers. In *2020 IEEE International Conference on Blockchain (Blockchain)* (pp. 291-299). IEEE.

Shi, S., He, D., Li, L., Kumar, N., Khan, M. K., & Choo, K. R. (2020). Applications of blockchain in ensuring the security and privacy of electronic health record systems: A survey. *Computers & Security, 97*, 101966.

Shi, W., Zhou, H., Li, J., Xu, W., Zhang, N., & Shen, X. (2018). Drone assisted vehicular networks: Architecture, challenges and opportunities. *IEEE Network, 32*(3), 130–137.

Shrestha, R., Bajracharya, R., Shrestha, A. P., & Nam, S. Y. (2020). A new type of blockchain for secure message exchange in VANET. *Digital Communications and Networks, 6*(2), 177–186. doi:10.1016/j.dcan.2019.04.003

Shrouf, F., Joaquin, B., Mere, O., & Miragliotta, G. (2014). Smart factories in Industry 4.0: A review of the concept and of energy management approached in production based on the Internet of Things paradigm. *Proceedings of the IEEE International Conference on Industrial Engineering and Engineering Management,* 679-701. 10.1109/IEEM.2014.7058728

Shukla, P. (2017). Ml-ids: A machine learning approach to detect wormhole attacks in internet of things. In 2017 Intelligent Systems Conference (IntelliSys), (pp. 234–240). IEEE. doi:10.1109/IntelliSys.2017.8324298

Sicari, S., Rizzardi, A., Miorandi, D., & Coen-Porisini, A. (2018). Reato: Reacting to denial of service attacks in the internet of things. *Computer Networks, 137,* 37–48. doi:10.1016/j.comnet.2018.03.020

Siegel, J. E., Erb, D. C., & Sarma, S. E. (2017). A survey of the connected vehicle landscape—Architectures, enabling technologies, applications, and development areas. *IEEE Transactions on Intelligent Transportation Systems, 19*(8), 2391–2406. doi:10.1109/TITS.2017.2749459

Sikorski, J. J., Haughton, J., & Kraft, M. (2017). Blockchain technology in the chemical industry: Machine-to-machine electricity market. *Applied Energy, 195,* 234–246. doi:10.1016/j.apenergy.2017.03.039

Singh, M., Rajan, M., Shivraj, V., & Balamuralidhar, P. (2015). Secure mqtt for internet of things (iot). In *2015 fifth international conference on communication systems and network technologies,* (pp. 746–751). IEEE.

Singh, M., Rajan, M. A., Shivraj, V. L., & Balamuralidhar, P. (2015). Secure MQTT for the Internet of things (IoT). *5th International Conference on Communication Systems and Network Technologies,* 746–751. 10.1109/CSNT.2015.16

Singh, P., Nayyar, A., Kaur, A., & Ghosh, U. (2020). Blockchain and fog based architecture for internet of everything in smart cities. *Future Internet, 12*(4), 61. doi:10.3390/fi12040061

Siriwardena, P. (2020). Securing apis with transport layer security (tls). In *Advanced API Security* (pp. 69–79). Springer. doi:10.1007/978-1-4842-2050-4_3

Sonar, K., & Upadhyay, H. (2014). A survey: Ddos attack on internet of things. *International Journal of Engineering Research and Development, 10*(11), 58–63.

Song, T., Li, R., Mei, B., Yu, J., Xing, X., & Cheng, X. (2017). A privacy preserving communication protocol for iot applications in smart homes. *IEEE Internet of Things Journal, 4*(6), 1844–1852. doi:10.1109/JIOT.2017.2707489

Soni, K. (2019, November 12). *Blockchain in Pharma Supply.* Minddeft. https://minddeft.com/blog/blockchain-in-pharma-supply-chain/

SOPHOS. (2015). *49 Busted in Europe for Man-In-The-Middle Bank Attacks.* https://nakedsecurity.sophos.com/2015/06/11/49-busted-in-europe-for-man-in-themiddle-bank-attacks/

Sovrin. (2018). https://sovrin.org/wp-content/uploads/2018/03/Sovrin-Protocol-and-Token-White-Paper.pdf

Sphere 10 Software. (2018). *Blockchain SQL.* http://blockchainsql.io/

Sreamr. (2017). *Streamr White Paper v2.0.* https://s3.amazonaws.com/streamr-public/ streamr-datacoin-whitepaper-2017-07-25-v1_0.pdf

Srinivas, J., Das, A. K., Wazid, M., & Kumar, N. (2018). *Anonymous lightweight chaotic map-based authenticated key agreement protocol for industrial internet of things. IEEE Trans*. Dependable Secure Comput.

Srpanj. (2019). *Guided Tour of Hyperledger Fabric and Hyperledger Indy*. https: //github.com/hyperledger/ursa

Statista, (2020) https://www.statista.com/statistics/647231/worldwide-blockchain-technology-market-size/

Stoyanova, M., Nikoloudakis, Y., Panagiotakis, S., Pallis, E., & Markakis, E. K. (2020). A survey on the internet of things (iot) forensics: Challenges, approaches, and open issues. *IEEE Communications Surveys and Tutorials, 22*(2), 1191–1221. doi:10.1109/COMST.2019.2962586

Su, J., Vasconcellos, D. V., Prasad, S., Sgandurra, D., Feng, Y., & Sakurai, K. (2018). Lightweight classification of iot malware based on image recognition. In *2018 IEEE 42Nd annual computer software and applications conference (COMPSAC)*, (vol. 2, pp. 664–669). IEEE. 10.1109/COMPSAC.2018.10315

Su, J., Vasconcellos, V. D., Prasad, S., Daniele, S., Feng, Y., & Sakurai, K. (2018). Lightweight classification of IoT malware based on image recognition. *IEEE 42nd Annual Computer Software and Applications Conference (COMPSAC), 2*, 664–669. doi:10.1109/TDSC.2018.2857811

Sun, X., Ng, D. W. K., Ding, Z., Xu, Y., & Zhong, Z. (2019). Physical layer security in uav systems: Challenges and opportunities. *IEEE Wireless Communications, 26*(5), 40–47. doi:10.1109/MWC.001.1900028

Tang, W. Ren, T., Deng, K., & Zhang, Y. (2019). Secure Data Aggregation of Lightweight E-Healthcare IoT Devices With Fair Incentives. *IEEE IoT Journal, 6*(5), 8714-8726.

Tang, H., Shi, Y., & Dong, P. (2019). Public blockchain evaluation using entropy and topsis. *Expert Systems with Applications, 117*, 204–210. doi:10.1016/j.eswa.2018.09.048

Tan, H., & Chung, I. (2020). Secure Authentication and Key Management With Blockchain in VANETs. *IEEE Access: Practical Innovations, Open Solutions, 8*, 2482–2498. doi:10.1109/ACCESS.2019.2962387

Tanwar, S., Parekh, K., & Evans, R. (2020). Blockchain-based electronic healthcare record system for healthcare 4.0 applications. *Journal of Information Security and Applications, 50*, 102407. doi:10.1016/j.jisa.2019.102407

Tan, Y., Liu, J., & Kato, N. (2020). Blockchain-based key management for heterogeneous flying ad-hoc network. *IEEE Transactions on Industrial Informatics*.

Thakkar, P., Nathan, S., & Viswanathan, B. (2018, September). Performance bench-marking and optimizing hyperledger fabric blockchain platform. In *2018 IEEE 26th International Symposium on Modeling, Analysis, and Simulation of Computer and Telecommunication Systems (MASCOTS)* (pp. 264-276). IEEE.

Tian, H., He, J., & Ding, Y. (2019). Medical data management on blockchain with privacy. *Journal of Medical Systems, 43*(2), 26.

Tigani, J., & Naidu, S. (2014). *Google BigQuery Analytics* (1st ed.). Wiley Publishing.

Tikhomirov, S., Voskresenskaya, E., Ivanitskiy, I., Takhaviev, R., Marchenko, E., & Alexandrov, Y. (2018, May). Smartcheck: Static analysis of ethereum smart contracts. In *Proceedings of the 1st International Workshop on Emerging Trends in Software Engineering for Blockchain* (pp. 9-16). Academic Press.

Toma, C., Talpiga, B., Boja, C., Popa, M. I., & Zurini, M. (2018). Secure IoT Supply Chain Management Solution Using Blockchain and Smart Contracts Technology, Innovative Security Solutions for Information Technology and Communications. *Lecture Notes in Computer Science, 11359*. https://blog.usejournal.com/how-can-blockchain-healthcare-solution-benefits-hospitals-and-patients-43fa6ce485a3

Tripathy, B. K., Jena, S. K., Reddy, V., Das, S., & Panda, S. K. (2020). A novel communication framework between manet and wsn in iot based smart environment. *International Journal of Information Technology*, 1–11.

Trufflesuite. (2021). https://www.trufflesuite.com/

Tseng, J. H., Liao, Y. C., Chong, B., & Liao, S. W. (2018). Governance on the drug supply chain via gcoin blockchain. *International Journal of Environmental Research and Public Health*, 15(6), 1055.

Uddin, M. A., Stranieri, A., Gondal, I., & Balasubramanian, V. (2021). A survey on the adoption of blockchain in iot: Challenges and solutions. *Blockchain: Research and Applications*, 100006.

Uddin, M. A., Stranieri, A., Gondal, I., & Balasubramanian, V. (2018). Continuous patient monitoring with a patient centric agent: A block architecture. *IEEE Access: Practical Innovations, Open Solutions*, 6, 32700–32726.

Varga, P., Plosz, S., Soos, G., & Hegedus, C. (2017). Security Threats and Issues in Automation IoT. *2017 IEEE 13th International Workshop on Factory Communication Systems (WFCS)*, 1–6. 10.1109/WFCS.2017.7991968

Vashchuk, O. & Shuwar, R. (2018). *Pros and cons of consensus algorithm proof of stake. Difference in the network safety in proof of work and proof of stake.* doi:10.1145/3154273.3154333

Vazirani, A. A., O'Donoghue, O., Brindley, D., & Meinert, E. (2020). Blockchain vehicles for efficient medical record management. *NPJ Digital Medicine*, 3(1), 1–5.

Vechain Team. (2018). *Vechain White Paper.* https://cdn.vechain.com/vechain_ico_ideas_of_ development_en.pdf

Vinayak, M. (2019). *FSCBlock: Designing financial smart contracts on permissioned and public blockchains* (Master's thesis). Department of Computer Science The University of Manitoba, Winnipeg, Canada.

Visconti, R. M. (2020). Portfolio of Intangibles, Smart Infrastructural Investments, and Royalty Companies. In *The Valuation of Digital Intangibles* (pp. 449–490). Palgrave Macmillan. doi:10.1007/978-3-030-36918-7_18

Vitale, F., Janzen, I., & Mcgrenere, J. (2018). Hoarding and Minimalism: Tendencies in Digital Data Preservation. In *2018 CHI Conference on Human Factors in Computing Systems* (pp. 1–12). ACM. 10.1145/3173574.3174161

Waltonchain. (2021). *Waltonchain white paper v2.0.* https://www.waltonchain.org/en/ Waltonchain_White_Paper_2.0_EN.pdf

Wan, J., Li, J., Imran, M., Li, D., & e-Amin, F. (2019). A blockchain-based solution for enhancing security and privacy in smart factory. *IEEE Transaction.*

Wang, J., Liu, Y., Niu, S., & Song, H. (2021). Lightweight blockchain assisted secure routing of swarm UAS networking. *Computer Communications*, 165, 131–140.

Wang, K., Yuan, L., Miyazaki, T., Chen, Y., & Zhang, Y. (2018). Jamming and Eavesdropping Defense in Green Cyber–Physical Transportation Systems Using a Stackelberg Game. *IEEE Transactions on Industrial Informatics*, 14(9), 4232–4242. doi:10.1109/TII.2018.2841033

Wang, Q., Zhu, X., Ni, Y., Gu, L., & Zhu, H. (2019b). *Blockchain for the IoT and industrial IoT: a review.* Internet Things.

Wang, Q., Zhu, X., Ni, Y., Gu, L., & Zhu, H. (2020). Blockchain for the iot and industrial iot: A review. *Internet of Things*, 10, 100081. doi:10.1016/j.iot.2019.100081

Wang, S., Ouyang, L., Yuan, Y., Ni, X., Han, X., & Wang, F.-Y. (2019a). Blockchain-enabled smart contracts: Architecture, applications, and future trends. *IEEE Transactions on Systems, Man, and Cybernetics. Systems*, 49(11), 2266–2277. doi:10.1109/TSMC.2019.2895123

Wang, S., Wang, J., Wang, X., Qiu, T., Yuan, Y., Ouyang, L., ... Wang, F. Y. (2018). Blockchain-powered parallel healthcare systems based on the ACP approach. *IEEE Transactions on Computational Social Systems, 5*(4), 942–950.

Wang, X., Zha, X., Ni, W., Liu, R. P., Guo, Y. J., Niu, X., & Zheng, K. (2019b). Survey on blockchain for Internet of Things. *Computer Communications, 136*, 10–29. doi:10.1016/j.comcom.2019.01.006

Wan, J., Tang, S., Shu, Z., Li, D., Wang, S., Imran, M., & Vasilakos, A. V. (2016). Software-defined industrial Internet of things in the context of industry 4.0. *IEEE Sensors Journal, 16*(20), 7373–7380. doi:10.1109/JSEN.2016.2565621

Wan, L., Eyers, D., & Zhang, H. (2019). Evaluating the Impact of Network Latency on the Safety of Blockchain Transactions. *2019 IEEE International Conference on Blockchain (Blockchain)*. 10.1109/Blockchain.2019.00033

Wei, S., Ge, L., Yu, W., Chen, G., Pham, K., Blasch, E., Shen, D., & Lu, C. (2014). Simulation study of unmanned aerial vehicle communication networks addressing bandwidth disruptions. In *Sensors and Systems for Space Applications VII* (Vol. 9085, p. 90850O). International Society for Optics and Photonics.

Wolfson, R. (2020, April 4). *Blockchain Provides Trusted Data to Counter Spread of Coronavirus*. https://cointelegraph.com/news/blockchain-provides-trusted-data-to-counter-spread-of-coronavirus

Wong, D. R., Bhattacharya, S., & Butte, A. J. (2019). Prototype of running clinical trials in an untrustworthy environment using blockchain. *Nature Communications, 10*(1), 1–8.

Wood, G. (2014). Ethereum: A secure decentralised generalised transaction ledger. *Ethereum project yellow paper, 151*(2014), 1-32.

Wood, G. (2014). Ethereum: A secure decentralised generalised transaction ledger. *Ethereum Project Yellow Paper, 151*(2014), 1-32.

Wood, G. (2014). Ethereum: A secure decentralised generalised transaction ledger. *Ethereum Project Yellow Paper, 151*(2014), 1–32.

World Economic Forum. (2015). *Deep shift technology tipping points and societal impact survey report*. http://www3.weforum.org/docs/WEF_GAC15_Technological_Tipping_Points_report_2015.pdf

Wu, Q., Mei, W., & Zhang, R. (2019). Safeguarding wireless network with uavs: A physical layer security perspective. *IEEE Wireless Communications, 26*(5), 12–18. doi:10.1109/MWC.001.1900050

Wurm, J., Hoang, K., & Arias, O., Sadeghi, A., & Jin, Y. (2016). Security analysis on consumer and industrial IoT devices. *21st Asia and South Pacific Design Automation Conference (ASP-DAC)*, 519–524. 10.1109/ASPDAC.2016.7428064

Wu, Y., Dai, H. N., Wang, H., & Choo, K. K. R. (2021). Blockchain-based privacy preservation for 5g-enabled drone communications. *IEEE Network, 35*(1), 50–56.

Xiao, W., Li, M., Alzahrani, B., Alotaibi, R., Barnawi, A., & Ai, Q. (2021). A Blockchain-Based Secure Crowd Monitoring System Using UAV Swarm. *IEEE Network, 35*(1), 108–115.

Xia, Q. I., Sifah, E. B., Smahi, A., Amofa, S., & Zhang, X. (2017). BBDS: Blockchain-based data sharing for electronic medical records in cloud environments. *Information, 8*(2), 44.

Xie, J., Tang, H., Huang, T., Yu, F. R., Xie, R., Liu, J., & Liu, Y. (2019). A Survey of Blockchain Technology Applied to Smart Cities: Research Issues and Challenges. *IEEE Communications Surveys and Tutorials, 21*(3), 2794–2830. doi:10.1109/COMST.2019.2899617

Xiong, Z., Zhang, Y., Niyato, D., Wang, P., & Han, Z. (2018). When mobile blockchain meets edge computing. *IEEE Communications Magazine, 56*(8), 33–39. doi:10.1109/MCOM.2018.1701095

Xu, C., Lin, H., Wu, Y., Guo, X., & Lin, W. (2019). An SDNFV-Based DDoS Defense Technology for Smart Cities. *IEEE Access: Practical Innovations, Open Solutions, 7,* 137856–137874. doi:10.1109/ACCESS.2019.2943146

Xu, H., Huang, W., Zhou, Y., Yang, D., Li, M., & Han, Z. (2021). Edge Computing Resource Allocation for Unmanned Aerial Vehicle Assisted Mobile Network with Blockchain Applications. *IEEE Transactions on Wireless Communications.*

Xu, J., Xue, K., Li, S., Tian, H., Hong, J., Hong, P., & Yu, N. (2019). Healthchain: A Blockchain-Based Privacy Preserving Scheme for Large-Scale Health Data. *IEEE Internet of Things Journal, 6*(5), 8770–8781. doi:10.1109/JIOT.2019.2923525

Xu, L. D., He, W., & Li, S. (2014). Internet of things in industries: A survey. *IEEE Transactions on Industrial Informatics, 10*(4), 2233–2243.

Xu, L. D., Xu, E. L., & Li, L. (2018). Industry 4.0: State of the art and future trends. *International Journal of Production Research, 56*(8), 2941–2962. doi:10.1080/00207543.2018.1444806

Xu, Y., Ren, J., Wang, G., Zhang, C., Yang, J., & Zhang, Y. (2019). *A blockchain-based non-repudiation network computing service scheme for industrial IoT. IEEE Transaction Industrial Informatics.*

Xu, Y., Ren, J., Wang, G., Zhang, C., Yang, J., & Zhang, Y. (2019). A blockchain-based nonrepudiation network computing service scheme for industrial iot. *IEEE Transactions on Industrial Informatics, 15*(6), 3632–3641. doi:10.1109/TII.2019.2897133

Yang, S., Chen, Z., Cui, L., Xu, M., Ming, Z., & Xu, K. (2019). CoDAG: An Efficient and Compacted DAG-Based Blockchain Protocol. In *2019 IEEE International Conference on Blockchain* (pp. 314-318). IEEE. 10.1109/Blockchain.2019.00049

Yang, W., Wang, S., Huang, X., & Mu, Y. (2019a). On the Security of an Efficient and Robust Certificateless Signature Scheme for IIoT Environments. *IEEE Access: Practical Innovations, Open Solutions, 7,* 91074–91079. doi:10.1109/ACCESS.2019.2927597

Yang, X., Karampatzakis, E., Doerr, C., & Kuipers, F. (2018). Security vulnerabilities in lorawan. In *2018 IEEE/ACM Third International Conference on Internet-of-Things Design and Implementation (IoTDI),* (pp. 129–140). IEEE. 10.1109/IoTDI.2018.00022

Yang, Y., Wu, L., Yin, G., Li, L., & Zhao, H. (2017). A survey on security and privacy issues in internet-of-things. *IEEE Internet of Things Journal, 4*(5), 1250–1258. doi:10.1109/JIOT.2017.2694844

Yang, Z., Yang, K., Lei, L., Zheng, K., & Leung, V. C. M. (2019b). Blockchain-based decentralized trust management in vehicular networks. *IEEE Internet of Things Journal, 6*(2), 1495–1505. doi:10.1109/JIOT.2018.2836144

Yan, Q., Huang, W., Luo, X., Gong, Q., & Yu, F. R. (2018). A multi-level DDoS mitigation framework for the industrial Internet of things. *IEEE Communications Magazine, 56*(2), 30–36. doi:10.1109/MCOM.2018.1700621

Yao, X., Kong, H., Liu, H., Qiu, T., & Ning, H. (2019). An attribute credential-based public-key scheme for fog computing in digital manufacturing. *IEEE Trans. Ind. Inf.*

Yap, K., Ali, E. E., & Chew, L. (2021). *The Need for Quality Assessment of mHealth Interventions.* Design and Quality Considerations for Developing Mobile Apps for Medication Management. doi:10.4018/978-1-7998-3832-6.ch004

Yaqoob, I., Salah, K., Jayaraman, R., & Al-Hammadi, Y. (2021). Blockchain for healthcare data management: Opportunities, challenges, and future recommendations. *Neural Computing & Applications,* 1–16.

Yazdinejad, A., Parizi, R. M., Srivastava, G., Dehghantanha, A., & Choo, K.-K. R. (2019). Energy efficient decentralized authentication in internet of underwater things using blockchain. In 2019 IEEE Globecom Workshops (GC Wkshps), (pp. 1–6). IEEE. doi:10.1109/GCWkshps45667.2019.9024475

Yin, D., Zhang, L., & Yang, K. (2018). A ddos attack detection and mitigation with software-defined internet of things framework. *IEEE Access: Practical Innovations, Open Solutions, 6*, 24694–24705. doi:10.1109/ACCESS.2018.2831284

Yue, X., Wang, H., Jin, D., Li, M., & Jiang, W. (2016). Healthcare data gateways: Found healthcare intelligence on blockchain with novel privacy risk control. *Journal of Medical Systems, 40*(10), 1–8.

Zarpelão, B. B., Miani, R. S., Kawakani, C. T., & de Alvarenga, S. C. (2017). A survey of intrusion detection in internet of things. *Journal of Network and Computer Applications, 84*, 25–37. doi:10.1016/j.jnca.2017.02.009

Zeadally, S., Siddiqui, F., & Baig, Z. (2019). 25 years of bluetooth technology. *Future Internet, 11*(9), 194. doi:10.3390/fi11090194

Zeng, P., Wang, X., Li, H., Jiang, F., & Doss, R. (2020). A Scheme of Intelligent Traffic Light System Based on Distributed Security Architecture of Blockchain Technology. *IEEE Access: Practical Innovations, Open Solutions, 8*, 33644–33657. doi:10.1109/ACCESS.2020.2972606

Zhang, N., Mi, X., Feng, X., Wang, X., Tian, Y., & Qian, F. (2018). *Understanding and Mitigating the Security Risks of Voice-Controlled Third-Party Skills on Amazon Alexa and Google Home*. Academic Press.

Zhang, N., Mi, X., Feng, X., Wang, X., Tian, Y., & Qian, F. (2018). *Understanding and mitigating the security risks of voice-controlled third-party skills on amazon alexa and google home*. arXiv preprint arXiv:1805.01525.

Zhang, P., Walker, M. A., White, J., Schmidt, D. C., & Lenz, G. (2017, October). Metrics for assessing blockchain-based healthcare decentralized apps. In *2017 IEEE 19th International Conference on e-Health Networking, Applications and Services (Healthcom)* (pp. 1-4). IEEE.

Zhang, X. D., Li, R., & Cui, B. (2018). A security architecture of VANET based on blockchain and mobile edge computing. *2018 1st IEEE International Conference on Hot Information-Centric Networking (HotICN)*.

Zhang, A., & Lin, X. (2018). Towards Secure and Privacy-Preserving Data Sharing in e-Health Systems via Consortium Blockchain. *Journal of Medical Systems, 42*(8), 140. doi:10.100710916-018-0995-5 PMID:29956061

Zhang, G., Wu, Q., Cui, M., & Zhang, R. (2019a). Securing uav communications via joint trajectory and power control. *IEEE Transactions on Wireless Communications, 18*(2), 1376–1389. doi:10.1109/TWC.2019.2892461

Zhang, H., Wang, J., & Ding, Y. (2019b). Blockchain-based decentralized and secure keyless signature scheme for smart grid. *Energy, 180*, 955–967. doi:10.1016/j.energy.2019.05.127

Zhang, K., Zhu, Y., Maharjan, S., & Zhang, Y. (2019b). Edge intelligence and blockchain empowered 5g beyond for the industrial internet of things. *IEEE Network, 33*(5), 12–19. doi:10.1109/MNET.001.1800526

Zhang, L., Lee, B., Ye, Y., & Qiao, Y. (2019, August). Ethereum Transaction Performance Evaluation Using Test-Nets. In *European Conference on Parallel Processing* (pp. 179-190). Springer.

Zhang, P., White, J., Schmidt, D. C., Lenz, G., & Rosenbloom, S. T. (2018). FHIRChain: Applying blockchain to securely and scalably share clinical data. *Computational and Structural Biotechnology Journal, 16*, 267–278.

Zhang, S., Zhang, H., Di, B., & Song, L. (2019). Cellular UAV-to-X communications: Design and optimization for multi-UAV networks. *IEEE Transactions on Wireless Communications, 18*(2), 1346–1359.

Zhang, X., & Chen, X. (2019). Data Security Sharing and Storage Based on a Consortium Blockchain in a Vehicular Ad-hoc Network. *IEEE Access: Practical Innovations, Open Solutions, 7*, 58241–58254. doi:10.1109/ACCESS.2018.2890736

Zhang, Y., Deng, R., Zheng, D., Li, J., Wu, P., & Cao, J. (2019a). *Efficient and Robust Certificateless Signature for Data Crowdsensing in Cloud-Assisted Industrial IoT*. IEEE Transaction Industry. doi:10.1109/TII.2019.2894108

Zhao, C., & Guan, Y. (2015) A graph-based investigation of bitcoin transactions. *11th IFIP WG 11.9 International Conference,* 79–95.

Zheng, K., Liu, Y., Dai, C., Duan, Y., & Huang, X. (2018, October). Model checking PBFT consensus mechanism in healthcare blockchain network. In *2018 9th International Conference on Information Technology in Medicine and Education (ITME)* (pp. 877-881). IEEE.

Zheng, P., Zheng, Z., Luo, X., Chen, X., & Liu, X. (2018, May). A detailed and real-time performance monitoring framework for blockchain systems. In *2018 IEEE/ACM 40th International Conference on Software Engineering: Software Engineering in Practice Track (ICSE-SEIP)* (pp. 134-143). IEEE.

Zheng, Z., Xie, S., Dai, H., Chen, X., & Wang, H. (2017). An overview of blockchain technology: Architecture, consensus, and future trends. In 2017 IEEE international congress on big data (BigData Congress). IEEE.

Zheng, Z., Xie, S., Dai, H., Chen, X., & Wang, H. (2017, June). An Overview of Blockchain Technology: Architecture, Consensus, and Future Trends. In *2017 IEEE international congress on big data (BigData Congress)* (pp. 557-564). IEEE.

Zheng, D., Jing, C., Guo, R., Gao, S., & Wang, L. (2019). A Traceable Blockchain-Based Access Authentication System With Privacy Preservation in VANETs. *IEEE Access: Practical Innovations, Open Solutions, 7,* 117716–117726. doi:10.1109/ACCESS.2019.2936575

Zheng, D., Wu, A., Zhang, Y., & Zhao, Q. (2018a). Efficient and privacy-preserving medical data sharing in internet of things with limited computing power. *IEEE Access: Practical Innovations, Open Solutions, 6,* 28019–28027. doi:10.1109/ACCESS.2018.2840504

Zheng, Z., Xie, S., Dai, H., Chen, X., & Wang, H. (2017). *An overview of blockchain technology: Architecture, consensus, and future trends. In 2017 IEEE international congress on big data (BigData congress).* IEEE.

Zheng, Z., Xie, S., Dai, H.-N., Chen, X., & Wang, H. (2018b). Blockchain challenges and opportunities: A survey. *International Journal of Web and Grid Services, 14*(4), 352–375. doi:10.1504/IJWGS.2018.095647

Zhou, L., Wang, L., & Sun, Y. (2018). MIStore: A blockchain-based medical insurance storage system. *Journal of Medical Systems, 42*(8), 1–17.

Zhou, R., Zhang, X., Du, X., Wang, X., Yang, G., & Guizani, M. (2018). File-centric multi-key aggregate keyword searchable encryption for industrial Internet of things. *IEEE Transactions on Industrial Informatics, 14*(8), 3648–3658. doi:10.1109/TII.2018.2794442

Zhou, T., Li, X., & Zhao, H. (2019). Med-PPPHIS: Blockchain-Based Personal Healthcare Information System for National Physique Monitoring and Scientific Exercise Guiding. *Journal of Medical Systems, 43*(9), 305. doi:10.100710916-019-1430-2 PMID:31410583

Zhou, W., & Piramuthu, S. (2018). IoT security perspective of a flexible healthcare supply chain. *Information Technology Management, 19*(3), 141–153. doi:10.100710799-017-0279-7

Zhou, Z., Feng, J., Zhang, C., Chang, Z., Zhang, Y., & Huq, K. M. S. (2018). SAGECELL: Software-defined space-air-ground integrated movingcells. *IEEE Communications Magazine, 56*(8), 92–99.

Ziegeldorf, J. H., Morchon, O. G., & Wehrle, K. (2014). *Privacy in the Internet of Things: Threats and Challenges.* https://arxiv.org/abs/1505.07683

Zorzo, A. F., Nunes, H. C., Lunardi, R. C., Michelin, R. A., & Kanhere, S. S. (2018). Dependable IoT using blockchain-based technology. In *2018 Eighth Latin-American Symposium on Dependable Computing* (pp. 1-9). IEEE.

About the Contributors

Adel Ben Mnaouer is currently a Professor at the Department of Computer Engineering and Computational Sciences at the Canadian University Dubai. Dr. Ben Mnaouer received his BSc degree in Computer Science from the "Ecole Supérieure des communications (SUP'COM) of Tunisia in 1985 and the MEng and PhD degrees in Electrical and Computer Engineering from the University of Fukui and from Yokohama National University, Japan, in 1993 and 1997 respectively. He has served as Associate Professor and Acting Dean (2010–2011) of the College of Computer Engineering and Information Technology at Dar Al Uloom University, Ryadh, Saudi Arabia, then as a Vice-Dean of research of the same College. He joined the Faculty of Engineering, Applied Science and Technology at the Canadian University as an Associate Professor in Sept 2012. His research interests are in the areas of protocol design and analysis of Wired and Wireless Networks, Internet of Things and Cyber-physical Systems, Blockchain applied to the Internet of Things, Cluster, Grid and Cloud Computing. Dr. Ben Mnaouer is the recipient of four major QNRF projects worth 3.7 million dollars focused on harnessing the power of wireless sensor networks in remote ubiquitous healthcare systems, in Air Quality Control, in Structural Health Monitoring and in developing new communications protocols that are better equipped to serve specific target application fields. He is active in Chairmanship, editorial board, TPC and organization of scores of top-class international conferences and Symposia. Dr. Ben Mnaouer is a Senior Member of the IEEE Communication Society since 2009.

Lamia Chaari Fourati is a professor at Computer Science and Multimedia Higher Institute), Sfax University, and researcher at Digital Research Center of Sfax (CRNS), Laboratory of Signals, systeMs, aRtificial Intelligence, neTworkS (SM@RTS). She focused her research activities on conception and validation of new protocols and mechanisms for emerging networks technologies. Her research activities are very important and up-to-date which are related to digital telecommunication networks, in particular wireless access networks, sensor networks, vehicular networks, Internet of things, 5G, software defined network, information centric network and wireless body area network, unmanned aerial vehicle, etc. In these areas, she is interested in problems such as quality of services provisioning (congestion control, admission control, resources allocations…), cyber security and ambient intelligence. Her scientific publications have met the interest of the scientific community and her work has been published in top-tier journals and conferences. She has more than 60 papers published in journals and more than 90 papers published in conferences. Prof. Lamia CHAARI FOURATI is the laureate for the Kwame Nkrumah Regional Awards for women 2016 (North Africa Region).

* * *

Hentati Aicha is a PhD student at National Engineering School of Sfax (ENIS), Tunisia. She received her Master's Degree in Computer Science and Multimedia from the Computer Science and Multimedia Higher Institute of Sfax (ISIMS), Tunisia, in 2014. She is a member of the Laboratory of Technology and Smart Systems (LT2S), Digital Research Center of Sfax (CRNS), Tunisia. Her scope of research ranges from data communications to secure networking, which are specially related to autonomous systems comprising of UAVs, drones systems, collaborative networking of technical and administrative assistants with complex operations in open ended open environments, and with high levels of independence and self-governing control and determination. The primary objective of her PhD research project is the design, implementation and validation of a collaborative inter-UAVs system for autonomous tracking of intruders and sabotagers. She is author and reviewer of many conferences and journal papers in these subject areas.

Samiha Ayed has received the B.S. and M.S. degrees in computer science from the National School of Computer Science of Manouba, Tunisia, respectively in 2005 and 2006. She got the Ph.D. degree in security of information systems from Telecom Bretagne, Rennes, France, in 2009. From 2012 to 2016, he was a Researcher with the SFIIS team of Telecom Bretagne. Since 2017, she has been an Associate Professor with the LIST3N-ERA team, University of Technology of Troyes.

Wiem Bekri is a Ph.D. student in the National School of Electronics and Telecommunications of Sfax, University of Sfax, Tunisia. In 2015 she obtained her Informatics science bachelor's degree from the Higher Institute of Informatics of Mahdia, University of Monastir, Tunisia. In 2019 she obtained her Master's degree in Enterprise System Engineering from the Higher Institute of Informatics and Multimedia, University of Sfax, Tunisia. She is currently a member of Laboratory of Signals, systeMs, aRtificial Intelligence and neTworkS (SM@RTS) in the Digital Research Centre of Sfax, Tunisia, and preparing her thesis regarding the IoT-SDN domain's security.

Henry Cabral Nunes is a Ph.D. candidate at the reliability and security group at PUCRS. During his master's developed his work in the blockchain area, with an emphasis on Smart Contracts. During his Ph.D. studies plans to extend his works to the privacy field. Henry has also interest in Security and Formal Methods.

Alfredo Cuzzocrea is currently Professor at the DIA Department, University of Calabria, Italy. Previously, he has been Researcher at the Institute of High Performance Computing and Networking of the Italian National Research Council, Italy, and Adjunct Professor at the University of Calabria, Italy. He is author or co-author of more than 350 papers in international conferences (including EDBT, CIKM, SSDBM, MDM, DaWaK, DOLAP), international journals (including JCSS, IS, KAIS, DKE, INS) and international books.

Volkan Dedeoglu is currently a postdoctoral research fellow in the Distributed Sensing Systems Group of CSIRO Data61. His current research focuses on blockchain-based IoT security and privacy. Volkan also holds an Adjunct Lecturer position at UNSW Sydney. Before joining Data61, Volkan worked as a postdoctoral research associate at Texas A&M University on physical layer security for communications. He designed error correcting codes for secure and reliable communications on compound channels. He completed his PhD in Telecommunications Engineering from University of South Australia in 2013. His

PhD research focused on energy efficient wireless sensor networks, data gathering, target tracking, cross-layer optimization, and distributed algorithms. He obtained MSc in Electrical and Computer Engineering from Koc University (Turkey, 2008), BSc in Electrical and Electronics Engineering from Bogazici University (Turkey, 2006), and B.A. in Public Administration from Anadolu University (Turkey, 2008).

Rima Grati has been an assistant professor at the College of Technological Innovation at Zayed University since autumn 2018, and an Assistant Professor at Emirates College of Technology since 2016. She earned her Ph.D. degree in Computer Science from the University of Tunisia, in 2016, and has a management information systems background for her Bachelor's and Master's degrees. Before earning her Ph.D., Dr. Rima served as a Lecturer at University of Sfax- Tunisia for many years. Dr. Rima's research interests are in the fields of Cloud computing, IoT, Business Process.

Achraf Haddaji received his electronics and telecommunications bachelor's degree from the Higher Institute of Applied Sciences and Technology of Mahdia, University of Monastir, Tunisia in 2018. He obtained his master's degree in computing and multimedia from the Higher Institute of Computer and Multimedia, University of Sfax, in 2020. Currently, he is pursuing a PhD degree from both The National School of Electronics and Telecommunications of Sfax, Tunisia, and the University of Technology of Troyes, France.

Sanaa Kaddoura is an assistant professor at Zayed University. She holds a PhD degree in computer science (2018) and a master degree in information systems (2011) from Beirut Arab University/Lebanon. She has 11 years of experience in teaching computer science courses for undergraduate students. Before joining Zayed University, she worked as a faculty member at Beirut Arab University. In addition, she was the team leader and IT engineer of the Online British Arabian School. Dr. Kaddoura research interest includes applications of artificial intelligence in computer security, natural Language processing and social networks analysis.

Salil S. Kanhere received his M.S. and Ph.D. degrees from Drexel University in Philadelphia. He is a Professor of Computer Science and Engineering at UNSW Sydney, Australia. His research interests include the IoT, blockchain, pervasive computing, cybersecurity and applied machine learning. He is a Senior Member of the IEEE and ACM, an Humboldt Research Fellow and an ACM Distinguished Speaker. He serves as the Editor in Chief of the Ad Hoc Networks journal and as Associate Editor of IEEE TNSM, COMCOM and PMC. He has served on the organising committee of several IEEE/ACM international conferences.

Thangavel M. is an Assistant Professor, presently affiliated to Department of Computer Science and Engineering, Institute of Technical Education & Research, Siksha 'O' Anusandhan (Deemed to be University), Bhubaneswar-751030, Odisha, India. He has completed the Ph.D. programme in Information and Communication Engineering under Anna University, Chennai, Tamilnadu, India in the year 2021. He presently holds 8.5 years of Teaching and Research experience. He graduated as a B.E. Computer Science and Engineering from M.A.M College of Engineering, Trichy (Anna University - Chennai) and as an M.E. Computer Science and Engineering from J.J. College of Engineering and Technology, Trichy (Anna University - Chennai). He is a Gold Medalist in UG and Anna University - First Rank Holder with Gold Medal in PG. His specialization is Cloud Computing, and Information Security. His Areas of Interest include DNA Cryptography, Ethical Hacking, Compiler Design, Computer Networks, Data Structures and High Performance Computing. He has published 10 articles in International Journals, 16 book chapters in International Publishers, 25 in the proceedings of International Conferences and 3 in the proceedings of national conferences /seminars. He has attended 95 Workshops / FDPs/Conferences in various Higher Learning Institutes like IIT, Anna University. He has organized 49 Workshops / FDPs /Contests/Industry based courses over the past 8 years of experience. He has been a delegate for Cyber Week 2017 organized by Tel Aviv University, Israel. He has been recognized by IIT Bombay; SAP CSR as SAP Award of Excellence with cash reward of Rs.5000/- for the best Participation in IITBombayX: FDPICT001x Use of ICT in Education for Online and Blended Learning. He shows interest in student counseling, in motivating for better placements and in helping them design value-based lifestyle.

Ramchandra Mangrulkar has received his PhD in Computer Science and Engineering from SGBAU Amravati in 2016 and currently he is working as an Associate Professor at the department of Computing Engineering at DJSCE Mumbai, Maharashtra, India. Prior to this, he was working Associate Professor and Head, department of Computer Engineering, Bapurao Deshmukh College of Engineering Sevagram. Maharashtra, India. Dr. Ramchandra Mangrulkar has published significant number of papers and book chapters in the field related journals and conferences and have also participated as a session chair in various conferences and conducted various workshops on Network Simulator and LaTeX. He also received certification of appreciation from DIG Special Crime Branch Pune and Superintendent of Police and broadcasting media gives wide publicity for the project work guided by him on the topic "Face Recognition System". He also received 3.5 lakhs grant under Research Promotion Scheme of AICTE for the project "Secured Energy Efficient Routing Protocol for Delay Tolerant Hybrid Network". He is active member of Board of Studies in various universities and autonomous institute in India.

Regio Michelin received M.S. and Ph.D. degrees in computer science from the Pontifical Catholic University of Rio Grande do Sul, Brazil, in 2014 and 2019, respectively. He is currently working as a research fellow at the Cyber Security Cooperative Research Centre (CSCRC), Australia. His research interests include blockchain, cybersecurity, and IoT.

Rim Moussa is currently a tenured associate professor at University of Carthage (ENI-Carthage, Tunisia). She is also habilitated as associate professor in Computer Science Engineering by the the French National Council of Universities. She received her M.Sc. (DEA127 -Computer Science: Intelligent Systems) and Ph.D in Distributed Databases from Université Paris IX Dauphine (France). She ensures both undergraduate and graduate lectures, related to distributed data management systems, Data Warehousing, NoSQL databases, Spatial databases, and Cloud Computing & HPC (Big Data, Apache Hadoop, Apache Spark). Her current research interests include Scalable and Distributed Data Management systems, Data warehousing, Big Data Architectures and Spatial Computing at scale.

Charles Neu is an associate of the Brazilian Computer Society (SBC). He holds a degree in Computer Science from the University of Santa Cruz do Sul (2005-2011) with overseas internship at Ostfalia University of Applied Sciences (Germany) (02.2010 - 08-2010), a Masters in Industrial Systems and Processes from the University of Santa Cruz do Sul (2012- 2013) with overseas internship at Ostfalia University of Applied Sciences (Germany) (08.2012 - 02-2013) and Ph.D. in Computer Science at Pontificial Catholic University of Rio Grande do Sul (PUCRS) with overseas internship at Ostfalia University of Applied Sciences (Germany, 2018) and Newcastle University (UK, 2018) . He is currently a Lecturer at the Computing Department, University of Santa Cruz do Sul, Brazil and a postdoc (assistant researcher) in digital forensics at PUCRS. He has experience in Computer Science, working mainly on the following topics: computer networks, communication systems, cryptography and network security.

Karthikeyan P. was born in Dindigul, Tamilnadu, India in 1981. He is currently working as an Associate Professor in Thiagarajar College of Engineering, Madurai from 2007 onwards. He has completed the Ph.D. programme in Information and Communication Engineering under Anna University, Chennai, Tamilnadu, India in the year 2015. He published 13 papers in refereed international journals and conferences. He received the B.E. degree in Computer Science and Engineering from Madurai Kamaraj University, Madurai, Tamilnadu, India in the year 2002. He also received his M.E. degree in Computer Science and Engineering from Anna University, Chennai, Tamilnadu, India in the year2004. His research interests include optimization algorithms, ad hoc networks, engineering education and mobile cloud computing.

Kamalendu Pal is with the Department of Computer Science, School of Mathematics, Computer Science and Engineering, City University London. Kamalendu received his BSc (Hons) degree in Physics from Calcutta University, India, Postgraduate Diploma in Computer Science from Pune, India; MSc degree in Software Systems Technology from Sheffield University, Postgraduate Diploma in Artificial Intelligence from Kingston University, MPhil degree in Computer Science from University College London, and MBA degree from University of Hull, United Kingdom. He has published dozens of research papers in international journals and conferences. His research interests include knowledge-based systems, decision support systems, computer integrated design, software engineering, and service-oriented computing. He is a member of the British Computer Society, the Institution of Engineering and Technology, and the IEEE Computer Society.

Avelino Zorzo is a member of the Brazilian Computer Society (SBC) and IEEE. Computer Science BSc from Universidade Federal do Rio Grande do Sul (1989), Computer Science MSc from Universidade Federal do Rio Grande do Sul (1994) and Computing Science PhD from University of Newcastle Upon Tyne (1999). Post doctorate at the Cybercrime and Computer Security Centre at the Newcastle University (2012). Education Director at the Brazilian Computing Society (2015-2017). Coordinator for Professional Post-graduate accreditation for the Ministry of Education in Brazil (2014-2021). Main research topics: security, fault tolerance, software testing and operating systems.

Index

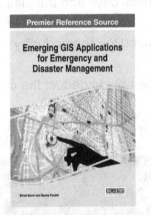
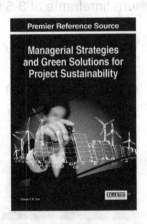

IGI Global Author Services

Providing a high-quality, affordable, and expeditious service, IGI Global's Author Services enable authors to streamline their publishing process, increase chance of acceptance, and adhere to IGI Global's publication standards.

Benefits of Author Services:

- **Professional Service:** All our editors, designers, and translators are experts in their field with years of experience and professional certifications.

- **Quality Guarantee & Certificate:** Each order is returned with a quality guarantee and certificate of professional completion.

- **Timeliness:** All editorial orders have a guaranteed return timeframe of 3-5 business days and translation orders are guaranteed in 7-10 business days.

- **Affordable Pricing:** IGI Global Author Services are competitively priced compared to other industry service providers.

- **APC Reimbursement:** IGI Global authors publishing Open Access (OA) will be able to deduct the cost of editing and other IGI Global author services from their OA APC publishing fee.

Author Services Offered:

English Language Copy Editing
Professional, native English language copy editors improve your manuscript's grammar, spelling, punctuation, terminology, semantics, consistency, flow, formatting, and more.

Scientific & Scholarly Editing
A Ph.D. level review for qualities such as originality and significance, interest to researchers, level of methodology and analysis, coverage of literature, organization, quality of writing, and strengths and weaknesses.

Figure, Table, Chart & Equation Conversions
Work with IGI Global's graphic designers before submission to enhance and design all figures and charts to IGI Global's specific standards for clarity.

Translation
Providing 70 language options, including Simplified and Traditional Chinese, Spanish, Arabic, German, French, and more.

Hear What the Experts Are Saying About IGI Global's Author Services

Learn More or Get Started Here:

For Questions, Contact IGI Global's Customer Service Team at cust@igi-global.com or 717-533-8845

IGI Global
PUBLISHER of TIMELY KNOWLEDGE
www.igi-global.com

Publisher of Peer-Reviewed, Timely, and
Innovative Academic Research Since 1988

IGI Global's Transformative Open Access (OA) Model:
How to Turn Your University Library's Database Acquisitions Into a Source of OA Funding

Well in advance of Plan S, IGI Global unveiled their OA Fee Waiver (Read & Publish) Initiative. Under this initiative, librarians who invest in IGI Global's InfoSci-Books and/or InfoSci-Journals databases will be able to subsidize their patrons' OA article processing charges (APCs) when their work is submitted and accepted (after the peer review process) into an IGI Global journal.

How Does it Work?

Step 1: **Library Invests in the InfoSci-Databases:** A library perpetually purchases or subscribes to the InfoSci-Books, InfoSci-Journals, or discipline/subject databases.

Step 2: **IGI Global Matches the Library Investment with OA Subsidies Fund:** IGI Global provides a fund to go towards subsidizing the OA APCs for the library's patrons.

Step 3: **Patron of the Library is Accepted into IGI Global Journal (After Peer Review):** When a patron's paper is accepted into an IGI Global journal, they option to have their paper published under a traditional publishing model or as OA.

Step 4: **IGI Global Will Deduct APC Cost from OA Subsidies Fund:** If the author decides to publish under OA, the OA APC fee will be deducted from the OA subsidies fund.

Step 5: **Author's Work Becomes Freely Available:** The patron's work will be freely available under CC BY copyright license, enabling them to share it freely with the academic community.

Note: This fund will be offered on an annual basis and will renew as the subscription is renewed for each year thereafter. IGI Global will manage the fund and award the APC waivers unless the librarian has a preference as to how the funds should be managed.

Hear From the Experts on This Initiative:

"I'm very happy to have been able to make one of my recent research contributions *freely available* along with having access to the *valuable resources* found within IGI Global's InfoSci-Journals database."

– Prof. Stuart Palmer,
Deakin University, Australia

"Receiving the support from IGI Global's OA Fee Waiver Initiative *encourages me to continue my research work without any hesitation*."

– Prof. Wenlong Liu, College of Economics and Management at Nanjing University of Aeronautics & Astronautics, China

Printed in the United States
by Baker & Taylor Publisher Services